History Of The Negro Race In America
Vol. 1

by

George Washington Williams

History Of The Negro Race In America
Vol. 1
by George Washington Williams

Copyright © 2023

All Rights reserved.

No part of this publication may be reproduced, stored in a retrieval system, or transmitted in any form or by any means, electronic, mechanical, photocopying or Otherwise, without the written permission of the publisher.
The author/editor asserts the moral right to be identified as the author/editor of this work.

ISBN: 978-93-59399-21-8

Published by

DOUBLE 9 BOOKS
2/13-B, Ansari Road
Daryaganj, New Delhi – 110002
info@double9books.com
www.double9books.com
Tel. 011-40042856

This book is under public domain

ABOUT THE AUTHOR

George Washington Williams (October 16, 1849 – August 2, 1891) was a Baptist clergyman, politician, lawyer, journalist, and author of African-American history. He moved to the Congo Free State (then owned by the monarch) in 1890 after being impressed by seeing monarch Leopold II of Belgium. In 1890, he sent an open letter to Leopold about the suffering of the region's native population at the hands of the king's agents, shocked by the widespread violent abuses and slavery forced on the Congolese. This letter, which popularized the term "crimes against humanity," sparked a worldwide outcry against the Congolese regime, which had caused millions of deaths. His brothers were John, Thomas, and Harry Lawsom Williams, and he was the oldest of four children. The boys' education was limited. Williams remained in a "house of refuge" for a period, where he learnt barbering, which was considered a competent and desirable occupation at the time. During the American Civil War, Williams ran away and enlisted in the Union Army under an assumed name at the age of 14; he fought in the final battles.

CONTENTS

PREFACE 9

Part I
    PRELIMINARY CONSIDERATIONS 15

CHAPTER I
    THE UNITY OF MANKIND 15

CHAPTER II
    THE NEGRO IN THE LIGHT OF PHILOLOGY,
    ETHNOLOGY, AND EGYPTOLOGY 26

CHAPTER III
    PRIMITIVE NEGRO CIVILIZATION 37

CHAPTER IV
    NEGRO KINGDOMS OF AFRICA 42

CHAPTER V
    THE ASHANTEE EMPIRE 50

CHAPTER VI
    THE NEGRO TYPE 60

CHAPTER VII
    AFRICAN IDIOSYNCRASIES 65

CHAPTER VIII
    LANGUAGES, LITERATURE, AND RELIGION 84

CHAPTER IX
    SIERRA LEONE 104

CHAPTER X
    THE REPUBLIC OF LIBERIA 116

CHAPTER XI
RÉSUMÉ 130

Part II
SLAVERY IN THE COLONIES[119] 138

CHAPTER XII
THE COLONY OF VIRGINIA 138

CHAPTER XIII
THE COLONY OF NEW YORK 157

CHAPTER XIV
THE COLONY OF MASSACHUSETTS 192

CHAPTER XV
THE COLONY OF MASSACHUSETTS,
—CONTINUED 246

CHAPTER XVI
THE COLONY OF MARYLAND 265

CHAPTER XVII
THE COLONY OF DELAWARE 276

CHAPTER XVIII
THE COLONY OF CONNECTICUT 279

CHAPTER XIX
THE COLONY OF RHODE ISLAND 290

CHAPTER XX
THE COLONY OF NEW JERSEY 313

CHAPTER XXI
THE COLONY OF SOUTH CAROLINA 320

CHAPTER XXII
THE COLONY OF NORTH CAROLINA 335

CHAPTER XXIII
THE COLONY OF NEW HAMPSHIRE 343

CHAPTER XXIV
THE COLONY OF PENNSYLVANIA 346

CHAPTER XXV
 THE COLONY OF GEORGIA 350

Part III
 THE NEGRO DURING THE REVOLUTION 358

CHAPTER XXVI
 MILITARY EMPLOYMENT OF NEGROES............................ 358

CHAPTER XXVII
 NEGROES AS SOLDIERS 406

CHAPTER XXVIII
 LEGAL STATUS OF THE NEGRO DURING
 THE REVOLUTION... 414

CHAPTER XXIX
 THE NEGRO INTELLECT.—BANNEKER
 THE ASTRONOMER.[611].— FULLER THE
 MATHEMATICIAN.—DERHAM THE PHYSICIAN 431

CHAPTER XXX
 SLAVERY DURING THE REVOLUTION 450

CHAPTER XXXI
 SLAVERY AS A POLITICAL AND LEGAL PROBLEM........ 461

APPENDIX 494

Part I
 PRELIMINARY CONSIDERATIONS. 494

Part II
 SLAVERY IN THE COLONIES. 521

INDEX 526

PREFACE

I was requested to deliver an oration on the Fourth of July, 1876, at Avondale, O. It being the one-hundredth birthday of the American Republic, I determined to prepare an oration on the *American Negro*. I at once began an investigation of the records of the nation to secure material for the oration. I was surprised and delighted to find that the historical memorials of the Negro were so abundant, and so creditable to him. I pronounced my oration on the Fourth of July, 1876; and the warm and generous manner in which it was received, both by those who listened to it and by others who subsequently read it in pamphlet form, encouraged me to devote what leisure time I might have to a further study of the subject.

I found that the library of the Historical and Philosophical Society of Ohio, and the great Americana of Mr. Robert Clarke containing about eight thousand titles, both in Cincinnati, offered peculiar advantages to a student of American history. For two years I spent what time I could spare from professional cares in studying the whole problem of the African slave-trade; the founding of the British colonies in North America; the slave problem in the colonies; the rupture between the colonies and the British Government; the war of the Revolution; the political structure of the Continental government and Confederation; the slavery question in local and national legislation; and then traced the slavery and anti-slavery question down to the Rebellion. I became convinced that a history of the Colored people in America was required, because of the ample historically trustworthy material at hand; because the Colored people themselves had been the most vexatious problem in North America, from the time of its discovery down to the present day; because that in every attempt upon the life of the nation, whether by foes from without or within, the Colored people had always displayed a matchless patriotism and an incomparable heroism in the cause of Americans; and because such a history [pg vi]would give the world more correct ideas of the Colored people, and incite the latter to greater effort in the struggle of citizenship and manhood. The single reason that there was no history of the Negro race would have been a sufficient reason for writing one.

The labor incident upon the several public positions held by me precluded an earlier completion of this task; and, finding it absolutely impossible to write while discharging public duties or practising law, I retired from the public service several years ago, and since that time have devoted all my energies to this work. It is now nearly seven years since I began this wonderful task.

I have been possessed of a painful sense of the vastness of my work from first to last. I regret that for the sake of pressing the work into a single volume, favorable to a speedy sale,—at the sacrifice of the record of a most remarkable people,—I found my heart unwilling, and my best judgment protesting.

In the preparation of this work I have consulted over twelve thousand volumes,—about one thousand of which are referred to in the footnotes,—and thousands of pamphlets.

After wide and careful reading, extending through three years, I conceived the present plan of this history. I divided it into nine parts. Two thoughts led me to prepare the chapters under the head of PRELIMINARY CONSIDERATIONS. First, The defenders of slavery and the traducers of the Negro built their pro-slavery arguments upon biblical ethnology and the curse of Canaan. I am alive to the fact, that, while I am a believer in the Holy Bible, it is not the best authority on ethnology. As far as it goes, it is agreeable to my head and heart. Whatever science has added I have gladly appropriated. I make no claim, however, to be a specialist. While the curse of Canaan is no longer a question of debate, yet nevertheless the folly of the obsolete theory should be thoroughly understood by the young men of the Negro race who, though voting now, were not born when Sumter was fired upon. Second, A growing desire among the enlightened Negroes in America to learn all that is possible from research concerning the antiquity of the race,—Africa, its inhabitants, and the development of the Negro governments of Sierra Leone and Liberia, led me to furnish something to meet a felt need. If the Negro slave desired his native land before the Rebellion, will not the free, intelligent, and reflective American Negro turn to Africa with its problems of geography [pg vii]and missions, now that he can contribute something towards the improvement of the condition of humanity? Editors and writers everywhere throughout the world should spell the word Negro with a capital N; and when referring to the race as Colored people employ a capital C. I trust this will be observed.

In PART II., SLAVERY IN THE COLONIES, I have striven to give a succinct account of the establishment and growth of slavery under the English Crown. It involved almost infinite labor to go to the records of "the original thirteen colonies." It is proper to observe that this part is one of great value and interest.

In PART III., THE NEGRO DURING THE REVOLUTION, I found much of an almost romantic character. Many traditions have been put down, and many obscure truths elucidated. Some persons may think it irreverent to tell the truth in the plain, homely manner that characterizes my narrative; but, while I have nothing to regret in this particular, I can assure them that I have been actuated by none other spirit than that of candor. Where I have used documents it was with a desire to escape the charge of superficiality. If, however, I may be charged with seeking to escape the labor incident to thorough digestion, I answer, that, while men with the reputation of Bancroft and Hildreth could pass unchallenged when disregarding largely the use of documents and the citation of authorities, I would find myself challenged by a large number of critics. Moreover I have felt it would be almost cruel to mutilate some of the very rare old documents that shed such peerless light upon the subject in hand.

I have brought the first volume down to the close of the eighteenth century, detailing the great struggle through which the slavery problem passed. I have given as fair an idea of the debate on this question, in the convention that framed the Constitution, as possible. It was then and there that the hydra of slavery struck its fangs into the Constitution; and, once inoculated with the poison of the monster, the government was only able to purify itself in the flames of a great civil war.

The second volume opens with the present century, and closes with the year 1880. Unable to destroy slavery by constitutional law, the best thought and effort of this period were directed against the extension of the evil into the territory beyond the Ohio, Mississippi, and Missouri rivers. But having placed three-fifths of the slave population under the Constitution, having pledged the Constitution to the protection of slave property, [pg viii]it required an almost superhuman effort to confine the evil to one section of the country. Like a loathsome disease it spread itself over the body politic until our nation became the eyesore of the age, and a byword among the nations of the world. The time came when our beloved country had to submit to heroic treatment, and the cancer of slavery was removed by the sword.

In giving an account of the *Anti-Slavery Agitation Movement*, I have found myself able to deal briefly with methods and results only. I have striven to honor all the multifarious measures adopted to save the Negro and the Nation. I have not attempted to write a history of the Anti-Slavery Movement. Many noble men and women have not even been mentioned. It should not be forgotten that this is a history of the Negro race; and as such I have not run into the topic discussed by the late Henry Wilson in his "Rise and Fall of the Slave Power."

In discussing the problem of the rendition of fugitive slaves by the Union army, I have given the facts with temperate and honest criticism. And, in recounting the sufferings Negro troops endured as prisoners of war in the hands of the Rebels, I have avoided any spirit of bitterness. A great deal of the material on the war I purchased from the MS. library of Mr. Thomas S. Townsend of New-York City. The questions of vital, prison, labor, educational, and financial statistics cannot fail to interest intelligent people of all races and parties. These statistics are full of comfort and assurance to the Negro as well as to his friends.

Every cabinet minister of the President wrote me full information upon all the questions I asked, and promptly too. The refusal of the general and adjutant-general of the army did not destroy my hope of getting some information concerning the Negro regiments in the regular army. I visited the Indian Territory, Kansas, Texas, and New Mexico, where I have seen the Ninth and Tenth Regiments of cavalry, and the Twenty-fourth Regiment of infantry. The Twenty-fifth Regiment of infantry is at Fort Randall, Dakota. These are among the most effective troops in the regular army. The annual desertions in white regiments of cavalry vary from ninety-eight to a hundred and eighteen; while in Negro regiments of cavalry the desertions only average from six to nine per annum. The Negro regiments are composed of young men, intelligent, faithful, brave. I heard but one complaint from the lips of a score of white officers I met, and that was that the Negroes sometimes struck their horses over the head. [pg ix]Every distinction in law has disappeared, except in the regular army. Here Negroes are excluded from the artillery service and engineer's department. It is wrong, and Congress should place these brave black soldiers upon the same footing as the white troops.

I have to thank Drs. George H. Moore and S. Austin Allibone, of the Lenox Library, for the many kind favors shown me while pursuing my studies in New-York City. And I am under very great obligations to Dr. Moore for his admirable "History of Early Slavery in Massachusetts," without which I should have been put to great inconvenience. To Mr. John Austin Stevens, late editor of "The Magazine of American History," who, during several months residence in New-York City, placed his private library and office at my service, and did every thing in his power to aid my investigations, I return my sincerest thanks. To the Librarians of the New-York Historical, Astor, and New-York Society Libraries, I return thanks for favors shown, and privileges granted. I am especially grateful to the Hon. Ainsworth R. Spofford, Librarian of Congress, for the manner in which he facilitated my researches during my sojourn in Washington. I had the use of many newspapers of the last century, and of other material to be found only in the Congressional Library.

To Sir T. Risely Griffith, Colonial Secretary and Treasurer of Sierra Leone, I am indebted for valuable statistics concerning that colony.

To the Assistant Librarian of the State Library of Ohio, the accomplished and efficient Miss Mary C. Harbough, I owe more than to any other person. Through her unwavering and untiring kindness and friendship, I have been enabled to use five hundred and seventy-six volumes from that library, besides newspaper files and Congressional Records. To Gov. Charles Foster, Chairman of the Board of Library Commissioners, I offer my profoundest thanks for the intelligent, active, and practical interest he has taken in the completion of this work. And to Major Charles Townsend, Secretary of State, I offer thanks for favors shown me in securing documents. To the Rev. J.L. Grover and his competent assistant, Mr. Charles H. Bell, of the Public Library of Columbus, I am indebted for the use of many works. They cheerfully rendered whatever aid they could, and for their kindness I return many thanks.

I am obliged to the Rev. Benjamin W. Arnett, Financial Secretary of the A.M.E. Church of the United States, for the statistics of his denomination. And to all persons who have sent me newspapers and pamphlets [pg x]I desire to return thanks. I am grateful to C.A. Fleetwood, an efficient clerk in the War Department, for statistics on the Freedmen's Bank. And, above all and more than all, I return my profoundest thanks to my heavenly Father for the inspiration, health, and money by which I have been enabled to complete this great task.

I have mentioned such Colored men as I thought necessary. To give a biographical sketch of all the worthy Colored men in the United States, would require more space than has been occupied in this work.

Not as the blind panegyrist of my race, nor as the partisan apologist, but from a love for *"the truth of history,"* I have striven to record the truth, the whole truth, and nothing but the truth. I have not striven to revive sectional animosities or race prejudices. I have avoided comment so far as it was consistent with a clear exposition of the truth. My whole aim has been to write a thoroughly trustworthy history; and what I have written, if it have no other merit, is reliable.

I commit this work to the public, white and black, to the friends and foes of the Negro, in the hope that the obsolete antagonisms which grew out of the relation of master and slave may speedily sink as storms beneath the horizon; and that the day will hasten when there shall be no North, no South, no Black, no White,—but all be American citizens, with equal duties and equal rights.

GEORGE W. WILLIAMS.

New York, November, 1882.

PART I
PRELIMINARY CONSIDERATIONS

CHAPTER I
THE UNITY OF MANKIND

The Biblical Argument.—One Race and One Language.—
One Blood.—The Curse of Canaan.

DURING the last half-century, many writers on ethnology, anthropology, and slavery have strenuously striven to place the Negro outside of the human family; and the disciples of these teachers have endeavored to justify their views by the most dehumanizing treatment of the Negro. But, fortunately for the Negro and for humanity at large, we live now in an epoch when race malice and sectional hate are disappearing beneath the horizon of a brighter and better future. The Negro in America is free. He is now an acknowledged factor in the affairs of the continent; and no community, state, or government, in this period of the world's history, can afford to be indifferent to his moral, social, intellectual, or political well-being.

It is proposed, in the first place, to call the attention to the absurd charge that the Negro does not belong to the human family. Happily, there are few left upon the face of the earth who still maintain this belief.

In the first chapter of the Book of Genesis it is clearly stated that "God created man," "male and female created he them;"[1] that "the Lord God formed man of the dust of the ground, and breathed into his nostrils the breath of life; and man became a living soul;"[2] and that "the Lord God took the man, and put him into the Garden of Eden to dress it and to keep it."[3] It is noticeable that the sacred historian, in every reference to Adam, speaks of him as "man;" and that the divine injunction to them was,—Adam and Eve,—"Be fruitful, and multiply, and replenish the earth, and subdue it; and have dominion over the fish of the sea, and over the fowl of the air, and over every living thing that moveth upon the earth."[4] As among the animals, so here in the higher order, there were two,—a pair,—"male and female," of the human species. We may begin with man, and run down the scale, and we are sure to find two of a kind, "male and female." This was the divine order. But they were to "be fruitful," were to "replenish the earth." That they did "multiply," we have the trustworthy testimony of God; and it was true that man and beast, fowl and fish, increased. We read that after their expulsion from the Garden of Eden, Eve bore Adam a family. Cain and Abel; and that they "peopled the earth."

After a number of years we find that wickedness increased in the earth; so much so that the Lord was provoked to destroy the earth with a flood, with the exception of Noah, his wife, his three sons and their wives,—eight souls in all.[5] Of the animals, two of each kind were saved.

But the most interesting portion of Bible history comes after the Flood. We then have the history of the confusion of tongues, and the subsequent and consequent dispersion of mankind. In the eleventh chapter and first verse of Genesis it is recorded: "And the whole earth was of one language, and of one speech." "The whole earth" here means all the inhabitants of the earth,—all mankind. The medium of communication was common. Everybody used one language. In the sixth verse occurs this remarkable language: "And the Lord said, Behold, the people is one, and they have all one language." Attention is called to this verse, because we have here the testimony of the Lord that "the people is one," and that the language of the people is one. This verse establishes two very important facts; i.e., there was but one nationality, and hence but one language. The fact that they had but one language furnishes reasonable proof that they were of one blood; and the historian has covered the whole question very carefully by recording the great truth that they were one people, and had but one language. The seventh, eighth, and ninth verses of the eleventh chapter are not irrelevant: "Go to, let us go down, and there confound their language, that they may not understand one another's speech. So the Lord scattered them abroad from thence upon the face of all the earth; and they left off to build the city. Therefore is the name of it called Babel; because the Lord did there confound the language of all the earth; and from thence did the Lord scatter them abroad upon the face of all the earth."

It was the wickedness of the people that caused the Lord to disperse them, to confound their speech, and bring to nought their haughty work. Evidently this was the beginning of different families of men,—different nationalities, and hence different languages. In the ninth verse it reads, that "from thence did the Lord scatter them abroad upon the face of all the earth." There is no ambiguity about this language. He did not only "confound their language," but "scattered them from thence," from Babel, "upon the face of all the earth." Here, then, are two very important facts: their *language* was *confused*, and they *were "scattered."* They were not only "scattered," they were "scattered *abroad upon the face of all* the earth." That is, they were dispersed very widely, sent into the various and remote parts of the earth; and their nationality received its being from the latitudes to which the divinely appointed wave of dispersion bore them; and their subsequent racial character was to borrow its tone and color from climateric influences. Three great families, the Shemitic, Hamitic, and Japhetic, were suddenly built up. Many other families, or tribes, sprang from these; but these were the three great heads of all subsequent races of men.

> "That the three sons of Noah overspread and peopled the whole earth, is so expressly stated in Scripture, that, had we not to argue against those who unfortunately disbelieve such evidence, we might here stop: let us, however, inquire how far the truth of this declaration is substantiated by other considerations. Enough has been said to show that there is a curious, if not a remarkable, analogy between the predictions of Noah on the future descendants of his three sons, and the actual state of those races which are generally supposed to have sprung from them. It may here be again remarked, that, to render the subject more clear, we have adopted the quinary arrangement of Professor Blumenbach: yet that Cuvier and other learned physiologists are of opinion that the primary varieties of the human form are more properly but three; viz., the Caucasian, Mongolian, and Ethiopian. This number corresponds with that of Noah's sons. Assigning, therefore, the Mongolian race to Japheth, and the Ethiopian to Ham, the Caucasian, the noblest race, will belong to Shem, the third son of Noah, himself descended from Seth, the third son of Adam. That the primary distinctions of the human varieties are but three, has been further maintained by the erudite Prichard; who, while he rejects the nomenclature both of Blumenbach and Cuvier, as implying absolute divisions, arranges the leading varieties of the human skull under three sections, differing from those of Cuvier only by name. That the three sons of Noah who were to 'replenish the earth,' and on whose progeny very opposite destinies were pronounced, should give birth to different races, is what might reasonably be conjectured; but

that the observation of those who do, and of those who do not, believe the Mosaic history, should tend to confirm truth, by pointing out in what these three races do actually differ, both physically and morally, is, to say the least, a singular coincidence. It amounts, in short, to a presumptive evidence, that a mysterious and very beautiful analogy pervades throughout, and teaches us to look beyond natural causes in attempting to account for effects apparently interwoven in the plans of Omnipotence."[6]

In the seventeenth chapter of the Acts of the Apostles, twenty-sixth verse, we find the following language: "And hath made of one blood all nations of men for to dwell on all the face of the earth, and hath determined the times before appointed, and the bounds of their habitation."[7] The Apostle Paul was a missionary. He was, at this time, on a mission to the far-famed city of Athens,—"the eye of Greece, and the fountain of learning and philosophy." He told the "men of Athens," that, as he travelled through their beautiful city, he had not been unmindful of its attractions; that he had not been indifferent to the claims of its citizens to scholarship and culture, and that among other things he noticed an altar erected to an unknown God. He went on to remark, that, great as their city and nation were, God, whose offspring they were, had created other nations, who lived beyond their verdant hills and swelling rivers. And, moreover, that God had created "all nations of men for to dwell on all the face of the earth" out "of one blood." He called their attention to the fact that God had fenced all the nations in by geographical boundaries,—had fixed the limits of their habitation.

We find two leading thoughts in the twenty-sixth verse; viz., that this passage establishes clearly and unmistakably the unity of mankind, in that God created them of one blood; second, he hath determined "the bounds of their habitation,"—hath located them geographically. The language quoted is very explicit. "He hath determined the bounds of their habitation," that is, "all the nations of men.[8] We have, then, the fact, that there are different "nations of men," and that they are all "of one blood," and, therefore, have a common parent. This declaration was made by the Apostle Paul, an inspired writer, a teacher of great erudition, and a scholar in both the Hebrew and the Greek languages.

It should not be forgotten either, that in Paul's masterly discussion of the doctrine of sin,—the fall of man,—he always refers to Adam as the "one man" by whom sin came into the world.[9] His Epistle to the Romans abounds in passages which prove very plainly the unity of mankind. The Acts of the Apostles, as well as the Gospels, prove the unity we seek to establish.

But there are a few who would admit the unity of mankind, and still insist that the Negro does not belong to the human family. It is so preposterous, that one has a keen sense of humiliation in the assured consciousness that he goes rather low to meet the enemies of God's poor; but it can certainly do no harm to meet them with the everlasting truth.

In the Gospel of Luke we read this remarkable historical statement: "And as they led him away, they laid hold upon one Simon, a Cyrenian, coming out of the country, and on him they laid the cross, that he might bear it after Jesus."[10] By referring to the map, the reader will observe that Cyrene is in Libya, on the north coast of Africa. All the commentators we have been able to consult, on the passage quoted below, agree that this man Simon was a Negro,—a black man. John Melville produced a very remarkable sermon from this passage.[11] And many of the most celebrated pictures of "The Crucifixion," in Europe, represent this Cyrenian as black, and give him a very prominent place in the most tragic scene ever witnessed on this earth. In the Acts of the Apostles we have a very full and interesting account of the conversion and immersion of the Ethiopian eunuch, "a man of Ethiopia, an eunuch of great authority under Candace, Queen of the Ethiopians, who had the charge of all her treasure, and had come to Jerusalem for to worship."[12] Here, again, we find that all the commentators agree as to the nationality of the eunuch: he was a Negro; and, by implication, the passage quoted leads us to the belief that the Ethiopians were a numerous and wealthy people. Candace was the queen that made war against Augustus Cæsar twenty years before Christ, and, though not victorious, secured an honorable peace.[13] She reigned in Upper Egypt,—up the Nile,—and lived at Meroe, that ancient city, the very cradle of Egyptian civilization.[14]

> "In the time of our Saviour (and indeed from that time forward), by Ethiopia was meant, in a general sense, the countries south of Egypt, then but imperfectly known; of one of which that Candace was queen whose eunuch was baptized by Philip. Mr. Bruce, on his return from Abyssinia, found in latitude 16° 38' a place called Chendi, where the reigning sovereign was then a queen; and where a tradition existed that a woman, by name Hendaque (which comes as near as possible to the Greek name Χανδακη), once governed all that country. Near this place are extensive ruins, consisting of broken pedestals and obelisks, which Bruce conjectures to be those of Meroe, the capital of the African Ethiopia, which is described by Herodotus as a great city in his time, namely, four hundred years before Christ; and where, separated from the rest of the world by almost impassable deserts, and

enriched by the commercial expeditions of their travelling brethren, the Cushites continued to cultivate, so late as the first century of the Christian era, some portions of those arts and sciences to which the settlers in the cities had always more or less devoted themselves."[15]

But a few writers have asserted, and striven to prove, that the Egyptians and Ethiopians are quite a different people from the Negro. Jeremiah seems to have understood that these people about whom we have been writing were Negroes,—we mean black. "Can the Ethiopian," asks the prophet, "change his skin, or the leopard his spots?" The prophet was as thoroughly aware that the Ethiopian was black, as that the leopard had spots; and Luther's German has for the word "Ethiopia," "Negro-land,"—the country of the blacks.[16] The word "Ethiop" in the Greek literally means "sunburn."

That these Ethiopians were black, we have, in addition to the valuable testimony of Jeremiah, the scholarly evidence of Herodotus, Homer, Josephus, Eusebius, Strabo, and others.

It will be necessary for us to use the term "Cush" farther along in this discussion: so we call attention at this time to the fact, that the Cushites, so frequently referred to in the Scriptures, are the same as the Ethiopians.

Driven from unscriptural and untenable ground on the unity of the races of mankind, the enemies of the Negro, falling back in confusion, intrench themselves in the curse of Canaan. "And Noah awoke from his wine, and knew what his younger son had done unto him. And he said, Cursed be Canaan; a servant of servants shall he be unto his brethren."[17] This passage was the leading theme of the defenders of slavery in the pulpit for many years. Bishop Hopkins says,—

> "The heartless irreverence which Ham, the father of Canaan, displayed toward his eminent parent, whose piety had just saved him from the Deluge, presented the immediate occasion for this remarkable prophecy; but the actual fulfilment was reserved for his posterity after they had lost the knowledge of God, and become utterly polluted by the abominations of heathen idolatry. The Almighty, foreseeing this total degradation of the race, ordained them to servitude or slavery under the descendants of Shem and Japheth, doubtless because he judged it to be their fittest condition. And all history proves how accurately the prediction has been accomplished, even to the present day."[18]

Now, the first thing to be done by those who adopt this view is, to prove, beyond a reasonable doubt, that Noah was inspired to pronounce this prophecy. Noah had been, as a rule, a righteous man. For more than a hundred years he had lifted up his voice against the growing wickedness of the world. His fidelity to the cause of God was unquestioned; and for his faith and correct living, he and his entire household were saved from the Deluge. But after his miraculous deliverance from the destruction that overcame the old world, his entire character is changed. There is not a single passage to show us that he continued his avocation as a preacher. He became a husbandman; he kept a vineyard; and, more than all, he drank of the wine and got drunk! Awaking from a state of inebriation, he knew that Ham had beheld his nakedness and "told his two brethren." But "Shem and Japheth took a garment, and laid it upon both their shoulders, and went backward, and covered the nakedness of their father; and their faces were backward, and they saw not their father's nakedness."[19] It is quite natural to suppose, that, humiliated and chagrined at his sinful conduct, and angered at the behavior of his son and grandson, Ham and Canaan, Noah expressed his disapprobation of Canaan. It was his desire, on the impulse of the moment, that Canaan should suffer a humiliation somewhat commensurate with his offence; and, on the other hand, it was appropriate that he should commend the conduct of his other sons, who sought to hide their father's shame. And all this was done without any inspiration. He simply expressed himself as a fallible man.

Bishop Hopkins, however, is pleased to call this a "prophecy." In order to prophesy, in the scriptural meaning of the word, a man must have the divine unction, and must be moved by the Holy Ghost; and, in addition to this, it should be said, that a true prophecy always comes to pass,—is sure of fulfilment. Noah was not inspired when he pronounced his curse against Canaan, for the sufficient reason that it was not fulfilled. He was not speaking in the spirit of prophecy when he blessed Shem and Japheth, for the good reason that their descendants have often been in bondage. Now, if these words of Noah were prophetic, were inspired of God, we would naturally expect to find all of Canaan's descendants in bondage, and all of Shem's out of bondage,—free! If this prophecy—granting this point to the learned bishop for argument's sake—has not been fulfilled, then we conclude one of two things; namely, these are not the words of God, or they have not been fulfilled. But they were not the words of prophecy, and consequently never had any divine authority. It was Canaan upon whom Noah pronounced the curse: and Canaan was the son of Ham; and Ham, it is said, is the progenitor of the Negro race. The Canaanites were not bondmen, but freemen,—powerful tribes when the Hebrews invaded their country; and from the Canaanites descended the bold and intelligent Carthaginians, as is admitted by the majority of writers on this subject. From Ham proceeded the Egyptians, Libyans, the Phutim, and the Cushim or Ethiopians, who, colonizing the African side of the Red Sea, subsequently extended themselves indefinitely to the west and south of that great continent. Egypt was called Chemia, or the country of Ham; and it has been thought that the Egyptian's deity, Hammon or Ammon, was a deification of Ham.[20] The Carthaginians were successful in numerous wars against the sturdy Romans. So in this, as in many other instances, the prophecy of Noah failed.

Following the chapter containing the prophecy of Noah, the historian records the genealogy of the descendants of Ham and Canaan. We will quote the entire account that we may be assisted to the truth.

> "And the sons of Ham; Cush, and Mizraim, and Phut, and Canaan; and the sons of Cush; Seba, and Havilah, and Sabtah, and Raamah, and Sabtechah: and the sons of Raamah; Sheba and Dedan. And Cush begat Nimrod: he began to be a mighty one in the earth. He was a mighty hunter before the Lord: wherefore it is said, Even as Nimrod the mighty hunter before the Lord. And the beginning of his kingdom was Babel, and Erech, and Accad, and Calneh, in the land of Shinar. Out of that land went forth Asshur, and builded Nineveh, and the city Rehoboth, and Calah, and Resen between Nineveh and Calah: the same is a great city. And Mizraim begat Ludim, and Anamim, and Lehabim, and Naphtuhim, and Pathrusim, and Casluhim (out of whom came Philistim), and Caphtorim. And Canaan begat Sidon his first-born, and Heth, and the Jebusite, and the Amorite, and the Girgasite, and the Hivite, and the Arkite, and the Sinite, and the Arvadite, and the Zemarite, and the Hamathite: and afterward were the families of the Canaanites spread abroad. And the border of the Canaanites was from Sidon, as thou comest to Gerar, unto Gaza; as thou goest, unto Sodom, and Gomorrah, and Admah, and Zeboim, even unto Lasha. These are the sons of Ham, after their families, after their tongues, in their countries, and in their nations."[21]

Here is a very minute account of the family of Ham, who it is said was to share the fate of his son Canaan, and a clear account of the children of Canaan. "Nimrod," says the record, "began to be a mighty one in the earth. He was a mighty hunter before the Lord.... And the beginning of his kingdom," etc. We find that Cush was the oldest son of Ham, and the father of Nimrod the "mighty one in the earth," whose "kingdom" was so extensive. He founded the Babylonian empire, and was the father of the founder of the city of Nineveh, one of the grandest cities of the ancient world. These wonderful achievements were of the children of Cush, the ancestor of the Negroes. It is fair to suppose that this line of Ham's posterity was not lacking in powers necessary to found cities and kingdoms, and maintain government.

Thus far we have been enabled to see, according to the Bible record, that the posterity of Canaan did not go into bondage; that it was a powerful people, both in point of numbers and wealth; and, from the number and character of the cities it built, we infer that it was an intellectual posterity. We conclude that thus far there is no evidence, from a biblical standpoint, that Noah's prophecy was fulfilled. But, notwithstanding the absence of scriptural proof as to the bondage of the children of Canaan, the venerable Dr. Mede says, "There never has been a son of Ham who has shaken a sceptre over the head of Japheth. Shem has subdued Japheth, and Japheth has subdued Shem; but Ham has never subdued either." The doctor is either falsifying the facts of history, or is ignorant of history. The Hebrews were in bondage in Egypt for centuries. Egypt was peopled by Misraim, the second son of Ham. Who were the Shemites? They were Hebrews! The Shemites were in slavery to the Hamites. Melchizedek, whose name was expressive of his character,—king of righteousness (or a righteous king), was a worthy priest of the most high God; and Abimelech, whose name imports parental king, pleaded the integrity of his heart and the righteousness of his nation before God, and his plea was admitted. Yet both these personages appear to have been Canaanites."[22] Melchizedek and Abimelech were Canaanites, and the most sacred and honorable characters in Old-Testament history. It was Abraham, a Shemite, who, meeting Melchizedek, a Canaanite, gave him a tenth of all his spoils. It was Nimrod, a Cushite, who "went to Asher, and built Nineveh," after subduing the Shemites, So it seems very plain that Noah's prophecy did not come true in every respect, and that it was not the word of God. "And God blessed Noah and his sons."[23] God pronounces his blessing upon this entire family, and enjoins upon them to "be fruitful and multiply, and replenish the earth." Afterwards Noah seeks to abrogate the blessing of God by his "cursed be Canaan." But this was only the bitter expression of a drunken and humiliated parent lacking divine authority. No doubt he and his other two sons conformed their conduct to the spirit of the curse pronounced, and treated the Hamites accordingly. The scholarly Dr. William Jones[24] says that Ham was the youngest son of Noah; that he had four sons, Cush, Misraim, Phut, and Canaan; and that they peopled Africa and part of Asia.[25] The Hamites were the offspring of Noah, and one of the three great families that have peopled the earth.[26]

FOOTNOTES:

[1] Gen. i. 27.

[2] Gen. ii. 7.

[3] Gen. ii. 15.

[4] Gen. i. 28.

[5] Gen. vi. 5sq.

[6] Encycl. of Geo., p. 255.

[7] If the Apostle Paul had asserted that all men resembled each other in the color of their skin and the texture of their hair, or even in their physiological make-up, he would have been at war with observation and critical investigation. But, having announced a wonderful truth in reference to the unity of the human race as based upon one blood, science comes to his support, and through the microscope reveals the corpuscles of the blood, and shows that the globule is the same in all human blood.

[8] Deut. xxxii. 8, 9: "When the Most High divided to the nations their inheritance, when he separated the sons of Adam, he set the bounds of the people according to the number of the children of Israel. For the Lord's portion is his people; Jacob is the lot of his inheritance."

[9] Rom. v. 12, 14-21.

[10] Luke xxiii, 26: Acts vi. 9, also second chapter, tenth verse. Matthew records the same fact in the twenty-seventh chapter, thirty-second verse. "And at they came out, they found a man of Cyrene, Simon by name: him they compelled to bear his cross."

[11] See Melville's Sermons.

[12] Acts viii. 27.

[13] Pliny says the Ethiopian government subsisted for several generations in the hands of queens whose name was Candace.

[14] See Liddell and Scott's Greek Lexicon.

[15] Jones's Biblical Cyclopædia, p. 311.

[16] The term Ethiope was anciently given to all those whose color was darkened by the sun.—Smyth's Unity of the Human Races, chap. i. p. 34.

[17] Gen. ix. 24, 25. See also the twenty-sixth and twenty-seventh verses.

[18] Bible Views of Slavery, p. 7.

[19] Gen. ix. 23.

[20] Plutarch, De Iside et Osiride. See also Dr. Morton, and Ethnological Journal, 4th No p. 172.

[21] Gen. x. 6-20.

[22] Dr. Bush.

[23] Gen. ix. I.

[24] Jones's Biblical Cyclopædia, p. 393. Ps. lxxviii. 51.

[25] Ps. cv. 23.

[26] If Noah's utterance were to be regarded as a prophecy, it applied only to the Canaanites, the descendants of Canaan, Noah's grandson. Nothing is said in reference to any person but Canaan in the supposed prophecy.

CHAPTER II
THE NEGRO IN THE LIGHT OF PHILOLOGY, ETHNOLOGY, AND EGYPTOLOGY

> Cushim and Ethiopia.—Ethiopians, White and Black.—Negro Characteristics.—The Dark Continent.—The Antiquity of the Negro.—Indisputable Evidence.—The Military and Social Condition of Negroes.—Cause of Color.—The Term Ethiopian.

THERE seems to be a great deal of ignorance and confusion in the use of the word "Negro;"[27] and about as much trouble attends the proper classification of the inhabitants of Africa. In the preceding chapter we endeavored to prove, not that Ham and Canaan were the progenitors of the Negro races,—for that is admitted by the most consistent enemies of the blacks,—but that the human race is one, and that Noah's curse was not a divine prophecy.

The term "Negro" seems to be applied chiefly to the dark and woolly-haired people who inhabit Western Africa. But the Negro is to be found also in Eastern Africa.[28] Zonaras says, "Chus is the person from whom the Cuseans are derived. They are the same people as the Ethiopians." This view is corroborated by Josephus,[29] Apuleius, and Eusebius. The Hebrew term "Cush" is translated Ethiopia by the Septuagint, Vulgate, and by almost all other versions, ancient and modern, as well as by the English version. "It is not, therefore, to be doubted that the term 'Cushim' has by the interpretation of all ages been translated by 'Ethiopians,' because they were also known by their black color, and their transmigrations, which were easy and frequent."[30] But while it is a fact, supported by both sacred and profane history, that the terms "Cush" and "Ethiopian" were used interchangeably, there seems to be no lack of proof that the same terms were applied frequently to a people who were not Negroes. It should be remembered, moreover, that there were nations who were black, and yet were not Negroes. And the only distinction amongst all these people, who are branches of the Hamitic family, is the texture of the hair. "But it is equally certain, as we have seen, that the term 'Cushite' is applied in Scripture to other branches of the same family; as, for instance, to the Midianites, from whom Moses selected his wife, and who could not have been Negroes. The term 'Cushite,' therefore, is used in Scripture as denoting nations who were not black, or in any respect Negroes, and also countries south of Egypt, whose inhabitants were Negroes; and yet both races are declared to be the descendants of Cush, the son of Ham. Even in Ezekiel's day the interior African nations were not of one race; for he represents Cush, Phut, Lud, and Chub, as either themselves constituting, or as being amalgamated with, 'a mingled people' (Ezek. xxx. 5); 'that is to say,' says Faber, 'it was a nation of Negroes who are represented as very numerous,—all the mingled people.'"[31]

The term "Ethiopia" was anciently given to all those whose color was darkened by the sun. Herodotus, therefore, distinguishes the Eastern Ethiopians who had straight hair, from the Western Ethiopians who had curly or woolly hair.[32]. They are a twofold people, lying extended in a long tract from the rising to the setting sun."[33]

The conclusion is patent. The words "Ethiopia" and "Cush" were used always to describe a black people, or the country where such a people lived. The term "Negro," from the Latin "niger" and the French "noir," means black; and consequently is a modern term, with all the original meaning of Cush and Ethiopia, with a single exception. We called attention above to the fact that all Ethiopians were not of the pure Negro type, but were nevertheless a branch of the original Hamitic family from whence sprang all the dark races. The term "Negro" is now used to designate the people, who, in addition to their dark complexion, have curly or woolly hair. It is in this connection that we shall use the term in this work.[34]

Africa, the home of the indigenous dark races, in a geographic and ethnographic sense, is the most wonderful country in the world It is thoroughly tropical. It has an area in English square miles of 11,556,600, with a population of 192,520,000 souls. It lies between the latitudes of 38° north and 35° south; and is, strictly speaking, an enormous peninsula, attached to Asia by the Isthmus of Suez. The most northern point is the cape, situated a little to the west of Cabo Blanco, and opposite Sicily, which lies in latitude 37° 20' 40" north, longitude 9° 41' east. Its southernmost point is Cabo d'Agulhas, in 34° 49' 15" south; the distance between these two points being 4,330 geographical, or about 5,000 English miles. The westernmost point is Cabo Verde, in longitude 17° 33' west; its easternmost, Cape Jerdaffun, in longitude 51° 21' east, latitude 10° 25' north, the distance between the two points being about the same as its length. The western coasts are washed by the Atlantic, the northern by the Mediterranean, and the eastern by the

Indian Ocean. The shape of this "dark continent" is likened to a triangle or to an Oval. It is rich in oils, ivory, gold, and precious timber. It has beautiful lakes and mighty rivers, that are the insoluble problems of the present times.

Of the antiquity of the Negro there can be no doubt. He is known as thoroughly to history as any of the other families of men. He appears at the first dawn of history, and has continued down to the present time. The scholarly Gliddon says, that "the hieroglyphical designation of 'KeSH,' exclusively applied to African races as distinct from the Egyptian, has been found by Lepsius as far back as the monuments of the sixth dynasty, 3000 B.C. But the great influx of Negro and Mulatto races into Egypt as captives dated from the twelfth dynasty; when, about the twenty-second century, B.C., Pharaoh SESOUR-TASEN extended his conquests up the Nile far into Nigritia. After the eighteenth dynasty the monuments come down to the third century, A.D., without one single instance in the Pharaonic or Ptolemaic periods that Negro labor was ever directed to any agricultural or utilitarian objects."[35] The Negro was found in great numbers with the Sukim, Thut, Lubin, and other African nations, who formed the strength of the army of the king of Egypt, Shishak, when he came against Rehoboam in the year 971 B.C.; and in his tomb, opened in 1849, there were found among his depicted army the exact representation of the genuine Negro race, both in color, hair, and physiognomy. Negroes are also represented in Egyptian paintings as connected with the military campaigns of the eighteenth dynasty. They formed a part of the army of Ibrahim Pacha, and were prized as gallant soldiers at Moncha and in South Arabia.[36] And Herodotus assures us that Negroes were found in the armies of Sesostris and Xerxes; and, at the present time, they are no inconsiderable part of the standing army of Egypt.[37] Herodotus states that eighteen of the Egyptian kings were Ethiopians.[38]

It is quite remarkable to hear a writer like John P. Jeffries, who evidently is not very friendly in his criticisms of the Negro, make such a positive declaration as the following:—

> "Every rational mind must, therefore, readily conclude that the African race has been in existence, as a distinct people, over four thousand two hundred years; and how long before that period is a matter of conjecture only, there being no reliable data upon which to predicate any reliable opinion."[39]

It is difficult to find a writer on ethnology, ethnography, or Egyptology, who doubts the antiquity of the Negroes as a distinct people. Dr. John C. Nott of Mobile, Ala., a Southern man in the widest meaning, in his "Types of Mankind," while he tries to make his book acceptable to Southern slaveholders, strongly maintains the antiquity of the Negro.

> "Ethnological science, then, possesses not only the authoritative testimonies of Lepsius and Birch in proof of the existence of Negro races during the twenty-fourth century, B.C., but, the same fact being conceded by all living Egyptologists, we may hence infer that these Nigritian types were contemporary with the earliest Egyptians."[40]

In 1829 there was a remarkable Theban tomb opened by Mr. Wilkinson, and in 1840 it was carefully examined by Harris and Gliddon. There is a most wonderful collection of Negro scenes in it. Of one of these scenes even Dr. Nott says,—

> "A Negress, apparently a princess, arrives at Thebes, drawn in a plaustrum by a pair of humped oxen, the driver and groom being red-colored Egyptians, and, one might almost infer, eunuchs. Following her are multitudes of Negroes and Nubians, bringing tribute from the upper country, as well as black slaves of both sexes and all ages, among which are some red children, whose fathers were Egyptians. The cause of her advent seems to have been to make offerings in the tomb of a 'royal son of KeSh—Amunoph,' who may have been her husband."[41]

It is rather strange that the feelings of Dr. Nott toward the Negro were so far mollified as to allow him to make a statement that destroys his heretofore specious reasoning about the political and social status of the Negro. He admits the antiquity of the Negro; but makes a special effort to place him in a servile state at all times, and to present him as a vanquished vassal before Ramses III. and other Egyptian kings. He sees no change in the Negro's condition, except that in slavery he is better fed and clothed than in his native home. But, nevertheless, the Negress of whom he makes mention, and the entire picture in the Theban tomb, put down the learned doctor's argument. Here is a Negro princess with Egyptian driver and groom, with a large army of attendants, going on a long journey to the tomb of her royal husband!

There is little room here to question the political and social conditions of the Negroes.[42] They either had enjoyed a long and peaceful rule, or by their valor in offensive warfare had won honorable place by conquest. And the fact that black slaves are mentioned does not in any sense invalidate the historical trustworthiness of the pictures found in this Theban tomb; for Wilkinson says, in reference to the condition of society at this period,—

"It is evident that both white and black slaves were employed as servants; they attended on the guests when invited to the house of their master; and, from their being in the families of priests as well as of the military chiefs, we may infer that they were purchased with money, and that the right of possessing slaves was not confined to those who had taken them in war. The traffic in slaves was tolerated by the Egyptians; and it is reasonable to suppose that many persons were engaged ... in bringing them to Egypt for public sale, independent of those who were sent as part of the tribute, and who were probably, at first, the property of the monarch; nor did any difficulty occur to the Ishmaelites in the purchase of Joseph from his brethren, nor in his subsequent sale to Potiphar on arriving in Egypt."

So we find that slavery was not, at this time, confined to any particular race of people. This Negro princess was as liable to purchase white as black slaves; and doubtless some were taken in successful wars with other nations, while others were purchased as servants.

But we have further evidence to offer in favor of the antiquity of the Negro. In Japan, and in many other parts of the East, there are to be found stupendous and magnificent temples, that are hoary with age. It is almost impossible to determine the antiquity of some of them, in which the idols are exact representations of woolly-haired Negroes, although the inhabitants of those countries to-day have straight hair. Among the Japanese, black is considered a color of good omen. In the temples of Siam we find the idols fashioned like unto Negroes.[43] Osiris, one of the principal deities of the Egyptians, is frequently represented as black.[44] Bubastis, also, the Diana of Greece, and a member of the great Egyptian Triad, is now on exhibition in the British Museum, sculptured in black basalt silting figure.[45] Among the Hindus, Kali, the consort of Siva, one of their great Triad; Crishna, the eighth incarnation of Vishnu; and Vishnu also himself, the second of the Trimerti or Hindu Triad, are represented of a black color.[46] Dr. Morton says,—

"The Sphinx may have been the shrine of the Negro population of Egypt, who, as a people, were unquestionably under our average size. Three million Buddhists in Asia represent their chief deity, Buddha, with Negro features and hair. There are two other images of Buddha, one at Ceylon and the other at Calanee, of which Lieut. Mahoney says, 'Both these statues agree in having crisped hair and long, pendent ear-rings,'"[47]

And the learned and indefatigable Hamilton Smith says,—

"In the plains of India are Nagpoor, and a ruined city without name at the gates of Benares (perhaps the real Kasi of tradition), once adorned with statues of a woolly-haired race."[48]

Now, these substantial and indisputable traces of the march of the Negro races through Japan and Asia lead us to conclude that the Negro race antedates all profane history. And while the great body of the Negro races have been located geographically in Africa, they have been, in no small sense, a cosmopolitan people. Their wanderings may be traced from the rising to the setting sun.

"The remains of architecture and sculpture in India seem to prove an early connection between that country and Africa.... The Pyramids of Egypt, the colossal statues described by Pausanias and others, the Sphinx, and the Hermes Canis, which last bears a strong resemblance to the Varaha Avatar, indicate the style of the same indefatigable workmen who formed the vast excavations of Canarah, the various temples and images of Buddha, and the idols which are continually dug up at Gaya or in its vicinity. These and other indubitable facts may induce no ill-grounded opinion, that Ethiopia and Hindustan were peopled or colonized by the same extraordinary race; in confirmation of which it may be added, that the mountaineers of Bengal and Benhar can hardly be distinguished in some of their features, particularly in their lips and noses, from the modern Abyssinians."[49]

There is little room for speculation here to the candid searcher after truth. The evidence accumulates as we pursue our investigations. Monuments and temples, sepulchred stones and pyramids, rise up to declare the antiquity of the Negro races. Hamilton Smith, after careful and critical investigation, reaches the conclusion, that the Negro type of man was the most ancient, and the indigenous race of Asia, as far north as the lower range of the Himalaya Mountains, and presents at length many curious facts which cannot, he believes, be otherwise explained.

"In this view, the first migrations of the Negro stock, coasting westward by catamarans, or in wretched canoes, and skirting South-western Asia, may synchronize with the earliest appearance of the Negro tribes of Eastern Africa, and just precede the more mixed races, which, like the Ethiopians of Asia, passed the Red Sea at the Straits of Bab-el-Mandeb, ascended the Nile, or crossed that river to the west."[50]

Taking the whole southern portion of Asia westward to Arabia, this conjecture—which likewise was a conclusion drawn, after patient research, by the late Sir T. Stanford Raffles—accounts, more satisfactorily than any other, for the Oriental habits, ideas, traditions, and words which can be traced among several of the present African tribes and in the South-Sea Islands. Traces of this black race are still found along the Himalaya range from the Indus to Indo-China, and the Malay peninsula, and in a mixed form all through the southern states to Ceylon.[51]

But it is unnecessary to multiply evidence in proof of the antiquity of the Negro. His presence in this world was coetaneous with the other families of mankind: here he has toiled with a varied fortune; and here under God—*his* God—he will, in the process of time, work out all the sublime problems connected with his future as a man and a brother.

There are various opinions rife as to the cause of color and texture of hair in the Negro. The generally accepted theory years ago was, that the curse of Cain rested upon this race; while others saw in the dark skin of the Negro the curse of Noah pronounced against Canaan. These two explanations were comforting to that class who claimed that they had a right to buy and sell the Negro; and of whom the Saviour said, "For they bind heavy burdens and grievous to be borne, and lay them on men's shoulders; but they themselves will not move them with one of their fingers."[52] But science has, of later years, attempted a solution of this problem. Peter Barrère, in his treatise on the subject, takes the ground that the bile in the human system has much to do with the color of the skin.[53] This theory, however, has drawn the fire of a number of European scholars, who have combated it with more zeal than skill. It is said that the spinal and brain matter are of a dark, ashy color; and by careful examination it is proven that the blood of Ethiopians is black. These facts would seem to clothe this theory with at least a shadow of plausibility. But the opinion of Aristotle, Strabo, Alexander, and Blumenbach is, that the climate, temperature, and mode of life, have more to do with giving color than any thing else. This is certainly true among animals and plants. There are many instances on record where dogs and wolves, etc., have turned white in winter, and then assumed a different color in the spring. If you start at the north and move south, you will find, at first, that the flowers are very white and delicate; but, as you move toward the tropics, they begin to take on deeper and richer hues until they run into almost endless varieties. Guyot argues on the other side of the question to account for the intellectual diversity of the races of mankind.

> "While all the types of animals and of plants go on decreasing in perfection, from the equatorial to the polar regions, in proportion to the temperatures, man presents to our view his purest, his most perfect type, at the very centre of the temperate continents,—at the centre of Asia, Europe, in the regions of Iran, of Armenia, and of the Caucasus; and, departing from this geographical centre in the three grand directions of the lands, the types gradually lose the beauty of their forms, in proportion to their distance, even to the extreme points of the southern continents, where we find the most deformed and degenerate races, and the lowest in the scale of humanity."[54]

The learned professor seeks to carry out his famous geographical argument, and, with great skill and labor, weaves his theory of the influence of climate upon the brain and character of man. But while no scholar would presume to combat the theory that plants take on the most gorgeous hues as one nears the equator, and that the races of mankind take on a darker color in their march toward the equator, certainly no student of Oriental history will assent to the unsupported doctrine, that the intensity of the climate of tropical countries affects the intellectual status of races. If any one be so prejudiced as to doubt this, let him turn to "Asiatic Researches," and learn that the dark races have made some of the most invaluable contributions to science, literature, civil-engineering, art, and architecture that the world has yet known. Here we find the cradle of civilization, ancient and remote.

Even changes and differences in color are to be noted in almost every community.

> "As we go westward we observe the light color predominating over the dark; and then, again, when we come within the influence of damp from the sea-air, we find the shade deepened into the general blackness of the coast population."

The artisan and farm-laborer may become exceedingly dark from exposure, and the sailor is frequently so affected by the weather that it is next to impossible to tell his nationality.

> "It is well known that the Biscayan women are a shining white, the inhabitants of Granada on the contrary dark, to such an extent, that, in this region, the pictures of the blessed Virgin and other saints are painted of the same color."[55]

The same writer calls attention to the fact, that the people on the Cordilleras, who live under the mountains towards the west, and are, therefore, exposed to the Pacific Ocean, are quite, or nearly, as fair in complexion as the Europeans; whereas, on the contrary, the inhabitants of the opposite side, exposed to the burning sun and scorching winds, are copper-colored. Of this theory of climateric influence we shall say more farther on.

It is held by some eminent physicians in Europe and America, that the color of the skin depends upon substances external to the *cutis vera*. Outside of the *cutis* are certain layers of a substance various in consistence, and scarcely perceptible: here is the home and seat of color; and these may be regarded as secretions from the vessels of the *cutis*. The dark color of the Negro principally depends on the substance interposed between the true skin and the scarf-skin. This substance presents different appearances: and it is described sometimes as a sort of organized network or reticular tissue; at others, as a mere mucous or slimy layer; and it is odd that these somewhat incompatible ideas are both conveyed by the term *reticulum mucosum* given to the intermediate portion of the skin by its orignal discoverer, Malpighi. There is, no doubt, something plausible in all the theories advanced as to the color and hair of the Negro; but it is verily all speculation. One theory is about as valuable as another.

Nine hundred years before Christ the poet Homer, speaking of the death of Memnon, killed at the siege of Troy, says, "He was received by his Ethiopians." This is the first use of the word Ethiopia in the Greek; and it is derived from the roots αιθω, "to burn," and ωψ, "face." It is safe to assume, that, when God dispersed the sons of Noah, he fixed the "bounds of their habitation," and, that, from the earth and sky the various races have secured their civilization. He sent the different nations into separate parts of the earth. He gave to each its racial peculiarities, and adaptability for the climate into which it went. He gave color, language, and civilization; and, when by wisdom we fail to interpret his inscrutable ways, it is pleasant to know that "he worketh all things after the counsel of his own mind."

FOOTNOTES:

[27] Edward W. Blyden, LL.D., of Liberia, says, "Supposing that this term was originally used as a phrase of contempt, is it not with us to elevate it? How often has it not happened that names originally given in reproach have been afterwards adopted as a title of honor by those against whom it was used?—Methodists, Quakers, etc. But as a proof that no

unfavorable signification attached to the word when first employed, I may mention, that, long before the slave-trade began, travellers found the blacks on the coast of Africa preferring to be called Negroes" (see Purchas' Pilgrimage ...). And in all the pre-slavetrade literature the word was spelled with a capital N. It was the slavery of the blacks which afterwards degraded the term. To say that the name was invented to degrade the race, some of whose members were reduced to slavery, is to be guilty of what in grammar is called a hysteron proteron. The disgrace became attached to the name in consequence of slavery; and what we propose to do is, now that slavery is abolished, to restore it to its original place and legitimate use, and therefore to restore the capital N."

[28] Prichard, vol. ii. p. 44.

[29] Josephus, Antiq., lib. 2, chap. 6.

[30] Poole.

[31] Smyth's Unity Human Races, chap. II, p. 41.

[32] Herodotus, vii., 69, 70. Ancient Univ. Hist., vol. xviii. pp. 254, 255.

[33] Strabo, vol. I. p. 60.

[34] It is not wise, to say the least, for intelligent Negroes in America to seek to drop the word "Negro." It is a good, strong, and healthy word, and ought to live. It should be covered with glory: let Negroes do it.

[35] Journal of Ethnology, No. 7, p. 310.

[36] Pickering's Races of Men, pp. 185-89.

[37] Burckhardt's Travels, p. 341.

[38] Euterpe, lib. 6.

[39] Jeffries's Nat. Hist. of Human Race, p. 315.

[40] Types of Mankind, p. 259.

[41] Types of Mankind, p. 262.

[42] Even in Africa it is found that Negroes possess great culture. Speaking of Sego, the capital of Bambara, Mr. Park says: "The view of this extensive city, the numerous, canoes upon the river, the crowded population, and the cultivated state of the surrounding country, formed altogether a

prospect of civilization and magnificence which I little expected to find in the bosom of Africa." See Park's Travels, chap. ii.

Mr. Park also adds, that the population of this city, Sego, is about thirty thousand. It had mosques, and even ferries were busy conveying men and horses over the Niger.

[43] See Ambassades Mémorables de la Companie des Indes orientales des Provinces Unies vers les Empereurs du Japan, Amst., 1680; and Kaempfer.

[44] Wilkinson's Egypt, vol. iii. p. 340.

[45] Coleman's Mythology of the Hindus, p. 91. Dr. William Jones, vol. iii., p. 377.

[46] Asiatic Researches, vol. vi. pp. 436-448.

[47] Heber's Narrative, vol. i. p. 254.

[48] Nat. Hist. of the Human Species, pp. 209, 214, 217.

[49] Asiatic Researches, vol. i. p 427. Also Sir William Jones, vol. iii. 3d disc.

[50] Nat. Hist. Human Species, p. 126.

[51] Prichard, pp. 188-219.

[52] Matt. xxiii. 4.

[53] Discours sur la cause physicale de la couleur des nègres.

[54] Earth and Man. Lecture x. pp. 254, 255.

[55] Blumenbach, p. 107.

CHAPTER III
PRIMITIVE NEGRO CIVILIZATION

The Ancient and High Degree of Negro Civilization.—Egypt, Greece, and Rome borrow from the Negro the Civilization that made them Great.—Cause of the Decline and Fall of Negro Civilization.—Confounding the Terms "Negro" and "African."

IT is fair to presume that God gave all the races of mankind civilization to start with. We infer this from the known character of the Creator. Before Romulus founded Rome, before Homer sang, when Greece was in its infancy, and the world quite young, "hoary Meroe" was the chief city of the Negroes along the Nile. Its private and public buildings, its markets and public squares, its colossal walls and stupendous gates, its gorgeous chariots and alert footmen, its inventive genius and ripe scholarship, made it the cradle of civilization, and the mother of art. It was the queenly city of Ethiopia,—for it was founded by colonies of Negroes. Through its open gates long and ceaseless caravans, laden with gold, silver, ivory, frankincense, and palm-oil, poured the riches of Africa into the capacious lap of the city. The learning of this people, embalmed in the immortal hieroglyphic, flowed adown the Nile, and, like spray, spread over the delta of that time-honored stream, on by the beautiful and venerable city of Thebes,—the city of a hundred gates, another monument to Negro genius and civilization, and more ancient than the cities of the Delta,—until Greece and Rome stood transfixed before the ancient glory of Ethiopia! Homeric mythology borrowed its very essence from Negro hieroglyphics; Egypt borrowed her light from the venerable Negroes up the Nile. Greece went to school to the Egyptians, and Rome turned to Greece for law and the science of warfare. England dug down into Rome twenty centuries to learn to build and plant, to establish a government, and maintain it. Thus the flow of civilization has been from the East—the place of light—to the West; from the Oriental to the Occidental. (God fixed the mountains east and west in Europe.)

> "Tradition universally represents the earliest men descending, it is true, from the high table-lands of this

continent; but it is in the low and fertile plains lying at their feet, with which we are already acquainted, that they unite themselves for the first time in natural bodies, in tribes, with fixed habitations, devoting themselves to husbandry, building cities, cultivating the arts,—in a word, forming well-regulated societies. The traditions of the Chinese place the first progenitors of that people on the high table-land, whence the great rivers flow: they mike them advance, station by station as far as the shores of the ocean. The people of the Brahmins come down from the regions of the Hindo-Khu, and from Cashmere, into the plains of the Indus and the Ganges; Assyria and Bactriana receive their inhabitants from the table-lands of Armenia and Persia.

"These alluvial plains, watered by their twin rivers, were better formed than all other countries of the globe to render the first steps of man, an infant still, easy in the career of civilized life. A rich soil, on which overflowing rivers spread every year a fruitful loam, as in Egypt, and one where the plough is almost useless, so movable and so easily tilled is it, a warm climate, finally, secure to the inhabitants of these fortunate regions plentiful harvests in return for light labor. Nevertheless, the conflict with the river itself and with the desert,—which, on the banks of the Euphrates, as on those of the Nile and the Indus, is ever threatening to invade the cultivated lands,—the necessity of irrigation, the inconstancy of the seasons, keep forethought alive, and give birth to the useful arts and to the sciences of observation. The abundance of resources, the absence of every obstacle, of all separation between the different parts of these vast plains, allow the aggregation of a great number of men upon one and the same space, and facilitate the formation of those mighty primitive states which amaze us by the grandeur of their proportions.

"Each of them finds upon its own soil all that is necessary for a brilliant exhibition of its resources. We see those nations come rapidly forward, and reach in the remotest antiquity a degree of culture of which the temples and the monuments of Egypt and of India, and the recently discovered palaces of Nineveh are living and glorious witnesses.

"Great nations, then, are separately formed in each of these areas, circumscribed by nature within natural limits. Each has its religion, its social principles, its civilization severally. But nature, as we have seen, has separated them; little intercourse is established between them; the social principle on which they are founded is exhausted by the very formation of the social state they enjoy, and is never renewed. A common life is wanting to them: they do not reciprocally share with each other their riches. With them movement is stopped: every thing becomes stable and tends to remain stationary.

"Meantime, in spite of the peculiar seal impressed on each of these Oriental nations by the natural conditions in the midst of which they live, they have, nevertheless some grand characteristics common to all, some family traits that betray the nature of the continent and the period of human progress to which they belong, making them known on the one side as Asiatic, and on the other side as primitive."[56]

Is it asked what caused the decline of all this glory of the primitive Negro? why this people lost their position in the world's history? Idolatry! Sin![57]

Centuries have flown apace, tribes have perished, cities have risen and fallen, and even empires, whose boast was their duration, have crumbled, while Thebes and Meroe stood. And it is a remarkable fact, that the people who built those cities are less mortal than their handiwork. Notwithstanding their degradation, their woes and wrongs, the perils of the forest and dangers of the desert, this remarkable people have not been blotted out. They still live, and are multiplying in the earth. Certainly they have been preserved for some wise purpose, in the future to be unfolded.

But, again, what was the cause of the Negro's fall from his high state of civilization? It was forgetfulness of God, idolatry! "Righteousness exalteth a nation; but sin is a reproach to any people."

The Negro tribes of Africa are as widely separated by mental, moral, physical, and social qualities as the Irish, Huns, Copts, and Druids are. Their location on the Dark Continent, their surroundings, and the amount of light that has come to them from the outside world, are the thermometer of their civilization. It is as manifestly improper to call all Africans Negroes as to call, Americans Indians.

"The Negro nations of Africa differ widely as to their manner of life and their characters, both of mind and body, in different parts of that continent, according as they have existed under different moral and physical conditions. Foreign culture, though not of a high degree, has been introduced among the population of some regions; while from others it has been shut out by almost impenetrable barriers, beyond which the aboriginal people remain secluded amid their mountains and forests, in a state of instinctive existence,—a state from which, history informs us, that human races have hardly emerged, until moved by some impulse from without. Neither Phoenician nor Roman culture seems to have penetrated into Africa beyond the Atlantic region and the desert. The activity and enthusiasm of the propagators of Islam have reached farther. In the fertile low countries beyond the Sahara, watered by rivers which descend northward from the central highlands, Africa has contained for centuries several Negro empires, originally founded by Mohammedans. The Negroes of this part of Africa are people of a very different description from the black pagan nations farther towards the South. They have adopted many of the arts of civilized society, and have subjected themselves to governments and political institutions. They practise agriculture, and have learned the necessary, and even some of the ornamental, arts of life, and dwell in towns of considerable extent; many of which are said to contain ten thousand, and even thirty thousand inhabitants,—a circumstance which implies a considerable advancement in industry and the resources of subsistence. All these improvements were introduced into the interior of Africa three or four centuries ago; and we have historical testimony, that in the region where trade and agriculture now prevail the population consisted, previous to the introduction of Islam, of savages as wild and fierce as the natives farther towards the south, whither the missionaries of that religion have never penetrated. It hence appears that human society has not been in all parts of Africa stationary and unprogressive from age to age. The first impulse to civilization was late in reaching the interior of that continent, owing to local circumstances which are easily understood; but, when it had once taken place, an improvement has resulted which is, perhaps, proportional to the early progress of human culture in other more favored regions of the world."[58]

But in our examination of African tribes we shall not confine ourselves to that class of people known as Negroes, but call attention to other tribes as well. And while, in this country, all persons with a visible admixture of Negro blood in them are considered Negroes, it is technically incorrect. For the real Negro was not the sole subject sold into slavery: very many of the noblest types of mankind in Africa have, through the uncertainties of war, found their way to the horrors of the middle passage, and finally to the rice and cotton fields of the Carolinas and Virginias. So, in speaking of the race in this country, in subsequent chapters, I shall refer to them as *colored people* or *Negroes*.

FOOTNOTES:

[56] Earth and Man, pp. 300-302.

[57] It is a remarkable fact, that the absence of salt in the food of the Eastern nations, especially the dark nations or races, has been very deleterious. An African child will eat salt by the handful, and, once tasting it, will cry for it. The ocean is the womb of nature; and the Creator has wisely designed salt as the savor of life, the preservative element in human food.

[58] Physical History of Mankind, vol. ii. pp. 45, 46.

CHAPTER IV
NEGRO KINGDOMS OF AFRICA

BENIN: Its Location.—Its Discovery by the Portuguese.—Introduction of the Catholic Religion.—The King as a Missionary,—His Fidelity to the Church Purchased by White Wife.—Decline of Religion.—Introduction of Slavery.—Suppression of the Trade by the English Government.—Restoration and Peace.

DAHOMEY: Its Location.—Origin of the Kingdom.—Meaning of the Name.—War.—Capture of the English Governor, and his Death.—The Military Establishment.—Women as Soldiers.—Wars and their Objects.—Human Sacrifices.—The King a Despot.—His Powers.—His Wives.—Polygamy.—Kingly Succession.—Coronation.—Civil and Criminal Law.—Revenue System.—Its Future.

YORUBA: Its Location.—Slavery and its Abolition.—Growth of the People of Abeokuta.—Missionaries and Teachers from Sierra Leone.—Prosperity and Peace attend the People.—Capacity of the People for Civilization.—Bishop Crowther.—His Influence.

BENIN

THE vast territory stretching from the Volta River on the west to the Niger in the Gulf of Benin on the east, the Atlantic Ocean on the south, and the Kong Mountains on the north, embraces the three powerful Negro kingdoms of Benin, Dahomey, and Yoruba. From this country, more than from any other part of Africa, were the people sold into American slavery. Two or three hundred years ago there were several very powerful Negro empires in Western Africa. They had social and political government, and were certainly a very orderly people. But in 1485 Alfonso de Aviro, a Portuguese, discovered Benin, the most easterly province; and as an almost immediate result the slave-trade was begun. It is rather strange, too, in the face of the fact, that, when De Aviro returned to the court of Portugal, an ambassador from the Negro king of Benin accompanied him for the purpose of requesting the presence of Christian missionaries among this people. Portugal became interested, and despatched Fernando Po to the Gulf of Benin; who, after discovering the island that bears his name, ascended the Benin River to Gaton, where he located a Portuguese colony. The Romish Church lifted her standard here. The brothers of the Society of Jesus, if they did not convert the king, certainly had him in a humor to bring all of his regal powers to bear upon his subjects to turn them into the Catholic Church. He actually took the contract to turn his subjects over to this Church! But this shrewd savage did not agree to undertake this herculean task for nothing. He wanted a white wife. He told the missionaries that he would deliver his subjects to Christianity for a white wife, and they agreed to furnish her. Some priests were sent to the Island of St. Thomas to hunt the wife. This island had, even at that early day, a considerable white population. A strong appeal was made to the sisters there to consider this matter as a duty to the holy Church. It was set forth as a missionary enterprise. After some contemplation, one of the sisters agreed to accept the hand of the Negro king. It was a noble act, and one for which she should have been canonized, but we believe never was.

The Portuguese continued to come. Gaton grew. The missionary worked with a will. Attention was given to agriculture and commerce. But the climate was wretched. Sickness and death swept the Portuguese as the fiery breath of tropical lightning. They lost their influence over the people. They established the slave-trade, but the Church and slave-pen would not agree. The inhuman treatment they bestowed upon the people gave rise to the gravest suspicions as to the sincerity of the missionaries. History gives us the sum total of a religious effort that was not of God. There isn't a trace of Roman Catholicism in that country, and the last state of that people is worse than the former.

The slave-trade turned the heads of the natives. Their cruel and hardened hearts assented to the crime of man-stealing. They turned aside from agricultural pursuits. They left their fish-nets on the seashore, their cattle uncared for, their villages neglected, and went forth to battle against their weaker neighbors. They sold their prisoners of war to slave-dealers on the coast, who gave them rum and tobacco as an exceeding great reward. When war failed to give from its bloody and remorseless jaws the victims for whom a ready market awaited, they turned to duplicity, treachery, and cruelty. "And men's worst enemies were those of their own household." The person suspicioned of witchcraft was speedily found guilty, and adjudged to slavery. The guilty and the innocent often shared the same fate. The thief, the adulterer, and the aged were seized by the rapacity that pervaded the people, and were hurled into the hell of slavery.

Now, as a result of this condition of affairs, the population was depleted, the people grew indolent and vicious, and finally the empire was rent with political feuds. Two provinces was the result. One still bore the name of Benin, the other was called Waree. The capital of the former contains about 38,000 inhabitants, and the chief town and island of Waree only contain about 16,000 of a population.

Finally England was moved to a suppression of the slave-trade at this point. The ocean is very calm along this coast, which enabled her fleets to run down slave-vessels and make prizes of them. This had a salutary influence upon the natives. Peace and quietness came as angels. A spirit of thrift possessed the people. They turned to the cultivation of the fields and to commercial pursuits. On the river Bonny, and along other streams, large and flourishing palm-oil marts sprang up; and a score or more of vessels are needed to export the single article of palm-oil. The morals of the people are not what they ought to be; but they have, on the whole, made wonderful improvement during the last fifty years.

DAHOMEY

This nation is flanked by Ashantee on the west, and Yoruba on the east; running from the seacoast on the south to the Kong mountains on the north. It is one hundred and eighty miles in width, by two hundred in breadth. Whydah is the principal town on the seacoast. The story runs, that, about two hundred and seventy-five years ago, Tacudons, chief of the Foys, carried a siege against the city of Abomey. He made a solemn vow to the gods, that, if they aided him in pushing the city to capitulate, he would build a palace in honor of the victory. He succeeded. He laid the foundations of his palace, and then upon them ripped open the bowels of Da. He called the building *Da-Omi*, which meant Da's belly. He took the title of King of Dahomey, which has remained until the present time. The neighboring tribes, proud and ambitious, overran the country, and swept Whydah and adjacent places with the torch and spear. Many whites fell into their hands as prisoners; all of whom were treated with great consideration, save the English governor of the above-named town. They put him to death, because, as they charged, he had incited and excited the people of Dahomey to resist their king.

This is a remarkable people. They are as cruel as they are cunning. The entire population is converted into an army: even women are soldiers. Whole regiments of women are to be found in the army of the king of Dahomey, and they are the best foot-regiments in the kingdom. They are drilled at stated periods, are officered, and well disciplined. The army is so large, and is so constantly employed in predatory raids upon neighboring tribes, that the consuming element is greater than the producing. The object of these raids was threefold: to get slaves for human sacrifices, to pour the blood of the victims on the graves of their ancestors yearly, and to secure human skulls to pave the court of the king and to ornament the walls about the palace! After a successful war, the captives are brought to the capital of the kingdom. A large platform is erected in the great market space, encircled by a parapet about three feet high. The platform blazes with rich clothes, elaborate umbrellas, and all the evidences of kingly wealth and splendor, as well as the spoils taken in battle. The king occupies a seat in the centre of the platform, attended by his imperturbable wives. The captives, rum, tobacco, and cowries are now ready to be thrown to the surging mob below. They have fought gallantly, and now clamor for their reward. "Feed us, king!" they cry, "feed us, king! for we are hungry!" and as the poor captives are tossed to the mob they are despatched without ceremony!

But let us turn from this bloody and barbarous scene. The king is the most absolute despot in the world. He is heir-at-law to all his subjects. He is regarded as a demigod. It is unlawful to indicate that the king eats, sleeps, or drinks. No one is allowed to approach him, except his nobles, who at a court levee disrobe themselves of all their elegant garments, and, prostrate upon the ground, they crawl into his royal presence. The whole people are the cringing lickspittles of the nobles in turn. Every private in the army is ambitious to please the king by valor. The king is literally monarch of all he surveys. He is proprietor of the land, and has at his disposal every thing animate or inanimate in his kingdom. He has about three thousand wives. [59] Every man who would marry must buy his spouse from the king; and, while the system of polygamy obtains everywhere throughout the kingdom, the subject must have care not to secure so many wives that it would appear that he is attempting to rival the king. The robust women are consigned to the military service. But the real condition of woman in this kingdom is slavery of the vilest type. She owns nothing. She is always in the market, and lives in a state of constant dread of being sold. When the king dies, a large number of his wives are sacrificed upon his grave. This fact inspires them to take good care of him! In case of death, the king's brother, then his nephew, and so on, take the throne. An inauguration generally lasts six days, during which time hundreds of human lives are sacrificed in honor of the new monarch.

The code of Dahomey is very severe. Witchcraft is punished with death; and in this regard stalwart old Massachusetts borrowed from the barbarian. Adultery is punished by slavery or sudden death. Thieves are also sold into slavery. Treason and cowardice and murder are punished by death. The civil code is as complicated as the criminal is severe. Over every village, is a Caboceer, equivalent to our mayor. He can convene a court by prostrating himself and kissing the ground. The court convenes, tries and condemns the criminal. If it be a death sentence, he is delivered to a man called the Milgan, or equivalent to our sheriff, who is the ranking officer in the state. If the criminal is sentenced to slavery, he is delivered to the Mayo, who is second in rank to the Milgan, or about like our turnkey or jailer. All sentences must be referred to the king for his approval; and all executions take place at the capital, where notice is given of the same by a public crier in the market-places.

The revenue system of this kingdom is oppressive. The majority of slaves taken in war are the property of the king. A tax is levied on each person or slave exported from the kingdom. In relation to domestic commerce, a tax is levied on every article of food and clothing. A custom-service is organized, and the tax-collectors are shrewd and exacting.

The religion of the people is idolatry and fetich, or superstition. They have large houses where they worship snakes; and so great is their reverence for the reptile, that, if any one kills one that has escaped, he is punished with death. But, above their wild and superstitious notions, there is an ever-present consciousness of a Supreme Being. They seldom mention the name of God, and then with fear and trembling.

> "The worship of God in the absurd symbol of the lower animals I do not wish to defend: but it is all that these poor savages can do; and is not that less impious than to speak of the Deity with blasphemous familiarity, as our illiterate preachers often do?"[60]

But this people are not in a hopeless condition of degradation.

> "The Wesleyan Missionary Society of England have had a mission-station at Badagry for some years, and not without some important and encouraging tokens of success.... The king, it is thought, is more favorable to Christian missions now than he formerly was."[61]

And we say Amen!

YORUBA

This kingdom extends from the seacoast to the river Niger, by which it is separated from the kingdom of Nufi. It contains more territory than either Benin or Dahomey. Its principal seaport is Lagos. For many years it was a great slave-mart, and only gave up the traffic under the deadly presence of English guns. Its facilities for the trade were great. Portuguese and Spanish slave-traders took up their abode here, and, teaching the natives the use of fire-arms, made a stubborn stand for their lucrative enterprise; but in 1852 the slave-trade was stopped, and the slavers driven from the seacoast. The place came under the English flag; and, as a result, social order and business enterprise have been restored and quickened. The slave-trade wrought great havoc among this people. It is now about fifty-five years since a few weak and fainting tribes, decimated by the slave-trade, fled to Ogun, a stream seventy-five miles from the coast, where they took refuge in a cavern. In the course of time they were joined by other tribes that fled before the scourge of slave-hunters. Their common danger gave them a commonality of interests. They were, at first, reduced to very great want. They lived for a long time on berries, herbs, roots, and such articles of food as nature furnished without money and without price; but, leagued together to defend their common rights, they grew bold, and began to spread out around their hiding-place, and engage in agriculture. Homes and villages began to rise, and the desert to blossom as the rose. They finally chose a leader,—a wise and judicious man by the name of Shodeke; and one hundred and thirty towns were united under one government. In 1853, less than a generation, a feeble people had grown to be nearly one hundred thousand (100,000); and Abeokuta, named for their cave, contains at present nearly three hundred thousand souls.

In 1839 some colored men from Sierra Leone, desirous of engaging in trade, purchased a small vessel, and called at Lagos and Badagry. They had been slaves in this country, and had been taken to Sierra Leone, where they had received a Christian education. Their visit, therefore, was attended with no ordinary interest. They recognized many of their friends and kindred, and were agreeably surprised at the wonderful change that had taken place in so short a time. They returned to Sierra Leone, only to inspire their neighbors with a zeal for commercial and missionary enterprise. Within three years, five hundred of the best colored people of Sierra Leone set out for Lagos and Badagry on the seacoast, and then moved overland to Abeokuta, where they intended to make their home. In this company of noble men were merchants, mechanics, physicians, school-teachers, and clergymen. Their people had fought for deliverance from physical bondage:

these brave missionaries had come to deliver them from intellectual and spiritual bondage. The people of Abeokuta gave the missionaries a hearty welcome. The colony received new blood and energy. School-buildings and churches rose on every hand. Commerce was revived, and even agriculture received more skilful attention. Peace and and plenty began to abound. Every thing wore a sunny smile, and many tribes were bound together by the golden cords of civilization, and sang their *Te Deum* together. Far-away England caught their songs of peace, and sent them agricultural implements, machinery, and Christian ministers and teachers. So, that, nowhere on the continent of Africa is there to be found so many renewed households, so many reclaimed tribes, such substantial results of a vigorous, Christian civilization.

The forces that quickened the inhabitants of Abeokuta were not all objective, exoteric: there were subjective and inherent forces at work in the hearts of the people. They were capable of civilization,—longed for it; and the first blaze of light from without aroused their slumbering forces, and showed them the broad and ascending road that led to the heights of freedom and usefulness. That they sought this road with surprising alacrity, we have the most abundant evidence. Nor did all the leaders come from abroad. Adgai, in the Yoruba language, but Crowther, in English, was a native of this country. In 1822 he was sold into slavery at the port of Badagry. The vessel that was to bear him away to the "land of chains and stocks" was captured by a British man-of-war, and taken to Sierra Leone. Here he came under the influence of Christian teachers. He proved to be one of the best pupils in his school. He received a classical education, fitted for the ministry, and then hastened back to his native country to carry the gospel of peace. It is rather remarkable, but he found his mother and several sisters still "in the gall of bitterness and in the bonds of iniquity." The son and brother became their spiritual teacher, and, ere long, had the great satisfaction of seeing them "clothed, in their right mind, and sitting at the feet of Jesus." His influence has been almost boundless. A man of magnificent physical proportions,—tall, a straight body mounted by a ponderous head, shapely, with a kind eye, benevolent face, a rich cadence in his voice,—the "black Bishop" Crowther is a princely looking man, who would attract the attention of cultivated people anywhere. He is a man of eminent piety, broad scholarship, and good works. He has translated the Bible into the Yoruba language, founded schools, and directed the energies of his people with a matchless zeal. His beautiful and beneficent life is an argument in favor of the possibilities of Negro manhood so long injured by the dehumanizing influences of slavery. Others have caught the inspiration that has made Bishop Crowther's life "as terrible as an army with banners" to the enemies of Christ and humanity, and are working to dissipate the darkness of that land of night.

FOOTNOTES:

[59] The king of Dahomey is limited to 3,333 wives! It is hardly fair to suppose that his majesty feels cramped under the ungenerous act that limits the number of his wives.

[60] Savage Africa, p. 51.

[61] Western Africa, p. 207.

CHAPTER V
THE ASHANTEE EMPIRE

Its Location and Extent.—Its Famous Kings.—The Origin of the Ashantees Obscure.—The War with Denkera.—The Ashantees against the Field conquer Two Kingdoms and annex them.—Death of Osai Tutu.—The Envy of the King of Dahomey.—Invasion of the Ashantee Country by the King of Dahomey.—His Defeat shared by his Allies.—Akwasi pursues the Army of Dahomey into its own Country.—Gets a Mortal Wound and suffers a Humiliating Defeat.—The King of Dahomey sends the Royal Kudjoh His Congratulations.—Kwamina deposed for attempting to introduce Mohammedanism into the Kingdom.—The Ashantees conquer the Mohammedans.—Numerous Wars.—Invasion of the Fanti Country.—Death of Sir Charles McCarthy.—Treaty.—Peace.

THE kingdom of Ashantee lies between the Kong Mountains and the vast country of the Fantis. The country occupied by the Ashantees was, at the first, very small; but by a series of brilliant conquests they finally secured a territory of three hundred square miles. One of their most renowned kings, Osai Tutu, during the last century, added to Ashantee by conquest the kingdoms of Sarem, Buntuku, Warsaw, Denkera, and Axim. Very little is known as to the origin of the Ashantees. They were discovered in the early part of the eighteenth century in the great valley between the Kong Mountains and the river Niger, from whence they were driven by the Moors and Mohammedan Negroes. They exchanged the bow for fire-arms, and soon became a warlike people. Osai Tutu led in a desperate engagement against the king of Denkera, in which the latter was slain, his army was put to rout, and large quantities of booty fell into the hands of the victorious Ashantees. The king of Axim unwittingly united his forces to those of the discomfited Denkera, and, drawing the Ashantees into battle again, sustained heavy losses, and was put to flight. He was compelled to accept the most exacting conditions of peace, to pay the king of the Ashantees four thousand ounces of gold to defray the expenses of the war, and have his territory made tributary to the conqueror. In a subsequent battle Osai Tutu was surprised and killed. His courtiers and wives were made prisoners, with much goods. This enraged the Ashantees, and they reeked vengeance on the heads of the inhabitants of Kromanti, who laid the disastrous ambuscade. They failed, however, to recover the body of their slain king; but many of his attendants were retaken, and numerous enemies, whom they sacrificed to the manes of their dead king at Kumasi.

After the death of the noble Osai Tutu, dissensions arose among his followers. The tribes and kingdoms he had bound to his victorious chariot-wheels began to assert their independence. His life-work began to crumble. Disorder ran riot; and, after a few ambitious leaders were convinced that the throne of Ashantee demanded brains and courage, they cheerfully made way for the coronation of Osai Opoko, brother to the late king. He was equal to the existing state of affairs. He proved himself a statesman, a soldier, and a wise ruler. He organized his army, and took the field in person against the revolting tribes. He reconquered all the lost provinces. He defeated his most valorous foe, the king of Gaman, after driving him into the Kong Mountains. When his jealous underlings sought his overthrow by conspiracy, he conquered them by an appeal to arms. His rule was attended by the most lasting and beneficent results. He died in 1742, and was succeeded by his brother, Osai Akwasi.

The fame and military prowess of the kings of the Ashantees were borne on every passing breeze, and told by every fleeing fugitive. The whole country was astounded by the marvellous achievements of this people, and not a little envy was felt among adjoining nations. The king of Dahomey especially felt like humiliating this people in battle. This spirit finally manifested itself in feuds, charges, complaints, and, laterally, by actual hostilities. The king of Dahomey felt that he had but one rival, the king of Ashantee. He felt quite sure of victory on account of the size, spirit, and discipline of his army. It was idle at this time, and was ordered to the Ashantee border. The first engagement took place near the Volta. The king of Dahomey had succeeded in securing an alliance with the armies of Kawaku and Bourony, but the valor and skill of the Ashantees were too much for the invading armies. If King Akwasi had simply maintained his defensive position, his victory would have been lasting; but, overjoyed at his success, he unwittingly pursued the enemy beyond the Volta, and carried war into the kingdom of Dahomey. Troops fight with great desperation in their own country. The Ashantee army was struck on its exposed flanks, its splendid companies of Caboceers went down before the intrepid Amazons. Back to the Volta, the boundary line between the two empires, fled the routed

Ashantees. Akwasi received a mortal wound, from which he died in 1752, when his nephew, Osai Kudjoh, succeeded to the throne.

Three brothers had held the sceptre over this empire, but now it passed to another generation. The new king was worthy of his illustrious family. After the days of mourning for his royal uncle were ended, before he ascended the throne, several provinces revolted. He at once took the field, subdued his recalcitrant subjects, and made them pay a heavy tribute. He won other provinces by conquest, and awed the neighboring tribes until an unobstructed way was open to his invincible army across the country to Cape Palmas. His fame grew with each military manoeuvre, and each passing year witnessed new triumphs. Fawning followed envy in the heart of the king of Dahomey; and a large embassy was despatched to the powerful Kudjoh, congratulating him upon his military achievements, and seeking a friendly alliance between the two governments. Peace was now restored; and the armies of Ashantee very largely melted into agricultural communities, and great prosperity came. But King Kudjoh was growing old in the service of his people; and, as he could no longer give his personal attention to public affairs, dissensions arose in some of the remote provinces. With impaired vision and feeble health he, nevertheless, put an army into the field to punish the insubordinate tribes; but before operations began he died. His grandson, Osai Kwamina, was designated as legal successor to the throne in 1781. He took a solemn vow that he would not enter the palace until he secured the heads of Akombroh and Afosee, whom he knew had excited and incited the people to rebellion against his grandfather. His vengeance was swift and complete. The heads of the rebel leaders were long kept at Juntas as highly prized relics of the reign of King Kwamina. His reign was brief, however. He was deposed for attempting to introduce the Mohammedan religion into the kingdom. Osai Apoko was crowned as his successor in 1797. The Gaman and Kongo armies attached themselves to the declining fortunes of the deposed king, and gave battle for his lost crown. It was a lost cause. The new king could wield his sword as well as wear a crown. He died of a painful sickness, and was succeeded by his son, Osai Tutu Kwamina, in 1800.

The new king was quite youthful,—only seventeen; but he inherited splendid qualities from a race of excellent rulers. He re-organized his armies, and early won a reputation for courage, sagacity, and excellent ability, extraordinary in one so young. He inherited a bitter feeling against the Mohammedans, and made up his mind to chastise two of their chiefs, Ghofan and Ghobago, and make the territory of Banna tributary to Ashantee. He invaded their country, and burned their capital. In an engagement fought at Kaha, the entire Moslem army was defeated and captured. The king of Ghofan was wounded and made prisoner, and died in the camp of the Ashantee army. Two more provinces were bound to the throne of Kwamina; and we submit that this is an historical anomaly, in that a pagan people subdued an army that emblazoned its banner with the faith of *the one God*!

The Ashantee empire had reached the zenith of its glory. Its flag waved in triumph from the Volta to Bossumpea, and the Kong Mountains had echoed the exploits of the veterans that formed the strength of its army. The repose that even this uncivilized people longed for was denied them by a most unfortunate incident.

Asim was a province tributary to the Ashantee empire. Two of the chiefs of Asim became insubordinate, gave offence to the king, and then fled into the country of the Fantis, one of the most numerous and powerful tribes on the Gold Coast. The Fantis promised the fugitives armed protection. There was no extradition treaty in those days. The king despatched friendly messengers, who were instructed to set forth the faults of the offending subjects, and to request their return. The request was contemptuously denied, and the messengers subjected to a painful death. The king of Ashantee invaded the country of the enemy, and defeated the united forces of Fanti and Asim. He again made them an offer of peace, and was led to believe it would be accepted. But the routed army was gathering strength for another battle, although Chibbu and Apontee had indicated to the king that the conditions of peace were agreeable. The king sent an embassy to learn when a formal submission would take place; and they, also, were put to death. King Osai Tutu Kwamina took "the great oath," and vowed that he would never return from the seat of war or enter his capital without the heads of the rebellious chiefs. The Ashantee army shared the desperate feelings of their leader; and a war was begun, which for cruelty and carnage has no equal in the annals of the world's history. Pastoral communities, hamlets, villages, and towns were swept by the red waves of remorseless warfare. There was no mercy in battle: there were no prisoners taken by day, save to be spared for a painful death at nightfall. Their groans, mingling with the shouts of the victors, made the darkness doubly hideous; and the blood of the vanquished army, but a short distance removed, ran cold at the thoughts of the probable fate that waited them on the morrow. Old men and old women, young men and young women, the rollicking children whose light hearts knew no touch of sorrow, as well as the innocent babes clinging to the agitated bosoms of their mothers,—unable to distinguish between friend or foe,—felt the cruel stroke of war. All were driven to an inhospitable grave in the place where the fateful hand of war made them its victims, or perished in the sullen waters of the Volta. For nearly a hundred miles "the smoke of their torment" mounted the skies. Nothing was left in the rear of the Ashantee army, not even cattle or buildings. Pursued by a fleet-footed and impartial disaster, the fainting Fantis and their terrified allies turned their faces toward the seacoast. And why? Perhaps this fleeing army had a sort of superstitious belief that the sea might help them. Then, again, they knew that there were many English on the Gold Coast; that they had forts and troops. They trusted, also, that the young king of the Ashantees would not follow his enemy under the British flag and guns. They were mistaken. The two revolting chiefs took refuge in the fort at Anamabo. On came the intrepid king, thundering at the very gates of the English fort. The village was swept with the hot breath of battle. Thousands perished before this invincible army. The English soldiers poured hot shot and musketry into the columns of the advancing army; but on they marched to victory with an impurturbable air, worthy of "the old guard" under Ney at Waterloo. Preparations were completed for blowing up the walls of the fort; and it would have been but a few hours until the king of Ashantee would have taken the governor's chair, had not the English capitulated. During the negotiations one of the offending chiefs made good his escape to a little village called Cape Coast; but the other was delivered up, and, having been taken back to Kumasi, was tortured to death. Twelve thousand persons fell in the engagement at Anamabo, and thousands of lives were lost in other engagements. This took place in 1807.

In 1811 the king of Ashantee sent an array to Elmina to protect his subjects against predatory bands of Fantis. Three or four battles were fought, and were invariably won by the Ashantee troops.

Barbarians have about as long memories as civilized races. They are a kind-hearted people, but very dangerous and ugly when they are led to feel that they have been injured. "*The great oath*" means a great deal; and the king was not happy in the thought that one of the insolent chiefs had found refuge in the town of Cape Coast, which was in the Fanti country. So in 1817 he invaded this country, and called at Cape Coast, and reduced the place to the condition of a siege. The English authorities saw the Fantis dying under their eyes, and paid the fine imposed by the King of Ashantee, rather than bury the dead inhabitants of the beleaguered town. The Ashantees retired.

England began to notice the Ashantees. They had proven themselves to be a most heroic, intelligent, and aggressive people. The Fantis lay stretched between them and the seacoast. The frequent invasion of this country, for corrective purposes as the Ashantees believed, very seriously interrupted the trade of the coast; and England began to feel it. The English had been defeated once in an attempt to assist the Fantis, and now thought it wise to turn attention to a pacific policy, looking toward the establishment of amicable relations between the Ashantees and themselves. There had never been any unpleasant relations between the two governments, except in the instance named. The Ashantees rather felt very kindly toward England, and for prudential and commercial reasons desired to treat the authorities at the coast with great consideration. They knew that the English gave them a market for their gold, and an opportunity to purchase manufactured articles that they needed. But the Fantis, right under the English flag, receiving a rent for the ground on which the English had their fort and government buildings, grew so intolerably abusive towards their neighbors, the Ashantees, that the British saw nothing before them but interminable war. It was their desire to avoid it if possible. Accordingly, they sent an embassy to the king of the Ashantees, consisting of Gov. James, of the fort at Akra, a Mr. Bowdich, nephew to the governor-in-chief at Cape Coast, a Mr. Hutchinson, and the surgeon of the English settlement, Dr. Teddlie. Mr. Bowdich headed the embassy to the royal court, where they were kindly received. A treaty was made. The rent that the Fantis had been receiving for ground occupied by the English—four ounces of gold per month—was to be paid to the king of Ashantee, as his by right of conquest. Diplomatic relations were to be established between the two governments, and Mr. Hutchinson was to remain at Kumasi as the British resident minister. He was charged with the carrying out of so much of the treaty as related to his government. The treaty was at once forwarded to the home government, and Mr. Dupuis was appointed consul of his Majesty's government to the court of Ashantee. A policy was outlined that meant the opening up of commerce with the distant provinces of the Ashantee empire along the Kong Mountains. In those days it took a long time to sail from England to the Gold Coast in Western Africa; and before Consul Dupuis reached the coast, the king of Ashantee was engaged in a war with the king of Gaman. The Ashantee army was routed. The news of the disaster was hailed by the Fantis on the coast with the most boisterous and public demonstrations. This gave the king of Ashantee offence. The British authorities were quite passive about the conduct of the Fantis, although by solemn treaty they had become responsible for their deportment. The Fantis grew very insulting and offensive towards the Ashantees. The king of the latter called the attention of the authorities at the Cape to the conduct of the Fantis, but no official action was taken. In the mean while Mr. Dupuis was not allowed to proceed on his mission to the capital of the Ashantees. Affairs began to assume a very threatening attitude; and only after the most earnest request was he permitted to proceed to the palace of the king of Ashantee. He received a hearty welcome at the court, and was entertained with the most lavish kindness. After long and painstaking consideration, a treaty was decided upon that was mutually agreeable; but the self-conceited and swaggering insolence of the British authorities on the coast put it into the waste basket. The commander of the British squadron put himself in harmony with the local authorities, and refused to give Consul Dupuis transportation to England for the commissioners of the Ashantee government, whom he had brought to the coast with the intention of taking to London with him.

A war-cloud was gathering. Dupuis saw it. He sent word to the king of Ashantee to remember his oath, and refrain from hostilities until he could communicate with the British government. The treaty stipulated for the recognition, by the British authorities, of the authority of the Ashantee king over the Fantis. Only those immediately around the fort were subject to English law, and then not to an extent to exempt them from tax imposed by the Ashantee authorities.

In the midst of these complications, Parliament, by a special act, abolished the charter of the African Company. This put all its forts, arsenals, and stations under the direct control of the crown. Sir Charles McCarthy was made governor-general of the British possessions on the Gold Coast, and took up his head-quarters at Cape Coast in March, 1822. Two months had passed now since Dupuis had sailed for England; and not a syllable had reached the king's messenger, who, all this time, had waited to hear from England. The country was in an unsettled state. Gov, McCarthy was not equal to the situation. He fell an easy prey to the fawning and lying Fantis. They received him as the champion of their declining fortunes, and did every thing in their power to give him an unfriendly opinion of the Ashantees. The king of the Ashantees began to lose faith in the British. His faithful messenger returned from the coast bearing no friendly tidings. The king withdrew his troops from the seacoast, and began to put his army upon a good war-footing. When all was in readiness a Negro sergeant in the British service was seized, and put to a torturous death. This was a signal for the grand opening. Of course the British were bound to demand redress. Sir Charles McCarthy was informed by some Fantis scouts that the king of Ashantee, at the head of his army, was marching for Cape Coast. Sir Charles rallied his forces, and went forth to give him battle. His object was to fight the king at a distance from the cape, and thus prevent him from devastating the entire country as in former wars. Sir Charles McCarthy was a brave man, and worthy of old England; but in this instance his courage was foolhardy. He crossed the Prah River to meet a wily and desperate foe. His troops were the worthless natives, hastily gathered, and were intoxicated with the hope of deliverance from Ashantee rule. He should have waited for the trained troops of Major Chisholm. This was his fatal mistake. His pickets felt the enemy early in the morning of the 21st of January, 1824. A lively skirmish followed. In a short time the clamorous war-horns of the advancing Ashantees were heard, and a general engagement came on. The first fighting began along a shallow stream. The Ashantees came up with the courage and measured tread of a well-disciplined army. They made a well-directed charge to gain the opposite bank of the stream, but were repulsed by an admirable bayonet charge from Sir Charles's troops. The Ashantees then crossed the stream above and below the British army, and fell with such desperation upon its exposed and naked flanks, that it was bent into the shape of a letter A, and hurled back toward Cape Coast in dismay. Wounded and exhausted, toward evening Sir Charles fled from his exposed position to the troops of his allies under the command of the king of Denkera. He concentrated his artillery upon the heaviest columns of the enemy; but still they came undaunted, bearing down upon the centre like an avalanche. Sir Charles made an attempt to retreat with his staff, but met instant death at the hands of the Ashantees. His head was removed from the body and sent to Kumasi. His heart was eaten by the chiefs of the army that they might imbibe his courage, while his flesh was dried and issued in small rations among the line-officers for the same purpose. His bones were kept at the capital of the Ashantee kingdom as national fetiches.[62]

Major Chisholm and Capt. Laing, learning of the disaster that had well-nigh swallowed up Sir Charles's army, retreated to Cape Coast. There were about thirty thousand troops remaining, but they were so terrified at the disaster of the day that they could not be induced to make a stand against the gallant Ashantees. The king of Ashantee, instead of following the routed army to the gates of Cape Coast, where he could have dealt it a death-blow, offered the English conditions of peace. Capt. Ricketts met the Ashantee messengers at Elmina, and heard from them the friendly messages of the king. The Ashantees only wanted the British to surrender Kudjoh Chibbu of the province of Denkera; but this fugitive from the Ashantee king, while negotiations were pending, resolved to rally the allied armies and make a bold stroke. He crossed the Prah at the head of a considerable force, and fell upon the Ashantee army in its camp. The English were charmed by this bold stroke, and sent a reserve force; but the whole army was again defeated by the Ashantees, and came back to Cape Coast in complete confusion.

The Ashantee army were at the gates of the town. Col. Southerland arrived with re-enforcements, but was beaten into the fort by the unyielding courage of the attacking force. A new king, Osai Ockote, arrived with fresh troops, and won the confidence of the army by marching right under the British guns, and hissing defiance into the face of the foe. The conflict that followed was severe, and destructive to both life and property. All the native and British forces were compelled to retire to the fort; while the Ashantee troops, inspired by the dashing bearing of their new king, closed in around them like tongues of steel. The invading army was not daunted by the belching cannon that cut away battalion after battalion. On they pressed for revenge and victory. The screams of fainting women and terrified children, the groans of the dying, and the bitter imprecations of desperate combatants,—a mingling medley,—swelled the great diapason of noisy battle. The eyes of the beleaguered were turned toward the setting sun, whose enormous disk was leaning against the far-away mountains, and casting his red and vermilion over the dusky faces of dead Ashantees and Fantis; and, imparting a momentary beauty to the features of the dead white men who fell so far away from home and friends, he sank to rest. There was a sad, far-off look in the eye of the impatient sailor who kept his lonely watch on the vessel that lay at rest on the sea. Night was wished for, prayed for, yearned for. It came at last, and threw its broad sable pinions over the dead, the dying, and the living. Hostilities were to be renewed in the morning; but the small-pox broke out among the soldiers, and the king of Ashantee retired.

Sir Neill Campbell was appointed governor-general at Cape Coast. One of his first acts was to call for all the chiefs of the Fantis, and give them to understand that hostilities between themselves and the king of Ashantee must stop. He then required Osai Ockoto to deposit four thousand ounces of gold ($72,000), as a bond to keep the peace. In case he provoked hostilities, the seventy-two thousand dollars were to be used to purchase ammunition with which to chastise him. In 1831 the king was obliged to send two of his royal family, Kwanta Missah, his own son, and Ansah, the son of the late king, to be held as hostages. These boys were sent to England, where they were educated, but are now residents of Ashantee.

Warsaw and Denkera, interior provinces, were lost to the Ashantee empire; but, nevertheless, it still remains one of the most powerful Negro empires of Western Africa.

The king of Ashantee has a fair government. His power is well-nigh absolute. He has a House of Lords, who have a check-power. Coomassi is the famous city of gold, situated in the centre of the empire. The communication through to the seacoast is unobstructed; and it is rather remarkable that the Ashantees are the only nation in Africa, who, living in the interior, have direct communication with the Caucasian. They have felt the somewhat elevating influence of Mohammedanism, and are not unconscious of the benefits derived by the literature and contact of the outside world. They are a remarkable people: brave, generous, industrious, and mentally capable. The day is not distant when the Ashantee kingdom will be won to the Saviour, and its inhabitants brought under the beneficent influences of Christian civilization.

FOOTNOTES:

[62] The following telegram shocks the civilized world. It serves notice on the Christians of the civilized world, that, in a large missionary sense, they have come far short of their duty to the "nations beyond," who sit in darkness and the shadow of death.

"Massacre Of Maidens. London, Nov. 10, 1881.—Advices from Cape Coast Castle report that the king of Ashantee killed two hundred young girls for the purpose of using their blood for mixing mortar for repair of one of the state buildings. The report of the massacre was received from a refugee chosen for one of the victims. Such wholesale massacres are known to be a custom with the king."—*Cinn. Commercial.*

CHAPTER VI
THE NEGRO TYPE

Climate the Cause.—His Geographical Theatre.—He is susceptible to Christianity and Civilization.

IF the reader will turn to a map of Africa, the Mountains of the Moon[63] will be found to run right through the centre of that continent. They divide Africa into two almost equal parts. In a dialectic sense, also, Africa is divided. The Mountains of the Moon, running east and west, seem to be nature's dividing line between two distinct peoples. North of these wonderful mountains the languages are numerous and quite distinct, and lacking affinity. For centuries these tribes have lived in the same latitude, under the same climatic influences, and yet, without a written standard, have preserved the idiomatic coloring of their tribal language without corruption. Thus they have eluded the fate that has overtaken all other races who without a written language, living together by the laws of affinity, sooner or later have found one medium of speech as inevitable as necessary.

But coming south of the Mountains of the Moon, until we reach the Cape of Good Hope, there is to be found one great family. Nor is the difference between the northern and southern tribes only linguistic. The physiological difference between these people is great. They range in color from the dead black up to pure white, and from the dwarfs on the banks of the Casemanche to the tall and giant-like Vei tribe of Cape Mount.

"The Fans which inhabit the mountain terraces are altogether of a different complexion from the seacoast tribes. Their hair is longer: that of the women hangs down in long braids to their shoulders, while the men have tolerably long two-pointed beards. It would be impossible to find such long hair among the coast tribes, even in a single instance.

"In the low, swampy land at the mouth of the Congo, one meets with typical Negroes; and there again, as one reaches a higher soil, one finds a different class of people.

"The Angolese resemble the Fula. They are scarcely ever black. Their hands and feet are exquisitely small; and in every way they form a contrast with the slaves of the Portuguese, who, brought for the most part from the Congo, are brutal and debased.

"I have divided Africa into three grand types,—the Ethiopian, the intermediate, and the Negro. In the same manner the Negro may be divided into three sub-classes:—

"The bronze-colored class: gracefully formed, with effeminate features, small hands and feet, long fingers, intelligent minds, courteous and polished manners. Such are the Mpongwe of the Gaboon, the Angolese, the Fanti of the Gold Coast, and most probably the Haoussa of the Niger, a tribe with which I am not acquainted.

"The black-skinned class: athletic shapes, rude manners, less intelligence, but always with some good faculties, thicker lips, broader noses, but seldom prognathous to any great degree. Such are the Wollof, the Kru-men, the Benga of Corisco, and the Cabinda of Lower Guinea, who hire themselves out as sailors in the Congo and in Angola precisely as do the Kru-men of North Guinea.

"Lastly, the typical Negroes: an exceptional race even among the Negroes, whose disgusting type it is not necessary to re-describe. They are found chiefly along the coast between the Casemanche and Sierra Leone, between Lagos and the Cameroons, in the Congo swamps, and in certain swampy plains and mountain-hollows of the interior."[64]

That climate has much to do with physical and mental character, we will not have to prove to any great extent. It is a fact as well established as any principle in pathology. Dr. Joseph Brown says,—

"It is observed that the natives of marshy districts who permanently reside in them lose their whole bodily and mental constitution, contaminated by the poison they inhale. Their aspect is sallow and prematurely senile, so that children are often wrinkled, their muscles flaccid, their hair lank, and frequently pale, the abdomen tumid, the stature stunted, and the intellectual and moral character low and degraded. They rarely attain what in more wholesome regions would be considered old age. In the marshy districts of certain countries,—for example, Egypt, Georgia, and Virginia,—the extreme term of life is stated to be forty in the latter place.... In portions of Brittany which adjoin the Loire, the extreme duration of life is fifty, at which age the inhabitant wears the aspect of eighty in a healthier district.

It is remarked that the inferior animals, and even vegetables, partake of the general deprivation; they are stunted and short-lived."

In his "Ashango Land," Paul B. du Chaillu devotes a large part of his fifteenth chapter to the Obongos, or Dwarfs. Nearly all African explorers and travellers have been much amazed at the diversity of color and stature among the tribes they met. This diversity in physical and mental character owes its existence to the diversity and perversity of African climate.

The Negro, who is but a fraction of the countless indigenous races of Africa, has been carried down to his low estate by the invincible forces of nature. Along the ancient volcanic tracts are to be found the Libyan race, with a tawny complexion, features quite Caucasian, and long black hair. On the sandstones are to be found an intermediate type, darker somewhat than their progenitors, lips thick, and nostrils wide at the base. Then comes the Negro down in the alluvia, with dark skin, woolly hair, and prognathous development.

> "The Negro forms an exceptional race in Africa. He inhabits that immense tract of marshy land which lies between the mountains and the sea, from Senegal to Benguela, and the low lands of the eastern side in the same manner. He is found in the parts about Lake Tchad, in Sennaar, along the marshy banks of rivers, and in several isolated spots besides."[65]

The true Negro inhabits Northern Africa. When his country, of which we know absolutely nothing, has been crowded, the nomadic portion of the population has poured itself over the mountain terraces, and, descending into the swamps, has become degraded in body and mind.

Technically speaking, we do not believe the Negro is a distinct species.

> "It is certain that the woolly hair, the prognathous development, and the deep black skin of the typical Negro, are not peculiar to the African continent."[66]

The Negro is found in the low, marshy, and malarious districts. We think the Negro is produced in a descending scale. The African who moves from the mountain regions down into the miasmatic districts may be observed to lose his stature, his complexion, his hair, and his intellectual vigor: he finally becomes the Negro. Pathologically considered, he is weak, sickly, and short-lived. His legs are slender and almost calf-less: the head is developed in the direction of the passions, while the whole form is destitute of symmetry.

> "It will be understood that the typical Negroes, with whom the slavers are supplied, represent the dangerous, the destitute, and diseased classes of African society. They

may be compared to those which in England fill our jails, our workhouses, and our hospitals. So far from being equal to us, the polished inhabitants of Europe, as some ignorant people suppose, they are immeasurably below the Africans themselves,

"The typical Negro is the true savage of Africa; and I must paint the deformed anatomy of his mind, as I have already done that of his body.

"The typical Negroes dwell in petty tribes, where all are equal except the women, who are slaves; where property is common, and where, consequently, there is no property at all; where one may recognize the Utopia of philosophers, and observe the saddest and basest spectacles which humanity can afford.

"The typical Negro, unrestrained by moral laws, spends his days in sloth, his nights in debauchery. He smokes hashish till he stupefies his senses or falls into convulsions; he drinks palm-wine till he brings on a loathsome disease; he abuses children, stabs the poor brute of a woman whose hands keep him from starvation, and makes a trade of his own offspring. He swallows up his youth in premature vice; he lingers through a manhood of disease, and his tardy death is hastened by those who no longer care to find him food.... If you wish to know what they have been, and to what we may restore them, look at the portraits which have been preserved of the ancient Egyptians: and in those delicate and voluptuous forms; in those round, soft features; in those long, almond-shaped, half-closed, languishing eyes; in those full pouting lips, large smiling mouths, and complexions of a warm and copper-colored tint,—you will recognize the true African type, the women-men of the Old World, of which the Negroes are the base, the depraved caricatures."[67]

But the Negro is not beyond the influences of civilization and Christianization. Hundreds of thousands have perished in the cruel swamps of Africa; hundreds of thousands have been devoured by wild beasts of the forests; hundreds of thousands have perished before the steady and murderous columns of stronger tribes; hundreds of thousands have perished from fever, small-pox, and cutaneous diseases; hundreds of thousands have been sold into slavery; hundreds of thousands have perished in the "middle-passage;" hundreds of thousands have been landed in this New World in the West: and yet hundreds of thousands are still swarming in the low and marshy lands of Western Africa. Poor as this material is, out of it we have made, here in the United States, six million citizens; and out of this cast-away material of Africa, God has raised up many children.

To the candid student of ethnography, it must be conclusive that the Negro is but the most degraded and disfigured type of the primeval African. And still, with all his interminable woes and wrongs, the Negro on the west coast of Africa, in Liberia and Sierra Leone, as well as in the southern part of the United States, shows that centuries of savagehood and slavery have not drained him of all the elements of his manhood. History furnishes us with abundant and specific evidence of his capacity to civilize and Christianize. We shall speak of this at length in a subsequent chapter.

FOOTNOTES:

[63] See Keith Johnson's Map of Africa, 1863.

[64] Savage Africa, pp. 403, 404.

[65] Savage Africa, p. 400.

[66] Savage Africa, p. 412.

[67] Savage Africa, p. 430.

CHAPTER VII
AFRICAN IDIOSYNCRASIES

Patriarchal Government.—Construction of Villages.—Negro Architecture.—Election of Kings.— Coronation Ceremony.—Succession.—African Queens.—Law, Civil and Criminal.—Priests.—Their Functions.—Marriage.—Warfare.—Agriculture.— Mechanic Arts.—Blacksmiths.

ALL the tribes on the continent of Africa are under, to a greater or less degree, the patriarchal form of government. It is usual for writers on Africa to speak of "kingdoms" and "empires;" but these kingdoms are called so more by compliment than with any desire to convey the real meaning that we get when the empire of Germany or kingdom of Spain is spoken of. The patriarchal government is the most ancient in Africa. It is true that great kingdoms have risen in Africa; but they were the result of devastating wars rather than the creation of political genius or governmental wisdom.

> "Pangola is the child or vassal of Mpende. Sandia and Mpende are the only independent chiefs from Kebrabasa to Zumbo, and belong to the tribe Manganja. The country north of the mountains, here in sight from the Zambesi, is called Senga, and its inhabitants Asenga or Basenga; but all appear to be of the same family as the rest of the Manganja and Maravi. Formerly all the Manganja were united under the government of their great chief, Undi, whose empire extended from Lake Shirwa to the River Loangwa; but after Undi's death it fell to pieces, and a large portion of it on the Zambesi was absorbed by their powerful Southern neighbors, the Bamjai. This has been the inevitable fate of every African empire from time immemorial. A chief of more than ordinary ability arises, and, subduing all his less powerful neighbors, founds a kingdom, which he governs more or less wisely till he dies. His successor, not having the talents of the conqueror, cannot retain the dominion, and some of the abler under-chiefs set up for themselves; and, in a few years, the remembrance only of the empire

remains. This, which may be considered as the normal state of African society, gives rise to frequent and desolating wars, and the people long in vain for a power able to make all dwell in peace. In this light a European colony would be considered by the natives as an inestimable boon to intertropical Africa. Thousands of industrious natives would gladly settle around it, and engage in that peaceful pursuit of agriculture and trade of which they are so fond; and, undistracted by wars or rumors of wars, might listen to the purifying and ennobling truths of the gospel of Jesus Christ. The Manganja on the Zambesi, like their countrymen on the Shire, are fond of agriculture; and, in addition to the usual varieties of food, cultivate tobacco and cotton in quantities more than equal to their wants. To the question, 'Would they work for Europeans?' an affirmative answer may be given; if the Europeans belong to the class which can pay a reasonable price for labor, and not to that of adventurers who want employment for themselves. All were particularly well clothed from Sandia's to Pangola's; and it was noticed that all the cloth was of native manufacture, the product of their own looms. In Senga a great deal of iron is obtained from the ore, and manufactured very cleverly."[68]

The above is a fair description of the internecine wars that have been carried on between the tribes in Africa, back "to a time whereof the memory of man runneth not to the contrary." In a preceding chapter we gave quite an extended account of four Negro empires. We call attention here to the villages of these people, and shall allow writers who have paid much attention to this subject to give their impressions. Speaking of a village of the Aviia tribe called Mandji, Du Chaillu says,—

"It was the dirtiest village I had yet seen in Africa, and the inhabitants appeared to me of a degraded class of Negroes. The shape and arrangement of the village were quite different from any thing I had seen before. The place was in the form of a quadrangle, with an open space in the middle not more than ten yards square; and the huts, arranged in a continuous row on two sides, were not more than eight feet high from the ground to the roof. The doors were only four feet high, and of about the same width, with sticks placed across on the inside, one above the other, to bar the entrance. The place for the fire was in the middle of the principal room, on each side of which was a little dark chamber; and on the floor was an *orala*, or stage, to smoke meat upon. In the middle of the yard was a hole dug in the ground for the reception of offal, from which a disgusting smell arose, the wretched inhabitants being too lazy or obtuse to guard against this by covering it with earth.

"The houses were built of a framework of poles, covered with the bark of trees, and roofed with leaves. In the middle of the village stood the public shed, or palaver-house,—a kind of town-hall found in almost all West-African villages. A large fire was burning in it, on the ground; and at one end of the shed stood a huge wooden idol, painted red and white, and rudely fashioned in the shape of a woman. The shed was the largest building in the village, for it was ten feet high, and measured fifteen feet by ten. It is the habit of the lazy negroes of these interior villages—at least, the men—to spend almost the whole day lying down under the palaver-shed, feeding their morbid imaginations with tales of witchcraft, and smoking their *condoquais*."

But all the villages of these poor children of the desert are not so untidy as the one described above. There is a wide difference in the sanitary laws governing these villages.

"The Ishogo villages are large. Indeed, what most strikes the traveller in coming from the seacoast to this inland country, is the large size, neatness, and beauty of the villages. They generally have about one hundred and fifty or one hundred and sixty huts, arranged in streets, which are very broad and kept remarkably clean. Each house has a door of wood which is painted in fanciful designs with red, white, and black. One pattern struck me as simple and effective; it was a number of black spots margined with white, painted in regular rows on a red ground. But my readers must not run away with the idea that the doors are like those of the houses of civilized people; they are seldom more than two feet and a half high. The door of my house was just twenty-seven inches high. It is fortunate that I am a short man, otherwise it would have been hard exercise to go in and out of my lodgings. The planks of which the doors are made are cut with great labor by native axes out of trunks of trees, one trunk seldom yielding more than one good plank. My hut, an average-sized dwelling, was twenty feet long and eight feet broad. It was divided into three rooms or compartments, the middle one, into which the door opened, being a little larger than the other two.... Mokenga is a beautiful village, containing about one hundred and sixty houses; they were the largest dwellings I had yet seen on the journey. The village was surrounded by a dense grove of plantain-trees, many of which had to be supported by poles, on account of the weight of the enormous bunches of plantains they bore. Little groves of lime-trees were scattered everywhere, and the limes, like so much golden fruit, looked beautiful amidst the dark foliage that surrounded them. Tall, towering palm-trees were scattered here and there. Above and behind the village was the dark green forest. The street was the broadest I ever saw in Africa; one part of it was about one hundred yards broad, and not a blade of grass could be seen in it. The Sycobii were building their nests everywhere, and made a deafening noise, for there were thousands and thousands of these little sociable birds."[69]

The construction of houses in villages in Africa is almost uniform, as far as our studies have led us.[70] Or, rather, we ought to modify this statement by saying there are but two plans of construction. One is where the houses are erected on the rectilinear, the other is where they are built on the circular plan. In the more warlike tribes the latter plan prevails. The hillsides and elevated places near the timber are sought as desirable locations for villages. The plan of architecture is simple. The diameter is first considered, and generally varies from ten to fifteen feet. A circle is drawn in the ground, and then long flexible sticks are driven into the earth. The builder, standing inside of the circle, binds the sticks together at the top; where they are secured together by the use of the "monkey-rope," a thick vine that stretches itself in great profusion from tree to tree in that country. Now, the reader can imagine a large umbrella with the handle broken off even with the ribs when closed up, and without any cloth,—nothing but the ribs left. Now open it, and place it on the ground before you, and you have a fair idea of the hut up to the present time. A reed thatching is laid over the frame, and secured firmly by parallel lashings about fifteen inches apart. The door is made last by cutting a hole in the side of the hut facing toward the centre of the contemplated circle of huts.[71] The door is about eighteen inches in height, and just wide enough to admit the body of the owner. The sharp points, after the cutting, are guarded by plaited twigs. The door is made of quite a number of stout sticks driven into the ground at equal distances apart, through which, in and out, are woven pliant sticks. When this is accomplished, the maker cuts off the irregular ends to make it fit the door, and removes it to its place. Screens are often used inside to keep out the wind: they are made so as to be placed in whatever position the wind is blowing. Some of these houses are built with great care, and those with domed roofs are elaborately decorated inside with beads of various sizes and colors.

The furniture consists of a few mats, several baskets, a milk-pail, a number of earthen pots, a bundle of assagais, and a few other weapons of war. Next, to guard against the perils of the rainy season, a ditch about two feet in width and of equal depth is made about the new dwelling. Now multiply this hut by five hundred, preserving the circle, and you have the village. The *palaver-house*, or place for public debates, is situated in the centre of the circle of huts. Among the northern and southern tribes, a fence is built around their villages, when they are called "kraals." The space immediately outside of the fence is cleared, so as to put an enemy at a disadvantage in an attack upon the village. Among the agricultural tribes, as, for example, the Kaffirs, they drive their cattle into the kraal, and for the young build pens.

The other method of building villages is to have one long street, with a row of houses on each side, rectangular in shape. They are about twenty-five or thirty feet in length, and about twelve to fifteen feet in width. Six or eight posts are used to join the material of the sides to. The roofs are flat. Three rooms are allowed to each house. The two end rooms are larger than the centre one, where the door opens out into the street. Sometimes these rooms are plastered, but it is seldom; and then it is in the case of the well-to-do class.[72]

We said, at the beginning of this chapter, that the government in Africa was largely patriarchal; and yet we have called attention to four great kingdoms. There is no contradiction here, although there may seem to be; for even kings are chosen by ballot, and a sort of a house of lords has a veto power over royal edicts.

"Among the tribes which I visited in my explorations I found but one form of government, which may be called the patriarchal. There is not sufficient national unity in any of the tribes to give occasion for such a despotism as prevails in Dahomey, and in other of the African nationalities. I found the tribes of equatorial Africa greatly dispersed, and, in general, no bond of union between parts of the same tribe. A tribe is divided up into numerous *clans*, and these again into numberless little villages, each of which last possesses an independent chief. The villages are scattered; are often moved for death or witchcraft, as I have already explained in the narrative; and not infrequently are engaged in war with each other.

"The chieftainship is, to a certain extent, hereditary, the right of succession vesting in the brother of the reigning chief or king. The people, however, and particularly the elders of the village, have a veto power, and can, for sufficient cause, deprive the lineal heir of his succession, and put in over him some one thought of more worth. In such cases the question is put to the vote of the village; and, where parties are equally divided as to strength, there ensue sometimes long and serious palavers before all can unite in a choice. The chief is mostly a man of great influence prior to his accession, and generally an old man when he gains power.

"His authority, though greater than one would think, judging from the little personal deference paid to him, is final only in matters of every-day use. In cases of importance, such as war, or any important removal, the elders of the village meet together and deliberate in the presence of the whole population, which last finally decide the question.

> "The elders, who possess other authority, and are always in the counsels of the chief, are the oldest members of important families in the village. Respect is paid to them on account of their years, but more from a certain regard for 'family,' which the African has very strongly wherever I have known him. These families form the aristocracy."[73]

Here are democracy and aristocracy blended somewhat. The king's power seems to be in deciding everyday affairs, while the weighty matters which affect the whole tribe are decided by the elders and the people. Mr. Reade says of such government,—

> "Among these equatorial tribes the government is patriarchal, which is almost equivalent to saying that there is no government at all. The tribes are divided into clans. Each clan inhabits a separate village, or group of villages; and at the head of each is a patriarch, the parody of a king. They are distinguished from the others by the grass-woven cap which they wear on their heads, and by the staff which they carry in their hands. They are always rich and aged: therefore they are venerated; but, though they can exert influence, they cannot wield power; they can advise, but they cannot command. In some instances, as in that of Quenqueza, King of the Rembo, the title and empty honors of royalty are bestowed upon the most influential patriarch in a district. This is a vestige of higher civilization and of ancient empire which disappears as one descends among the lower tribes."[74]

> "The African form of government is patriarchal, and, according to the temperament of the chief, despotic, or guided by the counsel of the elders of the tribe. Reverence for loyalty sometimes leads the mass of the people to submit to great cruelty, and even murder, at the hands of a despot or madman; but, on the whole, the rule is mild; and the same remark applies in a degree to their religion."[75]

When a new king is elected, he has first to repair to the pontiff's house, who—apropos of priests—is more important than the king himself. The king prostrates himself, and, with loud cries, entreats the favor of this high priest. At first the old man inside, with a gruff voice, orders him away, says he cannot be annoyed; but the king enumerates the presents he has brought him, and finally the door opens, and the priest appears, clad in white, a looking-glass on his breast, and long white feathers in his head. The king is sprinkled, covered with dust, walked over, and then, finally, the priest lies upon him. He has to swear that he will obey, etc.; and then he is allowed to go to the coronation. Then follow days and nights of feasting, and, among some tribes, human sacrifices.

The right of succession is generally kept on the male side of the family. The crown passes from brother to brother, from uncle to nephew, from cousin to cousin. Where there are no brothers, the son takes the sceptre. In all our studies on Africa, we have found only two women reigning. A woman by the name of Shinga ascended the throne of the Congo empire in 1640. She rebelled against the ceremonies, sought to be introduced by Portuguese Catholic priests, who incited her nephew to treason. Defeated in several pitched battles, she fled into the Jaga country, where she was crowned with much success. In 1646 she won her throne again, and concluded an honorable peace with the Portuguese. The other queen was the bloodthirsty Tembandumba of the Jagas. She was of Arab blood, and a cannibal by practice. She fought many battles, achieved great victories, flirted with beautiful young savages, and finally was poisoned.

The African is not altogether without law.

> "Justice appears, upon the whole, to be pretty fairly administered among the Makololo. A headman took some beads and a blanket from one of his men who had been with us; the matter was brought before the chief; and he immediately ordered the goods to be restored, and decreed, moreover, that no headman should take the property of the men who had returned. In theory all the goods brought back belonged to the chief; the men laid them at his feet, and

made a formal offer of them all: he looked at the articles, and told the men to keep them. This is almost invariably the case. Tuba Mokoro, however, fearing lest Sekeletu might take a fancy to some of his best goods, exhibited only a few of his old and least valuable acquisitions. Masakasa had little to show: he had committed some breach of native law in one of the villages on the way, and paid a heavy fine rather than have the matter brought to the doctor's ears. Each carrier is entitled to a portion of the goods in his bundle, though purchased by the chief's ivory; and they never hesitate to claim their rights; but no wages can be demanded from the chief if he fails to respond to the first application."[76]

We have found considerable civil and criminal law among the different tribes. We gave an account of the civil and criminal code of Dahomey in the chapter on that empire. In the Congo country all civil suits are brought before a judge. He sits on a mat under a large tree, and patiently hears the arguments pro and con. His decisions are final. There is no higher court, and hence no appeal. The criminal cases are brought before the Chitomé, or priest. He keeps a sacred fire burning in his house that is never suffered to go out. He is supported by the lavish and delicate gifts of the people, and is held to be sacred. No one is allowed to approach his house except on the most urgent business. He never dies, so say the people. When he is seriously sick his legal successor steals quietly into his house, and beats his brains out, or strangles him to death. It is his duty to hear all criminal cases, and to this end he makes a periodical circuit among the tribe. Murder, treason, adultery, killing the escaped snakes from the fetich-house,—and often stealing,—are punished by death, or by being sold into slavery. A girl who loses her standing, disgraces her family by an immoral act, is banished from the tribe. And in case of seduction the man is tied up and flogged. In case of adultery a large sum of money must be paid. If the guilty one is unable to pay the fine, then death or slavery is the penalty.

"Adultery is regarded by the Africans as a kind of theft. It is a vice, therefore, and so common that one might write a Decameron of native tales like those of Boccaccio. And what in Boccaccio is more poignant and more vicious than this song of the Benga, which I have often heard them sing, young men and women together, when no old men were present?—

'The old men young girls married.
The young girls made the old men fools;
For they love to kiss the young men in the dark,
Or beneath the green leaves of the plantain-tree.
The old men then threatened the young men,

And said, "You make us look like fools;
But we will stab you with our knives till your blood runs forth!"
"Oh, stab us, stab us!" cried the young men gladly,
"For then your wives will fasten up our wounds.""[77]

The laws of marriage among many tribes are very wholesome and elevating. When the age of puberty arrives, it is the custom in many tribes for the elderly women, who style themselves Negemba, to go into the forest, and prepare for the initiation of the igonji, or novice. They clear a large space, build a fire, which is kept burning for three days. They take the young woman into the fetich-house,—a new one for this ceremony,—where they go through some ordeal, that, thus far, has never been understood by men. When a young man wants a wife, there are two things necessary; viz., he must secure her consent, and then buy her. The apparent necessary element in African courtship is not a thing to be deprecated by the contracting parties. On the other hand, it is the sine qua non of matrimony. It is proof positive when a suitor gives cattle for his sweetheart, first, that he is wealthy; and, second, that he greatly values the lady he fain would make his bride. He first seeks the favor of the girl's parents. If she have none, then her next of kin, as in Israel in the days of Boaz. For it is a law among many tribes, that a young girl shall never be without a guardian. When the relatives are favorably impressed with the suitor, they are at great pains to sound his praise in the presence of the girl; who, after a while, consents to see him. The news is conveyed to him by a friend or relative of the girl. The suitor takes a bath, rubs his body with palm-oil, dons his best armor, and with beating heart and proud stride hastens to the presence of the fastidious charmer. She does not speak. He sits down, rises, turns around, runs, and goes through many exercises to show her that he is sound and healthy. The girl retires, and the anxious suitor receives the warm congratulations of the spectators on his noble bearing. The fair lady conveys her assent to the waiting lover, and the village rings with shouts of gladness. Next come the preliminary matters before the wedding. Marriage among most African tribes is a coetaneous contract. The bride is delivered when the price is paid by the bridegroom. No goods, no wife. Then follow the wedding and feasting, firing of guns, blowing of horns, music, and dancing.[78]

Polygamy is almost universal in Africa, and poor woman is the greater sufferer from the accursed system. It is not enough that she is drained of her beauty and strength by the savage passions of man: she is the merest abject slave everywhere. The young women are beautiful, but it is only for a brief season: it soon passes like the fragile rose into the ashes of premature old age. In Dahomey she is a soldier; in Kaffir-land she tends the herds, and builds houses; and in Congo without her industry man would starve. Everywhere man's cruel hand is against her. Everywhere she is the slave of his unholy passions.[79]

It is a mistaken notion that has obtained for many years, that the Negro in Africa is physically the most loathsome of all mankind. True, the Negro has been deformed by degradation and abuse; but this is not his normal condition. We have seen native Africans who were jet black, woolly-haired, and yet possessing fine teeth, beautiful features, tall, graceful, and athletic.

> "In reference to the status of the Africans among the nations of the earth, we have seen nothing to justify the notion that they are of a different 'breed' or 'species' from the most civilized. The African is a man with every attribute of human kind. Centuries of barbarism have had the same deteriorating effects on Africans as Prichard describes them to have had on certain of the Irish who were driven, some generations back, to the hills in Ulster and Connaught; and these depressing influences have had such moral and physical effects on some tribes, that ages probably will be required to undo what ages have done. This degradation, however, would hardly be given as a reason for holding any race in bondage, unless the advocate had sunk morally to the same low state. Apart from the frightful loss of life in the process by which, it is pretended, the Negroes are better provided for than in a state of liberty in their own country, it is this very system that perpetuates, if not causes, the unhappy condition with which the comparative comfort of some of them in slavery is contrasted.

"Ethnologists reckon the African as by no means the lowest of the human family. He is nearly as strong physically as the European; and, as a race, is wonderfully persistent among the nations of the earth. Neither the diseases nor the ardent spirits which proved so fatal to North-American Indians, South-Sea Islanders, and Australians, seem capable of annihilating the Negroes. Even when subjected to that system so destructive to human life, by which they are torn from their native soil, they spring up irrepressibly, and darken half the new continent. They are gifted by nature with physical strength capable of withstanding the sorest privations, and a lightheartedness which, as a sort of compensation, enables them to make the best of the worst situations. It is like that power which the human frame possesses of withstanding heat, and to an extent which we should never have known, had not an adventurous surgeon gone into an oven, and burnt his fingers with his own watch. The Africans have wonderfully borne up under unnatural conditions that would have proved fatal to most races.

> "It is remarkable that the power of resistance under calamity, or, as some would say, adaptation for a life of servitude, is peculiar only to certain tribes on the continent of Africa. Climate cannot be made to account for the fact that many would pine in a state of slavery, or voluntarily perish. No Krooman can be converted into a slave, and yet he is an inhabitant of the low, unhealthy west coast; nor can any of the Zulu or Kaffir tribes be reduced to bondage, though all these live on comparatively elevated regions. We have heard it stated by men familiar with some of the Kaffirs, that a blow, given even in play by a European, must be returned. A love of liberty is observable in all who have the Zulu blood, as the Makololo, the Watuta, and probably the Masai. But blood does not explain the fact. A beautiful Barotse woman at NHLe, on refusing to marry a man whom she did not like, was in a pet given by the headman to some Mambari slave-traders from Benguela. Seeing her fate, she seized one of their spears, and, stabbing herself, fell down dead."[80]

Dr. David Livingstone is certainly entitled to our utmost confidence in all matters that he writes about. Mr. Archibald Forbes says he has seen Africans dead upon the field of battle that would measure nine feet, and it was only a few months ago that we had the privilege of seeing a Zulu who was eight feet and eleven inches in height. As to the beauty of the Negro, nearly all African travellers agree.

"But if the women of Africa are brutal, the men of Africa are feminine. Their faces are smooth; their breasts are frequently as full as those of European women; their voices are never gruff or deep; their fingers are long; and they can be very proud of their rosy nails. While the women are nearly always ill-shaped after their girlhood, the men have gracefully moulded limbs, and always after a feminine type,—the arms rounded, the legs elegantly formed, without too much muscular development, and the feet delicate and small.

"When I first went ashore on Africa, viz., at Bathurst, I thought all the men who passed me, covered in their long robes, were women, till I saw one of the latter sex, and was thereby disenchanted.

"While no African's face ever yet reminded me of a man whom I had known in England, I saw again and again faces which reminded me of women; and on one occasion, in Angola, being about to chastise a *carregadore*, he sank on his knees as I raised my stick, clasped his hands, and looked up imploringly toward me,—was so like a young lady I had once felt an affection for, that, in spite of myself, I flung the stick away, fearing to commit a sacrilege.

"Ladies on reading this will open their eyes, and suppose that either I have very bad taste, or that I am writing fiction. But I can assure them that among the Angolas, and the Mpongwe, and the Mandingoes, and the Fula, I have seen men whose form and features would disgrace no petticoats,—not even satin ones at a drawing-room.

"While the women are stupid, sulky, and phlegmatic, the men are vivacious, timid, inquisitive, and garrulous beyond belief. They make excellent domestic servants, are cleanly, and even tedious in the nicety with which they arrange dishes on a table or clothes on a bed. They have also their friendships after the manner of woman, embracing one another, sleeping on the same mat, telling one another their secrets, betraying them, and getting terribly jealous of one another (from pecuniary motives) when they happen to serve the same master.

"They have none of that austerity, that reserve, that pertinacity, that perseverance, that strong-headed stubborn determination, or that ferocious courage, which are the common attributes of our sex. They have, on the other hand, that delicate tact, that intuition, that nervous imagination, that quick perception of character, which have become the proverbial characteristics of cultivated women. They know how to render themselves impenetrable; and if they desire to be perfidious, they wear a mask which few eyes can see through, while at the same time a certain sameness of purpose models their character in similar moulds. Their nature is an enigma: but solve it, and you have solved the race. They are inordinately vain: they buy looking-glasses; they will pass hours at their toilet, in which their wives must act as femmes de chambre; they will spend all their money on ornaments and dress, in which they can display a charming taste. They are fond of music, of dancing, and are not insensible to the beauties of nature. They are indolent, and have little ambition except to be admired and well spoken of. They are so sensitive that a harsh word will rankle in then hearts, and make them unhappy for a length of time; and they will strip themselves to pay the grills for their flattery, and to escape their satire. Though naturally timid, and loath to shed blood, they witness without horror the most revolting spectacles which their religion sanctions; and, though awed by us their superiors, a real injury will transform their natures, and they will take a speedy and merciless revenge.

"According to popular belief, the Africans are treacherous and hostile. The fact is, that all Africans are supposed to be Negroes, and that which is criminal is ever associated with that which is hideous. But, with the exception of some Mohammedan tribes toward the north, one may travel all over Africa without risking one's life. They may detain you, they may rob you, if you are rich; they may insult you, and refuse to let you enter their country, if you are poor: but your life is always safe till you sacrifice it by some imprudence.

"In ancient times the blacks were known to be so gentle to strangers that many believed that the gods sprang from them. Homer sings of the Ocean, father of the gods; and says that, when Jupiter wishes to take a holiday, he visits the sea, and goes to the banquets of the blacks,—a people humble, courteous, and devout."[81]

We have quoted thus extensively from Mr. Reade because he has given a fair account of the peoples he met. He is a good writer, but sometimes gets real funny!

It is a fact that all uncivilized races are warlike. The tribes of Africa are a vast standing army. Fighting seems to be their employment. We went into this matter of armies so thoroughly in the fourth chapter that we shall not have much to say here. The bow and arrow, the spear and assagai were the primitive weapons of African warriors; but they have learned the use of fire-arms within the last quarter of a century. The shield and assagai are not, however, done away with. The young Prince Napoleon, whose dreadful death the reader may recall, was slain by an assagai. These armies are officered, disciplined, and drilled to great perfection, as the French and English troops have abundant reason to know.

"The Zulu tribes are remarkable for being the only people in that part of Africa who have practised war in an European sense of the word. The other tribes are very good at bush fighting, and are exceedingly crafty at taking an enemy unawares, and coming on him before he is prepared for them. Guerilla warfare is, in fact, their only mode of waging battle; and, as is necessarily the case in such warfare, more depends on the exertion of individual combatants than on the scientific combinations of masses. But the Zulu tribe have, since the time of Dhaka, the great inventor of military tactics, carried on war in a manner approaching the notions of civilization.

"Their men are organized into regiments, each subdivided into companies, and each commanded by its own chief, or colonel; while the king, as commanding general, leads his forces to war, disposes them in battle-array, and personally directs their movements. They give an enemy notice that they are about to match against him, and boldly meet him in the open field. There is a military etiquette about them which some of our own people have been slow to understand. They once sent a message to the English commander that they would 'come and breakfast with him.' He thought it was only a joke, and was very much surprised when the Kaffirs, true to their promise, came pouring like a torrent over the hills, leaving him barely time to get his men under arms before the dark enemies arrived."[82]

And there are some legends told about African wars that would put the "Arabian Nights" to the blush.[83]

In Africa, as in districts of Germany and Holland, woman is burdened with agricultural duties. The soil of Africa is very rich,[84] and consequently Nature furnishes her untutored children with much spontaneous vegetation. It is a rather remarkable fact, that the average African warrior thinks it a degradation for him to engage in agriculture. He will fell trees, and help move a village, but will not go into the field to work. The women—generally the married ones—do the gardening. They carry the seed on their heads in a large basket, a hoe on their shoulder, and a baby slung on the back. They scatter the seed over the ground, and then break up the earth to the depth of three or four inches.

"Four or five gardens are often to be seen round a kraal, each situated so as to suit some particular plant. Various kinds of crops are cultivated by the Kaffirs, the principal being maize, millet, pumpkins, and a kind of spurious sugar-cane in great use throughout Southern Africa, and popularly known by the name of 'sweet-reed.' The two former constitute, however, the necessaries of life, the latter belonging rather to the class of luxuries. The maize, or, as it is popularly called when the pods are severed from the stem, 'mealies,' is the very staff of life to a Kaffir; as it is from the mealies that is made the thick porridge on which the Kaffir chiefly lives. If a European hires a Kaffir, whether as guide, servant, or hunter, he is obliged to supply him with a stipulated quantity of food, of which the maize forms the chief ingredient. Indeed, so long as the native of Southern Africa can get plenty of porridge and sour milk, he is perfectly satisfied with his lot. When ripe, the ears of maize are removed from the stem, the leafy envelope is stripped off, and they are hung in pairs over sticks until they are dry enough to be taken to the storehouse."[85]

The cattle are cared for by the men, and women are not allowed to engage in the hunt for wild animals. The cattle among the mountain and sandstone tribes are of a fine stock, but those of the tribes in the alluvia, like their owners, are small and sickly.

The African pays more attention to his weapons of offensive warfare than he does to his wives; but in many instances he is quite skilful in the handicrafts.

> "The Ishogo people are noted throughout the neighboring tribes for the superior quality and fineness of the bongos, or pieces of grass-cloth, which they manufacture. They are industrious and skilful weavers. In walking down the main street of Mokenga, a number of ouandjas, or houses without walls are seen, each containing four or five looms, with the weavers seated before them weaving the cloth. In the middle of the floor of the ouandjay a wood-fire is seen burning; and the weavers, as you pass by, are sure to be seen smoking their pipes, and chatting to one another whilst going on with their work. The weavers are all men, and it is men also who stitch the bongos together to make denguis or robes of them; the stitches are not very close together, nor is the thread very fine, but the work is very neat and regular, and the needles are of their own manufacture. The bongos are very often striped, and sometimes made even in check patterns; this is done by their dyeing some of the threads of the warp, or of both warp and woof, with various simple colors; the dyes are all made of decoctions of different kinds of wood, except for black, when a kind of iron ore is used. The bongos are employed as money in this put of Africa. Although called grass-cloth by me, the material is not made of grass, but of the delicate and firm cuticle of palm leaflets, stripped off in a dexterous manner with the fingers."[86]

Nearly all his mechanical genius seems to be exhausted in the perfection of his implements of war, and Dr. Livingstone is of the opinion, that when a certain perfection in the arts is reached, the natives pause. This, we think, is owing to their far remove from other nations. Livingstone says,—

"The races of this continent seem to have advanced to a certain point and no farther; their progress in the arts of working iron and copper, in pottery, basket-making, spinning, weaving, making nets, fish-hooks, spears, axes, knives, needles, and other things, whether originally invented by this people or communicated by another instructor, appears to have remained in the same rude state for a great number of centuries. This apparent stagnation of mind in certain nations we cannot understand, but, since we have in the latter ages of the world made what we consider great progress in the arts, we have unconsciously got into the way of speaking of some other races in much the same tone as that used by the Celestials in the Flowery Land. These same Chinese anticipated us in several most important discoveries, by as many centuries as we may have preceded others. In the knowledge of the properties of the magnet, the composition of gunpowder, the invention of printing, the manufacture of porcelain, of silk, and in the progress of literature, they were before us. But then the power of making further discoveries was arrested, and a stagnation of the intellect prevented their advancing in the path of improvement or invention."

Mr. Wood says,—

"The natives of Southern Africa are wonderful proficients in forging iron; and, indeed, a decided capability for the blacksmith's art seems to be inherent in the natives of Africa, from north to south, and from east to west. None of the tribes can do very much with the iron, but the little which they require is worked in perfection. As in the case with all uncivilized beings, the whole treasures of the art are lavished on their weapons; and so, if we wish to see what an African savage can do with iron, we must look at his spears, knives, and arrows—the latter, indeed, being but spears in miniature."

The blacksmith, then, is a person of some consequence in his village. He gives shape and point to the weapons by which game is to be secured and battles won. All seek his favor.

"Among the Kaffirs, a blacksmith is a man of considerable importance, and is much respected by the tribe. He will not profane the mystery of his craft by allowing uninitiated eyes to inspect his various processes, and therefore carries on his operations at some distance from the kraal. His first care is to prepare the bellows. The form which he uses prevails over a very large portion of Africa, and is seen, with some few modifications, even among the many islands of Polynesia. It consists of two leathern sacks, at the upper end of which is a handle. To the lower end of each sack is attached the hollow horns of some animal, that of the cow or eland being most commonly used; and when the bags are alternately inflated and compressed, the air passes out through the two horns.

"Of course the heat of the fire would destroy the horns if they were allowed to come in contact with it; and they are therefore inserted, not into the fire, but into an earthenware tube which communicates with the fire. The use of valves is unknown; but as the two horns do not open into the fire, but into the tube, the fire is not drawn into the bellows as would otherwise be the case. This arrangement, however, causes considerable waste of air, so that the bellows-blower is obliged to work much harder than would be the case if he were provided with an instrument that could conduct the blast directly to its destination. The ancient Egyptians used a bellows of precisely similar construction, except that they did not work them entirely by hand. They stood with one foot on each sack, and blew the fire by alternately pressing on them with the feet, and raising them by means of a cord fastened to their upper ends.

> "When the blacksmith is about to set to work, he digs a hole in the ground, in which the fire is placed; and then sinks the earthenware tube in a sloping direction, so that the lower end opens at the bottom of the hole, while the upper end projects above the level of the ground. The two horns are next inserted into the upper end of the earthenware tube; and the bellows are then fastened in their places, so that the sacks are conveniently disposed for the hands of the operator, who sits between them. A charcoal-fire is then laid in the hole, and is soon brought to a powerful heat by means of the bellows. A larger stone serves the purpose of an anvil, and a smaller stone does duty for a hammer. Sometimes the hammer is made of a conical piece of iron, but in most cases a stone is considered sufficient. The rough work of hammering the iron into shape is generally done by the chief blacksmith's assistants, of whom he has several, all of whom will pound away at the iron in regular succession. The shaping and finishing the article is reserved by the smith for himself. The other tools are few and simple, and consist of punches and rude pinchers made of two rods of iron.

"With these instruments the Kaffir smith can cast brass into various ornaments, Sometimes he pours it into a cylindrical mould, so as to make a bar from which bracelets and similar ornaments can be hammered, and sometimes he makes studs and knobs by forming their shape in clay moulds."[87]

Verily, the day will come when these warlike tribes shall beat their spears into pruning-hooks, and their assagais into ploughshares, and shall learn war no more! The skill and cunning of their artificers shall be consecrated to the higher and nobler ends of civilization, and the noise of battle shall die amid the music of a varied industry!

FOOTNOTES:

[68] Livingstone's Expedition to the Zambesi, pp. 216, 217.

[69] Ashango Land, pp. 288, 289, 291, 292.

[70] Western Africa, p. 257 sq.

[71] Through the Dark Continent, vol. i. p. 489.

[72] Uncivilized Races of Men, vol. i. chap, vii.

[73] Equatorial Africa, pp. 377, 378.

[74] Savage Africa, p. 216.

[75] Expedition to Zambesi, pp. 626, 627.

[76] Livingstone's Expedition to the Zambesi, pp. 307, 308.

[77] Savage Africa, p. 219.

[78] See Savage Africa, p. 207. Livingstone's Life-Work, pp. 47, 48. Uncivilized Races of Men, vol. 1. pp. 71-86; also Du Chaillu and Denham and Clappterton.

[79] Savage Africa, pp. 424, 425.

[80] Livingstone's Expedition to the Zambesi, pp 625, 626.

[81] Savage Africa, pp 426, 427.

[82] Uncivilized Races of Men, vol. i. p. 94.

[83] Through the Dark Continent, vol. i. p. 344 sq.; also vol. ii. pp. 87, 88.

[84] Livingstone's Zambesi, pp. 613-617.

[85] Uncivilized Races of Men, vol. i. p. 146.

[86] Ashango Land, pp 290, 291.

[87] Uncivilized Races of Men, vol. i. pp. 97, 98.

CHAPTER VIII
LANGUAGES, LITERATURE, AND RELIGION

Structure of African Languages.—The Mpongwe, Mandingo, and Grebo.—Poetry: Epic, Idyllic, and Miscellaneous.—Religions and Superstitions.

PHILOLOGICALLY the inhabitants of Africa are divided into two distinct families. The dividing line that Nature drew across the continent is about two degrees north of the equator. Thus far science has not pushed her investigations into Northern Africa; and, therefore, little is known of the dialects of that section. But from what travellers have learned of portions of different tribes that have crossed the line, and made their way as far as the Cape of Good Hope, we infer, that, while there are many dialects in that region, they all belong to one common family. During the Saracen movement, in the second century of the Christian era, the Arab turned his face toward Central Africa. Everywhere traces of his language and religion are to be found. He transformed whole tribes of savages. He built cities, and planted fields; he tended flocks, and became trader. He poured new blood into crumbling principalities, and taught the fingers of the untutored savage to war. His religion, in many places, put out the ineffectual fires of the fetich-house, and lifted the grovelling thoughts of idolaters heavenward. His language, like the new juice of the vine, made its way to the very roots of Negro dialects, and gave them method and tone. In the song and narrative, in the prayer and precept, of the heathen, the Arabic comes careering across each sentence, giving cadence and beauty to all.

On the heels of the Mohammedan followed the Portuguese, the tried and true servants of Rome, bearing the double swords and keys. Not so extensive as the Arab, the influence of the Portuguese, nevertheless, has been quite considerable.

All along the coast of Northern Guinea, a distance of nearly fifteen hundred miles,—from Cape Mesurado to the mouth of the Niger,—the Kree, Grebo, and Basa form one general family, and speak the Mandu language. On the Ivory Coast another language is spoken between Frisco and Dick's Cove. It is designated as the Av[)e]kw[)o]m language, and in its verbal and inflective character is not closely related to the Mandu. The dialects of Popo, Dahomey, Ashantee, and Akra are resolvable into a family or language called the Fantyipin. All these dialects, to a greater or less extent, have incorporated many foreign words,—Dutch, French, Spanish, English, Portuguese, and even many words from Madagascar. The language of the Gold and Ivory Coasts we find much fuller than those on the Grain Coast. Wherever commerce or mechanical enterprise imparts a quickening touch, we find the vocabulary of the African amplified. Susceptible, apt, and cunning, the coast tribes, on account of their intercourse with the outside world, have been greatly changed. We are sorry that the change has not always been for the better. Uncivilized sailors, and brainless and heartless speculators, have sown the rankest seeds of an effete Caucasian civilization in the hearts of the unsuspecting Africans. These poor people have learned to cheat, lie, steal; are capable of remarkable diplomacy and treachery; have learned well the art of flattery and extreme cruelty. Mr. Wilson says,—

> "The Sooahelee, or Swahere language, spoken by the aboriginal inhabitants of Zanzibar, is very nearly allied to the Mpongwe, which is spoken on the western coast in very nearly the same parallel of latitude. *One-fifth of the words of these two dialects are either the same, or so nearly so that they may easily be traced to the same root.*"

The Italics are our own. The above was written just a quarter of a century ago.

> "The language of Uyanzi seemed to us to be a mixture of almost all Central African dialects. Our great stock of native words, in all dialects, proved of immense use to me; and in three days I discovered, after classifying and comparing the words heard from the Wy-anzi with other African words, that I was tolerably proficient, at least for all practical purposes, in the Kiyanzi dialect."[88]

Mr. Stanley wrote the above in Africa in March, 1877. It was but a repetition of the experiences of Drs. Livingstone and Kirk, that, while the dialects west and south-west of the Mountains of the Moon are numerous, and apparently distinct, they are referable to one common parent. The Swahere language has held its place from the beginning. Closely allied to the Mpongwe, it is certainly one of great strength and beauty.

> "This great family of languages—if the Mpongwe dialect may be taken as a specimen—is remarkable for its beauty, elegance, and perfectly philosophical arrangements, as well as for its almost indefinite expansibility. In these respects it

not only differs essentially and radically from all the dialects north of the Mountains of the Moon, but they are such as may well challenge a comparison with any known language in the world."[89]

The dialects of Northern Africa are rough, irregular in structure, and unpleasant to the ear. The Mpongwe we are inclined to regard as the best of all the dialects we have examined. It is spoken, with but slight variations, among the Mpongwe, Ayomba, Oroungou, Rembo, Camma, Ogobay, Anenga, and Ngaloi tribes. A careful examination of several other dialects leads us to suspect that they, too, sustain a distant relationship to the Mpongwe.

Next to this remarkable language comes the Bakalai, with its numerous dialectic offspring, scattered amongst the following tribes: the Balengue, Mebenga, Bapoukow, Kombe, Mbiki, Mbousha, Mbondemo, Mbisho, Shekiani, Apingi, Evili, with other tribes of the interior.

The two families of languages we have just mentioned—the Mpongwe and the Bakalai—are distinguished for their system and grammatical structure. It is surprising that these unwritten languages should hold their place among roving, barbarous tribes through so many years. In the Mpongwe language and its dialects, the liquid and semi-vowel r is rolled with a fulness and richness harmonious to the ear. The Bakalai and its branches have no r; and it is no less true that all tribes that exclude this letter from their dialects are warlike, nomadic, and much inferior to the tribes that use it freely.

The Mpongwe language is spoken on each side of the Gabun, at Cape Lopez, and at Cape St. Catharin in Southern Guinea; the Mandingo, between Senegal and the Gambia; and the Grebo language, in and about Cape Palmas. It is about twelve hundred miles from Gabun to Cape Palmas, about two thousand miles from Gabun to Senegambia, and about six hundred miles from Cape Palmas to Gambia. It is fair to presume that these tribes are sufficiently distant from each other to be called strangers. An examination of their languages may not fail to interest.

It has been remarked somewhere, that a people's homes are the surest indications of the degree of civilization they have attained. It is certainly true, that deportment has much to do with the polish of language. The disposition, temperament, and morals of a people who have no written language go far toward giving their language its leading characteristics. The Grebo people are a well-made, quick, and commanding-looking people. In their intercourse with one another, however, they are unpolished, of sudden temper, and revengeful disposition.[90] Their language is consequently monosyllabic. A great proportion of Grebo words are of the character indicated. A few verbs will illustrate. Kba, carry; la, kill; ya, bring; mu, go; wa, walk; ni, do; and so on. This is true of objects, or nouns. Ge, farm; bro, earth; w[)e]nh, sun; tu, tree; gi, leopard; na, fire; yi, eye; bo, leg; lu, head; nu, rain; kai, house. The Grebo people seem to have no idea of syllabication. They do not punctuate; but, speaking with the rapidity with which they move, run their words together until a whole sentence might be taken for one word. If any thing has angered a Grebo he will say, "E ya mu kra wudi;" being interpreted, "It has raised a great bone in my throat." But he says it so quickly that he pronounces it in this manner, yamukroure. There are phrases in this language that are beyond the ability of a foreigner to pronounce. It has no contractions, and often changes the first and second person of the personal pronoun, and the first and second person plural, by lowering or pitching the voice. The orthography remains the same, though the significations of those words are radically different.

The Mpongwe language is largely polysyllabic. It is burdened with personal pronouns, and its adjectives have numerous changes in addition to their degrees of comparison. We find no inflections to suggest case or gender. The adjective *mpolo*, which means "large," carries seven or eight forms. While it is impossible to tell whether a noun is masculine, feminine, or neuter, they use one adjective for all four declensions, changing its form to suit each.

The following form of declensions will serve to impart a clearer idea of the arbitrary changes in the use of the adjective:

First Declension.	(Singular, nyare mpolu, a large cow.
	(Plural, inyare impolu, large cows.
Second Declension.	(Singular, egara evolu, a large chest.
	(Plural, gara volu, large chests.
Third Declension.	(Singular, idâmbe ivolu, a large sheep.
	(Plural, idâmbe ampolu, large sheep.
Fourth Declension.	(Singular, omamba ompolu, a large snake.
	(Plural, imamba impolu, large snakes.[91]

We presume it would be a difficult task for a Mpongwe to explain the arbitrary law by which such changes are made. And yet he is as uniform and strict in his obedience to this law as if it were written out in an Mpongwe grammar, and taught in every village.

His verb has four moods; viz., indicative, imperative, conditional, and subjunctive. The auxiliary particle gives the indicative mood its grammatical being. The imperative is formed from the present of the indicative by changing its initial consonant into its reciprocal consonant as follows:—

> *tonda*, to love.
> *ronda*, love thou.
> *denda*, to do.
> *lenda*, do thou.

The conditional mood has a form of its own; but the conjunctive particles are used as auxiliaries at the same time, and different conjunctive particles are used with different tenses. The subjunctive, having but one form, in a sentence where there are two verbs is used as the second verb.[92] So by the use of the auxiliary particles the verb can form the infinitive and potential mood. The Mpongwe verb carries four tenses,—present, past or historical, perfect past, and future. Upon the principle of alliteration the perfect past tense, representing an action as completed, is formed from the present tense by prefixing a, and by changing a-final into i: for example, t[)o]nda, "to love;" at[)o]ndi, "did love." The past or historical tense is derived from the imperative by prefixing a, and by changing a-final into i. Thus r[)o]nda, "love;" ar[)o]ndi, "have loved." The future tense is constructed by the aid of the auxiliary particle be, as follows: mi be t[)o]nda," I am going to love."

We have not been able to find a Mandingo grammar, except Mr. MacBrair's, which is, as far as we know, the only one in existence. We have had but little opportunity to study the structure of that language. But what scanty material we have at hand leads us to the conclusion that it is quite loosely put together. The saving element in its verb is the minuteness with which it defines the time of an action. The causative form is made by the use of a suffix. It does not use the verb "to go" or "come" in order to express a future tense. Numerous particles are used in the substantive verb sense. The Mandingo language is rather smooth. The letters v and z are not in it. About one-fifth of the verbs and nouns commence with vowels, and the noun always terminates in the letter o.

Here is a wide and interesting field for philologists: it should be cultivated.

The African's nature is as sunny as the climate he lives in. He is not brutal, as many advocates of slavery have asserted. It is the unanimous testimony of all explorers of, and travellers through, the Dark Continent, that the element of gentleness predominates among the more considerable tribes; that they have a keen sense of the beautiful, and are susceptible of whatever culture is brought within their reach. The Negro nature is not sluggish, but joyous and vivacious. In his songs he celebrates victories, and laughs at death with the complacency of the Greek Stoics.

"Rich man and poor fellow, all men must die:
Bodies are only shadows. Why should I be sad?"[93]

He can be deeply wrought upon by acts of kindness; and bears a friendship to those who show him favor, worthy of a better state of society. When Henry M. Stanley (God bless him! noble, brave soul!) was about emerging from the Dark Continent, he made a halt at Kabinda before he ended his miraculous journey at Zanzibar on the Pacific Ocean. He had been accompanied in his perilous journey by stout-hearted, brave, and faithful natives. Their mission almost completed, they began to sink into that listlessness which is often the precursor of death. They had been true to their master, and were now ready to die as bravely as they had lived. Read Mr. Stanley's account without emotion if you can:—

"'Do you wish to see Zanzibar, boys?' I asked.

"'Ah, it is far. Nay, speak not, master. We shall never see it,' they replied.

"'But you will die if you go on in this way. Wake up—shake yourselves—show yourselves to be men.'

"'Can a man contend with God? Who fears death? Let us die undisturbed, and be at rest forever,' they answered.

"Brave, faithful, loyal souls! They were, poor fellows, surrendering themselves to the benumbing influences of a listlessness and fatal indifference to life! Four of them died in consequence of this strange malady at Loanda, three more on board her Majesty's ship Industry, and one woman breathed her last the day after we arrived at Zanzibar. But in their sad death they had one consolation, in the words which they kept constantly repeating to themselves—

"'We have brought our master to the great sea, and he has seen his white brothers. La il Allah, il Allah! There is no God but God!' they said—and died.

"It is not without an overwhelming sense of grief, a choking in the throat, and swimming eyes, that I write of those days; for my memory is still busy with the worth and virtues of the dead. In a thousand fields of incident, adventure, and bitter trials, they had proved their stanch heroism and their fortitude; they had lived and endured nobly. I remember the enthusiasm with which they responded to my appeals; I remember their bold bearing during the darkest days; I remember the Spartan pluck, the indomitable courage, with which they suffered in the days of our adversity. Their voices again loyally answer me, and again I hear them address each other upon the necessity of standing by the 'master.' Their boat-song, which contained sentiments similar to the following:—

> 'The pale-faced stranger, lonely here,
> In cities afar, where his name is dear,
> Your Arab truth and strength shall show;
> He trusts in us, row, Arabs, row'—

despite all the sounds which now surround me, still charms my listening ear.[94] ...

"They were sweet and sad moments, those of parting. What a long, long, and true friendship was here sundered! Through what strange vicissitudes of life had they not followed me! What wild and varied scenes had we not seen together! What a noble fidelity these untutored souls had exhibited! The chiefs were those who had followed me to Ujiji in 1871; they had been witnesses of the joy of Livingstone at the sight of me; they were the men to whom I intrusted the safe-guard of Livingstone on his last and fatal journey, who had mourned by his corpse at Muilala, and borne the illustrious dead to the Indian Ocean.

> "And in a flood of sudden recollection, all the stormy period here ended rushed in upon my mind; the whole panorama of danger and tempest through which these gallant fellows had so stanchly stood by me—these gallant fellows now parting from me. Rapidly, as in some apocalyptic vision, every scene of strife with Man and Nature, through which these poor men and women had borne me company, and solaced me by the simple sympathy of common suffering, came hurrying across my memory; for each face before me was associated with some adventure or some peril, reminded me of some triumph or of some loss. What a wild, weird retrospect it was,—that mind's flash over the troubled past! so like a troublous dream!

"And for years and years to come, in many homes in Zanzibar, there will be told the great story of our journey, and the actors in it will be heroes among their kilt and kin. For me too they are heroes, these poor, ignorant children of Africa, for, from the first deadly struggle in savage Ituru to the last staggering rush into Embomma, they had rallied to my voice like veterans, and in the hour of need they had never failed me. And thus, aided by their willing hands and by their loyal hearts, the expedition had been successful, and the three great problems of the Dark Continent's geography had been fairly settled."[95]

How many times we have read this marvellous narrative of Stanley's march through the Dark Continent, we do not know; but we do know that every time we have read it with tears and emotion, have blessed the noble Stanley, and thanked God for the grand character of his black followers! There is no romance equal to these two volumes. The trip was one awful tragedy from beginning to end, and the immortal deeds of his untutored guards are worthy of the famous *Light Brigade*.

On the fourth day of August, 1877, Henry M. Stanley arrived at the village of Nsanda on his way to the ocean. He had in his command one hundred and fifteen souls. Foot-sore, travel-soiled, and hungry, his people sank down exhausted. He tried to buy food from the natives; but they, with an indifference that was painful, told them to wait until market-day. A foraging party scoured the district for food, but found none. Starvation was imminent. The feeble travellers lay upon the ground in the camp, with death pictured on their dusky features. Stanley called his boat-captains to his tent, and explained the situation. He knew that he was within a few days march of Embomma, and that here were located one Englishman, one Frenchman, one Spaniard, and one Portuguese. He told the captains that he had addressed a letter to these persons for aid; and that resolute, swift, and courageous volunteers were needed to go for the relief, — without which the whole camp would be transformed into a common graveyard. We will now quote from Mr. Stanley again in proof of the noble nature of the Negro:—

> "The response was not long coming; for Uledi sprang up and said, 'O master, don't talk more! I am ready now. See, I will only buckle on my belt, and I shall start at once, and nothing will stop me. I will follow on the track like a leopard.'

"'And I am one,' said Kachéché. 'Leave us alone, master. If there are white men at Embomma, we will find them out. We will walk and walk, and when we cannot walk we will crawl.'

"'Leave off talking men,' said Muini Pembé, 'and allow others to speak, won't you? Hear me, my master. I am your servant. I will outwalk the two. I will carry the letter, and plant it before the eyes of the white men.'

"'I will go too, sir,' said Robert.

"'Good! It is just as I should wish it; but, Robert, you cannot follow these three men. You will break down, my boy.'

"'Oh, we will carry him if he breaks down,' said Uledi. 'Won't we, Kachéché?'

"'*Inshallah!*' responded Kachéché decisively. 'We must have Robert along with us, otherwise the white men won't understand us.'"

What wonderful devotion! What sublime self-forgetfulness! The world has wept over such stories as Bianca and Héloise, and has built monuments that will stand,—

> "While Fame her record keeps,
> Or Homer paints the hallowed spot
> Where Valor proudly sleeps,"—

and yet these black heroes are unremembered. "I will follow the track like a leopard," gives but a faint idea of the strong will of Uledi; and Kachéché's brave words are endowed with all the attributes of that heroic *abandon* with which a devoted general hurls the last fragment of wasting strength against a stubborn enemy. And besides, there is something so tender in these words that they seem to melt the heart. "We will walk and walk, and when we cannot walk we will crawl!" We have never read but one story that approaches this narrative of Mr. Stanley, and that was the tender devotion of Ruth to her mother-in-law. We read it in the Hebrew to Dr. O.S. Stearns of Newton, Mass.; and confess that, though it has been many years since, the blessed impression still remains, and our confidence in humanity is strengthened thereby.

Here are a few white men in the wilds of Africa, surrounded by the uncivilized children of the desert. They have money and valuable instruments, a large variety of gewgaws that possessed the power of charming the fancy of the average savage; and therefore the whites would have been a tempting prey to the blacks. But not a hair of their head was harmed. The white men had geographical fame to encourage them in the struggle,— friends and loved ones far away beyond the beautiful blue sea. These poor savages had nothing to steady their purposes save a paltry sum of money as day-wages,—no home, no friends; and yet they were as loyal as if a throne were awaiting them. No, no! nothing waited on their heroic devotion to a magnificent cause but a lonely death when they had brought the "master" to the sea. When their stomachs, pinched by hunger; when their limbs, stiff from travel; when their eyes, dim with the mists of death; when every vital force was slain by an heroic ambition to serve the great Stanley; when the fires of endeavor were burnt to feeble embers,—then, and only then, would these faithful Negroes fail in the fulfilment of their mission, so full of peril, and yet so grateful to them, because it was in the line of duty.

Cicero urged virtue as necessary to effective oratory. The great majority of Negroes in Africa are both orators and logicians. A people who have such noble qualities as this race seems to possess has, as a logical necessity, the poetic element in a large degree.

In speaking of Negro poetry, we shall do so under three different heads; viz., the *Epic, Idyllic, Religious,* or miscellaneous.

The epic poetry of Africa, so far as known, is certainly worthy of careful study. The child must babble before it can talk, and all barbarians have a sense of the sublime in speech. Mr. Taine, in his "History of English Literature," speaking of early Saxon poetry, says,—

> "One poem nearly whole, and two or three fragments, are all that remain of this lay-poetry of England. The rest of the pagan current, German and barbarian, was arrested or overwhelmed, first by the influx of the Christian religion, then by the conquest of the Norman-French. But what remains more than suffices to show the strange and powerful poetic genius of the race, and to exhibit beforehand the flower in the bud.

> "If there has ever been anywhere a deep and serious poetic sentiment, it is here. They do not speak: they sing, or rather they shout. Each little verse is an acclamation, which breaks forth like a growl; their strong breasts heave with a groan of anger or enthusiasm, and a vehement or indistinct phrase or expression rises suddenly, almost in spite of them, to their lips. There is no art, no natural talent, for describing, singly and in order, the different parts of an object or an event. The fifty rays of light which every phenomenon emits in succession to a regular and well-directed intellect, come to them at once in a glowing and confused mass, disabling them by their force and convergence. Listen to their genuine war-chants, unchecked and violent, as became their terrible voices! To this day, at this distance of time, separated as they are by manners, speech, ten centuries, we seem to hear them still."[96]

This glowing description of the poetry of the primitive and hardy Saxon gives the reader an excellent idea of the vigorous, earnest, and gorgeous effusions of the African. Panda was king of the Kaffirs. He was considered quite a great warrior. It took a great many *isi-bongas* to describe his virtues. His chief *isi-bongas* was "O-Elephant." This was chosen to describe his strength and greatness. Mr. Wood gives an account of the song in honor of Panda:—

"1. Thou brother of the Tchaks, considerate forder,
2. A swallow which fled in the sky;
3. A swallow with a whiskered breast;
4. Whose cattle was ever in so huddled a crowd,
5. They stumble for room when they ran.
6. Thou false adorer of the valor of another,
7. That valor thou tookest at the battle of Makonko.
8. Of the stock of N'dabazita, ramrod of brass,
9. Survivor alone of all other rods;
10. Others they broke and left this in the soot,
11. Thinking to burn at some rainy cold day.
12. Thigh of the bullock of Inkakavini,
13. Always delicious if only 'tis roasted,
14. It will always be tasteless if boiled.
15. The woman from Mankeba is delighted;
16. She has seen the leopards of Jama,
17. Fighting together between the Makonko.
18. He passed between the Jutuma and Ihliza,
19. The Celestial who thundered between the Makonko.
20. I praisethee, O King! son of Jokwane, the son of Undaba,
21. The merciless opponent of every conspiracy.
22. Thou art an elephant, an elephant, an elephant.
23. All glory to thee, thou monarch who art black."

"The first isi-bonga, in line 1, alludes to the ingenuity with which Panda succeeded in crossing the river so as to escape out of the district where Dingan exercised authority. In the second line, 'swallow which fled in the sky' is another allusion to the secrecy with which he managed his flight, which left no more track than the passage of a swallow through the air. Lines 4 and 5 allude to the wealth, i.e., the abundance of cattle, possessed by Panda. Line 6 asserts that Panda was too humble minded, and thought more of the power of Dingan than it deserved; while line 7 offers as proof of this assertion, that, when they came to fight, Panda conquered Dingan. Lines 8 to 11 all relate to the custom of seasoning sticks by hanging them over the fireplaces in Kaffir huts. Line 14 alludes to the fact that meat is very seldom roasted by the Kaffirs, but is almost invariably boiled, or rather stewed, in closed vessels. In line 15 the 'woman from Mankebe' is

Panda's favorite wife. In line 19 'The Celestial' alludes to the name of the great Zulu tribe over which Panda reigned; the word 'Zulu' meaning celestial, and having much the same import as the same word when employed by the Chinese to denote their origin. Line 21 refers to the attempts of Panda's rivals to dethrone him, and the ingenious manner in which he contrived to defeat their plans by forming judicious alliances."

There is a daring insolence, morbid vanity, and huge description in this song of Panda, that make one feel like admitting that the sable bard did his work of flattery quite cleverly. It should not be forgotten by the reader, that, in the translation of these songs, much is lost of their original beauty and perspicuity. The following song was composed to celebrate the war triumphs of Dinga, and is, withal, exciting, and possessed of good movement. It is, in some instances, much like the one quoted above:—

"Thou needy offspring of Umpikazi,
Eyer of the cattle of men;
Bird of Maube, fleet as a bullet,
Sleek, erect, of beautiful parts;
Thy cattle like the comb of the bees;
O head too large, too huddled to move;
Devourer of Moselekatze, son of Machobana;
Devourer of 'Swazi, son of Sobuza;
Breaker of the gates of Machobana;
Devourer of Gundave of Machobana;
A monster in size, of mighty power;
Devourer of Ungwati of ancient race;
Devourer of the kingly Uomape;
Like heaven above, raining and shining."

The poet has seen fit to refer to the early life of his hero, to call attention to his boundless riches, and, finally, to celebrate his war achievements. It is highly descriptive, and in the Kaffir language is quite beautiful.

Tchaka sings a song himself, the ambitious sentiments of which would have been worthy of Alexander the Great or Napoleon Bonaparte. He had carried victory on his spear throughout all Kaffir-land. Everywhere the tribes had bowed their submissive necks to his yoke; everywhere he was hailed as king. But out of employment he was not happy. He sighed for more tribes to conquer, and thus delivered himself:—

"Thou hast finished, finished the nations!
Where will you go out to battle now?

Hey! where will you go out to battle now?
Thou hast conquered kings!
Where are you going to battle now?
Thou hast finished, finished the nations!
Where are you going to battle now?
Hurrah, hurrah, hurrah!
Where are you going to battle now?"

There is really something modern in this deep lament of the noble savage!

The following war song of the Wollof, though it lacks the sonorous and metrical elements of real poetry, contains true military aggressiveness, mixed with the theology of the fatalist.

A WAR SONG.

"I go in front. I fear not death. I am not afraid. If I die, I will take my blood to bathe my head.

"The man who fears nothing marches always in front, and is never hit by the murderous ball. The coward hides himself behind a bush, and is killed.

"Go to the battle. It is not lead that kills. It is Fate which strikes us, and which makes us die."

Mr. Reade says of the musicians he met up the Senegal,—

"There are three classes of these public minstrels,—1, those who play such vulgar instruments as the flute and drum; 2, those who play on the ballafond, which is the marimba of Angola and South America, and on the harp; 3, those who sing the legends and battle-songs of their country, or who improvise satires or panegyrics. This last class are dreaded, though despised. They are richly rewarded in their lifetime, but after death they are not even given a decent burial. If they were buried in the ground, it would become barren; if in the river, the water would be poisoned, and the fish would die: so they are buried in hollow trees.

The idyllic poetry of Africa is very beautiful in its gorgeous native dress. It requires some knowledge of their mythology in order to thoroughly understand all their figures of speech. The following song is descriptive of the white man, and is the production of a Bushman.

"In the blue palace of the deep sea
Dwells a strange creature:
His skin as white as salt;
His hair long and tangled as the sea-weed.

He is more great than the princes of the earth;
He is clothed with the skins of fishes,—
Fishes more beautiful than birds.
His house is built of brass rods;
His garden is a forest of tobacco.
On his soil white beads are scattered
Like sand-grains on the seashore."

The following idyl, extemporized by one of Stanley's black soldiers, on the occasion of reaching Lake Nyanza, possesses more energy of movement, perspicuity of style, and warm, glowing imagery, than any song of its character we have yet met with from the lips of unlettered Negroes. It is certainly a noble song of triumph. It swells as it rises in its mission of praise. It breathes the same victorious air of the song of Miriam: "*Sing ye to the Lord, for he hath triumphed gloriously; the horse and the rider hath he thrown into the sea.*" And in the last verse the child-nature of the singer riots like "The May Queen" of Tennyson.

THE SONG OF TRIUMPH.

"Sing, O friends, sing; the journey is ended:
Sing aloud, O friends; sing to the great Nyanza.
Sing all, sing loud, O friends, sing to the great sea;
Give your last look to the lands behind, and then turn to the sea.

Long time ago you left your lands,
Your wives and children, your brothers and your friends;
Tell me, have you seen a sea like this
Since you left the great salt sea?

CHORUS.

Then sing, O friends! sing; the journey is ended:
Sing aloud, O friend! sing to this great sea.

This sea is fresh, is good and sweet;
Your sea is salt, and bad, unfit to drink.
This sea is like wine to drink for thirsty men;
The salt sea—bah! it makes men sick.

Lift up your heads, O men, and gaze around;
Try if you can see its end.
See, it stretches moons away,
This great, sweet, fresh-water sea.

We come from Usukuma land,
The land of pastures, cattle, sheep and goats,
The land of braves, warriors, and strong men,
And, lo! this is the far-known Usukuma sea.

Ye friends, ye scorned at us in other days.
Ah, ha! Wangwana. What say ye now?
Ye have seen the land, its pastures and its herds,
Ye now see the far-known Usukuma sea.
Kaduma's land is just below;
He is rich in cattle, sheep, and goats.
The Msungu is rich in cloth and beads;
His hand is open, and his heart is free.

To-morrow the Msungu must make us strong
With meat and beer, wine and grain.
We shall dance and play the livelong day,
And eat and drink, and sing and play."

The religious and miscellaneous poetry is not of the highest order. One of the most remarkable men of the Kaffir tribe was Sicana, a powerful chief and a Christian. He was a poet, and composed hymns, which he repeated to his people till they could retain them upon their memories. The following is a specimen of his poetical abilities, and which the people are still accustomed to sing to a low monotonous air:—

"Ulin guba inkulu siambata tina
Ulodali bom' unadali pezula,
Umdala undala idala izula,
Yebinza inquinquis zixeliela.
Utika umkula gozizuline,
Yebinza inquinquis nozilimele.
Umze uakonana subiziele,
Umkokeli ua sikokeli tina,
Uenza infama zenza go bomi;
Imali inkula subiziele,
Wena wena q'aba inyaniza,
Wena wena kaka linyaniza,
Wena wena klati linyaniza;
Invena inh'inani subiziele,
Ugaze laku ziman' heba wena,
Usanhla zaku ziman' heba wena,
Umkokili ua, sikokeli tina:

Ulodali bom' uadali pezula,
Umdala uadala idala izula."

TRANSLATION.

"Mantle of comfort! God of love!
The Ancient One on high!
Who guides the firmament above,
The heavens, and starry sky;

Creator, Ruler, Mighty One;
The only Good, All-wise,—
To him, the great eternal God,
Our fervent prayers arise.

Giver of life, we call on him,
On his high throne above,
Our Rock of refuge still to be,
Of safety and of love;

Our trusty shield, our sure defence,
Our leader, still to be:
We call upon our pitying God,
Who makes the blind to see.

We supplicate the Holy Lamb
Whose blood for us was shed,
Whose feet were pierced for guilty man,
Whose hands for us have bled;

Even our God who gave us life,
From heaven, his throne above,
The great Creator of the world,
Father, and God of love."

When any person is sick, the priests and devout people consult their favorite spirits. At Goumbi, in Equatorial Africa, this ceremony is quite frequent. Once upon a time the king fell sick. Quengueza was the name of the afflicted monarch. Ilogo was a favorite spirit who inhabited the moon. The time to invoke the favor of this spirit is during the full moon. The moon, in the language of Equatorial Africa, is Ogouayli. Well, the people gathered in front of the king's house, and began the ceremony, which consisted chiefly in singing the following song:—

"*Ilogo, we ask thee!*
Tell who has bewitched the king!

> *Ilogo, we ask thee,*
> *What shall we do to cure the king?*
>
> *The forests are thine, Ilogo!*
> *The rivers are thine, Ilogo!*
>
> *The moon is thine!*
> *O moon! O moon! O moon!*
> *Thou art the house of Ilogo!*
> *Shall the king die? Ilogo!*
> *O Ilogo! O moon! O moon!"*[97]

In African caravans or processions, there is a man chosen to go in front and sing, brandishing a stick somewhat after the manner of our band-masters. The song is rather an indifferent howl, with little or no relevancy. It is a position much sought after, and affords abundant opportunity for the display of the voice. Such a person feels the dignity of the position. The following is a sample:—

> *"Shove him on!*
> *But is he a good man?*
> *No, I think he's a stingy fellow;*
> *Shove him on!*
> *Let him drop in the road, then.*
> *No, he has a big stick:*
> *Shove him on!*
> *Oh, matta-bicho! matta-bicho!*
> *Who will give me matta-bicho?"*

Of this song Mr. Reade says,—

"*Matta-bicho* is a bunda compound meaning *kill-worm*; the natives supposing that their entrails are tormented by a small worm, which it is necessary to kill with raw spirits. From the frequency of their demand, it would seem to be the worm that ever gnaws, and that their thirst is the fire which is never quenched."

The Griot, as we have already mentioned, sings for money. He is a most accomplished parasite and flatterer. He makes a study of the art. Here is one of his songs gotten up for the occasion.

I.

"The man who had not feared to pass the seas through a love of study and of science heard of the poor Griot. He had him summoned. He made him sing songs which made the echoes of the Bornou mountains, covered with palm-trees, ring louder and louder as the sounds flew over the summits of the trees.

II.

"The songs touched the heart of the great white man, and the dew of his magnificence fell upon the Griot's head. Oh! how can he sing the wonderful deeds of the Toubab? His voice and his breath would not be strong enough to sing that theme. He must be silent, and let the lion of the forest sing his battles and his victories.

III.

"Fatimata heard the songs of the Griot. She heard, too, the deeds which the Toubab had accomplished. She sighed, and covered her head with her robe. Then she turned to her young lover, and she said, 'Go to the wars; let the flying ball kill thee: for Fatimata loves thee no longer. The white man fills her thoughts.'"

The most beautiful nursery song ever sung by any mother, in any language, may be heard in the Balengi county, in Central Africa. There is wonderful tenderness in it,—tenderness that would melt the coldest heart. It reveals a bright spot in the heart-life of this people.[98]

> "*Why dost than weep, my child?*
> *The sky is bright; the sun is shining: why dost than weep?*
> *Go to thy father: he loves thee; go, tell him why thou weepest.*
> *What! thou weepest still! Thy father loves thee; I caress thee:*
> *yet still thou art sad.*
> *Tell me then, my child, why dost thou weep?*"

It is not so very remarkable, when we give the matter thought, that the African mother should be so affectionate and devoted in her relations to her children. The diabolical system of polygamy has but this one feeble apology to offer in Africa. The wives of one man may quarrel, but the children always find loving maternal arms ready to shelter their heads against the wrath of an indifferent and cruel father. The mother settles all the disputes of the children, and cares for them with a zeal and tenderness that would be real beautiful in many American mothers; and, in return, the children are very noble in their relations to their mothers. "Curse me, but do not speak ill of my mother," is a saying in vogue throughout nearly all Africa. The old are venerated, and when they become sick they are abandoned to die alone.

It is not our purpose to describe the religions and superstitions of Africa. [99] To do this would occupy a book. The world knows that this poor people are idolatrous,—"bow down to wood and stone." They do not worship the true God, nor conform their lives unto the teachings of the Saviour. They worship snakes, the sun, moon, and stars, trees, and water-courses. But the bloody human sacrifice which they make is the most revolting feature of their spiritual degradation. Dr. Prichard has gone into this subject more thoroughly than our time or space will allow.

"Nowhere can the ancient African religion be studied better than in the kingdom of Congo. Christianity in Abyssinia, and Mohammedanism in Northern Guinea, have become so mingled with pagan rites as to render it extremely difficult to distinguish between them.

> "The inhabitants of Congo, whom I take as a true type of the tribes of Southern Guinea generally, and of Southern Central Africa, believe in a supreme Creator, and in a host of lesser divinities. These last they represent by images; each has its temple, its priests, and its days of sacrifice, as among the Greeks and Romans."[100]

The false religions of Africa are but the lonely and feeble reaching out of the human soul after the true God.

FOOTNOTES:

[88] Stanley's Through the Dark Continent, vol. ii. pp. 320, 321; see, also, pp. 3, 78, 123, 245, 414.

[89] Western Africa, p. 455.

[90] Western Africa, p. 456.

[91] Western Africa, p. 470.

[92] Equatorial Africa, p. 531.

[93] Savage Africa, p. 212.

[94] Through the Dark Continent, vol. ii. pp, 470, 471.

[95] Through the Dark Continent, vol. ii. pp. 482, 483.

[96] History of English Literature, vol i. pp. 48. 49.

[97] Equatorial Africa, pp. 448, 449.

[98] On the intellectual faculties of the Negro, see Prichard, third ed., 1837, vol. ii. p. 346, sect. iii. Peschel's Races of Men, p. 462, sq., especially Blumenbach's Life and Works, p. 305, sq Western Africa, p. 379,—all of chap. xi.

[99] See Prichard, fourth ed., 1841, vol. 1. p. 197, sect. v. Moffat's Southern Africa; Uncivilized Races of Men, vol 1. pp. 183-219.

[100] Savage Africa, p. 287, sq.

CHAPTER IX
SIERRA LEONE

Its Discovery and Situation.—Natural Beauty.—Founding of a Negro Colony.—The Sierra Leone Company.—Fever and Insubordination.—It becomes an English Province—Character of its Inhabitants.—Christian Missions, etc.

SIERRA LEONE was discovered and named by Piedro de Cintra. It is a peninsula, about thirty miles in length by about twenty-five in breadth, and is situated 8° and 30' north latitude, and is about 13½° west longitude. Its topography is rather queer. On the south and west its mountains bathe their feet in the Atlantic Ocean, and on the east and north its boundaries are washed by the river and bay of Sierra Leone. A range of mountains, co-extensive with the peninsula,—forming its backbone,—rises between the bay of Sierra Leone and the Atlantic Ocean, from two to three thousand feet in altitude. Its outlines are as severe as Egyptian architecture, and the landscape view from east or west is charming beyond the power of description. Freetown is the capital, with about twenty thousand inhabitants, situated on the south side of Sierra Leone River, and hugged in by an amphitheatre of beautiful hills and majestic mountains.

"On the side of the hill [says Mr. Reed] which rises behind the town is a charming scene, which I will attempt to describe. You have seen a rural hamlet, where each cottage is half concealed by its own garden. Now convert your linden into graceful palm, your apples into oranges, your gooseberry-bushes into bananas, your thrush which sings in its wicker cage into a gray parrot whistling on a rail;... sprinkle this with strange and powerful perfumes; place in the west a sun flaming among golden clouds in a prussian-blue sea, dotted with white sails; imagine those mysterious and unknown sounds, those breathings of the earth-soul, with which the warm night of Africa rises into life,—and then you will realize one of those moments of poetry which reward poor travellers for long days and nights of naked solitude."[101]

In 1772 Lord Mansfield delivered his celebrated opinion on the case of the Negro man Sommersett, whose master, having abandoned him in a sick condition, afterwards sought to reclaim him. The decision was to the effect that no man, white or black, could set foot on British soil and remain a slave. The case was brought at the instance of Mr. Granville Sharp. The decision created universal comment. Many Negroes in New England, who had found shelter under the British flag on account of the proclamation of Sir Henry Clinton, went to England. Free Negroes from other parts— Jamaica, St. Thomas, and San Domingo—hastened to breathe the free air of the British metropolis. Many came to want, and wandered about the streets of London, strangers in a strange land. Granville Sharp, a man of great humanity, was deeply affected by the sad condition of these people. He consulted with Dr. Smeathman, who had spent considerable time in Africa; and they conceived the plan of transporting them to the west coast of Africa, to form a colony.[102] The matter was agitated in London by the friends of the blacks, and finally the government began to be interested. A district of about twenty square miles was purchased by the government of Naimbanna, king of Sierra Leone, on which to locate the proposed colony. About four hundred Negroes and sixty white persons, the greater portion of the latter being "women of the town,"[103] were embarked on "The Nautilus," Capt. Thompson, and landed at Sierra Leone on the 9th of May, 1787. The climate was severe, the sanitary condition of the place vile, and the habits of the people immoral. The African fever, with its black death-stroke, reaped a harvest; while the irregularities and indolence of the majority of the colonists, added to the deeds of plunder perpetrated by predatory bands of savages, reduced the number of the colonists to about sixty-four souls in 1791.

The dreadful news of the fate of the colony was borne to the philanthropists in England. But their faith in colonization stood as unblanched before the revelation as the Iron Duke at Waterloo. An association was formed under the name of "St. George's Bay," but afterwards took the name of the "Sierra Leone Company," with a capital stock of one million two hundred and fifty thousand dollars, with such humanitarians as Granville Sharp, Thornton, Wilberforce, and Clarkson among its directors. The object of the company was to push forward the work of colonization. One hundred Europeans landed at Sierra Leone in the month of February, 1792, and were followed in March by eleven hundred and thirty-one Negroes. A large number of them had served in the British army during the Revolutionary War in America, and, accepting the offer of the British Government, took land in this colony as a reward for services performed in the army. Another fever did its hateful work; and fifty or sixty Europeans, and many blacks, fell under its parching and consuming touch.[104] Jealous feuds rent the survivors, and idleness palsied every nerve of industry in the colony. In 1794 a French squadron besieged the place, and the people sustained a loss of about two hundred and fifty thousand dollars. Once more an effort was made to revive the place, and get its drowsy energies aroused in the discharge of necessary duties. Some little good began to show itself; but it was only the tender bud of promise, and was soon trampled under the remorseless heel of five hundred and fifty insurrectionary maroons from Jamaica and Nova Scotia.

The indifferent character of the colonists, and the hurtful touch of the climate, had almost discouraged the friends of the movement in England. It was now the year 1800. This vineyard planted by good men yielded "nothing but leaves." No industry had been developed, no substantial improvement had been made, and the future was veiled in harassing doubts and fears. The money of the company had almost all been expended. The company barely had the signs of organic life in it, but the light of a beautiful Christian faith had not gone out across the sea in stalwart old England. The founders of the colony believed that good management would make the enterprise succeed: so they looked about for a master hand to guide the affair. On the 8th of August, 1807, the colony was surrendered into the hands of the Crown, and was made an English colony. During the same year in which this transfer was made, Parliament declared the slave-trade piracy; and a naval squadron was stationed along the coast for the purpose of suppressing it. At the first, many colored people of good circumstances, feeling that they would be safe under the English flag, moved from the United States to Sierra Leone. But the chief source of supply of population was the captured slaves, who were always unloaded at this place. When the English Government took charge of Sierra Leone, the population was 2,000, the majority of whom were from the West Indies or Nova Scotia. In 1811 it was nearly 5,000; in 1820 it was 12,000; it 1833 it was 30,000; in 1835 it was 35,000; in 1844 it was 40,000; in 1869 it was 55,374, with but 129 white men. On the 31st of March, 1827, the slaves that had been captured and liberated by the English squadron numbered 11,878; of which there were 4,701 males above, and 1,875 under, fourteen years of age. There were 2,717 females above, and 1,517 under, the age of fourteen, besides 1,068 persons who settled in Freetown, working in the timber-trade.

With the dreadful scourge of slavery driven from the sea, the sanitary condition of the place greatly improved; and with a vigorous policy of order and education enforced, Sierra Leone began to bloom and blossom as a rose. When the slaver disappeared, the merchant-vessel came on her peaceful mission of commerce.

The annual trade-returns presented to Parliament show that the declared value of British and Irish produce and manufactures exported to the West Coast of Africa, arranged in periods of five years each, has been as follows:—

EXPORTS FROM GREAT BRITAIN.

1846-50 ... £2,773,408; or a yearly average of £554,681

1851-55 ... 4,314,752; " " " 862,950

1856-60 ... 5,582,941; " " " 1,116,588

1861-63 ... 4,216,045; " " " 1,405,348

IMPORTS

The same trade-returns show that the imports of African produce from the West Coast into Great Britain have been as follows. The "official value" is given before 1856, after that date the "computed real value" is given.

Official value, 1851-55 ... £4,154,725; average, £830,945

Computed real value, 1856-60 .. 9,376,251; " 1,875,250

" " " 1861-63 .. 5,284,611; " 1,761,537

The value of African produce has decreased during the last few years in consequence of the discovery of the petroleum or rock-oil in America. In 1864 between four and five thousand bales of cotton were shipped to England.

It is to be borne in mind, that under the system which existed when Sierra Leone, the Gambia, and Gold Coast settlements were maintained for the promotion of the slave-trade, the lawful commerce was only £20,000 annually, and that now the amount of tonnage employed in carrying legal merchandise is greater than was ever engaged in carrying slaves.[105] W. Winwood Reade visited Sierra Leone during the Rebellion in America; but, being somewhat prejudiced against the Negro, we do not expect any thing remarkably friendly. But we quote from him the view he took of the people he met there:—

"The inhabitants of the colony may be divided into four classes:—

"First, The street-venders, who cry cassada-cakes, palm-oil, pepper, pieces of beef, under such names, as *agedee, aballa, akalaray*, and which are therefore as unintelligible as the street-cries of London. This is the costermonger type.

"Second, The small market-people, who live in frame houses, sell nails, fish-hooks, tape, thread, ribbons, etc., and who work at handicrafts in a small way.

"Third, The shopkeepers, who inhabit frame houses on stone foundations, and within which one may see a sprinkling of mahogany, a small library of religious books, and an almost English atmosphere of comfort.

"Lastly, The liberated Africans of the highest grade, who occupy two-story stone houses enclosed all around by spacious piazzas, the rooms furnished with gaudy richness; and the whole their own property, being built from the proceeds of their ... thrift."

When England abolished the slave-trade on the West Coast of Africa, Christianity arose with healing in her wings. Until slavery was abolished in this colony, missionary enterprises were abortive; but when the curse was put under the iron heel of British prohibition, the Lord did greatly bless the efforts of the missionary. The Episcopal Church—"the Church of England"—was the first on the ground in 1808; but it was some years before any great results were obtained. In 1832 this Church had 638 communicants, 294 candidates for baptism, 684 sabbath-school pupils, and 1,388 children in day-schools. This Church carried its missionary work beyond its borders to the tribes that were "sitting in darkness;" and in 1850 had built 54 seminaries and schools, had 6,600 pupils, 2,183 communicants, and 7,500 attendants on public worship. It is pleasant to record that out of 61 teachers, 56 were native Africans! In 1865 there were sixteen missionary societies along the West Coast of Africa. Seven were American, six English, two German, and one West-Indian. These societies maintained 104 European or American missionaries, had 110 mission-stations, 13,000 scholars, 236 schools, 19,000 registered communicants; representing a Christian population of 60,000 souls.

The Wesleyan Methodists began their work in 1811; and in 1831 they had two missionaries, 294 members in their churches, and 160 pupils in school. They extended their missions westward to the Gambia, and eastward toward Cape Coast Castle, Badagry, Abbeokuta, and Kumasi; and in this connection, in 1850, had 44 houses of worship, 13 out-stations, 42 day-schools, 97 teachers, 4,500 pupils in day and sabbath schools, 6,000 communicants, 560 on probation, and 14,600 in attendance on public worship. In 1850 the population of Sierra Leone was 45,000; of which 36,000 were Christians, against 1,734 Mohammedans.

Sierra Leone represents the most extensive composite population in the world for its size. About one hundred different tribe are represented, with as many different languages or dialects. Bishop Vida, under direction of the British Parliament, gave special attention to this matter, and found not less than one hundred and fifty-one distinct languages, besides several dialects spoken in Sierra Leone. They were arranged under twenty-six groups, and yet fifty-four are unclassified that are distinct as German and French. "God makes the wrath of man to praise him, and the remainder thereof he will restrain." Through these numerous languages, poor benighted Africa will yet hear the gospel.

Some years ago Dr. Ferguson, who was once governor of the Sierra Leone colony, and himself a colored man, wrote and an extended account of the situation there, which was widely circulated in England and America at the time. It is so manifestly just and temperate in tone, so graphic and minute in description, that we reproduce it *in extenso*:—

> "1. Those most recently arrived are to be found occupying mud houses and small patches of ground in the neighborhood of one or other of the villages (the villages are about twenty in number, placed in different parts of the colony, grouped in three classes or districts; names, mountain, river, and sea districts.) The majority remain in their locations as agriculturists; but several go to reside in the neighborhood of Freetown, looking out for work as laborers, farm-servants, servant to carry wood and water, grooms, house-servants, etc.; others cultivate vegetables, rear poultry and pigs, and supply eggs, for the Sierra Leone market. Great numbers are found offering for sale in the public market and elsewhere a vast quantity of cooked edible substances—rice, corn and cassava cakes; heterogeneous compounds of rice and corn-flower, yams, cassava, palm-oil, pepper, pieces of beef, mucilaginous vegetables, etc., etc., under names quite unintelligible to a stranger, such as aagedee, aballa, akalaray, cabona, etc., etc., cries which are shouted along the streets of Freetown from morn till night. These, the lowest grade of liberated Africans, are a harmless and well-disposed people; there is no poverty among them, nor begging; their habits are frugal and industrious; their anxiety to possess money is remarkable: but their energies are allowed to run riot and be

wasted from the want of knowledge requisite to direct them in proper channels.

"2. Persons of grade higher than those last described are to be found occupying frame houses: they drive a petty trade in the market, where they expose for sale nails, fish-hooks, door-hinges, tape, thread, ribbons, needles, pins, etc. Many of this grade also look out for the arrival of canoes from the country laden with oranges, *kolas,* sheep, bullocks, fowls, rice, etc., purchase the whole cargo at once at the water-side, and derive considerable profit from selling such articles by retail in the market and over the town. Many of this grade are also occupied in curing and drying fish, an article which always sells well in the market, and is in great request by people at a distance from the water-side, and in the interior of the country. A vast number of this grade are tailors, straw-hat makers, shoemakers, cobblers, blacksmiths, carpenters, masons, etc. Respectable men of this grade meet with ready mercantile credits amounting from twenty pounds to sixty pounds; and the class is very numerous.

"3. Persons of grade higher than that last mentioned are found occupying frame houses reared on a stone foundation of from six to ten feet in height. These houses are very comfortable; they are painted outside and in; have piazzas in front and rear, and many of them all round; a considerable sprinkling of mahogany furniture of European workmanship is to be found in them; several books are to be seen lying about, chiefly of a religious character; and a general air of domestic comfort pervades the whole, which, perhaps more than any thing else, bears evidence of the advanced state of intelligence at which they have arrived. This grade is nearly altogether occupied in shopkeeping, hawking, and other mercantile pursuits. At sales of prize goods, public auctions, and every other place affording a probability of cheap bargains, they are to be seen in great numbers, where they club together in numbers of from three to six, seven, or more, to purchase large lots or unbroken bales. And the scrupulous honesty with which the subdivision of the goods is afterwards made cannot be evidenced more thoroughly than this: that, common as such transactions are, they have never yet been known to become the subject of controversy or litigation. The principal streets of Freetown, as well as the approaches to the town, are lined on each side by an almost continuous range of booths and stalls, among which almost every article of merchandise is offered for sale, and very commonly at a cheaper rate than similar articles are sold in the shops of the merchants.

"Two rates of profit are recognized in the mercantile transactions of the European merchants; namely, a wholesale and retail profit, the former varying from thirty to fifty per cent, the latter from fifty to one hundred per cent. The working of the retail trade in the hands of Europeans requires a considerable outlay in the shape of shop-rent, shopkeepers' and clerks' wages, etc. The liberated Africans were not slow in observing nor in seizing on the advantages which their peculiar position held out for the successful prosecution of the retail trade.

"Clubbing together, as before observed, and holding ready money in their hands the merchants are naturally anxious to execute for them considerable orders on such unexceptionable terms of payment while, on the other hand, the liberated Africans, seeing clearly their advantage, insist most pertinaciously on the lowest possible percentage of wholesale profit.

"Having thus become possessed of the goods at the lowest possible ready-money rate, then subsequent transactions are not closed with the expense of shop-rents, shopkeepers' and clerks' wages and subsistence, etc., etc., expenses unavoidable to Europeans. They are therefore enabled at once to undersell the European retail merchants, and to secure a handsome profit to themselves; a consummation the more easily attained, aided as it is by the extreme simplicity and abstemiousness of their mode of living, which contrast so favorably for them with the expensive and almost necessary luxuries of European life. Many of this grade possess huge canoes, with which they trade in the upper part of the river, along shore, and in the neighbouring rivers, bringing down rice, palm-oil, cam-wood, ivory, hides, etc.,

etc., in exchange for British manufactures. They are all in easy circumstances, readily obtaining mercantile credits from sixty pounds to two hundred pounds. Persons of this and the grade next to be mentioned evince great anxiety to become possessed of houses and lots in old Freetown. These lots are desirable because of their proximity to the market-place and the great thoroughfares, and also for the superior advantages which they allow for the establishment of their darling object,—'a retail store.' Property of this description has of late years become much enhanced in value, and its value is still increasing solely from the annually increasing numbers and prosperity of this and the next grade. The town-lots originally granted to the Nova-Scotian settlers and the Maroons are, year after year, being offered for sale by public auction, and in every case liberated Africans are the purchasers. A striking instance of their desire to possess property of this description, and of its increasing value, came under my immediate notice a few months ago.

"The gentlemen of the Church Missionary Society having been for some time looking about in quest of a lot on which to erect a new chapel, a lot suitable for the purpose was at length offered for sale by public auction, and at a meeting of the society's local committee, it was resolved, in order to secure the purchase of the property in question, to offer as high as sixty pounds. The clergyman delegated for this purpose, at my recommendation, resolved, on his own responsibility, to offer, if necessary, as high as seventy pounds; but to the surprise and mortification of us all, the lot was knocked down at upward of ninety pounds, and a liberated African was the purchaser. He stated very kindly that if he had known the society were desirous of purchasing the lot he would not have opposed them; he nevertheless manifested no desire of transferring to them the purchase, and even refused an advance of ten pounds on his bargain.

"4. Persons of the highest grade of liberated Africans occupy comfortable two story stone houses, enclosed all round with spacious piazzas. These houses are their own property and are built from the proceeds of their own industry. In several of them are to be seen mahogany chairs, tables, sofas, and four-post bedsteads, pier-glasses, floor-cloths, and other articles indicative of domestic comfort and accumulating wealth.

"Persons of this grade, like those last described, are almost wholly engaged in mercantile pursuits. Their transactions, however, are of greater magnitude and value, and their business is carried on with an external appearance of respectability commensurate with then superior pecuniary means: thus, instead of exposing their wares for sale in booths or stalls by the wayside, they are to be found in neatly fitted-up shops on the ground-floors of their stone dwelling houses.

"Many individual members of this grade have realized very considerable sums of money,—sums which, to a person not cognizant of the fact, would appear to be incredible. From the studied manner in which individuals conceal their pecuniary circumstances from the world, it is difficult to obtain a correct knowledge of the wealth of the class generally. The devices to which they have recourse in conducting a bargain are often exceedingly ingenious; and to be reputed rich might materially interfere with their success on such occasions. There is nothing more common than to hear a plea of poverty set up and most pertinaciously urged, in extenuation of the terms of a purchase, by persons whose outward condition, comfortable well-furnished houses, and large mercantile credits, indicate any thing but poverty.

"There are circumstances, however, the knowledge of which they cannot conceal, and which go far to exhibit pretty clearly the actual state of matters: such as, *First*, the facility with which they raise large sums of cash prompt' at public auctions. *Second*, the winding up of the estates of deceased persons. (Peter Newland, a liberated African, died a short time before I left the colony: and his estate realized, in houses, merchandise, and cash, upward of fifteen hundred pounds.) *Third*, the extent of their mercantile credits. I am well acquainted with an individual of this grade who is much courted and caressed by every European merchant in the colony, who has transactions in trade with all of them, and whose name, shortly before my departure from the colony, stood on the debtor side of the books of one of the principal merchants to the amount of nineteen hundred pounds, to which sum it had been reduced from three thousand pounds during the preceding two months. A highly respectable female has now, and has had for several years, the government contract for the supplying of fresh beef to the troops and the naval squadron; and I have not heard that on a single occasion there has been cause of complaint for negligence or non-fulfilment of the terms of the contract. *Fourth,* many of them at the present moment have their children being educated in England at their own expense. There is at Sierra Leone a very fine regiment of colonial militia, more than eight-tenths of which are liberated Africans. The amount of property which they have acquired is ample guaranty for their loyalty, should that ever be called in question. They turn out with great alacrity and cheerfulness on all occasions for periodical drill. But perhaps the most interesting point of view in which the liberated Africans are to be seen, and that which will render their moral condition most intelligible to those at a distance, is where they sit at the Quarter Sessions as petty, grand, and special jurors. They constitute a considerable part of the jury at every session, and I have repeatedly heard the highest legal authority in the colony express his satisfaction with their decisions."

But this account was written at the early sunrise of civilization in Sierra Leone. Now civilization is at its noonday tide, and the hopes of the most sanguine friends of the liberated Negro have been more than realized. How grateful this renewed spot on the edge of the Dark Continent would be to the weary and battle-dimmed vision of Wilberforce, Sharp, and other friends of the colony! And if they still lived, beholding the wonderful results, would they not gladly say, "Lord, now lettest thou thy servant depart in peace, according to thy word: for mine eyes have seen thy salvation which thou hast prepared before the face of all people; a light to lighten the Gentiles, and the glory of thy people Israel"?

FOOTNOTES:

[101] Savage Africa, p. 25.

[102] Précis sur l'Établissement des Colonies de Sierra Léona et de Boulama, etc. Par C.B. Wadström, pp. 3-28.

[103] Wadström Essay on Colonization, p. 220.

[104] This led to the sending of 119 whites, along with a governor, as counsellors, physicians, soldiers, clerks, overseers, artificers, settlers, and servants. Of this company 57 died within the year, 22 returned, and 40 remained. See Wadström, pp. 121, sq.

[105] See Livingstone's Zambesi, pp. 633, 634.

CHAPTER X
THE REPUBLIC OF LIBERIA

Liberia.—Its Location.—Extent.—Rivers and Mountains.—History of the First Colony.—The Noble Men who laid the Foundation of the Liberian Republic.—Native Tribes.—Translation of the New Testament into the Vei Language.—The Beginning and Triumph of Christian Missions to Liberia.—History of the Different Denominations on the Field.—A Missionary Republic of Negroes.—Testimony of Officers of the Royal Navy as to the Efficiency of the Republic in suppressing the Slave-Trade.—The Work of the Future.

THAT section of country on the West Coast of Africa known as Liberia, extending from Cape Palmas to Cape Mount, is about three hundred miles coastwise. Along this line there are six colonies of Colored people, the majority of the original settlers being from the United States. The settlements are Cape Palmas, Cape Mesurado, Cape Mount, River Junk, Basa, and Sinon. The distance between them varies from thirty-five to one hundred miles, and the only means of communication is the coast-vessels. Cape Palmas, though we include it under the general title of Liberia, was founded by a company of intelligent Colored people from Maryland. This movement was started by the indefatigable J.H.B. Latrobe and Mr. Harper of the Maryland Colonization Society. This society purchased at Cape Palmas a territory of about twenty square miles, in which there was at that time—more than a half-century ago—a population of about four thousand souls. Within two years from the time of the first purchase, this enterprising society held deeds from friendly proprietors for eight hundred square miles, embracing the dominions of nine kings, who bound themselves to the colonists in friendly alliance. This territory spread over both banks of the Cavally River, and from the ocean to the town of Netea, which is thirty miles from the mouth of the river. In the immediate vicinity of Cape Palmas,—say within an area of twenty miles,—there was a native population of twenty-five thousand. Were we to go toward the interior from the Cape about forty-five or fifty miles, we should find a population of at least seventy thousand natives, the majority of whom we are sure are anxious to enjoy the blessings of education, trade, civilization, and Christianity. The country about Cape Palmas is very beautiful and fertile. The cape extends out into the sea nearly a mile, the highest place being about one hundred and twenty-five feet. Looking from the beach, the ground rises gradually until its distant heights are crowned with heavy, luxuriant foliage and dense forest timber. And to plant this colony the Maryland Legislature appropriated the sum of two hundred thousand dollars! And the colony has done worthily, has grown rapidly, and at present enjoys all the blessings of a Christian community. Not many years ago it declared its independence.

But Liberia, in the proper use of the term, is applied to all the settlements along the West Coast of Africa that were founded by Colored people from the United States. It is the most beautiful spot on the entire coast. The view is charming in approaching this country, Rev. Charles Rockwell says,—

> "One is struck with the dark green hue which the rank and luxuriant growth of forest and of field everywhere presents. In this it respect it strongly resembles in appearance the dark forests of evergreens which line a portion of the coast of Eastern Virginia ... At different points there are capes or promontories rising from thirty to forty to one or two hundred feet above the level of the sea; while at other places the land, though somewhatuneven, has not, near the sea, any considerable hills. In some places near the mouths of the rivers are thickly wooded marshes; but on entering the interior of the country the ground gradually rises, the streams become rapid, and at the distance of twenty miles or more from the sea, hills, and beyond them mountains, are often met with."

The physical, social, and political bondage of the Colored people in America before the war was most discouraging. They were mobbed in the North, and sold in the South. It was not enough that they were isolated and neglected in the Northern States: they were proscribed by the organic law of legislatures, and afflicted by the most burning personal indignities. They had a few friends; but even their benevolent acts were often hampered by law, and strangled by caste-prejudice. Following the plans of Granville Sharp and William Wilberforce, Liberia was founded as a refuge to all Colored men who would avail themselves of its blessings.

Colonization societies sprang into being in many States, and large sums of money were contributed to carry out the objects of these organizations. Quite a controversy arose inside of anti-slavery societies, and much feeling was evinced; but the men who believed colonization to be the solution of the slavery question went forward without wavering or doubting. In March, 1820, the first emigrants sailed for Africa, being eighty-six in number; and in January, 1822, founded the town of Monrovia, named for President Monroe. Rev. Samuel J. Mills, while in college in 1806, was moved by the Holy Spirit to turn his face toward Africa as a missionary. His zeal for missionary labor touched the hearts of Judson, Newell, Nott, Hall, and Rice, who went to mission-fields in the East as early as 1812.[106] The American Colonization Society secured the services of the Rev. Samuel J. Mills and Rev. Ebenezer Burgess to locate the colony at Monrovia. Mr. Mills found an early, watery grave; but the report of Mr. Burgess gave the society great hope, and the work was carried forward.

The first ten years witnessed the struggles of a noble band of Colored people, who were seeking a new home on the edge of a continent given over to the idolatry of the heathen. The funds of the society were not as large as the nature and scope of the work demanded. Emigrants went slowly, not averaging more than 170 per annum,—only 1,232 in ten years: but the average from the first of January, 1848, to the last of December, 1852, was 540 yearly; and, in the single year of 1853, 782 emigrants arrived at Monrovia. In 1855 the population of Monrovia and Cape Palmas had reached about 8,000.

Going south from Monrovia for about one hundred miles, and inland about twenty, the country was inhabited by the Bassa tribe and its branches; numbering about 130,000 souls, and speaking a common language. "They were peaceful, domestic, and industrious; and, after fully supplying their own wants, furnish a large surplus of rice, oil, cattle, and other articles of common use, for exportation."[107] This tribe, like the Veis, of whom we shall make mention subsequently, have reduced their language to a written system. The New Testament has been translated into their language by a missionary, and they have had the gospel these many years in their own tongue.

The "Greybo language," spoken in and about Cape Palmas, has been reduced to a written form; and twenty thousand copies of eleven different works have been printed and distributed. There are about seventy-five thousand natives within fifty miles of Cape Palmas; and, as a rule, they desire to avail themselves of the blessings of civilization. The Veis occupy about fifty miles of seacoast; extending from Gallinas River, one hundred miles north of Monrovia, and extending south to Grand Mount. Their territory runs back from the seacoast about thirty miles, and they are about sixteen thousand strong.

This was a grand place to found a Negro state,—a *missionary republic*, as Dr. Christy terms it. When the republic rose, the better, wealthier class of free Colored people from the United States embarked for Liberia. Clergymen, physicians, merchants, mechanics, and school-teachers turned their faces toward the new republic, with an earnest desire to do something for themselves and race; and history justifies the hopes and players of all sincere friends of Liberia. Unfortunately, at the first, many white men were more anxious to get the Negro out of the country than to have him do well when out; and, in many instances, some unworthy Colored people got transportation to Liberia, of whom Americans were rid, but of whom Liberians could not boast. But the law of the survival of the fittest carried the rubbish to the bottom. The republic grew and expanded in every direction. From year to year new blood and fresh energy were poured into the social and business life of the people; and England, America, and other powers acknowledged the republic by sending resident ministers there.

The servants of Christ saw, at the earliest moment of the conception to build a black government in Africa, that the banner of the cross must wave over the new colony, if good were to be expected. The Methodist Church, with characteristic zeal and aggressiveness, sent with the first colonists several members of their denomination and two "local preachers;" and in March, 1833, the Rev. Melville B. Cox, an ordained minister of this church, landed at Monrovia. The mission experienced many severe trials; but the good people who had it in charge held on with great tenacity until the darkness began to give away before the light of the gospel. Nor did the Board of the Methodist Missionary Society in America lose faith. They appropriated for this mission, in 1851, $22,000; in 1852, $26,000; in 1853, $32,957; and in 1854, $32,957. In the report of the board of managers for 1851, the following encouraging statement occurs:—

> "All eyes are now turned toward this new republic on the western coast of Africa as the star of hope to the colored people both bond and free, in the United States. The republic is establishing and extending itself; and its Christian population is in direct contact with the natives, both Pagans and Mohammedans. Thus the republic has, indirectly, a powerful missionary influence, and its moral and religious condition is a matter of grave concern to the Church. Hence the Protestant Christian missions in Liberia are essential to the stability and prosperity of the republic, and the stability and prosperity of the republic are necessary to the protection and action of the missions. It will thus appear that the Christian education of the people is the legitimate work of the missions."

At this time (1851) they had an annual Conference, with three districts, with as many presiding elders, whose duty it was to visit all the churches and schools in their circuit. The Conference had 21 members, all of whom were colored men. The churches contained 1,301 members, of whom 115 were on probation, and 116 were natives. There were 20 week-day schools, with 839 pupils, 50 of whom were natives. Then there were seven schools among the natives, with 127 faithful attendants.

Bishop Scott, of the General Conference of the Methodist Episcopal Church, was, by order of his Conference, sent on an official visit to Liberia. He spent more than two months among the missions, and returned in 1853 much gratified with the results garnered in that distant field.

> "The government of the republic of Liberia, which is formed on the model of our own, and is wholly in the hands of colored men, seems to be exceedingly well administered. I never saw so orderly a people. I saw but one intoxicated colonist while in the country, and I heard not one profane word. The sabbath is kept with singular strictness, and the churches crowded with attentive and orderly worshippers."[108]

The above is certainly re-assuring, and had its due influence among Christian people at the time it appeared. At an anniversary meeting of the Methodist Church, held in Cincinnati, O., in the same year, 1853, Bishop Ames gave utterance to sentiments in regard to the character of the government of Liberia that quite shocked some pro-slavery people who held *"hired pews"* in the Methodist Church. His utterances were as brave as they were complimentary.

> "Nations reared under religious and political restraint are not capable of self-government, while those who enjoy only partially these advantages have set an example of such capability. We have in illustration of this a well-authenticated historical fact: we refer to the colored people of this country, who, though they have grown up under the most unfavorable circumstances, were enabled to succeed in establishing a sound republican government in Africa. They have given the most clear and indubitable evidence of their capability of self-government, and in this respect have shown a higher grade of manhood than the polished Frenchman himself."[109]

The Presbyterian Board of Missions sent Rev. J.B. Pinny into the field in 1833. In 1837, missions were established among the natives, and were blessed with very good results. In 1850 there were, under the management of this denomination, three congregations, with 116 members, two ordained ministers, and a flourishing sabbath school. A high-school was brought into existence in 1852, with a white gentleman, the Rev D.A. Wilson, as its principal. It was afterward raised into a college, and was always crowded.

The American Protestant-Episcopal Church raised its missionary standard in Liberia in 1836. The Rev John Payne was at the head of this enterprise, assisted by six other clergymen, until 1850, when he was consecrated missionary bishop for Africa. He was a white gentleman of marked piety, rare scholarship, and large executive ability. The station at Monrovia was under the care of the Rev. Alexander Crummell, an educated and eloquent preacher of the Negro race. There was an excellent training-school for religious and secular teachers; there are several boarding-schools for natives, with an average attendance of a hundred; and up to 1850 more than a thousand persons had been brought into fellowship with this church.

The Foreign Missionary Board of the Southern Baptist Convention in 1845 turned its attention to this fruitful field. In 1855, ten years after they began work, they had 19 religious and secular teachers, 11 day-schools, 400 pupils, and 484 members in their churches. There were 13 mission-stations, and all the teachers were colored men.

We have said, a few pages back in this chapter, that the Methodist Church was first on the field when the colony of Liberia was founded. We should have said one of the first; because we find, in "Gammell's History of the American Baptist Missions," that the Baptists were in this colony as missionaries in 1822, that under the direction of the Revs. Lot Carey and Collin Teage, two intelligent Colored Baptists, a church was founded. Mr. Carey was a man of most exemplary character. He had received an education in Virginia, where he had resided as a freeman for some years, having purchased his freedom by his personal efforts, and where also he was ordained in 1821.

"In September, 1826, he was unanimously elected vice-agent of the colony; and on the return of Mr. Ashmun to the United States, in 1828, he was appointed to discharge the duties of governor in the interim,—a task which he performed during the brief remnant of his life with wisdom, and with credit to himself. His death took place in a manner that was fearfully sudden and extraordinary. The natives of the country had committed depredations upon the property of the colony, and were threatening general hostilities. Mr. Carey, in his capacity as acting governor, immediately called out the military forces of the colony, and commenced vigorous measures for repelling the assault and protecting the settlements. He was at the magazine, engaged in superintending the making of cartridges, when by the oversetting of a lamp, a large mass of powder became ignited, and produced and explosion which resulted in the death of Mr. Carey, and seven others who were engaged with him. In this sudden and awful manner perished and extraordinary man,—one who in a higher sphere might have developed many of the noblest energies of character and who, even in the humble capacity of a missionary among his own benighted brethren, deserves a prominent place in the list of those who have shed lustre upon the African race.

> "At the period of Mr. Carey's death, the church of which he was the pastor contained a hundred members, and was in a highly flourishing condition. It was committed to the charge of Collin Teage, who now returned from Sierra Leone, and of Mr. Waring, one of its members, who had lately been ordained a minister. The influences which had commenced with the indefatigable founder of the mission continued to be felt long after he had ceased to live. The church an Monrovia was increased to two hundred member; and the power of the gospel was manifested in other settlements of the Colonization Society, and even among the rude natives of the coast, of whom nearly a hundred were converted to Christianity, and united with the several churches of the colony."[110]

We regret that statistics on Liberia are not as full as desirable; but we have found enough to convince us that the cause of religion, education, and republican government are in safe hands, and on a sure foundation. There are now more than three thousand and eighteen hundred children, seven hundred of whom are natives;[111] and in the day-schools are gathered about two thousand bright and promising pupils.

Many noble soldiers of the cross have fallen on this field, where a desperate battle has been waged between darkness and light, heathenism and religion, the wooden gods of men and the only true God who made heaven and earth. Many have been mortally touched by the poisonous breath of African fever, and, like the sainted Gilbert Haven, have staggered back to home and friends to die. Few of the white teachers have been able to remain on the field. During the first thirty years of missionary effort in the field, the mortality among the white missionaries was terrible. Up to 1850 the Episcopal Church had employed twenty white teachers, but only three of them were left. The rest died, or were driven home by the climate. Of nineteen missionaries sent out by the Presbyterian Church up to 1850, nine died, seven returned home, and but three remained. The Methodist Church sent out thirteen white teachers: six died, six returned home, and but one remained. Among the colored missionaries the mortality was reduced to a minimum. Out of thirty-one in the employ of the Methodist Church, only seven died natural deaths, and fourteen remained in the service. On this subject of mortality, Bishop Payne says,—

> "It is now very generally admitted, that Africa must be evangelized chiefly by her own children. It should be our object to prepare them, so far as we may, for their great work. And since colonists afford the most advanced material for raising up the needed instruments, it becomes us, in wise co-operation with Providence, to direct our efforts in the most judicious manner to them. To do this, the most important points should be occupied, to become in due time radiating centres of Christian influence to colonists and natives."[112]

In thirty-three years Liberia gained wonderfully in population, and, at the breaking-out of the Rebellion in the United States, had about a hundred thousand souls, besides the three hundred thousand natives in the vast territory over which her government is recognized. Business of every kind has grown up. The laws are wholesome; the law-makers intelligent and upright; the army and navy are creditable, and the republic is in every sense a grand success. Mr. Wilson says,—

> "Trade is the chosen employment of the great mass of the Liberians, and some of them have been decidedly successful in this vocation. It consists in the exchange of articles of American or European manufacture for the natural products of the country; of which palm oil, cam-wood, and ivory are the principal articles. Cam-wood is a rich dye-wood, and is brought to Monrovia on the shoulders of the natives from a great distance. It is worth in the European and American markets from sixty to eighty dollars per ton. The ivory of this region does not form an important item of commerce. Palm-oil is the main article of export, and is procured along the seacoast between Monrovia and Cape Palmas. The Liberian merchants own a number of small vessels, built by themselves, and varying in size from ten or fifteen to forty or fifty tons. These are navigated by the Liberian sailors, and are constantly engaged in bringing palm-oil to Monrovia, from whence it is again shipped in foreign vessels for Liverpool or New York. I made inquiry, during a short sojourn at this place in 1852 on my way to this country, about the amount of property owned by the wealthiest merchants of Monrovia, and learned that there were four or five who were worth from fifteen thousand to twenty thousand dollars, a large number who owned property to the amount of ten thousand dollars, and perhaps twelve or fifteen who were worth as much as five thousand dollars. The property of some of these may have increased materially since that time.

"The settlers along the banks of the St. Paul have given more attention to the cultivation of the soil. They raise sweet-potatoes, cassava, and plantains, for their own use, and also supply the Monrovia market with the same. Ground-nuts and arrow-root are also cultivated, but to a very limited extent. A few individuals have cultivated the sugar cane with success, and have manufactured a considerable quantity of excellent sugar and molasses. Some attention has been given to the cultivation of the coffee tree. It grows luxuriantly, and bears most abundantly. The flavor of the coffee is as fine as any in the world; and, if the Liberians would give the attention to it they ought, it would probably be as highly esteemed as any other in the world. It is easily cultivated, and requires little or no outlay of capital; and we are surprised that it has not already become an article of export. The want of disposition to cultivate the soil is, perhaps, the most discouraging feature in the prospects of Liberia. Mercantile pursuits are followed with zeal and energy, but comparatively few are willing to till the ground for the means of subsistence."

Liberia had its first constitution in 1825. It was drawn at the instance of the Colonization Society in the United States. It set forth the objects of the colony, defined citizenship, and declared the objects of the government. It remained in force until 1836. In 1839 a "Legislative Council" was created, and the constitution amended to meet the growing wants of the government. In 1847 Liberia declared herself an independent republic. The first article of the constitution of 1847 reads as follows:—

"Article I. Section I. All men are born equally free and independent, and among them natural, inherent and inalienable rights, are the rights of enjoying and defending *life* and Liberty."

This section meant a great deal to a people who had abandoned their homes in the United States, where a chief justice of the Supreme Court had declared that "a Negro has no rights which a white man is bound to respect,"—a country where the Federal Congress had armed every United-States marshal in all the Northern States with the inhuman and arbitrary power to apprehend, load with chains, and hurl back into the hell of slavery, every poor fugitive who sought to find a home in a professedly free section of "the *land of the free and the home of the brave*." These brave black pilgrims, who had to leave "the freest land in the world" in order to get their freedom, did not intend that the solemn and formal declaration of principles contained in their constitution should be reduced to a *reductio ad absurdum*, as those in the American Constitution were by the infamous *Fugitive-slave Law*. And in section 4 of their constitution they prohibit "the sum of all villanies"— *slavery*! The article reads:—

"There shall be no slavery within this republic. Nor shall any citizen of this republic, or any person resident therein, deal in slaves, either within or without this republic."

They had no measure of *compromise* by which slavery could be carried on beyond certain limits "for highly commercial and business interests of a portion of their fellow-citizens." Liberians might have grown rich by merely suffering the slave-trade to be carried on among the natives. The constitution fixed a scale of revenue, and levied a tariff on all imported articles. A customs-service was introduced, and many reforms enforced which greatly angered a few avaricious white men whose profession as *men-stealers* was abolished by the constitution. Moreover, there were others who for years had been trading and doing business along the coast, without paying any duties on the articles they exported. The new government incurred their hostility.

In April, 1850, the republic of Liberia entered into a treaty with England, and in article nine of said treaty bound herself to the suppression of the slave-trade in the following explicit language:—

"Slavery and the slave-trade being perpetually abolished in the republic of Liberia, the republic engages that a law shall be passed declaring it to be piracy for any *Liberian citizen* or vessel to be engaged or concerned in the slave-trade."

Notwithstanding the above treaty, the enemies of the republic circulated the report in England and America that the Liberian government was secretly engaged in the slave-trade. The friends of colonization in both countries were greatly alarmed by the rumor, and sought information in official quarters,—of men on the ground. The following testimony will show that the charge was malicious:—

"Capt. Arabian, R.N., in one of his despatches says, 'Nothing had been done more to suppress the slave-trade in this quarter than the constant intercourse of the natives with these industrious colonists;' and again, 'Their character is exceedingly correct and moral, their minds strongly impressed with religious feeling, and their domestic habits remarkably neat and comfortable.' 'wherever the influence of Liberia extends, the slave trade has been abandoned by the natives.'

"Lieut. Stott, R.N., in a letter to Dr. Hodgkin, dated July, 1840, says, it (Liberia) promises to be the only successful institution on the coast of Africa, keeping in mind its objects; viz., 'that of raising the African slave into a free man, the extinction of the slave-trade, and the religious and moral improvement of Africa;' and adds, 'The surrounding Africans are aware of the nature of the colony, taking refuge when persecuted by the few neighboring slave-traders. The remnant of a tribe has lately fled to and settled in the colony on land granted them. Between my two visits, a lapse of only a few days, four or five slaves sought refuge from their master, who was about to sell, or had sold, them to the only slave-factory on the coast. The native chiefs in the neighborhood have that respect for the colonists that they have made treaties for the abolition of the slave trade.'

"Capt. Irving, R.N., in a letter to Dr. Hodgkin, Aug 3, 1840, observes, 'You ask me if they aid in the slave-trade? I assure you, no! and I am sure the colonists would feel themselves much hurt should they know such a question could possibly arise in England. In my opinion it is the best and safest plan for the extinction of the slave-trade, and the civilization of Africa, for it is a well-known fact, that wherever their flag flies it is an eye-sore to the slave-dealers.'

"Capt. Herbert, R.N.: 'With regard to the present state of slave-taking in the colony of Liberia, I have never known one instance of a slave being owned or disposed of by a colonist. On the contrary, I have known them to render great facility to our cruisers in taking vessels engaged in that nefarious traffic.'

"Capt. Dunlop, who had abundant opportunities for becoming acquainted with Liberia during the years 1848-50, says, 'I am perfectly satisfied no such thing as domestic slavery exists in any shape amongst the citizens of the republic.'

"Commodore Sir Charles Hotham, commander-in-chief of her British Majesty's squadron on the western coast of Africa, in a letter to the Secretary of the Admiralty, dated April 7, 1847, and published in the Parliamentary Returns, says, 'On perusing the correspondence of my predecessors, I found a great difference of opinion existing as to the views and objects of the settlers; some even accusing the governor of lending himself to the slave-trade. After discussing the whole subject with officers and others best qualified to judge on the matter, I not only satisfied my own mind that there is no reasonable cause for such a suspicion, but further, that this establishment merits all the support we can give it, for it is only through their means that we can hope to improve the African race.' Subsequently, in 1849, the same officer gave his testimony before the House of Lords, in the following language: 'There is no necessity for the squadron watching the coast between Sierra Leone and Cape Palmas, as the liberian territory intervenes, and there the slave-trade has been extinguished.'"[113]

The government was firmly and wisely administered, and its friends everywhere found occasion for great pleasure in its marked success. While the government had more than a quarter of a million of natives under its care, the greatest caution was exercised in dealing with them legally. The system was not so complicated as our Indian system, but the duties of the officers in dealing with the uncivilized tribes were as delicate as those of an Indian agent in the United States.

"The history of a single case will illustrate the manner in which Liberia exerts her influence in preventing the native tribes from warring upon each other. The territory of Little Cape Mount, Grand Cape Mount, and Gallinas was purchased, three or four years since, and added to the Republic. The chiefs, by the term of sale, transferred the rights of sovereignty and of soil to Liberia, and bound themselves to obey her laws. The government of Great Britain had granted to Messrs. Hyde, Hodge, & Co., of London, a contract for the supply of laborers from the coast of Africa to the planters of her West India colonies. This grant was made under the rule for the substitution of apprentices, to supply the lack of labor produced by the emancipation of the slaves. The agents of Messrs. Hyde, Hodge, & Co. visited Grand Cape Mount, and made an offer of ten dollars per head to the chiefs for each person they could supply as emigrants for this object. The offer excited the cupidity of some of the chiefs; and to procure the emigrants and secure the bounty one of them, named Boombo, of Little Cape Mount, resorted to war upon several of the surrounding tribes. He laid waste the country, burned the towns and villages, captured and murdered many of the inhabitants, carried off hundreds of others, and robbed several factories in that legion belonging to merchants in Liberia. On the 26th of February, 1853, President Roberts issued his proclamation enjoining a strict observance of the law regulating passports, and forbidding the sailing of any vessel with emigrants without first visiting the port of Monrovia, where each passenger should be examined as to his wishes. On the 1st of March the president, with two hundred men, sailed for Little Cape Mount, arrested Boombo and fifty of his followers, summoned a council of the other chiefs at Monrovia for his trial on the 14th, and returned home with his prisoners. At the time appointed, the trial was held, Roombo was found guilty of 'high misdemeanor' and sentenced 'to make restitution, restoration, and reparation of goods stolen, people captured, and damages committed: to pay a fine of five hundred dollars, and be imprisoned for two years.' When the sentence was pronounced, the convict shed tears, regarding the ingredient of imprisonment in his sentence to be almost intolerable. These rigorous measures, adopted to maintain the authority of the government and majesty of the laws, have had a salutary influence upon the chiefs. No outbreaks have since occurred, and but little apprehension of danger for the future is entertained."[114]

The republic did a vast amount of good before the Great Rebellion in the United States, but since emancipation its population has been fed by the natives who have been educated and converted to Christianity. Professor David Christy, the great colonizationist, said in a lecture delivered in 1855,—

"If, then, a colony of colored men, beginning with less than a hundred, and gradually increasing to nine thousand, has in thirty years established an independent republic amidst a savage people, destroyed the slave-trade on six hundred miles of the African coast, put down the heathen temples in one of its largest counties, afforded security to all the missions within its limits, and now casts its shield over three hundred thousand native inhabitants, what may not be done in the next thirty years by colonization and missions combined, were sufficient means supplied to call forth all their energies?"

The circumstances that led to the founding of the Negro Republic in the wilds of Africa perished in the fires of civil war. The Negro is free everywhere; but the republic of Liberia stands, and should stand until its light shall have penetrated the gloom of Africa, and until the heathen shall gather to the brightness of its shining. May it stand through the ages as a Christian Republic, as a faithful light-house along the dark and trackless sea of African paganism!

FOOTNOTES:

[106] Ethiope, p. 197.

[107] Foreign Travel and Life at Sea, vol. ii. p. 359.

[108] Bishop Scott's Letter in the Colonization Herald, October, 1853.

[109] In Methodist Missionary Advocate, 1853.

[110] Gammell's History of the American Baptist Missions, pp. 248, 249.

[111] Edward W. Blyden, L.L.D., president of Liberia College, a West Indian, is a scholar of marvellous erudition, a writer of rare abilities, a subtle reasoner, a preacher of charming graces, and one of the foremost Negroes of the world. He is himself the best argument in favor of the Negro's capacity for Christian civilization. He ranks amongst the world's greatest linguists.

[112] Report of Bishop Payne, June 6, 1853.

[113] Colonization Herald, December, 1852.

[114] Ethiope, pp. 207, 208.

CHAPTER XI
RÉSUMÉ

The Unity of the Human Family re-affirmed.—God gave all Races of Men Civilization.—The Antiquity of the Negro beyond Dispute.—Idolatry the Cause of the Degradation of the American Races.—He has always had a Place in History, though Incidental.—Negro Type caused by Degradation.—Negro Empires an Evidence of Crude Ability for Self-Government.— Influence of the Two Christian Governments on the West Coast upon the Heathen.—Oration on Early Christianity in Africa.—The Duty of Christianity to evangelize Africa.

THE preceding ten chapters are introductory in their nature. We felt that they were necessary to a history of the Colored race in the United States. We desired to explain and explode two erroneous ideas,—the curse of Canaan, and the theory that the Negro is a distinct species,—that were educated into our white countrymen during the long and starless night of the bondage of the Negro. It must appear patent to every honest student of God's word, that the slavery interpretation of the curse of Canaan is without warrant of Scripture, and at war with the broad and catholic teachings of the New Testament. It is a sad commentary on American civilization to find even a few men like Helper, "Ariel," and the author of "The Adamic Race" still croaking about the inferiority of the Negro; but it is highly gratifying to know that they no longer find an audience or readers, not even in the South. A man never hates his neighbors until he has injured them. Then, in justification of his unjustifiable conduct, he uses slander for argument.

During the late war thousands of mouths filled with vituperative wrath against the colored race were silenced as in the presence of the heroic deeds of "the despised race," and since the war the obloquy of the Negro's enemies has been turned into the most fulsome praise.

We stand in line and are in harmony with history and historians — modern and ancient, sacred and profane—on the subject of the unity of the human family. There are, however, a few who differ; but their wild, incoherent, and unscholarly theories deserve the mercy of our silence.

It is our firm conviction, and it is not wholly unsupported by history, that the Creator gave all the nations arts and sciences. Where nations have turned aside to idolatry they have lost their civilization. The Canaanites, Jebusites, Hivites, etc., the idolatrous[115] nations inhabiting the land of Canaan, were the descendants of Canaan; and the only charge the Lord brought against them when he commanded Joshua to exterminate them was, that they were his enemies[116] in all that that term implies. The sacred record tells us that they were a warlike, powerful people,[117] living in walled cities, given to agriculture, and possessing quite a respectable civilization; but they were idolaters—God's enemies.

It is worthy of emphasis, that the antiquity of the Negro race is beyond dispute. This is a fact established by the most immutable historical data, and recorded on the monumental brass and marble of the Oriental nations of the most remote period of time. The importance and worth of the Negro have given him a place in all the histories of Egypt, Greece, and Rome. His position, it is true, in all history up to the present day, has been accidental, incidental, and collateral; but it is sufficient to show how he has been regarded in the past by other nations. His brightest days were when history was an infant; and, since he early turned from God, he has found the cold face of hate and the hurtful hand of the Caucasian against him. The Negro type is the result of degradation. It is nothing more than the lowest strata of the African race. Pouring over the venerable mountain terraces, an abundant stream from an abundant and unknown source, into the malarial districts, the genuine African has gradually degenerated into the typical Negro. His blood infected with the poison of his low habitation, his body shrivelled by disease, his intellect veiled in pagan superstitions, the noblest yearnings of his soul strangled at birth by the savage passions of a nature abandoned to sensuality,—the poor Negro of Africa deserves more our pity than our contempt.

It is true that the weaker tribes, or many of the Negroid type, were the chief source of supply for the slave-market in this country for many years; but slavery in the United States—a severe ordeal through which to pass to citizenship and civilization— had the effect of calling into life many a slumbering and dying attribute in the Negro nature. The cruel institution drove him from an extreme idolatry to an extreme religious exercise of his faith in worship. And now that he is an American citizen,—the condition and circumstances which rendered his piety appropriate abolished,—he is likely to move over to an extreme rationalism.

The Negro empires to which we have called attention are an argument against the theory that he is without government, and his career as a soldier[118] would not disgrace the uniform of an American soldier. Brave, swift in execution, terrible in the onslaught, tireless in energy, obedient to superiors, and clannish to a fault,—the abilities of these black soldiers are worthy of a good cause.

On the edge of the Dark Continent, Sierra Leone and Liberia have sprung up as light-houses on a dark and stormy ocean of lost humanity. Hundreds of thousands of degraded Negroes have been snatched from the vile swamps, and Christianity has been received and appreciated by them. These two Negro settlements have solved two problems; viz., the Negro's ability to administer a government, and the capacity of the native for the reception of education and Christian civilization. San Domingo and Jamaica have their lessons too, but it is not our purpose to write the history of the Colored people of the world. The task may be undertaken some time in the future, however.

It must be apparent to the interested friends of languishing Africa, that there are yet two more problems presented for our solution; and they are certainly difficult of solution. First, we must solve the problem of African geography; second, we must redeem by the power of the gospel, with all its attending blessings, the savage tribes of Africans who have never heard the beautiful song of the angels: "*Glory to God in the highest, and on earth peace, good-will toward men.*" That this work will be done we do not doubt. We have great faith in the outcome of the missionary work going on now in Africa; and we are especially encouraged by the wide and kindly interest awakened on behalf of Africa by the noble life-work of Dr. David Livingstone, and the thrilling narrative of Mr. Henry M. Stanley.

It is rather remarkable now, in the light of recent events, that we should have chosen a topic at the close of both our academic and theological course that we can see now was in line with this work so near our heart. The first oration was on "The Footsteps of the Nation," the second was "Early Christianity in Africa." Dr. Livingstone had just fallen a martyr to the cause of geography, and the orators and preachers of enlightened Christendom were busy with the virtues and worth of the dead. It was on the tenth day of June, 1874, that we delivered the last-named oration; and we can, even at this distance, recall the magnificent audience that greeted it, and the feeling with which we delivered it. We were the first Colored man who had ever taken a diploma from that venerable and world-famed institution (Newton Seminary, Newton Centre, Mass.), and therefore there was much interest taken in our graduation. We were ordained on the following evening at

Watertown, Mass.; and the original poem written for the occasion by our pastor, the Rev. Granville S. Abbott, D.D., contained the following significant verses:—

> "Ethiopia's hands long stretching,
> Mightily have plead with God;
> Plead not vainly: time is fetching
> Answers, as her faith's reward.
> God is faithful,
> Yea, and Amen is his word.
>
> Countless prayers, so long ascending,
> Have their answer here and now;
> Threads of purpose, wisely meeting
> In an ordination vow.
> Afric brother,
> To thy mission humbly bow."

The only, and we trust sufficient, apology we have to offer to the reader for mentioning matters personal to the author is, that we are deeply touched in reading the oration, after many years, in the original manuscript, preserved by accident. It is fitting that it should be produced here as bearing upon the subject in hand.

EARLY CHRISTIANITY IN AFRICA.

ORATION BY GEORGE W. WILLIAMS,

on the occasion of his graduation from newton theological seminary, newton centre, mass., june 10, 1874.

Africa was one of the first countries to receive Christianity. Simon, a Cyrenian, from Africa, bore the cross of Jesus for him to Calvary. There was more in that singular incident than we are apt to recognize, for the time soon came when Africa did indeed take up the Saviour's cross.

The African, in his gushing love, welcomed the new religion to his country and to his heart. He was willing to share its persecutions, and endure shame for the cross of Christ.

Africa became the arena in which theological gladiators met in dubious strife. It was the scene of some of the severest doctrinal controversies of the early Church. Here men and women, devoted to an idea, stood immovable, indomitable as the pyramids, against the severest persecution. Her sons swelled the noble army of martyrs and confessors. The eloquence of their shed blood has been heard through the centuries, and pleads the cause of the benighted to-day.

It was Africa that gave the Christian Church Athanasius and Origen, Cyprian, Tertullian, and Augustine, her greatest writers and teachers. Athanasius, the missionary of monachism to the West, was the indefatigable enemy of Arianism, the bold leader of the Catholic party at Alexandria, at the early age of thirty (30) elevated to its bishopric, one of the most important sees in the East. Ever conscientious and bold, the whole Christian Church felt his influence, while emperors and kings feared his power. His life was stormy, because he loved the truth and taught it in all boldness. He hated his own life for the truth's sake. He counted all things but loss, that he might gain Christ. He was often in perils by false brethren, was driven out into the solitary places of the earth,—into the monasteries of the Thebaid; and yet he endured as seeing Him who is invisible, looking for the reward of the promise, knowing that He who promised is faithful.

Origen was an Alexandrian by birth and culture, an able preacher, a forcible writer, and a theologian of great learning. His influence while living was great, and was felt long after his death.

In North Africa, Cyprian, the great writer of Church polity, a pastor and teacher of rare gifts, was the first bishop to lay down his life for the truth's sake. The shadows of fifteen centuries rest upon his name; but it is as fadeless to-day as when a weeping multitude followed him to his martyrdom, and exclaimed, "Let us die with our holy bishop."

The weary centuries intervene, and yet the student of Church polity is fascinated and instructed by the brilliant teachings of Cyprian. His bitterest enemies—those who have most acrimoniously assailed him—have at length recognized in him the qualities of a great writer and teacher; and his puissant name, sending its influence along the ages, attracts the admiration of the ecclesiastical scholars of every generation.

Tertullian, the leader of the Montanists, fiery, impulsive, the strong preacher, the vigorous writer, the bold controversialist, organized a sect which survived him, though finally disorganized through the influence of Augustine, the master theologian of the early Church, indeed of the Church universal.

Other fathers built theological systems that flourished for a season; but the system that Augustine established survived him, has survived the intervening centuries, and lives to-day.

Africa furnished the first dissenters from an established church,—the Donatists. They were the Separatists and Puritans of the early Church.

Their struggle was long, severe, but useless. They were condemned, not convinced; discomfited, not subdued; and the patient, suffering, indomitable spirit they evinced shows what power there is in a little truth held in faith.

Christianity had reached its zenith in Africa. It was her proudest hour. Paganism had been met and conquered. The Church had passed through a baptism of blood, and was now wholly consecrated to the cause of its Great Head. Here Christianity flowered, here it brought forth rich fruit in the lives of its tenacious adherents. Here the acorn had become the sturdy oak, under which the soldiers of the cross pitched their tents. The African Church had triumphed gloriously.

But, in the moment of signal victory, the Saracens poured into North Africa, and Mohammedanism was established upon the ruins of Christianity.

The religion of Christ was swept from its moorings, the saint was transformed into the child of the desert, and quiet settlements became bloody fields where brother shed brother's blood.

Glorious and sublime as was the triumph of Christianity in North Africa, we must not forget that only a narrow belt of that vast country, on the Mediterranean, was reached by Christianity. Its western and southern portions are yet almost wholly unknown. Her vast deserts, her mighty rivers, and her dusky children are yet beyond the reach of civilization; and her forests have been the grave of many who would explore her interior. To-day England stands by the new-made grave of the indomitable Livingstone,—her courageous son, who, as a missionary and geographer spent his best days and laid down his life in the midst of Africa.

For nearly three centuries Africa has been robbed of her sable sons. For nearly three centuries they have toiled in bondage, unrequited, in this youthful republic of the West. They have grown from a small company to be an exceedingly great people,—five millions in number. No longer chattels, they are human beings, no longer bondmen, they are freemen, with almost every civil disability removed.

Their weary feet now press up the mount of science. Their darkened intellect now sweeps, unfettered, through the realms of learning and culture. With his Saxon brother, the African slakes his insatiable thirstings for knowledge at the same fountain. In the Bible, he leads not only the one unalterable text, "Servants, obey your masters," but also, "Ye are all brethren." "God hath made of one blood all nations of men for to dwell on all the face of the earth." "He is no respecter of persons."

The Negro in this country has begun to enjoy the blessings of a free citizenship. Under the sunny sky of a Christian civilization he hears the clarion voices of progress about him, urging him onward and upward. From across the ocean, out of the jungles of Africa, come the voices of the benighted and perishing. Every breeze is freighted with a Macedonian call, "Ye men of the African race, come over and help us!"

> "Shall we, whose souls are lighted
> By wisdom from on high,—
> Shall we, to men benighted
> The lamp of life deny?"

God often permits evil on the ground of man's free agency, but he does not commit evil.

The Negro of this country can turn to his Saxon brothers and say, as Joseph said to his brethren who wickedly sold him, "As for you, ye meant it unto evil but God meant it unto good; that we, after learning your arts and sciences, might return to Egypt and deliver the rest of our brethren who are yet in the house of bondage."

That day will come! Her chains will be severed by the sword of civilization and liberty. Science will penetrate her densest forests, and climb her loftiest mountains, and discover her richest treasures. The Sun of righteousness, and the star of peace shall break upon her sin-clouded vision, and smile upon her renewed households The anthem of the Redeemer's advent shall float through her forests, and be echoed by her mountains. Those dusky children of the desert, who now wander and plunder, will settle to quiet occupations of industry. Gathering themselves into villages, plying the labors of handicraft and agriculture, they will become a well disciplined society, instead of being a roving, barbarous horde.

The sabbath bells will summon from scattered cottages smiling populations, linked together by friendship, and happy in all the sweetness of domestic charities. Thus the glory of her latter day shall be greater than at the beginning, *and Ethiopia shall stretch forth her hands unto God.*

It is our earnest desire and prayer, that the friends of missions in all places where God in his providence may send this history will give the subject of the civilization and Christianization of Africa prayerful consideration. The best schools the world can afford should be founded on the West Coast of Africa The native should be educated at home, and mission stations should be planted under the very shadow of the idol-houses of the heathen. The best talent and abundant means have been sent to Siam, China, and Japan. Why not send the best talent and needful means to Liberia, Sierra Leone, and Cape Palmas, that native missionaries may be trained for the outposts of the Lord? There is not a more promising mission-field in the world than Africa, and yet our friends in America take so little interest in this work! The Lord is going to save that Dark Continent, and it behooves his servants here to honor themselves in doing something to hasten the completion of this inevitable work! Africa is to be redeemed by the African, and the white Christians of this country can aid the work by munificent contributions. Will you do it, brethren? God help you!

FOOTNOTES:

[115] Deut. xii. 2, 3, also 30th verse.

[116] Deut. vi. 19.

[117] Deut. vii. 7.

[118] News comes to us from Egypt that Arabi Pacha's best artillerists are Negro soldiers.

PART II
SLAVERY IN THE COLONIES[119]

CHAPTER XII
THE COLONY OF VIRGINIA

1619-1775.

Introduction of the First Slaves.—"The Treasurer" and the Dutch Man-of-War.—The Correct Date.—The Number of Slaves.—Were there Twenty, or Fourteen?—Litigation about the Possession of the Slaves.—Character of the Slaves imported, and the Character of the Colonists.—Race Prejudices.—Legal Establishment of Slavery. Who are Slaves for Life.—Duties on Imported Slaves.—Political and Military Prohibitions against Negroes.—Personal Rights.—Criminal Laws against Slaves. Emancipation.—How brought about.—Free Negroes.—Their Rights.—Moral and Religious Training.—Population.—Slavery firmly established.

VIRGINIA was the mother of slavery as well as "the mother of Presidents." Unfortunate for her, unfortunate for the other colonies, and thrice unfortunate for the poor Colored people, who from 1619 to 1863 yielded their liberty, their toil,—unrequited,—their bodies and intellects to an institution that ground them to powder. No event in the history of North America has carried with it to its last analysis such terrible forces. It touched the brightest features of social life, and they faded under the contact of its poisonous breath. It affected legislation, local and national; it made and destroyed statesmen; it prostrated and bullied honest public sentiment; it strangled the voice of the press, and awed the pulpit into silent acquiescence; it organized the judiciary of States, and wrote decisions for judges; it gave States their political being, and afterwards dragged them by the fore-hair through the stormy sea of civil war; laid the parricidal fingers of Treason against the fair throat of Liberty,—and through all time to come no event will be more sincerely deplored than the introduction of slavery into the colony of Virginia during the last days of the month of August in the year 1619!

The majority of writers on American history, as well as most histories on Virginia, from Beverley to Howison, have made a mistake in fixing the date of the introduction of the first slaves. Mr. Beverley, whose history of Virginia was printed in London in 1772, is responsible for the error, in that nearly all subsequent writers—excepting the laborious and scholarly Bancroft and the erudite Campbell—have repeated his mistake. Mr. Beverley, speaking of the burgesses having "met the Governor and Council at James Town in May 1620," adds in a subsequent paragraph, "In August following a Dutch Man of War landed twenty Negroes for sale; which were the first of that kind that were carried into the country."[120] By "August following," we infer that Beverley would have his readers understand that this was in 1620. But Burk, Smith, Campbell, and Neill gave 1619 as the date.[121] But we are persuaded to believe that the first slaves were landed at a still earlier date. In Capt. John Smith's history, printed in London in 1629, is a mere incidental reference to the introduction of slaves into Virginia. He mentions, under date of June 25, that the "governor and councell caused Burgesses to be chosen in all places,"[122] which is one month later than the occurrence of this event as fixed by Beverley. Smith speaks of a vessel named "George" as having been "sent to Newfoundland" for fish, and, having started in May, returned after a voyage of "seven weeks." In the next sentence he says, "About the last of August came in a dutch man of warre that sold us twenty Negars."[123] Might not he have meant "about the end of last August" came the Dutch man-of-war, etc.? All historians, except two, agree that these slaves were landed in August, but disagree as to the year. Capt. Argall, of whom so much complaint was made by the Virginia Company to Lord Delaware,[124] fitted out the ship "Treasurer" at the expense of the Earl of Warwick, who sent him "an olde commission of hostility from the Duke of Savoy against the Spanyards," for a "filibustering" cruise to the West Indies.[125] And, "after several acts of hostility committed, and some purchase gotten, she returns to Virginia at the end of ten months or thereabouts."[126] It was in the early autumn of 1618,[127] that Capt. Edward (a son of William) Brewster was sent into banishment by Capt. Argall; and this, we think, was one of the last, if not the last official act of that arbitrary governor. It was certainly before this that the ship "Treasurer," manned "with the ablest men in the colony," sailed for "the Spanish dominions in the Western hemisphere." Under date of June 15, 1618, John Rolfe, speaking of the death of the Indian Powhatan, which took place in April, says, "Some private differences happened betwixt Capt. Bruster and Capt. Argall," etc. [128] Capt. John Smith's information, as secured from Master Rolfe, would lead to the conclusion that the difficulty which took place between Capt. Edward Brewster and Capt. Argall occurred in the spring instead of the autumn, as Neill says. If it be true that "The Treasurer" sailed in the early spring of 1618, Rolfe's statement as to the time of the strife between Brewster and Argall would harmonize with the facts in reference to the length of time the vessel was absent as recorded in Burk's history. But if Neill is correct as to the time of the quarrel,—for we maintain that it was about this time that Argall left the colony,—then his statement would tally with Burk's account of the time the vessel was on the cruise. If, therefore, she sailed in October, 1618, being absent ten months, she was due at Jamestown in August, 1619.

But, nevertheless, we are strangely moved to believe that 1618 was the memorable year of the landing of the first slaves in Virginia. And we have one strong and reliable authority on our side. Stith, in his history of Virginia, fixes the date in 1618.[129] On the same page there is an account of the trial and sentence of Capt. Brewster. The ship "Treasurer" had evidently left England in the winter of 1618. When she reached the Virginia colony, she was furnished with a new crew and abundant supplies for her cruise. Neill says she returned with booty and "a certain number of negroes." Campbell agrees that it was some time before the landing of the Dutch man-of-war that "The Treasurer" returned to Virginia. He says, "She returned to Virginia after some ten months with her booty, which consisted of captured negroes, who were not left in Virginia, because Capt. Argall had gone back to England, but were put on the Earl of Warwick's plantation in the Somer Islands."[130]

During the last two and one-half centuries the readers of the history of Virginia have been mislead as to these two vessels, the Dutch man-of-war and "The Treasurer." The Dutch man-of-war did land the first slaves; but the ship "Treasurer" was the first to bring them to this country, in 1618.

When in 1619 the Dutch man-of-war brought the first slaves to Virginia, Capt. Miles Kendall was deputy-governor. The man-of-war claimed to sail under commission of the Prince of Orange. Capt. Kendall gave orders that the vessel should not land in any of his harbors: but the vessel was without provisions; and the Negroes, fourteen in number, were tendered for supplies. Capt. Kendall accepted the slaves, and, in return, furnished the man-of-war with the coveted provisions. In the mean while Capt. Butler came and assumed charge of the affairs of the Virginia Company, and dispossessed Kendall of his slaves, alleging that they were the property of the Earl of Warwick. He insisted that they were taken from the ship "Treasurer,"[131] "with which the said Holland man-of-war had consorted." Chagrined, and wronged by

Gov. Butler, Capt. Kendall hastened back to England to lay his case before the London Company, and to seek equity. The Earl of Warwick appeared in court, and claimed the Negroes as his property, as having belonged to his ship, "The Treasurer." Every thing that would embarrass Kendall was introduced by the earl. At length, as a final resort, charges were formally preferred against him, and the matter referred to Butler for decision. Capt. Kendall did not fail to appreciate the gravity of his case, when charges were preferred against him in London, and the trial ordered before the man of whom he asked restitution! The case remained in statu quo until July, 1622, when the court made a disposition of the case. Nine of the slaves were to be delivered to Capt. Kendall, "and the rest to be consigned to the company's use." This decision was reached by the court after the Earl of Warwick had submitted the case to the discretion and judicial impartiality of the judges. The court gave instructions to Capt. Bernard, who was then the governor, to see that its order was enforced. But while the order of the court was in transitu, Bernard died. The earl, learning of the event, immediately wrote a letter, representing that the slaves should not be delivered to Kendall; and an advantage being taken—purely technical—of the omission of the name of the captain of the Holland man-of-war, Capt. Kendall never secured his nine slaves.

It should be noted, that while Rolfe, in Capt. Smith's history, fixes the number of slaves in the Dutch vessel at twenty,—as also does Beverley,—it is rather strange that the Council of Virginia, in 1623, should state that the commanding officer of the Dutch man-of-war told Capt. Kendall that "he had fourteen Negroes on board!"[132] Moreover, it is charged that the slaves taken by "The Treasurer" were divided up among the sailors; and that they, having been cheated out of their dues, asked judicial interference. [133] Now, these slaves from "The Treasurer" "were placed on the Earl of Warwick's lands in Bermudas, and there kept and detained to his Lordship's use." There are several things apparent; viz., that there is a mistake between the statement of the Virginia Council in their declaration of May 7, 1623, about the number of slaves landed by the man-of-war, and the statements of Beverley and Smith. And if Stith is to be relied upon as to the slaves of "The Treasurer" having been taken to the "Earl of Warwick's lands in Bermudas, and there kept," his lordship's claim to the slaves Capt. Kendall got from the Dutch man-of-war was not founded in truth or equity!

Whether the number was fourteen or twenty, it is a fact, beyond historical doubt, that the Colony of Virginia purchased the first Negroes, and thus opened up the nefarious traffic in human flesh. It is due to the Virginia Colony to say, that these slaves were forced upon them; that they were taken in exchange for food given to relieve the hunger of famishing sailors; that white servitude[134] was common, and many whites were convicts[135] from England; and the extraordinary demand for laborers may have deadened the moral sensibilities of the colonists as to the enormity of the great crime to which they were parties. Women were sold for wives,[136] and sometimes were kidnapped[137] in England and sent into the colony. There was nothing in the moral atmosphere of the colony inimical to the spirit of bondage that was manifest so early in the history of this people. England had always held her sceptre over slaves of some character: villeins in the feudal era, stolen Africans under Elizabeth and under the house of the Tudors; Caucasian children—whose German blood could be traced beyond the battle of Hastings—in her mines, factories, and mills; and vanquished Brahmans in her Eastern possessions. How, then, could we expect less of these "knights" and "adventurers" who "degraded the human race by an exclusive respect for the privileged classes"?[138]

The institution of slavery once founded, it is rather remarkable that its growth was so slow. According to the census of Feb. 16, 1624, there were but twenty-two in the entire colony.[139] There were eleven at Flourdieu Hundred, three in James City, one on James Island, one on the plantation opposite James City, four at Warisquoyak, and two at Elizabeth City. In 1648 the population of Virginia was about fifteen thousand, with a slave population of three hundred.[140] The cause of the slow increase of slaves was not due to any colonial prohibition. The men who were engaged in tearing unoffending Africans from their native home were some time learning that this colony was at this time a ready market for their helpless victims. Whatever feeling or scruple, if such ever existed, the colonists had in reference to the subject of dealing in the slave-trade, was destroyed at conception by the golden hopes of large gains. The latitude, the products of the soil, the demand for labor, the custom of the indenture of white servants, were abundant reasons why the Negro should be doomed to bondage for life.

The subjects of slavery were the poor unfortunates that the strong push to the outer edge of organized African society, where, through neglect or abuse, they are consigned to the mercy of avarice and malice. We have already stated that the weaker tribes of Africa are pushed into the alluvial flats of that continent; where they have perished in large numbers, or have become the prey of the more powerful tribes, who consort with slave-hunters. Disease, tribal wars in Africa, and the merciless greed of slave-hunters, peopled the colony of Virginia with a class that was expected to till the soil. African criminals, by an immemorial usage, were sold into slavery as the highest penalty, save death; and often this was preferred to bondage. Many such criminals found their way into the colony. To be bondmen among neighboring tribes at home was dreaded beyond expression; but to wear chains in a foreign land, to submit to the dehumanizing treatment of cruel taskmasters, was an ordeal that fanned into life the last dying ember of manhood and resentment.

The character of the slaves imported, and the pitiable condition of the white servants, produced rather an anomalous result. "Male servants, and slaves of both sex" were bound together by the fellowship of toil. But the distinction "made between them in their clothes and food"[141] drew a line, not between their social condition,—for it was the same,—but between their nationality. First, then, was social estrangement, next legal difference, and last of all political disagreement and strife. In order to oppress the weak, and justify the unchristian distinction between God's creatures, the persons who would bolster themselves into respectability must have the aid of law. Luther could march fearlessly to the Diet of Worms if every tile on the houses were a devil; but Macbeth was conquered by the remembrance of the wrong he had done the virtuous Duncan and the unoffending Banquo, long before he was slain by Macduff. A guilty conscience always needs a multitude of subterfuges to guard against dreaded contingencies. So when the society in the Virginia Colony had made up its mind that the Negroes in their midst were mere heathen,[142] they stood ready to punish any member who had the temerity to cross the line drawn between the races. It was not a mitigating circumstance that the white servants of the colony who came into natural contact with the Negroes were "disorderly persons," or convicts sent to Virginia by an order of the king of England. It was fixed by public sentiment and law that there should be no relation between the races. The first prohibition was made "September 17th, 1630." Hugh Davis, a white servant, was publicly flogged "before an assembly of Negroes and others," for defiling himself with a Negro. It was also required that he should confess as much on the following sabbath.[143]

In the winter of 1639, on the 6th of January, during the incumbency of Sir Francis Wyatt, the General Assembly passed the first prohibition against Negroes. "All persons," doubtless including fraternizing Indians, "except Negroes," were required to secure arms and ammunition, or be subject to a fine, to be imposed by "the Governor and Council."[144] The records are too scanty, and it is impossible to judge, at this remote day, what was the real cause of this law. We have already called attention to the fact that the slaves were but a mere fraction of the summa summarum of the population. It could not be that the brave Virginians were afraid of an insurrection! Was it another reminder that the "Negroes were heathen," and, therefore, not entitled to the privileges of Christian freemen? It was not the act of that government, which in its conscious rectitude "can put ten thousand to flight," but was rather the inexcusable feebleness of a diseased conscience, that staggers off for refuge "when no man pursueth."

Mr. Bancroft thinks that the "special tax upon female slaves"[145] was intended to discourage the traffic. It does not so seem to us. It seems that the Virginia Assembly was endeavoring to establish friendly relations with the Dutch and other nations in order to secure "trade." Tobacco was the chief commodity of the colonists. They intended by the act[146] of March, 1659, to guarantee the most perfect liberty "to trade with" them. They required, however, that foreigners should "give bond and pay the impost of tenn shillings per hogshead laid upon all tobacco exported to any fforreigne dominions." The same act recites, that whenever any slaves were sold for tobacco, the amount of imposts would only be "two shillings per hogshead," which was only the nominal sum paid by the colonists themselves. This act was passed several years before the one became a law that is cited by Mr. Bancroft. It seems that much trouble had been experienced in determining who were taxable in the colony. It is very clear that the LIV. Act of March, 1662, which Mr. Bancroft thinks was intended to discourage the importation of slaves by taxing female slaves, seeks only to determine who shall be taxable. It is a general law, declaring "that all male persons, of what age soever imported into this country shall be brought into lysts and be liable to the payment of all taxes, and all negroes, male and female being imported shall be accompted tythable, and all Indian servants male or female however procured being adjudged sixteen years of age shall be likewise tythable from which none shall be exempted."[147] Beverley says that "the male servants, and slaves of both sexes," were employed together. It seems that white women were so scarce as to be greatly respected. But female Negroes and Indians were taxable; although Indian children, unlike those of Negroes, were not held as slaves.[148] Under the LIV. Act there is but one class exempted from tax,—white females, and, we might add, persons under sixteen years of age.[149] So what Mr. Bancroft mistakes as repressive legislation against the slave-trade is only an exemption of white women, and intended to encourage their coming into the colony.

The legal distinction between slaves and servants was, "slaves for life, and servants for a time."[150] Slavery existed from 1619 until 1662, without any sanction in law. On the 14th of December, 1662, the foundations of the slave institution were laid in the old law maxim, "Partus sequitur ventrum,"—that the issue of slave mothers should follow their condition. [151] Two things were accomplished by this act; viz., slavery received the direct sanction of statutory law, and it was also made hereditary. On the 6th of March, 1655,—seven years before the time mentioned above,—an act was passed declaring that all Indian children brought into the colony by friendly Indians should not be treated as slaves,[152] but be instructed in the trades.[153] By implication, then, slavery existed legally at this time; but the act of 1662 was the first direct law on the subject. In 1670 a question arose as to whether Indians taken in war were to be servants for a term of years, or for life. The act passed on the subject is rather remarkable for the language in which it is couched; showing, as it does, that it was made to relieve the Indian, and fix the term of the Negro's bondage beyond a reasonable doubt. "It is resolved and enacted that all servants not being Christians imported into this colony by shipping shall be slaves for their lives; but what shall come by land shall serve, if boyes or girles, until thirty yeares of age, if men or women twelve yeares and no longer."[154] This remarkable act was dictated by fear and policy. No doubt the Indian was as thoroughly despised as the Negro; but the Indian was on his native soil, and, therefore, was a more dangerous[155] subject. Instructed by the past, and fearful of the future, the sagacious colonists declared by this act, that those who "shall come by land" should not be assigned to servitude for life. While this act was passed to define the legal status of the Indian, at the same time, and with equal force, it determines the fate of the Negro who is so unfortunate as to find his way into the colony. "All servants not being Christians imported into this colony by shipping shall be slaves for their lives." Thus, in 1670, Virginia, not abhorring the institution, solemnly declared that "all servants not christians"—heathen Negroes—coming into her "colony by shipping"—there was no other way for them to come!—should "be slaves for their lives!"

In 1682 the colony was in a flourishing condition. Opulence generally makes men tyrannical, and great success in business makes them unmerciful. Although Indians, in special acts, had not been classed as slaves, but only accounted "servants for a term of years," the growing wealth and increasing number of the colonists seemed to justify them in throwing off the mask. The act of the 3d of October, 1670, defining who should be slaves, was repealed at the November session of the General Assembly of 1682. Indians were now made slaves,[156] and placed upon the same legal footing with the Negroes. The sacred rite of baptism[157] did not alter the condition of children—Indian or Negro—when born in slavery. And slavery, as a cruel and inhuman institution, flourished and magnified with each returning year.

Encouraged by friendly legislation, the Dutch plied the slave-trade with a zeal equalled only by the enormous gains they reaped from the planters. It was not enough that faith had been broken with friendly Indians, and their children doomed by statute to the hell of perpetual slavery; it was not sufficient that the Indian and Negro were compelled to serve, unrequited, for their lifetime. On the 4th of October, 1705, "an act declaring the Negro, Mulatto, and Indian slaves, within this dominion, to be real estate,"[158] was passed without a dissenting voice. Before this time they had been denominated by the courts as chattels: now they were to pass in law as real estate. There were, however, several provisos to this act. Merchants coming into the colony with slaves, not sold, were not to be affected by the act until the slaves had actually passed in a bonâ-fide sale. Until such time their slaves were contemplated by the law as chattels. In case a master died without lawful heirs, his slaves did not escheat, but were regarded as other personal estate or property. Slave property was liable to be taken in execution for the payment of debts, and was recoverable by a personal action.[159]

The only apology for enslaving the Negroes we can find in all the records of this colony is, that they "were heathen." Every statute, from the first to the last, during the period the colony was under the control of England, carefully mentions that all persons—Indians and Negroes—who "are not Christians" are to be slaves. And their conversion to Christianity afterwards did not release them from their servitude.[160]

The act making Indian, Mulatto, and Negro slaves real property, passed in October, 1705, under the reign of Queen Anne, and by her approved, was "explained" and "amended" in February, 1727, during the reign of King George II. Whether the act received its being out of a desire to prevent fraud, like the "Statutes of Frauds," is beyond finding out. But it was an act that showed that slavery had grown to be so common an institution as not to excite human sympathy. And the attempt to "explain" and "amend" its cruel provisions was but a faint precursor of the evils that followed. Innumerable lawsuits grew out of the act, and the courts and barristers held to conflicting interpretations and constructions. Whether complaints were made to his Majesty, the king, the records do not relate; or whether he was moved by feelings of humanity is quite as difficult to understand. But on the 31st of October, 1751, he issued a proclamation repealing the act declaring slaves real estate.[161] The proclamation abrogated nine other acts, and quite threw the colony into confusion.[162] It is to be hoped that the king was animated by the noblest impulses in repealing one of the most dehumanizing laws that ever disgraced the government of any civilized people. The General Assembly, on the 15th of April, 1752, made an appeal to the king, "humbly" protesting against the proclamation. The law-makers in the colony were inclined to doubt the king's prerogative in this matter. They called the attention of his Majesty to the fact that he had given the "Governor" "full power and authority with the advice and consent of the council" to make needful laws; but they failed to realize fully that his Majesty, in accordance with the proviso contained in the grant of authority made to the governor and council of the colony, was using his veto. They recited the causes which induced them to enact the law, recounted the benefits accruing to his Majesty's subjects from the conversion of human beings into real property,[163] and closed with a touching appeal for the retention of the act complained of, so that slaves "might not at the same time be real estate in some respects, personal in others, and bothe in others!" History does not record that the brusque old king was at all moved by this earnest appeal and convincing argument of the Virginia Assembly.

In 1699 the government buildings at James City were destroyed. The General Assembly, in an attempt to devise means to build a new Capitol, passed an act on the 11th of April of the aforesaid year, fixing a "duty on servants and slaves imported"[164] into the colony. Fifteen shillings was the impost tax levied upon every servant imported, "not born in England or Wales, and twenty shillings for every Negro or other slave" thus imported. The revenue arising from this tax on servants and slaves was to go to the building of a new Capitol. Every slave-vessel was inspected by a customs-officer. The commanding officer of the vessel was required to furnish the names and number of the servants and slaves imported, the place of their birth, and pay the duty imposed upon each before they were permitted to be landed. This act was to be in force for the space of "three years from the publication thereof, and no longer."[165] But, in the summer of 1701, it was continued until the 25th day of December, 1703. The act was passed as a temporary measure to secure revenue with which to build the Capitol.[166] Evidently it was not intended to remain a part of the code of the colony. In 1732 it was revived by an act, the preamble of which leads us to infer that the home government was not friendly to its passage. In short, the act is preceded by a prayer for permission to pass it. Whatever may have been the feeling in England in reference to levying imposts upon servants and slaves, it is certain the colonists were in hearty accord with the spirit and letter of the act. It must be clear to every honest student of history, that there never was, up to this time, an attempt made to cure the growing evils of slavery. When a tax was imposed upon slaves imported, the object in view was the replenishing of the coffers of the colonial government. In 1734 another act was passed taxing imported slaves, because it had "been found very easy to the subjects of this colony, and no ways burthensome to the traders in slaves." The additional reason for continuing the law was, "that a competent revenue" might be raised "for preventing or lessening a poll-tax."[167] And in 1738, this law being "found, by experience, to be an easy expedient for raising a revenue towards the lessening a pooll-tax, always grievous to the people of this colony, and is in no way burthensom to the traders in slaves," it was re-enacted. In every instance, through all these years, the imposition of a tax on slaves imported into the colony had but one end in view,—the raising of revenue. In 1699 the end sought through the taxing of imported slaves was the building of the Capitol; in 1734 it was to lighten the burden of taxes on the subjects in the colony; but, in 1740, the object was to get funds to raise and transport troops in his Majesty's service.[168] The original duty remained; and an additional levy of five per centum was required on each slave imported, over and above the twenty shillings required by previous acts.

In 1742 the tax was continued, because it was "necessary" "to discharge the public debts."[169] And again, in 1745, it was still believed to be necessary "for supporting the public expense."[170] The act, in a legal sense, expired by limitation, but in spirit remained in full force until revived by the acts of 1752-53.[171] In the spring of 1755 the General Assembly increased the tax on imported slaves above the amount previously fixed by law.[172] The duty at this time was ten per centum on each slave sold into the colony. The same law was reiterated in 1757,[173] and, when it had expired by limitation, was revived in 1759, to be in force for "the term of seven years from thence next following."[174]

Encouraged by the large revenue derived from the tax imposed on servants and slaves imported into the colony from foreign parts, the General Assembly stood for the revival of the impost-tax. The act of 1699 required the tax at the hands of "the importer," and from as many persons as engaged in the slave-trade who were subjects of Great Britain, and residents of the colony; but the tax at length became a burden to them. In order to evade the law and escape the tax, they frequently went into Maryland and the Carolinas, and bought slaves, ostensibly for their own private use, but really to sell in the local market. To prevent this, an act was passed imposing a tax of twenty per centum on all such sales;[175] but there was a great outcry made against this act. Twenty per centum of the gross amount on each slave, paid by the person making the purchase, was a burden that planters bore with ill grace. The question of the reduction of the tax to ten per centum was vehemently agitated. The argument offered in favor of the reduction was three-fold; viz., "very burthensom to the fair purchaser," inimical "to the settlement and improvement of the lands" in the colony, and a great hinderance to "the importation of slaves, and thereby lessens the fund arising upon the duties upon slaves."[176] The reduction was made in May, 1760; and, under additional pressure, the additional duty on imported slaves to be "paid by the buyer" was taken off altogether.[177] But in 1766 the duty on imported slaves was revived;[178] and in 1772 an act was passed reviving the "additional duty" on "imported slaves, and was continued in force until the colonies threw off the British yoke in 1775."[179]

In all this epoch, from 1619 down to 1775, there is not a scrap of history to prove that the colony of Virginia ever sought to prohibit in any manner the importation of slaves. That she encouraged the traffic, we have abundant testimony; and that she enriched herself by it, no one can doubt.

During the period of which we have just made mention above, the slaves in this colony had no political or military rights. As early as 1639,[180] the Assembly excused them from owning or carrying arms; and in 1705 they were barred by a special act from holding or exercising "any office, ecclesiastical, civil, or military, or any place of publick trust or power,"[181] in the colony. If found with a "gun, sword, club, staff, or other weopon,"[182] they were turned over to the constable, who was required to administer "twenty lashes on his or her bare back." There was but one exception made. Where Negro and Indian slaves lived on the border or the colony, frequently harassed by predatory bands of hostile Indians, they could bear arms by first getting written license from their master;[183] but even then they were kept under surveillance by the whites.

Personal rights, we cannot see that the slaves had any. They were not allowed to leave the plantation on which they were held as chattel or real estate, without a written certificate or pass from their master, which was only granted under the most urgent circumstances.[184] If they dared lift a hand against any white man, or "Christian" (?) as they loved to call themselves, they were punished by thirty lashes; and if a slave dared to resist his master while he was correcting him, he could be killed; and the master would be guiltless in the eyes of the law.[185] If a slave remained on another plantation more than four hours, his master was liable to a fine of two hundred pounds of tobacco.[186] And if any white person had any commercial dealings with a slave, he was liable to imprisonment for one month without bail, and compelled to give security in the sum of ten pounds.[187] If a slave had earned and owned a horse and buggy, it was lawful to seize them;[188] and the church-warden was charged with the sale of the articles. Even with the full permission of his master, if a slave were found going about the colony trading any articles for his or master's profit, his master was liable to a fine of ten pounds; which fine went to the church-warden, for the benefit of the poor of the parish in which the slave did the trading.[189]

In all the matters of law, civil and criminal, the slave had no rights. Under an act of 1705, Catholics, Indian and Negro slaves, were denied the right to appear as "witnesses in any cases whatsoever," "not being Christians;"[190] but this was modified somewhat in 1732, when Negroes, Indians, and Mulattoes were admitted as witnesses in the trial of slaves. [191] In criminal causes the slave could be arrested, cast into prison, tried, and condemned, with but one witness against him, and sentenced without a jury. The solemnity and dignity of "trial by jury," of which Englishmen love to boast, was not allowed the criminal slave.[192] And, when a slave was executed, a value was fixed upon him; and the General Assembly was required to make an appropriation covering the value of the slave to indemnify the master.[193] More than five slaves meeting together, "to rebel or make insurrection" was considered "felony;" and they were liable to "suffer death, and be utterly excluded the benefit of clergy;"[194] but, where one slave was guilty of manslaughter in killing another slave, he was allowed the benefit of clergy.[195] In case of burglary by a slave, he was not allowed the benefit of the clergy, except "said breaking, in the case of a freeman, would be burglary."[196] And the only humane feature in the entire code of the colony was an act passed in 1772, providing that no slave should be condemned to suffer "unless four of the judges" before whom he is tried "concur."[197]

The free Negroes of the colony of Virginia were but little removed by law from their unfortunate brothers in bondage. Their freedom was the act of individuals, with but one single exception. In 1710 a few recalcitrant slaves resolved to offer armed resistance to their masters, whose treatment had driven them to the verge of desperation. A slave of Robert Ruffin, of Surry County, entered into the plot, but afterwards revealed it to the masters of the rebellious slaves. As a reward for his services, the General Assembly, on the 9th of October, 1710, gave him his manumission papers, with the added privilege to remain in the colony.[198] For the laws of the colony required "that no negro, mulatto, or indian slaves" should be set free "except for some meritorious services." The governor and council were to decide upon the merits of the services, and then grant a license to the master to set his slave at liberty.[199] If any master presumed to emancipate a slave without a license granted according to the act of 1723, his slave thus emancipated could be taken up by the church-warden for the parish in which the master of the slave resided, and sold "by public outcry." The money accruing from such sale was to be used for the benefit of the parish.[200] But if a slave were emancipated according to law, the General Assembly paid the master so much for him, as in the case of slaves executed by the authorities. But it was seldom that emancipated persons were permitted to remain in the colony. By the act of 1699 they were required to leave the colony within six months after they had secured their liberty, on pain of having to pay a fine of "ten pounds sterling to the church-wardens of the parish;" which money was to be used in transporting the liberated slave out of the country. [201] If slave women came in possession of their freedom, the law sought them out, and required of them to pay taxes;[202] a burden from which their white sisters, and even Indian women, were exempt.

If free Colored persons in the colony ever had the right of franchise, there is certainly no record of it. We infer, however, from the act of 1723, that previous to that time they had exercised the voting privilege. For that act declares "that no free negro shall hereafter have any vote at the election."[203] Perhaps they had had a vote previous to this time; but it is mere conjecture, unsupported by historical proof. Being denied the right of suffrage did not shield them from taxation. All free Negroes, male and female, were compelled to pay taxes.[204] They contributed to the support of the colonial government, and yet they had no voice in the government. They contributed to the building of schoolhouses, but were denied the blessings of education.

Free Negroes were enlisted in the militia service, but were not permitted to bear arms. They had to attend the trainings, but were assigned the most servile duties.[205] They built fortifications, pitched and struck tents, cooked; drove teams, and in some instances were employed as musicians. Where free Negroes were acting as housekeepers, they were allowed to have fire-arms in their possession;[206] and if they lived on frontier plantations, as we have made mention already, they were permitted to use arms under the direction of their employers.

In a moral and religious sense, the slaves of the colony of Virginia received little or no attention from the Christian Church. All intercourse was cut off between the races. Intermarrying of whites and blacks was prohibited by severe laws.[207] And the most common civilities and amenities of life were frowned down when intended for a Negro. The plantation was as religious as the Church, and the Church was as secular as the plantation. The "white christians" hated the Negro, and the Church bestowed upon him a most bountiful amount of neglect.[208] Instead of receiving religious instruction from the clergy, slaves were given to them in part pay for their ministrations to the whites,—for their "use and encouragement."[209] It was as late as 1756 before any white minister had the piety and courage to demand instruction for the slaves.[210] The prohibition against instruction for these poor degraded vassals is not so much a marvel after all. For in 1670, when the white population was forty thousand, servants six thousand,

and slaves two thousand, Sir William Berkeley, when inquired of by the home government as to the condition of education in the colony, replied:—

"The same course that is taken in England out of towns,— every man according to his ability instructing his children. We have forty-eight parishes, and our ministers are well paid, and by my consent should be better if they would pray oftener and preach less. But of all other commodities, so of this, the worst are sent us, and we had few that we could boast of, since the persecution of Cromwell's tyranny drove divers worthy men hither. But I thank God, there are no free schools nor printing, and I hope we shall not have these hundred years: for learning has brought disobedience and heresy and sects into the world; and printing has divulged them, and libels against the best government. God keep us from both!"[211]

Thus was the entire colony in ignorance and superstition, and it was the policy of the home government to keep out the light. The sentiments of Berkeley were applauded in official circles in England, and most rigorously carried out by his successor who, in 1682, with the concurrence of the council, put John Buckner under bonds for introducing the art of printing into the colony.[212] This prohibition continued until 1733. If the whites of the colony were left in ignorance, what must have been the mental and moral condition of the slaves? The ignorance of the whites made them the pliant tools of the London Company, and the Negroes in turn were compelled to submit to a condition "of rather rigorous servitude."[213] This treatment has its reflexive influence on the planters. Men fear most the ghosts of their sins, and for cruel deeds rather expect and dread "the reward in the life that now is." So no wonder Dinwiddie wrote the father of Charles James Fox in 1758: "We dare not venture to part with any of our white men any distance, as we must have a watchful eye over our negro slaves."

In 1648, as we mentioned some pages back, there were about three hundred slaves in the colony. Slow coming at first, but at length they began to increase rapidly, so that in fifty years they had increased one hundred per cent. In 1671 they were two thousand strong, and all, up to that date, direct from Africa. In 1715 there were twenty-three thousand slaves against seventy-two thousand whites.[214] By the year 1758 the slave population had increased to the alarming number of over one hundred thousand, which was a little less than the numerical strength of the whites.

During this period of a century and a half, slavery took deep root in the colony of Virginia, and attained unwieldy and alarming proportions.

It had sent its dark death-roots into the fibre and organism of the political, judicial, social, and religious life of the people. It was crystallized now into a domestic institution. It existed in contemplation of legislative enactment, and had high judicial recognition through the solemn forms of law. The Church had proclaimed it a "sacred institution," and the clergy had covered it with the sanction of their ecclesiastical office. There it stood, an organized system,—the dark problem of the uncertain future: more terrible to the colonists in its awful, spectral silence during the years of the Revolution than the victorious guns of the French and Continental armies, which startled the English lion from his hurtful hold at the throat of white men's liberties—black men had no country, no liberty—in this new world in the West. But, like the dead body of the Roman murderer's victim, slavery was a curse that pursued the colonists evermore.

FOOTNOTES:

[119] A Flemish favorite of Charles V. having obtained of his king a patent, containing an exclusive right of importing four thousand Negroes into America, sold it for twenty-five thousand ducats to some Genoese merchants, who first brought into a regular form the commerce for slaves between Africa and America.--Holmes's American Annals, vol. i. p. 35.

[120] R. Beverley's History of Virginia, pp. 35, 36.

[121] See Campbell, p. 144; Burk, vol. i. p. 326.

[122] Smith, vol. ii pp. 38, 39.

[123] Smith's History of Virginia, vol. ii. p. 39.

[124] Virginia Company of London, p. 117, sq.

[125] Campbell, p. 144.

[126] Burk, vol. I. p. 319.

[127] Neill, p. 120.

[128] Smith, vol. II. p. 37.

[129] There were two vessels, The Treasurer and the Dutch man-of-war; but the latter, no doubt, put the first slaves ashore.

[130] Campbell, p. 144.

[131] Burk, Appendix, p. 316, Declaration of Virginia Company, 7th May, 1623.

[132] See Burk, vol. i. p. 326.

[133] Stith, Book III. pp. 153, 154.

[134] Beverley, 235, sq.

[135] Campbell, 147.

[136] Beverley, p. 248.

[137] Court and Times of James First, ii. p. 108; also, Neill p. 121.

[138] Bancroft, vol. i. p. 468.

[139] Neill, p. 121.

[140] Hist. Tracts, vol. ii. Tract viii.

[141] Beverley, p. 236.

[142] Campbell, p. 145.

[143] Hening, vol. i. p. 146; also p. 552.

[144] Hening, vol. i. p 226.

[145] Bancroft, vol. i. p. 178.

[146] Hening, vol. i. p. 540.

[147] Ibid., vol. ii. p. 84.

[148] Hening, vol. i. p. 396.

[149] Burk, vol. ii. Appendix, p. xxiii.

[150] Beverley, p. 235.

[151] Hening, vol. ii. p. 170; see, also, vol. iii. p. 140.

[152] Beverley, p. 195.

[153] Hening, vol. i. p. 396.

[154] Ibid., vol. ii. p. 283.

[155] Campbell, p. 160; also Bacon's Rebellion.

[156] Hening, vol. ii. pp. 490, 491.

[157] Ibid., vol. ii. p. 260; see, also, vol. iii. p. 460.

[158] Ibid., vol. iii. p. 333.

[159] Hening, vol. iii. pp. 334, 335.

[160] Ibid., vol. iii. p. 448; see, also, vol. v. p. 548.

[161] Hildreth, in his History of the United States, says that the law making "Negroes, Mulattoes, and Indians" real

estate "continued to be the law so long as Virginia remained a British colony." This is a mistake, as the reader can see. The law was repealed nearly a quarter of a century before Virginia ceased to be a British colony.

[162] Hening, vol. v. p. 432, sq.

[163] Beverley, p. 98.

[164] Hening, vol. iii, pp. 193, 194.

[165] Hening, vol. iii. p. 195.

[166] Burk, vol. ii. Appendix, p. xxii.

[167] Hening, vol. iv. p. 394.

[168] Ibid., vol, v. pp. 92, 93.

[169] Ibid., vol. v. pp. 160, 161.

[170] Ibid., vol. v. pp. 318, 319.

[171] Ibid., vol. vi. pp. 217, 218.

[172] Ibid., vol. vii. p. 466.

[173] Ibid., vol. vii. p. 81.

[174] Ibid., vol. vii. p. 281.

[175] Hening, vol. vii, p. 338.

[176] Ibid., vol. vii. p. 363.

[177] Ibid., vol. vii. p. 383.

[178] Ibid., vol. viii. pp. 190, 191, 237, 336, 337.

[179] Ibid., vol. viii, pp. 530, 532.

[180] Ibid., vol. i. p. 226.

[181] Ibid., vol. iii. p. 251.

[182] Ibid., vol. iii. p. 459; also vol. iv. p. 131, vol. vi. p. 109, and vol. ii. p. 481.

[183] Hening., vol. vi. p. 110.

[184] Ibid., vol. ii. p. 481.

[185] Ibid., vol. ii p. 270.

[186] Ibid., vol. ii. p. 493.

[187] Ibid., vol. iii, p. 451.

[188] Ibid., vol. iii. pp. 459, 460.

[189] Ibid., vol. viii. p. 360.
[190] Ibid., vol. iii. p. 298.
[191] Ibid., vol. iv. p. 327.
[192] Ibid., vol. iii. p. 103.
[193] Ibid., vol. iii, p. 270, and vol. iv. p. 128.
[194] Hening, vol. iv. p. 126, and vol. vi. p. 104, sq.
[195] Ibid., vol. viii. p. 139.
[196] Ibid., vol. viii. p. 522.
[197] Ibid., vol. viii. p. 523.
[198] Ibid., vol. viii. pp. 536, 537.
[199] Ibid., vol. iv. p. 132.
[200] Ibid., vol. vi, p. 112.
[201] Hening, vol. iii. pp. 87, 88.
[202] Ibid., vol. ii. p. 267.
[203] Ibid., vol. iv. pp. 133, 134.
[204] Ibid., vol. iv, p. 133.
[205] Ibid., vol. vii. p. 95; and vol. vi. p. 533.
[206] Ibid., vol. iv. p. 131.
[207] Ibid., vol. iii. p. 87.
[208] Campbell, p. 529.
[209] Burk, vol. ii. Appendix, p. xiii.
[210] Foot's Sketches, First Series, p. 291.
[211] Hening, vol. ii. p. 517.
[212] Hening, vol. ii. p. 518.
[213] Campbell, p. 383.
[214] Chalmers's American Colonies, vol. ii. p. 7.

CHAPTER XIII
THE COLONY OF NEW YORK

1628-1775.
> Settlement of New York by the Dutch in 1609.—Negroes introduced into the Colony, 1628.—The Trade in Negroes increased.—Tobacco exchanged for Slaves and Merchandise. Government of the Colony.—New Netherland falls into the Hands of the English, Aug. 27, 1664.—Various Changes.—New Laws adopted.—Legislation.—First Representatives elected in 1683.—In 1702 Queen Anne instructs the Royal Governor in Regard to the Importation of Slaves.—Slavery Restrictions.—Expedition to effect the Conquest of Canada unsuccessful.—Negro Riot.—Suppressed by the Efficient Aid of Troops.—Fears of the Colonists.—Negro Plot of 1741.—The Robbery of Hogg's House.—Discovery of a Portion of the Goods.—The Arrest of Hughson, his Wife, and Irish Peggy.—Crimination and Recrimination.—The Breaking-out of Numerous Fires.—The Arrest of Spanish Negroes.—The Trial of Hughson.—Testimony of Mary Burton.—Hughson hanged.—The Arrest of Many Others implicated in the Plot.—The Hanging of Cæsar and Prince.—Quack and Cuffee burned at the Stake.—The Lieutenant-Governor's Proclamation.—Many White Persons accused of being Conspirators.—Description of Hughson's Manner of Swearing those having Knowledge of the Plot.—Conviction and Hanging of the Catholic Priest Ury.—The Sudden and Unexpected Termination of the Trial.—New Laws more Stringent toward Slaves adopted.

FROM the settlement of New York by the Dutch in 1609, down to its conquest by the English in 1664, there is no reliable record of slavery in that colony. That the institution was coeval with the Holland government, there can be no historical doubt. During the half-century that the Holland flag waved over the New Netherlands, slavery grew to such proportions as to be regarded as a necessary evil. As early as 1628 the irascible slaves from Angola,[215] Africa, were the fruitful source of wide-spread public alarm. A newly settled country demanded a hardy and energetic laboring class. Money was scarce, the colonists poor, and servants few. The numerous physical obstructions across the path of material civilization suggested cheap but efficient labor. White servants were few, and the cost of securing them from abroad was a great hindrance to their increase. The Dutch had possessions on the coast of Guinea and in Brazil, and hence they found it cheap and convenient to import slaves to perform the labor of the colony.[216]

The early slaves went into the pastoral communities, worked on the public highways, and served as valets in private families. Their increase was stealthy, their conduct insubordinate, and their presence a distressing nightmare to the apprehensive and conscientious.

The West India Company had offered many inducements to its patroons.[217] And its pledge to furnish the colonists with "as many blacks as they conveniently could," was scrupulously performed.[218] In addition to the slaves furnished by the vessels plying between Brazil and the coast of Guinea, many Spanish and Portuguese prizes were brought into the Netherlands, where the slaves were made the chattel property of the company. An urgent and extraordinary demand for labor, rather than the cruel desire to traffic in human beings, led the Dutch to encourage the bringing of Negro slaves. Scattered widely among the whites, treated often with the humanity that characterized the treatment bestowed upon the white servants, there was little said about slaves in this period. The majority of them were employed upon the farms, and led quiet and sober lives. The largest farm owned by the company was "cultivated by the blacks;"[219] and this fact was recorded as early as the 19th of April, 1638, by "Sir William Kieft, Director-General of New Netherland." And, although the references to slaves and slavery in the records of Amsterdam are incidental, yet it is plainly to be seen that the institution was purely patriarchal during nearly all the period the Hollanders held the Netherlands.

Manumission of slaves was not an infrequent event.[220] Sometimes it was done as a reward for meritorious services, and sometimes it was prompted by the holy impulses of humanity and justice. The most cruel thing done, however, in this period, was to hold as slaves in the service of the company the children of Negroes who were lawfully manumitted. "All their children already born, or yet to be born, remained obligated to serve the company as slaves." In cases of emergency the liberated fathers of these bond children were required to serve "by water or by land" in the defence of the Holland government.[221] It is gratifying, however, to find the recorded indignation of some of the best citizens of the New Netherlands against the enslaving of the children of free Negroes. It was severely denounced, as contrary to justice and in "violation of the law of nature." "How any one born of a free Christian mother" could, notwithstanding, be a slave, and be obliged to remain such, passed their comprehension.[222] It was impossible for them to explain it." And, although "they were treated just like Christians," the moral sense of the people could not excuse such a flagrant crime against humanity.[223]

Director-General Sir William Kieft's unnecessary war, "without the knowledge, and much less the order, of the XIX., and against the will of the Commonality there," had thrown the Province into great confusion. Property was depreciating, and a feeling of insecurity seized upon the people. Instead of being a source of revenue, New Netherlands, as shown by the books of the Amsterdam Chamber, had cost the company, from 1626 to 1644, inclusive, "over five hundred and fifty thousand guilders, deducting the returns received from there." It was to be expected that the slaves would share the general feeling of uneasiness and expectancy. Something had to be done to stay the panic so imminent among both classes of the colonists, bond and free. The Bureau of Accounts made certain propositions to the company calculated to act as a tonic upon the languishing hopes of the people. After reciting many methods by which the Province was to be rejuvenated, it was suggested "that it would be wise to permit the patroons, colonists, and other farmers to import as many Negroes from the Brazils as they could purchase for cash, to assist them on their farms; as (it was maintained) these slaves could do more work for their masters, and were less expensive, than the hired laborers engaged in Holland, and conveyed to New Netherlands, "by means of much money and large promises."[224]

Nor was the substitution of slave labor for white a temporary expedient. Again in 1661 a loud call for more slaves was heard.[225] In the October treaty of the same year, the Dutch yielded to the seductive offer of the English, "to deliver two or three thousand hogsheads of tobacco annually ... in return for negroes and merchandise." At the first the Negro slave was regarded as a cheap laborer,—a blessing to the Province; but after a while the cupidity of the English induced the Hollanders to regard the Negro as a coveted, marketable chattel.

> "In its scheme of political administration, the West-India Company exhibited too often a mercantile and selfish spirit; and in encouraging commerce in Negro slaves, it established an institution which subsisted many generations after its authority had ceased."[226]

The Dutch colony was governed by the Dutch and Roman law. The government was tripartite,—executive, legislative, and judicial,—all vested in, and exercised by, the governor and council. There seemed to be but little or no necessity for legislation on the slavery question. The Negro seemed to be a felt need in the Province, and was regarded with some consideration by the kind-hearted Hollanders. Benevolent and social, they desired to see all around them happy. The enfranchised African might and did obtain a freehold; while the Negro who remained under an institution of patriarchal simplicity, scarcely knowing he was in bondage, danced merrily at the best, in "kermis," at Christmas and Pinckster.[227] There were, doubtless, a few cases where the slaves received harsh treatment from their masters; but, as a rule, the jolly Dutch fed and clothed their slaves as well as their white servants. There were no severe rules to strip the Negroes of their personal rights,—such as social amusements or public feasts when their labors had been completed. During this entire period, they went and came among their class without let or hinderance. They were married, and given in marriage;[228] they sowed, and, in many instances, gathered an equitable share of the fruits of their labors. If there were no schools for them, there were no laws against an honest attempt to acquire knowledge at seasonable times. The Hollanders built their government upon the hearthstone, believing it to be the earthly rock of ages to a nation that would build wisely for the future. And while it is true that they regarded commerce as the life-blood of the material existence of a people, they nevertheless found their inspiration for multifarious duties in the genial sunshine of the family circle. A nation thus constituted could not habilitate slavery with all the hideous features it wore in Virginia and Massachusetts. The slaves could not escape the good influences of the mild government of the New Netherlands, nor could the Hollanders withhold the brightness and goodness of their hearts from their domestic slaves.

On the 27th of August, 1664, New Netherlands fell into the hands of the English; and the city received a new name,—New York, after the famous Duke of York. When the English colors were run up over Fort Amsterdam, it received a new name, "Fort James." In the twenty-four articles in which the Hollanders surrendered their Province, there is no direct mention of slaves or slavery. The only clause that might be construed into a reference to the slaves is as follows: "IV. If any inhabitant have a mind to remove himself, he shall have a year and six weeks from this day to remove himself, wife, children, *servants*, goods, and to dispose of his lands here." There was nothing in the articles of capitulation hostile to slavery in the colony.

During the reign of Elizabeth, the English government gave its royal sanction to the slave-traffic. "In 1562 Sir John Hawkins, Sir Lionel Duchet,

Sir Thomas Lodge, and Sir William Winter"—all "honorable men"—became the authors of the greatest curse that ever afflicted the earth. Hawkins, assisted by the aforenamed gentlemen, secured a ship-load of Africans from Sierra Leone, and sold them at Hispaniola. Many were murdered on the voyage, and cast into the sea. The story of this atrocity coming to the ears of the queen, she was horrified. She summoned Hawkins into her presence, in order to rebuke him for his crime against humanity. He defended his conduct with great skill and eloquence. He persuaded her Royal Highness that it was an act of humanity to remove the African from a bad to a better country, from the influences of idolatry to the influences of Christianity. Elizabeth afterwards encouraged the slave-trade.

So when New Netherlands became an English colony, slavery received substantial official encouragement, and the slave became the subject of colonial legislation.

The first laws under the English Government were issued under the patent to the Duke of York, on the 1st of March, 1665, and were known as "the Duke's Laws." It is rather remarkable that they were fashioned after the famous "Massachusetts Fundamentals," adopted in 1641. These laws have the following caption: *"Laws collected out of the several laws now in force in his majesty's American colonies and plantations."* The first mention of slavery is contained in a section under the caption of "Bond Slavery."

> "No Christian shall be kept in Bondslavery, villenage, or Captivity, Except Such who shall be Judged thereunto by Authority, or such as willing have sold or shall sell themselves, In which Case a Record of Such servitude shall be entered in the Court of Sessions held for that Jurisdiction where Such Masters shall Inhabit, provided that nothing in the Law Contained shall be to the prejudice of Master or Dame who have or shall by any Indenture or Covenant take Apprentices for Terme of Years, or other Servants for Term of years or Life."[229]

By turning to the first chapter on Massachusetts, the reader will observe that the above is the Massachusetts law of 1641 with but a very slight alteration. We find no reference to slavery directly, and the word slave does not occur in this code at all. Article 7, under the head of "Capital Laws," reads as follows: "If any person forcibly stealeth or carrieth away any mankind he shall be put to death."

On the 27th of January, 1683, Col. Thomas Dongan was sent to New York as its governor, and charged with carrying out a long list of instructions laid down by his Royal Highness the Duke of York. Gov. Dongan arrived in

New York during the latter part of August; and on the 13th of September, 1683, the council sitting at Fort James promulgated an order calling upon the people to elect representatives. On the 17th October, 1683, the General Assembly met for the first time at Fort James, in the city of New York. It is a great misfortune that the journals of both houses are lost. The titles of the Acts passed have been preserved, and so far we are enabled to fairly judge of the character of the legislation of the new assembly. On the 1st November, 1683, the Assembly passed "An Act for naturalizing all those of foreign nations at present inhabiting within this province and professing Christianity, and for encouragement for others to come and settle within the same."[230] This law was re-enacted in 1715, and provided, that "nothing contained in this Act is to be construed to discharge or set at liberty any servant, bondman or slave, but only to have relation to such persons as are free at the making hereof."[231]

So the mild system of domestic slavery introduced by the Dutch now received the sanction of positive British law. Most of the slaves in the Province of New York, from the time they were first introduced, down to 1664, had been the property of the West-India Company. As such they had small plots of land to work for their own benefit, and were not without hope of emancipation some day. But under the English government the condition of the slave was clearly defined by law and one of great hardships. On the 24th of October, 1684, an Act was passed in which slavery was for the first time regarded as a legitimate institution in the Province of New York under the English government.[232]

The slave-trade grew. New York began to feel the necessity of a larger number of slaves. In 1702 her "most gracious majesty," Queen Anne, among many instructions to the royal governor, directed that the people "take especial care, that God Almighty be devoutly and duly served," and that the "Royal African Company of England" "take especial care that the said Province may have a constant and sufficient supply of merchantable Negroes, at moderate rates."[233] It was a marvellous zeal that led the good queen to build up the Church of England alongside of the institution of human slavery. It was an impartial zeal that sought their mutual growth,—the one intended by our divine Lord to give mankind absolute liberty, the other intended by man to rob mankind of the great boon of freedom! But with the sanction of statutory legislation, and the silent acquiescence of the Church, the foundations of the institution of slavery were firmly laid in the approving conscience of a selfish public. Dazzled by prospective riches, and unscrupulous in the methods of accumulations, the people of the Province of New York clamored for more exacting laws by which to govern the slaves.[234] Notwithstanding Lord Cornbury had received the following instructions from the crown, "you shall endeavor to get a law passed for the restraining of any inhuman severity ... to find out the best means to facilitate and encourage the conversion of Negroes and Indians to the Christian religion," the Colonial Assembly (the same year, 1702) passed severe laws against the slaves. It was "An Act for regulating slaves," but was quite lengthy and specific. It was deemed "not lawful to trade with negro slaves," and the violation of this law was followed by fine and imprisonment. "Not above three slaves may meet together:" if they did they were liable to be whipped by a justice of the peace, or sent to jail. "A common whipper to be appointed," showed that the justices had more physical exercise than they cared for. "A slave not to strike a freeman," indicated that the slaves in New York as in Virginia were accounted as heathen. "Penalty for concealing slaves," and the punishment of Negroes for stealing, etc., were rather severe, but only indicated the temper of the people at that time.[235]

The recommendations to have Negro and Indian slaves baptized gave rise to considerable discussion and no little alarm. As was shown in the chapter on Virginia, the proposition to baptize slaves did not meet with a hearty indorsement from the master-class. The doctrine had obtained in most of the colonies, that a man was a freeman by virtue of his membership in a Christian church, and hence eligible to office. To escape the logic of this position, the dealer in human flesh sought to bar the door of the Church against the slave. But in 1706 *An Act to encourage the baptizing of Negro, Indian, and mulatto slaves,*" was passed in the hope of quieting the public mind on this question.

"Whereas divers of her Majesty's good Subjects, Inhabitants of this Colony, now are, and have been willing that such Negroe, Indian, and Mulatto Slaves, who belong to them, and desire the same, should be baptized, but are deterred and hindered therefrom by reason of a groundless Opinion that hath spread itself in this Colony, that by the baptizing of such Negro, Indian, or Mulatto Slave, they would become Free, and ought to be set at liberty. In order therefore to put an end to all such Doubts and scruples as have, or hereafter at any time may arise about the same—

"*Be it enacted, &c.*, that the baptizing of a Negro, Indian, or Mulatto Slave shall not be any cause or reason for the setting them or any of them at liberty.

"*And be it, &c.*, that all and every Negro, Indian, Mulatto and Mestee bastard child and children, who is, are, and shall be born of any Negro, Indian, or Mestee, shall follow the state and condition of the mother and be esteemed, reputed, taken and adjudged a slave and slaves to all intents and purposes whatsoever.

"Provided always, and be it, &c., That no slave whatsoever in this colony shall at any time be admitted as a witness for or against any freeman in any case, matter or cause, civil or criminal, whatsoever."[236]

So when the door of the Christian Church was opened to the Negro, he was to appear at the sacred altar with his chains on. Though emancipated from the bondage of Satan, he nevertheless remained the abject slave of the Christian colonists. Claiming spiritual kinship with Christ, the Negro could be sold at the pleasure of his master, and his family hearthstone trodden down by the slave-dealer. The humane feature of the system of slavery under the simple Dutch government, of allowing slaves to acquire an interest in the soil, was now at an end. The tendency to manumit faithful slaves called forth no approbation. The colonists grew cold and hard-fisted. They saw not God's image in the slave,—only so many dollars. There were no strong men in the pulpits of the colony who dared brave the avaricious spirit of the times. Not satisfied with colonial legislation, the municipal government of the city of New York passed, in 1710,[237] an ordinance forbidding Negroes, Indians, and Mulatto slaves from appearing "in the streets after nightfall without a lantern with a lighted candle in it."[238] The year before, a slave-market was erected at the foot of Wall Street, where slaves of every description were for sale. Negroes, Indians, and Mulattoes; men, women, and children; the old, the middle-aged, and the young,—all, as sheep in shambles, were daily declared the property of the highest cash-bidder. And what of the few who secured their freedom? Why, the law of 1712 declared that no Negro, Indian, or Mulatto that shall hereafter be set free "shall hold any land or real estate, but the same shall escheat."[239] There was, therefore, but little for the Negro in either state,—bondage or freedom. There was little in this world to allure him, to encourage him, to help him. The institution under which he suffered was one huge sepulchre, and he was buried alive.

The poor grovelling worm turns under the foot of the pedestrian. The Negro winched under his galling yoke of British colonial oppression.

A misguided zeal and an inordinate desire of conquest had led the Legislature to appropriate ten thousand pounds sterling toward an expedition to effect the conquest of Canada. Acadia had just fallen into the hands of Gov. Francis Nicholson without firing a gun, and the news had carried the New Yorkers off their feet. "On to Canada!" was the shibboleth of the adventurous colonists; and the expedition started. Eight transports, with eight hundred and sixty men, perished amid the treacherous rocks and angry waters of the St. Lawrence. The troops that had gone overland returned in chagrin. The city was wrapped in gloom: the Legislature refused to do any thing further; and here the dreams of conquest vanished. The city of New York was thrown on the defensive. The forts were repaired, and every thing put in readiness for an emergency. Like a sick man the colonists started at every rumor. On account of bad faith the Iroquois were disposed to mischief.

In the feeble condition of the colonial government, the Negro grew restless. At the first, as previously shown, the slaves were very few, but now, in 1712, were quite numerous. The Negro, the Quaker, and the Papist were a trinity of evils that the colonists most dreaded. The Negro had been badly treated; and an attempt on his part to cast off the yoke was not improbable, in the mind of the master-class. The fears of the colonists were at length realized. A Negro riot broke out. A house was burned, and a number of white persons killed; and, had it not been for the prompt and efficient aid of the troops, the city of New York would have been reduced to ashes.

Now, what was the condition of the slaves in the Christian colony of New York? They had no family relations: for a long time they lived together by common consent. They had no property, no schools, and, neglected in life, were abandoned to burial in a common ditch after death. They dared not lift their hand to strike a Christian or a Jew. Their testimony was excluded by the courts, and the power of their masters over their bodies extended sometimes to life and limb. This condition of affairs yielded its bitter fruit at length.

> "Here we see the effects of that blind and wicked policy which induced England to pamper her merchants and increase her revenues, by positive instructions to the governours of her colonies, strictly enjoining them (for the good of the African company, and for the emoluments expected from the assiento contract), to fix upon America a vast negro population, torn from their homes and brought hither by force. New York was at this time filled with negroes; every householder who could afford to keep servants, was surrounded by blacks, some pampered in indolence, all carefully kept in ignorance, and considered, erroneously, as creatures whom the white could not do without, yet lived in dread of. They were feared, from their numbers, and from a consciousness, however stifled, that they were injured and might seek revenge or a better condition."[240]

The Negro plot of 1741 furnishes the most interesting and thrilling chapter in the history of the colony of New York. Unfortunately for the truth of history, there was but one historian[241] of the affair, and he an interested judge; and what he has written should be taken cum grano salis. His book was intended to defend the action of the court that destroyed so many innocent lives, but no man can read it without being thoroughly convinced that the decision of the court was both illogical and cruel. There is nothing in this country to equal it, except it be the burning of the witches at Salem. But in stalwart old England the Popish Plot in 1679, started by Titus Oates, is the only occurrence in human history that is so faithfully reproduced by the Negro plot. Certainly history repeats itself. Sixty-two years of history stretch between the events. One tragedy is enacted in the metropolis of the Old World, the other in the metropolis of the New World. One was instigated by a perjurer and a heretic, the other by an indentured servant, in all probability from a convict ship. The one was suggested by the hatred of the Catholics, and the other by hatred of the Negro. And in both cases the evidence that convicted and condemned innocent men and women was wrung from the lying lips of doubtful characters by an overwrought zeal on the part of the legal authorities.

Titus Oates, who claimed to have discovered the "Popish Plot," was a man of the most execrable character. He was the son of an Anabaptist, took orders in the Church, and had been settled in a small living by the Duke of Norfolk. Indicted for perjury, he effected an escape in a marvellous manner. While a chaplain in the English navy he was convicted of practices not fit to be mentioned, and was dismissed from the service. He next sought communion with the Church of Rome, and made his way into the Jesuit College of St. Omers. After a brief residence among the students, he was deputed to perform a confidential mission to Spain, and, upon his return to St. Omers, was dismissed to the world on account of his habits, which were very distasteful to Catholics. He boasted that he had only joined them to get their secrets. Such a man as this started the cry of the Popish Plot, and threw all England into a state of consternation. A chemist by the name of Tongue, on the 12th of August, 1678, had warned the king against a plot that was directed at his life, etc. But the king did not attach any importance to the statement until Tongue referred to Titus Oates as his authority. The latter proved himself a most arrant liar while on the stand: but the people were in a credulous state of mind, and Oates became the hero of the hour;[242] and under his wicked influence many souls were hurried into eternity. Read Hume's account of the Popish Plot, and then follow the bloody narrative of the Negro plot of New York, and see how the one resembles the other.

> "Some mysterious design was still suspected in every enterprise and profession: arbitrary power and Popery were apprehended as the scope of all projects: each breath or rumor made the people start with anxiety: their enemies,

they thought, were in their very bosom, and had gotten possession of their sovereign's confidence. While in this timorous, jealous disposition, the cry of a plot all on a sudden struck their ears: they were wakened from their slumber, and like men affrighted and in the dark, took every figure for a spectre. The terror of each man became the source of terror to another. And a universal panic being diffused, reason and argument, and common-sense and common humanity, lost all influence over them. From this disposition of men's minds we are to account for the progress of the Popish Plot, and the credit given to it; an event which would otherwise appear prodigious and altogether inexplicable."[243]

On the 28th of February, 1741, the house of one Robert Hogg, Esq., of New-York City, a merchant, was robbed of some fine linen, medals, silver coin, etc. Mr. Hogg's house was situated on the corner of Broad and Mill Streets, the latter sometimes being called Jew's Alley. The case was given to the officers of the law to look up.

The population of New-York City was about ten thousand, about two thousand of whom were slaves. On the 18th of March the chapel in the fort took fire from some coals carelessly left by an artificer in a gutter he had been soldering. The roof was of shingles; and a brisk wind from the southeast started a fire, that was not observed until it had made great headway. In those times the entire populace usually turned out to assist in extinguishing fires; but this fire being in the fort, the fear of an explosion of the magazine somewhat checked their usual celerity on such occasions. The result was, that all the government buildings in the fort were destroyed. A militia officer by the name of Van Horne, carried away by the belief that the fire was purposely set by the Negroes, caused the beating of the drums and the posting of the "night watch." And for his vigilance he was nicknamed "Major Drum." The "Major's" apprehensions, however, were contagious. The fact that the governor reported the true cause of the fire to the Legislature had but little influence in dispossessing the people of their fears of a Negro plot. The next week the chimney of Capt. Warren's house near the fort took fire, but was saved with but slight damage. A few days after this the storehouse of a Mr. Van Zandt was found to be on fire, and it was said at the time to have been occasioned by the carelessness of a smoker. In about three days after, two fire alarms were sounded. One was found to be a fire in some hay in a cow-stable near a Mr. Quick's house. It was soon extinguished. The other alarm was on account of a fire in the kitchen loft of the dwelling of a Mr. Thompson. On the next day coals were discovered under the stables of a Mr. John Murray on Broadway. On the next morning an alarm called the people to the residence of Sergeant Burns, near the fort; and in a few hours the dwelling of a Mr. Hilton, near Fly Market, was found to be on fire. But the flames in both places were readily extinguished. It was thought that the fire was purposely set at Mr. Hilton's, as a bundle of tow was found near the premises. A short time before these strange fires broke out, a Spanish vessel, partly manned by Spanish Catholic Negroes, had been brought into the port of New York as a prize. All the crew that were Negroes were hurried into the Admiralty Court; where they were promptly condemned to slavery, and an order issued for their sale. The Negroes pleaded their freedom in another country, but had no counsel to defend them. A Capt. Sarly purchased one of these Negroes. Now, Capt. Sarly's house adjoined that of Mr. Hilton's; and so, when the latter's house was discovered to be on fire, a cry was raised, "The Spanish Negroes! The Spanish! Take up the Spanish Negroes!" Some persons took it upon themselves to question Capt. Sarly's Negro about the fires, and it is said that he behaved in an insolent manner; whereupon he was sent to jail. A magistrate gave orders to the constables to arrest and incarcerate the rest of the Spanish Negroes. The magistrates held a meeting the same day, in the afternoon; and, while they were deliberating about the matter, another fire broke out in Col. Phillipes's storehouse. Some of the white people cried "Negro! Negro!" and "Cuff Phillipes!" Poor Cuff, startled at the cry, ran to his master's house, from whence he was dragged to jail by an excited mob. Judge Horsemanden says,—

> "Many people had such terrible apprehensions on this occasion that several Negroes (many of whom had assisted to put out the fire) who were met in the streets, were hurried away to jail; and when they were there they were continued some time in confinement before the magistrates could spare time to examine into their several cases."[244]

Let the reader return now to the robbery committed in Mr. Hogg's house on the 28th of February. The officers thought they had traced the stolen goods to a public house on the North River, kept by a person named John Hughson. This house had been a place of resort for Negroes; and it was searched for the articles, but nothing was found. Hughson had in his service an indentured servant,—a girl of sixteen years,—named Mary Burton. She intimated to a neighbor that the goods were concealed in Hughson's house, but that it would be at the expense of her life to make this fact known. This information was made known to the sheriff, and he at once apprehended the girl and produced her before Alderman Banker. This benevolent officer promised the girl her freedom on the ground that she should tell all she knew about the missing property. For prudential reasons the Alderman ordered Mary Burton to be taken to the City Hall, corner Wall and Nassua

Streets. On the 4th of March the justices met at the City Hall. In the mean while John Hughson and his wife had been arrested for receiving stolen goods. They were now examined in the presence of Mary Burton. Hughson admitted that some goods had been brought to his house, produced them, and turned them over to the court. It appears from the testimony of the Burton girl that another party, dwelling in the house of the Hughson's, had taken part in receiving the stolen articles. She was a girl of bad character, called Margaret Sorubiero, alias Solinburgh, alias Kerry, but commonly called Peggy Carey. This woman had lived in the home of the Hughsons for about ten months, but at one time during this period had remained a short while at the house of John Rommes, near the new Battery, but had returned to Hughson's again. The testimony of Mary Burton went to show that a Negro by the name of Cæsar Varick, but called Quin, on the night in which the burglary was committed, entered Peggy's room through the window. The next morning Mary Burton saw "speckled linen" in Peggy's room, and that the man Varick gave the deponent two pieces of silver. She further testified that Varick drank two mugs of punch, and bought of Hughson a pair of stockings, giving him a lump of silver; and that Hughson and his wife received and hid away the linen.[245] Mr. John Varick (it was spelled Vaarck then), a baker, the owner of Cæsar, occupied a house near the new Battery, the kitchen of which adjoined the yard of John Romme's house. He found some of Robert Hogg's property under his kitchen floor, and delivered it to the mayor. Upon this revelation Romme fled to New Jersey, but was subsequently captured at Brunswick. He had followed shoemaking and tavern-keeping, and was, withal, a very suspicious character.

Up to this time nothing had been said about a Negro plot. It was simply a case of burglary. Hughson had admitted receiving certain articles, and restored them; Mr. Varick had found others, and delivered them to the mayor.

The reader will remember that the burglary took place on the 28th of February; that the justices arraigned the Hughsons, Mary Burton, and Peggy Carey on the 4th of March; that the first fire broke out on the 18th, the second on the 25th, of March, the third on the 1st of April, and the fourth and fifth on the 4th of April; that on the 5th of April coals were found disposed so as to burn a haystack, and that the day following two houses were discovered to be on fire.

On the 11th of April the Common Council met. The following gentlemen were present: John Cruger, Esq., mayor; the recorder, Daniel Horsemanden; aldermen, Gerardus Stuyvesant, William Romaine, Simon Johnson, John Moore, Christopher Banker, John Pintard, John Marshall; assistants, Henry Bogert, Isaac Stoutenburgh, Philip Minthorne, George Brinckerhoff, Robert

Benson, and Samuel Lawrence. Recorder Horsemanden suggested to the council that the governor be requested to offer rewards for the apprehension of the incendiaries and all persons implicated, and that the city pay the cost, etc. It was accordingly resolved that the lieutenant-governor be requested to offer a reward of one hundred pounds current money of the Province to any white person, and pardon, if concerned; and twenty pounds, freedom, and, if concerned, pardon to any slave (the master to be paid twenty-five pounds); and to any free Negro, Mulatto, or Indian, forty-five pounds and pardon, if concerned. The mayor and the recorder (Horsemanden), called upon Lieut.-Gov. Clark, and laid the above resolve before him.

The city was now in a state of great excitement. The air was peopled with the wildest rumors.

On Monday the 13th of April each alderman, assistant, and constable searched his ward. The militia was called out, and sentries posted at the cross-streets. While the troops were patrolling the streets, the aldermen were examining Negroes in reference to the origin of the fires. Nothing was found. The Negroes denied all knowledge of the fires or a plot.

On the 21st of April, 1741, the Supreme Court convened.[246] Judges Frederick Phillipse and Daniel Horsemanden called the grand jury. The members were as follows: Robert Watts, merchant, foreman; Jeremiah Latouche, Joseph Read, Anthony Rutgers, John M'Evers, John Cruger, jun., John Merrit, Adoniah Schuyler, Isaac DePeyster, Abraham Ketteltas, David Provoost, Rene Hett, Henry Beeckman, jun., David van Horne, George Spencer, Thomas Duncan, and Winant Van Zandt,—all set down as merchants,—a respectable, intelligent, and influential grand jury! Judge Phillipse informed the jury that the people "have been put into many frights and terrors," in regard to the fires; that it was their duty to use "all lawful means" to discover the guilty parties, for there was "much room to suspect" that the fires were not accidental. He told them that there were many persons in jail upon whom suspicion rested; that arson was felony at common law, even though the fire is extinguished, or goes out itself; that arson was a deep crime, and, if the perpetrators were not apprehended and punished, "who can say he is safe, or where will it end?" The learned judge then went on to deliver a moral lecture against the wickedness of selling "penny drams" to Negroes, without the consent of their masters. In conclusion, he charged the grand jury to present "all conspiracies, combinations and other offences."

It should be kept in mind that Mary Burton was only a witness in the burglary case already mentioned. Up to that time there had been no fires. The fires, and wholesale arrests of innocent Negroes, followed the robbery. But the grand jury called Mary Burton to testify in reference to the fires.

She refused to be sworn. She was questioned concerning the fires, but gave no answer. Then the proclamation of the mayor, offering protection, pardon, freedom, and one hundred pounds, was read. It had the desired effect. The girl opened her mouth, and spake all the words that the jury desired. At first she agreed to tell all she knew about the stolen goods, but would say nothing about the fires. This declaration led the jury to infer that she could, but would not say any thing about the fires. After a moral lecture upon her duty in the matter in the light of eternal reward, and a reiteration of the proffered reward that then awaited her wise decision, her memory brightened, and she immediately began to tell *all* she knew. She said that a Negro named Prince, belonging to a Mr. Auboyman, and Prince (Varick) brought the goods, stolen from Mr. Hogg's house, to the house of her master, and that Hughson, his wife, and Peggy (Carey) received them; further, that Cæsar, Prince, and Cuffee (Phillipse) had frequently met at Hughson's tavern, and discoursed about burning the fort; that they had said they would go down to the Fly (the east end of the city), and burn the entire place; and that Hughson and his wife had assented to these insurrectionary remarks, and promised to assist them. She added, by way of fulness and emphasis, that when a handful of wretched slaves, seconded by a miserable and ignorant white tavern-keeper, should have lain the city in ashes, and murdered eight or nine thousand persons,—then Cæsar should be governor, Hughson king, and Cuffee supplied with abundant riches! The loquacious Mary remembered that this intrepid trio had said, that when they burned the city it would be in the night, so they could murder the people as they came out of their homes. It should not be forgotten that *all* the fires broke out in the daytime!

It is rather remarkable and should be observed, that this wonderful witness stated that her master, John Hughson, had threatened to poison her if she told anybody that the stolen goods were in his house; that all the Negroes swore they would burn her if she told; and that, when they talked of burning the town during their meetings, there were no white persons present save her master, mistress, and Peggy Carey.

The credulous Horsemanden tells us that "the evidence of a conspiracy," not only to burn the city, but also "to destroy and murder the people," was most "astonishing to the grand jury!" But that any white person should confederate with slaves in such a wicked and cruel purpose was astounding beyond measure! And the grand jury was possessed of the same childlike faith in the ingenious narrative of the wily Mary. In their report to the judges, they set forth in strong terms their faith in the statements of the deponent, and required the presence of Peggy Carey. The extent of the delusion of the judges, jury, and people may be seen in the fact, that, immediately upon the report of the jury, the judges summoned the entire bar of the city of New York to meet them. The following gentlemen responded to the call: Messrs. Murray, Alexander, Smith, Chambers, Nichols, Lodge, and Jameson. All the lawyers were present except the attorney-general. By the act of 1712, "for preventing, suppressing and punishing the conspiracy and insurrection of negroes and other slaves,"[247] a justice of the peace could try the refractory slaves at once. But here was a deep, dark, and bloody plot to burn the city and murder its inhabitants, in which white persons were implicated. This fact led the learned judges to conclude it wise and prudent to refer this whole matter to the Supreme Court. And the generous offer of the entire bar of New-York City to assist, in turns, in every trial, should remain evermore an indestructible monument to their unselfish devotion to their city, the existence of which was threatened by less than a score of ignorant, penniless Negro slaves!

By the testimony of Mary Burton, Peggy Carey stood convicted as one of the conspirators. She had already languished in jail for more than a month. The judges thought it advisable to examine her in her cell. They tried to cajole her into criminating others; but she stoutly denied all knowledge of the fires, and said "that if she should accuse anybody of any such thing, she must accuse innocent persons, and wrong her own soul."

On the 24th of April, Cæsar Varick, Prince Auboyman, John Hughson, his wife, and Peggy Carey were arraigned for felony, and pleaded not guilty. Cæsar and Prince were first put on trial. As they did not challenge the jury, the following gentlemen were sworn: Messrs. Roger French, John Groesbeck, John Richard, Abraham Kipp, George Witts, John Thurman, Patrick Jackson, Benjamin Moore, William Hammersley, John Lashiere, Joshua Sleydall, and John Shurmer. "Guilty!" as charged in the indictment. They had committed the robbery, so said the jury.

On the 3d of May one Arthur Price, a common thief, was committed to jail for theft. He occupied a cell next to the notorious Peggy Carey. In order to bring himself into favor with the judges, he claimed to have had a conversation with Peggy through the hole in the door. Price says she told him that "she was afraid of those fellows" (the Negroes); that if they said any thing in any way involving her she would hang every one of them; that she did not care to go on the stand again unless she was called; that when asked if she intended to set the town on fire she said no; but she knew about the plot; that Hughson and his wife "were sworn with the rest;" that she was not afraid of "Prince, Cuff, Cæsar, and Fork's Negro—not Cæsar, but another," because they "were all true-hearted fellows." This remarkable conversation was flavored throughout with the vilest species of profanity. Notwithstanding this interview was between a common Irish prostitute and a wretched sneak-thief, it had great weight with the solemn and upright judges.

In the midst of this trial, seven barns were burnt in the town of Hackinsack. Two Negroes were suspected of the crime, but there was not the slightest evidence that they were guilty. But one of them said that he had discharged a gun at the party who set his master's barn on fire, but did not kill any one. The other one was found loading a gun with two bullets. This was enough to convict. They were burnt alive at a stake. This only added fuel to the flame of public excitement in New York.

On the 6th of May (Wednesday) two more arrests were made,—Hughson's daughter Sarah, suspected of being a confederate, and Mr. Sleydall's Negro Jack,—on suspicion of having put fire to Mr. Murray's haystack. On the same day the judges arraigned the white persons implicated in the case,—John Hughson, his wife, and Peggy Carey. The jury promptly found them guilty of "receiving stolen goods." "Peggy Carey," says Recorder Horsemanden, "seeming to think it high time to do something to recommend herself to mercy, made a voluntary confession." This vile, foul-mouthed prostitute takes the stand, and gives a new turn to the entire affair. She removes the scene of the conspiracy to another tavern near the new Battery, where John Romme had made a habit of entertaining, contrary to law, Negro slaves. Peggy had seen many meetings at this place, particularly in December, 1740. At that time she mentioned the following Negroes as being present: Cuff, Brash, Curacoa, Cæsar, Patrick, Jack, Cato; but her especial Cæsar Varick was not implicated! Romme administered an oath to all these Negroes, and then made a proposition to them; viz., that they should destroy the fort, burn the town, and bring the spoils to him. He engaged to divide with them, and take them to a new country, where he would give them their freedom. Mrs. Romme was present during this conversation; and, after the Negroes had departed, she and the deponent (Peggy) were sworn by Romme to eternal secrecy. Mrs. Romme denied swearing to the conspiracy, but acknowledged that her husband had received stolen goods, that he sold drams to Negroes who kept game-fowls there; but that never more than three Negroes came at a time. She absconded in great fright. It has been mentioned that Peggy Carey had lived at the tavern of John Romme for a short time, and that articles belonging to Mr. Hogg had been found under the kitchen floor of the house next to Romme's.

The judges evidently reasoned that all Negroes would steal, or that stealing was incident upon or implied by the condition of the slave. Then Romme kept a "tippling-house," and defied the law by selling "drams" to Negroes. Now, a man who keeps a "tippling-house" was liable to encourage a conspiracy.

A full list of the names of the persons implicated by Peggy was handed to the proper officers, and those wicked persons apprehended. They were brought before the redoubtable Peggy for identification. She accused them of being sworn conspirators. They all denied the charge. Then they were turned over to Mary Burton; and she, evidently displeased at Peggy's attempt to rival her in the favor of the powerful judges, testified that she knew them not. But it was vain. Peggy had the ear of the court, and the terror-stricken company was locked up in the jail. Alarmed at their helpless situation, the ignorant Negroes began "to accuse one another, as it would seem, by way of injuring an enemy and guarding themselves."

Cæsar and Prince, having been tried and convicted of felony, were sentenced to be hanged. The record says,—

> "Monday, 11th of May. Cæsar and Prince were executed this day at the gallows, according to sentence: they died very stubbornly, without confessing any thing about the conspiracy: and denied that they knew any thing about it to the last. The body of Cæsar was accordingly hung in chains."[248]

On the 13th of May, 1741, a solemn fast was observed; "because many houses and dwellings had been fired about our ears, without any discovery of the cause or occasion of them, which had put us into the utmost consternation." Excitement ran high. Instead of getting any light on the affair, the plot thickened.

On the 6th of May, Hughson, his wife, and Peggy Carey had been tried and found guilty, as has already been stated. Sarah Hughson, daughter of the Hughsons, was in jail. Mary Burton was the heroine of the hour. Her word was law. Whoever she named was produced in court. The sneak-thief, Arthur Price, was employed by the judges to perform a mission that was at once congenial to his tastes and in harmony with his criminal education. He was sent among the incarcerated Negroes to administer punch, in the desperate hope of getting more "confessions!" Next, he was sent to Sarah Hughson to persuade her to accuse her father and mother of complicity in the conspiracy. He related a conversation he had with Sarah, but she denied it to his teeth with great indignation. This vile and criminal method of securing testimony of a conspiracy never brought the blush to the cheek of a single officer of the law. "None of these things moved" them. They were themselves so completely lost in the general din and excitement, were so thoroughly convinced that a plot existed, and that it was their duty to prove it in some manner or other,—that they believed every thing that went to establish the guilt of any one.

Even a feeble-minded boy was arrested, and taken before the grand jury. He swore that he knew nothing of the plot to burn the town, but the kind magistrates told him that if he would tell the truth he should not be hanged. Ignorant as these helpless slaves were, they now understood "telling the truth" to mean to criminate some one in the plot, and thus gratify the inordinate hunger of the judges and jury for testimony relating to a "conspiracy." This Negro imbecile began his task of telling "what he knew," which was to be rewarded by allowing him to leave without being hung! He deposed that Quack desired him to burn the fort; that Cuffee said he would fire one house, Curacoa Dick another, and so on ad infinitum. He was asked by one of the learned gentlemen, "what the Negroes intended by all this mischief?" He answered, "To kill all the gentlemen and take their wives; that one of the fellows already hanged, was to be an officer in the Long Bridge Company, and the other, in the Fly Company."[249]

On the 25th of May a large number of Negroes were arrested. The boy referred to above (whose name was Sawney, or Sandy) was called to the stand again on the 26th, when he grew very talkative. He said that "at a meeting of Negroes he was called in and frightened into undertaking to burn the slip Market;" that he witnessed some of the Negroes in their attempts to burn certain houses; that at the house of one Comfort, he, with others, was sworn to secrecy and fidelity to each other; said he was never at either tavern, Hughson's nor Romme's; and ended his revelations by accusing a woman of setting fire to a house, and of murdering her child. As usual, after such confessions, more arrests followed. Quack and Cuffee were tried and convicted of felony, "for wickedly and maliciously conspiring with others to burn the town and murder the inhabitants." This was an occasion to draw forth the eloquence of the attorney-general; and in fervid utterance he pictured the Negroes as "monsters, devils, etc." A Mr. Rosevelt, the master of Quack, swore that his slave was home when the fire took place in the fort; and Mr. Phillipse, Cuffee's master, testified as much for his servant. But this testimony was not what the magistrates wanted: so they put a soldier on the stand who swore that Quack did come to the fort the day of the fire; that his wife lived there, and when he insisted on going in he (the sentry) knocked him down, but the officer of the guard passed him in. Lawyer Smith, "whose eloquence had disfranchised the Jews," was called upon to sum up. He thought too much favor had been shown the Negroes, in that they had been accorded a trial as if they were freemen; that the wicked Negroes might have been proceeded against in a most summary manner; that the Negro witnesses had been treated with too much consideration; that "the law requires no oath to be administered to them; and, indeed, it would be a profanation of it to administer it to a heathen in a legal form;" that "the monstrous ingratitude of this black tribe is what exceedingly aggravates their guilt;" that their condition as slaves was one of happiness and peace; that "they live without care; are commonly better fed and clothed than the poor of most Christian countries; they are indeed slaves," continued the eloquent and logical attorney, "but under the protection of the law: none can hurt them with impunity; but notwithstanding all the kindness and tenderness with which they have been treated among us, yet this is the second attempt of this same kind that this brutish and bloody species of mankind have made within one age!" Of course the jury knew their duty, and merely went through the form of going out and coming in immediately with a verdict of "guilty." The judge sentenced them to be chained to a stake and burnt to death,—"and the Lord have mercy upon your poor wretched souls." His Honor told them that "they should be thankful that their feet were caught in the net; that the mischief had fallen upon their own pates." He advised them to consider the tenderness and humanity with which they had been treated; that they were the most abject wretches, the very outcasts of the nations of the earth; and, therefore, they should look to their souls, for as to their bodies, they would be burnt.

These poor fellows were accordingly chained to the stake the next Sunday; but, before the fuel was lighted, Deputy Sheriff More and Mr. Rosevelt again questioned Quack and Cuffee, and reduced their confessions to paper, for they had stoutly protested their innocence while in court, in hope of being saved they confessed, in substance, that Hughson contrived to burn the town, and kill the people; that a company of Negroes voted Quack the proper person to burn the fort, because his wife lived there; that he did set the chapel on fire with a lighted stick; that Mary Burton had told the truth, and that she could implicate many more if she would, etc. All this general lying was done with the understanding that the confessors were to be reprieved until the governor could be heard from. But a large crowd had gathered to witness the burning of these poor Negroes, and they compelled the sheriff to proceed with the ceremonies. The convicted slaves were burned.

On the 1st of June the boy Sawney was again put upon the witness-stand. His testimony led to the arrest of more Negroes. He charged them with having been sworn to the plot, and with having sharp penknives with which to kill white men. One Fortune testified that he never knew of houses where conspirators met, nor did he know Hughson, but accuses Sawney, and Quack who had been burnt. The next witness was a Negro girl named Sarah. She was frightened out of her senses. She foamed at the mouth, uttered the bitterest imprecations, and denied all knowledge of a conspiracy. But the benevolent gentlemen who conducted the trial told her that others had said certain things in proof of the existence of a conspiracy, that the only way to save her life was to acknowledge that there had been a conspiracy to burn the town and kill the inhabitants. She then assented to all that was told her, and thereby implicated quite a number of Negroes; but, when her testimony was read to her, she again denied all. She was without doubt a fit subject for an insane-asylum rather than for the witness-stand, in a cause that involved so many human lives.

It will be remembered that John Hughson, his wife, and daughter had been in the jail for a long time. He now desired to be called to the witness-stand. He begged to be sworn, that in the most solemn manner he might deny all knowledge of the conspiracy, and exculpate his wife and child. But the modest recorder reminded him of the fact that he stood convicted as a felon already, that he and his family were doomed to be hanged, and that, therefore, it would be well for him to "confess all." He was sent back to jail unheard. Already condemned to be hung, the upright magistrates had Hughson tried again for "conspiracy" on the 4th of June! The indictments were three in number: First, that Hughson, his wife, his daughter, and Peggy Carey, with three Negroes, Cæsar, Prince, and Cuffee, conspired in March last to set fire to the house in the fort. Second, That Quack (already burnt) did set fire to and burn the house, and that the prisoners, Hughson, his wife, daughter Sarah, and Peggy, encouraged him so to do. Third, That Cuffee (already burnt) did set fire to Phillipse's house, and burnt it; and they, the prisoners, procured and encouraged him so to do. Hughson, his family, and Peggy pleaded not guilty to all the above indictments. The attorney-general delivered a spirited address to the jury, which was more forcible than elegant. He denounced the unlucky Hughson as "infamous, inhuman, an arch-rebel against God, his king, and his country,—a devil incarnate," etc. He was ably assisted by eminent counsel for the king,—Joseph Murray, James Alexander, William Smith, and John Chambers. Mary Burton was called again. She swore that Negroes used to go to Hughson's at night, eat and drink, and sometimes buy provisions; that Hughson did swear the Negroes to secrecy in the plot; that she herself had seen seven or eight guns and swords, a bag of shot, and a barrel of gunpowder at Hughson's house; that the prisoner told her he would kill her if she ever revealed any thing she knew or saw; wanted her to swear like the rest, offered her silk gowns, and gold rings,—but none of those tempting things moved the virtuous Mary. Five other witnesses testified that they heard Quack and Cuffee say to Hughson while in jail, "This is what you have brought us to." The Hughsons had no counsel, and but three witnesses. One of them testified that he had lived in Hughson's tavern about three months during the past winter, and had never seen Negroes furnished entertainment there. The two others said that they had never seen any evil in the man nor in his house, etc.

"William Smith, Esq." now took the floor to sum up. He told the jury that it was "black and hellish" to burn the town, and then kill them all; that John Hughson, by his complicity in this crime, had made himself blacker than the Negroes; that the credit of the witnesses was good, and that there was nothing left for them to do but to find the prisoners guilty, as charged in the indictment. The judge charged the jury, that the evidence against the prisoners "is ample, full, clear, and satisfactory. They were found guilty in twenty minutes, and on the 8th of June were brought into court to receive sentence. The judge told them that they were guilty of a terrible crime; that they had not only made Negroes their equals, but superiors, by waiting upon, keeping company with, entertaining them with meat, drink, and lodging; that the most amazing part of their conduct was their part in a plot to burn the town, and murder the inhabitants,—to have consulted with, aided, and abetted the "black seed of Cain," was an unheard of crime,—that although "with uncommon assurance they deny the fact, and call on God, as a witness of their innocence, He, out of his goodness and mercy, has confounded them, and proved their guilt, to the satisfaction of the court and jury." After a further display of forensic eloquence, the judge sentenced them "to be hanged by the neck 'till dead," on Friday, the 12th of June, 1741.

The Negro girl Sarah, referred to above, who was before the jury on the 1st of June in such a terrified state of body and mind, was re-called on the 5th of June. She implicated twenty Negroes, whom she declared were present at the house of Comfort, whetting their knives, and avowing that "they would kill white people." On the 6th of June, Robin, Cæsar, Cook, Cuffee, and Jack, another Cuffee, and Jamaica were arrested, and put upon trial on the 8th of June. It is a sad fact to record, even at this distance, that these poor blacks, without counsel, friends, or money, were tried and convicted upon the evidence of a poor ignorant, hysterical girl, and the "dying confession" of Quack and Cuffee, who "confessed" with the understanding that they should be free! Tried and found guilty on the 8th, without clergy or time to pray, they were burned at the stake the next day! Only Jack found favor with the court, and that favor was purchased by perjury. He was respited until it "was found how well he would deserve further favor." It was next to impossible to understand him, so two white gentlemen were secured to act as interpreters. Jack testified to having seen Negroes at Hughson's tavern; that "when they were eating, he said they began to talk about setting the houses on fire:" he was so good as to give the names of about fourteen Negroes whom he heard say that they would set their masters' houses on fire, and then rush upon the whites and kill them; that at one of these meetings there were five or six Spanish Negroes present, whose conversation he could not understand; that they waited a month and a half for the Spaniards and French to come, but when they came not, set fire to the fort. As usual, more victims of these confessors swelled the number already in the jail; which was, at this time, full to suffocation.

On the 19th of June the lieutenant-governor issued a proclamation of freedom to all who would "confess and discover" before the 1st of July. Several Indians were in the prison, charged with conspiracy. The confessions and discoveries were numerous. Every Negro charged with being an accomplice of the unfortunate wretches that had already perished at the stake began to accuse some one else of complicity in the plot. They all knew of many Negroes who were going to cut the white people's throats with penknives; and when the town was in flames they were to "meet at the end of Broadway, next to the fields!" And it must be recorded, to the everlasting disgrace of the judiciary of New York, that scores of ignorant, helpless, and innocent Negroes—and a few white people too—were convicted upon the confessions of the terror-stricken witnesses! There is not a court to-day in all enlightened Christendom that would accept as evidence—not even circumstantial—the incoherent utterances of these Negro "confessors." And yet an intelligent (?) New-York court thought the evidence "clear (?), and satisfactory!"

But the end was not yet reached. A new turn was to be given to the notorious Mary Burton. The reader will remember that she said that there never were any white persons present when the burning of the town was the topic of conversation, except her master and mistress and Peggy Carey. But on the 25th of June the budding Mary accused Rev. John Ury, a reputed Catholic priest, and a schoolmaster in the town, and one Campbell, also a school-teacher, of having visited Hughson's tavern with the conspirators.

On the 26th of June, nine more Negroes were brought before the court and arraigned. Seven pleaded guilty in the hope of a reprieve: two were tried and convicted upon the testimony of Mary Burton. Eight more were arraigned, and pleaded guilty; followed by seven more, some of whom pleaded guilty, and some not guilty. Thus, in one day, the court was enabled to dispose of twenty-four persons.

On the 27th of June, one Adam confessed that he knew of the plot, but said he was enticed into it by Hughson, three years before; that Hughson told him that he knew a man who could forgive him all his sins. So between John Hughson's warm rum, and John Ury's ability to forgive sin, the virtuous Adam found all his scruples overcome; and he took the oath. A Dr.

Hamilton who lodged at Holt's, and the latter also, are brought into court as accused of being connected with the plot. It was charged that Holt directed his Negro Joe to set fire to the play-house at the time he should indicate. At the beginning of the trial only four white persons were mentioned; but now they began to multiply, and barrels of powder to increase at a wonderful rate. The confessions up to this time had been mere repetitions. The arrests were numerous, and the jail crowded beyond its capacity. The poor Negroes implicated were glad of an opportunity to "confess" against some one else, and thereby save their own lives. Recorder Horsemanden says, "Now many negroes began to squeak, in order to lay hold of the benefit of the proclamation." He deserves the thanks of humanity for his frankness! For before the proclamation there were not more than seventy Negroes in jail; but, within eight days after it was issued, thirty more frightened slaves were added to the number. And Judge Horsemanden says, "'Twas difficult to find room for them, nor could we see any likelihood of stopping the impeachments." The Negroes turned to accusing white persons, and seven or eight were arrested. The sanitary condition of the prison now became a subject of grave concern. The judges and lawyers consulted together, and agreed to pardon some of the prisoners to make room in the jail. They also thought it prudent to lump the confessions, and thereby facilitate their work; but the confessions went on, and the jail filled up again.

The Spanish Negroes taken by an English privateer, and adjudged to slavery by the admiralty court, were now taken up, tried, convicted, and sentenced to be hung. Five others received sentence the same day.

The bloody work went on. The poor Negroes in the jail, in a state of morbid desperation, turned upon each other the blistering tongue of accusation. They knew that they were accusing each other innocently,—as many confessed afterwards,—but this was the last straw that these sinking people could see to catch at, and this they did involuntarily. "Victims were required; and those who brought them to the altar of Moloch, purchased their own safety, or, at least, their lives."

On the 2d of July, one Will was produced before Chief-Justice James DeLancy. He plead guilty, and was sentenced to be burnt to death on the 4th of July. On the 6th of July, eleven plead guilty. One Dundee implicates Dr. Hamilton with Hughson in giving Negroes rum and swearing them to the plot. A white man by the name of William Nuill deposed that a Negro— belonging to Edward Kelly, a butcher—named London swore by God that if he should be arrested and cast into the jail, he would hang or burn all the Negroes in New York, guilty or not guilty. On this same day five Negroes were hanged. One of them was "hung in chains" upon the same gibbet with Hughson. And the Christian historian says "the town was amused" on account of a report that Hughson had turned black and the Negro white! The vulgar and sickening description of the condition of the bodies, in which Mr. Horsemanden took evident relish, we withhold from the reader. It was rumored that a Negro doctor had administered poison to the convicts, and hence the change in the bodies after death.

In addition to the burning of the Negro Will, on the 4th of July, was the sensation created by his accusing two white soldiers, Kane and Kelly, with complicity in the conspiracy. Kane was examined the next day: said that he had never been to the house of John Romme; acknowledged that he had received a stolen silver spoon, given to his wife, and sold it to one Van Dype, a silversmith; that he never knew John Ury, etc. Knowing Mary Burton was brought forward,—as she always was when the trials began to lag,—and accused Kane. He earnestly denied the accusation at first, but finally confessed that he was at Hughson's in reference to the plot on two several occasions, but was induced to go there "by Corker, Coffin, and Fagan." After his tongue got limbered up, and his memory refreshed, he criminated Ury. He implicated Hughson's father and three brothers, Hughson's mother-in-law, an old fortune-teller, as being parties to the plot as sworn "to burn, and kill;" that Ury christened some of the Negroes, and even had the temerity to attempt to proselyte him, Kane; that Ury asked him if he could read Latin, could he read English; to both questions he answered no; that the man Coffin read to him, and descanted upon the benefits of being a Roman Catholic; that they could forgive sins, and save him from hell; and that if he had not gone away from their company they might have seduced him to be a Catholic; that one Conolly, on Governor's Island, admitted that he was "bred up a priest;" that one Holt, a dancing-master, also knew of the plot; and then described the mystic ceremony of swearing the plotters. He said, "There was a black ring made on the floor, about a foot and a half in diameter; and Hughson bid every one put off the left shoe and put their toes within the ring; and Mrs. Hughson held a bowl of punch over their heads, as the Negroes stood around the circle, and Hughson pronounced the oath above mentioned, (something like a freemason's oath and penalties,) and every negro severally repeated the oath after him, and then Hughson's wife fed them with a draught out of the bowl."

This was "new matter," so to speak, and doubtless broke the monotony of the daily recitals to which their honors had been listening all summer. Kane was about to deprive Mary Burton of her honors; and, as he could not write, he made his mark. A peddler named Coffin was arrested and examined. He denied all knowledge of the plot, never saw Hughson, never was at his place, saw him for the first time when he was executed; had never seen Kane but once, and then at Eleanor Waller's, where they drank beer together. But the court committed him. Kane and Mary Burton accused Edward Murphy. Kane charged David Johnson, a hatter, as one of the conspirators; while Mary Burton accuses Andrew Ryase, "little Holt," the dancing-master, John Earl, and seventeen soldiers,—all of whom were cast into prison.

On the 16th of July nine Negroes were arraigned: four plead guilty, two were sentenced to be burnt, and the others to be hanged. On the next day seven Negroes plead guilty. One John Schultz came forward, and made a deposition that perhaps had some little influence on the court and the community at large. He swore that a Negro man slave, named Cambridge, belonging to Christopher Codwise, Esq., did on the 9th of June, 1741, confess to the deponent, in the presence of Codwise and Richard Baker, that the confession he had made before Messrs. Lodge and Nichols was entirely false; viz., that he had confessed himself guilty of participating in the conspiracy; had accused a Negro named Cajoe through fear; that he had heard some Negroes talking together in the jail, and saying that if they did not confess they would be hanged; that what he said about Horsefield Cæsar was a lie; that he had never known in what section of the town Hughson lived, nor did he remember ever hearing his name, until it had become the town talk that Hughson was concerned in a plot to burn the town and murder the inhabitants.

This did not in the least abate the zeal of Mary Burton and William Kane. They went on in their work of accusing white people and Negroes, receiving the approving smiles of the magistrates. Mary Burton says that John Earl, who lived in Broadway, used to come to Hughson's with ten soldiers at a time; that these white men were to command the Negro companies; that John Ury used to be present; and that a man near the Mayor's Market, who kept a shop where she (Mary Burton) got rum from, a doctor, by nationality a Scotchman, who lived by the Slip, and another dancing-master, named Corry, used to meet with the conspirators at Hughson's tavern.

On the 14th of July, John Ury was examined, and denied ever having been at Hughson's, or knowing any thing about the conspiracy; said he never saw any of the Hughsons, nor did he know Peggy Carey. But William Kane, the soldier, insisted that Ury did visit the house of Hughson. Ury was again committed. On the next day eight persons were tried and convicted upon the evidence of Kane and Mary Burton. The jail was filling up again, and the benevolent magistrates pardoned fourteen Negroes. Then they turned their judicial minds to the case of William Kane vs. John Ury. First, he was charged with having counselled, procured, and incited a Negro slave, Quack, to burn the king's house in the fort: to which he pleaded not guilty. Second, that being a priest, made by the authority of the pretended See of

Rome, he had come into the Province and city of New York after the time limited by law against Jesuits and Popish priests, passed in the eleventh year of William III., and had remained for the space of seven months; that he had announced himself to be an ecclesiastical person, made and ordained by the authority of the See of Rome; and that he had appeared so to be by celebrating masses and granting absolution, etc. To these charges Ury pleaded not guilty, and requested a copy of the indictments, but was only allowed a copy of the second; and pen, ink, and paper grudgingly granted him. His private journal was seized, and a portion of its contents used as evidence against him. The following was furnished to the grand jury:—

> "Arrived at Philadelphia the 17th of February, 1738. At Ludinum, 5th March.—To Philadelphia, 29th April.—Began school at Burlington, 18th June. Omilta Jacobus Atherthwaite, 27th July.—Came to school at Burlington, 23d January, 1740.—Saw — —, 7th May.—At five went to Burlington, to Piercy, the madman.—Went to Philadelphia, 19th May.—Went to Burlington, 18th June.—At six in the evening to Penefack, to Joseph Ashton.—Began school at Dublin under Charles Hastie, at eight pounds a year, 31st July, — — , 15th October, — — , 27th ditto.—Came to John Croker (at the Fighting Cocks), New York, 2d November.—I boarded gratis with him, 7th November,—Natura Johannis Pool, 26th December.—I began to teach with John Campbell, 6th April, 1741.—Baptized Timothy Ryan, born 18th April, 1740, son of John Ryan and Mary Ryan, 18th May.—Pater Confessor Butler, two Anni, no sacramentum non confessio."[250]

On the 21st of July, Sarah Hughson, who had been respited, was put on the witness-stand again. There were some legal errors in the indictments against Ury, and his trial was postponed until the next term; but he was arraigned on a new indictment. The energies of the jury and judges received new life. Here was a man who was a Catholic,—or had been a Catholic,—and the spirit of religious intolerance asserted itself. Sarah Hughson remembered having seen Ury at her father's house on several occasions; had seen him make a ring with chalk on the floor, make all the Negroes stand around it, while he himself would stand in the middle, with a cross, and swear the Negroes. This was also "new matter:" nothing of this kind was mentioned in the first confession. But this was not all. She had seen Ury preach to the Negroes, forgive their sins, and baptize some of them! She said that Ury wanted her to confess to him, and that Peggy confessed to him in French.

On the 24th of July, Elias Desbroses, confectioner, being called, swore that Ury had come to his shop with one Webb, a carpenter, and inquired for sugar-bits, or wafers, and asked him "whether a minister had not his wafers of him? or, whether that paste, which the deponent showed him, was not made of the same ingredients as the Luthern minister's?" or words to that effect: the deponent told Ury that if he desired such things a joiner would make him a mould; and that when he asked him whether he had a congregation, Ury "waived giving him an answer."

On the 27th of July, Mr. Webb, the carpenter, was called to the witness-stand and testified as follows: That he had met Ury at John Croker's (at the Fighting Cocks), where he became acquainted with him; that he had heard him read Latin and English so admirably that he employed him to teach his child; that finding out that he was a school-teacher, he invited him to board at his house without charge; that he understood from him that he was a non-juring minister, had written a book that had drawn the fire of the Church, was charged with treason, and driven out of England, sustaining the loss of "a living" worth fifty pounds a year; that on religious matters the deponent could not always comprehend him; that the accused said Negroes were only fit for slaves, and to put them above that condition was to invite them to cut your throats. The observing Horsemanden was so much pleased with the above declaration, that he gives Ury credit in a footnote for understanding the dispositions of Negroes![251] Farther on Mr. Webb says, that, after one Campbell removed to Hughson's, Ury went thither, and so did the deponent on three different times, and heard him read prayers after the manner of the Church of England; but in the prayer for the king he only mentioned "our sovereign lord the King," and not "King George." He said that Ury pleaded against drunkenness, debauchery, and Deists; that he admonished every one to keep his own minister; that when the third sermon was delivered one Mr. Hildreth was present, when Ury found fault with certain doctrines, insisted that good works as well as faith were necessary to salvation; that he announced that on a certain evening he would preach from the text, "Upon this rock I will build my church, and the gates of hell shall not prevail against it; and whosoever sins ye remit, they are remitted, and whosoever sins ye retain, they are retained."

The judges, delighted with this flavor added to the usually dry proceedings, thought they had better call Sarah Hughson; that if she were grateful for her freedom she would furnish the testimony their honors desired. Sarah was accordingly called. She is recommended for mercy. She is, of course, to say what is put in her mouth, to give testimony such as the court desires. So the fate of the poor schoolmaster was placed in the keeping of the fateful Sarah.

On the 28th of July another grand jury was sworn, and, like the old one, was composed of merchants. The following persons composed it: Joseph Robinson, James Livingston, Hermanus Rutgers, jun., Charles LeRoux, Abraham Boelen, Peter Rutgers, Jacobus Roosevelt, John Auboyneau, Stephen Van Courtlandt, jun., Abraham Lynsen, Gerardus Duyckinck, John Provost, Henry Lane, jun., Henry Cuyler, John Roosevelt, Abraham DePeyster, Edward Hicks, Joseph Ryall, Peter Schuyler, and Peter Jay.[252]

Sarah Hughson had been pardoned. John Ury was brought into court, when he challenged some of the jury. William Hammersley, Gerardus Beekman, John Shurmur, Sidney Breese, Daniel Shatford, Thomas Behenna, Peter Fresneau, Thomas Willett, John Breese, John Hastier, James Tucker, and Brandt Schuyler were sworn to try him. Barring formalities, he was arraigned upon the old indictment; viz., felony, in inciting and exciting the Negro slave Quack to set fire to the governor's house. The king's counsel were the attorney-general, Richard Bradley, and Messrs. Murray, Alexander, Smith, and Chambers. Poor Ury had no counsel, no sympathizers. The attorney-general, in an opening speech to the jury, said that certain evidence was to be produced showing that the prisoner at the bar was guilty as charged in the indictment; that he had a letter that he desired to read to them, which had been sent to Lieut.-Gov. Clark, written by Gen. Oglethorpe ("the visionary Lycurgus of Georgia"), bearing date of the 16th of May. The following is a choice passage from the letter referred to:—

> "Some intelligence I had of a villanous design of a very extraordinary nature, and if true very important, viz., that the Spaniards had employed emissaries to burn all the magazines and considerable towns in the English North America, and thereby to prevent the subsisting of the great expedition and fleet in the West Indies; and for this purpose many priests were employed, who pretended to be physicians, dancing-masters, and other such kinds of occupations, and under that pretence to get admittance and confidence in families."[253]

The burden of his effort was the wickedness of Popery and the Roman-Catholic Church. The first witness called was the irrepressible Mary Burton. She began by rehearsing the old story of setting fire to the houses: but this time she varied it somewhat; it was not the fort that was to be burnt first, but Croker's, near a coffee-house, by the long bridge. She remembered the ring drawn with chalk, saw things in it that looked like rats (the good Horsemanden throws a flood of light upon this otherwise dark passage by telling his reader that it was the Negroes' black toes!); that she peeped in once and saw a black thing like a child, and Ury with a book in his hand, and at this moment she let a silver spoon drop, and Ury chased her, and would have caught her, had she not fallen into a bucket of water, and thus marvellously escaped! But the rule was to send this curious Mary to bed when any thing of an unusual nature was going on. Ury asked her some questions.

"*Prisoner.*—You say you have seen me several times at Hughson's, what clothes did I usually wear?

"*Mary Burton.*—I cannot tell what clothes you wore particularly.

"*Prisoner.*—That is strange, and know me so well?"

She then says several kinds, but particularly, or chiefly, a riding-coat, and often a brown coat, trimmed with black.

"*Prisoner.*—I never wore such a coat. What time of the day did I used to come to Hughson's?

> "M. Burton.—You used chiefly to come in the night-time, and when I have been going to bed I have seen you undressing in Peggy's room, as if you were to lie there; but I cannot say that you did, for you were always gone before I was up in the morning.

"*Prisoner.*—What room was I in when I called Mary, and you came up, as you said?

"*M. Burton.*—In the great room, up stairs.

"*Prisoner.*—What answer did the Negroes make, when I offered to forgive them their sins, as you said?

"*M. Burton.*—I don't remember."[254]

William Kane, the soldier, took the stand. He was very bold to answer all of Ury's questions. He saw him baptize a child, could forgive sins, and wanted to convert him! Sarah Hughson was next called, but Ury objected to her because she had been convicted. The judge informed him that she had been pardoned, and was, therefore, competent as a witness. Judge Horsemanden was careful to produce newspaper scraps to prove that the court of France had endeavored to create and excite revolts and insurrections in the English colonies, and ended by telling a pathetic story about an Irish schoolmaster in Ulster County who drank the health of the king of Spain![255] This had great weight with the jury, no doubt. Poor Ury, convicted upon the evidence of three notorious liars, without counsel, was left to defend himself. He addressed the jury in an earnest and intelligent manner. He showed where the evidence clashed; that the charges were not in harmony with his previous character, the silence of Quack and others already executed. He showed that Mr. Campbell took possession of the house that Hughson had occupied, on the 1st of May; that at that time Hughson and his wife were in jail, and Sarah in the house; that Sarah abused Campbell, and that he reproved her for the foul language she used; and that this furnished her with an additional motive to accuse him; that he never knew Hughson or any of the family. Mr. John Croker testified that Ury never kept company with Negroes, nor did he receive them at Croker's house up to the 1st of May, for all the plotting was done before that date; that he was a quiet, pious preacher, and an excellent schoolmaster; that he taught Webb's child, and always declared himself a non-juring clergyman of the Church of England. But the fatal revelation of this friend of Ury's was, that Webb made him a desk; and the jury thought they saw in it an altar for a Catholic priest! That was enough. The attorney-general told the jury that the prisoner was a Romish priest, and then proceeded to prove the exceeding sinfulness of that Church. Acknowledging the paucity of the evidence intended to prove him a priest, the learned gentleman hastened to dilate upon all the dark deeds of Rome, and thereby poisoned the minds of the jury against the unfortunate Ury. He was found guilty, and on the 29th of August, 1741, was hanged, professing his innocence, and submitting cheerfully to a cruel and unjust death as a servant of the Lord.[256]

The trials of the Negroes had continued, but were somewhat overshadowed by that of the reputed Catholic priest. On the 18th of July seven Negroes were hanged, including a Negro doctor named Harry. On the 23d of July a number of white persons were fined for keeping disorderly houses,—entertaining Negroes; while nine Negroes were, the same day, released from jail on account of a lack of evidence! On the 15th of August a Spanish Negro was hanged. On the 31st of August, Corry (the dancing-master), Ryan, Kelly, and Coffin—all white persons—were dismissed because no one prosecuted; while the reader must have observed that the evidence against them was quite as strong as that offered against any of the persons executed, by the lying trio Burton, Kane, and Sarah. But Mr. Smith the historian gives the correct reason why these trials came to such a sudden end.

> "The whole summer was spent in the prosecutions; every new trial led to further accusations: a coincidence of slight circumstances, was magnified by the general terror into violent presumptions; tales collected without doors, mingling with the proofs given at the bar, poisoned the minds of the jurors; and the sanguinary spirit of the day

suffered no check till Mary, the capital informer, bewildered by frequent examinations and suggestions, lost her first impressions, and began to touch characters, which malice itself did not dare to suspect."[257]

The 24th of September was solemnly set apart for public thanksgiving for the escape of the citizens from destruction!

As we have already said, this "Negro plot" has but one parallel in the history of civilization. It had its origin in a diseased public conscience, inflamed by religious bigotry, accelerated by hired liars, and consummated in the blind and bloody action of a court and jury who imagined themselves sitting over a powder-magazine. That a robbery took place, there was abundant evidence in the finding of some of the articles, and the admissions of Hughson and others; but there was not a syllable of competent evidence to show that there was an organized plot. And the time came, after the city had gotten back to its accustomed quietness, that the most sincere believers in the "Negro plot" were converted to the opinion that the zeal of the magistrates had not been "according to knowledge." For they could not have failed to remember that the Negroes were considered heathen, and, therefore, not sworn by the court; that they were not allowed counsel; that the evidence was indirect, contradictory, and malicious, while the trials were hasty and unfair. From the 11th of May to the 29th of August, one hundred and fifty-four Negroes were cast into prison; fourteen of whom were burnt, eighteen hanged, seventy-one transported, and the remainder pardoned. During the same space of time twenty-four whites were committed to prison; four of whom were executed, and the remainder discharged. The number arrested was one hundred and seventy-eight, thirty-six executed, and seventy-one transported! What a terrible tragedy committed in the name of law and Christian government! Mary Burton, the Judas Iscariot of the period, received her hundred pounds as the price of the blood she had caused to be shed; and the curtain fell upon one of the most tragic events in all the history of New York or of the civilized world.[258]

The legislature turned its attention to additional legislation upon the slavery question. Severe laws were passed against the Negroes. Their personal rights were curtailed until their condition was but little removed from that of the brute creation. We have gone over the voluminous records of the Province of New York, and have not found a single act calculated to ameliorate the condition of the slave.[259] He was hated, mistrusted, and feared. Nothing was done, of a friendly character, for the slave in the Province of New York, until threatening dangers from without taught the colonists the importance of husbanding all their resources. The war between the British colonies in North America and the mother country gave the Negro an opportunity to level, by desperate valor, a mountain of prejudice, and wipe out with his blood the dark stain of 1741. History says he did it.

FOOTNOTES:

[215] Brodhead's History of New York, vol. i. p. 184.

[216] O'Callaghan's History of New Netherlands, pp. 384, 385.

[217] Brodhead, vol. i. p. 194.

[218] Ibid, vol. i. pp. 196, 197.

[219] Dunlap's History of New York, vol. i. p, 58.

[220] O'Callaghan, p. 385.

[221] Van Tienhoven.

[222] Hildreth, vol. i. p. 441; also Hol. Doc., III. p. 351.

[223] Annals of Albany, vol. ii. pp. 55-60.

[224] O'Callaghan, p. 353. N.Y. Col. Docs., vol. ii, pp. 368, 369.

[225] Brodhead, vol. i. p. 697.

[226] Brodhead, vol. i. p. 746.

[227] Ibid., vol. i. p. 748.

[228] Valentine's Manual for 1861, pp. 640-664.

[229] New York Hist. Coll., vol. i. pp. 322, 323.

[230] Journals of Legislative Council, vol. i. p xii.

[231] Bradford's Laws, p. 125.

[232] Journals, etc., N.Y., vol. i. p. xiii.

[233] Dunlap's Hist, of N.Y., vol. i. p. 260,

[234] Booth's Hist, of N.Y., vol. i. p, 270-272.

[235] On the 22nd of March, 1680, the following proclamation was issued: "Whereas, several inhabitants within this city have and doe dayly harbour, entertain and countenance Indian and neger slaves in their houses, and to them sell and deliver wine, rum, and other strong liquors, for which they receive money or goods which by the said Indian and negro slaves is pilfered, purloyned, and stolen from their several masters, by which the publick peace is broken, and the damage of the master is produced, etc., therefore they are prohibited, etc.; and if neger or Indian slave make

application for these forbidden articles, immediate information is to be given to his master or to the mayor or oldest alderman."—Dunlap, vol. ii. Appendix, p. cxxviii.

[236] Bradford Laws, p. 81.

[237] The ordinance referred to was re-enacted on the 22d of April, 1731, and reads as follows: "No Negro, Mulatto, or Indian slave, above the age of fourteen, shall presume to appear in any of the streets, or in any other place of this city on the south side of Fresh Water, in the night time, above an hour after sunset, without a lanthorn and candle in it (unless in company with his owner or some white belonging to the family). Penalty, the watch-house that night; next day, prison, until the owner pays 4s, and before discharge, the slave to be whipped not exceeding forty lashes."—Dunlap, vol. ii. Appendix, p. clxiii.

[238] Booth, vol. i. p. 271.

[239] Hurd's Bondage and Freedom, vol. i. p. 281.

[240] Dunlap, vol. i. p. 323.

[241] Judge Daniel Horsemanden.

[242] Hume, vol. vi. pp. 171-212.

[243] Ibid., vol. vi. p. 171.

[244] Horsemanden's Negro Plot, p. 29.

[245] As far back as 1684 the following was passed against the entertainment of slaves: "No person to countenance or entertain any negro or Indian slave, or sell or deliver to them any strong liquor, without liberty from his master, or receive from them any money or goods; but, upon any offer made by a slave, to reveal the same to the owner, or to the mayor, under penalty of £5."—Dunlap, vol. ii. Appendix, p. cxxxiii.

[246] Horsemanden's Negro Plot, p. 33.

[247] Bradford's Laws, pp. 141-144.

[248] Horsemanden's Negro Plot, p. 60.

[249] The city of Now York was divided into parts at that time, and comprised two militia districts.

[250] Dunlap, vol. i. p. 344.

[251] Horsemanden's Negro Plot, p. 284.

[252] Horsemanden's Negro Plot, p. 286.

[253] Colonial Hist. of N.Y., vol. vi. p. 199.

[254] Horsemanden's Negro Plot, pp. 292, 293.

[255] Ibid., pp. 298, 299, note.

[256] Horsemanden's Negro Plot, pp. 221, 222.

[257] Smith's Hist. of N.Y., vol. ii. pp. 59, 60.

[258] "On the 6th of March, 1742, the following order was passed by the Common Council: 'Ordered, that the indentures of Mary Burton be delivered up to her, and that she be discharged from the remainder of her servitude, and three pounds paid her, to provide necessary clothing.' The Common Council had purchased her indentures from her master, and had kept her and them, until this time."—Dunlap, vol. ii. Appendix, p. clxvii.

[259] "On the 17th of November, 1767, a bill was brought into the House of Assembly "to prevent the unnatural and unwarrantable custom of enslaving mankind, and the importation of slaves into this province." It was changed into an act "for laying an impost on Negroes imported." This could not pass the governor and council; and it was afterward known that Benning I. Wentworth, the governor of New Hampshire, had received instructions not to pass any law "imposing duties on negroes imported into that province." Hutchinson of Massachusetts had similar instructions. The governor and his Majesty's council knew this at the time.

CHAPTER XIV
THE COLONY OF MASSACHUSETTS

1633-1775.

The Earliest Mentions of Negroes in Massachusetts.—Pequod Indians exchanged for Negroes.—Voyage of the Slave-Ship "Desire" in 1638.—Fundamental Laws adopted.—Hereditary Slavery.—Kidnapping Negroes.—Growth of Slavery in the Seventeenth Century.—Taxation of Slaves.—Introduction of Indian Slaves prohibited.—The Position of the Church respecting the Baptism of Slaves.—Slave Marriage.—Condition of Free Negroes.—Phillis Wheatley the African Poetess.—Her Life.—Slavery recognized in England in Order to be maintained in the Colonies.—The Emancipation of Slaves.—Legislation favoring the Importation of White Servants, but prohibiting the Clandestine Bringing-in of Negroes.—Judge Sewall's Attack on Slavery.—Judge Saffin's Reply to Judge Sewall.

HAD the men who gave the colony of Massachusetts its political being and Revolutionary fame known that the Negro—so early introduced into the colony as a slave—would have been in the future Republic for years the insoluble problem, and at last the subject of so great and grave economic and political concern, they would have committed to the jealous keeping of the chroniclers of their times the records for which the historian of the Negro seeks so vainly in this period. Stolen as he was from his tropical home; consigned to a servitude at war with man's intellectual and spiritual, as well as with his physical, nature; the very lowest of God's creation, in the estimation of the Roundheads of New England; a stranger in a strange land,—the poor Negro of Massachusetts found no place in the sympathy or history of the Puritan,—Christians whose deeds and memory have been embalmed in song and story, and given to an immortality equalled only by the indestructibility of the English language. The records of the most remote period of colonial history have preserved a silence on the question of Negro slavery as ominous as it is conspicuous. What data there are concerning the introduction of slavery are fragmentary, uncertain, and unsatisfactory, to say the least. There is but one work bearing the luminous stamp of historical trustworthiness, and which turns a flood of light on the dark records of the darker crime of human slavery in Massachusetts. And we are sure it is as complete as the ripe scholarship, patient research, and fair and fearless spirit of its author, could make it.[260]

The earliest mention of the presence of Negroes in Massachusetts is in connection with an account of some Indians who were frightened at a Colored man who had lost his way in the tangled path of the forest. The Indians, it seems, were "worse scared than hurt, who seeing a blackamore in the top of a tree looking out for his way which he had lost, surmised he was Abamacho, or the devil; deeming all devils that are blacker than themselves: and being near to the plantation, they posted to the English, and entreated their aid to conjure this devil to his own place, who finding him to be a poor wandering blackamore, conducted him to his master."[261] This was in 1633. It is circumstantial evidence of a twofold nature; i.e., it proves that there were Negroes in the colony at a date much earlier than can be fixed by reliable data, and that the Negroes were slaves. It is a fair presumption that this "wandering blackamore" who was conducted "to his master" was not the only Negro slave in the colony. Slaves generally come in large numbers, and consequently there must have been quite a number at this time.

Negro slavery in Massachusetts was the safety-valve to the pent-up vengeance of the Pequod Indians. Slavery would have been established in Massachusetts, even if there had been no Indians to punish by war, captivity, and duplicity. Encouraged by the British authorities, avarice and gain would have quieted the consciences of Puritan slave-holders. But the Pequod war was the early and urgent occasion for the founding of slavery under the foster care of a free church and free government! As the Pequod Indians would "not endure the yoke," would not remain "as servants,"[262] they were sent to Bermudas[263] and exchanged for Negroes,[264] with the hope that the latter would "endure the yoke" more patiently. The first importation of slaves from Barbados, secured in exchange for Indians, was made in 1637, the first year of the Pequod war, and was doubtless kept up for many years.

But in the following year we have the most positive evidence that New England had actually engaged in the slave-trade.

> "Mr. Pierce, in the Salem ship, the Desire, returned from the West Indies after seven months. He had been at Providence, and brought some cotton, and tobacco, and negroes, &c., from thence, and salt from Tertugos.... Dry fish and strong

liquors are the only commodities for those parts. He met there two men-of-war, sent forth by the lords, &c., of Providence with letters of mart, who had taken divers prizes from the Spaniard and many negroes."[265]

"The Desire" was built at Marblehead in 1636;[266] was of one hundred and twenty tons, and perhaps one of the first built in the colony. There is no positive proof that "The Mayflower," after landing the holy Pilgrim Fathers, was fitted out for a slave-cruise! But there is no evidence to destroy the belief that "The Desire" was built for the slave-trade. Within a few years from the time of the building of "The Desire," there were quite a number of Negro slaves in Massachusetts. "John Josselyn, Gen't" in his "Two Voyages to New England," made in "1638, 1663," and printed for the first time in 1674,[267] gives an account of an attempt to breed slaves in Massachusetts.

> "The Second of October, (1639) about 9 of the clock in the morning, Mr. Maverick's Negro woman came to my chamber window, and in her own Countrey language and tune sang very loud and shril, going out to her, she used a great deal of respect towards me, and willingly would have expressed her grief in English; but I apprehended it by her countenance and deportment, whereupon I repaired to my host, to learn of him the cause, and resolved to entreat him in her behalf, for that I understood before, that she had been a Queen in her own Countrey, and observed a very humble and dutiful garb used towards her by another Negro who was her maid. Mr. Maverick was desirous to have a breed of Negroes, and therefore seeing she would not yield by persuasions to company with a Negro young man he had in his house; he commanded him will'd she nill'd she to go to bed to her, which was no sooner done but she kickt him out again, this she took in high disdain beyond her slavery, and this was the cause of her grief."[268]

It would appear, at first blush, that slavery was an individual speculation in the colony; but the voyage of the ship "Desire" was evidently made with a view of securing Negro slaves for sale. Josselyn says, in 1627, that the English colony on the Island of Barbados had "in a short time increased to twenty thousand, besides Negroes."[269] And in 1637 he says that the New Englanders "sent the male children of Pequets to the Bermudus."[270] It is quite likely that many individuals of large means and estates had a few Negro slaves quite early,—perhaps earlier than we have any record; but as a public enterprise in which the colony was interested, slavery began as early as 1638. "It will be observed," says Dr. Moore, "that this first entrance into the slave-trade was not a private, individual speculation. It was the enterprise of the authorities of the colony. And on the 13th of March, 1639, it was ordered by the General Court "that 3l 8s should be paid Lieftenant Davenport for the present, for charge disbursed for the slaves, which, when they have earned it, hee is to repay it back againe." The marginal note is "Lieft. Davenport to keep ye slaves." (Mass. Rec. i. 253.[271]) So there can be no doubt as to the permanent establishment of the institution of slavery as early as 1639, while before that date the institution existed in a patriarchal condition. But there isn't the least fragment of history to sustain the haphazard statement of Emory Washburn, that slavery existed in Massachusetts "from the time Maverick was found dwelling on Noddle's Island in 1630."[272] We are sure this assertion lacks the authority of historical data. It is one thing for a historian to think certain events happened at a particular time, but it is quite another thing to be able to cite reliable authority in proof of the assertion. [273] But no doubt Mr. Washburn relies upon Mr. Palfrey, who refers his reader to Mr. Josselyn. Palfrey says, "Before Winthrop's arrival, there were two negro slaves in Massachusetts, held by Mr. Maverick, on Noddle's Island."[274] Josselyn gives the only account we have of the slaves on Noddle's Island. The incident that gave rise to this scrap of history occurred on the 2d of October, 1639. Winthrop was chosen governor in the year 1637. [275] It was in this year, on the 26th of February, that the slave-ship "Desire" landed a cargo of Negroes in the colony. Now, if Mr. Palfrey relies upon Josselyn for the historical trustworthiness of his statement that there were two Negroes in Massachusetts before Winthrop arrived, he has made a mistake. There is no proof for the assertion. That there were three Negroes on Noddle's Island, we have the authority of Josselyn, but nothing more. And if the Negro queen who kicked Josselyn's man out of bed had been as long in the island as Palfrey and Washburn indicate, she would have been able to explain her grief to Josselyn in English. We have no doubt but what Mr. Maverick got his slaves from the ship "Desire" in 1638, the same year Winthrop was inaugurated governor.

In Massachusetts, as in the other colonies, slavery made its way into individual families first; thence into communities, where it was clothed with the garment of usage and custom;[276] and, finally, men longing to enjoy the fruit of unrequited labor gave it the sanction of statutory law. There was not so great a demand for slaves in Massachusetts as in the Southern States; and yet they had their uses in a domestic way, and were, consequently, sought after. As early as 1641 Massachusetts adopted a body of fundamental laws. The magistrates,[277] armed with authority from the crown of Great Britain, had long exercised a power which well-nigh trenched upon the personal rights of the people. The latter desired a revision of the laws, and such modifications of the power and discretion of the magistrates as would be in sympathy with the spirit of personal liberty that pervaded the minds of the colonists. But while the people sought to wrest an arbitrary power from the unwilling hands of their judges, they found no pity in their hearts for the poor Negroes in their midst, who, having served as slaves because of their numerical weakness and the passive silence of justice, were now to become the legal and statutory vassals—for their life-time—of a liberty-loving and liberty-seeking people! In the famous "Body of Liberties" is to be found the first statute establishing slavery in the United States. It is as follows:—

> "It is ordered by this court, and the authority thereof; that there shall never be any bond slavery, villainage or captivity amongst us, unless it be lawful captives taken in just wars, as willingly sell themselves or are sold to us, and such shall have the liberties and christian usage which the law of God established in Israel concerning such persons doth morally require; provided this exempts none from servitude, who shall be judged thereto by authority."[278]

We have omitted the old spelling, but none of the words, as they appeared in the original manuscript. There isn't the shadow of a doubt but what this law has been preserved inviolate.[279]

There has been considerable discussion about the real bearing of this statute. Many zealous historians, in discussing it, have betrayed more zeal for the good name of the Commonwealth than for the truth of history. Able lawyers—and some of them still survive—have maintained, with a greater show of learning than of facts, that this statute abolished slavery in Massachusetts. But, on the other hand, there are countless lawyers who pronounce it a plain and unmistakable law, "creating and establishing slavery." An examination of the statute will help the reader to a clear understanding of it. To begin with, this law received its being from the existent fact of slavery in the colony. From the practice of a few holding Negroes as slaves, it became general and prodigious. Its presence in society called for lawful regulations concerning it. While it is solemnly declared "that there shall never be any bond slavery, villianage, or captivity" in the colony, there were three provisos; viz., "lawful captives taken in just wares," those who would "sell themselves or are sold to us," and such as "shall be judged thereto by authority." Under the foregoing conditions slavery was plainly established in Massachusetts. The "just wares" were the wars against the Pequod Indians. That these were made prisoners and slaves, we have the universal testimony of all writers on the history of Massachusetts. Just what class of people would "sell themselves" into slavery we are at a loss to know! We can, however, understand the meaning of the words, "or are sold to us." This was an open door for the traffic in human beings; for it made it lawful for to sell slaves to the colonists, and lawful for the latter to purchase them. Those who were "judged thereto by authority" were those in slavery already and such as should come into the colony by shipping.

This statute is wide enough to drive a load of hay through. It is not the work of a novice, but the labored and skilful product of great law learning.

"The law must be interpreted in the light of contemporaneous facts of history. At the time it was made (1641), what had its authors to provide for?

"1. Indian slaves—their captives taken in war.

"2. Negro slaves—their own importations of 'strangers,' obtained by purchase or exchange.

"3. Criminals—condemned to slavery as a punishment for offences.

"In this light, and only in this light, is their legislation intelligible and consistent. It is very true that the code of which this law is a part 'exhibits throughout the hand of the practised lawyer, familiar with the principles and securities of English Liberty;' but who had ever heard, at that time, of the 'common-law rights' of Indians and Negroes, or anybody else but Englishmen?

> "Thus stood the statute through the whole colonial period, and it was never expressly repealed. Based on the Mosaic code, it is an absolute recognition of slavery as a legitimate status, and of the right of one man to sell himself as well as that of another man to buy him. It sanctions the slave-trade, and the perpetual bondage of Indians and Negroes, their children and their children's children, and entitles Massachusetts to precedence over any and all the other colonies in similar legislation. It anticipates by many years any thing of the sort to be found in the statutes of Virginia, or Maryland, or South Carolina, and nothing like it is to be found in the contemporary codes of her sister colonies in New England."[280]

The subject had been carefully weighed; and, lacking authority for legalizing a crime against man, the Mosaic code was cited, and in accordance with its humane provisions, slaves were to be treated. But it was authority for slavery that the cunning lawyer who drew the statute was seeking, and not precedents to determine the kind of treatment to be bestowed upon the slave. Under it "human slavery existed for nearly a century and a half without serious challenge;"[281] and here, as well as in Virginia, it received the sanction of the Church and courts. It grew with its growth, and strengthened with its strength; until, as an organic institution, it had many defenders and few apologists.[282]

> "This article gives express sanction to the slave-trade, and the practice of holding Negroes and Indians in perpetual bondage, anticipating by many years any thing of the sort to be found in the statutes of Virginia or Maryland."[283]

And it is rather strange, in the light of this plain statute establishing and legalizing the purchase of slaves, that Mr. Washburn's statement, unsustained, should receive the public indorsement of so learned a body as the Massachusetts Historical Society!

> "But, after all [says Mr. Washburn], the laws on this subject, as well as the practice of the government, were inconsistent and anomalous, indicating clearly, that whether Colony or Province, so far as it felt free to follow its own inclinations, uncontrolled by the action of the mother country, Massachusetts was hostile to slavery as an institution!"[284]

No doubt Massachusetts was "inconsistent" in seeking liberty for her white citizens while forging legal chains for the Negro. And how far the colony "felt free to follow its own inclinations" Chief-Justice Parsons declares from the bench. Says that eminent jurist,—

> "Slavery was introduced into this country [Massachusetts] soon after its first settlement, and was tolerated until the ratification of the present Constitution—of 1780."[285]

So here we find an eminent authority declaring that slavery followed hard upon the heels of the Pilgrim Fathers, "and was tolerated" until 1780. Massachusetts "felt free" to tear from the iron grasp of the imperious magistrates the liberties of the people, but doubtless felt not "free" enough to blot out "the crime and folly of an evil time." And yet for years lawyers and clergymen, orators and statesmen, historians and critics, have stubbornly maintained, that, while slavery did creep into the colony, and did exist, it was "not probably by force of any law, for none such is found or known to exist."(?)[286]

Slavery having been firmly established in Massachusetts, the next step was to make it hereditary. This was done under the sanction of the highest and most solemn forms of the courts of law. It is not our purpose to give this subject the attention it merits, in this place; but in a subsequent chapter it will receive due attention. We will, however, say in passing, that it was the opinion of many lawyers in the last century, some of whom served upon the bench in Massachusetts, that children followed the condition of their mothers. Chief-Justice Parsons held that "the issue of the female slave, according to the maxim of the civil law, was the property of her master." And, subsequently, Chief-Justice Parker rendered the following opinion:—

> "The practice was ... to consider such issue as slaves, and the property of the master of the parents, liable to be sold and transferred like other chattels, and as assets in the hands of executors and administrators.... We think there is no doubt that, at any period of our history, the issue of a slave husband and a free wife would have been declared free. His children, if the issue of a marriage with a slave, would, immediately on their birth, become the property of his master, or of the master of the female slave."[287]

This decision is strengthened by the statement of Kendall in reference to the wide-spread desire of Negro slaves to secure free Indian wives, in order to insure the freedom of their children. He says,—

> "While slavery was supposed to be maintainable by law in Massachusetts, there was a particular temptation to Negroes for taking Indian wives, the children of Indian women being acknowledged to be free."[288]

We refer the reader, with perfect confidence, to our friend Dr. George H. Moore, who, in his treatment of this particular feature of slavery in Massachusetts, has, with great research, put down a number of zealous friends of the colony who have denied, with great emphasis, that any child was ever born into slavery there. Neither the opinion of Chief-Justice Dana, nor the naked and barren assertions of historians Palfrey, Sumner, and Washburn,—great though the men were,—can dispose of the *historical reality of hereditary slavery in Massachusetts*, down to the adoption of the Constitution of 1780.

The General Court of Massachusetts issued an order in 1645[289] for the return of certain kidnapped or stolen Negroes to their native country. It has been variously commented upon by historians and orators. The story runs, that a number of ships, plying between New-England seaport towns and Madeira and the Canaries, made it their custom to call on the coast of Guinea "to trade for negroes." Thus secured, they were disposed of in the slave-markets of Barbadoes and the West Indies. The New-England slave-market did not demand a large supply. Situated on a cold, bleak, and almost sterile coast, Massachusetts lacked the conditions to make slave-trading as lucrative as the Southern States; but, nevertheless, she disposed of quite a number, as the reader will observe when we examine the first census. A ship from the town of Boston consorted with "some Londoners" with the object of gaining slaves. Mr. Bancroft[290] says that "upon the Lord's day, invited the natives aboard one of their ships," and then made prisoners of such as came; which is not mentioned by Hildreth.[291] The latter writer says, that "on pretence of some quarrel with the natives," landed a small cannon called a "murderer," attacked the village on Sunday; and having burned the village, and killed many, made a few prisoners. Several of these prisoners fell to the Boston ship. On account of a disagreement between the captain and under officers of the ship, as well as the owners, the story of the above affair was detailed before a Boston court. Richard Saltonstall was one of the magistrates before whom the case was tried. He was moved by the recital of the cruel wrong done the Africans, and therefore presented a petition to the court, charging the captain and mate with the threefold crime of "murder," "man-stealing," and "sabbath-breaking."[292]

It seems that by the Fundamental Laws, adopted by the people in 1641, the first two offences were punishable by death, and all of them "capitall, by the law of God." The court doubted its jurisdiction over crimes committed on the distant coast of Guinea. But article ninety-one of "The Body of Liberties" determined who were lawful slaves,—those who sold themselves or were sold, "lawful captives taken in just wares," and those "judged thereto by authority." Had the unfortunate Negroes been purchased, there was no law in Massachusetts to free them from their owners; but having been kidnapped, unlawfully obtained, the court felt that it was its plain duty to bear witness against the "sin of man-stealing." For, in the laws adopted in 1641, among the "Capital Laws," at the latter part of article ninety-four is the following: "If any man stealeth a man, or mankind, he shall surely be put to death."[293] There is a marginal reference to Exod. xxi. 16. Dr. Moore does not refer to this in his elaborate discussion of statute on "bond slavery." And Winthrop says that the magistrates decided that the Negroes, "having been procured not honestly by purchase, but by the unlawful act of kidnaping," should be returned to their native country. That there was a criminal code in the colony, there can be no doubt; but we have searched for it in vain. Hildreth[294] says it was printed in 1649, but that there is now no copy extant.

The court issued an order about the return of the kidnapped Negroes, which we will give in full, on account of its historical value, and because of the difference of opinion concerning it.

> "The general court conceiving themselves bound by the first opportunity to bear witness against the heinous, and crying sin of man-stealing, as also to prescribe such timely redress for what is past, and such a law for the future, as may

sufficiently deter all others belonging to us to have to do in such vile and odious courses, justly abhorred of all good and just men, do order that the negro interpreter with others unlawfully taken, be by the first opportunity at the charge of the country for the present, sent to his native country (Guinea) and a letter with him of the indignation of the court thereabouts, and justice thereof, desiring our honored governor would please put this order in execution."[295]

This "protest against man-stealing" has adorned and flavored many an oration on the "position of Massachusetts" on the slavery question. It has been brought out "to point a moral and adorn a tale" by the proud friends of the Commonwealth; but the law quoted above against "man-stealing," the language of the "protest," the statute on "bond servitude," and the practices of the colonists for many years afterwards, prove that many have gloried, but not according to the truth.[296] When it came to the question of damages, the court said: "For the negars (they being none of his, but stolen) we thinke meete to allow nothing."[297]

So the decision of the court was based upon law,—the prohibition against "man-stealing." And it should not be forgotten that many of the laws of the colony were modelled after the Mosaic code. It is referred to, apologetically, in the statute of 1641; and no careful student can fail to read between the lines the desire there expressed to refer to the Old Testament as authority for slavery. Now, slaves were purchased by Abraham, and the New-England "doctors of the law" were unwilling to have slaves stolen when they could be bought[298] so easily. Dr. Moore says, in reference to the decision,—

"In all the proceedings of the General Court on this occasion, there is not a trace of anti-slavery opinion or sentiment, still less of anti-slavery legislation; though both have been repeatedly claimed for the honor of the colony."[299]

And Dr. Moore is not alone in his opinion; for Mr. Hildreth says this case "in which Saltonstall was concerned has been magnified by too precipitate an admiration into a protest on the part of Massachusetts against the African slave-trade. So far, however, from any such protest being made, at the very birth of the foreign commerce of New England the African slave-trade became a regular business."[300] There is now, therefore, no room to doubt but what the decision was rendered on a technical point of law, and not inspired by an anti-slavery sentiment.

As an institution, slavery had at first a stunted growth in Massachusetts, and did not increase its victims to any great extent until near the close of the seventeenth century. But when it did begin a perceptible growth, it made rapid and prodigious strides. In 1676 there were about two hundred slaves in the colony, and they were chiefly from Guinea and Madagascar.[301] In 1680 Gov. Bradstreet, in compliance with a request made by the home government, said that the slave-trade was not carried on to any great extent. They were introduced in small lots, and brought from ten to forty pounds apiece. He thought the entire number in the colony would not reach more than one hundred and twenty-five. Few were born in the colony, and none had been baptized up to that time.[302] The year 1700 witnessed an unprecedented growth in the slave-trade. From the 24th of January, 1698, to the 25th of December, 1707,[303] two hundred Negroes were imported into the colony,—quite as many as in the previous sixty years. In 1708 Gov. Dudley's report to the board of trade fixed the number of Negroes at five hundred and fifty, and suggested that they were not so desirable as white servants, who could be used in the army, and in time of peace turn their attention to planting. The prohibition against the Negro politically and in a military sense, in that section of the country, made him almost valueless to the colonial government struggling for deliverance from the cruel laws of the mother country. The white servant could join the "minute-men," plough with his gun on his back, go to the church, and, having received the blessing of the parish minister, could hasten to battle with the proud and almost boastful feelings of a Christian freeman! But the Negro, bond and free, was excluded from all these sacred privileges. Wronged, robbed of his freedom,—the heritage of all human kind,—he was suspicioned and contemned for desiring that great boon. On the 17th of February, 1720, Gov. Shute placed the number of slaves—including a few Indians—in Massachusetts at two thousand. During the same year thirty-seven males and sixteen females were imported into the colony.[304] We are unable to discover whether these were counted in the enumeration furnished by Gov. Shute or not. We are inclined to think they were included. In 1735 there were two thousand six hundred[305] bond and free in the colony; and within the next seventeen years the Negro population of Boston alone reached 1,541.[306]

In 1754 the colonial government found it necessary to establish a system of taxation. Gov. Shirley was required to inform the House of Representatives as to the different kinds of taxable property. And from a clause in his message, Nov. 19, 1754, on the one hundred and nineteenth page of the Journal, we infer two things; viz., that slaves were chattels or real estate, and, therefore, taxable. The governor says, "There is one part of the Estate, viz., the Negro slaves, which I am at a loss how to come at the knowledge of, without your assistance." In accordance with the request for assistance on this matter, the Legislature instructed the assessors of each town and district within the colony to secure a correct list of all Negro slaves, male and female, from sixteen years old and upwards, to be deposited in the office of the secretary of state.[307] The result of this enumeration was rather surprising; as it fixed the Negro population at 4,489,—quite an increase over the last enumeration. Again, in 1764-65, another census of the Negroes was taken; and they were found to be 5,779.

Here, as in Virginia, an impost tax was imposed upon all Negro slaves imported into the colony. We will quote section 3 of the Act of October, 1705, requiring duty upon imported Negroes; because many are disposed to discredit some historical statements about slavery in Massachusetts.

> "Sect. 3. And be it further enacted by the authority aforesaid, that from and after the first day of May, in the year one thousand seven hundred and six, every master of ship or vessel, merchant or other person, importing or bringing into this province any negroe or negroes, male or female, of what age soever, shall enter their number, names and sex in the impost office; and the master shall insert the same in the manifest of his lading, and shall pay to the commissioner and receiver of the impost, four pounds per head for every such negro, male or female; and as well the master, as the ship or vessel wherein they are brought, shall be security for payment of the said duty; and both or either of them shall stand charged in the law therefor to the commissioner, who may deny to grant a clearing for such ship or vessel, until payment be made, or may recover the same of the master, at the commissioner's election, by action of debt, bill, plaint or information in any of her majesty's courts of record within this province."[308]

A fine of eight pounds was imposed upon any person refusing or neglecting to make a proper entry of each slave imported, in the "Impost Office." If a Negro died within six weeks after his arrival, a drawback was allowed. If any slave was sold again into another Province or plantation within a year after his arrival, a drawback was allowed to the person who paid the impost duty. A subsequent and more stringent law shows that there was no desire to abate the traffic. In August, 1712, a law was passed "prohibiting the importation or bringing into the province any Indian servants or slaves;"[309] but it was only intended as a check upon the introduction of the Tuscaroras and other "revengeful" Indians from South Carolina.[310] Desperate Indians and insubordinate Negroes were the occasion of grave fears on the part of the colonists.[311] Many Indians had been cruelly dealt with in war; in peace, enslaved and wronged beyond their power of endurance. Their stoical nature led them to the performance of desperate deeds. There is kinship in suffering. There is an unspoken language in sorrow that binds hearts in the indissoluble fellowship of resolve. Whatever natural and national differences existed between the Indian and the Negro—one from the bleak coasts of New England, the other from the tropical coast of Guinea—were lost in the commonality of degradation and interest. The more heroic spirits of both races began to grow restive under the yoke. The colonists were not slow to observe this, and hence this law was to act as a restraint upon and against "their rebellion and hostilities." And the reader should understand that it was not an anti-slavery measure. It was not "hostile to slavery" as a system: it was but the precaution of a guilty and ever-gnawing public conscience.

Slavery grew. There was no legal obstacle in its way. It had the sanction of the law, as we have already shown, and what was better still, the sympathy of public sentiment. The traffic in slaves appears to have been more an object in Boston than at any period before or since. For a time dealers had no hesitation in advertising them for sale in their own names. At length a very few who advertised would refer purchasers to "inquire of the printer, and know further."[312] This was in 1727, fifteen years after the afore-mentioned Act became a law, and which many apologists would interpret as a specific and direct prohibition against slavery; but there is no reason for such a perversion of so plain an Act.

Slavery in Massachusetts, as elsewhere, in self-defence had to claim as one of its necessary and fundamental principles, that the slave was either *naturally* inferior to the other races, or that, by some fundamentally inherent law in the institution itself, the master was justified in placing the lowest possible estimate upon his slave property. "Property" implied absolute control over the thing possessed. It carried in its broad meaning the awful fact, not alone of ownership, but of the supremacy of the will of the owner. Mr. Addison says,—

> "What color of excuse can there be for the contempt with which we treat this part of our species, that we should not put them upon the common foot of humanity, that we should only set an insignificant fine upon the man who murders them; nay, that we should, as much as in us lies, cut them off from the prospect of happiness in another world, as well as in this, and deny them that which we look upon as the proper means for obtaining it?"[313]

None whatever! And yet the Puritans put the Negro slaves in their colony on a level with "horses and hogs." Let the intelligent American of to-day read the following remarkable note from Judge Sewall's diary, and then confess that facts are stranger than fiction.

> "1716. I essayed June 22, to prevent Indians and Negroes being rated with Horses and Hogs; but could not prevail. Col. Thaxter bro't it back, and gave as a reason of yr Nonagreement, They were just going to make a new valuation."[314]

It had been sent to the deputies, and was by them rejected, and then returned to the judge by Col. Thaxter. The House was "just going to make a New Valuation" of the property in the colony, and hence did not care to exclude slaves from the list of chattels,[315] in which they had always been placed.

"In 1718, all Indian, Negro, and Mulatto servants for life were estimated as other Personal Estate—viz.: Each male servant *for life* above fourteen years of age, at fifteen pounds value; each female servant for life, above fourteen years of age, at ten pounds value. The assessor might make abatement for cause of age or infirmity. Indian, Negro, and Mulatto Male servants *for a term of years* were to be numbered and rated as other Polls, and not as Personal Estate. In 1726, the assessors were required to estimate Indian, Negro, and Mulatto servants proportionably as other Personal Estate, according to their sound judgment and discretion. In 1727, the rule of 1718 was restored, but during one year only, for in 1728 the law was the same as that of 1726; and so it probably remained, including all such servants, as well for term of years as for life, in the ratable estates. We have seen the supply-bills for 1736, 1738, 1739, and 1740, in which this feature is the same.

> "And thus they continued to be rated with horses, oxen, cows, goats, sheep, and swine, until after the commencement of the War of the Revolution.[316]

On the 22d of April, 1728, the following notice appeared in a Boston newspaper:—

> "Two very likely Negro girls. Enquire two doors from the Brick Meetinghouse in Middle-street. At which place is to be sold women's stays, children's good callamanco stiffened-boddy'd coats, and childrens' stays of all sorts, and women's hoop-coats; all at very reasonable rates."[317]

So the "likely Negro girls" were mixed up in the sale of "women's stays" and "hoop-coats"! It was bad enough to "rate Negroes with Horses and Hogs," but to sell them with second-hand clothing was an incident in which is to be seen the low depth to which slavery had carried the Negro by its cruel weight. A human being could be sold like a cast-off garment, and pass without a bill of sale.[318] The announcement that a "likely Negro woman about nineteen years and a child about six months of age to be sold together or apart"[319] did not shock the Christian sensibilities of the people of Massachusetts. A babe six months old could be torn from the withered and famishing bosom of the young mother, and sold with other articles of merchandise. How bitter and how cruel was such a separation, mothers[320] only can know; and how completely lost a community and government are that regard with complacency a hardship so diabolical, the Christians of America must be able to judge.

The Church has done many cruel things in the name of Christianity. In the dark ages it filled the minds of its disciples with fear, and their bodies with the pains of penance. It burned Michael Servetus, and it strangled the scientific opinions of Galileo. And in stalwart old Massachusetts it thought it was doing God's service in denying the Negro slave the right of Christian baptism."

> "The famous French Code Noir of 1685 obliged every planter to have his Negroes baptized, and properly instructed in the doctrines and duties of Christianity. Nor was this the only important and humane provision of that celebrated statute, to which we may seek in vain for any parallel in British Colonial legislation."[321]

On the 25th of October, 1727, Matthias Plant[322] wrote, in answer to certain questions put to him by "the secretary of the Society for the Propagation of the Gospel," as follows:—

> "6. Negro slaves, one of them is desirous of baptism, but denied by her master, a woman of wonderful sense, and prudent in matters, of equal knowledge in Religion with most of her sex, far exceeding any of her own nation that ever yet I heard of."[323]

It was nothing to her master that she was "desirous of baptism," "of wonderful sense," "prudent in matters," and "of equal knowledge in religion with most of her sex!" She was a Negro slave, and as such was denied the blessings of the Christian Church.

> "The system of personal servitude was fast disappearing from Western Europe, where the idea had obtained that it was inconsistent with Christian duty for Christians to hold

Christians as slaves. But this charity did not extend to heathen and infidels. The same system of morality which held the possessions of unbelievers as lawful spoils of war, delivered over their persons also to the condition of servitude. Hence, in America, the slavery of the Indians, and presently of Negroes, whom experience proved to be much more capable of enduring the hardships of that condition."[324]

And those who were so fortunate as to secure baptism were not freed thereby.[325] In Massachusetts no Negro ever had the courage to seek his freedom through this door, and, therefore, there was no necessity for legislation there to define the question, but in the Southern colonies the law declared that baptism did not secure the liberty of the subject. As early as 1631 a law was passed admitting no man to the rights of "freemen" who was not a member of some church within the limits of the jurisdiction of the colony.[326] The blessings of a "freeman" were reserved for church-members only. Negroes were not admitted to the church, and, therefore, were denied the rights of a freeman.[327] Even the mother country had no bowels of compassion for the Negro. In 1677 the English courts held that a Negro slave was property.

> "That, being usually bought and sold among merchants as merchandise, and also being infidels, there might be a property in them sufficient to maintain trover."[328]

So as "infidels" the Negro slaves of Massachusetts were deprived of rights and duties belonging to a member of the Church and State.

> "Zealous for religion as the colonists were, very little effort was made to convert the Negroes, owing partly, at least, to a prevalent opinion that neither Christian brotherhood nor the law of England would justify the holding Christians as slaves. Nor could repeated colonial enactments to the contrary entirely root out this idea, for it was not supposed that a colonial statute could set aside the law of England."[329]

But the deeper reason the colonists had for excluding slaves from baptism, and hence citizenship, was twofold; viz., to keep in harmony with the Mosaic code in reference to "strangers" and "Gentiles," and to keep the door of the Church shut in the face of the slave; because to open it to him was to emancipate him in course of time. Religious and secular knowledge were not favorable to slavery. The colonists turned to the narrow, national spirit of the Old Testament, rather than to the broad and catholic spirit of the New Testament, for authority to withhold the mercies of the Christian religion from the Negro slaves in their midst.

The rigorous system of domestic slavery established in the colony of Massachusetts bore its bitter fruit in due season. It was impossible to exclude the slaves from the privileges of the Church and State without inflicting a moral injury upon the holy marriage relation. In the contemplation of the law the slave was a chattel, an article of merchandise. The custom of separating parent and child, husband and wife, was very clear proof that the marriage relation was either positively ignored by the institution of slavery, or grossly violated under the slightest pretext. All well-organized society or government rests upon this sacred relation. But slavery, with lecherous grasp and avaricious greed, trailed the immaculate robes of marriage in the moral filth of the traffic in human beings. True, there never was any prohibition against the marriage of one slave to another slave,—for they *tried* to breed slaves in Massachusetts!—but there never was any law encouraging the lawful union of slaves until after the Revolutionary War, in 1786. We rather infer from the following in the Act of October, 1705, that the marriage relation among slaves had been left entirely to the caprices of the master.

> "And no master shall unreasonably deny marriage to his Negro with one of the same nation; any law, usage or custom to the contrary notwithstanding."[330]

We have not been able to discover "any law" positively prohibiting marriage among slaves; but there was a custom denying marriage to the Negro, that at length received the weight of positive law. Mr. Palfrey says,—

> "From the reverence entertained by the fathers of New England for the nuptial tie, it is safe to infer that slave husbands and wives were never separated."[331]

We have searched faithfully to find the slightest justification for this inference of Mr. Palfrey, but have not found it. There is not a line in any newspaper of the colony, until 1710, that indicates the concern of the people in the lawful union of slaves. And there was no legislation upon the subject until 1786, when an "Act for the orderly Solemnization of Marriage" passed. That Negro slaves were united in marriage, there is abundant evidence, but not many in this period. It was almost a useless ceremony when "the customs and usages" of slavery separated them at the convenience of the owner. The master's power over his slaves was almost absolute. If he wanted to sell the children and keep the parents, his decision was not subject to any court of law. It was final. If he wanted to sell the wife of his slave man into the rice-fields of the Carolinas or into the West India Islands, the tears of the husband only exasperated the master. "The fathers of New England" had *no* reverence for the "nuptial tie" among their slaves, and, therefore, tore slave families asunder without the least compunction of conscience. "Negro children were considered an incumbrance in a family, and, when weaned, were given away like puppies," says the famous Dr. Belknap. But after the Act of 1705; "their banns were published like those of white persons;" and public sentiment began to undergo a change on the subject. The following Negro marriage was prepared by the Rev. Samuel Phillips of Andover. His ministry did not commence until 1710; and, therefore, this marriage was prepared subsequent to that date. He realized the need of something, and acted accordingly.

"You, Bob, do now, in ye Presence of God and these Witnesses, Take Sally to be your wife;

"Promising, that so far as shall be consistent with ye Relation which you now Sustain as a servant, you will Perform ye Part of an Husband towards her: And in particular, as you shall have ye Opportunity & Ability, you will take proper Care of her in Sickness and Health, in Prosperity & Adversity;

> "And that you will be True & Faithful to her, and will Cleave to her only, so long as God, in his Providence, shall continue your and her abode in Such Place (or Places) as that you can conveniently come together.—Do You thus Promise?

"You, Sally, do now, in ye Presence of God, and these Witnesses, Take Bob to be your Husband;

"Promising, that so far as your present Relation as a Servant shall admit, you will Perform the Part of a Wife towards him: and in particular,

"You Promise that you will Love him; And that as you shall have the Opportunity & Ability, you will take a proper Care of him in Sickness and Health; in Prosperity and Adversity:

"And you will cleave to him only, so long as God, in his Providence, shall continue his & your Abode in such Place (or Places) as that you can come together.—Do you thus Promise? I then, agreeable to your Request, and with ye Consent of your Masters & Mistresses, do Declare that you have License given you to be conversant and familiar together as Husband and Wife, so long as God shall continue your Places of Abode as aforesaid; And so long as you Shall behave yourselves as it becometh servants to doe:

"For you must both of you bear in mind that you remain still, as really and truly as ever, your Master's Property, and therefore it will be justly expected, both by God and Man, that you behave and conduct yourselves as Obedient and faithful Servants towards your respective Masters & Mistresses for the Time being:

"And finally, I exhort and Charge you to beware lest you give place to the Devil, so as to take occasion from the license now given you, to be lifted up with Pride, and thereby fall under the Displeasure, not of Man only, but of God also; for it is written, that God resisteth the Proud but giveth Grace to the humble.

"I shall now conclude with Prayer for you, that you may become good Christians, and that you may be enabled to conduct as such; and in particular, that you may have Grace to behave suitably towards each Other, as also dutifully towards your Masters & Mistresses, Not with Eye Service as Men pleasers, ye Servants of Christ doing ye Will of God from ye heart, &c.

["Endorsed] Negro Marriage."[332]

Where a likely Negro woman was courted by the slave of another owner, and wanted to marry, she was sold, as a matter of humanity, "with her wearing apparel" to the owner of the man. "A Bill of Sale of a Negro Woman Servant in Boston in 1724, recites that 'Whereas Scipio, of Boston aforesaid, Free Negro Man and Laborer, proposes Marriage to Margaret, the Negro Woman Servant of the said Dorcas Marshall [a Widow Lady of Boston]: Now to the Intent that the said Intended Marriage may take Effect, and that the said Scipio may Enjoy the said Margaret without any Interruption,' etc., she is duly sold, with her apparel, for Fifty Pounds."[333] Within the next twenty years the Governor and his Council found public opinion so modified on the question of marriage among the blacks, that they granted a Negro a divorce on account of his wife's adultery with a white man. But in Quincy's Reports, page 30, note, quoted by Dr. Moore, in 1758 the following rather loose decision is recorded: that the child of a female slave never married according to any of the forms prescribed by the laws of this land, by another slave, who "had kept her company with her master's consent," was not a bastard.

The Act of 1705 forbade any "christian" from marrying a Negro, and imposed a fine of fifty pounds upon any clergyman who should join a Negro and "christian" in marriage. It stood as the law of the Commonwealth until 1843, when it was repealed by an "Act relating to Marriage between Individuals of Certain Races."

As to the political rights of the Negro, it should be borne in mind, that, as he was excluded from the right of Christian baptism, hence from the Church; and as "only church-members enjoyed the rights of freemen, it is clear that the Negro was not admitted to the exercise of the duties of a freeman.[334] Admitting that there were instances where Negroes received the rite of baptism, it was so well understood as not entitling them to freedom or political rights, that it was never questioned during this entire period. Free Negroes were but little better off than the slaves. While they might be regarded as owning their own labor, political rights and ecclesiastical privileges were withheld from them.

"They became the objects of a suspicious legislation, which deprived them of most of the rights of freemen, and reduced them to a social position very similar, in many respects, to that which inveterate prejudice in many parts of Europe has fixed upon the Jews."

Though nominally free, they did not come under the head of "Christians." Neither freedom, nor baptism in the Church, could free them from the race-malice of the whites, that followed them like the fleet-footed "Furies." There were special regulations for free Negroes. The Act of 1703, forbidding slaves from being out at night after the hour of nine o'clock, extended to free Negroes.[335] In 1707 an Act was passed "regulating of free negroes."[336] It recites that "free negroes and mulattos, able of body, and fit for labor, who are not charged with trainings, watches, and other services,"[337] shall perform service equivalent to militia training. They were under the charge of the officer in command of the military company belonging to the district where they resided. They did fatigue-duty. And the only time, that, by law, the Negro was admitted to the trainings, was between 1652 and 1656. But there is no evidence that the Negroes took advantage of the law. Public sentiment is more potent than law. In May, 1656, the law of 1652, admitting Negroes to the trainings, was repealed.

> "For the better ordering and settling of severall cases in the military companyes within this jurisdiction, which, upon experience, are found either wanting or inconvenient, it is ordered and declared by this Court and the authoritie thereof, that henceforth no negroes or Indians, although servants to the English, shal be armed or permitted to trayne, and yt no other person shall be exempted from trayning but such as some law doth priveledge."[338]

And Gov. Bradstreet, in his report to the "Committee for Trade," made in May, 1680, says,—

> "We account all generally from Sixteen to Sixty that are healthfull and strong bodys, both House-holders and

Servants fit to beare Armes, except Negroes and slaves, whom wee arme not."[339]

The law of 1707—which is the merest copy of the Virginia law on the same subject—requires free Negroes to answer fire-alarms with the company belonging to their respective precincts. They were not allowed to entertain slave friends at their houses, without the permission of the owner of the slaves. To all prohibitions there was affixed severe fines in large sums of money. In case of a failure to pay these fines, the delinquent was sent to the House of Correction; where, under severe discipline, he was constrained to work out his fine at the rate of one shilling per day! If a Negro "presume to smite or strike any person of the English, or other Christian nation," he was publicly flogged by the justice before whom tried, at the discretion of that officer.

During this period the social condition of the Negroes, bond and free, was very deplorable. The early records of the town of Boston preserve the fact that one Thomas Deane, in the year 1661, was prohibited from employing a Negro in the manufacture of hoops, under a penalty of twenty shillings; for what reason is not stated.[340] No churches or schools, no books or teachers, they were left to the gloom and vain imaginations of their own fettered intellects. John Eliot "had long lamented it with a Bleeding and Burning Passion, that the English used their Negroes but as their Horses or their Oxen, and that so little care was taken about their immortal souls; he looked upon it as a Prodigy, that any wearing the Name of Christians should so much have the Heart of Devils in them, as to prevent and hinder the Instruction of the poor Blackamores, and confine the souls of their miserable Slaves to a Destroying Ignorance, merely for fear of thereby losing the Benefit of their Vassalage; but now he made a motion to the English within two or three Miles of him, that at such a time and place they would send their Negroes once a week unto him: For he would then Catechise them, and Enlighten them, to the utmost of his power in things of their Everlasting Peace; however, he did not live to make much progress in this undertaking."[341] The few faint voices of encouragement, that once in a great while reached them from the pulpit[342] and forum, were as strange music, mellowed and sweetened by the distance. The free and slave Negroes were separated by law, were not allowed to communicate together to any great extent. They were not allowed in numbers greater than three, and then, if not in the service of some white person, were liable to be arrested, and sent to the House of Correction.

> "The slave was the property of his master as much as his ox or his horse; he had no civil rights but that of protection from cruelty; he could acquire no property nor dispose

of any[343] without the consent of his master.... We think he had not the capacity to communicate a civil relation to his children, which he did not enjoy himself, except as the property of his master."[344]

With but small means the free Negroes of the colony were unable to secure many comforts in their homes. They were hated and dreaded more than their brethren in bondage. They could judge, by contrast, of the abasing influences of slavery. They were only nominally free; because they were taxed[345] without representation,—had no voice in the colonial government.

But, notwithstanding the obscure and neglected condition of the free Negroes, some of them by their industry, frugality, and aptitude won a place in the confidence and esteem of the more humane of the white population. Owning their own time, many of the free Negroes applied themselves to the acquisition of knowledge. Phillis Wheatley, though nominally a slave for some years, stood at the head of the intellectual Negroes of this period. She was brought from Africa to the Boston slave-market, where, in 1761, she was purchased by a benevolent white lady by the name of Mrs. John Wheatley. She was naked, save a piece of dirty carpet about her loins, was delicate of constitution, and much fatigued from a rough sea-voyage. Touched by her modest demeanor and intelligent countenance, Mrs. Wheatley chose her from a large company of slaves. It was her intention to teach her the duties of an ordinary domestic; but clean clothing and wholesome diet effected such a radical change in the child for the better, that Mrs. Wheatley changed her plans, and began to give her private instruction. Eager for learning, apt in acquiring, though only eight years old, she greatly surprised and pleased her mistress. Placed under the instruction of Mrs. Wheatley's daughter, Phillis learned the English language sufficiently well as to be able to read the most difficult portions of the Bible with ease and accuracy. This she accomplished in less than a year and a half. She readily mastered the art of writing; and within four years from the time she landed in the slave-market in Boston, she was able to carry on an extensive correspondence on a variety of topics.

Her ripening intellectual faculties attracted the attention of the refined and educated people of Boston, many of whom sought her society at the home of the Wheatleys. It should be remembered, that this period did not witness general culture among the masses of white people, and certainly no facilities for the education of Negroes. And yet some cultivated white persons gave Phillis encouragement, loaned her books, and called her out on matters of a literary character. Having acquired the principles of an English education, she turned her attention to the study of the Latin language,[346] and was able to do well in it. Encouraged by her success, she translated one of Ovid's tales. The translation was considered so admirable that it was published in Boston by some of her friends. On reaching England it was republished, and called forth the praise of many of the reviews.

Her manners were modest and refined. Her nature was sensitive and affectionate. She early gave signs of a deep spiritual experience,[347] which gave tone and character to all her efforts in composition and poetry. There was a charming vein of gratitude in all her private conversations and public utterances, which her owners did not fail to recognize and appreciate. Her only distinct recollection of her native home was, that every morning early her mother poured out water before the rising sun. Her growing intelligence and keen appreciation of the blessings of civilization overreached mere animal grief at the separation from her mother. And as she knew more of the word of God, she became more deeply interested in the condition of her race.

At the age of twenty her master emancipated her. Naturally delicate, the severe climate of New England, and her constant application to study, began to show on her health. Her friend and mother, for such she proved herself to be, Mrs. Wheatley, solicitous about her health, called in eminent medical counsel, who prescribed a sea-voyage. A son of Mrs. Wheatley was about to visit England on mercantile business, and therefore took Phillis with him. For the previous six years she had cultivated her taste for poetry; and, at this time, her reputation was quite well established. She had corresponded with persons in England in social circles, and was not a stranger to the English. She was heartily welcomed by the leaders of the society of the British metropolis, and treated with great consideration. Under all the trying circumstances of high social life, among the nobility and rarest literary genius of London, this redeemed child of the desert, coupled to a beautiful modesty the extraordinary powers of an incomparable conversationalist. She carried London by storm. Thoughtful people praised her; titled people dined her; and the press extolled the name of Phillis Wheatley, the African poetess.

Prevailed upon by admiring friends, in 1773[348] she gave her poems to the world. They were published in London in a small octavo volume of about one hundred and twenty pages, comprising thirty-nine pieces. It was dedicated to the Countess of Huntingdon, with a picture of the poetess, and a letter of recommendation signed by the governor and lieutenant-governor, with many other "respectable citizens of Boston."

TO THE PUBLIC.

As it has been repeatedly suggested to the publisher, by persons who have seen the manuscript, that numbers would be ready to suspect they were not really the writings of Phillis, he has procured the following attestation, from the most respectable characters in *Boston*, that none might have the least ground for disputing their *Original*.

We, whose Names are under-written, do assure the World, that the Poems specified in the following page were (as we verily believe) written by Phillis, a young Negro Girl, who was, but a few Years since, brought, an uncultivated Barbarian, from *Africa*, and has ever since been, and now is, under the disadvantage of serving as a Slave in a family in this town. She has been examined by some of the best judges, and is thought qualified to write them.

    His Excellency, Thomas Hutchinson, Governor.

    The Hon. Andrew Oliver, Lieutenant Governor.

Hon. Thomas Hubbard, | Rev. Charles Chauncy,

Hon. John Erving, | Rev. Mather Byles,

Hon. James Pitts, | Rev. Ed Pemberton,

Hon. Harrison Gray, | Rev. Andrew Elliot,

Hon. James Bowdoin, | Rev. Samuel Cooper,

John Hancock, Esq. | Rev. Samuel Mather,

Joseph Green, Esq. | Rev. John Moorhead,

Richard Cary, Esq. | Mr. John Wheatley, her master.

The volume has passed through several English and American editions, and is to be found in all first-class libraries in the country. Mrs. Wheatley sickened, and grieved daily after Phillis. A picture of her little ward, sent from England, adorned her bedroom; and she pointed it out to visiting friends with all the sincere pride of a mother. On one occasion she exclaimed to a friend, "See! Look at my Phillis! Does she not seem as though she would speak to me?" Getting no better, she sent a loving request to Phillis to come to her at as early a moment as possible. With a deep sense of gratitude to Mrs. Wheatley for countless blessings bestowed upon her, Phillis hastened to return to Boston. She found her friend and benefactor just living, and shortly had the mournful satisfaction of closing her sightless eyes. The husband and daughter followed the wife and mother quickly to the grave. Young Mr. Wheatley married, and settled in England. Phillis was alone in the world.

"She soon after received an offer of marriage from a respectable colored man, of Boston. The name of this individual was John Peters.[349] He kept a grocery in Court Street, and was a man of handsome person. He wore a wig, carried a cane, and quite acted out 'the gentleman.' In an evil hour, he was accepted; and, though he was a man of talents and information,—writing with fluency and propriety, and, at one period, reading law,—he proved utterly unworthy of the distinguished woman who honored him by her alliance."

Her married life was brief. She was the mother of one child, that died early. Ignorant of the duties of domestic life, courted and flattered by the cultivated, Peters's jealousy was at length turned into harsh treatment. Tenderly raised, and of a delicate constitution, Phillis soon went into decline, and died Dec. 5, 1784, in the thirty-first[350] year of her life, greatly beloved and sincerely mourned by all whose good fortune it had been to know of her high mental endowments and blameless Christian life.

Her influence upon the rapidly growing anti-slavery sentiment of Massachusetts was considerable. The friends of humanity took pleasure in pointing to her marvellous achievements, as an evidence of what the Negro could do under favorable circumstances. From a state of nudity in a slave-market, a stranger to the English language, this young African girl had won her way over the rough path of learning; had conquered the spirit of caste in the best society of conservative old Boston; had brought two continents to her feet in admiration and amazement at the rare poetical accomplishments of a child of Africa![351]

She addressed a poem to Gen. Washington that pleased the old warrior very much. We have never seen it, though we have searched diligently. Mr. Sparks says of it,—

"I have not been able to find, among Washington's papers the letter and poem addressed to him. They have doubtless been lost. From the circumstance of her invoking the muse in his praise, and from the tenor of some of her printed pieces, particularly one addressed to King George seven years before, in which she compliments him on the repeal of the Stamp Act, it may be inferred, that she was a Whig in politics after the American way of thinking; and it might be curious to see in what manner she would eulogize liberty and the rights of man, while herself, nominally at least, in bondage."[352]

Gen. Washington, in a letter to Joseph Reed, bearing date of the 10th of February, 1776, from Cambridge, refers to the letter and poem as follows:—

"I recollect nothing else worth giving you the trouble of, unless you can be amused by reading a letter and poem addressed to me by Miss Phillis Wheatley. In searching over a parcel of papers the other day, in order to destroy such as were useless, I brought it to light again. At first, with a view of doing justice to her poetical genius, I had a great mind to publish the poem; but not knowing whether it might not be considered rather as a mark of my own vanity, than as a compliment to her, I laid it aside,[353] till I came across it again in the manner just mentioned."[354]

This gives the world an "inside" view of the brave old general's opinion of the poem and poetess, but the "outside" view, as expressed to Phil's, is worthy of reproduction at this point.

CAMBRIDGE, 28 FEBRUARY, 1776.

Miss Phillis,—Your favor of the 26th of October did not reach my hands, till the middle of December. Time enough, you will say, to have given an answer ere this. Granted. But a variety of important occurrences, continually interposing to distract the mind and withdraw the attention, I hope will apologize for the delay, and plead my excuse for the seeming but not real neglect. I thank you most sincerely for your polite notice of me, in the elegant lines you enclosed; and however undeserving I may be of such encomium and panegyric, the style and manner exhibit a striking proof of your poetical talents; in honor of which, and as a tribute justly due to you, I would have published the poem, had I not been apprehensive, that, while I only meant to give the world this new instance of your genius, I might have incurred the imputation of vanity. This, and nothing else, determined me not to give it place in the public prints.

If you should ever come to Cambridge, or near head-quarters, I shall be happy to see a person so favored by the Muses, and to whom nature has been so liberal and beneficent in her dispensations.

I am, with great respect, your obedient, humble servant,

GEORGE WASHINGTON.[355]

This letter is a handsome compliment to the poetess, and does honor to both the head and heart of the general. His modesty, so characteristic, has deprived history of its dues. But it is consoling to know that the sentiments of the poem found a response in the patriotic heart of the *first soldier of the Revolution, and the Father of his Country*!

While Phillis Wheatley stands out as one of the most distinguished characters of this period, and who, as a Colored person, had no equal, yet she was not the only individual of her race of intellect and character. A Negro boy from Africa was purchased by a Mr. Slocum, who resided near New Bedford, Mass. After he acquired the language, he turned his thoughts to freedom, and in a few years, by working beyond the hours he devoted to his master, was enabled to buy himself from his master. He married an Indian woman named Ruth Moses, and settled at Cutterhunker, in the Elizabeth Islands, near New Bedford. In a few years, through industry and frugality, John Cuffe—the name he took as a freeman—was enabled to purchase a good farm of one hundred (100) acres. Every year recorded new achievements, until John Cuffe had a wide reputation for wealth, honesty, and intelligence. He applied himself to books, and secured, as the ripe fruit of his studious habits, a fair business education. Both himself and wife were Christian believers; and to lives of industry and increasing secular knowledge, they added that higher knowledge which makes alive to "everlasting life." Ten children were born unto them,—four boys and six girls. One of the boys, Paul Cuffe, became one of the most distinguished men of color Massachusetts has produced. The reader will be introduced to him in the proper place in the history. John Cuffe died in 1745, leaving behind, in addition to considerable property, a good name, which is of great price.[356]

Richard Dalton, Esq., of Boston, owned a Negro boy whom he taught to read any Greek writer without hesitancy. Mr. Dalton was afflicted with weak eyes; and his fondness for the classics would not allow him to forego the pleasure of them, and hence his Negro boy Cæsar was instructed in the Greek.[357] "The Boston Chronicle" of Sept. 21, 1769, contains the following advertisement: "To be sold, a Likely Little negroe boy, who can speak the French language, and very fit for a Valet."

With increasing evidence of the Negro's capacity for mental improvement, and fitness for the duties and blessings of a freeman, and the growing insolence and rigorous policy of the mother country, came a wonderful change in the colony. The Negroes were emboldened to ask for and claim rights as British subjects, and the more humane element among the whites saw in a relaxation of the severe treatment of the blacks security and immunity in war. But anti-slavery sentiment in Massachusetts was not born of a genuine desire to put down a wicked and cruel traffic in human beings. Two things operated in favor of humane treatment of the slaves,—an impending war, and the decision of Lord Mansfield in the Sommersett case. The English government was yearly increasing the burdens of the colonists. The country was young, its resources little known. The people were largely engaged in agricultural pursuits. There were no tariff laws encouraging or protecting the labor or skill of the people. Civil war seemed inevitable. Thoughtful men began to consider the question as to which party the Negroes of the colony would contribute their strength. It was no idle question to determine whether the Negroes were Tories or Whigs. As early as 1750 the questions as to the legality of holding Negroes in slavery in British colonies began to be discussed in England and New England. "What, precisely, the English law might be on the subject of slavery, still remained a subject of doubt."[358] Lord Holt held that slavery was a condition unknown to English law,—that the being in England was evidence of freedom. This embarrassed New-England planters in taking their slaves to England. The planters banded for their common cause, and secured the written opinion of Yorke and Talbot, attorney and solicitor general of England. They held that slaves could be held in England as well as in America; that baptism did not confer freedom: and the opinion stood as sound law for nearly a half-century.[359] The men in England who lived on the money wrung from the slave-trade, the members of the Royal African Company, came to the rescue of the institution of slavery. In order to maintain it by law in the American colonies, it had to be recognized in England. The people of Massachusetts took a lively interest in the question. In 1761, at a meeting "in the old court-house," James Otis,[360] in a speech against the "writs of assistance," struck a popular chord on the questions of "The Rights of the Colonies," afterwards published (1764) by order of the Legislature. He took the broad ground, "that the colonists, black and white, born here, are free-born British subjects and entitled to all the essential rights of such."[361] In 1766 Nathaniel Appleton and James Swan distinguished themselves in their defence of the doctrines of "liberty for all." It became the general topic of discussion in private and public, and country lyceums and college societies took it up as a subject of forensic disputation.[362] In the month of May, 1766, the representatives of the people were instructed to advocate the total abolition of slavery. And on the 16th of March, 1767, a resolution was offered to see whether the instructions should be adhered to, and was unanimously carried in the affirmative. But it should be remembered that British troops were in the colony, in the streets of Boston. The mutterings of the distant thunder of revolution could be heard. Public sentiment was greatly tempered toward the Negroes. On the 31st of May, 1609, the House of Representatives of Massachusetts resolved against the presence of troops, and besought the governor to remove them. His Excellency disclaimed any power under the circumstances to interfere. The House denounced a standing army in time of peace, without the consent of the General Court, as "without precedent, and unconstitutional."[363] In 1769 one of the courts of Massachusetts gave a decision friendly to a slave, who was the plaintiff. This stimulated the Negroes to an exertion for freedom. The entire colony was in a feverish state of excitement. An anonymous Tory writer reproached Bostonians for desiring freedom when they themselves enslaved others.

> "'What!' cries our good people here, 'Negro slaves in Boston! It cannot be.' It is nevertheless true. For though the Bostonians have grounded their rebellion on the 'immutable laws of nature,' yet, notwithstanding their resolves about freedom in their Town-meetings, they actually have in town 2,000 Negro slaves."[364]

These trying and exasperating circumstances were but the friendly precursors of a spirit of universal liberty.

In England the decision of Lord Mansfield in the Sommersett[365] case had encouraged the conscientious few who championed the cause of the slave. Charles Stewart, Esq., of Boston, Mass., had taken to London with him his Negro slave, James Sommersett. The Negro was seized with a sickness in the British metropolis, and was thereupon abandoned by his master. He afterwards regained his health, and secured employment. His master, learning of his whereabouts, had him arrested, and placed in confinement on board the vessel "Ann and Mary," Capt. John Knowls, commander, then lying in the Thames, but soon to sail for Jamaica, where Sommersett was to be sold.

> "On the 3rd of Dec., 1771, affidavits were made by Thomas Walklin, Elizabeth Cade, and John Marlow, that James Sommersett, a Negro, was confined in irons on board a ship called the Ann and Mary, John Knowls commander, lying in the Thames, and bound for Jamaica. Lord Mansfield, upon the prayer of the above subscribers, allowed a writ of habeas corpus, requiring the return of the body of Sommersett before his lordship with an explanation of the cause of his detention. On the 9th of Dec., Capt. Knowls produced the body of Sommersett in Court. Lord Mansfield, after a preliminary examination, referred the matter to the Court of King's Bench, and, therefore, took sureties, and bound Sommersett over 'till 'the 2nd day of the next Hillary term.'

At the time appointed the defendant with counsel, the reputed master of the Negro man Sommersett, and Capt. John Knowls, appeared before the court. Capt. Knowls recited the reasons that led him to detain Sommersett: whereupon the counsel for the latter asked for time in which to prepare an argument against the return. Lord Mansfield gave them until the 7th of February. At the time appointed Mr. Sergeant Davy and Mr. Sergeant Glynn argued against the return, and had further argument 'postponed' till Easter term,' when Mr. Mansfield, Mr. Alleyne, and Mr. Hargrave argued on the same side. 'The only question before us is whether the cause on the return is sufficient. If it is, the Negro must be remanded; if it is not, he must be discharged. The return states that the slave departed and refused to serve, whereupon he was kept to be sold abroad. So high an act of dominion must be recognized by the law of the country where it is used. The power of a master over his slave has been exceedingly different in different countries. The state of slavery is of such a nature that it is incapable of being introduced on any reasons, moral or political, but only by positive law, which preserves its force long after the reasons, occasions, and time itself from whence it was created is erased from memory. It is so odious that nothing can be suffered to support it but positive law. Whatever inconveniences, therefore, may follow from the decision, I cannot say this case is allowed or approved by the law of England, and therefore the black must be discharged.'"

The influence of this decision was wide-spread, and hurtful to slavery in the British colonies in North America. It poured new life into the expiring hopes of the Negroes, and furnished a rule of law for the advocates of "freedom for all." It raised a question of law in all the colonies as to whether the colonial governments could pass an Act legalizing that which was "contrary to English law."[366]

Notwithstanding the general and generous impulse for liberty, the indissoluble ties of avarice, and the greed for the unearned gains of the slave-trade, made public men conservate to conserve the interests of those directly interested in the inhuman traffic.

"In an age when the interests of trade guided legislation, this branch of commerce possessed paramount attractions. Not a statesman exposed its enormities; and, if Richard Baxter echoed the opinions of Puritan Massachusetts, if Southern drew tears by the tragic tale of Oronooko, if Steele awakened a throb of indignation by the story of Inkle and Yarico, if Savage and Shenstone pointed their feeble couplets with the wrongs of 'Afric's sable children,' if the Irish metaphysician Hutcheson, struggling for a higher system of morals, — justly stigmatized the traffic; yet no public opinion lifted its voice against it. English ships, fitted out in English cities, under the special favor of the royal family, of the ministry, and of parliament, stole from Africa, in the years from 1700 to 1750, probably a million and a half of souls, of whom one-eighth were buried in the Atlantic, victims of the passage; and yet in England no general indignation rebuked the enormity; for the public opinion of the age was obedient to materialism."[367]

Humane masters who desired to emancipate their slaves were embarrassed by a statute unfriendly to manumission. The Act of 1703[368] deterred many persons from emancipating their slaves on account of its unjust and hard requirements. And under it quite a deal of litigation arose. It required every master who desired to liberate his slave, before doing so, to furnish a bond to the treasurer of the town or place in which he resided, in a sum not less than fifty pounds.[369] This was to indemnify the town or place in case the Negro slave thus emancipated should, through lameness or sickness, become a charge. In case a master failed to furnish such security, his emancipated slaves were still contemplated by the law as in bondage, "notwithstanding any manumission or instrument of freedom to them made or given." Judge Sewall, in a letter to John Adams, cites a case in point.

"A man, by will, gives his Negro his liberty, and leaves him a legacy. The executor consents that the Negro shall be free, but refuseth to give bond to the selectmen to indemnify the town against any charge for his support in case he should become poor (without which, by the province law, he is not manumitted), or to pay him the legacy.

Query. Can he recover the legacy, and how?

I have just observed that in your last you desire me to say something towards discouraging you from removing to Providence; and you say, any thing will do. At present, I only say, you will do well enough where you are. I will explain myself, and add something further, in some future letter. I have not time to enlarge now, for which I believe you will not be inconsolably grieved. So, to put you out of pain, your hearty friend,

JONATHAN SEWALL."[370]

Mr. Adams replied as follows:—

"Now. *En mesure le manner*. The testator intended plainly that his negro should have his liberty and a legacy; therefore the law will presume that he intended his executor should do all that without which he could have neither. That this indemnification was not in the testator's mind, cannot be proved from the will any more than it could be proved, in the first case above, that the testator did not know a fee simple would pass a will without the word heirs; nor than, in the second case, that the devise of a trust, that might continue forever, would convey a fee-simple without the like words. I take it, therefore, that the executor of this will is, by implication, obliged to give bonds to the town treasurer, and, in his refusal, is a wrongdoer; and I cannot think he ought to be allowed to take advantage of his own wrong, so much as to allege this want of an indemnification to evade an action of the case brought for the legacy by the negro himself.

> But why may not the negro bring a special action of the case against the executor, setting forth the will, the devise of freedom and a legacy, and then the necessity of indemnification by the province law, and then a refusal to indemnify, and, of consequence, to set free and to pay the legacy?
>
> Perhaps the negro is free at common law by the devise. Now, the province law seems to have been made only to oblige the master to maintain his manumitted slave, and not to declare a manumission in the master's lifetime, or at his death, void. Should a master give his negro his freedom, under his hand and seal, without giving bond to the town, and should afterwards repent and endeavor to recall the negro into servitude, would not that instrument be a sufficient discharge against the master?"[371]

It is pleaded in extenuation of this Act, that it was passed to put a stop to the very prevalent habit of emancipating old and decrepit Negroes after there was no more service in them. If this be true, it reveals a practice more cruel than slavery itself.

In 1702 the representatives of the town of Boston were "desired to promote the encouraging the bringing of White servants and to put a period to Negroes being slaves."[372] This was not an anti-slavery measure, as some have wrongly supposed.[373] It was not a resolution or an Act: it was simply a request; and one that the "Representatives" did not grant for nearly a century afterwards.

"In 1718, a committee of both Houses prepared a bill entitled 'An Act for the Encouraging the Importation of White Male Servants, and the preventing the Clandestine bringing in of Negroes and Molattoes.'"

It was read in Council a first time on the 16th of June, and "sent down recommended" to the House; where it was also read a first time on the same day. The next day it was read a second time, and, "on the question for a third reading, decided in the negative."[374] In 1706 an argument or "Computation that the Importation of Negroes is not so profitable as that of White Servants," was published in Boston.[375] It throws a flood of light upon the Act mentioned above, and shows that the motives that inspired the people who wanted a period put to the holding of Negroes as slaves were grossly material and selfish. It was the first published article on the subject, and is worthy of reproduction in full. It is reprinted from "The Boston News-Letter," No. 112, June 10, 1706, in the New-York Historical Society.

"By last Year's Bill of Mortality for the Town of *Boston*, in *Number 100 News-Letter*, we are furnished with a List of 44 Negroes dead last year, which being computed one with another at 30*l*. per Head, amounts to the Sum of One Thousand three hundred and Twenty Pounds, of which we would make this Remark: That the Importing of Negroes into this or the Neighboring Provinces is not so beneficial either to the Crown or Country, as White Servants would be.

"For Negroes do not carry Arms to defend the Country as Whites do.

"Negroes are generally Eye-Servants, great Thieves, much addicted to Stealin And all things considered, it would conduce more to the g, Lying and Purloining.

"They do not People our Country as Whites would do whereby we should be strengthened against an Enemy.

"By Encouraging the Importing of White Men Servants, allowing somewhat to the Importer, most Husbandmen in the Country might be furnished with Servants for 8, 9, or 10*l*. a Head, who are not able to launch out 40 or 50*l*. for a Negro the now common Price.

"A Man then might buy a White Man Servant we suppose for 10*l*. to serve 4 years, and Boys for the same price to Serve 6, 8, or 10 years; If a White Servant die, the Loss exceeds not 10*l*. but if a Negro dies, 'tis a very great loss to the Husbandman; Three years Interest of the price of the Negro, will near upon if not altogether purchase a White Man Servant.

"If necessity call for it, that the Husbandman must fit out a Man against the Enemy; if he has a Negro he cannot send him, but if he has a White Servant, 'twill answer the end, and perhaps save his son at home.

"Were Merchants and Masters Encouraged as already said to bring in Men Servants, there needed not be such Complaint against Superiors Impressing our Children to the War, there would then be Men enough to be had without Impressing.

"The bringing in of such Servants would much enrich this Province, because Husbandmen would not only be able far better to manure what Lands are already under Improvement, but would also improve a great deal more that now lyes waste under Woods, and enable this Province to set about raising of Naval Stores, which would be greatly advantageous to the Crown of England, and this Province.

"For the raising of Hemp here, so as to make Sail-cloth and Cordage to furnish but our own shipping, would hinder the Importing it, and save a considerable sum in a year to make Returns for which we now do, and in time might be capacitated to furnish England not only with Sail-cloth and Cordage, but likewise with Pitch, Tar, Hemp, and other Stores which they are now obliged to purchase in Foreign Nations.

"Suppose the Government here should allow Forty Shillings per head for five years, to such as should Import every of these years 100 White Men Servants, and each to serve 4 years, the cost would be but 200*l*. a year, and a 1000*l*. for the 5 years. The first 100 Servants, being free the 4th year they serve the 5th for Wages, and the 6th there is 100 that goes out into the Woods, and settles a 100 Families to Strengthen and Baracado us from the Indians, and also a 100 Families more every year successively.

"And here you see that in one year the Town of Boston has lost 1320*l*. by 44 Negroes, which is also a loss to the Country in general, and for a less loss (if it may improperly be so called) for a 1000*l*. the Country may have 500 Men in 5 years time for the 44 Negroes dead in one year.

"A certain person within these 6 years had two Negroes dead computed both at 60*l*. which would have procured him six white Servants at 10*l*. per head to have Served 24 years, at 4 years apiece, without running such a great risque, and the Whites would have strengthened the Country, that Negroes do not.

"'Twould do well that none of those Servants be liable to be Impressed during their Service of Agreement at their first Landing.

"That such Servants being Sold or Transported out of this Province during the time of their Service, the Person that buys them be liable to pay 3*l*. into the Treasury."

Comment would be superfluous. It is only necessary for the reader to note that there is not a humane sentiment in the entire article.

But universal liberty was not without her votaries. All had not bowed the knee to Baal. The earliest friend of the Indian and the Negro was the scholarly, pious, and benevolent Samuel Sewall, at one time one of the judges of the Superior Court of Massachusetts, and afterwards the chief justice. He hated slavery with a righteous hatred, and early raised his voice and used his pen against it. He contributed the first article against slavery printed in the colony. It appeared as a tract, on the 24th of June, 1700, and was "Printed by Bartholomew Green and John Allen." It is withal the most remarkable document of its kind we ever saw. It is reproduced here to show the reader what a learned Christian judge thought of slavery one hundred and eighty-two years ago.

"THE SELLING OF JOSEPH A MEMORIAL.

"By the Hon'ble JUDGE SEWALL in New England.

"FORASMUCH *as* LIBERTY *is in real value next unto Life; None ought to part with it themselves, or deprive others of it, but upon most mature consideration.*

"The Numerousness of Slaves at this Day in the Province, and the Uneasiness of them under their Slavery, hath put many upon thinking whether the Foundation of it be firmly and well laid; so as to sustain the Vast Weight that is built upon it. It is most certain that all Men, as they are the Sons of Adam, are Co-heirs, and have equal Right unto Liberty, and all other outward Comforts of Life. GOD hath given the Earth [with all its commodities] unto the Sons of Adam, Psal., 115, 16. And hath made of one Blood all Nations of Men, for to dwell on all the face of the Earth, and hath determined the Times before appointed, and the bounds of their Habitation: That they should seek the Lord. Forasmuch then as we are the Offspring of GOD, &c. Acts, 17, 26, 27, 29. Now, although the Title given by the last ADAM doth infinitely better Men's Estates, respecting GOD and themselves; and grants them a most beneficial and inviolable Lease under the Broad Seal of Heaven, who were before only Tenants at Will; yet through the Indulgence of GOD to our First Parents after the Fall, the outward Estate of all and every of their Children, remains the same as to one another. So that Originally, and Naturally, there is no such thing as Slavery. Joseph was rightfully no more a slave to his Brethren, than they were to him; and they had no more Authority to Sell him, than they had to Slay him. And if they had nothing to do to sell him; the Ishmaelites bargaining with them, and paying down Twenty pieces of Silver, could not make a Title. Neither could Potiphar have any better Interest in him than the Ishmaelites had. Gen. 37, 20, 27, 28. For he that shall in this case plead Alteration of Property, seems to have forfeited a great part of his own claim to Humanity. There is no proportion between Twenty Pieces of Silver and LIBERTY. The Commodity itself is the Claimer. If Arabian Gold be imported in any quantities, most are afraid to meddle with it, though they might have it at easy rates; lest it should have been wrongfully taken from the Owners, it should kindle a fire to the Consumption of their whole Estate. 'Tis pity there should be more Caution used in buying a Horse, or a little lifeless dust, than there is in purchasing Men and Women: Whereas they are the Offspring of GOD, and their Liberty is,

... Auro pretiofior Omni.

"And seeing GOD hath said, *He that Stealeth a Man, and Selleth him, or if he be found in his Hand, he shall surely be put to Death.* Exod. 21, 16. This Law being of Everlasting Equity, wherein Man-Stealing is ranked among the most atrocious of Capital Crimes: What louder Cry can there be made of that Celebrated Warning

Caveat Emptor!

"And all things considered, it would conduce more to the Welfare of the Province, to have White Servants for a Term of Years, than to have Slaves for Life. Few can endure to hear of a Negro's being made free; and indeed they can seldom use their Freedom well; yet their continual aspiring after their forbidden Liberty, renders them Unwilling Servants. And there is such a disparity in their Conditions, Colour, and Hair, that they can never embody with us, & grow up in orderly Families, to the Peopling of the Land; but still remain in our Body Politick as a kind of extravasat Blood. As many Negro Men as there are among us, so many empty Places are there in our Train Bands, and the places taken up of Men that might make Husbands for our Daughters. And the Sons and Daughters of New England would become more like Jacob and Rachel, if this Slavery were thrust quite out of Doors. Moreover it is too well known what Temptations Masters are under, to connive at the Fornication of their Slaves; lest they should be obliged to find them Wives, or pay their Fines. It seems to be practically pleaded that they might be lawless; 'tis thought much of, that the Law should have satisfaction for their Thefts, and other Immoralities; by which means, Holiness to the Lord is more rarely engraven upon this sort of Servitude. It is likewise most lamentable to think, how in taking Negroes out of Africa, and selling of them here, That which GOD has joined together, Men do boldly rend asunder; Men from their Country, Husbands from their Wives, Parents from their Children. How horrible is the Uncleanness, Mortality, if not Murder, that the Ships are guilty of that bring great Crowds of these miserable Men and Women. Methinks when we are bemoaning the barbarous Usage of our Friends and Kinsfolk in Africa, it might not be unreasonable to enquire whether we are not culpable in forcing the Africans to become Slaves amongst ourselves. And it may be a question whether all the Benefit received by Negro Slaves will balance the Accompt of Cash laid out upon them; and for the Redemption of our own enslaved Friends out of Africa. Besides all the Persons and Estates that have perished there.

"Obj. 1. *These Blackamores are of the Posterity of Cham, and therefore are under the Curse of Slavery.* Gen. 9, 25, 26, 27.

"Ans. Of all Offices, one would not beg this; viz. Uncall'd for, to be an Executioner of the Vindictive Wrath of God; the extent and duration of which is to us uncertain. If this ever was a Commission; How do we know but that it is long since out of Date? Many have found it to their Cost, that a Prophetical Denunciation of Judgment against a Person or People, would not warrant them to inflict that evil. If it would, *Hazael* might justify himself in all he did against his master, and the *Israelites* from 2 *Kings* 8, 10, 12.

"But it is possible that by cursory reading, this Text may have been mistaken. For *Canaan* is the Person Cursed three times over, without the mentioning of *Cham*. Good Expositors suppose the Curse entailed on him, and that this Prophesie was accomplished in the Extirpation of the *Canaanites*, and in the Servitude of the *Gibeonites. Vide Pareum.* Whereas the Blackmores are not descended of *Canaan*, but of Cush. Psal. 68, 31. *Princes shall come out of Egypt* [Mizraim]. *Ethiopia* [Cush] *shall soon stretch out her hands unto God.* Under which Names, all *Africa* may be comprehended; and their Promised Conversion ought to be prayed for. *Jer.* 13, 23. *Can the Ethiopian change his Skin?* This shows that Black Men are the Posterity of *Cush*. Who time out of mind have been distinguished by their Colour. And for want of the true, *Ovid* assigns a fabulous cause of it.

> Sanguine tum credunt in corpora summa vocato
> Æthiopum populos nigrum traxisse colorem.   Metamorph. lib. 2.

"Obj. 2. *The* Nigers *are brought out of a Pagan Country, into places where the Gospel is preached.*

"Ans. Evil must not be done, that good may come of it. The extraordinary and comprehensive Benefit accruing to the Church of God, and to *Joseph* personally, did not rectify his Brethren's Sale of him.

"Obj. 3. *The Africans have Wars one with another: Our Ships bring lawful Captives taken in those wars.*

"Answ. For aught is known, their Wars are much such as were between *Jacob's* Sons and their Brother *Joseph*. If they be between Town and Town; Provincial or National: Every War is upon one side Unjust. An Unlawful War can't make lawful Captives. And by receiving, we are in danger to promote, and partake in their Barbarous Cruelties. I am sure, if some Gentlemen should go down to the *Brewsters* to take the Air, and Fish: And a stronger Party from *Hull* should surprise them, and sell them for Slaves to a Ship outward bound; they would think themselves unjustly dealt with; both by Sellers and Buyers. And yet 'tis to be feared, we have no other Kind of Title to our *Nigers. Therefore all things whatsoever ye would that men should do to you, do you even so to them: for this is the Law and the Prophets.* Matt. 7, 12.

"Obj. 4. Abraham *had Servants bought with his money and born in his House.*

"Ans. Until the Circumstances of *Abraham's* purchase be recorded, no Argument can be drawn from it. In the mean time, Charity obliges us to conclude, that He knew it was lawful and good.

"It is Observable that the *Israelites* were strictly forbidden the buying or selling one another for Slaves. *Levit.* 25. 39. 46. *Jer.* 34, 8-22. And God gaged His Blessing in lieu of any loss they might conceit they suffered thereby, *Deut.* 15. 18. And since the partition Wall is broken down, inordinate Self-love should likewise be demolished. God expects that Christians should be of a more Ingenuous and benign frame of Spirit. Christians should carry it to all the World, as the *Israelites* were to carry it one towards another. And for Men obstinately to persist in holding their Neighbours and Brethren under the Rigor of perpetual Bondage, seems to be no proper way of gaining Assurance that God has given them Spiritual Freedom. Our Blessed Saviour has altered the Measures of the ancient Love Song, and set it to a most Excellent New Tune, which all ought to be ambitious of Learning. Matt. 5. 43. 44. John 13. 34. These *Ethiopians*, as black as they are, seeing they are the Sons and Daughters of the First *Adam*, the Brethren and Sisters of the Last Adam, and the Offspring of God; They ought to be treated with a Respect agreeable.

"*Servitus perfecta voluntaria, inter Christianum & Christianum, ex parte servi patientis saepe est licita, quia est necessaria; sed ex parte domini agentis, & procurando & exercendo, vix potest esse licita; quia non convenit regulæ illi generali; Quaecunque volueritis ut faciant vobis homines, ita & vos facite eis. Matt. 7, 12.*

"*Perfecta servitus paenae, non potest jure locum habere, nisi ex delicto gravi quod ultimum supplicium aliquo modo meretur: quia Libertas ex naturali æstimatione proxime accedit ad vitam ipsam, & eidem a multis præferri solet.*

"Ames. Cas. Confc. Lib. 5. Cap. 23. Thes. 2. 3."

Judge Sewall's attack on slavery created no little stir in Boston; and the next year, 1701, Judge John Saffin, an associate of Judge Sewall, answered it in quite a lengthy paper.[376] Having furnished Judge Sewall's paper, it is proper that Judge Saffin's reply should likewise have a place here.

"JUDGE SAFFIN'S REPLY TO JUDGE SEWALL, 1701.

"A Brief and Candid Answer to a late Printed Sheet, *Entituled*, The Selling of Joseph.

"THAT Honourable and Learned Gentleman, the Author of a Sheet, Entituled, *The Selling of Joseph, A* Memorial, seems from thence to draw this conclusion, that because the Sons of *Jacob* did very ill in selling their Brother *Joseph* to the *Ishmaelites*, who were Heathens, therefore it is utterly unlawful to Buy and Sell Negroes, though among Christians; which Conclusion I presume is not well drawn from the Premises, nor is the case parallel; for it was unlawful for the *Israelites* to Sell their Brethren upon any account, or pretence whatsoever during life. But it was not unlawful for the Seed of *Abraham* to have Bond men, and Bond women either born in their House, or bought with their Money, as it is written of *Abraham, Gen.* 14. 14. & 21. 10. & *Exod.* 21. 16. & *Levit.* 25. 44. 45. 46 v. After the giving of the law: And in *Josh.* 9. 23. That famous Example of the *Gibeonites* is a sufficient proof where there no other.

"To speak a little to the Gentlemans first Assertion: That none ought to part with their Liberty themselves, or deprive others of it but upon mature consideration; a prudent exception, in which he grants, that upon some consideration a man may be deprived of his Liberty. And then presently in his next Position or Assertion he denies it, viz.: It is most certain, that all men as they are the Sons of Adam are Coheirs, and have equal right to Liberty, and all other Comforts of Life, which he would prove out of Psal. 115. 16. The Earth hath he given to the Children of Men. True, but what is all this to the purpose, to prove that all men have equal right to Liberty, and all outward comforts of this life; which Position seems to invert the Order that God hath set in the World, who hath Ordained different degrees and orders of men, some to be High and Honourable, some to be Low and Despicable; some to be Monarchs, Kings, Princes and Governours, Masters and Commanders, others to be Subjects, and to be Commanded; Servants of sundry sorts and degrees, bound to obey; yea, some to be born Slaves, and so to remain during their lives, as hath been proved. Otherwise there would be a meer parity among men, contrary to that of the Apostle, I. Cor. 12 from the 13 to the 26 verse, where he sets forth (by way of comparison) the different sorts and offices of the Members of the Body, indigitating that they are all of use, but not equal, and of Like dignity. So God hath set different Orders and Degrees of Men in the World, both in Church and Common weal. Now, if this Position of parity should be true, it would then follow that the ordinary Course of Divine Providence of God in the World should be wrong, and unjust, (which we must not dare to think, much less to affirm) and all the sacred Rules, Precepts and Commands of the Almighty which he hath given the Sons of Men to observe and keep in their respective Places, Orders and Degrees, would be to no purpose; which unaccountably derogate from the Divine Wisdom of the most High, who hath made nothing in vain, but hath Holy Ends in all his Dispensations to the Children of men.

"In the next place, this worthy Gentleman makes a large Discourse concerning the Utility and Conveniency to keep the one, and inconveniency of the other; respecting white and black Servants, which conduceth most to the welfare and benefit of this Province: which he concludes to be white men, who are in many respects to be preferred before Blacks; who doubts that? doth it therefore follow, that it is altogether unlawful for Christians to buy and keep Negro Servants (for this is the thesis) but that those that have them ought in Conscience to set them free, and so lose all the money they cost (for we must not live in any known sin) this seems to be his opinion; but it is a Question whether it ever was the Gentleman's practice? But if he could perswade the General Assembly to make an Act, That all that have Negroes, and do set them free, shall be Reimbursed out of the Publick Treasury, and that there shall be no more Negroes brought into the country; 'tis probable there would be more of his opinion; yet he would find it a hard task to bring the Country to consent thereto; for then the Negroes must be all sent out of the Country, or else the remedy would be worse than the disease; and it is to be feared that those Negroes that are free, if there be not some strict course taken with them by Authority, they will be a plague to this Country.

"*Again*, If it should be unlawful to deprive them that are lawful Captives, or Bondmen of their Liberty for Life being Heathens; it seems to be more unlawful to deprive our Brethren, of our own or other Christian Nations of the Liberty, (though but for a time) by binding them to Serve some Seven, Ten, Fifteen, and some Twenty Years, which oft times proves for their whole Life, as many have been; which in effect is the same in Nature, though different in the time, yet this was allow'd among the *Jews* by the Law of God; and is the constant practice of our own and other Christian Nations in the World: the which our Author by his Dogmatical Assertions doth condem as Irreligious; which is Diametrically contrary to the Rules and Precepts which God hath given the diversity of men to observe in their respective Stations, Callings, and Conditions of Life, as hath been observed.

"And to illustrate his Assertion our Author brings in by way of Comparison the Law of God against man Stealing, on pain of Death: Intimating thereby, that Buying and Selling of Negro's is a breach of that Law, and so deserves Death: A severe Sentence: But herein he begs the Question with a *Caveat Emptor*. For, in that very Chapter there is a Dispensation to the People of *Israel*, to have Bond men, Women and Children, even of their own Nation in some case; and Rules given therein to be observed concerning them; Verse the 4*th*. And in the before cited place, *Levit* 25. 44, 45, 46. Though the *Israelites* were forbidden (ordinarily) to make Bond men and Women of their own Nation, but of Strangers they might: the words run thus, verse 44. *Both thy Bond men, and thy Bond maids which thou shall have shall be of the Heathen, that are round about you: of them shall you Buy Bond men and Bond* *maids, &c.* See also, I *Cor.* 12, 13. Whether we be Bond or Free, which shows that in the times of the New Testament, there were Bond men also, &c.

> "In fine, The sum of this long Haurange, is no other, than to compare the Buying and Selling of Negro's unto the Stealing of Men, and the Selling of Joseph by his Brethren, which bears no proportion therewith, nor is there any congruiety therein, as appears by the foregoing Texts.

"Our Author doth further proceed to answer some Objections of his own framing, which he supposes some might raise.

"Object. 1. *That these Blackamores are of the Posterity of* Cham, *and therefore under the Curse of Slavery. Gen.* 9. 25, 26, 27. The which the Gentleman seems to deny, saying, *they ware the Seed of Canaan that were Cursed, &c.*

"*Answ.* Whether they were so or not, we shall not dispute: this may suffice, that not only the seed of *Cham* or *Canaan*, but any lawful Captives of other Heathen Nations may be made Bond men as hath been proved.

"Obj. 2. *That the Negroes are brought out of Pagan Countreys into places where the Gospel is preached.* To which he Replies, *that we must not doe Evil that Good may come of it.*

"*Ans.* To which we answer, That it is no Evil thing to bring them out of their own Heathenish Country, where they may have the knowledge of the True God, be Converted and Eternally saved.

"Obj. 3. *The* Africans *have Wars one with another*; our Ships bring lawful Captives taken in those Wars.

"To which our Author answers Conjecturally, and Doubtfully, *for aught we know*, that which may or may not be; which is insignificant, and proves nothing. He also compares the Negroes Wars, one Nation with another, with the Wars between *Joseph* and his Brethren. But where doth he read of any such War? We read indeed of a Domestick Quarrel they had with him, they envyed and hated *Joseph*; but by what is Recorded, he was meerly passive and meek as a Lamb. This Gentleman farther adds, *That there is not any War but is unjust on one side, &c.* Be it so, what doth that signify: We read of lawful Captives taken in the Wars, and lawful to be Bought and Sold without contracting the guilt of the *Agressors*; for which we have the example of *Abraham* before quoted; but if we must stay while both parties Warring are in the right, there would be no lawful Captives at all to be Bought; which seems to be rediculous to imagine, and contrary to the tenour of Scripture, and all Humane Histories on that subject.

"Obj. 4. *Abraham had Servants bought with his Money, and born in his House.* Gen. 14. 14. To which our worthy Author answers, *until the Circumstances of Abraham's purchase be recorded, no Argument can be drawn from it.*

"*Ans.* To which we Reply, this is also Dogmatical, and proves nothing. He farther adds, *In the mean time Charity Obliges us to conclude, that he knew it was lawful and good.* Here the gentleman yields the case; for if we are in Charity bound to believe *Abrahams* practice, in buying and keeping *Slaves* in his house to be lawful and good: then it follows, that our Imitation of him in this his Moral Action, is as warrantable as that of his Faith; *who is the Father of all them that believe.* Rom. 4. 16.

"In the close all, Our Author Quotes two more places of Scripture, viz., Levit. 25. 46, and Jer. 34. from the 8. to the 22. v. To prove that the people of Israel were strictly forbidden the Buying and Selling one another for Slaves: who questions that? and what is that to the case in hand? What a strange piece of Logick is this? 'Tis unlawful for Christians to Buy and Sell one another for slaves. Ergo, It is unlawful to Buy and Sell Negroes that are lawful Captiv'd Heathens.

"And after a Serious Exhortation to us all to Love one another according to the Command of Christ *Math.* 5, 43, 44. This worthy Gentleman concludes with this Assertion, *That these Ethiopians as Black as they are, seeing they are the Sons and Daughters of the first* Adam; *the Brethren and Sisters of the Second* Adam, *and the Offspring of God; we ought to treat them with a respect agreeable.*

"*Ans.* We grant it for a certain and undeniable verity, That all Mankind are the Sons and Daughters of *Adam*, and the Creatures of God: But it doth not therefore follow that we are bound to love and respect all men alike; this under favour we must take leave to deny, we ought in charity, if we see our Neighbour in want, to relieve them in a regular way, but we are not bound to give them so much of our Estates, as to make them equal with ourselves, because they are our Brethren, the Sons of *Adam*, no, not our own natural Kinsmen: We are Exhorted *to do good unto all, but especially to them who are of the Household of Faith,* Gal. 6. 10. And we are to love, honour and respect all men according to the gift of God that is in them. I may love my Servant well, but my Son better; Charity begins at home, it would be a violation of common prudence, and a breach of good manners, to treat a Prince like a Peasant. And this worthy Gentleman would deem himself much neglected, if we should show him no more Defference than to an ordinary Porter: And therefore these florid expressions, the Sons and Daughters of the First *Adam*, the Brethren and Sisters of the Second *Adam*, and the Offspring of God, seem to be misapplied to import and insinuate, that we ought to tender Pagan Negroes with all love, kindness, and equal respect as to the best of men.

"By all which it doth evidently appear both by Scripture and Reason, the practice of the People of God in all Ages, both before and after the giving of the Law, and in the times of the Gospel, that there were Bond men, Women and Children commonly kept by holy and good men, and improved in Service; and therefore by the Command of God, *Lev. 25, 44*, and their venerable Example, we may keep Bond men, and use them in our Service still; yet with all candour, moderation and Christian prudence, according to their state and condition consonant to the Word of God."

Judge Sewall had dealt slavery a severe blow, and opened up an agitation on the subject that was felt during the entire Revolutionary struggle. He became the great apostle of liberty, the father of the anti-slavery movement in the colony. He was the bold and stern John the Baptist of that period, "the voice of one crying in the wilderness" of bondage, to prepare the way for freedom.

The Quakers, or Friends as they were called, were perhaps the earliest friends of the slaves, but, like Joseph of Arimathæa, were "secretly" so, for fear of the "Puritans." But they early recorded their disapprobation of slavery as follows:—

26TH DAY OF YE 9TH MO. 1716.

> "An epistle from the last Quarterly Meeting was read in this, and ye matter referred to this meeting, viz., whether it is agreeable to truth for friends to purchase slaves and keep them term of liffe, was considered, and ye sense and judgment of this meeting is, that it is not agreeable to truth for friends to purchase slaves and hold them term of liffe.
>
> "Nathaniel Starbuck, junr is to draw out this meeting's judgment concerning friends not buying slaves and keeping them term of liffe, and send it to the next Quarterly Meeting, and to sign it in ye meeting's behalf."[377]

Considering the prejudice and persecution that pursued this good people, their testimony against slavery is very remarkable. In 1729-30 Elihu Coleman of Nantucket, a minister of the society of Friends, wrote a book against slavery, published in 1733, entitled, "A Testimony against that Anti-Christian Practice of making Slaves of men.[378] It was well written, and the truth fearlessly told for the conservative, self-seeking period he lived in. He says,—

"I am not unthoughtful of the ferment or stir that such discourse as this may make among some, who (like Demetrius of old) may say, by this craft we have our wealth, which caused the people to cry out with one voice, great is Diana of the Ephesians, whom all Asia and the world worship."

He examined and refuted the arguments put forth in defence of slavery, charged slaveholders with idleness, and contended that slavery was the mother of vice, at war with the laws of nature and of God. Others caught the spirit of reform, and the agitation movement gained recruits and strength every year. Felt says, "1765. Pamphlets and newspapers discuss the subjects of slavery with increasing zeal." The colonists were aroused. Men were taking one side or the other of a question of great magnitude. In 1767 an anonymous tract of twenty octavo pages against slavery made its appearance in Boston. It was written by Nathaniel Appleton, a co-worker with Otis, and an advanced thinker on the subject of emancipation. It was in the form of a letter addressed to a friend, and was entitled, "Considerations on Slavery." The Rev. Samuel Webster Salisbury published on the 2d of March, 1769, "An Earnest Address to my Country on Slavery." He opened his article with an argument showing the inconsistency of a Christian people holding slaves, pictured the evil results of slavery, and then asked,—

> "What then is to be done? Done! for God's sake break every yoke and let these oppressed ones go free without delay— let them taste the sweets of that liberty, which we so highly prize, and are so earnestly supplicating God and man to grant us: nay, which we claim as the natural right of every man. Let me beseech my countrymen to put on bowels of compassion for these their brethren (for so I must call them,) yea, let me beseech you for your own sake and for God's sake, to break every yoke and let the oppressed go free."[379]

Begun among the members of the bar and the pulpit, the common folk at length felt a lively interest in the subject of emancipation. An occasional burst of homely, vigorous eloquence from the pulpit on the duties of the hour inflamed the conscience of the pew with a noble zeal for a righteous cause. The afflatus of liberty sat upon the people as cloven tongues. Every village, town, and city had its orators whose only theme was emancipation. "The pulpit and the press were not silent, and sermons and essays in behalf of the enslaved Africans were continually making their appearance." The public conscience was being rapidly educated, and from the hills of Berkshire to the waters of Massachusetts Bay the fires of liberty were burning.

FOOTNOTES:

[260] George H. Moore, LL.D., for many years librarian of the New-York Historical Society, but at present the efficient superintendent of the Lenox Library, in his "Notes on the History of Slavery in Massachusetts," has summoned nearly all the orators and historians of Massachusetts to the bar of history. He leaves them open to one of three charges, viz., evading the truth, ignorance of it, or falsifying the record. And in addition to this work, which is authority, his "Additional Notes" glow with an energy and perspicuity of style which lead me to conclude that Dr. Moore works admirably under the spur, and that his refined sarcasm, unanswerable logic, and critical accuracy give him undisputed place amongst the ablest writers of our times.

[261] Wood's New-England Prospect, 1634, p. 77.

[262] Slavery in Mass., p. 7.

[263] Ibid., pp. 4, 5, and 6.

[264] Elliott's New-England Hist., pp. 167-205.

[265] Winthrop's Journal, Feb. 26, 1638, vol. i. p. 254; see, also, Felt, vol. ii. p. 230.

[266] Dr. Moore backs his statement as to the time The Desire was built by quoting from Winthrop, vol. i. p. 193. But there is a mistake somewhere as to the correct date. Winthrop says she was built in 1636; but I find in Mr. Drake's "Founders of New England," pp. 31, 32, this entry: "More (June) XXth, 1635. In the Desire de Lond. Pearce, and bond for New Eng. p'r cert, fro ij Justices of Peace and ministers of All Saints lionian in Northampton." If she sailed in 1635, she must have been built earlier.

[267] Dr. George H. Moore says Josselyn's Voyages were printed in 1664. This is an error. They were not published until ten years later, in 1674. In 1833 the Massachusetts Historical Society printed the work in the third volume and third series of their collection.

[268] Josselyn, p. 28.

[269] Ibid., p. 250.

[270] Ibid., p. 258.

[271] Slavery in Mass., p. 9.

[272] Mass. Hist Coll., vol. iv. 4th Series, p. 333, sq.

[273] Mr. Bancroft (Centenary Edition, vol. i. p. 137) says, "The earliest importation of Negro slaves into New England was made in 1637, from Providence Isle, in the Salem ship Desire." But Winthrop (vol. i. p. 254, under date of the 26th of February, 1638) says, "The Desire returned from

the West Indies after seven months." He also states (ibid., p. 193) that The Desire was "built at Marblehead in 1636." But this may or may not be true according to the old method of keeping time.

[274] Palfrey's Hist. of N.E., vol. ii. p. 30, note.

[275] Josselyn, p. 257.

[276] Elliott's New-England Hist., vol. ii. pp. 57, 58.

[277] Hildreth, vol. i, p. 270, sq.

[278] Ancient Charters and Laws of Mass., pp. 52, 23.

[279] Slavery in Mass., p. 13, note.

[280] Slavery in Mass., pp. 18, 19.

[281] Ibid., p. 12.

[282] Elliott's New-England Hist., vol. i. p. 383.

[283] Hildreth, vol. i. p. 278.

[284] Mass. Hist. Coll., vol. iv. 4th Series, p. 334.

[285] Quoted by Dr. Moore, p. 20.

[286] Commonwealth vs. Aves, 18 Pickering, p. 208.

[287] Andover vs. Canton, Mass. Reports, 551, 552, quoted by Dr. Moore.

[288] Kendall's Travels, vol. ii. p. 179.

[289] The following note, if it refers to the kidnapped Negroes, gives an earlier date,—"29th May, 1644. Mr. Blackleach his petition about the Mores was consented to, to be committed to the eldrs, to enforme us of the mind of God herein, & then further to consider it."—Mass. Records, vol. ii. p. 67.

[290] Bancroft, Centennial edition, vol. i. p. 137.

[291] Hildreth, vol. i. p. 282.

[292] The petition is rather a remarkable paper, and is printed below. It is evident that the judge was in earnest. And yet the court, while admitting the petition, tried the case on only one ground, man-stealing.

To the honored general court. The oath I took this yeare att my enterance upon the place of assistante was to this effect: That I would truly endeavour the advancement of the gospell and the good of the people of this plantation (to the best of my skill) dispencing justice equally and impartially (according to the laws of God and this land) in all cases wherein I act by virtue of my place. I conceive myself called by virtue of my place to act (according to this oath) in the case concerning the negers taken by captain Smith and Mr. Keser;

wherein it is apparent that Mr. Keser gave chace to certaine negers; and upon the same day tooke divers of them; and at another time killed others; and burned one of their townes. Omitting several misdemeanours, which accompanied these acts above mentioned, I conceive the acts themselves to bee directly contrary to these following laws (all of which are capitall by the word of God; and two of them by the lawes of this jurisdiction).

The act (or acts) of murder (whether by force or fraude) are expressly contrary both to the law of God, and the law of this country.

The act of stealing negers, or taking them by force (Whether it be considered as theft or robbery) is (as I conceive) expressly contrary, both to the law of God, and the law of this country.

The act of chaceing the negers (as aforesayde) upon the sabbath day (being a servile worke and such as cannot be considered under any other heade) is expressly capitall by the law of God.

These acts and outrages being committed where there was noe civill government, which might call them to accompt, and the persons, by whom they were committed beeing of our jurisdiction, I conceive this court to bee the ministers of God in this case, and therefore my humble request is that the severall offenders may be imprisoned by the order of this court, and brought into their deserved censure in convenient time; and this I humbly crave that soe the sinn they have committed may be upon their own heads, and not upon ourselves (as otherwise it will.)

Yrs in all christean observance,

Richard Saltonstall.

The house of deputs thinke meete that this petition shall be granted, and desire our honored magistrats concurrence herein.

Edward Rawson.

—COFFIN'S *NEWBURY*, PP. 335, 336.

[293] Laws Camb., 1675, p. 15.

[294] Hildreth, vol. i. p. 368.

[295] Coffin, p. 335.

[296] Drake (p. 288) says, "This act, however, was afterwards repealed or disregarded."

[297] Mass. Records, vol ii. p 129.

[298] Moore, Appendix, 251, sq.

[299] Slavery in Mass., p. 30.

[300] Hildreth, vol. i. p, 282.

[301] Slavery in Mass., p. 49. See, also, Drake's Boston, p. 441, note.

[302] Mass. Hist. Coll., vol. viii. 3d Series, p. 337.

[303] Slavery in Mass., p. 50.

[304] Coll. Amer. Stat. Asso., vol. i. p. 586.

[305] Douglass's British Settlements, vol. i. p. 531.

[306] Drake, p. 714. I cannot understand how Dr. Moore gets 1,514 slaves in Boston in 1742, except from Douglass. His "1742" should read 1752, and his "1,514" slaves should read 1,541 slaves.

[307] "There is a curious illustration of 'the way of putting it' in Massachusetts, in Mr. Felt's account of this 'census of slaves,' in the Collections of the American Statistical Association, vol. i. p, 208. He says that the General Court passed this order 'for the purpose of having an accurate account of slaves in our Commonwealth, as a subject in which the people were becoming much interested, relative to the cause of liberty!" There is not a particle of authority for this suggestion—such a motive for their action never existed anywhere but in the imagination of the writer himself!"—Slavery in Mass., p. 51, note.

[308] Ancient Charters and Laws of Mass., p. 748.

[309] Ibid.

[310] Slavery in Mass., p. 61.

[311] Hildreth, vol. ii. pp. 269, 270.

[312] Drake's Boston, p. 574.

[313] Spectator, No. 215, Nov. 6, 1711.

[314] Slavery in Mass., p. 64.

[315] "In the inventory of the estate of Samuel Morgaridge, who died in 1754, I find,

'Item, three negroes   £133, 6s., 8d.

Item, flax   £12, 2s., 8.'

"In the inventory of Henry Rolfe's estate, taken in April, 1711, I find the following, namely,

'Fifteen sheep, old and young £3, 15.

An old gun	2
An old Negroe man	10 0

£13 7s.'"

--Coffin, p. 188.

[316] Slavery in Mass., pp. 64, 65.

[317] Drake, 583, note.

[318] Here is a sample of the sales of those days: "In 1716, Rice Edwards, of Newbury, shipwright, sells to Edmund Greenleaf 'my whole personal estate with all my goods and chattels as also one negro man, one cow, three pigs with timber, plank, and boards." —Coffin, p. 337.

[319] New-England Weekly Journal, No. 267, May 1, 1732.

[320] A child one year and a half old—a nursing child sold from the bosom of its mother!—and for life!—Coffin, p. 337.

[321] Slavery in Mass., p. 96. Note.

[322] Eight years after this, on the 22d of June, 1735, Mr. Plant records in his diary: "I wrote Mr. Salmon of Barbadoes to send me a Negro." (Coffin, p. 338.) It doesn't appear that the reverend gentleman was opposed to slavery!

[323] Note quoted by Dr. Moore, p. 58.

[324] Hildreth, vol. i. p. 44.

[325] "For they tell the Negroes, that they must believe in Christ, and receive the Christian faith, and that they must receive the sacrament, and be baptized, and so they do; but still they keep them slaves for all this."—MACY'S Hist. of Nantucket, pp. 280, 281.

[326] Ancient Charters and Laws of Mass., p. 117.

[327] Mr. Palfrey relies upon a single reference in Winthrop for the historical trustworthiness of his statement that a Negro slave could be a member of the church. He thinks, however, that this "presents a curious question," and wisely reasons as follows: "As a church-member, he was eligible to the political franchise, and, if he should be actually invested with it, he would have a part in making laws to govern his master,—laws with which his master, if a non-communicant, would have had no concern except to obey them. But it is improbable that the Court would have made a slave—while a slave—a member of the Company, though he were a communicant.—Palfrey, vol. ii. p. 30. Note.

[328] Butts vs. Penny, 2 Lev., p. 201; 3 Kib., p. 785.

[329] Hildreth, vol. ii. p. 426.

[330] Ancient Charters and Laws of Mass., p. 748.

[331] Palfrey, vol. ii. p. 30. Note.

[332] Hist. Mag., vol. v., 2d Series, by Dr. G.H. Moore.

[333] Slavery in Mass., p. 57, note.

[334] I use the term freeman, because the colony being under the English crown, there were no citizens. All were British subjects.

[335] Ancient Charters and Laws of Mass., p. 746.

[336] Ibid., p. 386.

[337] Mr. Palfrey is disposed to hang a very weighty matter on a very slender thread of authority. He says, "In the list of men capable of bearing arms, at Plymouth, in 1643, occurs the name of 'Abraham Pearse, the Blackmoore,' from which we infer ... that Negroes were not dispensed from military service in that colony" (History of New England, vol. ii. p. 30, note). This single case is borne down by the laws and usages of the colonists on this subject. Negroes as a class were absolutely excluded from the military service, from the commencement of the colony down to the war with Great Britain.

[338] Slavery in Mass., Appendix, p. 243.

[339] Mass. Hist. Soc. Coll., vol. viii. 3d Series, p. 336.

[340] Lyman's Report, 1822.

[341] Mather's Magnalia, Book III., p. 207. Compare also p. 209.

[342] Elliott's New-England Hist., vol. ii. p. 165.

[343] Mr. Palfrey comes again with his single and exceptional case, asking us to infer a rule therefrom. See History of New England, note, p. 30.

[344] Chief-Justice Parker, in Andover vs. Canton, 13 Mass. p. 550.

[345] Slavery in Mass., p. 62.

[346] Mott's Sketches, p. 17.

[347] At the early age of sixteen, in the year 1770, Phillis was baptized into the membership of the society worshipping in the "Old South Meeting-House." The gifted, eloquent, and noble Dr. Sewall was the pastor. This was an exception to the rule, that slaves were not baptized into the Church.

[348] All writers I have seen on this subject—and I think I have seen all—leave the impression that Miss Wheatley's poems were first published in London. This is not true. The first published poems from her pen were issued in Boston in 1770. But it was a mere pamphlet edition, and has long since perished.

[349] All the historians but Sparks omit the given name of Peters. It was John.

[350] The date usually given for her death is 1780, while her age is fixed at twenty-six. The best authority gives the dates above, and I think they are correct.

[351] "Her correspondence was sought, and it extended to persons of distinction even in England, among whom may be named the Countess of Huntingdon, Whitefield, and the Earl of Dartmouth."—Sparks's Washington, vol. iii. p. 298, note.

[352] Sparks's Washington, vol iii. p. 299, note.

[353] This destroys the last hope I have nursed for nearly six years that the poem might yet come to light. Somehow I had overlooked this note.

[354] Sparks's Washington, vol iii. p. 288.

[355] Ibid., vol. iii. pp. 297, 298.

[356] Armistead's A Tribute to the Negro, pp. 460, 461.

[357] Douglass, vol. ii. p. 345, note.

[358] Hildreth, vol. ii. p. 426.

[359] Pearce vs. Lisle, Ambler, 76.

[360] It may sound strangely in the ears of some friends and admirers of the gifted John Adams to hear now, after the lapse of many years, what he had to say of the position Otis took. His mild views on slavery were as deserving of scrutiny as those of the elder Quincy. Mr. Adams says: "Nor were the poor negroes forgotten. Not a Quaker in Philadelphia, or Mr. Jefferson, of Virginia, ever asserted the rights of negroes in stronger terms. Young as I was, and ignorant as I was, I shuddered at the doctrine he taught; and I have all my lifetime shuddered, and still shudder, at the consequences that may be drawn from such premises. Shall we say, that the rights of masters and servants clash, and can be decided only by force? I adore the idea of gradual abolitions! But who shall decide how fast or how slowly these abolitions shall be made?"

[361] Hildreth, vol. ii. pp. 564, 565.

[362] Coffin says, "In October of 1773, an action was brought against Richard Greenleaf, of Newburyport, by Cæsar [Hendrick], a colored man, whom he claimed as his slave, for holding him in bondage. He laid the damages at fifty pounds. The council for the plaintiff, in whose favor the jury brought in their verdict and awarded him eighteen pounds' damages and costs, was John Lowell, Esq., afterward Judge Lowell. This case excited much interest, as it was the first, if not the only one of the kind, that ever occurred in the county."

[363] Hildreth, vol. ii, pp. 550, 551.

[364] Drake, p. 729, note.

[365] I use the English spelling,—Sommersett.

[366] Hildreth, vol. ii. p. 567.

[367] Bancroft, 12th ed. vol. iii. p. 412.

[368] Ancient Charters and Laws of Mass., pp. 745, 746.

[369] The following is from Felt's Salem, vol. ii. pp. 415, 416, and illustrates the manner in which the law was complied with: "1713. Ann, relict of Governor Bradstreet, frees Hannah, a negro servant. 1717, Dec. 21. William and Samuel Upton, of this town, liberate Thomas, who has faithfully served their father, John Upton, of Reading. They give security to the treasurer, that they will meet all charges, which may accrue against the said black man. 1721, May 27. Elizur Keyser does the same for his servant, Cato, after four years more, and then the latter was to receive two suits of clothes.... 1758, June 5. The heirs of John Turner, having freed two servants, Titus and Rebeckah, give bonds to the selectmen, that they shall be no public charge."

[370] John Adams's Works, vol. i. p. 51.

[371] Adams's Works, vol. i. p. 55.

[372] Drake, p. 525.

[373] The late Senator Sumner, in a speech delivered on the 28th of June, 1854, refers to this as "the earliest testimony from any official body against negro slavery." Even the weight of the senator's assertion cannot resist the facts of history. The "resolve" instructing the "representatives" was never carried; but, on the contrary, the next Act was the law of 1703 restricting manumission!

[374] Journal H. of R., 15, 16. General Court Records, x. 282.

[375] Slavery in Mass., p. 106.

[376] It was thought to be lost for some years, until Dr. George H. Moore secured a copy from George Brinley, Esq., of Hartford, Conn., and reproduced it in his Notes.

[377] History of Nantucket, p. 281.

[378] Coffin, p. 338; also History of Nantucket, pp. 279, 280.

[379] Coffin, p. 338.

CHAPTER XV
THE COLONY OF MASSACHUSETTS,— CONTINUED

1633-1775.

The Era of Prohibitory Legislation against Slavery.—Boston instructs her Representatives to vote against the Slave-Trade.—Proclamation issued by Gov. Dummer against the Negroes, April 13, 1723.—Persecution of the Negroes.—"Suing for Liberty."—Letter of Samuel Adams to John Pickering, jun., on Behalf of Negro Memorialists.—A Bill for the Suppression of the Slave-Trade passes.—Is vetoed by Gov. Gage, and fails to become a Law.

THE time to urge legislation on the slavery question had come. Cultivated at the first as a private enterprise, then fostered as a patriarchal institution, slavery had grown to such gigantic proportions as to be regarded as an unwieldy evil, and subversive of the political stability of the colony. Men winked at the "day of its small things," and it grew. Little legislation was required to regulate it, and it began to take root in the social and political life of the people. The necessities for legislation in favor of slavery increased. Every year witnessed the enactment of laws more severe, until they appeared as scars upon the body of the laws of the colony. To erase these scars was the duty of the hour.

It was now 1755. More than a half-century of agitation and discussion had prepared the people for definite action. Manumission and petition were the first methods against slavery. On the 10th of March, 1755, the town of Salem instructed their representative, Timothy Pickering, to petition the General Court against the importation of slaves.[380] The town of Worcester, in June, 1765, instructed their representative to "use his influence to obtain a law to put an end to that unchristian and impolitic practice of making slaves of the human species, and that he give his vote for none to serve in His Majesty's Council, who will use their influence against such a law."[381] The people of Boston, in the month of May, 1766, instructed their representatives as follows:—

"And for the total abolishing of slavery among us, that you move for a law to prohibit the importation and the purchasing of slaves for the future."[382]

And in the following year, 1767, on the 16th of March, the question was put as to whether the town should adhere to its previous instructions in favor of the suppression of the slave-trade, and passed in the affirmative. Nearly all the towns, especially those along the coast, those accessible by mails and newspapers, had recorded their vote, in some shape or other, against slavery. The pressure for legislation on the subject was great. The country members of the Legislature were almost a unit in favor of the passage of a bill prohibiting the further importation of slaves. The opposition came from the larger towns, but the opposers were awed by the determined bearing of the enemies of the slave-trade. The scholarship, wealth, and piety of the colony were steadily ranging to the side of humanity.

On the 13th of March, 1767, a bill was introduced in the House of Representatives "to prevent the unwarrantable and unlawful Practice or Custom of inslaving Mankind in this Province, and the importation of slaves into the same."[383] It was read the first time, when a dilatory motion was offered that the bill lie over to the next session, which was decided in the negative. An amendment was offered to the bill, limiting it "to a certain time," which was carried; and the bill made a special order for a second reading on the following day. It was accordingly read on the 14th, when a motion was made to defer it for a third reading to the next "May session." The friends of the bill voted down this dilatory motion, and had the bill made the special order of the following Monday,—it now being Saturday. On Sunday there must have been considerable lobbying done, as can be seen by the vote taken on Monday. After it was read, and the debate was concluded, it was "Ordered that the Matter subside, and that Capt. Sheaffe, Col. Richmond, and Col. Bourne, be a Committee to bring in a Bill for laying a Duty of Impost on slaves importing into this Province."[384] This was a compromise, that, as will be seen subsequently, impaired the chances of positive and wholesome legislation against slavery. The original bill dealt a double blow: it struck at the slave-trade in the Province, and levelled the institution already in existence. But some secret influences were set in operation, that are forever hidden from the searching eye of history; and the friends of liberty were bullied or cheated. There was no need of a bill imposing an impost tax on slaves imported, for such a law had been in existence for more than a half-century. If the tax were not heavy enough, it could have been increased by an amendment of a dozen lines. On the 17th the substitute was brought in by the special committee appointed by the Speaker the previous day. The rules requiring bills to be read on three several days were suspended, the bill ordered to a first and second reading, and then made the special order for eleven o'clock on the next day, Wednesday, the 18th. The motion to lie on the table until the "next May" was defeated. An amendment was then offered to limit the life of the bill to one year, which was carried, and the bill recommitted. On the afternoon of the same day it was read a third time, and placed on its passage with the amendment. It passed, was ordered engrossed, and was "sent up by Col. Bowers, Col. Gerrish, Col. Leonard, Capt. Thayer, and Col. Richmond." On the 19th of March it was read a first time in the council. On the 20th it was read a second time, and passed to be engrossed "as taken into a new draft." When it reached the House for concurrence, in the afternoon of the same day, it was "Read and unanimously non-concurred, and the House adhere to their own vote, sent up for concurrence."[385]

Massachusetts has gloried much and long in this Act to prohibit "the Custom of enslaving mankind;" but her silver-tongued orators and profound statesmen have never possessed the courage to tell the plain truth about its complete failure. From the first it was harassed by dilatory motions and amendments directed to its life; and the substitute, imposing an impost tax on imported slaves for one year, showed plainly that the friends of the original bill had been driven from their high ground. It was like applying for the position of a major-general, and then accepting the place of a corporal. It was as though they had asked for a fish, and accepted a serpent instead. It seriously lamed the cause of emancipation. It filled the slaves with gloom, and their friends with apprehension. On the other hand, those who profited by barter in flesh and blood laughed secretly to themselves at the abortive attempt of the anti-slavery friends to call a halt on the trade. They took courage. For ten weary years the voices lifted for the freedom of the slave were few, faint, and far between. The bill itself has been lost. What its subject-matter was, is left to uncertain and unsatisfactory conjecture. All we know is from the title just quoted. But it was, nevertheless, the only direct measure offered in the Provincial Legislature against slavery during the entire colonial period, and came nearest to passage of any. But "a miss is as good as a mile!"

It was now the spring season of 1771. Ten years had flown, and no one in all the Province of Massachusetts had had the courage to attempt legislation friendly to the slave. The scenes of the preceding year were fresh in the minds of the inhabitants of Boston. The blood of the martyrs to liberty was crying from the ground. The "red coats" of the British exasperated the people. The mailed hand, the remorseless steel finger, of English military power was at the throat of the rights of the people. The colony was gasping for independent political life. A terrible struggle for liberty was imminent.

The colonists were about to contend for all that men hold dear,—their wives, their children, their homes, and their country. But while they were panting for an untrammelled existence, to plant a free nation on the shores of North America, they were robbing Africa every year of her sable children, and condemning them to a bondage more cruel than political subjugation. This glaring inconsistency imparted to reflecting persons a new impulse toward anti-slavery legislation.

In the spring of 1771 the subject of suppressing the slave-trade was again introduced into the Legislature. On the 12th of April a bill "To prevent the Importation of slaves from Africa" was introduced, and read the first time, and, upon the question "When shall the bill be read again?" was ordered to a second reading on the day following at ten o'clock. Accordingly, on the 13th, the bill was read a second time, and postponed till the following Tuesday morning. On the 16th it was recommitted. On the 19th of the same month a "Bill to prevent the Importation of Negro slaves into this Province" was read a first time, and ordered to a second reading "to-morrow at eleven o'clock." On the following day it was read a second time, and made the special order for three o'clock on the following Monday. On the 22d, Monday, it was read a third time, and placed upon its passage and engrossed. On the 24th it passed the House. When it reached the Council James Otis proposed an amendment, and a motion prevailed that the bill lie upon the table. But it was taken from the table, and the amendment of Otis was concurred in by the House. It passed the Council in the latter part of April, but failed to receive the signature of the governor, on the ground that he was "not authorized by Parliament."[386] The same reason for refusing his signature was set up by Gen. Gage. Thus the bill failed. Gov. Hutchinson gave his reasons to Lord Hillsborough, secretary of state for the colonies. The governor thought himself restrained by "instructions" to colonial governors "from assenting to any laws of a new and unusual nature." In addition to the foregoing, his Excellency doubted the lawfulness of the legislation to which the "scruple upon the minds of the people in many parts of the province" would lead them; and that he had suggested the propriety of transmitting the bill to England to learn "his Majesty's pleasure" thereabouts. Upon these reasons Dr. Moore comments as follows:—

"These are interesting and important suggestions. It is apparent that at this time there was no special instruction to the royal governor of Massachusetts, forbidding his approval of acts against the slave-trade. Hutchinson evidently doubted the genuineness of the 'chief motive' which was alleged to be the inspiration of the bill, the 'meerly moral' scruple against slavery; but his reasonings furnish a striking illustration of the changes which were going on in public opinion, and the gradual softening of the harsher features of slavery under their influence. The non-importation agreement throughout the Colonies, by which America was trying to thwart the commercial selfishness of her rapacious Mother, had rendered the provincial viceroys peculiarly sensitive to the slightest manifestation of a disposition to approach the sacred precincts of those prerogatives by which King and Parliament assumed to bind their distant dependencies: and the 'spirit of non-importation' which Massachusetts had imperfectly learned from New York was equally offensive to them, whether it interfered with their cherished 'trade with Africa,' or their favorite monopolies elsewhere."

Discouraged by the failure of the House and General Court to pass measures hostile to the slave-trade, the people in the outlying towns began to instruct their representatives, in unmistakable language, to urge the enactment of repressive legislation on this subject. At a town meeting in Salem on the 18th of May, 1773,[387] the representatives were instructed to prevent, by appropriate legislation, the further importation of slaves into the colony, as "repugnant to the natural rights of mankind, and highly prejudicial to the Province." On the very next day, May 19, 1773, at a similar meeting in the town of Leicester, the people gave among other instructions to Thomas Denny, their representative, the following on the question of slavery:—

> "And, as we have the highest regard for (so as even to revere the name of) liberty, we cannot behold but with the greatest abhorrence any of our fellow-creatures in a state of slavery.
>
> "Therefore we strictly enjoin you to use your utmost influence that a stop maybe put to the slave-trade by the inhabitants of this Province; which, we apprehend, may be effected by one of these two ways: either by laying a heavy duty on every negro imported or brought from Africa or elsewhere into this Province; or by making a law, that every negro brought or imported as aforesaid should be a free man or woman as soon as they come within the jurisdiction of it; and that every negro child that shall be born in said government after the enacting such law should be free at the same age that the children of white people are; and, from the time of their birth till they are capable of earning their living, to be maintained by the town in which they are born, or at the expense of the Province, as shall appear most reasonable.
>
> "Thus, by enacting such a law, in process of time will the blacks become free; or, if the Honorable House of Representatives shall think of a more eligible method, we

shall be heartily glad of it. But whether you can justly take away or free a negro from his master, who fairly purchased him, and (although illegally; for such is the purchase of any person against their consent unless it be for a capital offence) which the custom of this country has justified him in, we shall not determine; but hope that unerring Wisdom will direct you in this and all your other important undertakings."[388]

Medford instructed the representative to "use his utmost influence to have a final period put to that most cruel, inhuman and unchristian practice, the slave-trade." At a town meeting the people of Sandwich voted, on the 18th of May, 1773, "that our representative is instructed to endeavor to have an Act passed by the Court, to prevent the importation of slaves into this country, and that all children that shall be born of such Africans as are now slaves among us, shall, after such Act, be free at 21 yrs. of age."[389]

This completes the list of towns that gave instructions to their representatives, as far as the record goes. But there doubtless were others; as the towns were close together, and as the "spirit of liberty was rife in the land."

The Negroes did not endure the yoke without complaint. Having waited long and patiently for the dawn of freedom in the colony in vain, a spirit of unrest seized them. They grew sullen and desperate. The local government started, like a sick man, at every imaginary sound, and charged all disorders to the Negroes. If a fire broke out, the "Negroes did it," — in fact, the Negroes, who were not one-sixth of the population, were continually committing depreciations against the whites! On the 13th of April, 1723, Lieut.-Gov. Dummer issued a proclamation against the Negroes, which contained the following preamble:—

"Whereas, within some short time past, many fires have broke out within the town of Boston, and divers buildings have thereby been consumed: which fires have been designedly and industriously kindled by some villanous and desperate negroes, or other dissolute people, as appears by the confession of some of them (who have been examined by the authority), and many concurring circumstances; and it being vehemently suspected that they have entered into a combination to burn and destroy the town, I have therefore thought fit, with the advice of his Majesty's council, to issue forth this proclamation," etc.

On Sunday, the 18th of April, 1723, the Rev. Joseph Sewall preached a sermon suggested "by the late fires yt have broke out in Boston, supposed to be purposely set by ye negroes." The town was greatly exercised. Everybody regarded the Negroes with distrust. Special measures were demanded to insure the safety of the town. The selectmen of Boston passed "nineteen articles" for the regulation of the Negroes. The watch of the town was increased, and the military called out at the sound of every fire-alarm "to keep the slaves from breaking out"! In August, 1730, a Negro was charged with burning a house in Malden; which threw the entire community into a panic. In 1755 two Negro slaves were put to death for poisoning their master, John Codman of Charlestown. One was hanged, and the other burned to death. In 1766 all slaves who showed any disposition to be free were "transported and exchanged for small negroes."[390] In 1768 Capt. John Willson, of the Fifty-ninth Regiment, was accused of exciting the slaves against their masters; assuring them that the soldiers had come to procure their freedom, and that, "with their assistance, they should be able to drive the Liberty Boys to the Devil." The following letter from Mrs. John Adams to her husband, dated at the Boston Garrison, 22d September, 1774, gives a fair idea of the condition of the public pulse, and her pronounced views against slavery.

> "There has been in town a conspiracy of the negroes. At present it is kept pretty private, and was discovered by one who endeavored to dissuade them from it. He being threatened with his life, applied to Justice Quincy for protection. They conducted in this way, got an Irishman to draw up a petition to the Governor [Gage], telling him they would fight for him provided he would arm them, and engage to liberate them if he conquered. And it is said that he attended so much to it, as to consult Percy upon it, and one Lieutenant Small has been very busy and active. There is but little said, and what steps they will take in consequence of it I know not. I wish most sincerely there was not a slave in the province; it always appeared a most iniquitous scheme to me to fight ourselves for what we are daily robbing and plundering from those who have as good a right to freedom as we have. You know my mind upon this subject."[391]

The Negroes of Massachusetts were not mere passive observers of the benevolent conduct of their white friends. They were actively interested in the agitation going on in their behalf. Here, as in no other colony, the Negroes showed themselves equal to the emergencies that arose, and capable of appreciating the opportunities to strike for their own rights. The Negroes in the colony at length struck a blow for their liberty. And it was not the wild, indiscriminate blow of Turner, nor the military measure of Gabriel; not the remorseless logic of bludgeon and torch,—but the sober, sensible efforts of men and women who believed their condition abnormal, and slavery prejudicial to the largest growth of the human intellect. The eloquence of Otis, the impassioned appeals of Sewall, and the zeal of Eliot had rallied the languishing energies of the Negroes, and charged their hearts with the divine passion for liberty. They had learned to spell out the letters of freedom, and the meaning of the word had quite ravished their fainting souls. They had heard that the royal charter declared all the colonists British subjects; they had devoured the arguments of their white friends, and were now prepared to act on their own behalf. The slaves of Greece and Rome, it is true, petitioned the authorities for a relaxation of the severe laws that crushed their manhood; but they were captives from other nations, noted for government and a knowledge of the science of warfare. But it was left to the Negroes of Massachusetts to force their way into counts created only for white men, and win their cause!

On Wednesday, Nov. 5, 1766, John Adams makes the following record in his diary:—

> "5. Wednesday. Attended Court; heard the trial of an action of trespass, brought by a mulatto woman, for damages, for restraining her of her liberty. This is called suing for liberty; the first action that ever I knew of the sort, though I have heard there have been many."[392]

So as early as 1766 Mr. Adams records a case of "suing for liberty;" and though it was the first he had known of, nevertheless, he had "heard there have been many." *How* many of these cases were in Massachusetts it cannot be said with certainty, but there were "many." The case to which Mr. Adams makes reference was no doubt that of Jenny Slew *vs.* John Whipple, jun., cited by Dr. Moore. It being the earliest case mentioned anywhere in the records of the colony, great interest attaches to it.

> "Jenny Slew of Ipswich in the County of Essex, spinster, Pltff., agst. John Whipple, Jun., of said Ipswich Gentleman, Deft., in a Plea of Trespass that the said John on the 29th day of January, A.D. 1762, at Ipswich aforesaid with force and arms took her the said Jenny, held and kept her in servitude as a slave in his service, and has restrained her of her liberty from that time to the fifth of March last without any lawful right & authority so to do and did her other injuries against the peace & to the damage of said Jenny Slew as she saith the sum of twenty-five pounds. This action was first brought at last March Court at Ipswich when & where the parties appeared & the case was continued by order of Court to the then next term when and where

the Pltff appeared & the said John Whipple Jun, came by Edmund Trowbridge, Esq. his attorney & defended when he said that there is no such person in nature as Jenny Slew of Ipswich aforesaid, Spinster, & this the said John was ready to verify wherefore the writ should be abated & he prayed judgment accordingly which plea was overruled by the Court and afterwards the said John by the said Edmund made a motion to the Court & praying that another person might endorse the writ & be subject to cost if any should finally be for the Court but the Court rejected the motion and then Deft. saving his plea in abatement aforesaid said that he is not guilty as the plaintiff contends, & thereof put himself on the Country, & then the cause was continued to this term, and now the Pltff. reserving to herself the liberty of joining issue on the Deft's plea aforesaid in the appeal says that the defendant's plea aforesaid is an insufficient answer to the Plaintiff's declaration aforesaid and by law she is not held to reply thereto & she is ready to verify wherefore for want of a sufficient answer to the Plaintiff's declaration aforesaid she prays judgment for her damages & costs & the defendant consenting to the waiving of the demurrer on the appeal said his plea aforesaid is good & because the Pltff refuses to reply thereto He prays judgment for his cost. It is considered by the Court that the defendant's plea in chief aforesaid is good & that the said John Whipple recover of the said Jenny Slew costs tax at the Pltff appealed to the next Superior Court of Judicature to be holden for this County & entered into recognizance with sureties as the law directs for prosecuting her appeal to effect." Records of the Inferior Court of C.C.P., Vol.—, (Sept. 1760 to July 1766), page 502.

"Jenny Slew of Ipswich, in the County of Essex, Spinster, Appellant, versus John Whipple, Jr. of said Ipswich, Gentleman Appellee from the judgment of an Inferior Court of Common Pleas held at Newburyport within and for the County of Essex on the last Tuesday of September 1765 when and where the appellant was plaint., and the appellee was defendant in a plea of trespass, for that the said John upon the 29th day of January, A.D. 1762, at Ipswich aforesaid with force and arms took her the said Jenny held & kept her in servitude as a slave in his service & has restrained her of her liberty from that time to the fifth of March 1765 without any lawful right or authority so to do & did other injuries against the Peace & to the damage of the said Jenny Slew, as she saith, the sum of twenty-five pounds, at which Inferior Court, judgment was rendered upon the demurrer then that the said John Whipple recover against the said Jenny Slew costs. This appeal was brought forward at the Superior Court of Judicature &c., holden at Salem, within & for the County of Essex on the first Tuesday of last November, from whence it was continued to the last term of this Court for this County by consent & so from thence unto this Court, and now both parties appeared & the demurrer aforesaid being waived by consent & issue joined upon the plea tendered at said Inferior Court & on file. The case after full hearing was committed to a jury sworn according to law to try the same who returned their verdict therein upon oath, that is to say, they find for appellant reversion of the former judgment four pounds money damage & costs. It's therefore considered by the Court, that the former judgment be reversed & that the said Slew recover against the said Whipple the sum of four pounds lawful money of this Province damage & costs taxed 9*l*. 9*s*. 6*d*.

"Exon. issued 4 Dec. 1766." *Records of the Superior Court of Judicature (vol.* 1766-7), *page* 175.

The next of the "freedom cases," in chronological order, was the case of Newport vs. Billing, and was doubtless the one in which John Adams was engaged in the latter part of September, 1768.[393] It was begun in the Inferior Court, where the decision was against the slave, Amos Newport. The plaintiff took an appeal to the highest court in the colony; and that court gave as its solemn opinion, "that the said Amos [Newport] was not a freeman, as he alleged, but the proper slave of the said Joseph [Billing]."[394] It should not be lost sight of, that not only the Fundamental laws of 1641, but the highest court in Massachusetts, held, as late as 1768, that there was property in man!

The case of James vs. Lechmere is the one "which has been for more than half a century the grand cheval de bataille of the champions of the historic fame of Massachusetts."[395] Richard Lechmere resided in Cambridge, and held to servitude for life a Negro named "James." On the 2d of May, 1769, this slave began an action in the Inferior Court of Common Pleas. The action was "in trespass for assault and battery, and imprisoning and holding the plaintiff in servitude from April 11, 1758, to the date of the writ." The judgment of the Inferior Court was adverse to the slave; but on the 31st of October, 1769, the Superior Court of Suffolk had the case settled by compromise. A long line of worthies in Massachusetts have pointed with pride to this decision as the legal destruction of slavery in that State. But it "is shown by the records and files of Court to have been brought up from the Inferior Court by sham demurrer, and, after one or two continuances, settled by the parties."[396] The truth of history demands that the facts be given to the world. It will not be pleasant for the people of Massachusetts to have this delusion torn from their affectionate embrace. It was but a mere historical chimera, that ought not to have survived a single day; and, strangely enough, it has existed until the present time among many intelligent people. This case has been cited for the last hundred years as having settled the question of bond servitude in Massachusetts, when the fact is, there was no decision in this instance! And the claim that Richard Lechmere's slave James was adjudged free "upon the same grounds, substantially, as those upon which Lord Mansfield discharged Sommersett," is absurd and baseless.[397] For on the 27th of April, 1785 (thirteen years after the famous decision), Lord Mansfield himself said, in reference to the Sommersett case, "that his decision went no farther than that the master cannot by force compel the slave to go out of the kingdom." Thirty-five years of suffering and degradation remained for the Africans after the decision of Lord Mansfield. His lordship's decision was rendered on the 22d of June, 1772; and in 1807, thirty-five years afterwards, the British government abolished the slave-trade. And then, after twenty-seven years more of reflection, slavery was abolished in English possessions. So, sixty-two years after Lord Mansfield's decision, England emancipated her slaves! It took only two generations for the people to get rid of slavery under the British flag. How true, then, that "facts are stranger than fiction"!

In 1770 John Swain of Nantucket brought suit against Elisha Folger, captain of the vessel "Friendship," for allowing a Mr. Roth to receive on board his ship a Negro boy named "Boston," and for the recovery of the slave. This was a jury-trial in the Court of Common Pleas. The jury brought in a verdict in favor of the slave, and he was "manumitted by the magistrates." John Swain took an appeal from the decision of the Nantucket Court to the Supreme Court of Boston, but never prosecuted it.[398] In 1770, in Hanover, Plymouth County, a Negro asked his master to grant him his freedom as his right. The master refused; and the Negro, with assistance of counsel, succeeded in obtaining his liberty.[399]

> "In October of 1773, an action was brought against Richard Greenleaf, of Newburyport, by Cæsar [Hendrick,] a colored man, whom he claimed as his slave, for holding him in bondage. He laid the damages at fifty pounds. The counsel for the plaintiff, in whose favor the jury brought in their verdict and awarded him eighteen pounds damages and costs, was John Lowell, esquire, afterward judge Lowell. This case excited much interest, as it was the first, if not the only one of the kind, that ever occurred in the county."[400]

This case is mentioned in full by Mr. Dane in his "Abridgment and Digest of American Law," vol. ii. p. 426.

In the Inferior Court of Common Pleas, in the county of Essex, July term in 1774, a Negro slave of one Caleb Dodge of Beverly brought an action against his master for restraining his liberty. The jury gave a verdict in favor of the Negro, on the ground that there was "no law of the Province to hold a man to serve for life."[401] This is the only decision we have been able to find based upon such a reason. The jury may have reached this conclusion from a knowledge of the provisions of the charter of the colony; or they may have found a verdict in accordance with the charge of the court. The following significant language in the charter of the colony could not have escaped the court:—

"That all and every of the subjects of us, our heirs and successors, which go to and inhabit within our said province and territory, and every of their children which shall happen to be born there, or on the seas in going thither, or returning from thence, shall have and enjoy all liberties and immunities of free and natural subjects within the dominions of us, our heirs and successors, to all intents, constructions, and purposes whatsoever, as if they and every of them were born within our realm of England."

The Rev. Dr. Belknap, speaking of these cases which John Adams speaks of as "suing for liberty," gives an idea of the line of argument used by the Negroes:—

> "On the part of the blacks it was pleaded, that the royal charter expressly declared all persons born or residing in the province, to be as free as the King's subjects in Great Britain; that by the laws of England, no man could be deprived of his liberty but by the judgment of his peers; that the laws of the province respecting an evil existing, and attempting to mitigate or regulate it, did not authorize it; and, on some occasions, the plea was, that though the slavery of the parents be admitted, yet no disability of that kind could descend to children."[402]

The argument pursued by the masters was,—

> "The pleas on the part of the masters were, that the negroes were purchased in open market, and bills of sale were produced in evidence; that the laws of the province recognized slavery as existing in it, by declaring that no person should manumit his slave without giving bond for his maintenance."[403]

It is well that posterity should know the motives that inspired judges and juries to grant these Negroes their prayer for liberty.

"In 1773, etc., some slaves did recover against their masters; but these cases are no evidence that there could not be slaves in the Province, for sometimes masters permitted their slaves to recover, to get clear of maintaining them as *paupers* when old and infirm; the effect, as then generally understood, of a judgment against the master on this point of slavery; hence, a very feeble defence was often made by the masters, especially when sued by the old or infirm slaves, as the masters could not even manumit their slaves, without indemnifying their towns against their maintenance, as town paupers."

And Chief-Justice Parsons, in the case of Winchendon *vs.* Hatfield, in error, says, —

> "Several negroes, born in this country of imported slaves demanded their freedom of their masters by suit at law, and obtained it by a judgment of court. The defence of the master was feebly made, for such was the temper of the times, that a restless discontented slave was worth little; and when his freedom was obtained in a course of legal proceedings, the master was not holden for his future support, if he became poor."

Thus did the slaves of Massachusetts fill their mouths with arguments, and go before the courts. The majority of them, aged and infirm, were allowed to gain their cause in order that their masters might be relieved from supporting their old age. The more intelligent, and, consequently, the more determined ones, were allowed to have their freedom from prudential reasons, more keenly felt than frankly expressed by their masters. In some instances, however, noble, high-minded Christians, on the bench and on juries, were led to their conclusions by broad ideas of justice and humanity. But the spirit of the age was cold and materialistic. With but a very few exceptions, the most selfish and constrained motives conspired to loose the chains of the bondmen in the colony.

The slaves were not slow to see that the colonists were in a frame of mind to be persuaded on the question of emancipation. Their feelings were at white heat in anticipation of the Revolutionary struggle, and the slaves thought it time to strike out a few sparks of sympathy.

On the 25th of June, 1773, a petition was presented to the House of Representatives, and read before that body during the afternoon session. It was the petition "of Felix Holbrook, and others, Negroes, praying that they may be liberated from a state of Bondage, and made Freemen of this Community, and that this Court would give and grant to them some part of the unimproved Lands belonging to the Province, for a settlement, or relieve them in such other Way as shall seem good and wise upon the Whole." After its reading, a motion prevailed to refer it to a select committee for consideration, with leave to report at any time. It was therefore "ordered, that Mr. Hancock, Mr. Greenleaf, Mr. Adams, Capt. Dix, Mr. Pain, Capt. Heath, and Mr. Pickering consider this Petition, and report what may be proper to be done."[404] It was a remarkably strong committee. There were the patriotic Hancock, the scholarly Greenleaf, the philosophic Pickering, and the eloquent Samuel Adams. It was natural that the Negro petitioners should have expected something. Three days after the committee was appointed, on the 28th of June, they recommended "that the further Consideration of the Petition be referred till next session." The report was adopted, and the petition laid over until the "next session."[405]

But the slaves did not lose heart. They found encouragement among a few noble spirits, and so were ready to urge the Legislature to a consideration of their petition at the next session, in the winter of 1774. The following letter shows that they were anxious and earnest.

"SAMUEL ADAMS TO JOHN PICKERING, JR.

"BOSTON, JANY. 8, 1774.

"Sir,—

> As the General Assembly will undoubtedly meet on the 26th of this month, the Negroes whose petition lies on file, and is referred for consideration, are very solicitous for the Event of it, and having been informed that you intended to consider it at your leisure Hours in the Recess of the Court, they earnestly wish you would compleat a Plan for their Relief. And in the meantime, if it be not too much Trouble, they ask it as a favor that you would by a Letter enable me to communicate to them the general outlines of your Design. I am, with sincere regard," etc.[406]

It is rather remarkable, that on the afternoon of the first day of the session,—Jan. 26, 1774,—the "Petition of a number of Negro Men, which was entered on the Journal of the 25th of June last, and referred for Consideration to this session," was "read again, together with a Memorial of the same Petitioners, and Ordered, that Mr. Speaker, Mr. Pickering, Mr. Hancock, Mr. Adams, Mr. Phillips, Mr. Pain, and Mr. Greenleaf consider the same, and report."[407] The public feeling on the matter was aroused. It was considered as important as, if not more important than, any measure before the Legislature.

The committee were out until March, considering what was best to do about the petition. On the 2d of March, 1774, they reported to the House "a Bill to prevent the Importation of Negroes and others as slaves into this Province," when it was read a first time. On the 3d of March it was read a second time in the morning session; in the afternoon session, read a third time, and passed to be engrossed. It was then sent up to the Council to be concurred in, by Col. Gerrish, Col. Thayer, Col. Bowers, Mr. Pickering and Col. Bacon.[408] On the next day the bill "passed in Council with Amendments,"[409] and was returned to the House. On the 5th of March the House agreed to concur in Council amendments, and on the 7th of March passed the bill as amended. On the day following it was placed upon its passage in the Council, and carried. It was then sent down to the governor to receive his signature, in order to become the law of the Province. That official's approval was withheld, and the reason given was, "the secretary said (on returning the approved bills) that his Excellency had not had time to consider the other Bills that had been laid before him."[410]

It is quite fortunate that the bill was preserved;[411] for it is now, in the certain light of a better civilization, a document of great historic value.

"ANNO REGNI REGIS GEORGII TERTII &c. DECIMO QUARTO.

"An Act to prevent the importation of Negroes or other Persons as Slaves into this Province, and the purchasing them within the same, *and for making provision for relief of the children of such as are already subjected to slavery Negroes Mulattoes & Indians born within this Province.*

"Whereas the Importation of Persons as Slaves into this Province has been found detrimental to the interest of his Majesty's subjects therein; And it being apprehended that the abolition thereof will be beneficial to the Province—

"*Be it therefore Enacted* by the Governor Council and House of Representatives that whoever shall after the Tenth Day of April next import or bring into this Province by Land or Water any Negro or other Person or Persons whether Male or Female as a Slave or Slaves shall for each and every such Person so imported or brought into this Province forfeit and pay the sum of one hundred Pounds to be recovered by presentment or indictment of a Grand Jury and when so recovered to be to his Majesty for the use of this Government or by action of debt in any of his Majesty's Courts of Record and in case of such recovery the one moiety thereof to be to his majesty for the use of this Government the other moiety to the Person or Persons who shall sue for the same.

"*And be it further Enacted* that from and after the Tenth Day of April next any Person or Persons that shall purchase any Negro or other Person or Persons as a Slave or Slaves imported or brought into this Province as aforesaid shall forfeit and pay for every Negro or other Person so purchased Fifty Pounds to be recovered and disposed of in the same way and manner as before directed.

"*And be it further Enacted* that every Person, concerned in importing or bringing into this Province, or purchasing any such Negro or other Person or Persons as aforesaid within the same; who shall be unable, or refuse, to pay the Penalties or forfeitures ordered by this Act; shall for every such offence suffer Twelve months' imprisonment without Bail or mainprise.

"*Provided* allways that nothing in this act contained shall extend to subject to the Penalties aforesaid the Masters, Mariners, Owners or Freighters of any such Vessel or Vessels, as before the said Tenth Day of April next shall have sailed from any Port or Ports in this Province, for any Port or Ports not within this Government, for importing or bringing into this Province any Negro or other Person or Persons as Slaves who in the prosecution of the same voyage may be imported or brought into the same. *Provided* he shall not offer them or any of them for sale.

"*Provided* also that this act shall not be construed to extend to any such Person or Persons, occasionally hereafter coming to reside within this Province, or passing thro' the same, who may bring such Negro or other Person or Persons as necessary servants into this Province provided that the stay or residence of such Person or Persons shall not exceed Twelve months or that such Person or Persons within said time send such Negro or other Person or Persons out of this Province there to be and remain, and also that during said Residence such Negro or other Person or Persons shall not be sold or alienated within the same.

" ∀ *And be it further Enacted and declared that nothing in this act contained shall extend or be construed to extend for retaining or holding in perpetual servitude any Negro or other Person or Persons now inslaved within this Province but that every such Negro or other Person or Persons shall be intituled to all the Benefits such Negro or other Person or Persons might by Law have been intituled to, in case this act had not been made.*

"In the House of Representatives March 2, 1774. Read a first & second Time. March 3, 1774. Read a third Time & passed to be engrossed. Sent up for concurrence.

T. Cushing, *Spkr.*

"In Council March 3, 1774. Read a first time. 4. Read a second Time and passed in Concurrence to be Engrossed with the Amendment at dele ∀ the whole Clause. Sent down for concurrence.

Thos. Flucker, Secry.

In the House of Representatives March 4, 1774. Read and concurred.

T. Cushing, *Spkr.*"

Like all other measures for the suppression of the slave-trade, this bill failed to become a law. If Massachusetts desired to free herself from this twofold cross of woe,—even if her great jurists could trace the law that justified the abolition of the curse, in the pages of the royal charter,—were not the British governors of the Province but conserving the corporation interests of the home government and the members of the Royal African Company? By the Treaty of Utrecht, England had agreed to furnish the Spanish West Indies with Negroes for the space of thirty years. She had aided all her colonies to establish slavery, and had sent her navies to guard the vessels that robbed Africa of five hundred thousand souls annually. [412] This was the cruel work of England. For all her sacrifices in the war, the millions of treasure she had spent, the blood of her children so prodigally shed, with the glories of Blenheim, of Ramillies, of Oudenarde and Malplaquet, England found her consolation and reward in seizing and enjoying, as the lion's share of results of the grand alliance against the Bourbons, the exclusive right for thirty years of selling African slaves to the Spanish West Indies and the coast of America![413] Why should Gov. Hutchinson sign a bill that was intended to choke the channel of a commerce in human souls that was so near the heart of the British throne?

Gov. Hutchinson was gone, and Gen. Gage was now governor. He convened the General Court at Salem, in June, 1774. On the 10th of June the same bill that Gov. Hutchinson had refused to sign was introduced, with a few immaterial changes, and pushed to a third reading, and engrossed the same day. It was called up on the 16th of June, and passed. It was sent up to the Council, where it was read a third time, and concurred in. But the next day the General Court was dissolved! And over the grave of this, the last attempt at legislation to suppress the slave-trade in Massachusetts, was written: "*Not to have been consented* to by the governor"!

These repeated efforts at anti-slavery legislation were strategic and politic. The gentlemen who hurried those bills through the House and Council, almost regardless of rules, knew that the royal governors would never affix their signatures to them. But the colonists, having put themselves on record, could appeal to the considerate judgment of the impatient Negroes; while the refusal of the royal governors to give the bills the force of law did much to drive the Negroes to the standard of the colonists. In the long night of darkness that was drawing its sable curtains about the colonial government, the loyalty of the Negroes was the lonely but certain star that threw its peerless light upon the pathway of the child of England so soon to be forced to lift its parricidal hand against its rapacious and cruel mother.

FOOTNOTES:

[380] Felt, vol. ii. p. 416.

[381] Newspaper Literature, vol. i. p. 31.

[382] Lyman's Report, quoted by Dr. Moore.

[383] House Journal, p. 387.

[384] Ibid.

[385] House Journals; see, also, Gen. Court Records, May, 1763, to May, 1767, p. 485.

[386] Slavery in Mass., pp. 131, 132.

[387] Felt, vol. ii. pp. 416, 417.

[388] Hist. of Leicester, pp. 442, 443.

[389] Freeman's Hist. of Cape Cod, vol. ii. pp. 114, 115.

[390] Boston Gazette, Aug. 17, 1761.

[391] Letters of Mrs. Adams, p. 20.

[392] Adams's Works, vol. ii. p. 200.

[393] Adams's Works, vol. ii, p. 213.

[394] Records, 1768, fol., p. 284.

[395] This is the case referred to by the late Charles Sumner in his famous speech in answer to Senator Butler of South Carolina; see also Slavery in Mass., p. 115, 116; Washburn's Judicial Hist. of Mass., p. 202; Mass. Hist. Soc. Proc., 1863-64, p. 322.

[396] Records, 1769, fol. p. 196. Gray in Quincy's Reports, p. 30, note, quoted by Dr. Moore.

[397] Slavery in Mass., pp. 115, 116, note.

[398] Lyman's Report, 1822.

[399] Slavery in Mass., p. 118.

[400] Hist. of Newbury, p. 339.

[401] The Watchman's Alarm, p. 28, note; also Slavery in Mass., p. 119.

[402] Mass. Hist Soc. Coll., vol. iv. 1st Series, pp. 202, 203.

[403] Hildreth, vol. ii. p. 564.

[404] House Journal, p. 85, quoted by Dr. Moore.

[405] House Journal, p. 94.

[406] Slavery in Mass., p. 136.

[407] House Journal, p. 104.

[408] House Journal p. 224.

[409] Ibid., p. 226.

[410] House Journal, Gen Court Records, xxx. pp. 248, 264; also, Slavery in Mass, p. 137.

[411] Mass. Archives, Domestic Relations, 1643-1774, vol. ix. p. 457.

[412] Ethiope, p. 12.

[413] Bolingbroke, pp. 346-348.

CHAPTER XVI
THE COLONY OF MARYLAND

1634-1775.

Maryland under the Laws of Virginia until 1630.—First Legislation on the Slavery Question in 1637-38—Slavery established by Statute in 1663—The Discussion of Slavery.—An Act passed encouraging the Importation of Negroes and White Slaves in 1671.—An Act laying an Impost on Negroes and White Servants imported into the Colony.—Duties imposed on Rum and Wine.—Treatment of Slaves and Papists.—Convicts imported into the Colony—An Attempt to justify the Convict-Trade.—Spirited Replies.—The Laws of 1723, 1729, 1752.—Rights of Slaves—Negro Population in 1728.—Increase of Slavery in 1750—No Efforts made to prevent the Evils of Slavery.—The Revolution nearing.—New Life for the Negroes.

UP to the 20th of June, 1630, the territory that at present constitutes the State of Maryland was included within the limits of the colony of Virginia. During that period the laws of Virginia obtained throughout the entire territory.

In 1637[414] the first assembly of the colony of Maryland agreed upon a number of bills, but they never became laws. The list is left, but nothing more. The nearest and earliest attempt at legislation on the slavery question to be found is a bill that was introduced "for punishment of ill servants." During the earlier years of the existence of slavery in Virginia, the term "servant" was applied to Negroes as well as to white persons. The legal distinction between slaves and servants was, "servants for a term of years,"—white persons; and "servants for life,"—Negroes. In the first place, there can be no doubt but what Negro slaves were a part of the population of this colony from its organization;[415] and, in the second place, the above-mentioned bill of 1637 for the "punishment of ill servants" was intended, doubtless, to apply to Negro servants, or slaves. So few were they in number, that they were seldom referred to as "slaves." They were "servants;" and that appellation dropped out only when the growth of slavery as an institution, and the necessity of specific legal distinction, made the Negro the only person that was suited to the condition of absolute property.

In 1638 there was a list of bills that reached a second reading, but never passed. There was one bill "for the liberties of the people," that declared "all Christian inhabitants (slaves only excepted) to have and enjoy all such rights, liberties, immunities, privileges and free customs, within this province, as any natural born subject of England hath or ought to have or enjoy in the realm of England, by force or virtue of the common law or statute law of England, saving in such cases as the same are or may be altered or changed by the laws and ordinances of this province."[416] There is but one mention made of "slaves" in the above Act, but in none of the other Acts of 1638. There are certain features of the Act worthy of special consideration. The reader should keep the facts before him, that by the laws of England no Christian could be held in slavery; that in the Provincial governments the laws were made to conform with those of the home government; that, in specifying the rights of the colonists, the Provincial assemblies limited the immunities and privileges conferred by the Magna Charta upon British subjects, to Christians; that Negroes were considered heathen, and, therefore, denied the blessings of the Church and State; that even where Negro slaves were baptized, it was held by the courts in the colonies, and was the law-opinion of the solicitor-general of Great Britain, that they were not ipso facto free;[417] and that, where Negroes were free, they had no rights in the Church or State. So, while this law of 1638 did not say that Negroes should be slaves, in designating those who were to enjoy the rights of freemen, it excludes the Negro, and thereby fixes his condition as a slave by implication. If he were not named as a freeman, it was the intention of the law-makers that he should remain a bondman,—the exception to an established rule of law.[418]

In subsequent Acts reference was made to "servants," "fugitives," "runaways," etc.; but the first statute in this colony establishing slavery was passed in 1663. It was *"An Act concerning negroes and other slaves."* It enacts section one:—

"All negroes or other slaves within the province, and all negroes and other slaves to be hereafter imported into the province, shall serve *durante vita*; and all children born of any negro or other slave, shall be slaves as their fathers were for the term of their lives."

Section two:—

"And forasmuch as divers freeborn *English* women, forgetful of their free condition, and to the disgrace of our nation, do intermarry with negro slaves, by which also divers suits may arise, touching the issue of such women, and a great damage doth befall the master of such negroes, for preservation whereof for deterring such free-born women from such shameful matches, *be it enacted,* &c.: That whatsoever free-born woman shall intermarry with any slave, from and after the last day of the present assembly, shall serve the master of such slave during the life of her husband; and that all the issue of such free-born women, so married, shall be slaves as their fathers were."

Section three:—

"And be it further enacted, that all the issues of English, or other free-born women, that have already married negroes, shall serve the master of their parents, till they be thirty years of age and no longer."[419]

Section one is the most positive and sweeping statute we have ever seen on slavery. It fixes the term of servitude for the longest time man can claim,—the period of his earthly existence,—and dooms the children to a service from which they were to find discharge only in death. Section two was called into being on account of the intermarriage of white women with slaves. Many of these women had been indentured as servants to pay their passage to this country, some had been sent as convicts, while still others had been apprenticed for a term of years. Some of them, however, were very worthy persons. No little confusion attended the fixing of the legal status of the issue of such marriages; and it was to deter Englishwomen from such alliances, and to determine the status of the children before the courts, that this section was passed. Section three was clearly an ex post facto law: but the public sentiment of the colony was reflected in it; and it stood, and was re-enacted in 1676.

Like Virginia, the colony of Maryland found the soil rich, and the cultivation of tobacco a profitable enterprise. The country was new, and the physical obstructions in the way of civilization numerous and formidable. Of course all could not pursue the one path that led to agriculture. Mechanic and trade folk were in great demand. Laborers were scarce, and the few that could be obtained commanded high wages. The Negro slave's labor could be made as cheap as his master's conscience and heart were small. Cheaper labor became the cry on every hand, and the Negro was the desire of nearly all white men in the colony.[420] In 1671 the Legislature passed "An Act encouraging the importation of negroes and slaves into" the colony, which was followed by another and similar Act in 1692. Two motives inspired the colony to build up the slave-trade; viz., to have more laborers, and to get something for nothing. And, as soon as Maryland was known to be a good market for slaves, the traffic increased with wonderful rapidity. Slaves soon became the bone and sinew of the working-force of the colony. They were used to till the fields, to fell the forests, to assist mechanics, and to handle light crafts along the water-courses. They were to be found in all homes of opulence and refinement; and, unfortunately, their presence in such large numbers did much to lower honorable labor in the estimation of the whites, and to enervate women in the best white society. While the colonists persuaded themselves that slavery was an institution indispensable to the colony, its evil effects soon became apparent. It were impossible to engage the colony in the slave-trade, and escape the bad results of such an inhuman enterprise. It made men cruel and avaricious.

It was the motion of individuals to have legislative encouragement tendered the venders of human flesh and blood; but the time came when the government of the colony saw that an impost tax upon the slaves imported into the colony would not impair the trade, while it would aid the government very materially. In 1696 "An Act laying an imposition on negroes, slaves and while persons imported" into the colony was passed. It is plain from the reading of the caption of the above bill, that it was intended to reach three classes of persons; viz., Negro servants, Negro slaves, and white servants. The word "imported" means such persons as could not pay their passage, and were therefore indentured to the master of the vessel. When they arrived, their time was hired out, if they were free, for a term of years, at so much per year;[421] but if they were slaves the buyer had to pay all claims against this species of property before he could acquire a fee simple in the slave. Some historians have too frequently misinterpreted the motive and aim of the colonial Legislatures in imposing an impost tax upon Negroes and other servants imported into their midst. The fact that the law applied to white persons does not aid in an interpretation that would credit the makers of the act with feelings of humanity. A people who could buy and sell wives did not hesitate to see in the indentured white servants property that ought to be taxed. Why not? These white servants represented so many dollars invested, or so many years of labor in prospect! So all persons imported into the colony of Maryland, "Negroes, slaves, and white persons," were taxed as any other marketable article. A swift and remorseless civilization against the stolid forces of nature made men indiscriminate and cruel in their impulses to obtain. Public sentiment had been formulated into law: the law contemplated "servants and slaves" as chattel property; and the political economists of the Province saw in this species of property rich gains for the government. It was condition, circumstances, that made the servant or slave; but at length it was nationality, color.

When, on the threshold of the eighteenth century, "white indentured" servants were rapidly ceasing to exist under color or sanction of law, religious bigotry and ecclesiastical intolerance joined hands with the supporters of Negro slavery in a crusade[422] against the Irish Catholics. In 1704 the Legislature passed "An Act imposing three pence per gallon on rum and wine, brandy and spirits, and twenty shillings per poll for negroes, for raising a supply to defray the public charge of this province, and twenty shillings, per poll, on Irish servants, to prevent the importing too great a number of Irish papist into this province." Although this Act was intended to remain on the statute-books only three years, its life was prolonged by a supplemental Act, and it disgraced the colony for twenty-one years. As in New York, so here, the government regarded the slave and Papist with feelings of hatred and fear. The former was only suited to a condition of perpetual bondage, the latter to be ostracized and driven out from before the face of the exclusive Protestants of that period. Both were cruelly treated; one on account of his face, the other on account of his faith.

> "Unfortunately for the professors of the Catholic religion, by the force of circumstances which it is not necessary to detail, their religious persuasions became identified, in the public mind, with opposition to the principles of the revolution. Their political disfranchisement was the consequence. Charles Calvert, the deposed proprietary, shared the common fate of his Catholic brethren. Sustained and protected by the crown in the enjoyment of his mere private rights, the general jealousy of Catholic power denied him the government of the province."[423]

A knowledge of the antecedents of the master-class will aid the reader to a more accurate conception of the character of the institution of slavery in the colony of Maryland.

It is not very pleasing for the student of history at this time to remember that the British colonies in North America received into their early life the worst poison of European society,—the criminal element. From the first the practice of transporting convicts into the colonies obtained. And, during the reign of George I., statutes were passed "authorizing transportation as a commutation punishment for clergyable felonies." These convicts were transported by private shippers, and then sold into the colony; and thus it became a gainful enterprise. From 1700 until 1760 this nefarious and pestiferous traffic greatly increased. At length it became, as already indicated, the subject of a special impost tax. Three or four hundred convicts were imported into the colony annually, and the people began to complain. [424] In "The Maryland Gazette" of the 30th of July, 1767, a writer attempted to show that the convict element was not to be despised, but was rather a desirable addition to the Province. He says,—

"I suppose that for these last thirty years, communibus annis, there have been at least 600 convicts per year imported into this province: and these have probably gone into 400 families."

After answering some objections to their importation because of the contagious diseases likely to be communicated by them, he further remarks,—

"This makes at least 400 to one, that they do no injury to the country in the way complained of: and the people's continuing to buy and receive them so constantly, shows plainly the general sense of the country about the matter; notwithstanding a few gentlemen seem so angry that convicts are imported here at all, and would, if they could, by spreading this terror, prevent the people's buying them. I confess I am one, says he, who think a young country cannot be settled, cultivated, and improved, without people of some sort: and that it is much better for the country to receive convicts than slaves. The wicked and bad amongst them, that come into this province, mostly run away to the northward; mix with their people, and pass for honest men: whilst those more innocent, and who came for very small offences, serve their times out here, behave well, and become useful people."

This attempt to justify the *convict trade* elicited two able and spirited replies over the signatures of "Philanthropos" and "C.D." appearing in "Green's Gazette" of 20th of August, 1767, in which the writer of the first article is handled "with the gloves off."

"His remarks [says Philanthropos] remind me of the observation of a great philosopher, who alleges that there is a certain race of men of so selfish a cast, that they would even set a neighbour's house on fire, for the convenience of roasting an egg at the blaze. That these are not the reveries of fanciful speculatists, the author now under consideration is in a great measure a proof; for who, but a man swayed with the most sordid selfishness, would endeavor to disarm the people of all caution against such imminent danger, lest their just apprehensions should interfere with his little schemes of profit? And who but such a man would appear publicly as an advocate for the importation of felons, the scourings of jails, and the abandoned outcasts of the British nation, as a mode in any sort eligible for peopling a young country?"

In another part of his reply he remarks,—

"In confining the indignation because of their importation to a few, and representing that the general sense of the people is in favor of this vile importation, he is guilty of the most shameful misrepresentation and the grossest calumny upon the whole province. What opinion must our mother country, and our sister colonies, entertain of our virtue, when they see it confidently asserted in the Maryland Gazette, that we are fond of peopling our country with the most abandoned profligates in the universe? Is this the way to purge ourselves from that false and bitter reproach, so commonly thrown upon us, that we are the descendants of convicts? As far as it has lain in my way to be acquainted with the general sentiments of the people upon this subject, I solemnly declare, that the most discerning and judicious amongst them esteem it the greatest grievance imposed upon us by our mother country."

The writer felt that a young country could not be settled "without people of some sort," and that it was better to secure "convicts than slaves." Upon what grounds precisely this defender of buying convict labor based his conclusion that he would rather have "convicts than slaves" is not known. It could not have been that he believed the convicts of England more industrious or skilful than Negro slaves? Or, had he theoretical objections to slavery as a permanent institution? Perhaps the writer had himself graduated from the criminal class! But there were gentlemen who differed with him, and couched their objections to the convict system of importation in very vigorous English. On the 20th of August, 1767, two articles appeared in "Greene's Gazette." Says one of these writers, —

"For who, but a man swayed with the most sordid selfishness, would endeavor to disarm the people of all caution against such imminent danger, lest their just apprehensions should interfere with his little schemes of profit? And who but such a man would appear publicly as an advocate for the importation of felons, the scourings of jails, and the abandoned outcasts of the British nation, as a mode in any sort eligible for peopling a young country?"

There can be no doubt but that many of the convicts thus imported, having served out their time, in a brief season became slave-drivers and slave-owners. With hearts reduced to flinty hardness in the fires of unrestrained passions, the convict element, as it became absorbed in the great free white population of the Province,[425] created a most positive sentiment in favor of a cruel code for the government of the Negro slave. There were two motives that inspired the ex-convict to cruelty to the Negro:

to divert attention from himself, and to persuade himself, in his doubting mind, that the Negro was inferior to him by nature. It was, no doubt, a great undertaking; but the findings of such a court must have been comforting to an anxious conscience! The result can be judged. Maryland made a slave-code, which, for cruelty and general inhumanity, has no equal in the South. [426] The Maryland laws of 1715 contained, in chapter forty-four, an act with one hundred and thirty-five sections relating to Negro slaves. A most rigorous pass-system was established. By section six, no Negro or other servant was allowed to leave the county without a pass under the seal of the county in which their master resided; for which pass the slave or other servant was compelled to pay ten pounds of tobacco, or one shilling in money. If such persons were apprehended, a justice of the peace could impose such fines and inflict such punishment as were fixed by the law applying to runaways. By the Act of 1723, chapter fifteen, under the caption of "An Act to prevent the tumultuous meeting and other irregularities of negroes and other slaves," the severity of the laws was increased tenfold. According to section four, a Negro or other slave who had the temerity to strike a white person, was to have his ears "cropt on order of a Justice." Section six denies slaves the right of possession of property: they could not own cattle. Section seven gave authority to any white man to kill a Negro who resisted an attempt to arrest him; and by a supplemental Act of 1751, chapter fourteen, the owner of a slave thus killed was to be paid out of the public treasury. In 1729 an Act was passed providing, that upon the conviction of certain crimes, Negroes and other slaves shall be not only hanged, but the body should be quartered, and exposed to public view. When slaves grew old and infirm in the service of their masters, and the latter were inspired by a desire to compliment the faithfulness of their servants by emancipation, the law came in and forbade manumission by the "last will or testament," or the making free in any way of Negro slaves. It was a temporary Act, passed in 1752, void of every element of humanity; and yet it stood as the law of the colony for twenty long years.

In 1748 the Negro population of Maryland was thirty-six thousand, and still rapidly increasing.

"By a 'very accurate census,' taken this year, this was found to be the number of white inhabitants in Maryland:—

	FREE.	SERVANTS.	CONVICTS.	TOTAL.
Men	24,058	3,576	1,507	29,141
Women	23,521	1,824	386	25,731

Boys	26,637	1,048	67	27,752
Girls	24,141	422	21	24,584
	98,357	6,870	1,981	107,208

"By the same account the total number of mulattoes in Maryland amounted to 3,592; and the total number of Negroes, to 42,764. Pres. Stiles' MS. It was reckoned (say the authors of Univ. Hist.), that above 2,000 Negro slaves were annually imported into Maryland."[427]

In 1756 the blacks had increased to 46,225, and in 1761 to 49,675. There was nothing in the laws to prohibit the instruction of Negroes, and yet no one dared to brave public sentiment on that point. The churches gave no attention or care to the slaves. During the first half or three-quarters of a century there was an indiscriminate mingling and marrying among the Negroes and white servants; and, although this was forbidden by rigid statutes, it went on to a considerable extent. The half-breed, or Mulatto, population increased;[428] and so did the number of free Negroes. The contact of these two elements—of slaves and convicts—was neither prudent nor healthy. The Negroes suffered from the touch of the moral contagion of this effete matter driven out of European society. Courted as rather agreeable companions by the convicts at first, the Negro slaves were at length treated worse by the ex-convicts than by the most intelligent and opulent slave-dealers in all the Province. And with no rights in the courts, incompetent to hold an office of any kind, the free Negroes were in almost as disagreeable a situation as the slaves.

From the founding of the colony of Maryland in 1632 down to the Revolutionary War, there is no record left us that any effort was ever made to cure the most glaring evils of slavery. For the Negro this was one long, starless night of oppression and outrage. No siren's voice whispered to him of a distant future, propitious and gracious to hearts almost insensible to a throb of joy, to minds unconscious of the feeblest rays of light. Being absolute property, it was the right of the master to say how much food, or what quantity of clothing, his slave should have. There were no rules by which a slave could claim the privilege of ceasing from labor at the close of the day. No, the master had the same right to work his slaves after nightfall as to drive his horse morning, noon, and night. Poor clothes, rough and scanty diet, wretched quarters, overworked, neglected in body and mind, the Negroes of Maryland had a sore lot.

The Revolution was nearing. Public attention was largely occupied with the Stamp Act and preparations for hostilities. The Negro was left to toil on; and, while at this time there was no legislation sought for slavery, there was nothing done that could be considered hostile to the institution. The Negroes hailed the mutterings of the distant thunders of revolution as the precursor of a new era to them. It did furnish an opportunity for them in Maryland to prove themselves patriots and brave soldiers. And how far their influence went to mollify public sentiment concerning them, will be considered in its appropriate place. Suffice it now to say, that cruel and hurtful, unjust and immoral, as the institution of slavery was, it had not robbed the Negro of a lofty conception of the fundamental principles that inspired white men to resist the arrogance of England; nor did it impair his enthusiasm in the cause that gave birth to a new republic amid the shock of embattled arms.

FOOTNOTES:

[414] Dr. Abiel Holmes, in his American Annals, vol. ii. p. 5, says, "Maryland now contained about thirty-six thousand persons, of white men from sixteen years of age and upwards, and negroes male, and female from sixteen to sixty." I infer from this statement that slavery was in existence in Maryland in 1634; and I cannot find any thing in history to lead me to doubt but that slavery was born with the colony.

[415] Cabinet Cyclopædia, vol. i. p. 61.

[416] See Bacon's Laws, also Holmes's Annals, vol. i. p. 250.

[417] The following appeared in the Plantation Laws, printed in London in 1705: "Where any negro or slave, being in servitude or bondage, is or shall become Christian, and receive the sacrament of baptism, the same shall not nor ought not to be deemed, adjudged or construed to be a manumission or freeing of any such negro or slave, or his or her issue, from their servitude or bondage, but that notwithstanding they shall at all times hereafter be and remain in servitude and bondage as they were before baptism, any opinion, matter or thing to the contrary notwithstanding."

[418] McSherry's Hist. of Maryland, p. 86.

[419] Freedom and Bondage, vol. i. p. 249.

[420] McMahon's Hist. of Maryland, vol. i. p. 274.

[421] The following form was used for a long time in Maryland for binding out a servant.

This Indenture *made the — — day of — — in the — — yeere of our Soveraigne Lord King* Charles, *&c betweene — — of the one party,* and *— — on the other party,* Witnesseth, *that the said — — doth hereby covenant promise, and grant, to* and with the said — — his *Executors and Assignes, to serve him from the day of the date hereof, untill his first and next arrivall in* Maryland: *and after for and during the tearme of* — — *yeeres, in such service and imployment, as the said* — — *or his assignee shall there imploy him, according to the custome of the Countrey in the like kind. In consideration whereof, the said* — — *doth promise and grant, to and with the said* — — *to pay for his passing, and to find him with Meat, Drinke, Apparell and Lodging, with other necessaries during the said terme; and at the end of the said terme, to give him one whole yeeres provision of Corne, and fifty acres of Land, according to the order of the countrey. In witnesse whereof, the said* — — *hath hereunto put his hand and seate, the day and yeere above written.*

Sealed and delivered in the presence of — —

—*Relation of the State of Maryland*, pp. 62, 63.

[422] Modern Traveller, vol. i. pp. 122, 123.

[423] McMahon's Maryland, vol. i. p. 278.

[424] 1st Pitkin's United States, p. 133.

[425] McMahone says of this convict element: "The pride of this age revolts at the idea of going back to such as these, for the roots of a genealogical tree; and they, whose delight it would be, to trace their blood through many generations of stupid, sluggish, imbecile ancestors, with no claim to merit but the name they carry down, will even submit to be called 'novi homines,' if a convict stand in the line of ancestry."

[426] With perhaps the single exception of South Carolina, of which the reader will learn more farther on.

[427] American Annals.

[428] Dr. Holmes says, "The total number of mulattoes in Maryland amounted to 3,592," in 1755.

CHAPTER XVII
THE COLONY OF DELAWARE

1636-1775.

The Territory of Delaware settled in part by Swedes and Danes, anterior to the Year 1638.—The Duke of York transfers the Territory of Delaware to William Penn.—Penn grants the Colony the Privilege of Separate Government.—Slavery introduced on the Delaware as early as 1636.—Complaint against Peter Alricks for using Oxen and Negroes belonging to the Company.—The First Legislation on the Slavery Question in the Colony.—An Enactment of a Law for the Better Regulation of Servants.—An Act restraining Manumission.

ANTERIOR to the year 1638, the territory now occupied by the State of Delaware was settled in part by Swedes and Danes. It has been recorded of them that they early declared that it was "not lawful to buy and keep slaves."[429] But the Dutch claimed the territory. When New Netherlands was ceded to the Duke of York, Delaware was occupied by his representatives. On the 24th of August, 1682, the Duke transferred that territory to William Penn.[430] But in 1703 Penn surrendered the old form of government, and gave the Delaware counties the privilege of a separate administration under the Charter of Privileges. Delaware inaugurated a legislature, but remained under the Council and Governor of Pennsylvania. But slavery made its appearance on the Delaware as early as 1636.[431]

> "At this early period there appears to have been slavery on the Delaware. As one Coinclisse was 'condemned, on the 3d of February, to serve the company with the blacks on South River for wounding a soldier at Fort Amsterdam. He was also to pay a fine to the fiscal, and damages to the wounded soldier.' On the 22d, a witness testifying in the case of Governor Van Twiller, (the governor of New Neitherlands before Kieft,) who was charged with neglect and mismanagement of the company's affairs, said that 'he

had in his custody for Van Twiller, at Fort Hope and Nassau, twenty-four to thirty goats, and that three negroes bought by the director in 1636, were since employed in his private service.' Thus it will be seen that slavery was introduced on the Delaware as early as 1636, though probably not in this State, as the Dutch at that time had no settlement here."[432]

And on the 15th of September, 1657, complaint was made that Peter Alricks had "used the company's oxen and negroes;" thus showing that there were quite a number of Negroes in the colony at the time mentioned. In September, 1661, there was a meeting between Calvert, D'Hinoyossa, Peter Alricks, and two Indian chiefs, to negotiate terms of peace. At this meeting the Marylanders agreed to furnish the Dutch annually three thousand hogsheads of tobacco, provided the Dutch would "supply them with negroes and other commodities."[433] Negroes were numerous, and an intercolonial traffic in slaves was established.

The first legislation on the slavery question in the colony of Delaware was had in 1721. "*An Act for the trial of Negroes*" provided that two justices and six freeholders should have full power to try "negro and mulatto slaves" for heinous offences. In case slaves were executed, the Assembly paid the owner two-thirds the value of such slave. It forbade convocations of slaves, and made it a misdemeanor to carry arms. During the same year an Act was passed punishing adultery and fornication. In case of children of a white woman by a slave, the county court bound them out until they were thirty-one years of age. In 1739 the Legislature passed an Act for the better regulation of servants and slaves, consisting of sixteen articles. It provided that no indentured servant should be sold into another government without the approval of at least one justice. Such servant could not be assigned over except before a justice. If a person manumitted a slave, good security was required: if he failed to do this, the manumission was of no avail. If free Negroes did not care for their children, they were liable to be bound out. In 1767 the Legislature passed another Act restraining manumission. It recites:—

> "Section 2. And be it enacted by the honorable John Penn, esq. with his Majesty's royal approbation, Lieutenant Governor and Commander in Chief of the counties of New-Castle, Kent and Sussex, upon Delaware, and province of Pennsylvania, under the honorable Thomas Penn and Richard Penn, esquires, true and absolute proprietaries of the said counties and province, by and with the advice and consent of the Representatives of the freemen of the said counties, in General Assembly met, and by the authority

of the same, That if any master or mistress shall, by will or otherwise, discharge or set free any Mulatto or Negro slave or slaves; he or she, or his or her executors or administrators, at the next respective County Court of Quarter Sessions, shall enter into a recognizance with sufficient sureties, to be taken in the name of the Treasurer of the said county for the time being, in the sum of Sixty Pounds for each slave so set free, to indemnify the county from any charge they or any of them may be unto the same, in case of such Negro or Mulattoe's being sick, or otherwise rendered incapable to support him or herself; and that until such recognizance be given, no such Negro or Mulatto shall be deemed free."[434]

The remainder of the slave code in this colony was like unto those of the other colonies, and therefore need not be described. Negroes had no rights, ecclesiastical or political. They had no property, nor could they communicate a relation of any character. They had no religious or secular training, and none of the blessings of home life. Goaded to the performance of the most severe tasks, their only audible reply was an occasional growl. It sent a feeling of terror through their inhuman masters, and occasioned them many ugly dreams.

FOOTNOTES:

[429] Dr. Stevens in his History of Georgia, vol. i. p. 288, says, "In the Swedish and German colony, which Gustavus Adolphus planted in Delaware, and which in many points resembled the plans of the Trustees, negro servitude was disallowed." But he gives no authority, I regret.

[430] See Laws of Delaware, vol. i. Appendix, pp. 1-4.

[431] Albany Records, vol. ii, p. 10.

[432] Vincent's History of Delaware, p. 159.

[433] Ibid., p. 381.

[434] Laws of Delaware, vol. i. p. 436.

CHAPTER XVIII
THE COLONY OF CONNECTICUT

1646-1775.

The Founding of Connecticut, 1631-36.—No Reliable Data given for the Introduction of Slaves.—Negroes were first introduced by Ship during the Early Years of the Colony.—"Committee for Trade and Foreign Plantations."—Interrogating the Governor as to the Number of Negroes in the Colony in 1680.—The Legislature (1690) passes a Law pertaining to the Purchase and Treatment of Slaves and Free Persons.—An Act passed by the General Court in 1711, requiring Persons manumitting Slaves to maintain them.—Regulating the Social Conduct of Slaves in 1723.—The Punishment of Negro, Indian, and Mulatto Slaves, for the Use of Profane Language, in 1630.—Lawfulness of Indian and Negro Slavery recognized by Code, Sept. 5, 1646.—Limited Rights of Free Negroes in the Colony.—Negro Population in 1762.—Act against Importation of Slaves, 1774.

ALTHOUGH the colony of Connecticut was founded between the years 1631 and 1636, there are to be found no reliable data by which to fix the time of the introduction of slavery there.[435] Like the serpent's entrance into the Garden of Eden, slavery entered into this colony stealthily; and its power for evil was discovered only when it had become a formidable social and political element. Vessels from the West Coast of Africa, from the West Indies, and from Barbadoes, landed Negroes for sale in Connecticut during the early years of its settlement. And for many years slavery existed here, without sanction of law, it is true, but perforce of custom. Negroes were bought as laborers and domestics, and it was a long time before their number called for special legislation. But, like a cancer, slavery grew until there was not a single colony in North America that could boast of its ability to check the dreadful curse. When the first slaves were introduced into this colony, can never be known; but, that there were Negro slaves from the beginning, we have the strongest historical presumption. For nearly two decades there was no reference made to slavery in the records of the colony.

In 1680 "the Committee for Trade and Foreign Plantations" addressed to the governors of the North-American plantations or colonies a series of questions. Among the twenty-seven questions put to Gov. Leete of Connecticut, were two referring to Negroes. The questions were as follows:—

"17. What number of English, Scotch, Irish or Forreigners have (for these seaven yeares last past, or any other space of time) come yearly to plant and inhabit within your Corporation. And also, what Blacks and Slaves have been brought in within the said time, and att what rates?

> "18. What number of Whites, Blacks or Mulattos have been born and christened, for these seaven yeares last past, or any other space of time, for as many yeares as you are able to state on account of?"[436]

To these the governor replied as follows:—

> "17. Answ. For English, Scotts and Irish, there are so few come in that we cannot give a certain accot. Som yeares come none; sometimes, a famaly or two, in a year. And for Blacks, there comes sometimes 3 or 4 in a year from Barbadoes; and they are sold usually at the rate of 22li. a piece, sometimes more and sometimes less, according as men can agree with the master of vessels, or merchants that bring them hither.

> "18. Answ. We can give no accot. of the perfect number of either born; but fewe blacks; and but two blacks christened, as we know of."[437]

It is evident that the number of slaves was not great at this time, and that they were few and far between. The sullen and ofttimes revengeful spirit of the Indians had its effect upon the few Negro slaves in the colony. Sometimes they were badly treated by their masters, and occasionally they would run away. The country was new, the settlements scattered; and slavery as an institution, at this time and in this colony, in its infancy. The spirit of insubordination among the slave population seemed to call aloud for legislative restriction. In October, 1690, the Legislature passed the following bill:—

> "Whereas many persons of this Colony doe for their necessary use purchase negroe seruants, and often times the sayd seruants run away to the great wronge, damage and disapoyntment of their masters and owners, for prevention

of which for [221] the future, as much as II may be, it is ordered by this Court that Whateuer negroe or negroes shall hereafter, at any time, be fownd wandring out of the towne bownds or place to which they doe belong, without a ticket or pass from the authority, or their masters or owners, shall be stopt and secured by any of the inhabitants, or such as shall meet with them, and brought before the next authority to be examined and returned to their owners, who shall sattisfy for the charge if any be; and all ferrymen within this Colony are hereby required not to suffer any negroe without such certificate, to pass over their ferry by assisting them therein, upon the penalty of twenty shillings, to be payd as a fine to the county treasury, and to be leuyed upon theire estates for non-payment in way of distresse by warrant from any one Assistant or Comr. This order to be observed as to vagrant and susspected persons fownd wandring from town to town, hauveing no passes; such to be seized for examination and farther disspose by the authority; and if any negroes are free and for themselves, travelling without such ticket or certificate, they to bear the charge themselves of their takeing up."[438]

The general air of complaint that pervades the above bill leads to the conclusion that it was required by an alarming state of affairs. The pass-system was a copy from the laws of the older colonies where slavery had long existed. By implication free Negroes had to secure from the proper authorities a certificate of freedom; and the bill required them to carry it, or pay the cost of arrest.

One of the most palpable evidences of the humanity of the Connecticut government was the following act passed in May, 1702:—

"Whereas it is observed that some persons in this Colonie having purchased Negro or Malatta Servants or Slaves, after they have spent the pricipall part of their time and strength in their masters service, doe sett them at liberty, and the said slaves not being able to provide necessaries for themselves may become a charge and burthen to the towns where they have served: for prevention whereof,

"It is ordered and enacted by this Court and the authority thereof: That every person in this Colonie that now is or hereafter shall be owner of a negro or mulatta servant or slave, and after some time of his or her being taken into imployment in his or her service, shall sett such servant or slave at liberty to provide for him or herselfe, if afterwards such servant or slave shall come to want, every such servant shall be relieved at the onely cost and charge of the person in whose service he or she was last reteined or taken, and by whome sett at liberty, or at the onely cost and charge of his or her heirs, executors or administrators, any law, usage or custome to the contrary notwithstanding."[439]

Massachusetts had acted and did act very cowardly about this matter. But Connecticut showed great wisdom and humanity in making a just and equitable provision for such poor and decrepit slaves as might find themselves turned out to charity after a long life of unrequited toil. Slavery was in itself "the sum of all villanies," — the blackest curse that ever scourged the earth. To buy and sell human beings; to tear from the famishing breast of the mother her speechless child; to separate the husband from the wife of his heart; to wring riches from the unpaid toil of human beings; to tear down the family altar, and let lecherous beasts, who claim the name of "Christian," run over defenceless womanhood as swine over God's altar!— is there any thing worse, do you ask? Yes! To work a human being from youth to old age, to appropriate the labor of that being exclusively, to rob it of the blessings of this life, to poison every domestic charity, to fetter the intellect by the power of fatal ignorance, to withhold the privileges of the gospel of love; and then, when the hollow cough comes under an inclement sky, when the shadows slant, when the hand trembles, when the gait is shuffling, when the ear is deaf, the eye dim, when desire faileth, — then to turn that human being out to die is by far the profoundest crime man can be guilty of in his dealings with mankind! And slavery had so hardened men's hearts, that the above act was found to be necessary to teach the alphabet of human kindness. No wonder human forbearance was strained to its greatest tension when masters, thus liberating their slaves, assumed the lofty air of humanitarians who had actually done a noble act in manumitting a slave!

In 1708 the General Court was called upon to legislate against the commercial communion that had gone on between the slaves and free persons in an unrestricted manner for a long time. Slaves would often steal articles of household furniture, wares, clothing, etc., and sell them to white persons. And, in order to destroy the ready market this wide-spread kleptomania found, an Act was passed making it a misdemeanor for a free person to purchase any article from slaves. It is rather an interesting law, and is quoted in full.

"Whereas divers rude and evil minded persons for the sake of filthie lucre do frequently receive from Indians, malattoes and negro servants, money and goods stolen or obteined by other indirect and unlawful means, thereby incouraging such servants to steal from their masters and others: for redress whereof,

> [35] Be it enacted by the Governour, Council and Representatives, in General Court assembled, and by the authoritie of the same, That every free person whomsoever, which shall presume either openly or privately to buy or receive of or from any Indian, molato or negro servant or slave, any goods, money, merchandize, wares, or provisions, without order from the master or mistress of such servant or slave, every person so offending and being thereof convicted, shall be sentenced to restore all such money, goods, wares, merchandizes, or provisions, unto the partie injured, in specie, (if not altered,) and also forfeit to the partie double the value thereof over and above, or treble the value where the same are disposed of or made away. And if the person so offending be unable, or shall not make restitution as awarded, then to be openly whipt with so many stripes (not exceeding twentie,) as the court or justices that have cognizance of such offence shall order, or make satisfaction by service. And the Indian, negro, or molatto servant or slave, of or from whom such goods, money, wares, merchandizes or provisions shall be received or bought, if it appear to be stolen, or that shall steal any money, goods, or chattells, and be thereof convicted, although the buyer or receiver be not found, shall be punished by whipping not exceeding thirtie stripes, and the money, goods or chattels shall be restored to the partie injured, if it be found. And every assistant and justice of peace in the countie where such offence is committed, is hereby authorized to hear and determine all offences against this law, provided the damage exceed not the sum of fortie shillings."[440]

On the same day another act was passed, charging that as Mulatto and Negro slaves had become numerous in parts of the colony, destined to become insubordinate, abusive of white people, etc., and is as follows:—

"And whereas negro and molatto servants or slaves are become numerous in some parts of this Colonie, and are very apt to be turbulent, and often quarrelling with white people to the great disturbance of the peace:

> "It is therefore ordered and enacted by the Governour, Council and Representatives, in General Court assembled, and by the authoritie of the same, That if any negro or malatto servant or slave disturb the peace, or shall offer to strike any white person, and be thereof convicted, such negro or malatto servant or slave shall be punished by whipping, at the discretion of the court, assistant or justice of the peace that shall have cognizance thereof, not exceeding thirtie stripes for one offence."[441]

In 1711 the General Court of Connecticut Colony signally distinguished itself by the passage of an act in harmony with that of 1702. It was found that indentured servants as well as slaves had been made the victims of the cruel policy of turning slaves and servants out into the world without means of support after they had become helpless, or had served out their time. This class of human beings had been cast aside, like a squeezed lemon, to be trodden under the foot of men. The humane and thoughtful men of the colony demanded a remedy at law, and it came in the following admirable bill:—

"An Act relating to Slaves, and such in particular as shall happen to become Servants for Time.

> "It is ordered and enacted by the Governour, Council and Representatives, in General Court assembled, and by the authority of the same, That all slaves set at liberty by their owners, and all negro, malatto, or Spanish Indians, who are servants to masters for time, in case they come to want, after they shall be so set at liberty, or the time of their said service be expired, shall be relieved by such owners or masters respectively, their heirs, executors, or administrators; and upon their, or either of their refusal so to do, the said slaves and servants shall be relieved by the selectmen of the towns to which they belong, and the said selectmen shall recover of the said owners or masters, their heirs, executors, or administrators, all the charge and cost they were at for such relief, in the usual manner as in the case of any other debts."[442]

In 1723 an Act was passed regulating the social conduct, and restricting the personal rights, of slaves. The slaves were quite numerous at this time, and hence the colonists deemed it proper to secure repressive legislation. It is strange how anticipatory the colonies were during the zenith of the slavery institution! They were always expecting something of the slaves. No doubt they thought that it would be but the normal action of goaded humanity if the slaves should rise and cut their masters' throats. The colonists lived in mortal dread of their slaves, and the character of the legislation was but the thermometer of their fear. This Act was a slight indication of the unrest of the people of this colony on the slavery question:—

"[376] An Act to prevent The Disorder of Negro And Indian Servants and Slaves in the Night Season.

"*Be it enacted by the Governour, Council and Representatives, in General Court assembled, and by the authority of the same,* That from and after the publication of this act, if any negro or Indian servant or slave shall be found abroad from home in the night season, after nine of the clock, without special order from his or their master or mistress, it shall be lawful for any person or persons to apprehend and secure such negro or Indian servant or slave so offending, and him or them bring before the next assistant or justice of peace; which assistant or justice of peace shall have full power to pass sentence upon such negro or Indian servant or slave so offending, and order him or them to be publickly whipt on his or their naked body, not exceeding ten stripes, and pay cost of court, except his or their master or mistress shall redeem them by paying a fine not exceeding twenty shillings.

> "And it is hereby enacted by the authority aforesaid, That if any such negro or Indian servant or slave as abovesaid shall have entertainment in any house after nine of the clock as aforesaid, except to do any business they may be sent upon, the head of the family that entertaineth or tolerates them in his or their house, or any the dependencies thereof, and being convicted thereof before any one assistant or justice of the peace, who shall have power to hear and determine the same, shall forfeit the sum of twenty shillings, one-half to the complainer and the other half to the treasury of the town where the offence is committed; any law or usage to the contrary notwithstanding. And that it shall be the duty of the several grand-jurors and constables and tything-men, to make diligent enquiry into and present of all breaches of this act."[443]

The laws regulating slavery in the colony of Connecticut, up to this time, had stood, and been faithfully enforced. There had been a few infractions of the law, but the guilty had been punished. And in addition to statutory regulation of slaves, the refractory ones were often summoned to the bar of public opinion and dealt with summarily. Individual owners of slaves felt themselves at liberty to use the utmost discretion in dealing with this species of their property. So on every hand the slave found himself scrutinized, suspicioned, feared, hated, and hounded by the entire community of whites who were by law a perpetual *posse comitatus*. The result of too great vigilance and severe censorship was positive and alarming. It made the slave desperate. It intoxicated him with a malice that would brook no restraint. It is said that the use of vigorous adjectives and strong English is a relief to one in moments of trial. But even this was denied the oppressed slaves in Connecticut; for in May, 1730, a bill was passed punishing them for using strong language.

"An Act for the Punishment of Negroes, Indian and Mulatto Slaves, for Speaking Defamatory Words.

> "Be it enacted by the Governour, Council and Representatives, in General Court assembled, and by the authority of the same, That if any Negro, Indian or Molatto slave shall utter, publish and speak such words of any person that would by law be actionable if the same were uttered, published or spoken by any free person of any other, such Negro, Indian or Molatto slave, being thereof convicted before any one assistant or justice of the peace, (who are hereby impowred to hear and determine the same,) shall be punished by whipping, at the discretion of the assistant or justice before whom the tryal is, (respect being had to the circumstances of the case,) not exceeding forty stripes. And the said slave, so convict, shall be sold to defray all charges arising thereby, unless the same be by his or their master or mistress paid and answered, &c."[444]

The above act is the most remarkable document in this period of its kind. And yet there are two noticeable features in it: viz., the slave is to be proceeded against the same as if he were a free person; and he was to be entitled to offer evidence, enter his plea, and otherwise defend himself against the charge. This was more than was allowed in any of the other colonies.

On the 9th of September, 1730, Gov. J. Talcott, in a letter to the "Board of Trade," said that there were "about 700 Indian and Negro slaves" in the colony. The most of these were Negro slaves. For on the 8th of July, 1715, a proclamation was issued by the governor against the importation of Indians;[445] and on the 13th of October, 1715, a bill was passed "prohibiting the Importation or bringing into" the colony any Indian slaves. It was an exact copy of the Act of May, 1712, passed in the colony of Massachusetts.

The colony of Connecticut never established slavery by direct statute; but in adopting a code which was ordered by the General Court of Hartford to be "copied by the secretary into the book of public records," it gave the institution legal sanction. This code was signed on the 5th of September, 1646. It recognized the lawfulness of Indian and Negro slavery. This was done under the confederacy of the "United Colonies of New England."[446] For some reason the part of the code recognizing slavery is omitted from the revised laws of 1715. In this colony, as in Massachusetts, only members of the church, "and living within the jurisdiction," could be admitted to the rights of freemen. In 1715 an Act was passed requiring persons who desired to become "freemen of this corporation," to secure a certificate from the selectmen that they were "persons of quiet and peaceable behavior and civil conversation, of the age of twenty-one years, and freeholders." This provision excluded all free Negroes. It was impossible for one to secure such a certificate. Public sentiment alone would have frowned upon such an innovation upon the customs and manners of the Puritans. On the 17th of May, 1660, the following Act was passed: "It is ordered by this court, that neither Indian nor negar servts shall be required to traine, watch or ward in the Collo:"[447]

To determine the status of the Negro here, this Act was necessary. He might be free, own his own labor; but if the law excluded him from the periodical musters and trainings, from the church and civil duties, his freedom was a mere misnomer. It is difficult to define the rights of a free Negro in this colony. He was restricted in his relations with the slaves, and in his intercourse with white people was regarded with suspicion. If he had, in point of law, the right to purchase property, the general prejudice that confronted him on every hand made his warmest friends judiciously conservative. There were no provisions made for his intellectual or spiritual growth. He was regarded by both the religious and civil government, under which he lived, as a heathen. Even his accidental conversion could not change his condition, nor mollify the feelings of the white Christians (?) about him. Like the wild animal, he was possessed with the barest privilege of getting something to eat. Beyond this he had nothing. Everywhere he turned, he felt the withering glance of a suspicious people. Prejudice and prescriptive legislation cast their dark shadows on his daily path; and the conscious superiority of the whites consigned him to the severest drudgery for his daily bread. The recollection of the past was distressing, the trials and burdens of the present were almost unbearable, while the future was one shapeless horror to him.

Perhaps the lowly and submissive acquiescence of the Negroes, bond and free, had a salutary effect upon the public mind. There is something awfully grand in an heroic endurance of undeserved pain. The white Christians married, and were given in marriage; they sowed and gathered rich harvests; they bought and built happy homes; beautiful children were born unto them; they built magnificent churches, and worshipped the true God: the present was joyous, and the future peopled with sublime anticipation. The contrast of these two peoples in their wide-apart conditions must have made men reflective. And added to this came the loud thunders of the Revolution. Connecticut had her orators, and they touched the public heart with the glowing coals of patriotic resolve. They felt the insecurity of their own liberties, and were now willing to pronounce in favor of the liberty of the Negroes. The inconsistency of asking for freedom, praying for freedom, fighting for freedom, and dying for freedom, when they themselves held thousands of human beings in bondage the most cruel the world ever knew, helped the cause of the slave. In 1762 the Negro population of this colony was four thousand five hundred and ninety.[448] Public sentiment was aroused on the slavery question; and in October, 1774, the following prohibition was directed at slavery:—

> "Act against importation of slaves—"No Indian, negro, or mulatto slave shall at any time hereafter be brought or imported into this State, by sea or land, from any place or places whatsoever, to be disposed of, left or sold, within this State."[449]

The above bill was brief, but pointed; and showed that Connecticut was the only one of the New-England colonies that had the honesty and courage to legislate against slavery. And the patriotism and incomparable valor of the Negro soldiers of Connecticut, who proudly followed the Continental flag through the fires of the Revolutionary War, proved that they were worthy of the humane sentiment that demanded the Act of 1774.

FOOTNOTES:

[435] In the Capital Laws of Connecticut, passed on the 1st of December, 1642, the tenth law reads as follows. "10. If any man stealeth a man or mankind, he shall be put to death. Ex. 21 16." But this was the law in Massachusetts, and yet slavery existed there for one hundred and forty-three (143) years.

[436] Conn. Col. Recs., 1678-89, p. 293.

[437] Ibid., p. 298.
[438] Conn Col Recs., 1689-1706, p. 40
[439] Ibid. 1689-1706, pp. 375, 376.
[440] Conn. Col. Recs., 1706-16, p. 52.
[441] Ibid., pp 51, 53.
[442] Conn. Col. Recs., 1706-16, p. 233.
[443] Conn. Col. Recs., 1717-25, pp. 390, 391.
[444] Ibid., 1726-35, p. 290.
[445] Conn. Col. Recs., 1706-16, pp. 515, 516.
[446] Hazard, State Papers, vol. ii. pp. 1-6.
[447] Conn. Col. Recs., vol. i. p. 349.
[448] Pres. Stiles's MSS.
[449] Freedom and Bondage, vol. i. pp. 272, 273.

CHAPTER XIX
THE COLONY OF RHODE ISLAND

1647-1775.

Colonial Government in Rhode Island, May, 1647.—An Act passed to abolish Slavery in 1652, but was never enforced.—An Act specifying what Times Indian and Negro Slaves should not appear in the Streets.—An Impost-Tax on Slaves (1708).—Penalties imposed on Disobedient Slaves.—Anti Slavery Sentiment in the Colonies receives Little Encouragement.—Circular Letter from the Board of Trade to the Governor of the English Colonies, relative to Negro Slaves.—Governor Cranston's Reply.—List of Militia-Men, including White and black Servants.—Another Letter from the Board of Trade.—An Act preventing Clandestine Importations and Exportations of Passengers, Negroes, or Indian Slaves.—Masters of Vessels required to report the Names and Number of Passengers to the Governor.—Violation of the Impost-Tax Law on Slaves punished by Severe Penalties.—Appropriation by the General Assembly, July 5, 1715, from the Fund derived from the Impost Tax, for the paving of the Streets of Newport.—An Act passed disposing of the Money raised by Impost-Tax.—Impost-Law repealed, May, 1732.—An Act relating to freeing Mulatto and Negro Slaves passed 1728—An Act passed preventing Masters of Vessels from carrying Slaves out of the Colony, June 17, 1757.—Eve of the Revolution.—An Act prohibiting Importation of Negroes into the Colony in 1774.—The Population of Rhode Island in 1730 and 1774.

INDIVIDUAL Negroes were held in bondage in Rhode Island from the time of the formation of the colonial government there, in May, 1647, down to the close of the eighteenth century. Like her sister colonies, she early took the poison of the slave-traffic into her commercial life, and found it a most difficult political task to rid herself of it. The institution of slavery was never established by statute in this colony; but it was so firmly rooted five years after the establishment of the government, that it required the positive and explicit prohibition of law to destroy it. On the 19th of May, 1652, the General Court passed the following Act against slavery. It is the earliest positive prohibition against slavery in the records of modern nations.

> "Whereas, there is a common course practiced amongst English men to buy negers, to that end they may have them for service or slaves forever; for the preventinge of such practices among us, let it be ordered, that no blacke mankind or white being forced by covenant bond, or otherwise, to serve any man or his assighnes longer than ten yeares, or until they come to bee twentie-four yeares of age, if they bee taken in under fourteen, from the time of their cominge within the liberties of this Collonie. And at the end or terme of ten yeares to sett them free, as the manner is with the English servants. And that man that will not let them goe free, or shall sell them away elsewhere, to that end that they may bee enslaved to others for a long time, hee or they shall forfeit to the Collonie forty pounds."[450]

The above law was admirable, but there was lacking the public sentiment to give it practical force in the colony. It was never repealed, and yet slavery flourished under it for a century and a half. Mr. Bancroft says, "The law was not enforced, but the principle lived among the people."[451] No doubt the principle lived among the people; but, practically, they did but little towards emancipating their slaves until the Revolutionary War cloud broke over their homes. There is more in the statement Mr. Bancroft makes than the casual reader is likely to discern.

The men who founded Rhode Island, or Providence Plantation as it was called early, were of the highest type of Christian gentlemen. They held advanced ideas on civil government and religious liberty. They realized, to the full, the enormity of the sinfulness of slavery; but while they hesitated to strike down what many men pronounced a necessary social evil, it grew to be an institution that governed more than it could be governed. The institution was established. Slaves were upon the farms, in the towns, and in the families, of those who could afford to buy them. The population of the colony was small; and to manumit the slaves in whom much money was invested, or to suddenly cut off the supply from without, was more than the colonists felt able to perform. The spirit was willing, but the flesh was weak.

For a half-century there was nothing done by the General Court to check or suppress the slave-trade, though the Act of 1652 remained the law of the colony. The trade was not extensive. No vessels from Africa touched at Newport or Providence. The source of supply was Barbadoes; and, occasionally, some came by land from other colonies. Little was said for or against slavery during this period. It was a question difficult to handle. The sentiment against it was almost unanimous. It was an evil; but how to get rid of it, was the most important thing to be considered. During this period of perplexity, there was an ominous silence on slavery. The conservatism of the colonists produced the opposite in the Negro population. They began to think and talk about their "rights." The Act of 1652 had begun to bear fruit. At the expiration of ten years' service, slaves began to demand their freedom-papers. This set the entire Negro class in a state of expectancy. Their eagerness for liberty was interpreted by the more timid among the whites as the signal for disorder. A demand was made for legislation that would curtail the personal liberties of the Negroes in the evenings. It is well to produce the Act of Jan. 4, 1703, that the reader may see the similarity of the laws passed in the New-England colonies against Negroes:—

"An Act to restrict negroes and Indians for walking in unseasonable times in the night, and at other times not allowable.

"Voted, Be it enacted by this Assembly and the authority thereof, and it is hereby enacted, If any negroes or Indians, either freemen, servants, or slaves, do walk in the streets of the town of Newport, of any other town in this Collony, after nine of the clock of the night, without a certificate from their masters, or some English person of said family with them, or some lawfull excuse for the same, that it shall be lawfull for any person to take them up and deliver them to a Constable, to be secured, or see them secured, till the next morning, and then to be brought before some Justice of the Peace in said town, to be dealt withall, according to the recited Act, which said Justice shall cause said person or persons so offending, to be whipped at the publick whipping post in said town, not exceeding fifteen stripes upon their naked backs, except their incorrigible behavior require more. And all free negroes and free Indians to be under the same penalty, without a lawful excuse for their so being found walking in the streets after such unseasonable time of night.

> "And be it further enacted, All and every house keeper, within said town or towns or Collony, that shall entertain men's servants, either negroes or Indians, without leave of their masters or to whom they do belong, after said set time of the night before mentioned, and being convicted of the same before any one Justice of the Peace, he or they shall pay for each his defect five shillings in money, to be for the use of the poor in the town where the person lives; and if refused

to be paid down, to be taken by distraint by a warrant to any one Constable, in said town; any Act to the contrary notwithstanding."[452]

It is rather remarkable that this Act should prohibit free Negroes and free Indians from walking the streets after nine o'clock. In this particular this bill had no equal in any of the other colonies. This act seemed to be aimed with remarkable precision at the Negroes as a class, both bond and free. The influence of free Negroes upon the slaves had not been in harmony with the condition of the latter; and the above Act was intended as a reminder, in part, to free Negroes and Indians. It went to show that there was but little meaning in the word "free," when placed before a Negro's name. No such restriction could have been placed upon the personal rights of a white colonist; for, under the democratical government of the colony, a subject was greater than the government. No law could stand that was inimical to his rights as a freeman. But the free Negro had no remedy at law. He was literally between two conditions, bondage and freedom.

Attention has been called to the fact, that the Act of 1652 was never enforced. In April, 1708, an Act, laying an impost-tax upon slaves imported into the colony, was passed which really gave legal sanction to the slave-trade.[453] The following is the Act referred to:—

"And it is further enacted by the authority aforesaid, that whereas, by an act of Assembly, in February last past, concerning the importing negroes, one article of said act, expressing that three pounds money shall be paid into the treasury for each negro imported into this colony; but upon exporting such negro in time limited in said act, said three pounds were to be drawn out of the treasury again by the importer:

> "It is hereby enacted, that said sum for the future, shall not be drawn out, but there continued for the use in said act expressed; any act to the contrary, notwithstanding."[454]

The Act referred to as having passed "in February last past," cannot be found.[455] But, from the one quoted above, it is to be inferred that two objects were aimed at, viz.: First, under the codes of Massachusetts and Virginia, a drawback was allowed to an importer of a Negro who exported him within a stated time: the Rhode-Island Act of "February" had allowed importers this privilege. Second, notwithstanding the loud-sounding Act of 1652, this colony was not only willing to levy an impost-tax upon all slaves imported, but, in her greed for "blood money," even denied the importer the mean privilege, in exporting his slave, of drawing his rebate! The consistency of Rhode Island must have been a jewel that the other colonies did not covet.

The last section of the Act of 1703 was directed against "house keepers," who were to be fined for entertaining Negro or Indian slaves after nine o'clock. In 1708 another Act was passed, supplemental to the one of 1703, and added stripes as a penalty for non-payment of fines. Many white persons in the larger towns had grown rather friendly towards the slaves; and, even where they did not speak out in public against the enslavement of human beings, their hearts led them to the performance of many little deeds of kindness. They discovered many noble attributes in the Negro character, and were not backward in expressing their admiration. When summoned before a justice, and fined for entertaining Negroes after nine o'clock, they paid the penalty with a willingness and alacrity that alarmed the slave-holding caste. This was regarded as treason. Some could not pay the fine, and, hence, went free. The new Act intended to remedy this. It was as follows:—

"An Act to prevent the entertainment of Negroes, &c.

"Whereas, there is a law in this colony to suppress any persons from entertaining of negro slaves or Indian servants that are not their own, in their houses, or unlawfully letting them have strong drink, whereby they were damnified, such persons were to pay a fine of five shillings, and so by that means go unpunished, there being no provision made [of] what corporeal punishment they should have, if they have not wherewith to pay:

> "Therefore, it is now enacted, that any such delinquent that shall so offend, if he or she shall not have or procure the sum of ten shillings for each defect, to be paid down before the authority before whom he or she hath been legally convicted, he or she shall be by order of said authority, publicly whipped upon their naked back, not exceeding ten stripes; any act to the contrary, notwithstanding. "[456]

It is certain that what little anti-slavery sentiment there was in the British colonies in North America during the first century of their existence received no encouragement from Parliament. From the beginning, the plantations in this new world in the West were regarded as the hotbeds in which slavery would thrive, and bring forth abundant fruit, to the great gain of the English government. All the appointments made by the crown were expected to be in harmony with the plans to be carried out in the colonies. From the settlement of Jamestown down to the breaking out of the war, and the signing of the Declaration of Independence, not a single one of the royal governors ever suffered his sense of duty to the crowned heads to be warped by local views on "the right of slavery." The Board of

Trade was untiring in its attention to the colonies. And no subject occupied greater space in the correspondence of that colossal institution than slavery. The following circular letter, addressed to the governors of the colonies, is worthy of reproduction here, rather than in the Appendix. It is a magnificent window, that lets the light in upon a dark subject. It gives a very fair idea of the profound concern that the home government had in foreign and domestic slavery.

"CIRCULAR LETTER FROM THE BOARD OF TRADE TO THE GOVERNORS OF THE ENGLISH COLONIES, RELATIVE TO NEGRO SLAVES.

"APRIL 17, 1708.

"Sir: Some time since, the Queen was pleased to refer to us a petition relating to the trade of Africa, upon which we have heard what the Royal African Company, and the separate traders had to offer; and having otherwise informed ourselves, in the best manner we could, of the present state of that trade, we laid the same before Her Majesty. The consideration of that trade came afterwards into the house of commons, and a copy of our report was laid before the house; but the session being then too far spent to enter upon a matter of so great weight, and other business intervening, no progress was made therein. However, it being absolutely necessary that a trade so beneficial to the kingdom should be carried on to the greatest advantage, there is no doubt but the consideration thereof will come early before the Parliament at their next meeting; and as the well supplying of the plantations and colonies with sufficient numbers of negroes at reasonable prices, is in our opinion the chief point to be considered in regard to that trade, and as hitherto we have not been able to know how they have been supplied by the company, or by separate traders, otherwise than according to the respective accounts given by them, which for the most part are founded upon calculations made from their exports on one side and the other, and do differ so very much, that no certain judgment can be made upon those accounts.

> "Wherefore, that we may be able at the next meeting of the Parliament to lay before both houses when required, an exact and authentic state of that trade, particularly in regard to the several plantations and colonies: we do hereby desire and strictly require you, that upon the receipt hereof, you do inform yourself from the proper officers or otherwise, in the best manner you can, what number of negroes have been yearly imported directly from Africa into Jamaica,

since the 24th of June, 1698, to the 25th of December, 1707, and at what rate per head they have been sold each year, one with another, distinguishing the numbers that have been imported on account of the Royal African Company, and those which have been imported by separate traders; as likewise the rates at which such negroes have been sold by the company and by separate traders. We must recommend it to your care to be as exact and diligent therein as possibly you can, and with the first opportunity to transmit to us such accounts as aforesaid, that they may arrive here in due time, as also duplicates by the first conveyance.

"And that we may be the better able to make a true judgment of the present settlement of that trade, we must further recommend it to you to confer with some of the principal planters and inhabitants within your government touching that matter, and to let us know how the negro trade was carried on, and the island of Jamaica supplied with negroes till the year 1698, when that trade was laid open by act of Parliament; how it has been carried on, and negroes supplied since that time, or in what manner they think the said trade may best be managed for the benefit of the plantations.

"We further desire you will inform us what number of ships, if any, are employed from Jamaica to the coast of Africa in the negro trade, and how many separate traders are concerned therein.

"Lastly, whatever accounts you shall from time to time send us touching these matters of the negro trade, we desire that the same may be distinct, and not intermixed with other matters; and that for the time to come, you do transmit to us the like half yearly accounts of negroes, by whom imported and at what rates sold; the first of such subsequent accounts, to begin from Christmas, 1707, to which time those now demanded, are to be given. So we bid you heartily farewell,

"Your very loving friends,

"Stamford,
Herbert,
Ph. Meadows,
I. Pulteney,
R. Monckton.

"P.S. We expect the best account you can give us, with that expedition which the shortness of the time requires.

> "Memorandum. This letter, mutatis mutandis, was writ to the Governors of Barbadoes, the Leeward Islands, Bermuda, New York, New Jersey, Maryland, the President of the Council of Virginia, the Governor of New Hampshire and the Massachusetts Bay, the Deputy Governor of Pennsylvania, the Lords proprietors of Carolina, the Governors and Companies of Connecticut and Rhode Island."[457]

The good Queen of England was interested in the traffic in human beings; and although the House of Commons was too busy to give attention to "a matter of so great weight," the "Board of Trade" felt that it was "absolutely necessary that a trade so beneficial to the kingdom should be carried on to the greatest advantage." England never gave out a more cruel document than the above circular letter. To read it now, under the glaring light of the nineteenth century, will almost cause the English-speaking people of the world to doubt even "the truth of history." Slavery did not exist at sufferance. It was a crime against the weak, ignorant, and degraded children of Africa, systematically perpetrated by an organized Christian government, backed by an army that grasped the farthest bounds of civilization, and a navy that overshadowed the oceans.

The reply of the governor of Rhode Island was not as encouraging as their lordships could have wished.

GOVERNOR CRANSTON'S REPLY.

"May it please your Lordships: In obedience to your Lordships' commands of the 15th of April last, to the trade of Africa.

"We, having inspected into the books of Her Majesty's custom, and informed ourselves from the proper officers thereof, by strict inquiry, can lay before your Lordships no other account of that trade than the following, viz:

"1. That from the 24th of June, 1698, to the 25th of December, 1707, we have not had any negroes imported into this colony from the coast of Africa, neither on the account of the Royal African Company, or by any of the separate traders.

"2. That on the 30th day of May, 1696, arrived at this port from the coast of Africa, the brigantine Seaflower, Thomas Windsor, master, having on board her forty-seven negroes, fourteen of which he disposed of in this colony, for betwixt £30 and £35 per head; the rest he transported by land for Boston, where his owners lived.

"3. That on the 10th of August, the 19th and 28th of October, in the year 1700, sailed from this port three vessels, directly for the coast of Africa; the two former were sloops, the one commanded by Nicho's Hillgroue, the other by Jacob Bill; the last a ship, commanded by Edwin Carter, who was part owner of the said three vessels, in company with Thomas Bruster, and John Bates, merchants, of Barbadoes, and separate traders from thence to the coast of Africa; the said three vessels arriving safe to Barbadoes from the coast of Africa, where they made the disposition of their negroes.

"4. That we have never had any vessels from the coast of Africa to this colony, nor any trade there, the brigantine above mentioned, excepted.

"5. That the whole and only supply of negroes to this colony, is from the island of Barbadoes; from whence is imported one year with another, betwixt twenty and thirty; and if those arrive well and sound, the general price is from £30 to £40 per head.

"According to your Lordships' desire, we have advised with the chiefest of our planters, and find but small encouragement for that trade to this colony; since by the best computation we can make, there would not be disposed in this colony above twenty or thirty at the most, annually, the reasons of which are chiefly to be attributed to the general dislike our planters have for them, by reason of then turbulent and unruly tempers.

"And that most of our planters that are able and willing to purchase any of them, are supplied by the offspring of those they have already, which increase daily; and that the inclination of our people in general, is to employ white servants before Negroes.

"Thus we have given our Lordships a true and faithful account of what hath occurred, relating to the trade of Africa from this colony; and if, for the future, our trade should be extended to those parts, we shall not fail transmitting accounts thereof according to your Lordships' orders, and that at all times, be ready to show ourselves,

"Your Lordships' obedient servant,

"Samuel Cranston, Governor.

"Newport, on Rhode Island, December 5, 1708."[458]

So in nine years there had been no Negro slaves imported into the colony; that in 1696 fourteen had been sold to the colonists for between thirty pounds and thirty-five pounds apiece; that this was the only time a vessel direct from the coast of Africa had touched in this colony; that the supply of Negro slaves came from Barbadoes, and that the colonists who would purchase slaves were supplied by the offspring of those already in the plantation; and that the colonists preferred white servants to black slaves. The best that can be said of Gov. Cranston's letter is, it was very respectful in tone. The following table was one of the enclosures of the letter. It is given in full on account of its general interest:—

"A list of the number of freemen and militia, with the servants, white and black, in the respective towns; as also the number of inhabitants in Her Majesty's colony of Rhode Island, &c., December the 5th, 1708.

Towns.	Freemen.	Militia.	White Servants.	Black Servants.	Total Number Of Inhabitants
Newport	190	358	20	220	2,203
Providence	241	283	6	7	1,446
Portsmouth	98	104	8	40	628
Warwick	80	95	4	10	480
Westerly	95	100	5	20	570
New Shoreham	38	47	—	6	208
Kingstown	200	282	—	85	1,200
Jamestown	33	28	9	32	206
Greenwich	40	65	3	6	240
Total	1,015	1,362	56	426	7,181

"It is to be understood that all men within this colony, from the age of sixteen to the age of sixty years, are of the militia, so that all freemen above and under said ages are inclusive in the abovesaid number of the militia.

"As to the increase or decrease of the inhabitants within five years last past, we are not capable to give an exact account, by reason there was no list ever taken before this (the militia excepted), which hath increased since the 14th of February, 1704-5 (at which time a list was returned to your Lordships), the number of 287.

"Samuel Cranston, Governor.

"Newport, on Rhode Island, December the 5th, 1708."[459]

The Board of Trade replied to Gov. Cranston, under date of "Whitehall, January 16th, 1709-10.," saying they should be glad to hear from him "in regard to Negroes," etc.[460]

The letter of inquiry from the Board of Trade imparted to slave-dealers an air of importance and respectability. The institution was not near so bad as it had been thought to be; the royal family were interested in its growth; it was a gainful enterprise; and, more than all, as a matter touching the conscience, the Bible and universal practice had sanctified the institution. To attempt to repeal the Act of 1652 would have been an occasion unwisely furnished for anti-slavery men to use to a good purpose. The bill was a dead letter, and its enemies concluded to let it remain on the statute-book of the colony.

The experiment of levying an impost-tax upon Negro slaves imported into the colony had proved an enriching success. After 1709 the slave-trade became rather brisk. As the population increased, public improvements became necessary,—there were new public buildings in demand, roads to be repaired, bridges to be built, and the poor and afflicted to be provided for. To do all this, taxes had to be levied upon the freeholders. A happy thought struck the leaders of the government. If men would import slaves, and the freemen of the colony would buy them, they should pay a tax as a penalty for their sin.[461] And the people easily accommodated their views to the state of the public treasury.

Attention has been called already to the impost Act of 1708. On the 27th of February, 1712, the General Assembly passed "An Act for preventing clandestine importations and exportations of passengers, or negroes, or Indian slaves into or out of this colony," etc. The Act is quite lengthy. It required masters of vessels to report to the governor the names and number of all passengers landed into the colony, and not to carry away any person without a pass or permission from the governor, upon pain of a fine of fifty pounds current money of New England. Persons desiring to leave the colony had to give public notice for ten days in the most public place in the colony;

and it specifies the duties of naval officers, and closes with the following in reference to Negro slaves, calling attention to the impost Act of 1708.—

"It was then and there enacted, that for all negroes imported into this colony, there shall be £3 current money, of New England, paid into the general treasury of this colony for each negro, by the owner or importer of said negro; reference being had unto the said act will more fully appear.

"But were laid under no obligation by the said act, to give an account to the Governor what negroes they did import, whereby the good intentions of said act were wholly frustrated and brought to no effect, and by the clandestinely hiding and conveying said negroes out of the town into the country, where they lie concealed:

"For the prevention of which for the future, it is hereby enacted by the authority aforesaid, that from and after the publication of this act, all masters of vessels that shall come into the harbor of Newport, or into any port of this government, that hath imported any negroes or Indian slaves, shall, before he puts on shore in any port of this government, or in the town of Newport, any negroes or Indian slaves, or suffers any negroes or Indian slaves to be put on shore by any person whatsoever, from on board his said vessel, deliver unto the naval officer in the town of Newport, a fair manifest under his hand, which shall specify the full number of negroes and Indian slaves he hath imported in his said vessel, of what sex, with their names, the names of their owners, or of those they are consigned to; to the truth of which manifest so given in, the said master shall give his corporal oath, or solemn engagement unto the said naval officer, who is hereby empowered to administer the same unto him, which said manifest being duly sworn unto, the said naval officer shall make a fair entry thereof in a book, which shall be prepared for that use, whereunto the said mister shall set his hand....

"And when the said master hath delivered his said manifest and sworn to it, as abovesaid, and before he hath landed on shore, or suffer to be landed, any negroes or Indian slaves as aforesaid, he, the said master, shall pay to the naval officer the sum of £3 current money, of New England, for each negro; and the sum of forty shillings of the like money for each Indian that shall be by him imported into this colony, or that shall be brought into this colony in the vessel whereof he is master.

> "But if he hath not ready money to pay down, as aforesaid, he shall then give unto the said naval officer a bill, as the law directs, to pay unto him the full sum above mentioned, for each and every negro and Indian imported as above said, which bill shall run payable in ten days from the entering

the manifest as above said; and if at the end of the ten days, the said master shall refuse to pay the full contents of his bill, that then the said naval officer shall deliver the said bill unto the Governor, or in his absence, to the next officer of the peace, as aforesaid who shall immediately proceed with the said master in the manner above said, by committing of him to Her Majesty's jail, where he shall remain without bail or mainprize, until he hath paid unto the naval officer, for the use of this colony, double the sum specified in his said bill, and all charges that shall accrue thereby; which money shall be paid out by the said naval officer, as the General Assembly of this colony shall order the same.

"And it is further enacted, that the naval officer who now is, and who ever shall be for the future put into said office, shall at his entering into the said office, take his engagement to the faithful performance of the above said acts. And for his encouragement, shall have such fees as are hereafter mentioned at the end of this act.

"And for the more effectual putting in execution those acts, and that none may plead ignorance:

"It is enacted by the authority aforesaid, that all masters of vessels trading to this government, shall give bond, with sufficient surety in the naval office, for the sum of £50, current money of New England."[462]

We have omitted a large portion of the bill, because of its length; but have quoted sufficient to give an excellent idea of the marvellous caution taken by the good Christians of Rhode Island to get every cent due them on account of the slave trade, which their prohibition did not prohibit. It was a carefully drawn bill for those days.

The diligence of the public officers in the seaport town of Newport was richly rewarded. The slave-trade now had the sanction and regulation of colonial law. The demand for Negro laborers was not affected in the least, while traders did not turn aside on account of three pounds per head tax upon every slave sold into Rhode Island. On the 5th of July, 1715, the General Assembly appropriated a portion of the fund derived from the impost-tax on imported Negroes to repairing the streets; and then strengthened and amplified the original law on impost-duties, etc. The following is the Act:—

"This Assembly, taking into consideration that Newport is the metropolitan town in this colony, and that all the courts of judicature within this colony are held there; and also, that it is the chief market town in the government; and that it hath very miry streets, especially that leading from the ferry, or landing place, up to the colony house, so that the members of the courts are very much discommoded therewith, and is a great hindrance to the transporting of provisions, &c., in and out of the said towns, to the great loss of the inhabitants thereof: —

"Therefore, be it enacted by this present Assembly, and by the authority thereof it is enacted, that the sum of £289 17s. 3d., now lying in the naval officer's hand, (being duties paid to this colony for importing of slaves), shall be, and is hereby granted to the town of Newport, towards paving the streets of Newport, from the ferry place, up to the colony house, in said Newport; to be improved by their directors, such as they shall, at their quarter meetings appoint for the same.

"And whereas, there was an act of Assembly, made at Newport in the year 1701-2, for the better preventing of fraud, and cozen, in paying the duties for importing of negro and Indian slaves into this colony, and the same being found in some clauses deficient, for the effecting of the full intent and purpose thereof: —

"Therefore, it is hereby enacted by the authority aforesaid, that every master of ship, or vessel, merchant or other person or persons, importing or bringing into this colony any negro slave or slaves of what age soever, shall enter their number, names, and sex in the naval office; and the master shall insert the same in the manifest of his lading, and shall pay to the naval officer in Newport, £3 per head, for the use of this colony, for every negro, male or female, so imported, or brought in. And every such master, merchant, or other person, refusing or neglecting to pay the said duty within ten days after they are brought ashore in said colony, then the said naval officer, on knowledge thereof, shall enter an action and sue [for] the recovery of the same, against him or them, in an action of debt, in any of His Majesty's courts of record, within this colony.

"And if any master of ship or vessel, merchant or others, shall refuse or neglect to make entry, as aforesaid, of all negroes imported in such ship or vessel, or be convicted of not entering the full number, such master, merchant, or other person, shall forfeit and pay the sum of £6, for every one that he shall refuse or neglect to make entry, of one moiety thereof to His Majesty, for and towards the support of the government of this colony; and the other moiety to him or them that shall inform or sue for the same; to be recovered by the naval officer in manner as above said.

"And also, all persons that shall bring any negro or negroes into this colony, from any of His Majesty's provinces adjoining, shall in like manner enter the number, names and sex, of all such negroes, in the above said office, under the penalty of the like forfeiture, as above said, and to be recovered in like manner by the naval officer, and shall pay into the said office within the time above limited, the like sum of £3 per head; and for default of payment, the same to be recovered by the naval officer in like manner as aforesaid.

"Provided always, that if any gentleman, who is not a resident in this colony, and shall pass through any part thereof, with a waiting man or men with him, and doth not reside in this colony six months, then such waiting men shall be free from the above said duty; the said gentleman giving his solemn engagement, that they are not for sale; any act or acts, clause or clauses of acts, to the contrary hereof, in any ways, notwithstanding.

> "Provided, that none of the clauses in the aforesaid act, shall extend to any masters or vessels, who import negroes into this colony, directly from the coast of Africa.

"And it is further enacted by the authority aforesaid, that the money raised by the impost of negroes, as aforesaid, shall be disposed of as followeth, viz.:

"The one moiety of the said impost money to be for the use of the town of Newport, to be disposed of by the said town towards paving the streets of said town, and for no other use whatsoever, for and during the full time of seven years from the publication of this act, and that £60 of said impost money be for, and towards the erecting of a substantial bridge over Potowomut river, at or near the house of Ezekiel Hunt, in East Greenwich, and to no other use whatsoever.

> "And that Major Thomas Frye and Capt. John Eldredge be the persons appointed to order and oversee the building of said bridge, and to render an account thereof, to the Assembly, and the said Major Frye and Capt. Eldredge to be paid for their trouble and pains, out of the remaining part of said impost money, and the remainder of said impost money to be disposed of as the Assembly shall from time to time see fit."[463]

And in October, 1717, the following order passed the assembly:—

> "It is ordered by this Assembly, that the naval officer pay out of the impost money on slaves, £100, to the overseer that oversees the paving of the streets of Newport, to be improved for paying the charges of paving said streets."[464]

The fund accruing from the impost-duty on slaves was regarded with great favor everywhere, especially in Newport. It had cleaned her streets and lightened the burdens of taxation which rested so grievously upon the freeholders. There was no voice lifted against the iniquitous traffic, and the conscience of the colony was at rest. In June, 1729, the following Act was passed:—

"An Act disposing of the money raised in this colony on importing negro slaves into this colony.

"Forasmuch as there is an act of Assembly made in this colony the 27th day of February, A.D. 1711, laying a duty of £3 per head on all slaves imported into this colony, as is in said act is expressed; and several things of a public nature requiring a fund to be set apart for carrying them on:—

> "Be it therefore enacted by the General Assembly, and by the authority of the same it is enacted and declared, that henceforward all monies that shall be raised in this colony by the aforesaid account, on any slaves imported into this colony, shall be employed, the one moiety thereof for the use of the town of Newport, towards paving and amending the streets thereof, and the other moiety, for, and towards the support, repairing and mending the great bridges on the main, in the country roads, and for no other use whatsoever; any thing in the aforesaid act to the contrary, in anywise notwithstanding."[465]

It is wonderful how potential the influence of money is upon mankind. The sentiments of the good people had been scattered to the winds; and they had found a panacea for the violated convictions of the wrong of slavery in the reduction of their taxes, new bridges, and cleansed streets. Conscience had been bribed into acquiescence, and the iniquity thrived. There were those who still endeavored to escape the vigilance of the naval officers, and save the three pounds on each slave. But the diligence and liberality of the authorities were not to be outdone by the skulking stinginess of Negro-smugglers. On the 18th of June, 1723, the General Assembly passed the following order:—

> "Voted, that Mr. Daniel Updike, the attorney general, be, and he hereby is ordered, appointed and empowered to gather in the money due to this colony, for the importation of negroes, and to prosecute, sue and implead such person or persons as shall refuse to pay the same; and that he be allowed five shillings per head, for every slave that shall

be hereafter imported into this colony, out of the impost money; and that he be also allowed ten per cent. more for all such money as he shall recover of the outstanding debts; and in all respects to have the like power as was given to the naval officer by the former act."[466]

The above illustrates the spirit of the times. There was a mania for this impost-tax upon stolen Negroes, and the law was to be enforced against all who sought to evade its requirements. But the Assembly had a delicate sense of equity, as well as an inexorable opinion of the precise demands of the law in its letter and spirit. On the 19th of June, 1716, the following was passed:—

"It is ordered by this Assembly, that the duty of two sucking slaves imported into this colony by Col. James Vaughan, of Barbadoes, be remitted to the said James Vaughan."[467]

It was not below the dignity of the Legislature of the colony of Rhode Island to pass a bill of relief for Col. Vaughan, and refund to him the six pounds he had paid to land his two sucking Negro baby slaves! In June, 1731, the naval officer, James Cranston, called the attention of the Assembly to the case of one Mr. Royall,—who had imported forty-five Negroes into the colony, and after a short time sold sixteen of them into the Province of Massachusetts Bay, where there was also an impost-tax,—and asked directions. The Assembly replied as follows:—

"Upon consideration whereof, it is voted and ordered, that the duty to this colony of the said sixteen negroes transported into the Massachusetts Bay, as aforesaid, be taken off and remitted; but that he collect the duty of the other twenty-nine."[468]

But the zeal of the colony in seeking the enforcement of the impost-law created a strong influence against it from without; and by order of the king the entire law was repealed in May, 1732.[469]

The cruel practice of manumitting aged and helpless slaves became so general in this plantation, that the General Assembly passed a law regulating it, in February, 1728. It was borrowed very largely from a similar law in Massachusetts, and reads as follows:—

"An Act relating to freeing mulatto and negro slaves.

"Forasmuch, as great charge, trouble and inconveniences have arisen to the inhabitants of divers towns in this colony, by the manumitting and setting free mulatto and negro slaves; for remedying whereof, for the future,—

"Be it enacted by the General Assembly of this colony, and by the authority of the same it is enacted, that no mulatto or negro slave, shall be hereafter manumitted, discharged or set free, or at liberty, until sufficient security be given to the town treasurer of the town or place where such person dwells, in a valuable sum of not less than £100, to secure and indemnify the town or place from all charge for, or about such mulatto or negro, to be manumitted and set at liberty, in case he or she by sickness, lameness or otherwise, be rendered incapable to support him or herself.

> "And no mulatto or negro hereafter manumitted, shall be deemed or accounted free, for whom security shall not be given as aforesaid, but shall be the proper charge of their respective masters or mistresses, in case they should stand in need of relief and support; notwithstanding any manumission or instrument of freedom to them made and given; and shall be liable at all times to be put forth to service by the justices of the peace, or wardens of the town."[470]

It is very remarkable that there were no lawyers to challenge the legality of such laws as the above, which found their way into the statute books of all the New-England colonies. There could he no conditional emancipation. If a slave were set at liberty, why he was free, and, if he afterwards became a pauper, was entitled to the same care as a white freeman. But it is not difficult to see that the status of a free Negro was difficult of definition. When the Negro slave grew old and infirm, his master no longer cared for him, and the public was protected against him by law. Death was his most beneficent friend.

In October, 1743, a widow lady named Comfort Taylor, of Bristol County, Massachusetts Bay, sued and obtained judgment against a Negro named Cuff Borden for two hundred pounds, and cost of suit "for a grievous trespass." Cuff was a slave. An ordinary execution would have gone against his person: he would have been imprisoned, and nothing more. In view of this condition of affairs, Mrs. Taylor petitioned the General Assembly of Rhode Island, praying that authority be granted the sheriff to sell Cuff, as other property, to satisfy the judgment. The Assembly granted her prayer as follows:—

> "Upon consideration whereof, it is voted and resolved, that the sheriff of the said county of Newport, when he shall receive the execution against the said negro Cuff, be, and he is hereby fully empowered to sell said negro Cuff as other personal estate: and after the fine of £20 be paid into the general treasury, and all other charges deducted out of the

price of said negro, the remainder to be appropriated in said satisfying said execution."[471]

This case goes to show that in Rhode Island Negro slaves were rated, at law, as chattel property, and could be taken in execution to satisfy debts as other personal property.

A great many slaves availed themselves of frequent opportunities of going away in privateers and other vessels. With but little before them in this life, they were even willing to risk being sold into slavery at some other place, that they might experience a change. They made excellent seamen, and were greatly desired by masters of vessels. This went on for a long time. The loss to the colony was great; and the General Assembly passed the subjoined bill as a check to the stampede that had become quite general: —

> "An Act to prevent the commanders of privateers, or masters of any other vessels, from carrying slaves out of this colony.

"Whereas, it frequently happens that the commanders of privateers, and masters of other vessels, do carry off slaves that are the property of inhabitants of this colony, and that without the privity or consent of their masters or mistresses; and whereas, there is no law of this colony for remedying so great an evil, —

"Be it therefore enacted by this General Assembly, and by the authority of the same, it is enacted, that from and after the publication of this act, if any commander of a private man of war, or master of a merchant ship or other vessel, shall knowingly carry away from, or out of this colony, a slave or slaves, the property of any inhabitant thereof, the commander of such privateer, or the master of the said merchant ship or vessel, shall pay, as a fine, the sum of £500, to be recovered by the general treasurer of this colony for the time being, by bill, plaint, or information in any court of record within this colony.

"And be it further enacted by the authority aforesaid, that the owner or owners of any slave or slaves that may be carried away, as aforesaid, shall have a right of action against the commander of the said privateer, or master of the said merchant ship or vessel, or against the owner or owners of the same, in which the said slave or slaves is, or are carried away, and by the said action or suit, recover of him or them, double damages.

"And whereas, disputes may arise respecting the knowledge that the owner or owners, commanders or masters of the said private men of war, merchant ships or vessels may have of any slave or slaves being on board a privateer, or merchant ship or vessel, —

"Be it therefore further enacted, and by the authority aforesaid, it is enacted, that when any owner or owners of any slave or slaves in this colony, shall suspect that a slave or slaves, to him, her or them belonging, is, or are, on board any private man of war, or merchant ship or vessel, the owner or owners of such slave or slaves may make application, either to the owner or owners, or to the commander or master of the said ship or vessel, before its sailing, and inform him or them thereof, which being done in the presence of one or more substantial witness or witnesses, the said information or application shall amount to, and be construed, deemed and taken to be a full proof of his or their knowledge thereof, provided, the said slave or slaves shall go in any such ship or vessel.

"And be it further enacted by the authority aforesaid, that if the owner or owners of any slave or slaves in this colony, or any other person or persons, legally authorized by the owner or owners of a slave or slaves, shall attempt to go on board any privateer, or a merchant ship or vessel, to search for his, her or their slave or slaves, and the commander or master of such ship or vessel, or other officer or officers on board the same, in the absence of the commander or master, shall refuse to permit such owner or owners of a slave or slaves, or other person or persons, authorized, as aforesaid, to go on board and search for the slave or slaves by him, her or them missed, or found absent, such refusal shall be deemed, construed, and taken to be full proof that the owner or owners, commander or master of the said privateer or other ship or vessel, hath, or have a real knowledge that such slave or slaves is, or are on board.

"And this act shall be forthwith published, and therefrom have, and take force and effect, in and throughout this colony.

"Accordingly the said act was published by the beat of drum, on the 17th day of June, 1757, a few minutes before noon, by

"THO. WARD, Secretary."[472]

The education of the Negro slave in this colony was thought to be inimical to the best interests of the master class. Ignorance was the *sine qua non* of slavery. The civil government and ecclesiastical establishment ground him, body and spirit, as between "the upper and nether millstones." But the Negro was a good listener, and was not unconscious of what was going on around him. He was neither blind nor deaf.

The fires of the Revolutionary struggle began to melt the frozen feelings of the colonists towards the slaves. When they began to feel the British lion clutching at the throat of their own liberties, the bondage of the Negro stared them in the face. They knew the Negro's power of endurance, his personal courage, his admirable promptitude in the performance of difficult tasks, and his desperate spirit when pressed too sharply. The thought of such an ally for the English army, such an element in their rear, was louder in their souls than the roar of the enemy's guns. The act of June, 1774, shows how deeply the people felt on the subject.

> "An Act prohibiting the importation of Negroes into this Colony.

Whereas, the inhabitants of America are generally engaged in the preservation of their own rights and liberties, among which, that of personal freedom must be considered as the greatest; as those who are desirous of enjoying all the advantages of liberty themselves, should be willing to extend personal liberty to others;—

"Therefore, be it enacted by this General Assembly, and by the authority thereof it is enacted, that for the future, no negro or mulatto slave shall be brought into this colony; and in case any slave shall hereafter be brought in, he or she shall be, and are hereby, rendered immediately free, so far as respects personal freedom, and the enjoyment of private property, in the same manner as the native Indians.

"Provided, nevertheless, that this law shall not extend to servants of persons travelling through this colony, who are not inhabitants thereof, and who carry them out with them, when they leave the same.

"Provided, also, that nothing in this act shall extend, or be deemed to extend, to any negro or mulatto slave, belonging to any inhabitant of either of the British colonies, islands or plantations, who shall come into this colony, with an intention to settle or reside, for a number of years, therein; but such negro or mulatto, so brought into this colony, by such person inclining to settle or reside therein, shall be, and remain, in the same situation, and subject in like manner to their master or mistress, as they were in the colony or plantation from whence they removed.

> "Provided, nevertheless, that if any person, so coming into this colony, to settle or reside, as aforesaid, shall afterwards remove out of the same, such person shall be obliged to carry all such negro or mulatto slaves, as also all such as shall be born from them, out of the colony with them.
> "Provided, also, that nothing in this act shall extend, or be deemed to extend, to any negro or mulatto slave brought from the coast of Africa, into the West Indies, on board any vessel belonging to this colony, and which negro or mulatto

slave could not be disposed of in the West Indies, but shall be brought into this colony.

"Provided, that the owner of such negro or mulatto slave give bond to the general treasurer of the said colony, within ten days after such arrival in the sum of £100, lawful money, for each and every such negro or mulatto slave so brought in, that such negro or mulatto slave shall be exported out of the colony, within one year from the date of such bond; if such negro or mulatto be alive, and in a condition to be removed.

"Provided, also, that nothing in this act shall extend, or be deemed to extend, to any negro or mulatto slave that may be on board any vessel belonging to this colony, now at sea, in her present voyage."[473]

In 1730 the population of Rhode Island was, whites, 15,302; Indians, 985; Negroes, 1,648; total, 17,935. In 1749 there were 28,439 whites, and 3,077 Negroes. Indians were not given this year. In 1756 the whites numbered 35,939, the Negroes 4,697. In 1774 Rhode Island contained 9,439 families, Newport had 9,209 inhabitants. The whites in the entire colony numbered 54,435, the Negroes, 3,761, and the Indians, 1,482.[474] It will be observed that the Negro population fell off between the years 1749 and 1774. It is accounted for by the fact mentioned before,—that many ran away on ships that came into the Province.

The Negroes received better treatment at this time than at any other period during the existence of the colony. There was a general relaxation of the severe laws that had been so rigidly enforced. They took great interest in public meetings, devoured with avidity every scrap of news regarding the movements of the Tory forces, listened with rapt attention to the patriotic conversations of their masters, and when the storm-cloud of war broke were as eager to fight for the independence of North America as their masters.

FOOTNOTES:

[450] R.I. Col. Recs., vol. i. p. 243.

[451] Bancroft, vol. i. 5th ed. p. 175.

[452] R.I. Col. Recs., vol. iii. pp. 492, 493.

[453] There is no law making the manufacturing of whiskey legal in the United States; and yet the United-States government makes laws to regulate the business, and collects a revenue from it. It exists by and with the consent of the government, and, in a sense, is legal.

[454] R.I. Col. Recs., vol. iv. p. 34.

[455] I have searched diligently for the Act of February, among the Rhode-Island Collections and Records, but have not found it. It was evidently more comprehensive than the above Act.

[456] R.I. Col. Recs., vol iv. p. 50.

[457] R.I. Col. Recs, vol. iv. pp. 53, 54.

[458] R.I. Coll. Recs., vol. iv. pp. 54, 55.

[459] R.I. Col. Recs., vol iv. p. 59.

[460] J. Carter Brown's Manuscripts, vol. viii. Nos. 506, 512.

[461] It was a specious sort of reasoning. I learn that the bank over on the corner is to be robbed to-night at twelve o'clock. Shall I go and rob it at ten o'clock; because, if I do not do so, another person will, two hours later?

[462] R.I. Col. Recs., vol. iv. pp. 133-135.

[463] R.I. Col. Recs., vol. iv. pp. 191-193.

[464] R.I. Col. Recs., vol. iv p. 225.

[465] R.I. Col. Recs., vol. iv. pp. 423, 424.

[466] Ibid., p. 330.

[467] Ibid., vol. iv. p. 209.

[468] R.I. Col. Recs., vol. iv. p. 454.

[469] Ibid., vol. iv. p. 471.

[470] Ibid., vol. iv. pp. 415, 416.

[471] R.I. Col. Recs., vol. v. pp. 72, 73.

[472] R.I. Col. Recs., vol vi. pp. 64, 65.

[473] R.I. Col. Recs., vol. vii. pp. 251, 252.

[474] American Annals, vol ii. pp. 107,155, 156, 184, and 265.

CHAPTER XX
THE COLONY OF NEW JERSEY

1664-1775.

New Jersey passes into the Hands of the English.—Political Powers conveyed to Berkeley and Carteret.—Legislation on the Subject of Slavery during the Eighteenth Century.—The Colony divided into East and West Jersey.—Separate Governments.—An Act concerning Slavery by the Legislature of East Jersey.—General Apprehension respecting the rising of Negro and Indian Slaves.—East and West Jersey surrender their Rights of Government to the Queen.—An Act for regulating the Conduct of Slaves.—Impost-Tax of Ten Pounds levied upon each Negro imported into the Colony.—The General Court passes a Law regulating the Trial of Slaves.—Negroes ruled out of the Militia Establishment upon Condition.—Population of the Jerseys in 1738 and 1745.

THE colony of New Jersey passed into the control of the English in 1664; and the first grant of political powers, upon which the government was erected, was conveyed by the Duke of York to Berkeley and Carteret during the same year. In the "Proprietary Articles of Concession," the words *servants, slaves, and Christian servants* occur. It was the intention of the colonists to draw a distinction between "*servants for a term of years,*" and "*servants for life,*" between white servants and black slaves, between Christians and pagans.

When slavery was introduced into Jersey is not known.[475] There is no doubt but that it made its appearance there almost as early as in New Netherlands. The Dutch, the Quakers, and the English held slaves. But the system was milder here than in any of the other colonies. The Negroes were scattered among the families of the whites, and were treated with great humanity. Legislation on the subject of slavery did not begin until the middle of the eighteenth century, and it was not severe. Before this time, say three-quarters of a century, a few Acts had been passed calculated to protect the slave element from the sin of intoxication. In 1675 an Act passed, imposing fines and punishments upon any white person who should transport, harbor, or entertain "apprentices, servants, or slaves." It was perfectly natural that the Negroes should be of a nomadic disposition. They had no homes, no wives, no children,—nothing to attach them to a locality. Those who resided near the seacoast watched, with unflagging interest, the coming and going of the mysterious white-winged vessels. They hung upon the storied lips of every fugitive, and dreamed of lands afar where they might find that liberty for which their souls thirsted as the hart for the waterbrook. Far from their native country, without the blessings of the Church, or the warmth of substantial friendship, they fell into a listless condition, a somnolence that led them to stagger against some of the regulations of the Province. Their wandering was not inspired by any subjective, inherent, generic evil: it was but the tossing of a weary, distressed mind under the dreadful influences of a hateful dream. And what little there is in the early records of the colony of New Jersey is at once a compliment to the humanity of the master, and the docility of the slave.

In 1676 the colony was divided into East and West Jersey, with separate governments. The laws of East Jersey, promulgated in 1682, contained laws prohibiting the entertaining of fugitive servants, or trading with Negroes. The law respecting fugitive servants was intended to destroy the hopes of runaways in the entertainment they so frequently obtained at the hands of benevolent Quakers and other enemies of "indenture" and slavery. The law-makers acted upon the presumption, that as the Negro had no property, did not own himself, he could not sell any article of his own. All slaves who attempted to dispose of any article were regarded with suspicion. The law made it a misdemeanor for a free person to purchase any thing from a slave, and hence cut off a source of revenue to the more industrious slaves, who by their frugality often prepared something for sale.

In 1694 "an Act concerning slaves" was passed by the Legislature of East Jersey. It provided, among other things, for the trial of "negroes and other slaves, for felonies punishable with death, by a jury of twelve persons before three justices of the peace; for theft, before two justices; the punishment by whipping." Here was the grandest evidence of the high character of the white population in East Jersey. In every other colony in North America the Negro was denied the right of "trial by jury," so sacred to Englishmen. In Virginia, Maryland, Massachusetts, Connecticut,—in all the colonies,—the Negro went into court convicted, went out convicted, and was executed, upon the frailest evidence imaginable. But here in Jersey the only example of justice was shown toward the Negro in North America. "Trial by jury" implied the right to be sworn, and give competent testimony. A Negro slave, when on trial for his life, was accorded the privilege of being tried by twelve honest white colonists before three justices of the peace. This was in striking contrast with the conduct of the colony of New York, where Negroes were arrested upon the incoherent accusations of dissolute whites and terrified blacks. It gave the Negroes a new and an anomalous position in the New World. It banished the cruel theory of Virginia, New York, and Connecticut, that the Negro was a pagan, and therefore should not be sworn in courts of justice, and threw open a wide door for his entrance into a more hopeful state than he had, up to that time, dared to anticipate. It allowed him to infer that his life was a little more than that of the brute that perisheth; that he could not be dragged by malice through the forms of a trial, without jury, witness, counsel, or friend, to an ignominious death, that was to be regretted only by his master, and his regrets to be solaced by the Legislature paying "the price;" that the law regarded him as a man, whose life was too dear to be committed to the disposition of irascible men, whose prejudices could be mollified only in extreme cruelty or cold-blooded murder. It had much to do toward elevating the character of the Negro in New Jersey. It first fired his heart with the noble impulse of gratitude, and then led him to hope. And how much that little word means! It causes the soul to spread its white pinions to every favoring breeze, and hasten on to a propitious future. And then the fact that Negroes had rights acknowledged by the statutes, and respectfully accorded them by the courts, had its due influence upon the white colonists. The men, or class of men, who have rights not challenged, command the respect of others. The fact clothes them with dignity as with a garment. And then, by the inevitable logic of the position of the courts of East Jersey, the colonists were led to the conclusion that the Negroes among them had other rights. And, as it has been said already, they received better treatment here than in any other colony in the country.

In West Jersey happily the word "slave" was omitted from the laws. Only servants and runaway servants were mentioned, and the selling of rum to Negroes and Indians was strictly forbidden.

The fear of insurrection among Indians and Negroes was general throughout all of the colonies. One a savage, and the other untutored, they knew but two manifestations,—gratitude and revenge. It was deemed a wise precaution to keep these unfortunate people as far removed from the exciting influences of rum as possible. Chapter twenty-three of a law passed in West Jersey in 1676, providing for publicity in judicial proceedings, concludes as follows:—

> "That all and every person and persons inhabiting the said province, shall, as far as in us lies, be free from oppression and slavery."[476]

In 1702 the proprietors of East and West Jersey surrendered their rights of government to the queen. The Province was immediately placed with New York, and the government committed to the hands of Lord Cornbury. [477] In 1704 "An Act for regulating negroe, Indian and mulatto slaves within the province of New Jersey," was introduced, but was tabled and disallowed. The Negroes had just cause for the fears they entertained as to legislation directed at the few rights they had enjoyed under the Jersey government. Their fellow-servants over in New York had suffered under severe laws, and at that time had no privilege in which they could rejoice. In 1713 the following law was passed:—

> "An act for regulating slaves. (1 Nev. L., c. 10.) Sect. 1. Against trading with slaves. 2. For arrest of slaves being without pass. 3. Negro belonging to another province, not having license, to be whipped and committed to jail. 4. Punishment of slaves for crimes to be by three or more justices of the peace, with five of the principal freeholders, without a grand jury; seven agreeing, shall give judgment. 5. Method in such causes more particularly described. Provides that 'the evidence of Indian, negro, or mulatto slaves shall be admitted and allowed on trials of such slaves, on all causes criminal.' 6. Owner may demand a jury. 7, 8. Compensation to owners for death of slave. 9. A slave for attempting to ravish any white woman, or presuming 'to assault or strike any free man or woman professing Christianity,' any two justices have discretionary powers to inflict corporal punishment, not extending to life or limb. 10. Slaves, for stealing, to be whipped. 11. Penalties on justices, &c., neglecting duty. 12. Punishment for concealing, harboring, or entertaining slaves of others. 13. Provides that no Negro, Indian, or mulatto that shall thereafter be made free, shall hold any real estate in his own right, in fee simple or fee tail. 14. 'And whereas it is found by experience that free Negroes are an idle, slothful people, and prove very often a charge to the place where they are,' enacts that owners manumitting, shall give security, &c."[478]

Nearly all the humane features of the Jersey laws were supplanted by severe prohibitions, requirements, and penalties. The trial by jury was construed to mean that one Negro's testimony was good against another Negro in a trial for a felony, allowing the owner of the slave to demand a jury. Humane masters were denied the right to emancipate their slaves, and the latter were prohibited from owning real property in fee simple or fee tail. Having stripped the Negro of the few rights he possessed, the General Court, during the same year, went on to reduce him to absolute property, and levied an impost-tax of ten pounds upon every Negro imported into the colony, to remain in force for seven years.

In 1754 an Act provided, that in the borough of Elizabeth any white servant or servants, slave or slaves, which shall "be brought before the Mayor, &c., by their masters or other inhabitant of the Borough, for any misdemeanor rude or disorderly behavior, may be committed to the workhouse to hard labor and receive correction not exceeding thirty lashes."[479] This Act was purely local in character, and indiscriminate in its application to every class of servants. It was nothing more than a police regulation, and as such was a wholesome law.

In 1768 the General Court passed An Act to regulate the trial of slaves for murder and other crimes and to repeal so much of an act, &c. Sections one and two provided for the trial of slaves by the ordinary higher criminal courts. Section three provided that the expenses incurred in the execution of slaves should be levied upon all the owners of able-bodied slaves in the county, by order of the justices presiding at the trial. Section four repealed sections four, five, six, and seven of the Act of 1713. This was significant. It portended a better feeling toward the Negroes, and illumined the dark horizon of slavery with the distant light of hope. A strong feeling in favor of better treatment for Negro slaves made itself manifest at this time. When the Quaker found the prejudice against himself subsiding, he turned, like a good Samaritan, to pour the wine of human sympathy into the lacerated feelings of the Negro. Private instruction was given to them in many parts of Jersey. The gospel was expounded to them in its beauty and simplicity, and produced its good fruit in better lives.

The next year, 1769, a mercenary spirit inspired and secured the passage of another Act levying a tax upon imported slaves, and requiring persons manumitting slaves to give better securities. It reads,—

> "Whereas duties on the importation of negroes in several of the neighboring colonies hath, on experience, been found beneficial in the introduction of sober industrious foreigners, to settle under his Majesty's allegiance, and the promoting a spirit of industry among the inhabitants in general, in order therefore to promote the same good designs in this government and that such as purchase slaves may contribute some equitable proportion of the public burdens."[480]

How an impost-tax upon imported slaves would be "beneficial in the introduction of sober industrious foreigners," is not easily perceived;

and how it would promote "a spirit of industry among the inhabitants in general," is a problem most difficult of solution. But these were the lofty reasons that inspired the General Court to seek to fill the coffers of the Province with money drawn from the slave-lottery, where human beings were raffled off to the highest bidders in the colony. The cautious language in which the Act was couched indicated the sensitive state of the public conscience on slavery at that time. They were afraid to tell the truth. They did not dare to say to the people: We propose to repair the streets of your towns, the public roads, and lighten the burden of taxation, by saying to men-stealers, we will allow you to sell your cargoes of slaves into this colony provided you share the spoils of your superlative crime! No, they had to tell the people that the introduction of Negro slaves, upon whom there was a tax, would entice sober and industrious white people to come among them, and would quicken the entire Province with a spirit of thrift never before witnessed!

In 1760 the Negro was ruled out of the militia establishment upon a condition. The law provided against the enlistment of any "young man under the age of twenty-one years, or any slaves who are so for terms of life, or apprentices," without leave of their masters. This was the mildest prohibition against the entrance of the slave into the militia service in any of the colonies. There is nothing said about the employment of the free Negroes in this service; and it is fair to suppose, in view of the mild character of the laws, that they were not excluded. In settlements where the German and Quaker elements predominated, the Negro found that his "lines had fallen unto him in pleasant places, and that he had a goodly heritage." In the coast towns, and in the great centres of population, the white people were of a poorer class. Many were adventurers, cruel and unscrupulous in their methods. The speed with which the people sought to obtain a competency wore the finer edges of their feeling to the coarse grain of selfishness; and they not only drew themselves up into the miserable rags of their own selfish aggrandizements as far as all competitors were concerned, but regarded slavery with imperturbable complacency.

In 1738 the population of the Jerseys was, whites, 43,388; blacks, 3,981. In 1745 the whites numbered 56,797, and the blacks, 4,606.[481]

FOOTNOTES:

[475] It is unfortunate that there is no good history of New Jersey. The records of the Historical Society of that State are not conveniently printed, nor valuable in colonial data.

[476] Freedom and Bondage, vol. i. p. 283.

[477] The following were the instructions his lordship received, concerning the treatment of Negro slaves: "You shall endeavour to get a law past for the restraining of any inhuman severity, which by ill masters or overseers may be used towards their Christian servants and their slaves, and that provision be made therein that the wilfull killing of Indians and negroes may be punished with death, and that a fit penalty be emposed for the maiming of them."—Freedom and Bondage, vol. i. p. 280, note.

[478] Freedom and Bondage, vol. i. p. 284.

[479] Hurd, vol. i. p. 285.

[480] Hurd, vol. i. p 285.

[481] American Annals, vol. ii. pp. 127, 143.

CHAPTER XXI
THE COLONY OF SOUTH CAROLINA

1665-1775.

The Carolinas receive two Different Charters from the Crown of Great Britain.—Era of Slavery Legislation.—Law establishing Slavery.—The Slave Population of this Province regarded as Chattel Property.—Trial of Slaves.—Increase of Slave Population.—The Increase in the Rice-Trade.—Severe Laws regulating the Private and Public Conduct of Slaves.—Punishment of Slaves for running away.—The Life of Slaves regarded as of Little Consequence by the Violent Master Class.—An Act empowering two Justices of the Peace to investigate Treatment of Slaves.—An Act prohibiting the Overworking of Slaves.—Slave-Market at Charleston.—Insurrection.—A Law authorizing the carrying of Fire-Arms among the Whites.—The Enlistment of Slaves to serve in Time of Alarm.—Negroes admitted to the Militia Service.—Compensation to Masters for the Loss of Slaves killed by the Enemy or who desert.—Few Slaves manumitted.—From 1754-76, Little Legislation on the Subject of Slavery.—Threatening War between England and her Provincial Dependencies.—The Effect upon Public Sentiment.

THE Carolinas received two different charters from the crown of Great Britain. The first was witnessed by the king at Westminster, March 24, 1663; the second, June 30, 1665. The last charter was surrendered to the king by seven of the eight proprietors on the 25th July, 1729. The government became regal; and the Province was immediately divided into North and South Carolina by an order of the British Council, and the boundaries between the two governments fixed.

There were Negro slaves in the Carolinas from the earliest days of their existence. The era of slavery legislation began about the year 1690. The first Act for the "Better Ordering of Slaves" was "read three times and passed, and ratified in open Parliament, the seventh day of February, Anno Domini, 1690." It bore the signatures of Seth Sothell, G. Muschamp, John Beresford, and John Harris. It contained fifteen articles of the severest character. On the 7th of June, 1712, the first positive law establishing slavery passed, and was signed.[482] The entire Act embraced thirty-five sections. Section one is quoted in full because of the interest that centres in it in connection with the problem of slavery legislation in the colonies.

> "1. Be it therefore enacted, by his Excellency, William, Lord Craven, Palatine, and the rest of the true and absolute Lords and Proprietors of this Province, by and with the advice and consent of the rest of the members of the General Assembly, now met at Charlestown, for the South-west part of this Province, and by the authority of the same, That all negroes, mulatoes, mustizoes or Indians, which at any time heretofore have been sold, or now are held or taken to be, or hereafter shall be bought and sold for slaves, are hereby declared slaves; and they, and their children, are hereby made and declared slaves, to all intents and purposes; excepting all such negroes, mulatoes, mustizoes or Indians, which heretofore have been, or hereafter shall be, for some particular merit, made and declared free, either by the Governor and council of this Province, pursuant to any Act or law of this Province, or by their respective owners or masters; and also, excepting all such negroes, mulatoes, mustizoes or Indians, as can prove they ought not to be sold for slaves. And in case any negro, mulatoe, mustizoe or Indian, doth lay claim to his or her freedom upon all or any of the said accounts, the same shall be finally heard and determined by the Governor and council of this Province."[483]

The above section was re-enacted into another law, containing forty-three sections, passed on the 23d of February, 1722. Virginia declared that children should follow the condition of their mothers, but never passed a law in any respect like unto this most remarkable Act. South Carolina has the unenviable reputation of being the only colony in North America where by positive statute the Negro was doomed to perpetual bondage.[484] On the 10th of May, 1740, an act regulating slaves, containing fifty sections, recites:—

> "Whereas, in his Majesty's plantations in America, slavery his been introduced and allowed, and the people commonly called negroes, Indians, mulattoes and mustizoes, have been deemed absolute slaves, and the subjects of property in the hands of particular persons, the extent of whose power over such slaves ought to be settled and limited by positive

laws, so that the slave may be kept in due subjection and obedience, and the owners and other persons having the care and government of slaves may be restrained from exercising too great rigour and cruelty over them, and that the public peace and order of this Province may be preserved: We pray your most sacred Majesty that it may be enacted."[485]

The first section of this Act was made more elaborate than any other law previously passed. It bore all the marks of ripe scholarship and profound law learning. The first section is produced here:—

"1. And be it enacted, by the honorable William Bull, Esquire, Lieutenant Governor and Commander-in-chief, by and with the advice and consent of his Majesty's honorable Council, and the Commons House of Assembly of this Province, and by the authority of the same, That all negroes and Indians, (free Indians in amity with this government, and negroes, mulattoes and mustizoes, who are now free, excepted,) mulattoes or mustizoes who now are, or shall hereafter be, in this Province, and all their issue and offspring, born or to be born, shall be, and they are hereby declared to be, and remain forever hereafter, absolute slaves, and shall follow the condition of the mother, and shall be deemed, held, taken, reputed and adjudged in law, to be chattels personal, in the hands of their owners and possessors, and their executors, administrators and assigns, to all intents, constructions and purposes whatsoever; provided always, that if any negro, Indian, mulatto or mustizo, shall claim his or her freedom, it shall and may be lawful for such negro, Indian, mulatto or mustizo, or any person or persons whatsoever, on his or her behalf, to apply to the justices of his Majesty's court of common pleas, by petition or motion, either during the sitting of the said court, or before any of the justices of the same court, at any time in the vacation; and the said court, or any of the justices thereof, shall, and they are hereby fully impowered to, admit any person so applying to be guardian for any negro, Indian, mulatto or mustizo, claiming his, her or their freedom; and such guardians shall be enabled, entitled and capable in law, to bring an action of trespass in the nature of ravishment of ward, against any person who shall claim property in, or who shall be in possession of, any such negro, Indian, mulatto or mustizo; and the defendant shall and may plead the general issue on such action brought, and the special matter may and shall be given in evidence, and upon a general or special verdict found, judgment shall be given according to the very right of the cause, without having any regard to any defect in the proceedings, either in form or substance; and if judgment shall be given for the plaintiff, a special entry shall be made, declaring that the ward of the plaintiff is free, and the jury shall assess damages which the plaintiff's ward hath sustained, and the court shall give judgment, and award execution, against the defendant for such damage, with full costs of suit; but in case judgment shall be given for the defendant, the said court is hereby fully impowered to inflict such corporal punishment, not extending to life or limb, on the ward of the plaintiff, as they, in their discretion, shall think fit; provided always, that in any action or suit to be brought in pursuance of the direction of this Act, the burthen of the proof shall lay on the plaintiff, and it shall be always presumed that every negro, Indian, mulatto and mustizo, is a slave, unless the contrary can be made appear, the Indians in amity with this government excepted, in which case the burthen of the proof shall lye on the defendant; provided also, that nothing in this Act shall be construed to hinder or restrain any other court of law or equity in this Province, from determining the property of slaves, or their right of freedom, which now have cognizance or jurisdiction of the same, when the same shall happen to come in judgment before such courts, or any of them, always taking this Act for their direction therein."[486]

The entire slave population of this Province was regarded as chattel property, absolutely. They could be seized in execution as in the case of other property, but not, however, if there were other chattels available. In case of "burglary, robbery, burning of houses, killing or stealing of any meat or other cattle, or other petty injuries, as maiming one of the other, stealing of fowls, provisions, or such like trespass or injuries," a justice of the peace was to be informed. He issued a warrant for the arrest of the offender or offenders, and summoned all competent witnesses. After examination, if found guilty, the offender or offenders were committed to jail. The justice then notified the justice next to him to be associated with him in the trial. He had the authority to fix the day and hour of the trial, to summon witness, and "three discreet and sufficient freeholders." The justices then swore the "freeholders," and, after they had tried the case, had the authority to pronounce the sentence of death, "or such other punishment" as they felt meet to fix. "The solemnity of a jury" was never accorded to slaves. "Three freeholders" could dispose of human life in such cases, and no one could hinder.[487] The confession of the accused slave, and the testimony of another slave, were "held for good and convincing evidence in all petty larcenies or trespasses not exceeding forty shillings." In the case of a Negro on trial for his life, "the oath of Christian evidence" was required, or the "positive evidence of two Negroes or slaves," in order to convict.

The increase of slaves was almost phenomenal. The rice-trade had grown to enormous proportions. The physical obstruction gave away rapidly before the incessant and stupendous efforts of Negro laborers. The colonists held out most flattering inducements to Englishmen to emigrate into the Province. The home government applauded the zeal and executive abilities of the local authorities. Attention was called to the necessity of legislation for the government of the vast Negro population in the colony. The code of South Carolina was without an example among the civilized governments of modern times. It was unlawful for any free person to inhabit or trade with Negroes.[488] Slaves could not leave the plantation on which they were owned, except in livery, or armed with a pass, signed by their master, containing the name of the possessor. For a violation of this regulation they were whipped on the naked back. No man was allowed to conduct a "plantation, cow-pen or stock," that shall be six miles distant from his usual place of abode, and wherein six Negroes were employed, without one or more white persons were residing on the place.[489] Negro slaves found on another plantation than the one to which they belonged, "on the Lord's Day, fast days, or holy-days," even though they could produce passes, were seized and whipped. If a slave were found "keeping any horse, horses, or neat cattle," any white man, by warrant, could seize the animals, and sell them through the church-wardens; and the money arising from such sale was devoted to the poor of the parish in which said presumptuous slaves resided. If more than seven slaves were found travelling on the highway, except accompanied by a white man, it was lawful for any white man to apprehend each and every one of such slaves, and administer twenty lashes upon their bare back. No slave was allowed to hire out his time. Some owners of slaves were poor, and, their slaves being trusty and industrious, permitted them to go out and get whatever work they could, with the understanding that the master was to have the wages. An Act was passed in 1735, forbidding such transactions, and fining the persons who hired slaves who had no written certificate from their masters setting forth the terms upon which the work was to be done. No slave could hire a house or plantation. No amount of industry could make him an exception to the general rule. If he toiled faithfully for years, amassed a fortune for his master, earned quite a competence for himself during the odd moments he caught from a busy life, and then, with acknowledged character and business tact, he sought to hire a plantation or buy a house, the law came in, and pronounced it a misdemeanor, for which both purchaser and seller had to pay in fines, stripes, and imprisonment. A slave could not keep in his own name, or that of his master, any kind of a house of entertainment. He was even prohibited by law from selling corn or rice in the Province. The penalty was a fine of forty shillings, and the forfeiture of the articles for sale. They could not keep a boat or canoe.

The cruelties of the code are without a parallel, as applied to the correction of Negro slaves.

"If any negro or Indian slave [says the act of Feb. 7, 1690] shall offer any violence, by stricking or the like, to any white person, he shall for the first offence be severely whipped by the constable, by order of any justice of peace; and for the second offence, by like order, shall be severely whipped, his or her nose slit, and face burnt in some place; and for the third offence, to be left to two justices and three sufficient freeholders, to inflict death, or any other punishment, according to their discretion."

As the penalties for the smallest breach of the slave-code grew more severe, the slaves grew more restless and agitated. Sometimes under great fear they would run away for a short time, in the hope that their irate masters would relent. But this, instead of helping, hindered and injured the cause of the slaves. Angered at the conduct of their slaves, the master element, having their representatives on the floor of the Assembly, secured the passage of the following brutal law:—

> "That every slave of above sixteen years of age, that shall run away from his master, mistress or overseer, and shall so continue for the space of twenty days at one time, shall, by his master, mistress, overseer or head of the family's procurement, for the first offence, be publicly and severely whipped, not exceeding forty lashes; and in case the master, mistress, overseer, or head of the family, shall neglect to inflict such punishment of whipping, upon any negro or slave that shall so run away, for the space of ten days, upon complaint made thereof, within one month, by any person whatsoever, to any justice of the peace, the said justice of the peace shall, by his warrant directed to the constable, order the said negro or slave to be publicly and severely whipped, the charges of such whipping, not exceeding twenty shillings, to be borne by the person neglecting to have such

runaway negro whipped, as before directed by this Act. And in case such negro or slave shall run away a second time, and shall so continue for the space of twenty days, he or she, so offending, shall be branded with the letter R, on the right cheek. And in case the master, mistress, overseer, or head of the family, shall neglect to inflict the punishment upon such slave running away the second time, the person so neglecting shall forfeit the sum of ten pounds, and upon any complaint made by any person, within one month, to any justice of the peace, of the neglect of so punishing any slave for running away the second time, such justice shall order the constable to inflict the same punishment upon such slave, or cause the same to be done, the charges thereof, not exceeding thirty shillings, to be borne by the person neglecting to have the punishment inflicted. And in case such negro or slave shall run away the third time, and shall so continue for the space of thirty days, he or she, so offending, for the third offence, shall be severely whipped, not exceeding forty lashes, and shall have one of his ears cut off; and in case the master, mistress, overseer or head of the family, shall neglect to inflict the punishment upon such slave running away the third time, the person so neglecting shall forfeit the sum of twenty pounds, and upon any complaint made by any person, within two months, to any justice of the peace, of the neglect of the so punishing any slave for running away the third time, the said justice shall order the constable to inflict the same punishment upon such slave, or cause the same to be done, the charges thereof, not exceeding forty shillings, to be borne by the person neglecting to have the punishment inflicted. And in case such male negro or slave shall run away the fourth time, and shall so continue for the space of thirty days, he, so offending, for the fourth offence, by order or procurement of the master, mistress, overseer or head of the family, shall be gelt; and in case the negro or slave that shall be gelt, shall die, by reason of his gelding, and without any neglect of the person that shall order the same, the owner of the negro or slave so dying, shall be paid for him, out of the public treasury. And if a female slave shall run away the fourth time, then she shall, by order of her master, mistress or overseer, be severely whipped, and be branded on the left cheek with the letter R, and her left ear cut off. And if the owner, if in this Province, or in case of his absence, if his agent, factor or attorney, that hath the charge of the negro or slave, by this Act required to be gelt, whipped, branded and the ear cut off, for the fourth time of running away, shall neglect to have the same done and executed, accordingly as the same is ordered by this Act, for the space of twenty days after such slave is in his or their custody, that then such owner shall lose his property to the said slave, to him or them that will sue for the same, by information, at any time within six months, in the court of common pleas in this Province. And every person who shall so recover a slave by information, for the reasons aforesaid, shall, within twenty days after such recovery, inflict such punishment upon such slave as his former owner or head of a family ought to have done, and for neglect of which he lost his property to the said slave, or for neglect thereof shall forfeit fifty pounds; and in case any negro slave so recovered by information, and gelt, shall die, in such case, the slave so dying shall not be paid for out of the public treasury. And in case any negro or slave shall run away the fifth time, and shall so continue by the space of thirty days at one time, such slave shall be tried before two justices of the peace and three freeholders, as before directed by this Act in case of murder, and being by them declared guilty of the offence, it shall be lawful for them to order the cord of one of the slave's legs to be cut off above the heel, or else to pronounce sentence of death upon the slave, at the discretion of the said justices; and any judgment given after the first offence, shall be sufficient conviction to bring the offenders within the penalty for the second offence; and after the second, within the penalty of the third; and so for the inflicting the rest of the punishments."[490]

If any slave attempted to run away from his or her master, and go out of the Province, he or she could be tried before two justices and three freeholders, and sentenced to suffer a most cruel death. If it could be proved that any Negro, free or slave, had endeavored to persuade or entice any other Negro to run off out of the Province, upon conviction he was punished with forty lashes, and branded on the forehead with a red hot iron, "that the mark thereof may remain." If a white man met a slave, and demanded of him to show his ticket, and the slave refused, the law empowered the white man "to beat, maim, or assault; and if such Negro or slave" could not "be taken, to kill him," if he would not "shew his ticket."

The cruel and barbarous code of the slave-power in South Carolina produced, in course of time, a re-action in the opposite direction. The large latitude that the law gave to white people in their dealings with the hapless slaves made them careless and extravagant in the use of their authority. It educated them into a brood of tyrants. They did not care any more for the life of a Negro slave than for the crawling worm in their path. Many white men who owned no slaves poured forth their wrathful invectives and cruel blows upon the heads of innocent Negroes with the slightest pretext. They pushed, jostled, crowded, and kicked the Negro on every occasion. The young whites early took their lessons in abusing God's poor and helpless children; while an overseer was prized more for his brutal powers—to curse, beat, and torture—than for any ability he chanced to possess for business management. The press and pulpit had contemplated this state of affairs until they, too, were the willing abettors in the most cruel system of bondage that history has recorded. But no man wants his horse driven to death, if it is a beast. No one cares to have every man that passes kick his dog, even if it is not the best dog in the community. It is his dog, and that makes all the difference in the world. The men who did the most cruel things to the slaves they found in their daily path were, as a rule, without slaves or any other kind of property. They used their authority unsparingly. Common-sense taught the planters that better treatment of the slaves meant better work, and increased profits for themselves. A small value was finally placed upon a slave's life,—fifty pounds. Fifty pounds paid into the public treasury by a man who, "of wantonness, or only of bloody-mindedness, or cruel intention," had killed "a negro or other slave of his own," was enough to appease the public mind, and atone for a cold-blooded murder! If he killed another man's slave, the law demanded that he pay fifty pounds current money into the public treasury, and the full price of the slave to the owner, but was "not to be liable to any other punishment or forfeiture for the same."[491] The law just referred to, passed in 1712, was re-enacted in 1722. One change was made in it: i.e., if a white servant, having no property, killed a slave, three justices could bind him over to the master whose slave he killed to serve him for five years. This law had a wholesome effect upon irresponsible white men, who often presumed upon their nationality, having neither brains, money, nor social standing, to punish slaves.

In 1740, May 10, the following Act became a law, showing that there had been a wonderful change in public sentiment rejecting the treatment of slaves:—

> "XXXVII. And whereas, cruelty is not only highly unbecoming those who profess themselves christians but is odious in the eyes of all men who have any sense of virtue or humanity;

therefore, to restrain and prevent barbarity being exercised towards slaves, Be it enacted by the authority aforesaid, That if any person or persons whosoever, shall wilfully murder his own slave, or the slave of any other person every such person shall, upon conviction thereof, forfeit and pay the sum of seven hundred pounds current money, and shall be rendered, and is hereby declared altogether and forever incapable of holding, exercising, enjoying or receiving the profits of any office, place or employment, civil or military, within this Province: And in case any such person shall not be able to pay the penalty and forfeitures hereby inflicted and imposed, every such person shall be sent to any of the frontier garrisons of this Province, or committed to the work house in Charlestown, there to remain for the space of seven years, and to serve or to be kept at hard labor. And in case the slave murdered shall be the property of any other person than the offender, the pay usually allowed by the public to the soldiers of such garrison, or the profits of the labor of the offender, if committed to the work house in Charlestown shall be paid to the owner of the slave murdered. And if any person shall, on a sudden heat of passion, or by undue correction, kill his own slave, or the slave of any other person, he shall forfeit the sum of three hundred and fifty pounds, current money. And in case any person or persons shall wilfully cut out the tongue, put out the eye, castrate, or cruelly scald, burn, or deprive any slave of any limb or member, or shall inflict any other cruel punishment, other than by whipping or beating with a horse-whip, cow-skin, switch or small stick or by putting irons on, or confining or imprisoning such slave, every such person shall, for every such offence, forfeit the sum of one hundred pounds, current money."[492]

It may be said truthfully that the slaves in the colony of South Carolina were accorded treatment as good as that bestowed upon horses, in 1750. But their social condition was most deplorable. The law positively forbid the instruction of slaves, and the penalty was "one hundred pounds current money." For a few years Saturday afternoon had been allowed them as a day of recreation, but as early as 1690 it was forbidden by statute. In the same year an Act was passed declaring that slaves should "have convenient clothes, once every year; and that no slave" should "be free by becoming a christian,[493] but as to payments of debts" were "deemed and taken as all other goods and chattels." Their houses were searched every fortnight "for runaway slaves" and "stolen goods." Druggists were not allowed to employ a Negro to handle medicines, upon pain of forfeiting twenty pounds current money for every such offence. Negroes were not allowed to practise medicine, nor administer drugs of any kind, except by the direction of some white person. Any gathering of Negroes could be broken up at the discretion of a justice living in the district where the meeting was in session.

Poor clothing and insufficient food bred wide-spread discontent among the slaves, and attracted public attention.[494] Many masters endeavored to get on as cheaply as possible in providing for their slaves. In 1732 the Legislature passed an Act empowering two justices of the peace to inquire as to the treatment of slaves on the several plantations; and if any master neglected his slaves in food and raiment, he was liable to a fine of not more than fifty shillings. In May, 1740, an Act was passed requiring masters to see to it that their slaves were not overworked. The time set for them to work, was "from the 25th day of March to the 25th day of September," not "more than fifteen hours in four-and-twenty;" and "from the 25th day of September to the 25th day of March," not "more than fourteen hours in four-and-twenty."

The history of the impost-tax on slaves imported into the Province of South Carolina is the history of organized greed, ambition, and extortion. Many were the gold sovereigns that were turned into the official coffers at Charleston! With a magnificent harbor, and a genial climate, no city in the South could rival it as a slave-market. With an abundant supply from without, and a steady demand from within, the officials at Charleston felt assured that high impost-duties could not interfere with the slave-trade; while the city would be a great gainer by the traffic, both mediately and immediately.

Sudden and destructive insurrections were the safety-valves to the institution of slavery. A race long and cruelly enslaved may endure the yoke patiently for a season: but like the sudden gathering of the summer clouds, the pelting rain, the vivid, blinding lightning, the deep, hoarse thundering, it will assert itself some day; and then it is indeed a day of judgment to the task-masters! The Negroes in South Carolina endured a most cruel treatment for a long time; and, when "the day of their wrath" came, they scarcely knew it themselves, much less the whites. Florida was in the possession of the Spaniards. Its governor had sent out spies into Georgia and South Carolina, who held out very flattering inducements to the Negroes to desert their masters and go to Florida. Moreover, there was a Negro regiment in the Spanish service, whose officers were from their own race. Many slaves had made good their escape, and joined this regiment. It was allowed the same uniform and pay as the Spanish soldiers had. The colony of South Carolina was fearing an enemy from without, while behold their worst enemy was at their doors! In 1740 some Negroes assembled themselves together at a town called Stone, and made an attack upon two young men, who were guarding a warehouse, and killed them. They seized the arms and ammunition, effected an organization by electing one of their number captain; and, with boisterous drums and flying banners, they marched off "like a disciplined company." They entered the house of one Mr. Godfrey, slew him, his wife, and child, and then fired his dwelling. They next took up their march towards Jacksonburgh, and plundered and burnt the houses of Sacheveral, Nash, Spry, and others. They killed all the white people they found, and recruited their ranks from the Negroes they met. Gov. Bull was "returning to Charleston from the southward, met them, and, observing them armed, quickly rode out of their way."[495] In a march of twelve miles, they had wrought a work of great destruction. News reached Wiltown, and the militia were called out. The Negro insurrectionists were intoxicated with their triumph, and drunk from rum they had taken from the houses they had plundered. They halted in an open field to sing and dance; and, during their hilarity, Capt. Bee, at the head of the troops of the district, fell upon them, and, having killed several, captured all who did not make their escape in the woods.

The Province was thrown into intense excitement. The Legislature called attention to the insurrection,[496] and declared legal some very questionable and summary acts. In 1743 the people had not recovered from the fright they received from the insurrection. On the 7th of May, 1743, an Act was passed requiring every white male inhabitant, who resorted "to any church or any other public place of divine worship, within" the Province to "carry with him a gun or a pair of horse pistols, in good order and fit for service, with at least six charges of gun-powder and ball," upon pain of paying "twenty shillings."

As there was a law against teaching slaves to read and write, there were no educated preachers. If a Negro desired to preach to his fellow-slaves, he had to secure written permission from his master. While Negroes were sometimes baptized into the communion of the Church,—usually the Episcopal Church,—they were allowed only in the gallery, or organ-loft, of white congregations, in small numbers. No clergyman ventured to break unto this benighted people the bread of life. They were abandoned to the superstitions and religious fanaticisms incident to their condition.

In 1704 an Act was passed "for raising and enlisting such slaves as shalt be thought serviceable to this Province in time of Alarms." It required, within thirty days after the publication of the Act, that the commanders of military organizations throughout the Province should appoint "five freeholders," "sober and discreet men," who were to make a complete list of all the able-bodied slaves in their respective districts. Three of them were competent to decide upon the qualifications of a slave. After the completion of the list, the freeholders mentioned above notified the owners to appear before them upon a certain day, and show cause why their slaves should not be chosen for the service of the colony. The slaves were then enlisted, and their masters charged with the duty of arming them "with a serviceable lance, hatchet or gun, with sufficient amunition and hatchets, according to the conveniency of the said owners, to appear under the colours of the respective captains, in their several divisions, throughout" the Province, for the performance of such "public service" as required. If an owner refused to equip or permit his slave to respond to alarms, he was fined five pounds for each neglect, which was to be paid to the captain of the company to which the slave belonged. If a slave were killed by the enemy "in the line of duty," the owner of such slave was paid out of the public treasury such sum of money as three freeholders, under oath, should award. The Negroes did admirably; and four years later, on the 24th of April, 1708, the Legislature re-enacted the bill making them militia-men. The last Act contained ten sections, and bears evidence of the pleasure the whites took in the employment of Negroes as their defenders. If a Negro were taken prisoner by the enemy, and effected his escape back into the Province, he was emancipated. And if a Negro captured and killed an enemy, he was emancipated, but if wounded himself, was set free at the public expense. If he deserted to the enemy, his master was paid for his loss.

Few slaves were manumitted. The law required that masters who emancipated their slaves should make provisions for transporting them out of the Province. If they were found in the Province twelve months after they were set free, the manumission was considered void, except approved by the Legislature.

From 1754 till 1776 there was little legislation on the subject of slavery. The pressure from without made men conservative about slavery, and radical on the question of the rights and liberties of the colonies. The threatening war between England and her provincial dependencies made men humane and patriotic; and during these years of anxiety and excitement, the weary slaves breathed a better atmosphere, and enjoyed the rare sensation of confidence and benevolence.

FOOTNOTES:

[482] An eminent lawyer, chief justice of the Supreme Court of the State of——, and a warm personal friend of mine, recently said to me, during an

afternoon stroll, that he never knew that slavery was ever established by statute in any of the British colonies in North America.

[483] Statutes of S.C., vol. vii. p. 352.

[484] Virginia made slavery statutory as did other colonies, but we have no statute so explicit as the above. But slavery was slavery in all the colonies, cruel and hurtful.

[485] Statutes of S.C., vol. vii. p. 397.

[486] Statutes of S.C., vol. vii. pp. 397, 398.

[487] Ibid., vol. vii. pp. 343, 344.

[488] This Act, passed on the 16th of March, 1696, was made "perpetual" on the 12th of December, 1712. It remained throughout the entire period. See Statutes of S.C., vol. ii, p. 598.

[489] Statutes of S.C., vol. vii. p. 363.

[490] Statutes of S.C., vol. vii. pp. 359, 360.

[491] Statutes of S.C., vol. vii. 363.

[492] Ibid., vol vii. pp. 410. 411.

[493] The following is the Act of the 7th of June, 1690. "XXXIV Since charity, and the christian religion, which we profess, obliges us to wish well to the souls of all men, and that religion may not be made a pretence to alter any man's property and right, and that no person may neglect to baptize their negroes or slaves, or suffer them to be baptized, for fear that thereby they should be manumitted and set free, Be it therefore enacted by the authority aforesaid, that it shall be, and is hereby declared, lawful for any negro or Indian slave, or any other slave or slaves whatsoever, to receive and profess the christian faith, and be thereinto baptized; but that notwithstanding such slave or slaves shall receive and profess the Christian religion, and be baptized, he or they shall not thereby be manumitted or set free, or his or their owner, master or mistress lose his or their civil right, property, and authority over such slave or slaves, but that the slave or slaves, with respect to his servitude shall remain and continue in the same state and condition that he or they was in before the making of this act." — Statutes of S.C., vol. vii. pp 364, 365.

[494] In 1740 an Act was passed requiring masters to provide "sufficient clothing" for their slaves.

[495] Hist. S.C. and Georgia, vol. ii. p. 73.

[496] Statutes of S.C., vol. vii. p. 416.

CHAPTER XXII
THE COLONY OF NORTH CAROLINA

1669-1775.

The Geographical Situation of North Carolina Favorable to the Slave-Trade.—The Locke Constitution adopted.—William Sayle commissioned Governor.—Legislative Career of the Colony.—The Introduction of the Established Church of England into the Colony.—The Rights of Negroes controlled absolutely by their Masters.—An Act respecting Conspiracies.—The Wrath of Ill-natured Whites visited upon their Slaves.—An Act against the Emancipation of Slaves.—Limited Rights of Free Negroes.

THE geographical situation of North Carolina was favorable to the slave-trade.

Through the genius of Shaftesbury, and the subtle cunning of John Locke, Carolina received, and for a time adopted, the most remarkable constitution ever submitted to any people in any age of the world. The whole affair was an insult to humanity, and in its fundamental elements bore the palpable evidences of the cruel conclusions of an exclusive philosophy. "No elective franchise could be conferred upon a freehold of less than fifty acres," while all executive power was vested in the proprietors themselves. Seven courts were controlled by forty-two counsellors, twenty-eight of whom held their places through the gracious favor of the proprietary and "the nobility." Trial by jury was concluded by the opinions of the majority.

> "The instinct of aristocracy dreads the moral power of a proprietary yeomanry; the perpetual degradation of the cultivators of the soil was enacted. The leet-men, or tenants, holding ten acres of land at a fixed rent, were not only destitute of political franchises, but were adscripts to the soil, 'under the jurisdiction of their lord, without appeal;' and it was added, 'all the children of leet-men shall be leet-men, and so to all generations.'"[497]

The men who formed the rank and file of the yeomanry of the colony of North Carolina were ill prepared for a government launched upon the immense scale of the Locke Constitution. The hopes and fears, the feuds and debates, the vexatious and insoluble problems, of the political science of government which had clouded the sky of the most astute and ambitous statesmen of Europe, were dumped into this remarkable instrument. The distance between the people and the nobility was sought to be made illimitable, and the right to govern was based upon permanent property conditions. Hereditary wealth was to go arm in arm with political power.

The constitution was signed on the 21st of July, 1669, and William Sayle was commissioned as governor. The legislative career of the Province began in the fall of the same year; and history must record that it was one of the most remarkable and startling North America ever witnessed. The portions of the constitution which refer to the institution of slavery are as follows:—

"97th. But since the natives of that place, who will be concerned in our plantation, are utterly strangers to Christianity, whose idolatry, ignorance or mistake, gives us no right to expel or use them ill; and those who remove from other parts to plant there, will unavoidably be of different opinions, concerning matters of religion, the liberty whereof they will expect to have allowed them, and it will not be reasonable for us on this account to keep them out; that civil peace may be obtained amidst diversity of opinions, and our agreement and compact with all men, may be duly and faithfully observed; the violation whereof, upon what pretence soever, cannot be without great offence to Almighty God, and great scandal to the true religion which we profess; and also that Jews, Heathens and other dissenters from the purity of the Christian religion, may not be scared and kept at a distance from it, but by having an opportunity of acquainting themselves with the truth and reasonableness of its doctrines, and the peaceableness and inoffensiveness of its professors, may by good usage and persuasion, and all those convincing methods of gentleness and meekness, suitable to the rules and design of the gospel, be won over to embrace, and unfeignedly receive the truth; therefore any seven or more persons agreeing in any religion, shall constitute a church or profession, to which they shall give some name, to distinguish it from others....

"101st. No person above seventeen years of age, shall have any benefit or protection of the law, or be capable of any place of profit or honor, who is not a member of some church or profession, having his name recorded in some one, and but one religious record, at once....

"107th. Since charity obliges us to wish well to the souls of all men, and religion ought to alter nothing in any man's civil estate or right, it shall be lawful for slaves as well as others, to enter themselves and be of what church or profession any of them shall think best, and thereof be as fully members as any freemen. But yet no slave shall hereby be exempted from that civil dominion his master hath over him, but be in all things in the same state and condition he was in before....

> "110th. Every freeman of Carolina, shall have absolute power and authority over his negro slaves, of what opinion or religion soever."[498]

Though the Locke Constitution was adopted by the proprietaries, March 1, 1669, it may be doubted whether it ever had the force of law, as it was never ratified by the local Legislature. Article one hundred and ten, granting absolute power and authority to a master over his Negro slave, is without a parallel in the legislation of the colonies. And while the slave might enter the Christian Church, and his humanity thereby be recognized, it was strangely inconsistent to place his life at the disposal of brutal masters, who "neither feared God nor regarded man."

The Negro slaves in North Carolina occupied the paradoxical position of being eligible to membership in the Christian Church, and the absolute property of their white brothers. In the second draught of the constitution, signed in March, 1670, against the eloquent protest of John Locke, the section on religion was amended so as, while tolerating every religious creed, to declare "the Church Of England" the only true Orthodox Church, and the national religion of the Province. This, in the face of the fact that the great majority of all the Christians who flocked to the New World were dissenters, separatists, and nonconformists, can only be explained in the light of the burning zeal of the Church of England to out-Herod Herod,— to carry the Negroes into the communion of the State church for political purposes. It was the most sordid motive that impelled the churchmen to open the church to the slave. His membership did not change his condition, nor secure him immunity from the barbarous treatment the institution of slavery bestowed upon its helpless victims.

In the eyes of the law the Negro, being absolute property, had no rights, except those temporarily delegated by the master; and he acted in the relation of an agent. Negro slaves were not allowed "to raise horses, cattle or hogs;" and if any stock were found in their possession six months after the passage of the Act of 1741, they were to be seized by the sheriff of the county, and sold by the church-wardens of the parish. The profits arising from such sales went, one half to the parish, the other half to the informer.[499] A slave was not suffered to go off of the plantation where he was appointed to live, without a pass signed by his master or the overseer. There was an exception made in the case of Negroes wearing liveries. Negro slaves were not allowed the use of fire-arms or other weapons, except they were armed with a certificate from their master granting the coveted permission. If they hunted with arms, not having a certificate, any Christian could apprehend them, seize the weapons, deliver the slave to the first justice of the peace; who was authorized to administer, without ceremony, twenty lashes upon his or her bare back, and send him or her home. The master had to pay the cost of arrest and punishment. The one exception to this law was, that one Negro on each plantation or in each district could carry a gun to shoot game for his master and protect stock, etc.; but his certificate was to be in his possession all the time. If a Negro went from the plantation on which he resided, to another plantation or place, he was required by statute to travel in the most generally frequented road. If caught in another road, not much travelled, except in the company of a white man, it was lawful for the man who owned the land through which he was passing to seize him, and administer not more than forty lashes. If Negroes visited each other in the night season,—the only time they could visit,—the ones who were found on another plantation than their master's were punished with lashes on their naked back, not exceeding forty; while the Negroes who had furnished the entertainment received twenty lashes for their hospitality. In case any slave, who had not been properly fed and clothed by his master, was convicted of stealing cattle, hogs, or corn from another man, an action of trespass could be maintained against the master in the general or county court, and damages recovered.[500]

Here, as in the other colonies, the greatest enemy of the colonists was an accusing conscience. The people started at every breath of rumor, and always imagined their slaves conspiring to cut their throats. There was nothing in the observed character of the slaves to justify the wide-spread consternation that filled the public mind. Nor was there any occasion to warrant the passage of the Act of 1741, respecting conspiracies among slaves. It is a remarkable document, and is produced here.

> "XLVII. And be it further enacted by the authority aforesaid, That if any number of negroes or other slaves, that is to say, three, or more, shall, at any time hereafter, consult, advise or conspire to rebel or make insurrection, or shall plot or conspire the murder of any person or persons whatsoever, every such consulting, plotting or conspiring, shall be adjudged and deemed felony; and the slave or slaves convicted thereof, in manner herein after directed, shall suffer death.

"XLVIII. *And be it further enacted by the authority aforesaid,*'That every slave committing such offence, or any other crime or misdemeanor, shall forthwith be committed by any justice of the peace, to the common jail of the county within which the said offence shall be committed, there to be safely kept; and that the sheriff of such county, upon such commitment, shall forthwith certify the same to any Justice in the commission for the said court for the time being, resident in the county, who is thereupon required and directed to issue a summons for two or more Justices of the said court, and four freeholders, such as shall have slaves in the said county, which said three Justices and four freeholders, owners of slaves, are hereby impowered and required upon oath, to try all manner of crimes and offences, that shall be committed by any slave or slaves, at the court house of the county, and to take for evidence, the confession of the offender, the oath of one or more credible witnesses, or such testimony of negroes, mulattoes or Indians, bond or free, with pregnant circumstances, as to them shall seem convincing, without the solemnity of a jury; and the offender being then found guilty, to pass such judgment upon such offender, according to their discretion, as the nature of the crime or offence shall require; and on such judgment, to award execution.

"XLIX. *Provided always, and be it enacted*, That it shall and may be lawful for each and every Justice, being in the commission of the peace for the county where any slave or slaves shall be tried, by virtue of this act, (who is owner of slaves) to sit upon such trial, and act as a member of such court though he or they be not summoned thereto; anything herein before contained to the contrary, in any wise, notwithstanding.

"L. And to the end such negro, mulatto or Indian, bond or free, not being christians, as shall hereafter be produced as an evidence on the trial of any slave or slaves, for capital or other crimes, may be under the greater obligation to declare the truth; *Be it further enacted*, There where any such negro, mulatto or Indian, bond or free, shall, upon due proof made, or pregnant circumstances, appearing before any county court within this government, be found to have given a false testimony, every such offender shall, without further trial, be ordered, by the said court, to have one ear nailed to the pillory, and there stand for the space of one hour, and the said ear to be cut off, and thereafter the other ear nailed in like manner, and cut off, at the expiration of one other hour: and moreover, to order every such offender thirty-nine lashes, well laid on, on his or her bare back, at the common whipping post.

"LI. *And be it further enacted by the authority aforesaid*, That at every such trial of slaves committing capital or other offences, the first person in commission sitting on such trial, shall, before the examination of every negro, mulatto or Indian, not being a christian, charge such to declare the truth.

> "LII. Provided always, and it is hereby intended, That the master, owner or overseer of any slave, to be arraigned and tried by virtue of this act, may appear at the trial, and make what just defence he can for such slave or slaves; so that such defence do not relate to any formality in the proceeding on the trial."[501]

The manner of conducting the trials of Negroes charged with felony or misdemeanor was rather peculiar. Upon one or more white persons' testimony, or the evidence of Negroes and Indians, bond or free, the unfortunate defendant, "without the solemnity of a jury," before three justices and four freeholders, could be hurried through a trial, convicted, sentenced to die a dreadful death, and then be executed without the officiating presence of a minister of the gospel.

The unprecedented discretion allowed to masters in the government led to the most tragic results. Men were not only reckless of the lives of their own slaves, but violent toward those belonging to others. If a Negro showed the least independence in conversation with a white man, he could be murdered in cold blood; and it was only a case of a contumacious slave getting his dues. But men became so prodigal in the exercise of this authority that the public became alarmed, and the Legislature called a halt on the master-class. At first the Legislature paid for the slaves who were destroyed by the consuming wrath of ill-natured whites, but finally allowed an action to lie against the persons who killed a slave. This had a tendency to reduce the number of murdered slaves; but the fateful clause in the Locke Constitution had educated a voracious appetite for blood, and the extremest cruel treatment continued without abatement.

The free Negro population was very small in this colony. The following act on manumission differs so widely from the law on this point in the other colonies, that it is given as an illustration of the severe character of the legislation of North Carolina against the emancipation of Negroes.

> "LVI. And be it further enacted by the authority aforesaid, That no Negro or mulatto slaves shall be set free, upon any

pretence whatsoever, except for meritorious services, to be adjudged and allowed of by the county court, and Licence thereupon first had and obtained: and that where any slave shall be set free by his or her master or owner, otherwise than is herein before directed, it shall and may be lawful for the church-wardens of the parish wherein such negro, mulatto or Indian, shall be found, at the expiration of six months, next alter his or her being set free, and they are hereby authorized and required, to take up and sell the said negro, mulatto or Indian, as a slave, at the next court to be held for the said county, at public vendue: and the monies arising by such sale, shall be applied to the use of the parish, by the vestry thereof: and if any negro, mulatto or Indian slave, set free otherwise than is herein directed, shall depart this province, within six months next after his or her freedom, and shall afterwards return into this government, it shall and may be lawful for the churchwardens of the parish where such negro or mulatto shall be found, at the expiration of one month, next after his or her return into this government to take up such negro or mulatto, and sell him or them, as slaves, at the next court to be held for the county, at public vendue; and the monies arising thereby, to be applied, by the vestry, to the use of the parish, as aforesaid."[502]

The free Negroes were badly treated. They were not allowed any communion with the slaves. A free Negro man was not allowed to marry a white woman, nor even a Negro slave woman without the consent of her master. If he formed an alliance with a white woman, her offspring were bound out, or sold by the church-wardens, until they obtained their majority. [503] If the white woman were an indentured servant, she was constrained to serve an additional year. If she were a free woman, she was sold for two years by the church-wardens. Free Negroes were greatly despised and shunned by both slaves and white people.

As a conspicuous proof of the glaring hypocrisy of the "nobility," who, in the constitution, threw open the door of the Church to the Negro, it should be said, that, during the period from the founding of the Province down to the colonial war, no attempt was ever made, through the ecclesiastical establishment, to dissipate the dark clouds of ignorance that enveloped the

Negro's mind. They were left in a state of ignorance and crime. The gravest social evils were winked at by masters, whose lecherous examples were the occasion for the most grievous offending of the slaves. The Mulattoes and other free Negroes were taxed. They had no place in the militia, nor could they claim the meanest rights of the humblest "leetman."

FOOTNOTES:

[497] Bancroft, vol. ii., 5th ed. p. 148.

[498] Statutes of S.C., vol. i. pp. 53-55.

[499] Public Acts of N.C., vol. i. p. 64.

[500] This is an instance of humanity in the North-Carolina code worthy of special note. It stands as the only instance of justice toward the overworked and under-fed slaves of the colony.

[501] Public Acts of N.C., p.65.

[502] Public Acts of N.C., p. 66.

[503] The Act of 1741 says, "until 31 years of age."

CHAPTER XXIII
THE COLONY OF NEW HAMPSHIRE

1679-1775.

The Provincial Government of Massachusetts exercises Authority over the State of New Hampshire at its Organization.—Slavery existed from the Beginning.—The Governor releases a Slave from Bondage.—Instruction against Importation of Slaves.—Several Acts regulating the Conduct of Servants.—The Indifferent Treatment of Slaves.—The Importation of Indian Servants forbidden.—An Act checking the Severe Treatment of Servants and Slaves.—Slaves in the Colony until the Commencement of Hostilities.

ANTERIOR to the year 1679, the provincial government of Massachusetts exercised authority over the territory that now comprises the State of New Hampshire. It is not at all improbable, then, that slavery existed in this colony from the beginning of its organic existence. As early as 1683 it was set upon by the authorities as a wicked and hateful institution. On the 14th of March, 1684, the governor of New Hampshire assumed the responsibility of releasing a Negro slave from bondage. The record of the fact is thus preserved:—

> "The governor tould Mr. Jaffery's negro hee might goe from his master, hee would clere him under hande and sele, so the fello no more attends his master's consernes."[504]

It may be inferred from the above, that the royal governor of the Province felt the pressure of public sentiment on the question of anti-slavery. While this colony copied its criminal code from Massachusetts, its people seemed to be rather select, and, on the question of human rights, far in advance of the people of Massachusetts. The twelfth article was: "If any man stealeth mankind he shall be put to death or otherwise grievously punished." The entire code—the first one—was rejected in England as "fanatical and absurd."[505] It was the desire of this new and feeble colony to throw every obstacle in the way of any legal recognition of slavery. The governors of all the colonies received instruction in regard to the question of slavery, but the governor of New Hampshire had received an order from the crown to have the tax on imported slaves removed. The royal instructions, dated June 30, 1761, were as follows:—

> "You are not to give your assent to, or pass any law imposing duties on negroes imported into New Hampshire."[506]

New Hampshire never passed any law establishing slavery, but in 1714 enacted several laws regulating the conduct of servants. One was *An Act to prevent disorder in the night*:—

> "Whereas great disorders, insolencies, and burglaries are ofttimes raised and committed in the night time by Indian, negro and mulatto servants and slaves, to the disquiet and hurt of her Majesty's good subjects, for the prevention whereof Be it, &c.—that no Indian, negro or mulatto servant or slave may presume to be absent from the families where they respectively belong, or be found abroad in the night time after nine o'clock; unless it be upon errand for their respective masters."[507]

The instructions against the importation of slaves were in harmony with the feelings of the great majority of the people. They felt that slavery would be a hinderance rather than a help to them, and in the selection of servants chose white ones. If the custom of holding men in bondage had become a part of the institutions of Massachusetts,—so like a cancer that it could not be removed without endangering the political and commercial life of the colony,—the good people of New Hampshire, acting in the light of experience, resolved, upon the threshold of their provincial life, to oppose the introduction of slaves into their midst. The first result was, that they learned quite early that they could get on without slaves; and, second, the traders in human flesh discovered that there was no demand for slaves in New Hampshire. Even nature fought against the crime; and Negroes were found to be poorly suited to the climate, and, of course, were an expensive luxury in that colony.

But, nevertheless, there were slaves in New Hampshire. The majority of them had gone in during the time the colony was a part of the territory of Massachusetts. They had been purchased by men who regarded them as indispensable to them. They had lived long in many families; children had been born unto them, and in many instances they were warmly attached to their owners. But all masters were not alike. Some treated their servants and slaves cruelly. The neglect in some cases was worse than stripes or overwork. Some were poorly clad and scantily fed; and, thus exposed to the inclemency of the severe climate, many were precipitated into premature graves. Even white and Indian servants shared this harsh treatment. The Indians endured greater hardships than the Negroes. They were more lofty in their tone, more sensitive in their feelings, more revengeful in their disposition. They were both hated and feared, and the public sentiment against them was very pronounced. A law, passed in 1714, forbid their importation into the colony under a heavy penalty.

In 1718 it was found necessary to pass a law to check the severe treatment inflicted upon servants and slaves. *An Act for restraining inhuman severities* recited, —

> "Fort the prevention and restraining of inhuman severities which by evil masters or overseers, may be used towards their Christian servants, that from and after the publication hereof, if any man smite out the eye or tooth of his man servant or maid servant, or otherwise maim or disfigure them much, unless it be by mere casualty, he shall let him or her go free from his service, and shall allow such further recompense as the court of quarter sessions shall adjudge him. 2. That if any person or persons whatever in this province shall wilfully kill his Indian or negroe servant or servants he shall be punished with death."[508]

There were slaves in New Hampshire down to the breaking-out of the war in the colonies, but they were only slaves in name. Few in number, widely scattered, they felt themselves closely identified with the interests of the colonists.

FOOTNOTES:

[504] Belknap's Hist. of N.H., vol. i. p. 333.

[505] Hildreth, vol. i. p. 501.

[506] Gordon's Hist. of Am. Rev., vol. v. Letter 2.

[507] Freedom and Bondage, vol. i. p. 266.

[508] Freedom and Bondage, vol. i. p. 267.

CHAPTER XXIV
THE COLONY OF PENNSYLVANIA

1681-1775.

Organization of the Government of Pennsylvania.—The Swedes and Dutch plant Settlements on the Western Bank of the Delaware River.—The Governor of New York seeks to exercise Jurisdiction over the Territory of Pennsylvania.—The First Laws agreed upon in England.—Provisions of the Law.—Memorial against Slavery draughted and adopted by the Germantown Friends.—William Penn presents a Bill for the Better Regulation of Servants.—An Act preventing the Importation of Negroes and Indians.—Rights of Negroes.—A Duty laid upon Negroes and Mulatto Slaves.—The Quaker the Friend of the Negro.—England begins to threaten her Dependencies in North America.—The People of Pennsylvania reflect upon the Probable Outrages their Negroes might commit.

LONG before there was an organized government in Pennsylvania, the Swedes and Dutch had planted settlements on the western bank of the Delaware River. But the English crown claimed the soil; and the governor of New York, under patent from the Duke of York, sought to exercise jurisdiction over the territory. On the 11th of July, 1681, "Conditions and Concessions were agreed upon by William Penn, Proprietary," and the persons who were "adventurers and purchasers in the same province." Provision was made for the punishment of persons who should injure Indians, and that the planter injured by them should "not be his own judge upon the Indian." All controversies arising between the whites and the Indians were to be settled by a council of twelve persons,—six white men and six Indians.

The first laws for the government of the colony were agreed upon in England, and in 1682 went into effect. Provision was made for the registering of all servants, their full names, amount of wages paid, and the time when they received their remuneration. It was strictly required that servants should not be kept beyond the time of their indenture, should be kindly treated, and the customary outfit furnished at the time of their freedom.

The baneful custom of enslaving Negroes had spread through every settlement in North America, and was even "tolerated in Pennsylvania under the specious pretence of the religious instruction of the slave."[509] In 1688 Francis Daniel Pastorius draughted a memorial against slavery, which was adopted by the Germantown Friends, and by them sent up to the Monthly Meeting, and thence to the Yearly Meeting at Philadelphia.[510] The original document was found by Nathan Kite of Philadelphia in 1844. [511] It was a remarkable document, and the first protest against slavery issued by any religious body in America. Speaking of the slaves, Pastorius asks, "Have not these negroes as much right to fight for their freedom as you have to keep them slaves?" He believed the time would come,—

> "When, from the gallery to the farthest seat,
> Slave and slave-owner shall no longer meet,
> But all sit equal at the Master's feet."

He regarded the "buying, selling, and holding men in slavery, as inconsistent with the Christian religion." When his memorial came before the Yearly Meeting for action, it confessed itself "unprepared to act," and voted it "not proper then to give a positive judgment in the case." In 1696 the Yearly Meeting pronounced against the further importation of slaves, and adopted measures looking toward their moral improvement. George Keith, catching the holy inspiration of humanity, with a considerable following, denounced the institution of slavery "as contrary to the religion of Christ, the rights of man, and sound reason and policy."[512]

While these efforts were, to a certain extent, abortive, yet, nevertheless, the Society of the Friends made regulations for the better treatment of the enslaved Negroes. The sentiment thus created went far toward deterring the better class of citizens from purchasing slaves. To his broad and lofty sentiments of humanity, the pious William Penn sought to add the force of positive law. The published views of George Fox, given at Barbadoes in 1671, in his "Gospel Family Order, being a short discourse concerning the ordering of Families, both of Whites, Blacks, and Indians," had a salutary effect upon the mind of Penn. In 1700 he proposed to the Council "the necessitie of a law [among others] about ye marriages of negroes." The bill was referred to a joint committee of both houses, and they brought in a bill "for regulating Negroes in their Morals and Marriages &c." It reached a second reading, and was lost.[513] Penn regarded the teaching of Negroes the sanctity of the marriage relation as of the greatest importance to the colony, and the surest means of promoting pure morals. Upon what grounds it was rejected is not known. He presented, at the same session of the Assembly, another bill, which provided "for the better regulation of servants in this province and territories." He desired the government of slaves to be prescribed and regulated by law, rather than by the capricious whims of masters. No servant was to be sold out of the Province without giving his consent, nor could he be assigned over except before a justice of the peace. It provided for a regular allowance to servants at the expiration of their time, and required them to serve five days extra for every day's absence from their master without the latter's assent. A penalty was fixed for concealing runaway slaves, and a reward offered for apprehending them. No free person was allowed to deal with servants, and justices and sheriffs were to be punished for neglecting their duties in the premises.

In case a Negro was guilty of murder, he was tried by two justices, appointed by the governor, before six freeholders. The manner of procedure was prescribed, and the nature of the sentence and acquittal. Negroes were not allowed to carry a gun or other weapons. Not more than four were allowed together, upon pain of a severe flogging. An Act for raising revenue was passed, and a duty upon imported slaves was levied, in 1710. In 1711-12, an Act was passed "to prevent the importation of negroes and Indians" into the Province. A general petition for the emancipation of slaves by law was presented to the Legislature during this same year; but the wise law-makers replied, that "it was neither just nor convenient to set them at liberty." The bill passed on the 7th of June, 1712, but was disapproved by Great Britain, and was accordingly repealed by an Act of Queen Anne, Feb. 20, 1713. In 1714 and 1717, Acts were passed to check the importation of slaves. But the English government, instead of being touched by the philanthropic endeavors of the people of Pennsylvania, was seeking, for purposes of commercial trade and gain, to darken the continent with the victims of its avarice.

Negroes had no political rights in the Province. Free Negroes were prohibited from entertaining Negro or Indian slaves, or trading with them. Masters were required, when manumitting slaves, to furnish security, as in the other colonies. Marriages between the races were forbidden. Negroes were not allowed to be abroad after nine o'clock at night.

In 1773 the Assembly passed *"An Act making perpetual the Act entitled, An Act for laying a duty on negroes and mulatto slaves,"* etc., and added ten pounds to the duty. The colonists did much to check the vile and inhuman traffic; but, having once obtained a hold, it did eat like a canker. It threw its dark shadow over personal and collective interests, and poisoned the springs of human kindness in many hearts. It was not alone hurtful to the slave: it transformed and blackened character everywhere, and fascinated those who were anxious for riches beyond the power of moral discernment. Here, however, as in New Jersey, the Negro found the Quaker his practical friend; and his upper and better life received the pruning advice, refining and elevating influence, of a godly people. But intelligence in the slave was an occasion of offending, and prepared him to realize his deplorable situation. So to enlighten him was to excite in him a deep desire for liberty, and, not unlikely, a feeling of revenge toward his enslavers. So there was really danger in the method the guileless Friends adopted to ameliorate the condition of the slaves.

When England began to breathe out threatenings against her contumacious dependencies in North America, the people of Pennsylvania began to reflect upon the probable outrages their Negroes would, in all probability, commit. They inferred that the Negroes would be their enemy because they were their slaves. This was the equitable findings of a guilty conscience. They did not dare expect less than the revengeful hate of the beings they had laid the yoke of bondage upon; and verily they found themselves with "fears within, and fightings without."

FOOTNOTES:

[509] Gordon's History of Penn., p. 114.

[510] Whittier's Penn. Pilgrim, p. viii.

[511] The memorial referred to was printed in extenso in The Friend, vol. xviii. No 16.

[512] Minutes of Yearly Meeting, Watson's MS. Coll. Bettle's notices of N.S. Minutes, Penn. Hist. Soc.

[513] Colonial Rec., vol. i. pp. 598, 606. See also Votes of Assembly, vol. i. pp. 120-122.

CHAPTER XXV
THE COLONY OF GEORGIA

1732-1775.

Georgia once included in the Territory of Carolina.—The Thirteenth Colony planted in North America by the English Government.—Slaves ruled out altogether by the Trustees.—The Opinion of Gen. Oglethorpe concerning Slavery.—Long and Bitter Discussion in Regard to the Admission of Slavery into the Colony.—Slavery introduced.—History of Slavery in Georgia.

GEORGIA was once included in the territory of Carolina, and extended from the Savannah to the St. John's River. A corporate body, under the title of "The Trustees for establishing the Colony of Georgia," was created by charter, bearing date of June 9, 1732. The life of their trust was for the space of twenty-one years. The rules by which the trustees sought to manage the infant were rather novel; but as a discussion of them would be irrelevant, mention can be made only of that part which related to slavery. Georgia was the last colony—the thirteenth—planted in North America by the English government. Special interest centred in it for several reasons, that will be explained farther on.

The trustees ruled out slavery altogether. Gen. John Oglethorpe, a brilliant young English officer of gentle blood, the first governor of the colony, was identified with "the Royal African Company, which alone had the right of planting forts and trading on the coast of Africa." He said that "slavery is against the gospel, as well as the fundamental law of England. We refused, as trustees, to make a law permitting such a horrid crime." Another of the trustees, in a sermon preached on Sunday, Feb. 17, 1734, at St. George's Church, Hanover Square, London, declared, "Slavery, the misfortune, if not the dishonor, of other plantations, is absolutely proscribed. Let avarice defend it as it will, there is an honest reluctance in humanity against buying and selling, and regarding those of our own species as our wealth and possessions." Beautiful sentiments! Eloquent testimony against the crime of the ages! At first blush the student of history is apt to praise the sublime motives of the "trustees," in placing a restriction against the slave-trade. But the declaration of principles quoted above is not borne out by the facts of history. On this point Dr. Stevens, the historian of Georgia, observes, "Yet in the official publications of that body [the trustees], its inhibition is based only on political and prudential, and not on humane and liberal grounds, and even Oglethorpe owned a plantation and negroes near Parachucla in South Carolina, about forty miles above Savannah."[514] To this reliable opinion is added:—

> "The introduction of slaves was prohibited to the colony of Georgia for some years, not from motives of humanity, but for the reason it was encouraged elsewhere, to wit: the interest of the mother country. It was a favorite idea with the 'mother country,' to make Georgia a protecting blanket for the Carolinas, against the Spanish settlements south of her, and the principal Indian tribes to the west; to do this, a strong settlement of white men was sought to be built up, whose arms and interests would defend her northern plantations. The introduction of slaves was held to be unfavorable to this scheme, and hence its prohibition. During the time of the prohibition, Oglethorpe himself was a slave holder in Carolina."[515]

The reasons that led the trustees to prohibit slavery in the colony are put thus tersely.—

> "1st. Its expense: which the poor emigrant would be entirely unable to sustain, either in the first cost of a negro, or his subsequent keeping. 2d. Because it would induce idleness and render labour degrading. 3d. Because the settlers, being freeholders of only fifty-acre lots, requiring but one or two extra hands for their cultivation, the German servants would be a third more profitable than the blacks. Upon the last original design I have mentioned, in planting this colony, they also based an argument against their admission, viz., that the cultivation of silk and wine, demanding skill and nicety, rather than strength and endurance of fatigue, the whites were better calculated for such labour than the negroes. These were the prominent arguments, drawn from the various considerations of internal and external policy, which influenced the Trustees in making this prohibition.

Many of them, however, had but a temporary bearing, none stood the test of experience."[516]

It is clear, then, that the founders of the colony of Georgia were not moved by the noblest impulses to prohibit slavery within their jurisdiction. In the chapter on South Carolina, attention was called to the influence of the Spanish troops in Florida on the recalcitrant Negroes in the Carolinas, the Negro regiment with subalterns from their own class, and the work of Spanish emissaries among the slaves. The home government thought it wise to build up Georgia out of white men, who could develop its resources, and bear arms in defence of British possessions along an extensive border exposed to a pestiferous foe. But the Board of Trade soon found this an impracticable scheme, and the colonists themselves began to clamor "for the use of negroes."[517] The first petition for the introduction and use of Negro slaves was offered to the trustees in 1735. This prayer was promptly and positively denied, and for fifteen years they refused to grant all requests for the use of Negroes. They adhered to their prohibition in letter and spirit. Whenever and wherever Negroes were found in the colony, they were sold back into Carolina. In the month of December, 1738, a petition, addressed to the trustees, including nearly all the names of the foremost colonists, set forth the distressing condition into which affairs had drifted under the enforcement of the prohibition, and declared that "the use of negroes, with proper limitations, which, if granted, would both occasion great numbers of white people to come here, and also to render us capable to subsist ourselves, by raising provisions upon our lands, until we could make some produce fit for export, in some measure to balance our importations." But instead of securing a favorable hearing, the petition drew the fire of the friends of the prohibition against the use of Negroes. On the 3d of January, 1739, a petition to the trustees combating the arguments of the above-mentioned petition, and urging them to remain firm, was issued at Darien. This was followed by another one, issued from Ebenezer on the 13th of March, in favor of the position occupied by the trustees. A great many Scotch and German people had settled in the colony; and, familiar with the arts of husbandry, they became the ardent supporters of the trustees. James Habersham, the "dear fellow-traveller," of Whitefield, exclaimed, —

> "I once thought, it was unlawful to keep negro slaves, but I am now induced to think God may have a higher end in permitting them to be brought to this Christian country, than merely to support their masters. Many of the poor slaves in America have already been made freemen of the heavenly Jerusalem, and possibly a time may come when many thousands may embrace the gospel, and thereby be brought

into the glorious liberty of the children of God. These, and other considerations, appear to plead strongly for a limited use of negroes; for, while we can buy provisions in Carolina cheaper than we can here, no one will be induced to plant much."

But the trustees stood firm against the subtle cunning of the politicians, and the eloquent pleadings of avarice.

On the 7th October, 1741, a large meeting was held at Savannah, and a petition drawn, in which the land-holders and settlers presented their grievances to the English authorities in London. On the 26th of March, 1742, Mr. Thomas Stephens, armed with the memorial, as the agent of the memorialists, sailed for London. While the document ostensibly set forth their wish for a definition of "the tenure of the lands," really the burden of the prayer was for "*Negroes*." He presented the memorial to the king, and his Majesty referred it to a committee of the "Lords of Council for Plantation Affairs." This committee transferred a copy of the memorial to the trustees, with a request for their answer. About this time Stephens presented a petition to Parliament, in which he charged the trustees with direliction of duty, improper use of the public funds, abuse of their authority, and numerous other sins against the public welfare. It created a genuine sensation. The House resolved to go into a "committee of the whole," to consider the petitions and the answer of the trustees. The answer of the trustees was drawn by the able pen of the Earl of Egmont, and by them warmly approved on the 3d of May, and three days later was read to the House of Commons. A motion prevailed "that the petitions do lie upon the table," for the perusal of the members, for the space of one week. At the expiration of the time fixed, Stephens appeared, and all the petitions of the people of Georgia to the trustees in reference to "the tenure of lands," and for "the use of negroes," were laid before the honorable body. In the committee of the whole the affairs of the colony were thoroughly investigated; and, after a few days session, Mr. Carew reported a set of resolutions, being the sense of the committee after due deliberation upon the matters before them:—

> "That the province of Georgia, in America, by reason of its situation, may be an useful barrier to the British provinces on the continent of America against the French and Spaniards, and Indian nations in their interests; that the ports and harbors within the said province may be a good security to the trade and navigation of this kingdom, that the said province, by reason of the fertility of the soil, the healthfulness of the climate, and the convenience of the rivers, is a proper place for establishing a settlement,

and may contribute greatly to the increasing trade of this kingdom; that it is very necessary and advantageous to this nation that the colony of Georgia should be preserved and supported; that it will be an advantage to the colony of Georgia to permit the importation of rum into the said colony from any of the British colonies; that the petition of Thomas Stephens contains false, scandalous and malicious charges, tending to asperse the characters of the Trustees for Establishing the Colony of Georgia, in America."

When the resolution making the importation of rum lawful reached a vote, it was amended by adding, "As also the use of negroes, who may be employed there with advantage to the colony, under proper regulations and restrictions." It was lost by a majority of nine votes. A resolution prevailed calling Thomas Stephens to the bar of the House, "to be reprimanded on his knees by Mr. Speaker," for his offence against the trustees.

On the next day Stephens, upon his bended knees at the bar of the House of Commons, before the assembled statesmen of Great Britain, was publicly reprimanded by the speaker, and discharged after paying his fees. Thus ended the attempt of the people of the colony of Georgia to secure permission, over the heads of the trustees, to introduce slaves into their service.

The dark tide of slavery influence was dashing against the borders of the colony. The people were discouraged. Business was stagnated. Internal dissatisfaction and factional strife wore hard upon the spirit of a people trying to build up and develop a new country. Then the predatory incursions of the Spaniards, and the threatening attitude of the Indians, unnerved the entire Province. In this state of affairs white servants grew insolent and insubordinate. Those whose term of service expired refused to work. In this dilemma many persons boldly put the rule of the trustees under foot, and hired Negroes from the Carolinas. At length the trustees became aware of the clandestine importation of Negroes into the colony, and thereupon gave the magistrates a severe reproval. On the 2d of October, 1747, they received the following reply:—

> "We are afraid, sir, from what you have wrote in relation to negroes, that he Honourable Trustees have been misinformed as to our conduct relating thereto; for we can with great assurance assert, that this Board has always acted an uniform part in discouraging the use of negroes in this colony, well knowing it to be disagreeable to the Trustees, as well as contrary to an act existing for the prohibition of

them, and always give it in charge to those whom we had put in possession of lands, not to attempt the introduction or use of negroes. But notwithstanding our great caution, some people from Carolina, soon after settling lands on the Little Ogeechee, found means of bringing and employing a few negroes on the said lands, some time before it was discovered to us, upon which they thought it high time to withdraw them, for fear of being seized, and soon after withdrew themselves and families out of the colony, which appeals to us at present to be the resolution of divers others."[518]

It was charged that the law-officers knew of the presence of Negroes in Georgia; that their standing and constant toast was, "*the one thing needful*" (Negroes); and that they themselves had surreptitiously aided in the procurement of Negroes for the colony. The supporters of the colonists grew less powerful as the struggle went forward. The most active grew taciturn and conservative. The advocates of Negro labor became bolder, and more acrimonious in debate; and at length the champions of exclusive white labor shrank into silence, appalled at the desperation of then opponents. The Rev. Martin Bolzius, one of the most active supporters of the trustees, wrote those gentlemen on May 3, 1748:—

"Things being now in such a melancholy state, I must humbly beseech your honors, not to regard any more our of our friend's petitions against negroes."

The Rev. George Whitefield and James Habersham used their utmost influence upon the trustees to obtain a modification of the prohibition against "the use of negroes." On the 6th of December, 1748, Rev. Whitefield, speaking of a plantation and Negroes he had purchased, wrote the trustees:—

> "Upwards of five thousand pounds have been expended in that undertaking, and yet very little proficiency made in the cultivation of my tract of land, and that entirely owing to the necessity I lay under of making use of white hands. Had a negro been allowed, I should now have had a sufficiency to support a great many orphans, without expending above half the sum which has been laid out. An unwillingness to let so good a design drop, and having a rational conviction that it must necessarily, if some other method was not fixed upon to prevent it—these two considerations, honoured gentlemen, prevailed on me about two years ago, through the bounty of my good friends, to purchase a plantation in South Carolina, where negroes are allowed. Blessed be God,

this plantation has succeeded; and though at present I have only eight working hands, yet in all probability there will be more raised in one year, and with a quarter the expense, than has been produced at Bethesda for several years last past. This confirms me in the opinion I have entertained for a long time, that Georgia never can or will be a flourishing province without negroes are allowed."[519]

The sentiment in favor of the importation of Negro slaves had become well-nigh unanimous. The trustees began to waver. On the 10th of January, 1749, another petition was presented to the trustees. It was carefully drawn, and set forth the restrictions under which slaves should be introduced. On the 16th of May following, it was read to the trustees; and they resolved to have it "presented to His Majesty in council." They also asked that the prohibition against the introduction of Negroes, passed in "1735, be repealed." The Earl of Shaftesbury, at the head of a special committee, draughted a bill repealing the prohibition. On the 26th of October, 1749, a large and influential committee of twenty-seven drew up and signed a petition urging the immediate introduction of slavery, with certain limitations. The paper was duly attested, and returned to the trustees. The opposition to the introduction of slavery into the colony of Georgia had been conquered; and, after a long and bitter struggle, slavery was firmly and legally established in this the last Province of the English in the Western world. The colonists were jubilant.

The charter under which the trustees acted expired by limitation in 1752, and a new form of government was established under the Board of Trade. The royal commission appointed a governor and council. One of the first ordinances enacted by them was one whereby "all offences committed by slaves were to be tried by a single justice, without a jury, who was to award execution, and, in capital cases, to set a value on the slave, to be paid out of the public treasury." At the first session of the Assembly in 1755, a law was passed *"for the regulation and government of slaves."* In 1765 an Act was passed establishing a pass system, and the rest of the legislation in respect to slaves was a copy of the laws of South Carolina.

The history of slavery in Georgia during this period is unparalleled and incomparably interesting. It illustrates the power of the institution, and shows that there was no Province sufficiently independent of its influence so as to expel it from its jurisdiction. Like the Angel of Death that passed through Egypt, there was no colony that it did not smite with its dark and destroying pinions. The dearest, the sublimest, interests of humanity were prostrated by its defiling touch. It shut out the sunlight of human kindness; it paled the fires of hope; it arrested the development of the branches of men's better natures, and peopled their lower being with base and consuming desires; it placed the "Golden Rule" under the unholy heel of time-servers and self-seekers; it made the Church as secular as the Change, and the latter as pious as the former: it was a gigantic system, at war with the civilization of the Roundheads and Puritans, and an intolerable burden to a people who desired to build a new nation in this New World in the West.

FOOTNOTES:

[514] Stephens's Journal, vol. iii. p. 281.

[515] Freedom and Bondage, vol. i. p. 310, note.

[516] Stevens's Hist. of Georgia, vol. i. p. 289.

[517] Bancroft, vol. iii. 12th ed. p. 427.

[518] Stevens's Hist. of Georgia, vol. i. p. 307.

[519] Whitefield's Works, vol. ii. pp. 90, 105, 208.

PART III
THE NEGRO DURING THE REVOLUTION

CHAPTER XXVI
MILITARY EMPLOYMENT OF NEGROES

1775-1780.

"Many black soldiers were in the service during all stages of the war."—SPARKS.

The Colonial States in 1715.—Ratification of the Non-Importation Act by the Southern Colonies.—George Washington presents Resolutions against Slavery, in a Meeting at Fairfax Court-House, Va.—Letter written by Benjamin Franklin to Dean Woodward, pertaining to Slavery.—Letter to the Freemen of Virginia from a Committee, concerning the Slaves brought from Jamaica.—Severe Treatment of Slaves in the Colonies modified.—Advertisement in "The Boston Gazette" of the Runaway Slave Crispus Attucks.—The Boston Massacre.—Its Results.—Crispus Attucks shows his Loyalty.—His Spirited Letter to the Tory Governor of the Province.—Slaves admitted into the Army.—The Condition of the Continental Army.—Spirited Debate in the Continental Congress, over the Draught of a Letter to Gen. Washington.—Instructions to discharge all Slaves and Free Negroes in his Army.—Minutes of the Meeting held at Cambridge.—Lord Dunmore's Proclamation.—Prejudice in the Southern Colonies.—Negroes in Virginia flock to the British Army.—Caution to the Negroes printed in a Williamsburg Paper.—The Virginia Convention answers the

Proclamation of Lord Dunmore.—Gen. Greene, in a Letter to Gen. Washington, calls Attention to the raising of a Negro Regiment on Staten Island.—Letter from a Hessian Officer.—Connecticut Legislature on the Subject of Employment of Negroes as Soldiers.—Gen. Varnum's Letter to Gen. Washington, suggesting the Employment of Negroes, sent to Gov. Cooke.—The Governor refers Varnum's Letter to the General Assembly.—Minority Protest against enlisting Slaves to serve in the Army.—Massachusetts tries to secure Legal Enlistments of Negro Troops.—Letter of Thomas Kench to the Council and House of Representatives, Boston, Mass.—Negroes serve in White Organizations until the Close of the American Revolution.—Negro Soldiers serve in Virginia.—Maryland employs Negroes.—New York passes an Act providing for the Raising of two Colored Regiments.—War in the Middle and Southern Colonies.—Hamilton's Letter to John Jay.—Col. Laurens's Efforts to raise Negro Troops in South Carolina.—Proclamation of Sir Henry Clinton inducing Negroes to desert the Rebel Army.—Lord Cornwallis issues a Proclamation offering Protection to all Negroes seeking his Command,—Col. Laurens is called to France on Important Business.—His Plan for securing Black Levies for the South upon his Return.—His Letters to Gen. Washington in Regard to his Fruitless Plans.—Capt David Humphreys recruits a Company of Colored Infantry in Connecticut.—Return of Negroes in the Army in 1778.

 THE policy of arming the Negroes early claimed the anxious consideration of the leaders of the colonial army during the American Revolution. England had been crowding her American plantations with slaves at a fearful rate; and, when hostilities actually began, it was difficult to tell whether the American army or the ministerial army would be able to secure the Negroes as allies. In 1715 the royal governors of the colonies gave the Board of Trade the number of the Negroes in their respective colonies. The slave population was as follows:—

NEGROES.		NEGROES.	
New Hampshire	150	Maryland	9,500
Massachusetts	2,000	Virginia	23,000
Rhode Island	500	North Carolina	3,700
Connecticut	1,500	South Carolina	10,500

New York   4,000 | ------

New Jersey   1,500 | Total   58,850

Pennsylvania and Delaware   2,500 |

Sixty years afterwards, when the Revolution had begun, the slave population of the thirteen colonies was as follows:—

NEGROES.		NEGROES.	
Massachusetts	3,500	Maryland	80,000
Rhode Island	4,373	Virginia	165,000
Connecticut	5,000	North Carolina	75,000
New Hampshire	629	South Carolina	110,000
New York	15,000	Georgia	16,000
New Jersey	7,600		-------
Pennsylvania	10,000	Total	501,102
Delaware	9,000		

Such a host of beings was not to be despised in a great military struggle. Regarded as a neutral element that could be used simply to feed an army, to perform fatigue duty, and build fortifications, the Negro population was the object of fawning favors of the white colonists. In the Non-Importation Covenant, passed by the Continental Congress at Philadelphia, on the 24th of October, 1774, the second resolve indicated the feeling of the representatives of the people on the question of the slave-trade:—

> "2. We will neither import nor purchase, any slave imported after the first day of December next; after which time, we will wholly discontinue the slave-trade, and will neither be concerned in it ourselves, nor will we hire our vessels, nor sell our commodities or manufactures to those who are concerned in it."[520]

It, with the entire covenant, received the signatures of all the delegates from the twelve colonies.[521] The delegates from the Southern colonies were greatly distressed concerning the probable attitude of the slave element. They knew that if that ignorant mass of humanity were inflamed by some act of strategy of the enemy, they might sweep their homes and families from the face of the earth. The cruelties of the slave-code, the harsh treatment of Negro slaves, the lack of confidence in the whites everywhere manifested among the blacks,—as so many horrid dreams, harassed the minds of slaveholders by day and by night. They did not even possess the courage to ask the slaves to remain silent and passive during the struggle between England and themselves. The sentiment that adorned the speeches of orators, and graced the writings of the colonists, during this period, was "the equality of the rights of all men." And yet the slaves who bore their chains under their eyes, who were denied the commonest rights of humanity, who were rated as chattels and real property, were living witnesses to the insincerity and inconsistency of this declaration. But it is a remarkable fact, that all the Southern colonies, in addition to the action of their delegates, ratified the Non-Importation Covenant. The Maryland Convention on the 8th of December, 1774; South Carolina Provincial Congress on the 11th January, 1775; Virginia Convention on the 22d March, 1775; North Carolina Provincial Congress on the 23d of August, 1775; Delaware Assembly on the 25th of March, 1775 (refused by Gov. John Penn); and Georgia,—passed the following resolves thereabouts:—

"1. *Resolved*, That this Congress will adopt, and carry into execution, all and singular the measures and recommendations of the late Continental Congress.

"4. *Resolved*, That we will neither import or [nor] purchase any slave imported from Africa or elsewhere after this date."

Meetings were numerous and spirited throughout the colonies, in which, by resolutions, the people expressed their sentiments in reference to the mother country. On the 18th of July, 1774, at a meeting held in Fairfax Court-House, Virginia, a series of twenty-four resolutions was presented by George Washington, chairman of the committee on resolutions, three of which were directed against slavery.

"17 *Resolved*. That it is the opinion of this meeting, that, during our present difficulties and distress, no slaves ought to be imported into any of the British colonies on this continent; and we take this opportunity of declaring our most earnest wishes to see an entire stop for ever put to such a wicked, cruel, and unnatural trade....

"21. *Resolved*, That it is the opinion of this meeting, that this and the other associating colonies should break off all trade, intercourse, and dealings with that colony, province, or town, which shall decline, or refuse to agree to, the plan which shall be adopted by the General Congress....

"24. *Resolved*, That George Washington and Charles Broadwater, lately elected our representatives to serve in the General Assembly, be appointed to attend the Convention at Williamsburg on the first day of August next, and present these resolves, as the sense of the people of this county upon the measures proper to be taken in the present alarming and dangerous situation of America."

Mr. Sparks comments upon the resolutions as follows:—

"The draught, from which the resolves are printed, I find among Washington's papers, in the handwriting of George Mason, by whom they were probably drawn up; yet, as they were adopted by the Committee of which Washington was chairman, and reported by him as moderator of the meeting, they may be presumed to express his opinions, formed on a perfect knowledge of the subject, and after cool deliberation. This may indeed be inferred from his letter to Mr. Bryan Fairfax, in which he intimates a doubt only as to the article favoring the idea of a further petition to the king. He was opposed to such a step, believing enough had been done in this way already; but he yielded the point in tenderness to the more wavering resolution of his associates.

"These resolves are framed with much care and ability, and exhibit the question then at issue, and the state of public feeling, in a manner so clear and forcible as to give them a special claim to a place in the present work, in addition to the circumstance of their being the matured views of Washington at the outset of the great Revolutionary struggle in which he was to act so conspicuous a part....

> "Such were the opinions of Washington, and his associates in Virginia, at the beginning of the Revolutionary contest. The seventeenth resolve merits attention, from the pointed manner in which it condemns the slave trade."[522]

Dr. Benjamin Franklin, in a letter to Dean Woodward, dated April 10, 1773, says,—

> "I have since had the satisfaction to learn that a disposition to abolish slavery prevails in North America, that many of the Pennsylvanians have set their slaves at liberty; and that even the Virginia Assembly have petitioned the king for permission to make a law for preventing the importation of more into that Colony. This request, however, will probably not be granted as their former laws of that kind have always been repealed, and as the interest of a few merchants here has more weight with Government than that of thousands at a distance."[523]

Virginia gave early and positive proof that she was in earnest on the question of non-importation. One John Brown, a merchant of Norfolk, broke the rules of the colony by purchasing imported slaves, and was severely rebuked in the following article:—

"'TO THE FREEMEN OF VIRGINIA:

"'COMMITTEE CHAMBER, NORFOLK, MARCH 6, 1775

"'Trusting to your sure resentment against the enemies of your country, we, the committee, elected by ballot for the Borough of Norfolk, hold up for your just indignation Mr. John Brown, merchant of this place.

"'On Thursday, the 2d of March, this committee were informed of the arrival of the brig Fanny, Capt. Watson, with a number of slaves for Mr. Brown: and, upon inquiry, it appeared they were shipped from Jamaica as his property, and on his account; that he had taken great pains to conceal their arrival from the knowledge of the committee; and that the shipper of the slaves, Mr. Brown's correspondent, and the captain of the vessel, were all fully apprised of the Continental prohibition against that article.

"'From the whole of this transaction, therefore, we, the committee for Norfolk Borough, do give it as our unanimous opinion, that the said John Brown, has wilfully and perversely violated the Continental Association to which he had with his own hand subscribed obedience, and that, agreeable to the eleventh article, we are bound forthwith to publish the truth of the case, to the end that all such foes to the rights of British America may be publicly known and universally contemned as the enemies of American liberty, and that every person may henceforth break off all dealings with him.'"

And the first delegation from Virginia to Congress in August, 1774, had instructions as follows, drawn by Thomas Jefferson:—

> "For the most trifling reasons, and sometimes for no conceivable reason at all, his Majesty has rejected laws of the most salutary tendency. The abolition of domestic slavery is the great object of desire in those Colonies, where it was, unhappily, introduced in their infant state. But, previous to the enfranchisement of the slaves we have, it is necessary to exclude all further importations from Africa. Yet our repeated attempts to effect this by prohibitions, and by imposing duties which might amount to a prohibition, have been hitherto defeated by his Majesty's negative; thus preferring the immediate advantages of a few British corsairs to the lasting interests of the American States, and to the rights of human nature, deeply wounded by this infamous practice."[524]

It is scarcely necessary to mention the fact, that there were several very cogent passages in the first draught of the Declaration of Independence that were finally omitted. The one most pertinent to this history is here given:—

> "He has waged cruel war against human nature itself, violating its most sacred rights of life and liberty in the persons of a distant people who never offended him; captivating and carrying them into slavery in another hemisphere, or to incur miserable death in their transportation thither. This piratical warfare, the opprobrium of Infidel powers, is the warfare of the Christian king of Great Britain. Determined to keep open a market where men should be bought and sold, he has prostituted his negative for suppressing every legislative attempt to prohibit or to restrain this execrable commerce. And, that this assemblage of horrors might want no fact of distinguished die, he is now exciting those very people to rise in arms among us, and to purchase that liberty of which he has deprived them, by murdering the people on whom he also obtruded them; thus paying off former crimes committed against the liberties of one people with crimes which he urges them to commit against the lives of another. [525]

The solicitude concerning the slavery question was not so great in the Northern colonies. The slaves were not so numerous as in the Carolinas and other Southern colonies. The severe treatment of slaves had been greatly modified, the spirit of masters toward them more gentle and conciliatory, and the public sentiment concerning them more humane. Public discussion of the Negro question, however, was cautiously avoided. The failure of attempted legislation friendly to the slaves had discouraged their friends, while the critical situation of public affairs made the supporters of slavery less aggressive. On the 25th of October, 1774, an effort was made in the Provincial Congress of Massachusetts to re-open the discussion, but it failed. The record of the attempt is as follows:—

> "Mr. Wheeler brought into Congress a letter directed to Doct. Appleton, purporting the propriety, that while we are attempting to free ourselves from our present embarrassments, and preserve ourselves from slavery, that we also take into consideration the state and circumstances of the negro slaves in this province. The same was read, and it was moved that a committee be appointed to take the same into consideration. After some debate thereon, the question

was put, whether the matter now subside, and it passed in the affirmative."[526]

Thus ended the attempt to call the attention of the people's representatives to the inconsistency of their doctrine and practice on the question of the equality of human rights. Further agitation of the question, followed by the defeat of just measures in the interest of the slaves, was deemed by many as dangerous to the colony. The discussions were watched by the Negroes with a lively interest; and failure led them to regard the colonists as their enemies, and greatly embittered them. Then it was difficult to determine just what would be wisest to do for the enslaved in this colony. The situation was critical: a bold, clear-headed, loyal-hearted man was needed.

On Tuesday, Oct. 2, 1750, "The Boston Gazette, or Weekly Journal," contained the following advertisement:—

"RAN-away from his master *William Brown* of *Framingham*, on the 30th of *Sept.* last, a Molatto Fellow, about 27 Years of Age, named *Crispas*, 5 Feet 2 Inches high, short curl'd Hair, his Knees nearer together than common; had on a light colour'd Bear-skin Coat, plain brown Fustian Jacket, or brown all-Wool one, new Buckskin Breeches, blue Yarn Stockings, and a checked woolen Shirt.

"Whoever shall take up said Run-away, and convey him to his abovesaid Master, shall have *ten Pounds*, old Tenor Reward, and all necessary Charges paid. And all Masters of Vessels and others, are hereby cautioned against concealing or carrying off said Servant on Penalty of the Law. Boston, October 2, 1750."

During the month of November,—the 13th and 20th,—a similar advertisement appeared in the same paper; showing that the "Molatto Fellow" had not returned to his master.

Twenty years later "Crispas's" name once more appeared in the journals of Boston. This time he was not advertised as a runaway slave, nor was there reward offered for his apprehension. His soul and body were beyond the cruel touch of master; the press had paused to announce his apotheosis, and to write the name of the Negro patriot, soldier, and martyr to the ripening cause of the American Revolution, in fadeless letters of gold,—Crispus Attucks!

On March 5, 1770, occurred the Boston Massacre; and, while it was not the real commencement of the Revolutionary struggle, it was the bloody drama that opened the most eventful and thrilling chapter in American history. The colonists had endured, with obsequious humility, the oppressive acts of Britain, the swaggering insolence of the ministerial troops, and the sneers of her hired minions. The aggressive and daring men had found themselves hampered by the conservative views of a large class of colonists, who feared lest some one should take a step not exactly according to the law. But while the "wise and prudent" were deliberating upon a legal method of action, there were those, who, "made of sterner stuff," reasoned right to the conclusion, that they had rights as colonists that ought to be respected. That there was cause for just indignation on the part of the people towards the British soldiers, there is no doubt. But there is reason to question the time and manner of the assault made by the citizens. Doubtless they had "a zeal, but not according to knowledge." There is no record to controvert the fact of the leadership of Crispus Attucks. A manly-looking fellow, six feet two inches in height, he was a commanding figure among the irate colonists. His enthusiasm for the threatened interests of the Province, his loyalty to the teachings of Otis, and his willingness to sacrifice for the cause of equal rights, endowed him with a courage, which, if tempered with better judgment, would have made him a military hero in his day. But consumed by the sacred fires of patriotism, that lighted his path to glory, his career of usefulness ended at the beginning. John Adams, as the counsel for the soldiers, thought that the patriots Crispus Attucks led were a "rabble of saucy boys, negroes, mulattoes, &c.," who could not restrain their emotion. Attucks led the charge with the shout, "The way to get rid of these soldiers is to attack the main-guard; strike at the root: this is the nest." A shower of missiles was answered by the discharge of the guns of Capt. Preston's company. The exposed and commanding person of the intrepid Attucks went down before the murderous fire. Samuel Gray and Jonas Caldwell were also killed, while Patrick Carr and Samuel Maverick were mortally wounded.

 The scene that followed beggared description. The people ran from their homes and places of business into the streets, white with rage. The bells rang out the alarm of danger. The bodies of Attucks and Caldwell were carried into Faneuil Hall, where their strange faces were viewed by the largest gathering of people ever before witnessed. Maverick was buried from his mother's house in Union Street, and Gray from his brother's residence in Royal Exchange Lane. But Attucks and Caldwell, strangers in the city, without relatives, were buried from Faneuil Hall, so justly called "the Cradle of Liberty." The four hearses formed a junction in King Street; and from thence the procession moved in columns six deep, with a long line of coaches containing the first citizens of Boston. The obsequies were witnessed by a very large and respectful concourse of people. The bodies were deposited in one grave, over which a stone was placed bearing this inscription:—

"Long as in Freedom's cause the wise contend,
Dear to your country shall your fame extend;
While to the world the lettered stone shall tell
Where Caldwell, Attucks, Gray and Maverick fell."

Who was Crispus Attucks? A Negro whose soul, galling under the destroying influence of slavery, went forth a freeman, went forth not only to fight for *his* liberty, but to give his life as an offering upon the altar of *American liberty*. He was not a madcap, as some would have the world believe. He was not ignorant of the issues between the American colonies and the English government, between the freemen of the colony and the dictatorial governors. Where he was during the twenty years from 1750 to 1770, is not known; but doubtless in Boston, where he had heard the fiery eloquence of Otis, the convincing arguments of Sewall, and the tender pleadings of Belknap. He had learned to spell out the fundamental principles that should govern well-regulated communities and states; and, having come to the rapturous consciousness of his freedom in fee simple, the brightest crown God places upon mortal man, he felt himself neighbor and friend. His patriotism was not a mere spasm produced by sudden and exciting circumstances. It was an education; and knowledge comes from experience; and the experience of this black hero was not of a single day. Some time before the memorable 5th of March, Crispus addressed the following spirited letter to the Tory governor of the Province:—

"To Thomas Hutchinson: *Sir*,—You will hear from us with astonishment. You ought to hear from us with horror. You are chargeable before God and man, with our blood. The soldiers were but passive instruments, mere machines; neither moral nor voluntary agents in our destruction, more than the leaden pellets with which we were wounded. You was a free agent. You acted, coolly, deliberately, with all that premeditated malice, not against us in particular, but against the people in general, which, in the sight of the law, is an ingredient in the composition of murder. You will hear further from us hereafter.

CRISPUS ATTUCKS."[527]

This was the declaration of war. It was fulfilled. The world has heard from him; and, more, the English-speaking world will never forget the noble daring and excusable rashness of Attucks in the holy cause of liberty! Eighteen centuries before he was saluted by death and kissed by immortality, another Negro bore the cross of Christ to Calvary for him. And when the colonists were staggering wearily under their cross of woe, a Negro came to the front, and bore that cross to the victory of glorious martyrdom!

And the people did not agree with John Adams that Attucks led "a motley rabble," but a band of patriots. Their evidence of the belief they entertained was to be found in the annual commemoration of the "5th of March," when orators, in measured sentences and impassioned eloquence, praised the hero-dead. In March, 1775, Dr. Joseph Warren, who a few months later, as Gen. Warren, made Bunker Hill the shrine of New-England patriotism, was the orator. On the question of human liberty, he said,—

"That personal freedom is the natural right of every man, and that property, or an exclusive right to dispose of what he has honestly acquired by his own labor, necessarily arises therefrom, are truths which common sense has placed beyond the reach of contradiction. And no man, or body of men, can, without being guilty of flagrant injustice, claim a right to dispose of the persons or acquisitions of any other man, or body of men, unless it can be proved that such a right has arisen from some compact between the parties, in which it has been explicitly and freely granted."

These noble sentiments were sealed by his blood at Bunker Hill, on the 17th of June, 1775, and are the amulet that will protect his fame from the corroding touch of centuries of time

The free Negroes of the Northern colonies responded to the call "to arms" that rang from the placid waters of Massachusetts Bay to the verdant hills of Berkshire, and from Lake Champlain to the upper waters of the Hudson. Every Northern colony had its Negro troops, not as separate organizations,—save the black regiment of Rhode Island,—but scattered throughout all of the white organizations of the army. At the first none but free Negroes were received into the army; but before peace came Negroes were not only admitted, they were purchased, and sent into the war, with an offer of freedom and fifty dollars bounty at the close of their service. On the 29th of May, 1775, the "Committee of Safety" for the Province of Massachusetts passed the following resolve against the enlistment of Negro slaves as soldiers:—

> "Resolved, That it is the opinion of this committee, as the contest now between Great Britain and the colonies respects the liberties and privileges of the latter, which the colonies are determined to maintain, that the admission of any persons, as soldiers, into the army now raising, but only such as are freemen, will be inconsistent with the principles that are to be supported, and reflect dishonor on this colony, and that no slaves be admitted into this army upon any consideration whatever."[528]

On Tuesday, the 6th of June, 1775, "A resolve of the committee of safety, relative to the [admission] of slaves into the army was read, and ordered to lie on the table for further consideration."[529] But this was but another evidence of the cold, conservative spirit of Massachusetts on the question of other people's rights.

The Continental army was in bad shape. Its arms and clothing, its discipline and efficiency, were at such a low state as to create the gravest apprehensions and deepest solicitude. Gen. George Washington took command of the army in and around Boston, on the 3d of July, 1775, and threw his energies into the work of organization. On the 10th of July he issued instructions to the recruiting-officers of Massachusetts Bay, in which he forbade the enlistment of any "negro," or "any Person who is not an American born, unless such Person has a Wife and Family and is a settled resident in this Country."[530] But, nevertheless, it is a curious fact, as Mr. Bancroft says, "the roll of the army at Cambridge had from its first formation borne the names of men of color." "Free negroes stood in the ranks by the side of white men. In the beginning of the war they had entered the provincial army; the first general order which was issued by Ward, had required a return, among other things, of the 'complexion' of the soldiers; and black men like others were retained in the service after the troops were adopted by the continent." There is no room to doubt. Negroes were in the army from first to last, but were there in contravention of law and positive prohibition.[531]

On the 29th of September, 1775, a spirited debate occurred in the Continental Congress, over the draught of a letter to Gen. Washington, reported by Lynch, Lee, and Adams. Mr. Rutledge of South Carolina moved that the commander-in-chief be instructed to discharge all slaves and free Negroes in his army. The Southern delegates supported him earnestly, but his motion was defeated. Public attention was called to the question, and at length the officers of the army debated it. The following minute of a meeting held at Cambridge preserves and reveals the sentiment of the general officers of the army on the subject:—

"At a council of war, held at head-quarters, October 8th, 1775, present: His Excellency, General Washington; Major-Generals Ward, Lee, and Putnam Brigadier-Generals Thomas, Spencer, Heath, Sullivan, Greene, and Gates—the question was proposed:

"'Whether it will be advisable to enlist any negroes in the new army? or whether there be a distinction between such as are slaves and those who are free?'

"It was agreed unanimously to reject all slaves; and, by a great majority, to reject negroes altogether."

Ten days later, Oct. 18, 1775, a committee of conference met at Cambridge, consisting of Dr. Franklin, Benjamin Harrison, and Thomas Lynch, who conferred with Gen. Washington, the deputy-governors of Connecticut and Rhode Island, and the Committee of the Council of Massachusetts Bay. The object of the conference was the renovation and improvement of the army. On the 23d of October, the employment of Negroes as soldiers came before the conference for action, as follows:—

"Ought not negroes to be excluded from the new enlistment, especially such as are slaves? all were thought improper by the council of officers."

"*Agreed* that they be rejected altogether"

In his General Orders, issued from headquarters on the 12th of November, 1775, Washington said,—

> "Neither negroes, boys unable to bear arms, nor old men unfit to endure the fatigues of the campaign, are to be enlisted."[532]

But the general repaired this mistake the following month. Lord Dunmore had issued a proclamation declaring "all indented servants, negroes, or others (appertaining to rebels) free." Fearing lest many Negroes should join the ministerial army, in General Orders, 30th December, Washington wrote:—

"As the General is informed that numbers of free negroes are desirous of enlisting he gives leave to the recruiting officers to entertain them, and promises to lay the matter before the Congress, who, he doubts not, will approve of it."

Lord Dunmore's proclamation is here given:—

"*By his Excellency the Right Honorable* John, *Earl of* Dunmore, *his Majesty's Lieutenant and Governor-General of the Colony and Dominion of Virginia, and Vice-Admiral of the same,*—

"A PROCLAMATION.

> "As I have ever entertained hopes that an accommodation might have taken place between Great Britain and this Colony, without being compelled by my duty to this most disagreeable but now absolutely necessary step, rendered so by a body of armed men, unlawfully assembled, firing on his Majesty's tenders; and the formation of an army, and that

army now on their march to attack his Majesty's troops, and destroy the well-disposed subject of this Colony: To defeat such treasonable purposes, and that all such traitors and their abettors may be brought to justice, and that the peace and good order of this Colony may be again restored, which the ordinary course of the civil law is unable to effect, I have thought fit to issue this my Proclamation; hereby declaring, that until the aforesaid good purposes can be obtained, I do, in virtue of the power and authority to me given by his Majesty, determine to execute martial law, and cause the same to be executed, throughout this Colony. And, to the end that peace and good order may the sooner be restored, I do require every person capable of bearing arms to resort to his Majesty's standard, or be looked upon as traitors to his Majesty's Crown and Government, and thereby become liable to the penalty the law inflicts upon such offences,— such as forfeiture of life, confiscation of lands, &c., &c. And I do hereby further declare all indented servants, negroes, or others (appertaining to Rebels,) free, that are able and willing to bear arms, they joining his Majesty's troops, as soon as may be, for the more speedily reducing this Colony to a proper sense of their duty to his Majesty's crown and dignity. I do further order and require all his Majesty's liege subjects to retain their quit-rents, or any other taxes due, or that may become due, in their own custody, till such time as peace may be again restored to this at present most unhappy country, or demanded of them, for their former salutary purposes, by officers properly authorized to receive the same.

"Given under my hand, on board the Ship *William*, off *Norfolk*, the seventh day of November, in the sixteenth year of his Majesty's reign.

"Dunmore.

"GOD SAVE THE KING!"[533]

On account of this, on the 31st of December, Gen. Washington wrote the President of Congress as follows:—

"It has been represented to me, that the free negroes, who have served in this army, are very much dissatisfied at being discarded. As it is to be apprehended, that they may seek employ in the ministerial army, I have presumed to depart from the resolution respecting them, and have given license for their being enlisted. If this is disapproved of by Congress, I will put a stop to it."[534]

This letter was referred to a committee consisting of Messrs. Wythe, Adams, and Wilson. On the 16th of January, 1776, they made the following report:—

"That the free negroes who have served faithfully in the army at Cambridge may be re-enlist—therein, but no others."[535]

This action on the part of Congress had reference to the army around Boston, but it called forth loud and bitter criticism from the officers of the army at the South. In a letter to John Adams, dated Oct. 24, 1775, Gen. Thomas indicated that there was some feeling even before the action of Congress was secured. He says,—

"I am sorry to hear that any prejudices should take place in any Southern colony, with respect to the troops raised in this. I am certain the insinuations you mention are injurious, if we consider with what precipitation we were obliged to collect an army. In the regiments at Roxbury, the privates are equal to any that I served with in the last war; very few old men, and in the ranks very few boys. Our fifers are many of them boys. We have some negroes; but I look on them, in general, equally serviceable with other men for fatigue; and, in action, many of them have proved themselves brave.

"I would avoid all reflection, or any thing that may tend to give umbrage; but there is in this army from the southward a number called riflemen, who are as indifferent men as I ever served with. These privates are mutinous, and often deserting to the enemy; unwilling for duty of any kind; exceedingly vicious; and, I think, the army here would be as well without as with them. But to do justice to their officers, they are, some of them, likely men."

The Dunmore proclamation was working great mischief in the Southern colonies. The Southern colonists were largely engaged in planting, and, as they were Tories, did not rush to arms with the celerity that characterized the Northern colonists. At an early moment in the struggle, the famous Rev. Dr. Hopkins of Rhode Island wrote the following pertinent extract:—

"God is so ordering it in his providence, that it seems absolutely necessary something should speedily be done with respect to the slaves among us, in order to our safety, and to prevent their turning against us in out present struggle, in order to get their liberty. Our oppressors have planned to gain the blacks, and induce them to take up arms against us, by promising them liberty on this condition; and this plan they are prosecuting to the utmost of their power, by which means they have persuaded numbers to join them. And should we attempt to restrain them by force and severity, keeping a strict guard over them, and punishing them severely who shall be detected in attempting to join our opposers, this will only be making bad worse, and serve to render our inconsistence, oppression, and cruelty more criminal, perspicuous, and shocking, and bring down the righteous vengeance of Heaven on our heads. The only way pointed out to prevent this threatening evil is to set the blacks at liberty ourselves by some public acts and laws, and then give them proper encouragement to labor, or take arms in the defence of the American cause, as they shall choose. This would at once be doing them some degree of justice, and defeating our enemies in the scheme that they are prosecuting."[536]

On Sunday, the 24th of September, 1775, John Adams recorded the following conversation, that goes to show that Lord Dunmore's policy was well matured:—

"In the evening, Mr. Bullock and Mr. Houston, two gentlemen from Georgia, came into our room, and smoked and chatted the whole evening. Houston and Adams disputed the whole time in good humor. They are both dabs at disputation, I think. Houston, a lawyer by trade, is one of course, and Adams is not a whit less addicted to it than the lawyers. The question was, whether all America was not in a state of war, and whether we ought to confine ourselves to act upon the defensive only? He was for acting offensively, next spring or this fall, if the petition was rejected or neglected. If it was not answered, and favorably answered, he would be for acting against Britain and Britons, as, in open war, against French and Frenchmen; fit privateers, and take their ships anywhere. These gentlemen give a melancholy account of the State of Georgia and South Carolina. They say that if one thousand regular troops should land in Georgia, and their commander be provided with arms and clothes enough, and proclaim freedom to all the negroes who would join his camp, twenty thousand negroes would join it from the two Provinces in a fortnight. The negroes have a wonderful art of communicating intelligence among themselves; it will run several hundreds of miles in a week or fortnight. They say, their only security is this; that all the king's friends, and tools of government, have large plantations, and property in negroes; so that the slaves of the Tories would be lost, as well as those of the Whigs."[537]

The Negroes in Virginia sought the standards of the ministerial army, and the greatest consternation prevailed among the planters. On the 27th of November, 1775, Edmund Pendleton wrote to Richard Lee that the slaves were daily flocking to the British army.

> "The Governour, hearing of this, marched out with three hundred and fifty soldiers, Tories and slaves, to Kemp's Landing, and after setting up his standard, and issuing his proclamation, declaring all persons Rebels who took up arms for the country, and inviting all slaves, servants, and apprentices to come to him and receive arms, he proceeded to intercept Hutchings and his party, upon whom he came by surprise, but received, it seems, so warm a fire, that the ragamuffins gave way. They were, however, rallied on discovering that two companies of our militia gave way; and left Hutchings and Dr. Reid with a volunteer company, who maintained their ground bravely till they were overcome by numbers, and took shelter in a swamp. The slaves were sent in pursuit of them; and one of Col. Hutchings's own, with another, found him. On their approach, he discharged his pistol at his slave, but missed him; and was taken by them, after receiving a wound in his face with a sword. The number taken or killed, on either side, is not ascertained. It is said the Governour went to Dr. Reid's shop, and, after taking the medicines and dressings necessary for his wounded men, broke all the others to pieces. Letters mention that slaves flock to him in abundance; but I hope it is magnified."[538]

But the dark stream of Negroes that had set in toward the English troops, where they were promised the privilege of bearing arms and their freedom, could not easily be stayed. The proclamation of Dunmore received the criticism of the press, and the Negroes were appealed to and urged to stand by their "true friends." A Williamsburg paper, printed on the 23d of November, 1775, contained the following well-written plea:—

"CAUTION TO THE NEGROES.

"The second class of people for whose sake a few remarks upon this proclamation seem necessary is the Negroes. They have been flattered with their freedom, if they be able to bear arms, and will speedily join Lord Dunmore's troops. To none, then, is freedom promised, but to such as are able to do Lord Dunmore service. The aged, the infirm, the women and children, are still to remain the property of their masters,—of masters who will be provoked to severity, should part of their slaves desert them. Lord Dunmore's declaration, therefore, is a cruel declaration to the Negroes. He does not pretend to make it out of any tenderness to them, but solely upon his own account; and, should it meet with success, it leaves by far the greater number at the mercy of an enraged and injured people. But should there be any amongst the Negroes weak enough to believe that Lord Dunmore intends to do them a kindness, and wicked enough to provoke the fury of the Americans against their defenceless fathers and mothers, their wives, their women and children, let them only consider the difficulty of effecting their escape, and what they must expect to suffer if they fall into the hands of the Americans. Let them further consider what must be their fate should the English prove conquerors. If we can judge of the future from the past, it will not be much mended. Long have the Americans, moved by compassion and actuated by sound policy, endeavored to stop the progress of slavery. Our Assemblies have repeatedly passed acts, laying heavy duties upon imported Negroes; by which they meant altogether to prevent the horrid traffick. But their humane intentions have been as often frustrated by the cruelty and covetousness of a set of English merchants, who prevailed upon the King to repeal our kind and merciful acts, little, indeed, to the credit of his humanity. Can it, then, be supposed that the Negroes will be better used by the English, who have always encouraged and upheld this slavery, than by their present masters, who pity their condition; who wish, in general, to make it as easy and comfortable as possible; and who would, were it in their power, or were they permitted, not only prevent any more Negroes from losing their freedom, but restore it to such as have already unhappily lost it? No: the ends of Lord

Dunmore and his party being answered, they will either give up the offending Negroes to the rigor of the laws they have broken, or sell them in the West Indies, where every year they sell many thousands of their miserable brethren, to perish either by the inclemency of weather or the cruelty of barbarous masters. Be not then, ye Negroes, tempted by this proclamation to ruin yourselves. I have given you a faithful view of what you are to expect; and declare before God, in doing it, I have considered your welfare, as well as that of the country. Whether you will profit by my advice, I cannot tell; but this I know, that, whether we suffer or not, if you desert us, you most certainly will."[539]

But the Negroes had been demoralized, and it required an extraordinary effort to quiet them. On the 13th of December, the Virginia Convention put forth an answer to the proclamation of Lord Dunmore. On the 14th of December a proclamation was issued "offering pardon to such slaves as shall return to their duty within ten days after the publication thereof." The following; was their declaration:—

"*By the Representatives of the People of the Colony and Dominion of Virginia, assembled in General Convention,*

"A DECLARATION.

"Whereas Lord Dunmore, by his Proclamation dated on board the ship 'William,' off Norfolk, the seventh day of November, 1775, hath offered freedom to such able-bodied slaves as are willing to join him, and take up arms against the good people of this Colony, giving thereby encouragement to a general insurrection, which may induce a necessity of inflicting the severest punishments upon those unhappy people, already deluded by his base and insidious arts, and whereas, by an act of the General Assembly now in force in this Colony, it is enacted, that all negro or other slaves, conspiring to rebel or make insurrection, shall suffer death, and be excluded all benefit of clergy;—we think it proper to declare, that all slaves who have been or shall be seduced, by his Lordship's Proclamation, or other arts, to desert their masters' service, and take up arms against the inhabitants of this Colony, shall be liable to such punishment as shall hereafter be directed by the General Convention. And to the end that all such who have taken this unlawful and wicked step may return in safety to their duty, and escape the punishment due to their crimes, we hereby promise pardon to them, they surrendering themselves to Colonel William Woodford or any other commander of our troops, and not appearing in arms after the publication hereof. And we do further earnestly recommend it to all humane and benevolent persons in this Colony to explain and make known this our offer of mercy to those unfortunate people."[540]

Gen. Washington was not long in observing the effects of the Dunmore proclamation. He began to fully realize the condition of affairs at the South, and on Dec. 15 wrote Joseph Reed as follows:—

"If the Virginians are wise, that arch-traitor to the rights of humanity, Lord Dunmore, should be instantly crushed, if it takes the force of the whole army to do it; otherwise, like a snow-ball in rolling, his army will get size, some through fear, some through promises, and some through inclination, joining his standard but that which renders the measure indispensably necessary is the negroes; for, if he gets formidable, numbers of them will be tempted to join who will be afraid to do it without."[541]

The slaves themselves were not incapable of perceiving the cunning of Lord Dunmore. England had forced slavery upon the colonists against their protest, had given instructions to the royal governors concerning the increase of the traffic, and therefore could not be more their friends than the colonists. The number that went over to the enemy grew smaller all the while, and finally the British were totally discouraged in this regard. Lord Dunmore was unwilling to acknowledge the real cause of his failure to secure black recruits, and so he charged it to the fever.

"LORD DUNMORE TO THE SECRETARY OF STATE.
[No. 1]

"SHIP 'DUNMORE,' IN ELIZABETH RIVER, VIRGINIA,

30TH MARCH, 1776

"Your Lordship will observe by my letter, No. 34, that I have been endeavouring to raise two regiments here—one of white people, the other of black. The former goes on very slowly, but the latter very well, and would have been in great forwardness, had not a fever crept in amongst them, which earned off a great many very fine fellows."

[No. 3]

"Ship 'Dunmore,' In Gwin's Island Harbour, Virginia,

June 26, 1776.

"I am extremely sorry to inform your Lordship, that that fever, of which I informed you in my letter No. 1, has proved a very malignant one, and has carried off an incredible number of our people, especially the blacks. Had it not been for this horrid disorder, I am satisfied I should have had two thousand blacks, with whom I should have had no doubt of penetrating into the heart of this Colony."[542]

While the colonists felt, as Dr. Hopkins had written, that something ought to be done toward securing the services of the Negroes, yet their representatives were not disposed to legislate the Negro into the army. He was there, and still a conservative policy was pursued respecting him. Some bold officers took it upon themselves to receive Negroes as soldiers. Gen. Greene, in a letter to Gen. Washington, called attention to the raising of a Negro regiment on Staten Island.

"Camp On Long Island,

July 21, 1776, two o'clock.

"Sir; Colonel Hand reports seven large ships are coming up from the Hook to the Narrows.

"A negro belonging to one Strickler, at Gravesend was taken prisoner (as he says) last Sunday at Coney Island. Yesterday he made his escape, and was taken prisoner by the rifle-guard. He reports eight hundred negroes collected on Staten Island, this day to be formed into a regiment.

"I am your Excellency's most obedient, humble servant,

"N. GREENE.

"To his Excellency Gen. Washington, Headquarters, New York."[543]

To the evidence already produced as to the indiscriminate employment of Negroes as soldiers in the American army, the observations of a foreign officer are added. Under date of the 23d of October, 1777, a Hessian officer wrote:[544]—

> "From here to Springfield, there are few habitations which have not a negro family dwelling in a small house near by. The negroes are here as fruitful as other cattle. The young ones are well foddered, especially while they are still calves. Slavery is, moreover, very gainful. The negro is to be considered just as the bond-servant of a peasant. The negress does all the coarse work of the house, and the little black young ones wait on the little white young ones. The negro can take the field, instead of his master; and therefore no regiment is to be seen in which there are not negroes in abundance: and among them there, are able-bodied, strong, and brave fellows. Here, too, there are many families of free negroes, who live in good houses, have property, and live just like the rest of the inhabitants."[545]

In the month of May, 1777, the Legislature of Connecticut sought to secure some action on the subject of the employment of Negroes as soldiers."

"In May, 1777, the General Assembly of Connecticut appointed a Committee 'to take into consideration the state and condition of the negro and mulatto slaves in this State, and what may be done for their emancipation.' This Committee, in a report presented at the same session (signed by the chairman, the Hon. Matthew Griswold of Lyme), recommended—

> "'That the effective negro and mulatto slaves be allowed to enlist with the Continental battalions now raising in this State, under the following regulations and restrictions; viz., that all such negro and mulatto slaves as can procure, either by bounty, hire, or in any other way, such a sum to be paid to their masters as such negro or mulatto shall be judged to be reasonably worth by the selectmen of the town where such negro or mulatto belongs, shall be allowed to enlist into either of said battalions, and shall thereupon be, de facto, free and emancipated; and that the master of such negro or mulutto shall be exempted from the support and maintenance of such negro or mulatto, in case such negro or mulatto shall hereafter become unable to support and maintain himself.

"'And that, in case any such negro or mulatto slave shall be disposed to enlist into either of said battalions during the [war], he shall be allowed so to do: and such negro or mulatto shall be appraised by the selectmen of the town to which he belongs, and his master shall be allowed to receive the bounty to which such slave may be entitled and also one-half of the annual wages of such slave during the time he shall continue in said service; provided, however, that said master shall not be allowed to receive such part of said wages after he shall have received so much as amounts, together with the bounty, to the sum at which he was appraised.'"

In the lower house the report was put over to the next session, but when it reached the upper house it was rejected.

"You will see by the Report of Committee, May, 1777, that General Varnum's plan for the enlistment of slaves had been anticipated in Connecticut; with this difference, that Rhode Island *adopted* it, while Connecticut did *not*.

> "The two States reached nearly the same results by different methods. The unanimous declaration of the officers at Cambridge, in the winter of 1775, against the enlistment of slaves,—confirmed by the Committee of Congress,—had some weight, I think, with the Connecticut Assembly, so far as the formal enactment of a law authorized such enlistments was in question. At the same time, Washington's license to continue the enlistment of negroes was regarded as a rule of action both by the selectmen in making up, and by the State Government in accepting, the quota of the towns. The process of draughting, in Connecticut, was briefly this: The able-bodied men, in each town, were divided into 'classes:' and each class was required to furnish one or more men, as the town's quota required, to answer a draught. Now, the Assembly, at the same session at which the proposition for enlisting slaves was rejected (May, 1777), passed an act providing that any two men belonging to this State, 'who should procure an able-bodied soldier or recruit to enlist into either of the Continental battalions to be raised from this State,' should themselves be exempted from draught during the continuance of such enlistment. Of recruits or draughted men thus furnished, neither the selectmen nor commanding officers questioned the color or the civil status: white and black, bond and free, if 'able-bodied,' went on the roll together, accepted as the representatives of their

'class,' or as substitutes for their employers. At the next session (October, 1777), an act was passed which gave more direct encouragement to the enlistment of slaves. By this existing law, the master who emancipated a slave was not released from the liability to provide for his support. This law was now so amended, as to authorize the selectmen of any town, on the application of the master,—after 'inquiry into the age, abilities, circumstances, and character' of the servant or slave, and being satisfied 'that it was likely to be consistent with his real advantage, and that it was probable that he would be able to support himself,'—to grant liberty for his emancipation, and to discharge the master 'from any charge or cost which may be occasioned by maintaining or supporting the servant or slave made free as aforesaid.' This enactment enabled the selectmen to offer an additional inducement to enlistment for making up the quota of the town. The slave (or servant for term of years) might receive his freedom; the master might secure exemption from draught, and a discharge from future liabilities, to which he must otherwise have been subjected. In point of fact, some hundreds of blacks—slaves and freemen—were enlisted, from time to time, in the regiments of the State troops and of the Connecticut line. How many, it is impossible to tell: for, from first to last, the company or regimental rolls indicate no distinctions of color. The name is the only guide, and, in turning over the rolls of the Connecticut line, the frequent recurrence of names which were exclusively appropriated to negroes and slaves, shows how considerable was their proportion of the material of the Connecticut army; while such surnames as 'Liberty.' 'Freeman,' 'Freedom,' &c, by scores, indicate with what anticipations, and under what inducements, they entered the service.

As to the efficiency of the service they rendered, I can say nothing from the records, except what is to be gleaned from scattered files such as one of the petitions I send you. So far as my acquaintance extends, almost every family has its traditions of the good and faithful service of a black servant or slave, who was killed in battle, or served through the war, and came home to tell stories of hard fighting, and draw his pension. In my own native town,—not a large one,—I remember five such pensioners, three of whom, I believe, had been slaves, and, in fact, were slaves to the day of their death; for (and this explains the uniform action of the General Assembly on petitions for emancipation) neither the towns nor the State were inclined to exonerate the master, at a time when slavery was becoming unprofitable, from the obligation to provide for the old age of his slave."[546]

Gen. Varnum, a brave and intelligent officer from Rhode Island, early urged the employment of Negro soldiers. He communicated his views to Gen. Washington, and he referred the correspondence to the governor of Rhode Island.

GEN. WASHINGTON TO GOV. COOKE.

HEADQUARTERS, 2D JANUARY, 1778

Sir:—Enclosed you will receive a copy of a letter from General Varnum to me, upon the means which might be adopted for completing the Rhode Island troops to their full proportion in the Continental army. I have nothing to say in addition to what I wrote the 29th of the last month on this important subject, but to desire that you will give the officers employed in this business all the assistance in your power.

I am with great respect, sir,

Your most obedient servant,

G. Washington.

"To Governor Cooke."[547]

The letter of Gen. Varnum to Gen. Washington, in reference to the employment of Negroes as soldiers, is as follows:—

GEN. VARNUM TO GEN. WASHINGTON.

"CAMP, JANUARY 2D, 1778.

"Sir:—The two battalions from the State of Rhode Island being small, and there being a necessity of the state's furnishing an additional number to make up their proportion in the Continental army; the field officers have represented to me the propriety of making one temporary battalion from the two, so that one entire corps of officers may repair to Rhode Island, in order to receive and prepare the recruits for the field. It is imagined that a battalion of negroes can be easily raised there. Should that measure be adopted, or recruits obtained upon any other principle, the service will be advanced. The field officers who go upon this command, are Colonel Greene, Lieutenant Colonel Olney, and Major Ward; seven captains, twelve lieutenants, six ensigns, one paymaster, one surgeon and mates, one adjutant and one chaplain.

"I am your Excellency's most obedient servant,

"J.M. Varnum.

"To His Excellency General Washington."[548]

Gov. Cooke wrote Gen. Washington as follows:—

"STATE OF RHODE ISLAND, &C,

"PROVIDENCE, JANUARY 19TH, 1778.

"Sir:—Since we had the honor of addressing Your Excellency by Mr. Thompson, we received your favor of the 2d of January current, enclosing a proposition of Gen. Varnum's for raising a battalion of negroes.

"We in our letter of the 15th current, of which we send a duplicate, have fully represented our present circumstances, and the many difficulties we labor under, in respect to our filling up the Continental battalions. In addition thereto, will observe, that we have now in the state's service within the government, two battalions of infantry, and a regiment of artillery who are enlisted to serve until the 16th day of March next; and the General Assembly have ordered two battalions of infantry, and a regiment of artillery, to be raised, to serve until the 16th of March, 1779. So that we have raised and kept in the field, more than the proportion of men assigned us by Congress.

"The General Assembly of this state are to convene themselves on the second Monday of February next, when your letters will be laid before them, and their determination respecting the same, will be immediately transmitted to Your Excellency.

"I have the honor to be, &c.,

"Nicholas Cooke.

"To Gen. Washington."[549]

The governor laid the above letters before the General Assembly, at their February session; and the following act was passed:—

"Whereas, for the preservation of the rights and liberties of the United States, it is necessary that the whole powers of government should be exerted in recruiting the Continental battalions; and whereas, His Excellency Gen. Washington hath enclosed to this state a proposal made to him by Brigadier General Varnum, to enlist into the two battalions, raising by this state, such slaves as should be willing to enter into the service; and whereas, history affords us frequent precedents of the wisest, the freest, and bravest nations having liberated their slaves, and enlisted them as soldiers to fight in defence of their country; and also whereas, the enemy, with a great force, have taken possession of the capital, and of a greater part of this state; and this state is obliged to raise a very considerable number of troops for its own immediate defence, whereby it is in a manner rendered impossible for this state to furnish recruits for the said two battalions, without adopting the said measure so recommended.

"It is voted and resolved, that every able-bodied negro, mulatto, or Indian man slave, in this state, may enlist into either of the said two battalions, to serve during the continuance of the present war with Great Britain.

"That every slave, so enlisting, shall be entitled to, and receive, all the bounties, wages, and encouragements, allowed by the Continental Congress, to any soldier enlisting into their service.

"It is further voted and resolved, that every slave, so enlisting, shall, upon his passing muster before Col. Christopher Greene, be immediately discharged from the service of his master or mistress, and be absolutely free, as though he had never been encumbered with any kind of servitude or slavery.

"And in case such slave shall, by sickness or otherwise, be rendered unable to maintain himself, he shall not be chargeable to his master or mistress; but shall be supported at the expense of the state.

"And whereas, slaves have been, by the laws, deemed the property of their owners, and therefore compensation ought to be made to the owners for the loss of their service,—

"It is further voted and resolved, that there be allowed, and paid by this state, to the owner, for every such slave so enlisting, a sum according to his worth; at a price not exceeding £120 for the most valuable slave; and in proportion for a slave of less value.

"Provided, the owner of said slave shall deliver up to the officer, who shall enlist him, the clothes of the said slave; or otherwise he shall not be entitled to said sum.

"And for settling and ascertaining the value of such slaves,—

"It is further voted and resolved, that a committee of five be appointed, to wit:

"One from each county; any three of whom, to be a quorum, to examine the slaves who shall be so enlisted, after they shall have passed muster, and to set a price upon each slave according to his value, as aforesaid.

> "It is further voted and resolved, that upon any ablebodied negro, mulatto, or Indian slave, enlisting as aforesaid, the officer who shall so enlist him, after he shall have passed muster, as aforesaid, shall deliver a certificate thereof, to the master or mistress of said negro, mulatto, or Indian slave; which shall discharge him from the service of his said master or mistress, as aforesaid.
>
> "It is further voted and resolved, that the committee who shall estimate the value of any slave, as aforesaid, shall give a certificate of the sum at which he may be valued, to the owner of said slave; and the general treasurer of this state is hereby empowered and directed to give unto the said owner of the said slave, his promissory note, as treasurer, as aforesaid, for the sum of money at which he shall be valued, as aforesaid, payable on demand, with interest at the rate of six per cent. per annum; and that said notes, which shall be so given, shall be paid with the money which is due to this state, and is expected from Congress; the money which has been borrowed out of the general treasury, by this Assembly, being first re-placed."[550]

This measure met with some opposition, but it was too weak to effect any thing. The best thing the minority could do was to enter a written protest.

"PROTEST AGAINST ENLISTING SLAVES TO SERVE IN THE ARMY.

"We, the subscribers, beg leave to dissent from the vote of the lower house, ordering a regiment of negroes to be raised for the Continental service, for the following reasons, viz.:

"1st. Because, in our opinion, there is not a sufficient number of negroes in the state, who would have an inclination to enlist, and would pass muster, to constitute a regiment; and raising several companies of blacks, would not answer the purposes intended; and therefore the attempt to constitute said regiment would prove abortive, and be a fruitless expense to the state.

"2d. The raising such a regiment, upon the footing proposed, would suggest an idea and produce an opinion in the world, that the state had purchased a band of slaves to be employed in the defence of the rights and liberties of our country, which is wholly inconsistent with those principles of liberty and constitutional government, for which we are so ardently contending; and would be looked upon by the neighboring states in a contemptible point of view, and not equal to their troops; and they would therefore be unwilling that we should have credit for them, as for an equal number of white troops; and would also give occasion to our enemies to suspect that we are not able to procure our own people to oppose them in the field; and to retort upon us the same kind of ridicule we so liberally bestowed upon them, on account of Dunmore's regiment of blacks; or possibly might suggest to them the idea of employing black regiments against us.

"3d. The expense of purchasing and enlisting said regiment, in the manner proposed, will vastly exceed the expenses of raising an equal number of white men; and at the same time will not have the like good effect.

> "4th. Great difficulties and uneasiness will arise in purchasing the negroes from their masters; and many of the masters will not be satisfied with any prices allowed.

"JOHN NORTHUP,
GEORGE PIERCE,
JAMES BABCOK, JR.,
SYLVESTER GARDNER,
OTHNIEL GORTON,
SAMUEL BABCOCK." [551]

Upon the passage of the Act, Gov. Cooke hastened to notify Gen. Washington of the success of the project.

"PROVIDENCE, FEBRUARY 23D, 1778.

> "Sir:—I have been favored with your Excellency's letter of the [3d instant,][552] enclosing a proposal made to you by General Varnum, for recruiting the two Continental battalions raised by this state.

"I laid the letter before the General Assembly at their session, on the second Monday in this month; who, considering the pressing necessity of filling up the Continental army, and the peculiarly difficult circumstances of this state, which rendered it in a manner impossible to recruit our battalions in any other way, adopted the measure.

"Liberty is given to every effective slave to enter the service during the war; and upon his passing muster, he is absolutely made free, and entitled to all the wages, bounties and encouragements given by Congress to any soldier enlisting into their service. The masters are allowed at the rate of £120, for the most valuable slave; and in proportion to those of less value.

"The number of slaves in this state is not great; but it is generally thought that three hundred, and upwards, will be enlisted.

"I am, with great respect, sir,

"Your Excellency's most obedient, humble servant,

"Nicholas Cooke.

"To Gen. Washington."[553]

Where masters had slaves in the army, they were paid an annual interest on the appraised value of the slaves, out of the public treasury, until the end of the military service of such slaves.[554] If owners presented certificates from the committee appointed to appraise enlisted Negroes, they were paid in part or in full in "Continental loan-office certificates."[555]

The reader will remember, that it has been already shown that Negroes, both bond and free, were excluded from the militia of Massachusetts; and, furthermore, that both the Committee of Safety and the Provincial Congress had opposed the enlistment of Negroes. The first move in the colony to secure legal enlistments and separate organizations of Colored troops was a communication to the General Assembly of Massachusetts, 3d of April, 1778.

"To the Honorable Council, and House of Representatives, Boston, or at Roxbury.

"Honored Gentlemen,—At the opening of this campaign, our forces should be all ready, well equipped with arms and ammunition, with clothing sufficient to stand them through the campaign, their wages to be paid monthly, so as not to give the soldiery so much reason of complaint as it is the general cry from the soldiery amongst whom I am connected.

"We have accounts of large re-enforcements a-coming over this spring against us; and we are not so strong this spring, I think, as we were last. Great numbers have deserted; numbers have died, besides what is sick, and incapable of duty, or bearing arms in the field.

"I think it is highly necessary that some new augmentation should be added to the army this summer,—all the re-enforcements that can possibly be obtained. For now is the time to exert ourselves or never; for, if the enemy can get no further hold this campaign than they now possess, we [have] no need to fear much from them hereafter.

"A re-enforcement can quick be raised of two or three hundred men. Will your honors grant the liberty, and give me the command of the party? And what I refer to is negroes. We have divers of them in our service, mixed with white men. But I think it would be more proper to raise a body by themselves, than to have them intermixed with the white men; and their ambition would entirely be to outdo the white men in every measure that the fortune of war calls a soldier to endure. And I could rely with dependence upon them in the field of battle, or to any post that I was sent to defend with them; and they would think themselves happy could they gain their freedom by bearing a part of subduing the enemy that is invading our land, and clear a peaceful inheritance for their masters, and posterity yet to come, that they are now slaves to.

"The method that I would point out to your Honors in raising a detachment of negroes;—that a company should consist of a hundred, including commissioned officers; and that the commissioned officers should be white, and consist of one captain, one captain-lieutenant, two second lieutenants; the orderly sergeant white; and that there should be three sergeants black, four corporals black, two drums and two fifes black, and eighty-four rank and file. These should engage to serve till the end of the war, and then be free men. And I doubt not, that no gentleman that is a friend to his country will disapprove of this plan, or be against his negroes enlisting into the service to maintain the cause of freedom, and suppress the worse than savage enemies of our land.

"I beg your Honors to grant me the liberty of raising one company, if no more. It will be far better than to fill up our battalions with runaways and deserters from Gen. Burgoyne's army, who, after receiving clothing and the bounty, in general make it their business to desert from us. In the lieu thereof, if they are [of] a mind to serve in America, let them supply the families of those gentlemen where those negroes belong that should engage.

"I rest, relying on your Honor's wisdom in this matter, as it will be a quick way of having a re-enforcement to join the grand army, or to act in any other place that occasion shall require; and I will give my faith and assurance that I will act upon honor and fidelity, should I take the command of such a party as I have been describing.

"So I rest till your Honors shall call me; and am your very humble and obedient servant,

"Thomas Kench,

"In Col. Craft's Regiment of Artillery, now on Castle Island.

"Castle Island, April 3, 1778."

A few days later he addressed another letter to the same body.

"*To the Honorable Council in Boston.*

"The letter I wrote before I heard of the disturbance with Col. Seares, Mr. Spear, and a number of other gentlemen, concerning the freedom of negroes, in Congress Street. It is a pity that riots should be committed on the occasion, as it is justifiable that negroes should have their freedom, and none amongst us be held as slaves, as freedom and liberty is the grand controversy that we are contending for; and I trust, under the smiles of Divine Providence, we shall obtain it, if all our minds can be united; and putting the negroes into the service will prevent much uneasiness, and give more satisfaction to those that are offended at the thoughts of their servants being free.

"I will not enlarge, for fear I should give offence; but subscribe myself

"Your faithful servant,

"Thomas Kench.

"Castle Island, April 7, 1778."[556]

On the 11th of April the first letter was referred to a joint committee, with instructions "to consider the same, and report." On the 17th of April, "a resolution of the General Assembly of Rhode Island for enlisting Negroes in the public service" was referred to the same committee. In the Militia Act of 1775, the exceptions were, "Negroes, Indians, and mulattoes." By the act of May, 1776, providing for the re-enforcement of the American army, it was declared that, "Indians, negroes, and mulattoes, shall not be held to take up arms or procure any person to do it in their room." By another act, passed Nov. 14, 1776, looking toward the improvement of the army, "Negroes, Indians, and mulattoes" were excluded. During the year 1776 an order was issued for taking the census of all males above sixteen, but excepted "Negroes, Indians, and mulattoes." But after some reverses to the American army, Massachusetts passed a resolve on Jan. 6, 1777, "for raising every seventh man to complete our quota," "without any exceptions, save the people called Quakers." This was the nearest Massachusetts ever got toward recognizing Negroes as soldiers. And on the 5th of March, 1778, Benjamin Goddard, for the selectmen, Committee of Safety, and militia officers of the town of Grafton, protested against the enlistment of the Negroes in his town.

It is not remarkable, in view of such a history, that Massachusetts should have hesitated to follow the advice of Thomas Kench. On the 28th of April, 1778, a law was draughted following closely the Rhode-Island Act. But no separate organization was ordered; and, hence, the Negroes served in white organizations till the close of the American Revolution.

There is nothing in the records of Virginia to show that there was ever any legal employment of Negroes as soldiers; but, from the following, it is evident that free Negroes *did* serve, and that there was no prohibition against them, providing they showed their certificates of freedom:—

> "And whereas several negro slaves have deserted from their masters, and under pretence of being free men have enlisted as soldiers: For prevention whereof, Be it enacted, that it shall not be lawful for any recruiting officer within this commonwealth to enlist any negro or mulatto into the service of this or either of the United States, until such negro or mulatto shall produce a certificate from some justice of the peace for the county wherein he resides that he is a free man."[557]

Maryland employed Negroes as soldiers, and sent them into regiments with white soldiers. John Cadwalder of Annapolis, wrote Gen. Washington on the 5th of June, 1781, in reference to Negro soldiers, as follows:—

> "We have resolved to raise, immediately, seven hundred and fifty negroes, to be incorporated with the other troops; and a bill is now almost completed."[558]

The legislature of New York, on the 20th of March, 1781, passed the following Act, providing for the raising of two regiments of blacks:—

> "Sect. 6.—And be it further enacted by the authority aforesaid, that any person who shall deliver one or more of his or her able-bodied male slaves to any warrant officer, as afore said, to serve in either of the said regiments or independent corps, and produce a certificate thereof, signed by any person authorized to muster and receive the men to be raised by virtue of this act, and produce such certificate to the Surveyor-General, shall, for every male slave so entered and mustered as aforesaid, be entitled to

the location and grant of one right, in manner as in and by this act is directed; and shall be, and hereby is, discharged from any future maintenance of such slave, any law to the contrary notwithstanding: And such slave so entered as aforesaid, who shall serve for the term of three years or until regularly discharged, shall, immediately after such service or discharge, be, and is hereby declared to be, a free man of this State."[559]

The theatre of the war was now transferred from the Eastern to the Middle and Southern colonies. Massachusetts alone had furnished, and placed in the field, 67,907 men; while all the colonies south of Pennsylvania, put together, had furnished but 50,493,—or 8,414 less than the single colony of Massachusetts.[560] It was a difficult task to get the whites to enlist at the South. Up to 1779, nearly all the Negro soldiers had been confined to the New-England colonies. The enemy soon found out that the Southern colonies were poorly protected, and thither he moved. The Hon. Henry Laurens of South Carolina, an intelligent and observing patriot, wrote Gen. Washington on the 16th of March, 1779, concerning the situation at the South:—

"Our affairs [he wrote] in the Southern department are more favorable than we had considered them a few days ago; nevertheless, the country is greatly distressed, and will be more so unless further reinforcements are sent to its relief. Had we arms for three thousand such black men as I could select in Carolina, I should have no doubt of success in driving the British out of Georgia, and subduing East Florida, before the end of July."[561]

Gen. Washington sent the following conservative reply:—

"The policy of our arming slaves is in my opinion a moot point, unless the enemy set the example. For, should we begin to form battalions of them, I have not the smallest doubt, if the war is to be prosecuted, of their following us in it, and justifying the measure upon our own ground. The contest then must be, who can arm fastest. And where are our arms? Besides, I am not clear that a discrimination will not render slavery more irksome to those who remain in it. Most of the good and evil things in this life are judged of by comparison; and I fear a comparison in this case will be productive of much discontent in those, who are held in servitude. But, as this is a subject that has never employed much of my thoughts, these are no more than the first crude ideas that have struck me upon the occasion."[562]

The gifted and accomplished Alexander Hamilton, a member of Washington's military family, was deeply interested in the plan suggested by the Hon. Henry Laurens, whose son was on Washington's staff. Col. John Laurens was the bearer of the following remarkable letter from Hamilton to John Jay, President of Congress.

"HEADQUARTERS, MARCH 14, 1779.

"To John Jay.

"Dear Sir,—Col. Laurens who will have the honor of delivering you this letter, is on his way to South Carolina, on a project which I think, in the present situation of affairs there, is a very good one, and deserves every kind of support and encouragement. This is, to raise two, three, or four battalions of negroes, with the assistance of the government of the State, by contributions from the owners in proportion to the number they possess. If you should think proper to enter upon the subject with him, he will give you a detail of his plan. He wishes to have it recommended by Congress to the State: and, as an inducement, that they should engage to take those battalions into Continental pay.

"It appears to me, that an expedient of this kind, in the present state of Southern affairs, is the most rational that can be adopted, and promises very important advantages. Indeed, I hardly see how a sufficient force can be collected in that quarter without it; and the enemy's operations there are growing infinitely more serious and formidable. I have not the least doubt that the negroes will make very excellent soldiers with proper management; and I will venture to pronounce, that they cannot be put into better hands than those of Mr. Laurens. He has all the zeal, intelligence, enterprise, and every other qualification, necessary to succeed in such an undertaking. It is a maxim with some great military judges, that, with sensible officers, soldiers can hardly be too stupid; and, on this principle, it is thought that the Russians would make the best troops in the world, if they were under other officers than their own. The King of Prussia is among the number who maintain this doctrine; and has a very emphatic saying on the occasion, which I do not exactly recollect. I mention this because I hear it frequently objected to the scheme of embodying negroes, that they are too stupid to make soldiers. This is so far from appearing to me a valid objection, that I think their want of cultivation (for their natural faculties are probably as good as ours), joined to that habit of subordination which they acquire from a life of servitude, will make them sooner become soldiers than our white inhabitants. Let officers be men of sense and sentiment; and the nearer the soldiers approach to machines, perhaps the better.

"I foresee that this project will have to combat much opposition from prejudice and self-interest. The contempt we have been taught to entertain for the blacks makes us fancy many things that are founded neither in reason nor experience; and an unwillingness to part with property of so valuable a kind will furnish a thousand arguments to show the impracticability or pernicious tendency of a scheme which requires such a sacrifice. But it should be considered, that, if we do not make use of them in this way, the enemy probably will; and that the best way to counteract the temptations they will hold out will be to offer them ourselves. An essential part of the plan is to give them their freedom with their muskets. This will secure their fidelity, animate their courage, and, I believe, will have a good influence upon those who remain, by opening a door to their emancipation. This circumstance, I confess, has no small weight in inducing me to wish the success of the project, for the dictates of humanity, and true policy, equally interest me in favor of this unfortunate class of men.

"With the truest respect and esteem,

"I am, Sir, your most obedient servant,

"ALEX. HAMILTON."[563]

The condition of the Southern States became a matter of Congressional solicitude. The letter of Col. Hamilton was referred to a special committee on the 29th of March, 1779. It was represented that South Carolina especially was in great danger. The white population was small; and, while there were some in the militia service, it was thought necessary to keep as large a number of whites at home as possible. The fear of insurrection, the desertion[564] of Negroes to the enemy, and the exposed condition of her border, intensified the anxiety of the people. The only remedy seemed to lie in the employment of the more fiery spirits among the Negroes as the defenders of the rights and interests of the colonists. Congress rather hesitated to act,—it was thought that that body lacked the authority to order the enlistment of Negroes in the States,—and therefore recommended to "the states of South Carolina and Georgia, if they shall think the same expedient, to take measures immediately for raising three thousand able-bodied negroes." After some consideration the following plan was recommended by the special committee, and adopted:—

"IN CONGRESS, MARCH 29, 1779.

"The Committee, consisting of Mr. Burke, Mr. Laurens, Mr. Armstrong, Mr. Wilson, and Mr. Dyer, appointed to take into consideration the circumstances of the Southern States, and the ways and means for their safety and defence, report,—

"That the State of South Carolina, as represented by the delegates of the said State and by Mr. Huger, who has come hither at the request of the Governor of the said State, on purpose to explain the particular circumstances thereof, is unable to make any effectual efforts with militia, by reason of the great proportion of citizens necessary to remain at home to prevent insurrections among the negroes, and to prevent the desertion of them to the enemy.

"That the state of the country, and the great numbers of those people among them, expose the inhabitants to great danger from the endeavors of the enemy to excite them either to revolt or desert.

"That it is suggested by the delegates of the said State and by Mr. Huger, that a force might be raised in the said State from among the negroes, which would not only be formidable to the enemy from their numbers, and the discipline of which they would very readily admit, but would also lessen the danger from revolts and desertions, by detaching the most vigorous and enterprising from among the negroes.

"That, as this measure may involve inconveniences peculiarly affecting the States of South Carolina and Georgia, the Committee are of the opinion that the same should be submitted to the governing powers of the said States; and if the said powers shall judge it expedient to raise such a force, that the United States ought to defray the expense thereof: whereupon,

"Resolved, That it be recommended to the States of South Carolina and Georgia, if they shall think the same expedient, to take measures immediately for raising three thousand able-bodied negroes.

"That the said negroes be formed into separate corps, as battalions, according to the arrangements adopted for the main army, to be commanded by white commissioned and non-commissioned officers.

"That the commissioned officers be appointed by the said States.

"That the non-commissioned officers may, if the said States respectively shall think proper, be taken from among the non-commissioned officers and soldiers of the Continental battalions of the said States respectively.

"That the Governors of the said States, together with the commanding officer of the Southern army, be empowered to incorporate the several Continental battalions of their States with each other respectively, agreeably to the arrangement of the army, as established by the resolutions of May 27, 1778; and to appoint such of the supernumerary officers to command the said negroes as shall choose to go into that service.

"Resolved, That Congress will make provision for paying the proprietors of such negroes as shall be enlisted for the service of the United States during the war a full compensation for the property, at a rate not exceeding one thousand dollars for each active, able bodied negro man of standard size, not exceeding thirty-five years of age, who shall be so enlisted and pass muster.

"That no pay or bounty be allowed to the said negroes, but that they be clothed and subsisted at the expense of the United States.

> "That every negro who shall well and faithfully serve as a soldier to the end of the present war, and shall then return his arms, be emancipated, and receive the sum of fifty dollars."[565]

Congress supplemented the foregoing measure by commissioning young Col. Laurens to carry forward the important work suggested. The gallant young officer was indeed worthy of the following resolutions:—

"Whereas John Laurens, Esq., who has heretofore acted as aide-de-camp to the Commander-in-chief, is desirous of repairing to South Carolina, with a design to assist in defence of the Southern States;—

> "Resolved, That a commission of lieutenant-colonel be granted to the said John Laurens, Esq."[566]

He repaired to South Carolina, and threw all his energies into his noble mission. That the people did not co-operate with him, is evidenced in the following extract from a letter he subsequently wrote to Col. Hamilton:—

> "Ternant will relate to you how many violent struggles I have had between duty and inclination,—how much my heart was with you, while I appeared to be most actively employed here. But it appears to me, that I should be inexcusable in the light of a citizen, if I did not continue my utmost efforts

for carrying the plan of the black levies into execution, while there remain the smallest hopes of success."[567]

The enemy was not slow in discovering the division of sentiment among the colonists as to the policy of employing Negroes as soldiers. And the suspicions of Gen. Washington, indicated to Henry Laurens, in a letter already quoted, were not groundless. On the 30th of June, 1779, Sir Henry Clinton issued a proclamation to the Negroes. It first appeared in "The Royal Gazette" of New York, on the 3d of July, 1779.

"By his Excellency Sir Henry Clinton, K.B. General and Commander-in-chief of all his Majesty's Forces within the Colonies laying on the Atlantic Ocean, from Nova Scotia to West-Florida, inclusive, &c., &c., &.

"PROCLAMATION.

"Whereas the enemy have adopted a practice of enrolling NEGROES among their Troops, I do hereby give notice That all negroes taken in arms, or upon any military Duty, shall be purchased for [*the public service at*] a stated Price; the money to be paid to the Captors.

"But I do most strictly forbid any Person to sell or claim Right over any negroe, the property of a Rebel, who may take Refuge with any part of this Army: And I do promise to every negroe who shall desert the Rebel Standard, full security to follow within these Lines, any Occupation which he shall think proper.

"Given under my Hand, at Head-Quarters, Phillipsburgh, the 30th day of June, 1779.

"H. Clinton.

"By his Excellency's command,

"JOHN SMITH, SECRETARY."

The proclamation had effect. Many Negroes, weary of the hesitancy of the colonists respecting acceptance of their services, joined the ministerial army. On the 14th of February, 1780, Col. Laurens wrote Gen. Washington, from Charleston, S.C., as follows:—

> "Private accounts say that General Prevost is left to command at Savannah; that his troops consist of the Hessians and Loyalists that were there before, re-enforced by a corps of blacks and a detachment of savages. It is generally reported that Sir Henry Clinton commands the present expedition."[568]

Lord Cornwallis also issued a proclamation, offering protection to all Negroes who should seek his command. But the treatment he gave them, as narrated by Mr. Jefferson in a letter to Dr. Gordon, a few years after the war, was extremely cruel, to say the least.

> "Lord Cornwallis destroyed all my growing crops of corn and tobacco; he burned all my barns, containing the same articles of the last year, having first taken what corn he wanted; he used, as was to be expected, all my stock of cattle, sheep, and hogs, for the sustenance of his army, and carried off all the horses capable of service; of those too young for service he cut the throats; and he burned all the fences on the plantation, so as to leave it an absolute waste. He carried off also about thirty slaves. Had this been to give them freedom, he would have done right; but it was to consign them to inevitable death from the small-pox and putrid fever, then raging in his camp. This I knew afterwards to be the fate of twenty-seven of them. I never had news of the remaining three, but presume they shared the same fate. When I say that Lord Cornwallis did all this, I do not mean that he carried about the torch in his own hands, but that it was all done under his eye; the situation of the house, in which he was, commanding a view of every part of the plantation, so that he must have seen every fire. I relate these things on my own knowledge, in a great degree, as I was on the ground soon after he left it. He treated the rest of the neighborhood somewhat in the same style, but not with that spirit of total extermination with which he seemed to rage over my possessions. Wherever he went, the dwelling-houses were plundered of every thing which could be carried off. Lord Cornwallis's character in England would forbid the belief that he shared in the plunder; but that his table was served with the plate thus pillaged from private houses, can be proved by many hundred eye-witnesses. From an estimate I made at that time, on the best information I could collect, I suppose the State of Virginia lost, under Lord Cornwallis's hand, that year, about thirty thousand slaves; and that, of these, twenty-seven thousand died of the small-pox and camp-fever, and the rest were partly sent to the West Indies and exchanged for rum, sugar, coffee, and fruit; and partly sent to New York, from whence they went, at the peace, either to Nova Scotia or to England. From this last place, I

believe, they have been lately sent to Africa. History will never relate the horrors committed by the British Army in the Southern States of America."[569]

Col. Laurens was called from the South, and despatched to France on an important mission in 1780. But the effort to raise Negro troops in the South was not abandoned.

On the 13th of March, 1780, Gen. Lincoln, in a letter to Gov. Rutledge of South Carolina, dated at Charleston, urged the importance of raising a Negro regiment at once. He wrote,—

"Give me leave to add once more, that I think the measure of raising a black corps a necessary one; that I have great reason to believe, if permission is given for it, that many men would soon be obtained. I have repeatedly urged this matter, not only because Congress have recommended it, and because it thereby becomes my duty to attempt to have it executed, but because my own mind suggests the utility and importance of the measure, as the safety of the town makes it necessary."

James Madison saw in the emancipation and arming of the Negroes the only solution of the vexatious Southern problem. On the 20th of November, 1780, he wrote Joseph Jones as follows:—

"Yours of the 18th came yesterday. I am glad to find the Legislature persist in their resolution to recruit their line of the army for the war; though, without deciding on the expediency of the mode under their consideration, would it not be as well to liberate and make soldiers at once of the blacks themselves, as to make them instruments for enlisting white soldiers? It would certainly be more consonant with the principles of liberty, which ought never to be lost sight of in a contest for liberty: and, with white officers and a majority of white soldiers, no imaginable danger could be feared from themselves, as there certainly could be none from the effect of the example on those who should remain in bondage; experience having shown that a freedman immediately loses all attachment and sympathy with his former fellow-slaves."[570]

The struggle went on between Tory and Whig, between traitor and patriot, between selfishness and the spirit of noble consecration to the righteous cause of the Americans. Gen. Greene wrote from North Carolina on the 28th of February, 1781, to Gen. Washington as follows:—

"The enemy have ordered two regiments of negroes to be immediately embodied, and are drafting a great proportion of the young men of that State [South Carolina], to serve during the war."[571]

Upon his return to America, Col. Laurens again espoused his favorite and cherished plan of securing black levies for the South. But surrounded and hindered by the enemies of the country he so dearly loved, and for the honor and preservation of which he gladly gave his young life, his plans were unsuccessful. In two letters to Gen. Washington, a few months before he fell fighting for his country, he gave an account of the trials that beset his path, which he felt led to honorable duty. The first bore date of May 19, 1782.

"The plan which brought me to this country was urged with all the zeal which the subject inspired, both in our Privy Council and Assembly; but the single voice of reason was drowned by the howlings of a triple-headed monster, in which prejudice, avarice, and pusillanimity were united. It was some degree of consolation to me, however, to perceive that truth and philosophy had gained some ground; the suffrages in favor of the measure being twice as numerous as on a former occasion. Some hopes have been lately given me from Georgia; but I fear, when the question is put, we shall be outvoted there with as much disparity as we have been in this country.

"I earnestly desire to be where any active plans are likely to be executed, and to be near your Excellency on all occasions in which my services can be acceptable. The pursuit of an object which, I confess, is a favorite one with me, because I always regarded the interests of this country and those of the Union as intimately connected with it, has detached me more than once from your family; but those sentiments of veneration and attachment with which your Excellency has inspired me, keep me always near you, with the sincerest and most zealous wishes for a continuance of your happiness and glory."[572]

The second was dated June 12, 1782, and breathes a despondent air:—

"The approaching session of the Georgia Legislature, and the encouragement given me by Governor Howley, who has a decisive influence in the counsels of that country, induce me to remain in this quarter for the purpose of taking new measures on the subject of our black levies. The arrival of Colonel Baylor, whose seniority entitles him to the command of the light troops, affords me ample leisure for pursuing the business in person; and I shall do it with all the tenacity of a man making a last effort on so interesting an occasion."[573]

Washington's reply showed that he, too, had lost faith in the patriotism of the citizens of the South to a great degree. He wrote his faithful friend:—

> "I must confess that I am not at all astonished at the failure of your plan. That spirit of freedom, which, at the commencement of this contest, would have gladly sacrificed every thing to the attainment of its object, has long since subsided, and every selfish passion has taken its place. It is not the public but private interest which influences the generality of mankind; nor can the Americans any longer boast an exception. Under these circumstances, it would rather have been surprising if you had succeeded; nor will you, I fear, have better success in Georgia."[574]

Although the effort of the Legislature of Connecticut to authorize the enlistment of Negroes in 1777 had failed, many Negroes, as has been shown, served in regiments from that State; and a Negro company was organized. When white officers refused to serve in it, the gallant David Humphreys volunteered his services, and became the captain.

> "In November, 1782, he was, by resolution of Congress, commissioned as a Lieutenant-Colonel, with order that his commission should bear date from the 23d of June, 1780, when he received his appointment as aide-de-camp to the Commander-in-chief. He had, when in active service, given the sanction of his name and influence in the establishment of a company of colored infantry, attached to Meigs', afterwards Butler's, regiment, in the Connecticut line. He continued to be the nominal captain of that company until the establishment of peace."[575]

The following was the roster of his company:—

"Captain,

DAVID HUMPHREYS.

Privates,

Jack Arabus, Brister Baker, John Ball,
John Cleveland, Cæsar Bagdon, John McLean,
Phineas Strong, Gamaliel Terry, Jesse Vose,
Ned Fields, Lent Munson, Daniel Bradley,
Isaac Higgins, Heman Rogers, Sharp Camp,
Lewis Martin, Job Cæsar, Jo Otis.
Cæsar Chapman, John Rogers, James Dinah,
Peter Mix, Ned Freedom, Solomon Sowtice,
Philo Freeman, Ezekiel Tupham, Peter Freeman,
Hector Williams, Tom Freeman, Cato Wilbrow,
Juba Freeman, Congo Zado, Cuff Freeman,
Cato Robinson, Peter Gibbs, Juba Dyer,
Prince George, Prince Johnson, Andrew Jack,
Prince Crosbee, Alex. Judd, Peter Morando,
Shubael Johnson, Pomp Liberty, Peter Lion,
Tim Cæsar, Cuff Liberty, Sampson Cuff,
Jack Little, Pomp Cyrus, Dick Freedom,
Bill Sowers, Harry Williams, Pomp McCuff."[576]
Dick Violet, Sharp Rogers,

But notwithstanding the persistent and bitter opposition to the employment of slaves, from the earliest hours of the Revolutionary War till its close, Negroes, bond and free, were in all branches of the service. It is to be regretted that the exact number cannot be known. Adjutant-Gen. Scammell made the following official return of Negro soldiers in the main army, under Washington's immediate command, two months after the battle of Monmouth; but the Rhode-Island regiment, the Connecticut, New York, and New-Hampshire troops are not mentioned. Incomplete as it is, it is nevertheless official, and therefore correct as far as it goes.

RETURN OF NEGROES IN THE ARMY, 24th Aug., 1778.

BRIGADES.	Present.	Sick Absent.	On Command.	Total.
North Carolina	42	10	6	58

Woodford	36	3	1	40
Muhlenburg	64	26	8	98
Smallwood	20	3	1	24
2d Maryland	43	15	2	60
Wayne	2	—	—	60
2d Pennsylvania	[33]	[1]	[1]	[35]
Clinton	33	2	4	39
Parsons	117	12	19	148
Huntington	56	2	4	62
Nixon	26	—	1	27
Patterson	64	13	12	89
Late Learned	34	4	8	46
Poor	16	7	4	27
Total	586	98	71	755

ALEX. SCAMMELL, ADJ.-GEN.[577]

It is gratifying to record the fact, that the Negro was enrolled as a soldier in the war of the American Revolution. What he did will be recorded in the following chapter.

FOOTNOTES:

[520] Journal of the Continental Congress.

[521] The Hon. Peter Force, in an article to The National Intelligencer, Jan. 16 and 18, 1855, says: "Southern colonies, jointly with all the others, and separately each for itself, did agree to prohibit the importation of slaves, voluntarily and in good faith." Georgia was not represented in this Congress, and, therefore, could not sign.

[522] Sparks's Washington, vol. ii. pp. 488-495.

[523] Sparks's Franklin, vol. viii, p. 42.

[524] Jefferson's Works, vol. i. p. 135.

[525] Ibid., pp. 23,24.

[526] Journals of the Provincial Congress of Mass., p. 29.

[527] Adams's Works, vol. ii. p. 322.

[528] Journals of the Provincial Congress of Mass., p. 553.

[529] Ibid., p. 302.

[530] The following is a copy of Gen. Gates's order to recruiting-officers:—

"You are not to enlist any deserter from the Ministerial Army, or any stroller, negro, or vagabond, or person suspected of being an enemy to the liberty of America, nor any under eighteen years of age.

"As the cause is the best that can engage men of courage and principle to take up arms, so it is expected that none but such will be accepted by the recruiting officer. The pay, provision, &c., being so ample, it is not doubted but that the officers sent upon this service will, without delay, complete their respective corps, and march the men forthwith to camp.

"You are not to enlist any person who is not an American born, unless such person has a wife and family, and is a settled resident in this country. The persons you enlist must be provided with good and complete arms."

—Moore's DIARY OF THE AMERICAN REVOLUTION, VOL. I. P. 110.

[531] The Provincial Congress of South Carolina, Nov 20, 1775, passed the following resolve:—"On motion,Resolved, That the colonels of the several regiments of militia throughout the Colony have leave to enroll such a number of able male slaves, to be employed as pioneers and laborers, as public exigencies may require; and that a daily pay of seven shillings and sixpence be allowed for the service of each such slave while actually employed."

—AMERICAN ARCHIVES, 4TH SERIES, VOL. IV P. 6.

[532] Sparks's Washington, vol. iii. p. 155, note.

[533] Force's American Archives, 4th Series, vol. iii. p. 1,385.

[534] Spark's Washington, vol. iii. p. 218.

[535] Journals of Congress, vol ii. p. 26.

[536] Hopkins's Works, vol. ii. p. 584.

[537] Works of John Adams, vol. ii p. 428.

[538] Force's American Archives, 4th Series, vol. iv. p. 202.

[539] Force's American Archives, 4th Series, vol. iii. p. 1,387.

[540] Force's American Archives, 4th Series, vol. iv. pp. 84, 85.

[541] Life and Correspondence of Joseph Reed, vol. i. p. 135.

[542] Force's American Archives, 5th Series, vol. ii. pp 160, 162.

[543] Force's American Archives, 5th Series, vol. i p. 486.

[544] During a few months of study in New-York City, I came across the above in the library of the N.Y. Hist. Soc.

[545] Schloezer's Briefwechsel, vol. iv. p. 365.

[546] An Historical Research (Livermore), pp. 114-116.

[547] R.I. Col. Recs., vol. viii. p. 640.

[548] R.I. Col. Recs., vol. viii. p. 641.

[549] Ibid., vol. viii. p. 524.

[550] R.I. Col. Recs., vol viii. pp. 358-360.

[551] R.I. Col. Recs., vol. viii. p. 361.

[552] This is evidently a mistake, as Washington's letter was dated Jan. 2, as the reader will see.

[553] R.I. Col. Recs., vol. viii. p. 526.

[554] Ibid., p. 376.

[555] Ibid., p. 465.

[556] MSS. Archives of Mass., vol. cxcix. pp. 80, 84.

[557] Hening, vol. ix. 280.

[558] Sparks's Correspondence of the American Revolution, vol. iii. p. 331.

[559] Laws of the State of New York, chap. xxxiii. (March 20, 1781, 4th Session).

[560] The American Loyalist, p. 30, second edition.

[561] Sparks's Washington, vol. vi p. 204, note.

[562] Ibid., vol. vi. p. 204.

[563] Life of John Jay, by William Jay, vol. II. pp. 31, 32.

[564] Ramsay, the historian of South Carolina says, "It has been computed by good judges, that, between 1775 and 1783, the State of South Carolina lost twenty-five thousand negroes."

[565] Secret Journals of Congress, vol. i. pp. 107-110.

[566] Journals of Congress, vol. v. p. 123.

[567] Works of Hamilton, vol. i. pp. 114, 115.

[568] Sparks's Correspondence of the American Revolution, vol. ii. p. 402.

[569] Jefferson's Works, vol ii. p. 426.

[570] Madison Papers, p. 68.

[571] Sparks's Correspondence of the American Revolution, vol. iii. p. 246.

[572] Sparks's Correspondence of the American Revolution, vol. iii. p. 506.

[573] Ibid., p. 515.

[574] Sparks's Washington, vol. viii. pp. 322, 323.

[575] Biographical Sketch in "The National Portrait Gallery of Distinguished Americans."

[576] Colored Patriots of the Revolution, p. 134.

[577] This return was discovered by the indefatigable Dr. George H. Moore. It is the only document of the kind in existence.

CHAPTER XXVII
NEGROES AS SOLDIERS

1775-1783.

The Negro as a Soldier.—Battle of Bunker Hill—Gallantry of Negro Soldiers.—Peter Salem, the Intrepid Black Soldier.—Bunker-hill Monument.—The Negro Salem Poor distinguishes himself by Deeds of Desperate Valor.—Capture of Gen. Lee.—Capture of Gen. Prescott—Battle of Rhode Island.—Col. Greene commands a Negro Regiment.—Murder of Col. Greene in 1781.—The Valor of the Negro Soldiers.

AS soldiers the Negroes went far beyond the most liberal expectations of their stanchest friends. Associated with white men, many of whom were superior gentlemen, and nearly all of whom were brave and enthusiastic, the Negro soldiers of the American army became worthy of the cause they fought to sustain. Col. Alexander Hamilton had said, *"their natural faculties are as good as ours;"* and the assertion was supported by their splendid behavior on all the battle-fields of the Revolution. Endowed by nature with a poetic element, faithful to trusts, abiding in friendships, bound by the golden threads of attachment to places and persons, enthusiastic in personal endeavor, sentimental and chivalric, they made hardy and intrepid soldiers. The daring, boisterous enthusiasm with which they sprang to arms disarmed racial prejudice of its sting, and made friends of foes.

Their cheerfulness in camp, their celerity in the performance of fatigue-duty, their patient endurance of heat and cold, hunger and thirst, and their bold efficiency in battle, made them welcome companions everywhere they went. The officers who frowned at their presence in the army at first, early learned, from experience, that they were the equals of any troops in the army for severe service in camp, and excellent fighting in the field.

The battle of Bunker Hill was one of the earliest and most important of the Revolution. Negro soldiers were in the action of the 17th of June, 1775, and nobly did their duty. Speaking of this engagement, Bancroft says,—

> "Nor should history forget to record that, as in the army at Cambridge, so also in this gallant band, the free negroes of the colony had their representatives."[578]

Two Negro soldiers especially distinguished themselves, and rendered the cause of the colonists great service. Major Pitcairn was a gallant officer of the British marines. He led the charge against the redoubt, crying exultingly, "The day is ours!" His sudden appearance and his commanding air at first startled the men immediately before him. They neither answered nor fired, probably not being exactly certain what was next to be done. At this critical moment, a Negro soldier stepped forward, and, aiming his musket directly at the major's bosom, blew him through.[579] Who was this intrepid black soldier, who at a critical moment stepped to the front, and with certain aim brought down the incarnate enemy of the colonists? What was his name, and whence came he to battle? His name was Peter Salem, a private in Col Nixon's regiment of the Continental Army.

> "He was born in Framingham [Massachusetts], and was held as a slave, probably until he joined the army: whereby, if not before, he became free. ... Peter served faithfully as a soldier, during the war."[580]

Perhaps Salem was then a slave: probably he thought of the chains and stripes from whence he had come, of the liberty to be purchased in the ordeals of war, and felt it his duty to show himself worthy of his position as an American soldier. He proved that his shots were as effective as those of a white soldier, and that he was not wanting in any of the elements that go to make up the valiant soldier. Significant indeed that a Negro was the first to open the hostilities between Great Britain and the colonies,—the first to pour out his blood as a precious libation on the altar of a people's rights; and that here, at Bunker Hill, when the crimson and fiery tide of battle seemed to be running hard against the small band of colonists, a Negro soldier's steady musket brought down the haughty form of the arch-rebel, and turned victory to the weak! England had loaded the African with chains, and doomed him to perpetual bondage in the North-American colonies; and when she came to forge political chains, in the flames of fratricidal war, for an English-speaking people, the Negro, whom she had grievously wronged, was first to meet her soldiers, and welcome them to a hospitable grave.

Bunker-hill Monument has a charm for loyal Americans; and the Negro, too, may gaze upon its enduring magnificence. It commemorates the deeds, not of any particular soldier, but all who stood true to the principles of equal rights and free government on that memorable "17th of June."

> "No name adorns the shaft; but ages hence, though our alphabets may become as obscure as those which cover the monuments, of Nineveh and Babylon, its uninscribed surface (on which monarchs might be proud to engrave their titles) will perpetuate the memory of the 17th of June. It is the monument of the day, of the event, of the battle of Bunker Hill; of all the brave men who shared its perils,— alike of Prescott and Putnam and Warren, the chiefs of the day, and the colored man, Salem, who is reported to have shot the gallant Pitcairn, as he mounted the parapet. Cold as the clods on which it rests, still as the silent heavens to which it soars, it is yet vocal, eloquent, in their undivided praise."[581]

The other Negro soldier who won for himself rare fame and distinguished consideration in the action at Bunker Hill was Salem Poor. Delighted with his noble bearing, his superior officers could not refrain from calling the attention of the civil authorities to the facts that came under their personal observation. The petition that set forth his worth as a brave soldier is still preserved in the manuscript archives of Massachusetts:—

"To the Honorable General Court of the Massachusetts Bay.

"The subscribers beg leave to report to your Honorable House (which we do in justice to the character of so brave a man), that, under our own observation, we declare that a negro man called Salem Poor, of Col. Frye's regiment, Capt. Ames' company, in the late battle at Charlestown, behaved like an experienced officer, as well as an excellent soldier. To set forth particulars of his conduct would be tedious. We would only beg leave to say, in the person of this said negro centres a brave and gallant soldier. The reward due to so great and distinguished a character, we submit to the Congress.

"Jona. Brewer, Col.	Eliphalet Bodwell, Sgt.
Jona. Brewer, Col.	Eliphalet Bodwell, Sgt.
Thomas Nixon, Lt.-Col.	Josiah Foster, Lieut.
Wm. Prescott, Colo.	Ebenr. Varnum, 2d Lieut.
Ephm. Corey, Lieut.	Wm. Hudson Ballard, Cpt.

Joseph Baker, Lieut.
Joshua Row, Lieut.
Jonas Richardson, Capt.
"Cambridge, Dec. 5, 1775.

William Smith, Cap.
John Morton, Sergt.[?]
Lieut. Richard Welsh.

"In Council, Dec. 21, 1775.—Read, and sent down.

"PEREZ MORTON, DEP'Y SEC'Y."[582]

How many other Negro soldiers behaved with cool and determined valor at Bunker Hill, it is not possible to know. But many were there; they did their duty as faithful men, and their achievements are the heritage of the free of all colors under our one flag. Col. Trumbull, an artist as well as a soldier, who was stationed at Roxbury, witnessed the engagement from that elevation. Inspired by the scene, when it was yet fresh in his mind, he painted the historic picture of the battle in 1786. He represents several Negroes in good view, while conspicuous in the foreground is the redoubtable Peter Salem. Some subsequent artists—mere copyists—have sought to consign this black hero to oblivion, but 'tis vain. Although the monument at Bunker Hill "does not bear his name, the pencil of the artist has portrayed the scene, the pen of the impartial historian has recorded his achievement, and the voice of the eloquent orator has resounded his valor."

Major Samuel Lawrence "at one time commanded a company whose rank and file were all Negroes, of whose courage, military discipline, and fidelity he always spoke with respect. On one occasion, being out reconnoitring with this company, he got so far in advance of his command, that he was surrounded, and on the point of being made prisoner by the enemy. The men, soon discovering his peril, rushed to his rescue, and fought with the most determined bravery till that rescue was effectually secured. He never forgot this circumstance, and ever after took especial pains to show kindness and hospitality to any individual of the colored race who came near his dwelling."[583]

Gen. Lee, of the American army, was captured by Col. Harcourt of the British army. It was regarded as a very distressing event; and preparations were made to capture a British officer of the same rank, so an exchange could be effected. Col. Barton of the Rhode-Island militia, a brave and cautious officer, was charged with the capture of Major-Gen. Prescott, commanding the royal army at Newport. On the night of the 9th of July, 1777, Col. Barton, with forty men, in two boats with muffled oars, evaded the enemy's boats, and, being taken for the sentries at Prescott's head-quarters, effected that officer's capture—a Negro taking him. The exploit was bold and successful.

> "They landed about five miles from Newport, and three-quarters of a mile from the house, which they approached cautiously, avoiding the main guard, which was at some distance. The Colonel went foremost, with a stout, active negro close behind him, and another at a small distance; the rest followed so as to be near, but not seen.
>
> "A single sentinel at the door saw and hailed the Colonel; he answered by exclaiming against, and inquiring for, rebel prisoners, but kept slowly advancing. The sentinel again challenged him, and required the countersign. He said he had not the countersign, but amused the sentry by talking about rebel prisoners, and still advancing till he came within reach of the bayonet, which, he presenting, the Colonel suddenly struck aside and seized him. He was immediately secured, and ordered to be silent, on pain of instant death. Meanwhile, the rest of the men surrounding the house, the negro, with his head, at the second stroke forced a passage into it, and then into the landlord's apartment. The landlord at first refused to give the necessary intelligence; but, on the prospect of present death he pointed to the General's chamber, which being instantly opened by the negro's head, the Colonel calling the General by name, told him he was a prisoner."[584]

Another account was published by a surgeon of the army, and is given here:—

> "Albany, Aug. 3, 1777.—The pleasing information is received here that Lieut.-Col. Barton, of the Rhode-Island militia, planned a bold exploit for the purpose of surprising and taking Major-Gen. Prescott, the commanding officer of the royal army at Newport. Taking with him, in the night, about forty men, in two boats, with oars muffled, he had the address to elude the vigilance of the ships-of-war and guard-boats: and, having arrived undiscovered at the quarters of Gen. Prescott, they were taken for the sentinels; and the general was not alarmed till his captors were at the door of his lodging-chamber, which was fast closed. A negro man, named Prince, instantly thrust his beetle head through

the panel door; and seized his victim while in bed.... This event is extremely honorable to the enterprising spirit of Col. Barton, and is considered as ample retaliation for the capture of Gen. Lee by Col. Harcourt. The event occasions great joy and exultation, as it puts in our possession an officer of equal rank with Gen. Lee, by which means an exchange may be obtained. Congress resolved that an elegant sword should be presented to Col. Barton for his brave exploit."[585]

Col. Barton evidently entertained great respect for the valor and trustworthiness of the Negro soldier whom he made the chief actor in a most hazardous undertaking. It was the post of honor; and the Negro soldier Prince discharged the duty assigned him in a manner that was entirely satisfactory to his superior officer, and crowned as one of the most daring and brilliant *coups d'état* of the American Revolution.

The battle of Rhode Island, fought on the 29th of August, 1778, was one of the severest of the Revolution. Newport was laid under siege by the British. Their ships-of-war moved up the bay on the morning of the action, and opened a galling fire upon the exposed right flank of the American army; while the Hessian columns, stretching across a chain of the "highland," attempted to turn Gen. Greene's flank, and storm the advanced redoubt. The heavy cannonading that had continued since nine in the morning was now accompanied by heavy skirmishing; and the action began to be general all along the lines. The American army was disposed in three lines of battle; the first extended in front of their earthworks on Butt's Hill, the second in rear of the hill, and the third as reserve a half-mile in the rear of the advance line. At ten o'clock the battle was at white heat. The British vessels kept up a fire that greatly annoyed the Americans, but imparted courage to the Hessians and British infantry. At length the foot columns massed, and swept down the slopes of Anthony's Hill with the impetuosity of a whirlwind. But the American columns received them with the intrepidity and coolness of veterans. The loss of the enemy was fearful.

> "Sixty were found dead in one spot. At another, thirty Hessians were buried in one grave. Major-Gen. Greene commanded on the right. Of the four brigades under his immediate command, Varnum's, Glover's, Cornell's and Greene's, all suffered severely, but Gen. Varnum's perhaps the most. A third time the enemy, with desperate courage and increased strength, attempted to assail the redoubt, and would have carried it but for the timely aid of two continental battalions despatched by Sullivan to support his

almost exhausted troops. It was in repelling these furious onsets, that the newly raised black regiment, under Col. Greene, distinguished itself by deeds of desperate valor. Posted behind a thicket in the valley, they three times drove back the Hessians who charged repeatedly down the hill to dislodge them; and so determined were the enemy in these successive charges, that the day after the battle the Hessian colonel, upon whom this duty had devolved, applied to exchange his command and go to New York, because he dared not lead his regiment again to battle, lest his men should shoot him for having caused them so much loss."[586]

A few years later the Marquis de Chastellux, writing of this regiment, said,—

"The 5th [of January, 1781] I did not set out till eleven, although I had thirty miles' journey to Lebanon. At the passage to the ferry, I met with a detachment of the Rhode-Island regiment, the same corps we had with us all the last summer, but they have since been recruited and clothed. The greatest part of them are negroes or mulattoes; but they are strong, robust men, and those I have seen had a very good appearance.'"[587]

On the 14th of May, 1781, the gallant Col. Greene was surprised and murdered at Point's Bridge, New York, but it was not effected until his brave black soldiers had been cut to pieces in defending their leader. It was one of the most touching and beautiful incidents of the war, and illustrates the self-sacrificing devotion of Negro soldiers to the cause of American liberty.

At a meeting of the Congregational and Presbyterian Anti-Slavery Society, at Francestown, N.H., the Rev. Dr. Harris, himself a Revolutionary soldier, spoke thus complimentarily of the Rhode-Island Negro regiment:—

"Yes, a regiment of *negroes*, fighting for *our* liberty and independence,— not a white man among them but the officers,—stationed in this same dangerous and responsible position. Had they been unfaithful, or driven away before the enemy, all would have been lost. *Three times in succession* were they attacked, with most desperate valor and fury, by well disciplined and veteran troops, and *three times* did they successfully repel the assault, and thus preserve our army from capture. They fought through the war. They were brave, hardy troops. They helped to gain our liberty and independence."

From the opening to the closing scene of the Revolutionary War; from the death of Pitcairn to the surrender of Cornwallis; on many fields of strife and triumph, of splendid valor and republican glory; from the hazy dawn of unequal and uncertain conflict, to the bright morn of profound peace; through and out of the fires of a great war that gave birth to a new, a grand republic,—the Negro soldier fought his way to undimmed glory, and made for himself a magnificent record in the annals of American history. Those annals have long since been committed to the jealous care of the loyal citizens of the Republic black men fought so heroically to snatch from the iron clutches of Britain.

FOOTNOTES:

[578] Bancroft, vol. vii., 6th ed., p. 421.

[579] An Historical Research, p. 93.

[580] History of Leicester, p. 267.

[581] Orations and Speeches of Everett, vol. iii. p. 529.

[582] MS. Archives of Massachusetts, vol. clxxx, p. 241.

[583] Memoir of Samuel Lawrence, by Rev. S.K. Lothrop, D.D., pp. 8, 9.

[584] Frank Moore's Diary of the American Revolution, vol. i. p. 468.

[585] Thatcher's Military Journal, p. 87.

[586] Arnold's History of Rhode Island, vol. ii. pp. 427, 428.

[587] Chastellux' Travels, vol. i. p. 454; London, 1789.

CHAPTER XXVIII
LEGAL STATUS OF THE NEGRO DURING THE REVOLUTION

1775-1783.

The Negro was Chattel or Real Property.—His Legal Status during his New Relation as a Soldier—Resolution introduced in the Massachusetts House of Representatives to prevent the selling of Two Negroes captured upon the High Seas—The Continental Congress appoints a Committee to consider what should be done with Negroes taken by Vessels of War in the Service of the United Colonies.—Confederation of the New States.—Spirited Debate in Congress respecting the Disposal of Recaptures.—The Spanish Ship "Victoria" captures an English Vessel having on Board Thirty-four Negroes taken from South Carolina.—The Negroes recaptured by Vessels belonging to the State of Massachusetts.—They are delivered to Thomas Knox, and conveyed to Castle Island.—Col. Paul Revere has Charge of the Slaves on Castle Island—Massachusetts passes a Law providing for the Security, Support, and Exchange of Prisoners brought into the State.—Gen Hancock receives a Letter from the Governor of South Carolina respecting the Detention of Negroes—In the Provincial Articles between the United States of America and His Britannic Majesty, Negroes were rated as Property.—And also in the Definite Treaty of Peace between the United States of America and His Britannic Majesty.—And also in the Treaty of Peace of 1814, between His Britannic Majesty and the United States, Negroes were designated as Property.—Gen. Washington's Letter to Brig-Gen Rufus Putnam in regard to a Negro in his Regiment claimed by Mr. Hobby.—Enlistment in the Army did not always work a Practical Emancipation.

WHEN the Revolutionary War began, the legal status of the Negro slave was clearly defined in the courts of all the colonies. He was either chattel or real property. The question naturally arose as to his legal status during his new relation as a soldier. Could he be taken as property, or as a prisoner of war? Was he booty, or was he entitled to the usage of civilized warfare,—a freeman, and therefore to be treated as such?

The Continental Congress, Nov. 25, 1775, passed a resolution recommending the several colonial legislatures to establish courts that should give jurisdiction to courts, already in existence, to dispose of "cases of capture." In fact, and probably in law, Congress exercised power in cases of appeal. Moreover, Congress had prescribed a rule for the distribution of prizes. But, curiously enough, Massachusetts, in 1776, passed an Act declaring, that, in case captures were made by the forces of the colony, the local authorities should have complete jurisdiction in their distribution; but, when prizes or captives were taken upon colonial territory by the forces of the United Colonies, the distributions should be made in accordance with the laws of Congress. This was but a single illustration of the divided sovereignty of a crude government. That there was need of a uniform law upon this question, there could be no doubt, especially in a war of the magnitude of the one that was then being waged.

On the 13th of September, 1776, a resolution was introduced into the Massachusetts House of Representatives, "to prevent the sale of two negro men lately brought into this state, as prisoners taken on the high seas, and advertised to be sold at Salem, the 17th inst., by public auction."[588] The resolve in full is here given:—

"In The House Of Representatives, Sept. 13, 1776:

"Whereas this House is credibly informed that two negro men lately brought into this State as prisoners taken on the High Seas are advertised to be sold at Salem, the 17th instant, by public auction,

"*Resolved*, That the selling and enslaving the human species is a direct violation of the natural rights alike vested in all men by their Creator, and utterly inconsistent with the avowed principles on which this and the other United States have carried their struggle for liberty even to the last appeal, and therefore, that all persons connected with the said negroes be and they hereby are forbidden to sell them or in any manner to treat them otherways than is already ordered for the treatment of prisoners of war taken in the same vessel or others in the like employ and if any sale of the said negroes shall be made, it is hereby declared null and void.

"Sent up for concurrence.

"Saml. Freeman, Speaker, P.T.

"In Council, Sept. 14, 1776. Read and concurred as taken into a new draught. Sent down for concurrence.

"John Avery, Dpy. Secy.

"In the House of Representatives, Sept. 14, 1776. Read and non-concurred, and the House adhere to their own vote. Sent up for concurrence.

"J. Warren, Speaker.

"In Council, Sept. 16, 1776. Read and concurred as now taken into a new draft. Sent down for concurrence.

"John Avery, Dpy. Secy.

"In the House of Representatives, Sept. 16, 1779. Read and concurred.

"J. Warren, Speaker.

"Consented to.

"Jer. Powell,	Jabez Fisher,
W. Sever,	B. White,
B. Greenleaf,	Moses Gill,
Caleb Cushing,	Dan'l Hopkins,
B. Chadbourn,	Benj. Austin,
John Whetcomb,	Wm. Phillips,
Eldad Taylor,	D. Sewall,
S. Holten,	Dan'l Hopkins."

On the Journal of the House, p. 106, appears the following record,—

"David Sewall, Esq., brought down the resolve which passed the House yesterday, forbidding the sale of two negroes, with the following vote of Council thereon, viz *In Council*, Sept. 14, 1776. Read and concurred, as taken into a new draught. Sent down for concurrence. Read and non-concurred, and the House adhere to their own vote. Sent up for concurrence."

The resolve, as it originally appeared, was dragged through a tedious debate, non-concurred in by the House, recommitted, remodelled, and sent back, when it finally passed.

"LXXXIII. Resolve forbidding the sale of two Negroes brought in as Prisoners; Passed September 14, [16th,] 1776.

"Whereas this Court is credibly informed that two Negro Men lately taken on the High Seas, on board the sloop *Hannibal,* and brought into this State as Prisoners, are advertized to be sold at *Salem,* the 17th instant, by public Auction:

"Resolved, That all Persons concerned with the said Negroes be, and they are hereby forbidden to sell them, or in any manner to treat them otherwise than is already ordered for the Treatment of Prisoners taken in like manner; and if any Sale of the said Negroes shall be made it is hereby declared null and void, and that whenever it shall appear that any Negroes are taken on the High Seas and brought as Prisoners into this State, they shall not be allowed to be Sold, nor treated any otherwise than as Prisoners are ordered to be treated who are taken in like Manner."[589]

It looked like a new resolve. The pronounced and advanced sentiment in favor of the equal rights of all created beings had been taken out, and it appeared now as a war measure, warranted upon military policy. This is the only chaplet that the most devout friends of Massachusetts can weave out of her acts on the Negro problem during the colonial period, to place upon her brow. It attracted wide-spread and deserved attention.

During the following month, on the 14th of October, 1776, the Continental Congress appointed a special committee, Messrs. Lee, Wilson, and Hall, "to consider what is to be done with Negroes taken by vessels of war, in the service of the United States." Here was a profound legal problem presented for solution. According to ancient custom and law, slaves came as the bloody logic of war. War between nations was of necessity international; but while this truth had stood through many centuries, the conversion of the Northern nations of Europe into organized society greatly modified the old doctrine of slavery. Coming under the enlightening influences of modern international law, war captives could not be reduced to slavery.[590] This doctrine was thoroughly understood, doubtless, in the North-American colonies as in Europe. But the almost universal doctrine of property in the Negro, and his status in the courts of the colonies, gave the royal army great advantage in the appropriation of Negro captives, under the plea that they were "property," and hence legitimate "spoils of war;" while, on the part of the colonists, to declare that captured Negroes were entitled to the treatment of "prisoners of war," was to reverse a principle of law as old as their government. It was, in fact, an abandonment of the claim of property in the Negro. It was a recognition of his rights as a soldier, a bestowal of the highest favors known in the treatment of captives of war.[591] But there was another difficulty in the way. Slavery had been recognized in the venerable memorials of the most remote nations. This condition was coeval with the history of all nations, but nowhere regarded as a relation of a local character. It grew up in social compacts, in organized communities of men, and in great and powerful states. It was recognized in private international law; and the relation of master and slave was guarded in their local habitat, and respected wherever found.[592] And this relation, this property in man, did not cease because the slave sought another nation, for it was recognized in all the commercial transactions of nations. Now, upon this principle, the colonists were likely to claim their right to property in slaves captured.

The confederation of the new States was effected on the 1st of March, 1781. Art. IX. gave the "United States in Congress assembled" the exclusive authority of making laws to govern the disposal of all captures made by land or water; to decide which were legal; how prizes taken by the land or naval force of the government should be appropriated, and the right to establish courts of competent jurisdiction in such case, etc. The first legislation under this article was an Act establishing a court of appeals on the 4th of June, 1781. It was discussed on the 25th of June, and again, on the 17th of July, took up a great deal of time, but was recommitted. The committee were instructed to prepare an ordinance regulating the proceedings of the admiralty cases, in the several States, in instances of capture; to codify all resolutions and laws upon the subject; and to request the States to enact such provisions as would be in harmony with the reserved rights of the Congress in such cases as were specified in the Ninth Article. Accordingly, on the 21st of September, 1781, the committee reported to Congress the results of their labor, in a bill on the subject of captures. Upon the question of agreeing to the following section, the yeas and nays were demanded by Mr. Mathews of South Carolina:—

"On the recapture by a citizen of any negro, mulatto, Indian, or other person from whom labor or service is lawfully claimed by *another citizen*, specific restitution shall be adjudged to the claimant, whether the original capture shall have been made on land or water, a reasonable salvage being paid by the claimant to the recaptor, not exceeding one-fourth part of the value of such labor or service, to be estimated according to the laws of the State *of which the claimant shall be a citizen*: but if the service of such negro, mulatto, Indian or other person, captured below high-water mark, shall not be legally claimed *by a citizen of these United States*, he shall be set at liberty."

The delegates from North Carolina, Delaware, New Jersey, and Connecticut, refrained from voting; South Carolina voted in the negative: but it was carried by twenty-eight yeas, against two nays. After a spirited debate, continuing through several days, and having received several amendments, it finally passed on Dec. 4, 1781, as follows:—

"On the recapture by a citizen of any negro, mulatto, Indian, or other person, from whom labor or service is lawfully claimed by *a State or a citizen of a State*, specific restitution shall be adjudged to the claimant, whether the original capture shall have been made on land or water, *and without regard to the time of possession by the enemy*, a reasonable salvage being paid by the claimant to the recaptor, not exceeding 1-4th of the value of such labor or service, to be estimated according to the laws of the State *under which the claim shall be made*.

"But if the service of such negro, mulatto, Indian, or other person, captured below high water mark, shall not be legally claimed *within a year and a day from the sentence of the Court*, he shall be set at liberty."

It should be carefully observed that the above law refers only to *recaptures*. It would be interesting to know the views the committee entertained in reference to slaves captured by the ministerial army. Nothing was said about this interesting feature of the case. Why Congress did not claim proper treatment of the slaves captured by the enemy while in the service of the United Colonies, is not known. Doubtless its leaders saw where the logic of such a position would lead them. The word "another" was left out of the original measure, and was made to read, in the one that passed, *"a State or citizen;"* as if it were feared that, by implication, a Negro would be recognized as a *citizen*.

By the proclamation of Sir Henry Clinton, already mentioned in the preceding chapter, Negroes were threatened with sale for "the public service;" and Mr. Jefferson in his letter to Mr. Gordon (see preceding chapter), says the enemy sold the Negroes captured in Virginia into the West Indies. After the capture of Stony Point by Gen. Wayne, concerning two Negroes who fell into his hands, he wrote to Lieut.-Col. Meigs from New Windsor on the 25th of July, 1779, as follows:—

"The wish of the officers to free the three Negroes after a few Years Service meets my most hearty approbation but as the Chance of War or other Incidents may prevent the officer [owner] from Compling with the Intention of the Officers it will be proper for the purchaser or purchasers to sign a Condition in the Orderly Book.

> " ... I wou'd cheerfully join them in their Immediate Manumission—if a few days makes no material difference I could wish the sale put off until a Consultation may be had, & the opinion of the Officers taken on this Business."[593]

In June, 1779, a Spanish ship called "Victoria" sailed from Charleston, S.C., for Cadiz. During the first part of her voyage she was run down by a

British privateer; but, instead of being captured, she seized her assailant, and found on board thirty-four Negroes, whom the English vessel had taken from plantations in South Carolina. The Spaniards got the Negroes on board their ship, disabled the English vessel, and then dismissed her. Within a few days she was taken by two British letters-of-marque, and headed for New York. During her passage thither she was re-captured by the "Hazard" and "Tyrannicide," armed vessels in the service of Massachusetts, and taken into the port of Boston. By direction of the Board of War she was ordered into the charge of Capt. Johnson, and was unloaded on the 21st of June. The Board of War reported to the Legislature that there were thirty-four Negroes "taken on the high seas and brought into the state." On the 23d of June [1780] the Legislature ordered "that Gen. Lovell, Capt. Adams, and Mr. Cranch, be a committee to consider what is proper to be done with a number of negroes brought into port in the prize ship called the[594] Lady Gage."[595] On the 24th of June, "the committee appointed to take into consideration the state and circumstances of a number of negroes lately brought into the port of Boston, reported a resolve directing the Board of War to inform our delegates in Congress of the state of facts relative to them, to put them into the barracks on Castle Island, and cause them to be supplied and employed."[596] The resolve passed without opposition.

"CLXXX. *Resolve on the Representation of the Board of War respecting a number of negroes captured and brought into this State.* Passed June 24, 1779.

"On the representation made to this Court by the Board of War respecting a number of negroes brought into the Port of Boston, on board the Prize Ship Victoria:

"*Resolved*, that the Board of War be and they are hereby directed forthwith to write to our Delegates in Congress, informing them of the State of Facts relating to said Negroes, requesting them to give information thereof to the Delegates from the State of *South Carolina*, that so proper measures may be taken for the return of said Negroes, agreeable to their desire.

> "And it is further Resolved, that the Board of War be and they hereby are directed to put the said Negroes, in the mean time, into the barracks on Castle Island in the Harbor of Boston, and cause them to be supplied with such Provision and Clothing as shall be necessary for their comfortable support, putting them under the care and direction of some Prudent person or Persons, whose business it shall be to see that the able-bodied men may be usefully employed during their stay in carrying on the Fortifications on said Island, or

elsewhere within the said Harbor; and that the Women be employed according to their ability in Cooking, Washing, etc. And that the said Board of War keep an exact Account of their Expenditures in supporting said Negroes."[597]

The Negroes were delivered to Thomas Knox on the 28th of June, and were conveyed "to Castle Island pr. Order of Court." The Board of War voted the "34 Negroes delivered" rations. Lieut.-Col. Paul Revere was instructed to "issue to the Negroes at Castle Island—1 lb. of Beef, 1 lb. of Rice pr. day." The following letter is not without interest:—

"WAR OFFICE, 28 JUNE, 1779.

"Lt.-Col. Revere,

"Agreeable to a Resolve of Court we send to Castle Island and place under your care the following Negroes, viz.:

[19] Men,

[10] Women,

[5] Children,

lately brought into this Port in the Spanish retaken Ship Victoria. The Men are to be employed on the Fortifications there or elsewhere in the Harbor, in the most useful manner, and the Women and Children, according to their ability, in Cooking, Washing, etc. They are to be allowed for their subsistence One lb. of Beef, and one lb. of Rice per day each, which Commissary Salisbury will furnish upon your order, and this to continue until our further orders.

"*By Order of the Board.*"

In accordance with the order of the Legislature, made on the 24th of June, the president of the Board of War, Samuel P. Savage, wrote a letter to the Massachusetts delegates in Congress, dated "War Office June 29th 1779," calling attention to the re-captured Negroes. The letter closed with the following:—

"Every necessary for the speedy discharge of these people, we have no doubt you will take, that as much expense as possible may be saved to those who call themselves their owners."

The writer was at pains to enumerate, in his letter, such slaves as he was enabled to locate.

"5 Men 4 Women 4 Boys 1 Girl belonging to Mr. Wm. Vryne.

"9 Men 1 Woman belonging to Mr. Anthony Pawley.

"1 Man belonging to Mr. Thomas Todd.

"2 Men 3 Women belonging to Mr. Henry Lewis.

"2 Men 2 Women belonging to Mr. William Pawley.

"One of the negroes is an elderly sensible man, calls himself James, and says he is free, which we have no reason to doubt the truth of. He also says that he with the rest of the Negroes were taken from a place called Georgetown."[598]

Pending the action of the *lawful* owners of these captives, the council instructed the commandant of Castle Island, Col. Paul Revere, to place out to service, in different towns, some of the Negroes, with the understanding that they should be delivered up to the authorities on their order. Some were delivered to gentlemen who desired them as servants. But in the fall of 1779 quite a number were still on the island, as may be seen by the following touching letter:—

"Boston, Octr. 12. 1779. A Return of ye Negroes at Castle Island, Viz.:

"NEGRO MEN.

"1. ANTHONY.	6. BOBB.	11. JUNE.
2. PARTRICK.	7. ANTHONEY.	12. RHODICK.
3. PADDE.	8. ADAM.	13. JACK.
4. ISAAC.	9. JACK.	14. FULLER.
5. QUASH.	10. GYE.	15. LEWIS.

"The above men are stout fellows.

"NEGRO BOYS.

"NO. 1. SMART.
      2. RICHARD.

"Boys very small.

"NEGRO WOOMEN.	NEGRO GIRLS.
"NO. 1. KITTEY.	NO. 1. LYSETT.
2. LUCY.	2. SALLY
3. MILLEY.	3. MERCY.
4. LANDER.	
"Pretty large.	Rather stout. "Gentlemen.

"The Scituation of these Negroes is pitiable with respect to Cloathing.

"I am, Gent.

"Your very hum. Servt.

"JOHN HANCOCK."[599]

"OCT. 12, 1779."

In the mean time some of the reputed owners of the Negroes at Castle Island had come from Charleston, S.C., to secure their property. When they arrived in Boston they secured the services of John Codman, Isaac Smith, and William Smith, who on the 15th of November, 1779, petitioned the Council for the "restitution" of slaves taken by a British privateer, and retaken by two armed vessels of Massachusetts. A committee was appointed to consider the petitions, and report what action should be taken in the matter. Two days later another petition was presented to the Council by one John Winthrop, "praying that certain negroes, who were brought into this state by the Hazard and Tyrannicide, may be delivered to him." It was referred to the committee appointed on the 15th of November. On the 18th of November, "Jabez Fisher, Esq., brought down a report of the Committee of both Houses on the petition of Isaac Smith, being by way of resolve, directing the Board of War to deliver so many of the negroes therein mentioned, as are now alive. Passed in Council, and sent down for concurrence." The order of the House is, "Read and concurred, as taken into a new draught. Sent up for concurrence."

It is printed among the resolves of November, 1779.

"XXXI. Resolve relinquishing this state's claim to a number of Negroes, passed November 18, 1779.

"Whereas a number of negroes were re-captured and brought into this State by the armed vessels Hazard and Tyrannicide, and have since been supported at the expense of this State, and as the original owners of said Negroes now apply for them:

> "Therefore Resolved, That this Court hereby relinquish and give up any claim they may have upon the said owners for re-capturing said negroes: Provided they pay to the Board of War of this State the expence that has arisen for the support and clothing of the Negroes aforesaid."[600]

On the 12th of April, 1780, Massachusetts passed an Act providing more effectually "for the security, support, and exchange of prisoners of war brought into the State." It declares that

> "All Prisoners of War, whether captured by the Army or Navy of the United States, or armed Ships or Vessels of any of the United States, or by the Subjects, Troops, Ships, or Vessels of War of this State, and brought into the same, or cast on shore by shipwreck on the coast thereof ... all such prisoners, so brought in or cast on shore (including Indians, Negroes, and Molatoes) be treated in all respects as prisoners of war to the United States, any law or resolve or this Court to the contrary notwithstanding."[601]

The above Act was passed in compliance with a resolution of Congress, Jan. 13, 1780; and it repealed an Act of 1777, that made no provisions for the capture of Negroes.

On the 23d of January, 1784, Gov. Hancock sent a message to the Legislature, transmitting correspondence received dining the adjournment of the Legislature from Oct 28, 1783, to Jan. 21, 1784. Calling the attention of the Legislature to this correspondence, he referred to a letter from "His Excellency the Governor of South Carolina, respecting the detention of some Negroes here, belonging to the subjects of that state. I have communicated it to the Judges of the Supreme Judicial Court—their observations upon it are with the Papers. I have made no reply to the letter, judging it best to have your decision upon it."[602] The same papers on the same day were read in the Senate, and a joint committee of both houses was appointed. The committee reported to both branches of the Legislature on the 23d of March, 1784, and the report was adopted. A request was made of the governor to furnish copies of the opinions of the judges, etc.

"CLXXI. Order requesting the Governor to write to Governor *Guerard* of *South Carolina*, inclosing the letter of the Judges of the Supreme Judicial Court, March, 23d, 1784.

"*Ordered*, that his Excellency the Governor be requested to write to His Excellency *Benjamin Guerard*, Governor of *South Carolina*, inclosing for the information of Governor Guerard, the letter of the Judges of the Supreme Judicial Court of this Commonwealth, with the copy in the said letter referred to, upon the subject of Governor *Guerard's* letter, dated the sixth October, 1783."

The papers referred to seem to have been lost, but extracts are here produced:—

"Governor Guerard To Governor Hancock, 6th October, 1783.

> Extract. "That such adoption is favoring rather of the Tyranny of Great Britain which occasioned her the loss of these States—that no act of British Tyranny could exceed the encouraging the negroes from the State owning them to desert their owners to be emancipated—that it seems arbitrary and domination—assuming for the Judicial Department of any one State, to prevent a restoration voted by the Legislature and ordained by Congress. That the liberation of our negroes disclosed a specimen of Puritanism I should not have expected from gentlemen of my Profession."

Memorandum. "He had demanded fugitives, carried off by the British, captured by the North, and not given up by the interference of the Judiciary.' Governor Hancock referred the subject to the Judges."

"Judges Cushing And Sargent To Governor Hancock, Boston, Dec. 20, 1783.

> Extract. "How this determination is an attack upon the spirit, freedom, dignity, independence, and sovereignty of South Carolina, we are unable to conceive. That this has any connection with, or relation to Puritanism, we believe is above yr Excellency's comprehension as it is above ours. We should be sincerely sorry to do any thing inconsistent with the Union of the States, which is and must continue to be the basis of our Liberties and Independence; on the contrary we wish it may be strengthened, confirmed, and endure for ever."[603]

By the Treaty of Peace in 1783, Negroes were put in the same category with horses and other articles of property.[604]

> "Negroes [says Mr. Hamilton], by the laws of the States, in which slavery is allowed, are personal property. They,

therefore, on the principle of those laws, like horses, cattle and other movables, were liable to become booty—and belonged to the enemy, [captor] as soon as they came into his hands. Belonging to him, he was free either to apply them to his own use, or set them at liberty. If he did the latter, the grant was irrevocable, restitution was impossible. Nothing in the laws of nations or in those of Great Britain, will authorize the resumption of liberty, once granted to a human being."[605]

On the 6th of May, 1783, Gen. Washington wrote Sir Guy Carleton:—

"In the course of our conversation on this point, I was surprised to hear you mention, that an embarkation had already taken place, in which a large number of negroes had been carried away. Whether this conduct is consonant to, or how far it may be deemed an infraction of the treaty, is not for me to decide. I cannot, however, conceal from you, that my private opinion is, that the measure is totally different from the letter and spirit of the treaty. But waiving the discussion of the point, and leaving its decision to our respective sovereigns; I find it my duty to signify my readiness, in conjunction with your Excellency, to enter into any agreement, or take any measures, which may be deemed expedient, to prevent the future carrying away of any negroes, or other property of the American inhabitants."[606]

In his reply, dated New York, May 12, 1783, Sir Guy Carleton says,—

"I enclose a copy of an order, which I have given out to prevent the carrying away any negroes or other property of the American inhabitants."[607]

It is clear, that notwithstanding the Act of the Massachusetts Legislature, and in the face of the law of Congress on the question of recaptures, Gen. Washington, the Congress of the United Colonies, and subsequently of the United States, regarded Negroes as *property* from the beginning to the end of the war. The following treaties furnish abundant proof that Negroes were regarded as property during the war, by the American government:—

"Provisional Articles Between the United States of America and His Britannic Majesty.

"Agreed upon by and between Richard Oswald, Esquire the Commissioner of His Britannic Majesty, for treating of Peace with the

Commissioners of the United States of America, in behalf of his said Majesty, on one part, and John Adams, Benjamin Franklin, John Jay and Henry Laurens, four of the Commissioners of the said States, etc., etc., etc.

"Article VII. * * * All prisoners on both sides shall be set at liberty, and His Britannic Majesty shall with all convenient speed, and without causing any destruction, or carrying away any '*negroes or other property*' of the American inhabitants, withdraw all his armies, garrisons and fleets from the said United States, and from every port, place and harbour within the same.* * *

"Done at Paris, Nov 30, 1782.

"Richard Oswald, [l.s.]

"John Adams, [l.s.]

"B. Franklin, [l.s.]

"John Jay, [l.s.]

"HENRY LAURENS, [L.S.]"[608]

"Definite treaty of peace, between the united states of america and his britannic majesty.

"Article VII. * * * And His Britannic Majesty shall, with all convenient speed, and without causing any destruction, or carrying away any '*negroes or other property*' of the American inhabitants, withdraw all his armies, etc., etc., etc.* * *

"Done at Paris, Sept. 3, 1783.

"D Hartley. [l.s.]

"John Adams, [l.s.]

"B. Franklin, [l.s.]

"JOHN JAY, [L.S.]"[609]

"Treaty of peace and amity, between his britannic majesty and the united states of america,

"[Ratified and confirmed by and with the advice and consent of the Senate, Feb. 11, 1815.]

"Article I. * * * Shall be restored without delay, and without causing any destruction, or carrying away any of the artillery or other public property originally captured in the said forts or places, and which shall remain therein upon the exchange of the ratifications of this treaty, or any '*slaves or other private property.*' * * * *

"Done, in triplicate, at Ghent, Dec. 24, 1814.

> "Gambier, [l.s.]
>
> "Henry Goulburn, [l.s.]
>
> "William Adams, [l.s.]
>
> "John Ouincy Adams, [l.s.]
>
> "J.A. Bayard, [l.s.]
>
> "H. Clay, [l.s.]
>
> "Jona. Russell, [l.s.]
>
> "ALBERT GALLATIN. [L.S.]"[610]

It was not a difficult matter to retake Negroes captured by the enemy, and then treat them as prisoners of war. But no officer in the American army, no member of Congress, had the moral courage to proclaim that property ceased in a man the moment he donned the uniform of a Revolutionary soldier, and that all Negro soldiers captured by the enemy should be treated as prisoners of war. So, all through the war with Britain, the Negro soldier was liable to be claimed as property; and every bayonet in the army was at the command of the master to secure his property, even though it had been temporarily converted into an heroic soldier who had defended the country against its foes. The unprecedented spectacle was to be witnessed, of a master hunting his slaves under the flag of the nation. And at the close of hostilities many Negro soldiers were called upon to go back into the service of their masters; while few secured their freedom as a reward for their valor. The following letter of Gen. Washington, addressed to Brig.-Gen. Rufus Putnam, afterwards printed at Marietta, O., from his papers, indicates the regard the Father of his Country had for the rights of the master, though those rights were pushed into the camp of the army where many brave Negroes were found; and it also illustrates the legal strength of such a claim:—

"HEAD QUARTERS, FEB. 2, 1783.

"Sir,—Mr. Hobby having claimed as his property a negro man now serving in the Massachusetts Regiment, you will please to order a court of inquiry, consisting of five as respectable officers as can be found in your brigade, to examine the validity of the claim, the manner in which the person in question came into service, and the propriety of his being discharged or retained in service. Having inquired into the matter, with all the attending circumstances, they will report to you their opinion thereon; which you will report to me as soon as conveniently may be.

"I am, Sir, with great respect,
"Your most obedient servant,

"G. Washington.

"P.S.—All concerned should be notified to attend.
"Brig.-Gen. Putnam."

Enlistment in the army did not work a practical emancipation of the slave, as some have thought. Negroes were rated as chattel property by both armies and both governments during the entire war. This is the cold fact of history, and it is not pleasing to contemplate. The Negro occupied the anomalous position of an American slave and an American soldier. He was a soldier in the hour of danger, but a chattel in time of peace.

FOOTNOTES:

[588] Felt says, in History of Salem, vol. ii. p. 278: "Sept. 17 [1776]. At this date two slaves, taken on board of a prize, were to have been sold here; but the General Court forbid the sale, and ordered such prisoners to be treated like all others."

[589] Resolves, p. 14. Quoted by Dr. Moore from the original documents.

[590] Mr. Motley, "Rise of Dutch Republic," vol. i. p. 151, says that in the sixteenth century, in wars between European states, the captor had a property in his prisoner, which was assignable.

[591] Law of Fiefdom and Bondage, vol. i. p. 158.

[592] Mr. Hurd says, "In ascribing slavery to the law of nations it is a very common error to use that term not in the sense of universal jurisprudence—the Roman jus gentium-but in the modern sense of public international law, and to give the custom of enslaving prisoners of war, in illustration: as if the legal condition of other slaves who had never been taken in war were

not equally jure gentium according to the Roman jurisprudence" See Mr. Webster's speech, 7th March, 1830; Works, vol. v. p. 329.

[593] Dawson's Stony Point, pp. 111, 118.

[594] Dr. Moore thinks this the wrong name. The resolve proves it.

[595] House Journal, p. 60.

[596] Ibid, pp. 63, 64.

[597] Resolves, p. 51.

[598] Mass. Archives, vol. cli., pp. 202-294.

[599] The indefatigable Dr. George H. Moore copied the letter from the original manuscript. The portions in Italics are in the handwriting of Hancock. I have been placed under many obligations to my friend Dr. Moore.

[600] Resolves, p. 131.

[601] Laws, 1780, chap. v. pp. 283, 284.

[602] Journal, vol. iv. pp. 308, 309.

[603] From Mr. Bancroft's MSS., America, 1783, vol. ii. Quoted by Dr. Moore.

[604] Sparks's Washington, vol. viii. p. 428, note.

[605] Works of Hamilton, vol. vii. p. 191.

[606] Sparks's Washington, vol. viii. pp. 431,432.

[607] Sparks's Washington, vol. viii, Appendix, p. 544.

[608] U.S. Statutes at large, vol. viii, pp. 54, 57.

[609] Ibid., pp. 80, 83.

[610] U.S. Statutes at large, vol. viii. p. 218.

CHAPTER XXIX
THE NEGRO INTELLECT.—BANNEKER THE ASTRONOMER.[611].— FULLER THE MATHEMATICIAN.—DERHAM THE PHYSICIAN

Statutory Prohibition against the Education of Negroes.— Benjamin Banneker, the Negro Astronomer and Philosopher.—His Antecedents—Young Banneker as a Farmer and Inventor—The Mills of Ellicott & Co.—Banneker cultivates his Mechanical Genius and Mathematical Tastes.—Banneker's first Calculation of an Eclipse submitted for Inspection in 1789.—His Letter to Mr Ellicott.—The Testimony of a Personal Acquaintance of Banneker as to his Upright Character.—His Home becomes a Place of Interest to Visitors.—Record of his Business Transactions.—Mrs. Mason's Visit to him.—She addresses him in Verse.— Banneker replies by Letter to her.—Prepares his First Almanac for Publication in 1792.—Title of his Almanac—Banneker's Letter to Thomas Jefferson.—Thomas Jefferson's Reply.— Banneker invited to accompany the Commissioners to run the Lines of the District of Columbia.—Banneker's Habits of studying the Heavenly Bodies.—Minute Description given to his Sisters in Reference to the Disposition of his Personal Property after Death.—His Death.—Regarded as the most Distinguished Negro of his Time.—Fuller the Mathematician, or "The Virginia Calculator."—Fuller of African Birth, but stolen and sold as a Slave into Virginia.— Visited by Men of Learning.—He was pronounced to be a Prodigy in the Manipulation of Figures.—His Death.— Derham the Physician.—Science of Medicine regarded as the most Intricate Pursuit of Man.—Early Life of James Derham.—His Knowledge of Medicine, how acquired.— He becomes a Prominent Physician in New Orleans.—Dr. Rush gives an Account of an Interview with him.—What the Negro Race produced by their Genius in America.

FROM the moment slavery gained a foothold in North America until the direful hour that witnessed its dissolution amid the shock of embattled arms, learning was the forbidden fruit that no Negro dared taste. Positive and explicit statutes everywhere, as fiery swords, drove him away hungry from the tree of intellectual life; and all persons were forbidden to pluck the fruit for him, upon pain of severe penalties. Every yearning for intellectual food was answered by whips and thumb-screws.

But, notwithstanding the state of almost instinctive ignorance in which slavery held the Negro, there were those who occasionally astounded the world with the brightness of their intellectual genius. There were some Negroes whose minds ran the gauntlet of public proscription on one side and repressive laws on the other, and safely gained eminence in astronomy, mathematics, and medicine.

BANNEKER THE ASTRONOMER.

Benjamin Banneker, the Negro astronomer and philosopher, was born in Maryland, on the 9th of November, 1731. His maternal grandmother was a white woman, a native of England, named Molly Welsh. She came to Maryland in a shipload of white emigrants, who, according to the custom of those days, were sold to pay their passage. She served her master faithfully for seven years, when, being free, she purchased a small farm, at a nominal price. Soon after she bought two Negro slaves from a ship that had come into the Chesapeake Bay, and began life anew. Both of these Negroes proved to be men of more than ordinary fidelity, industry, and intelligence. One of them, it was said, was the son of an African king. She gave him his freedom, and then married him. His name was Banneker.[612] Four children were the fruit of this union; but the chief interest centres in only one,—a girl, named Mary. Following the example of her mother, she also married a native of Africa: but both tradition and history preserve an unbroken silence respecting his life, with the single exception that, embracing the Christian religion, he was baptized "Robert Banneker;" and the record of his death is thus preserved, in the family Bible: "Robert Banneker departed this life, July ye 10th 1759." Thus it is evident that he took his wife's surname. Benjamin Banneker was the only child of Robert and Mary Banneker.

Young Benjamin was a great favorite with his grandmother, who taught him to read. She had a sincere love of the Sacred Scriptures, which she did not neglect to inculcate into the youthful heart of her grandson. In the neighborhood,—at that time an almost desolate spot,—a school was conducted where the master admitted several Colored children, with the whites, to the benefits of his instructions. It was a "pay school," and thither young Banneker was sent at a very tender age. His application to his studies was equalled by none. When the other pupils were playing, he found great pleasure in his books. How long he remained in school, is not known.

His father purchased a farm of one Richard Gist, and here he spent the remnant of his days.

When young Banneker had obtained his majority, he gave attention to the various interests of farm-life. He was industrious, intelligent in his labors, scrupulously neat in the management of his grounds, cultivated a valuable garden, was gentle in his treatment of stock,—horses, cows, etc.,— and was indeed comfortably situated. During those seasons of leisure which come to agriculturists, he stored his mind with useful knowledge. Starting with the Bible, he read history, biography, travels, romance, and such works on general literature as he was able to borrow. His mind seemed to turn with especial satisfaction to mathematics, and he acquainted himself with the most difficult problems.

He had a taste also for mechanics. He conceived the idea of making a timepiece, a clock, and about the year 1770 constructed one. With his imperfect tools, and with no other model than a borrowed watch, it had cost him long and patient labor to perfect it, to make the variation necessary to cause it to strike the hours, and produce a concert of correct action between the hour, the minute, and the second machinery. He confessed that its regularity in pointing out the progress of time had amply rewarded all his pains in its construction.[613]

In 1773 Ellicott & Co. built flour-mills in a valley near the banks of the Patapsco River. Banneker watched the mills go up; and, when the machinery was set in motion, looked on with interest, as he had a splendid opportunity of observing new principles of mechanism. He made many visits to the mills, and became acquainted with their proprietors; and, till the day of his death, he found in the Ellicotts kind and helpful friends.

After a short time the Ellicotts erected a store, where, a little later, a post-office, was opened. To this point the farmers and gentlemen, for miles around, used to congregate. Banneker often called at the post-office, where, after overcoming his natural modesty and diffidence, he was frequently called out in conversations covering a variety of topics. His conversational powers, his inexhaustible fund of information, and his broad learning (for those times and considering his circumstances), made him the connoisseur of that section. At times he related, in modest terms, the difficulties he was constrained to encounter in order to acquire the knowledge of books he had, and the unsatisfied longings he still had for further knowledge. His fame as a mathematician was already established, and with the increasing facilities of communication his accomplishments and achievements were occupying the thought of many intelligent people.

"By this time he had become very expert in the solution of difficult mathematical problems, which were then, more than in this century, the amusement of persons of leisure, and they were frequently sent to him from scholars residing in different parts of our country who wished to test his capacity. He is reported to have been successful in every case, and, sometimes, he returned with his answers, questions of his own composition conveyed in rhyme."

The following question was propounded to Mr. George Ellicott, and was solved by Benjamin Hallowell of Alexandria.

> "A Cooper and Vintner sat down for a talk,
> Both being so groggy, that neither could walk,
> Says Cooper to Vintner, 'I'm the first of my trade,
> There's no kind of vessel, but what I have made,
> And of any shape, Sir,—just what you will,—
> And of any size, Sir,—from a ton to a gill!'
> 'Then,' says the Vintner, 'you're the man for me,—
> Make me a vessel, if we can agree.
> The top and the bottom diameter define,
> To bear that proportion as fifteen to nine;
> Thirty-five inches are just what I crave,
> No more and no less, in the depth, will I have;
> Just thirty-nine gallons this vessel must hold,—
> Then I will reward you with silver or gold,—
> Give me your promise, my honest old friend?'
> 'I'll make it to-morrow, that you may depend!'
> So the next day the Cooper his work to discharge,
> Soon made the new vessel, but made it too large:—
> He took out some staves, which made it too small,
> And then cursed the vessel, the Vintner and all.
> He beat on his breast, 'By the Powers!'—he swore,
> He never would work at his trade any more!
> Now my worthy friend, find out, if you can,
> The vessel's dimensions and comfort the man!
>
> "Benjamin Banneker.

The greater diameter of Banneker's tub must be 24.746 inches; the less diameter, 14.8476 inches.

He was described by a gentleman who had often met him at Ellicott's Mills as "of black complexion, medium stature, of uncommonly soft and gentlemanly manners and of pleasing colloquial powers."

Fortunately Mr. George Ellicott was a gentleman of exquisite literary taste and critical judgment. He discovered in Banneker the elements of a cultivated gentleman and profound scholar. He threw open his library to this remarkable Negro, loaded him with books and astronomical instruments, and gave him the emphatic assurance of sympathy and encouragement. He occasionally made Banneker a visit, when he would urge upon him the importance of making astronomical calculations for almanacs. Finally, in the spring of 1789, Banneker submitted to Mr. Ellicott his first projection of an eclipse. It was found to contain a slight error; and, having kindly pointed it out, Mr. Ellicott received the following reply from Banneker:—

LETTER OF BENJAMIN BANNEKER TO GEORGE ELLICOTT.

"Sir,—I received your letter at the hand of Bell but found nothing strange to me In the Letter Concerning the number of Eclipses, the according to authors the Edge of the penumber only touches the Suns Limb in that Eclips, that I left out of the Number—which happens April 14th day, at 37 minutes past 7 o'clock in the morning, and is the first we shall have; but since you wrote to me, I drew in the Equations of the Node which will cause a small Solar Defet, but as I did not intend to publish, I was not so very peticular as I should have been, but was more intent upon the true method of projecting; a Solar Eclips—It is an easy matter for us when a Diagram is laid down before us, to draw one in resemblance of it, but it is a hard matter for young Tyroes in Astronomy, when only the Elements for the projection is laid down before him to draw his diagram with any degree of Certainty.

"Says the Learned Leadbetter, the projection, I shall here describe, is that mentioned by Mr. Flamsted. When the sun is in Cancer, Leo, Virgo, Libra, Scorpio or, Sagitary, the Axes of the Globe must lie to the right hand of the Axes of the Ecliptic, but when the sun is in Capricorn, Aquarius, Pisces, Aries, Taurus, or Gemini, then to the left.

"Says the wise author Ferguson, when the sun is in Capercorn, Aquarius, Pisces, Aries, Taurus, and Gemeni, the Northern half of the Earths Axes lies to the right hand of the Axes of the Ecliptic and to the left hand, whilst the Sun is on the other six signs.

"Now Mr. Ellicott, two such learned gentlemen as the above mentioned, one in direct opposition to the other, stagnates young beginners, but I hope the stagnation will not be of long duration, for this I observe that Leadbetter counts the time on the path of Vertex 1, 2, 3 &c. from the right to the left hand or from the consequent to the antecedent,—But Ferguson on the path of Vertex counts the time 1, 2, 3 &c. from the left to the right hand, according to the order of numbers, so that that is regular, shall compensate for irregularity. Now sir if I can overcome this difficulty I doubt not being able to calculate a Common Almanac—Sir no more

"But remain your faithful friend,

"B. Banneker.

"Mr. George Ellicott, *Oct. 13th, 1789.*"

His mother, an active, intelligent, slight-built Mulatto, with long black hair, had exercised a tender but positive influence over him. His character, so far as is known, was without blemish, with the single exception of an occasional use of ardent spirits. He found himself conforming too frequently to the universal habit of the times, social drinking. Liquors and wines were upon the tables and sideboards of the best families, and wherever Banneker went it confronted him. He felt his weakness in this regard, and resolved to abstain from the use of strong drink. Some time after returning from a visit to Washington, in company with the commissioners who laid out the District of Columbia, he related to his friends that during the entire absence from home he had abstained from the use of liquors; adding, "I feared to trust myself even with wine, lest it should steal away the little sense I have." On a leaf of one of his almanacs, appears the following in his own handwriting:—

"Evil communications corrupt good manners, I hope to live to hear, that good communication corrects 'bad manners.'"

He had a just appreciation of his own strength. He hated vice of every kind; and, while he did not connect himself to any church, he was deeply attached to the *Society of Friends*. He was frequently seen in their meeting-house. He usually occupied the rear bench, where he would sit with uncovered head, leaning upon his staff, wrapt in profound meditation. The following letter addressed to Mr. J. Saurin Norris shows that his character was upright:—

"In the year 1800, I commenced my engagements in the store of Ellicott's Mills, where my first acquaintance with Benjamin Banneker began. He often came to the store to purchase articles for his own use; and, after hearing him converse, I was always anxious to wait upon him. After making his

With the use of Mayer's Tables, Ferguson's Astronomy, and Leadbeater's Lunar Tables, Banneker had made wonderful progress in his astronomical investigations. He prepared his first almanac for publication in 1792. Mr. James McHenry became deeply interested in him, and, convinced of his talent in this direction, wrote a letter to the firm of Goddard & Angell, publishers of almanacs, in Baltimore. They became the sole publishers of Banneker's almanacs till the time of his death. In an editorial note in the first almanac, they say,—

"They feel gratified in the opportunity of presenting to the public, through their press, what must be considered as an extraordinary effort of genius; a complete and accurate Ephemeris for the year 1792, calculated by a sable descendant of Africa," etc.

And they further say,—

"That they flatter themselves that a philanthropic public, in this enlightened era, will be induced to give their patronage and support to this work, not only on account of its intrinsic merits, (it having met the approbation of several of the most distinguished astronomers of America, particularly the celebrated Mr. Rittenhouse,) but from similar motives to those which induced the editors to give this calculation the preference,—the ardent desire of drawing modest merit from obscurity, and controverting the long-established illiberal prejudice against the blacks."

The title of his almanac is given below as a matter of historic interest.

> "Benjamin Banneker's Pennsylvania, Delaware, Virginia, and Maryland Almanac and Ephemeris, for the year of our Lord 1792, being Bissextile or leap year, and the sixteenth year of American Independence, which commenced July 4, 1776; containing the motions of the Sun and Moon, the true places and aspects of the Planets, the rising and setting of the Sun, and the rising, setting, and southing, place and age of the Moon, &c. The Lunations, Conjunctions, Eclipses, Judgment of the Weather, Festivals, and remarkable days."

He had evidently read Mr. Jefferson's Notes on Virginia; and touched by the humane sentiment there exhibited, as well as saddened by the doubt expressed respecting the intellect of the Negro, Banneker sent him a copy of his first almanac, accompanied by a letter which pleaded the cause of his race, and in itself, was a refutation of the charge that the Negro had no intellectual outcome.

"MARYLAND, BALTIMORE COUNTY, AUGUST 19, 1791.

To right or left, if they should swerve,
Their blemishes would not appear,
Beyond their lives a single year.—
But thou, a man exalted high,
Conspicuous in the world's keen eye,
On record now, thy name's enrolled,
And future ages will be told,—
There lived a man named Banneker,
An African Astronomer!—
Thou need'st to have a special care,
Thy conduct with thy talent square,
That no contaminating vice,
Obscure thy lustre in our eyes."

During the following year Banneker sent the following letter to his good friend Mrs. Mason:—

"AUGUST 26TH, 1797.

"Dear Female Friend:—

"I have thought of you every day since I saw you last, and of my promise in respect of composing some verses for your amusement, but I am very much indisposed, and have been ever since that time. I have a constant pain in my head, a palpitation in my flesh, and I may say I am attended with a complication of disorders, at this present writing, so that I cannot with any pleasure or delight, gratify your curiosity in that particular, at this present time, yet I say my will is good to oblige you, if I had it in my power, because you gave me good advice, and edifying language, in that piece of poetry which you was pleased to present unto me, and I can but love and thank you for the same; and if ever it should be in my power to be serviceable to you, in any measure, your reasonable requests, shall be armed with the obedience of,

"Your sincere friend and well-wisher,

"Benjamin Banneker.

"Mrs. Susanna Mason.

"N.B. The above is mean writing, done with trembling hands. B.B."

"'Sold on the 2nd of April, 1795, to Buttler, Edwards & Kiddy, the right of an Almanac, for the year 1796, for the sum of 80 dollars, equal to £30.

"'On the 30th of April, 1795, lent John Ford five dollars. £1 17s. 6d.

"'12th of December, 1797, bought a pound of candles at 1s. 8d.

"'Sold to John Collins 2 qts. of dried peaches 6d. "1 qt. mead 4d.

"'On the 26th of March, came Joshua Sanks with 3 or 4 bushels of turnips to feed the cows.

"'13th of April, 1803, planted beans and sowed cabbage seed.'

"He took down from a shelf a little book, wherein he registered the names of those, by whose visits he felt particularly honored, and recorded my mother's name upon the list; he then, diffidently, but very respectfully, requested her acceptance of one of his Almanacs in manuscript."

Within a few days after this visit Mrs. Mason addressed him in a poetical letter, which found its way into the papers of the section, and was generally read. The subjoined portions are sufficient to exhibit the character of the effusion. The admonitory lines at the end doubtless refer to his early addiction to strong drink.

"*An Address to Benjamin Banneker, an African Astronomer, who presented the Author with a Manuscript Almanac in 1796.*"

"Transmitted on the wings of Fame,
Thine *eclat* sounding with thy name,
Well pleased, I heard, ere 'twas my lot
To see thee in thy humble cot.
That genius smiled upon thy birth,
And application called it forth;
That times and tides thou could'st presage,
And traverse the Celestial stage,
Where shining globes their circles run,
In swift rotation round the sun;
Could'st tell how planets in their way,
Mspan>From order ne'er were known to stray.
Sun, moon and stars, when they will rise,
When sink below the upper skies,
When an eclipse shall veil their light,
And hide their splendor from our sight.

Some men whom private walks pursue,
Whom fame ne'er ushered into view,
May run their race, and few observe

purchases, he usually went to the part of the store where George Ellicott was in the habit of sitting to converse with him about the affairs of our Government and other matters. He was very precise in conversation and exhibited deep reflection. His deportment whenever I saw him, appeared to be perfectly upright and correct, and he seemed to be acquainted with every thing of importance that was passing in the country.

"I recollect to have seen his Almanacs in my father's house, and believe they were the only ones used in the neighborhood at the time. He was a large man inclined to be fleshy, and was far advanced in years, when I first saw him, I remember being once at his house, but do not recollect any thing about the comforts of his establishment, nor of the old clock, about which you enquired. He was fond of, and well qualified, to work out abstruse questions in arithmetic. I remember, he brought to the store, one which he had composed himself, and presented to George Ellicott for solution. I had a copy which I have since lost; but the character and deportment of the man being so wholly different from any thing I had ever seen from one of his color, his question made so deep an impression on my mind I have ever since retained a perfect recollection of it, except two lines, which do not alter the sense. I remember that George Ellicott, was engaged in making out the answer, and cannot now say that he succeeded, but have no doubt he did. I have thus, briefly given you my recollections of Benjamin Banneker. I was young when he died, and doubtless many incidents respecting him, have, from the time which has since elapsed, passed from my recollection:

"CHARLES W. DORSEY, OF ELKRIDGE."

After the death of his mother, Banneker dwelt alone until the day of his death, having never married, his manners were gentle and engaging, his benevolence proverbial. His home became a place of great interest to visitors, whom he always received cordially, and treated hospitably all who called.

"We found the venerable star-gazer," says the author of the Memoir of Susanna Mason, "under a wide spreading pear tree, leaden with delicious fruit; he came forward to meet us, and bade us welcome to his lowly dwelling. It was built of logs, one story in height, and was surrounded by an orchard. In one corner of the room, was suspended a clock of his own construction, *which* was a true hearald of departing hours. He was careful in the little affairs of life as well as in the great matters. He kept record of all his business transactions, literary and domestic. The following extracts from his Account Book exhibit his love for detail.

"Sir,

"I am fully sensible of the greatness of the freedom I take with you on the present occasion; a liberty which seemed scarcely allowable, when I reflected on that distinguished and dignified station in which you stand, and the almost general prejudice which is so prevalent in the world against those of my complexion.

"It is a truth too well attested, to need a proof here, that we are a race of beings, who have long laboured under the abuse and censure of the world; that we have long been looked upon with an eye of contempt; and considered rather as brutish than human, and scarcely capable of mental endowments.

"I hope I may safely admit, in consequence of the report which has reached me, that you are a man far less inflexible in sentiments of this nature, than many others, that you are measurably friendly and well disposed towards us; and that you are willing to lend your aid and assistance for our relief from those many distresses, and numerous calamities, to which we are reduced.

"If this is founded in truth, I apprehend you will embrace every opportunity to eradicate that train of absurd and false ideas and opinions, which so generally prevail with respect to us: and that your sentiments are concurrent with mine, which are, that one universal Father hath given being to us all; that He hath not only made us all of one flesh, but that He hath also, without partiality, afforded us all the same sensations, and endowed us all with the same faculties; and that however variable we may be in society or religion, however diversified in situation or in colour, we are all of the same family, and stand in the same relation to Him.

"If these are sentiments of which you are fully persuaded, you cannot but acknowledge, that it is the indispensable duty of those, who maintain for themselves the rights of human nature, and who profess the obligations of Christianity, to extend their powers and influence to the relief of every part of the human race, from whatever burden or oppression they may unjustly labour under: and this, I apprehend, a full conviction of the truth and obligation of these principles should lead all to.

"I have long been convinced, that if your love for yourselves, and for those inestimable laws which preserved to you the rights of human nature, was founded on sincerity you could not but be solicitous, that every individual, of whatever rank or distinction, might with you equally enjoy the blessings thereof; neither could you rest satisfied short of the most active effusion of your exertions, in order to their promotion from any state of degradation, to which the unjustifiable cruelty and barbarism of men may have reduced them.

"I freely and cheerfully acknowledge, that I am of the African race, and in that colour which is natural to them, of the deepest dye; and it is under a sense of the most profound gratitude to the Supreme Ruler of the Universe, that I now confess to you, that I am not under that state of tyrannical thraldom, and inhuman captivity, to which too many of my brethren are doomed, but that I have abundantly tasted of the fruition of those blessings, which proceed from that free and unequalled liberty with which you are favoured; and which I hope you will willingly allow you have mercifully received, from the immediate hand of that Being from whom proceedeth every good and perfect gift.

"Suffer me to recall to your mind that time, in which the arms of the British crown were exerted, with every powerful effort, in order to reduce you to a state of servitude: look back, I entreat you, on the variety of dangers to which you were exposed; reflect on that period in which every human aid appeared unavailable, and in which even hope and fortitude wore the aspect of inability to the conflict, and you cannot but be led to a serious and grateful sense of your miraculous and providential preservation; you cannot but acknowledge, that the present freedom and tranquility which you enjoy, you have mercifully received, and that it is the peculiar blessing of heaven.

"This, Sir, was a time when you cleary saw into the injustice of a state of Slavery, and in which you had just apprehensions of the horrors of its condition. It was then that your abhorrence thereof was so excited, that you publicly held forth this true and invaluable doctrine, which is worthy to be recorded and remembered in all succeeding ages: 'We hold these truths to be self-evident, that all men are created equal; that they are endowed by their Creator with certain inalienable rights, and that among these are, life, liberty, and the pursuit of happiness.'

"Here, was a time in which your tender feelings for yourselves had engaged you thus to declare; you were then impressed with proper ideas of the great violation of liberty, and the free possession of those blessings, to which you were entitled by nature; but, sir, how pitiable is it to reflect, that although you were so fully convinced of the benevolence of the Father of Mankind, and of his equal and impartial distribution of these rights and privileges which he hath conferred upon them, that you should at the same time counteract his mercies, in detaining by fraud and violence, so numerous a part of my brethren under groaning captivity and cruel oppression, that you should at the same time be found guilty of that most criminal act, which you professedly detested in others, with respect to yourselves.

"Your knowledge of the situation of my brethren is too extensive to need a recital here; neither shall I presume to prescribe methods by which they may be relieved, otherwise than by recommending to you and all others, to wean yourselves from those narrow prejudices which you have imbibed with respect to them, and as Job proposed to his friends, 'put your soul in their soul's stead;' thus shall your hearts be enlarged with kindness and benevolence towards them; and thus shall you need neither the direction of myself or others in what manner to proceed herein.

> "And now, sir, although my sympathy and affection for my brethren hath caused my enlargement thus far, I ardently hope, that your candour and generosity will plead with you in my behalf, when I state that it was not originally my design; but having taken up my pen in order to present a copy of an almanac which I have calculated for the succeeding year, I was unexpectedly led thereto.

"This calculation is the production of my arduous study, in my advanced stage of life: for having long had unbounded desires to become acquainted with the secrets of nature, I have had to gratify my curiosity herein through my own assiduous application to astronomical study, in which I need not recount to you the many difficulties and disadvantages which I have had to encounter.

"And although I had almost declined to make my calculation for the ensuing year, in consequence of the time which I had allotted for it being taken up at the federal territory, by the request of Mr. Andrew Ellicott, yet I industriously applied myself thereto, and hope I have accomplished it with correctness and accuracy. I have taken the liberty to direct a copy to you, which I humbly request you will favourably receive; and although you may have the opportunity of perusing it after its publication, yet I desire to send it to you in manuscript previous thereto, that thereby you might not only have an earlier inspection, but that you might also view it in my own handwriting.

"And now, sir, I shall conclude, and subscribe myself, with the most profound respect,

"Your most obedient humble servant,

"Benjamin Banneker."

Mr. Jefferson, who was Secretary of State under President Washington, sent the great Negro the following courteous reply:—

"PHILADELPHIA, AUG. 30, 1791.

"Sir,—I thank you sincerely for your letter of the 19th instant, and for the almanac it contained. Nobody wishes more than I do to see such proofs as you exhibit, that Nature has given to our black brethren talents equal to those of the other colors of men, and that the appearance of a want of them is owing only to the degraded condition of their existence, both in Africa and America. I can add, with truth, that no one wishes more ardently to see a good system commenced for raising the condition, both of their body and mind, to what it ought to be, as fast as the imbecility of their present existence, and other circumstances which cannot be neglected, will admit. I have taken the liberty of sending your almanac to Monsieur de Condorcet, Secretary of the Academy of Sciences, at Paris, and members of the Philanthropic Society, because I considered it a document to which your whole color had a right, for their justification against the doubts which have been entertained of them,

"I am, with great esteem, sir,

"Your most obedient servant,

"Tho. Jefferson.

"Mr. Benjamin Banneker, near Ellicott's

Lower Mills, Baltimore county."[614]

The only time Banneker was ever absent from his home any distance was when "the Commissioners to run the lines of the District of Columbia"— then known as the "Federal Territory"—invited him to accompany them upon their mission. Mr. Norris says:—

"Banneker's deportment throughout the whole of this engagement, secured their respect, and there is good authority for believing, that his endowments led the commissioners to overlook the color of his skin, to converse with him freely, and enjoy the clearness and originality of his remarks on various subjects. It is a fact, that they honored him with an invitation to a daily seat at their table; but this, with his usual modesty, he declined. They then ordered a side table laid for him, in the same apartment with themselves. On his return, he called to give an account of his engagements, at the house of one of his friends. He arrived on horseback, dressed in his usual costume;—full suit of drab cloth, surmounted by a broad brimmed beaver hat. He seemed to have been re-animated by the presence of the eminent men with whom he had mingled in the District, and gave a full account of their proceedings."

His habits of study were rather peculiar. At nightfall, wrapped in a great cloak, he would lie prostrate upon the ground, where he spent the night in contemplation of the heavenly bodies. At sunrise he would retire to his dwelling, where he spent a portion of the day in repose. But as he seemed to require less sleep than most people, he employed the hours of the afternoons in the cultivation of his garden, trimming of fruit-trees, or in observing the habits and flight of his bees. When his service and attention were not required out-doors, he busied himself with his books, papers, and mathematical instruments, at a large oval table in his house. The situation of Banneker's dwelling was one which would be admired by every lover of nature, and furnished a fine field for the observation of celestial phenomena. It was about half a mile from the Patapsco River, and commanded a prospect of the near and distant hills upon its banks, which have been so justly celebrated for their picturesque beauty. A never-failing spring issued from beneath a large golden-willow tree in the midst of his orchard.[615] The whole situation was charming, inspiring, and no doubt helped him in the solution of difficult problems.

There is no reliable data to enlighten us as to the day of his death; but it is the opinion of those who lived near him, and their descendants, that he died in the fall of 1804. It was a bright, beautiful day, and feeling unwell he walked out on the hills to enjoy the sunlight and air. During his walk he came across a neighbor, to whom he complained of being sick. They both returned to his house, where, after lying down upon his couch, he became speechless, and died peacefully. During a previous sickness he had charged his sisters, Minta Black and Molly Morten, that, so soon as he was dead, all the books, instruments, etc., which Mr. Ellicott had loaned him, should be taken back to the benevolent lender; and, as a token of his gratitude, all his manuscripts containing all his almanacs, his observations and writings on various subjects, his letter to Thomas Jefferson, and that gentleman's reply, etc., were given to Mr. Ellicott.[616] On the day of his death, faithful to the instructions of their brother, Banneker's sisters had all the articles moved to Mr. Ellicott's house; and their arrival was the first sad news of the astronomer's death. To the promptness of these girls in carrying out his orders is the gratitude of the friends of science due for the preservation of the results of Banneker's labors. During the performance of the last sad rites at the grave, two days after his death, his house was discovered to be on fire. It burnt so rapidly that it was impossible to save any thing: so his clock and other personal property perished in the flames. He had given to one of his sisters a feather-bed, upon which he had slept for many years; and she, fortunately and thoughtfully, removed it when he died, and prized it as the only memorial of her distinguished brother. Some years after, she had occasion to open the bed, when she discovered a purse of money—another illustration of his careful habits and frugality.

Benjamin Banneker was known favorably on two continents, and at the time of his death was the most intelligent and distinguished Negro in the United States.

FULLER THE MATHEMATICIAN.

One of the standing arguments against the Negro was, that he lacked the faculty of solving mathematical problems. This charge was made without a disposition to allow him an opportunity to submit himself to a proper test. It was equivalent to putting out a man's eyes, and then asserting boldly that he cannot see; of manacling his ankles, and charging him with the inability to run. But notwithstanding all the prohibitions against instructing the Negro, and his far remove from intellectual stimulants, the subject to whom attention is now called had within his own untutored intellect the elements of a great mathematician.

Thomas Fuller, familiarly known as the Virginia Calculator, was a native of Africa. At the age of fourteen he was stolen, and sold into slavery in Virginia, where he found himself the property of a planter residing about four miles from Alexandria. He did not understand the art of reading or writing, but by a marvellous faculty was able to perform the most difficult calculations. Dr. Benjamin Rush of Philadelphia, Penn., in a letter addressed to a gentleman residing in Manchester, Eng., says that hearing of the phenomenal mathematical powers of "Negro Tom," he, in company with other gentlemen passing through Virginia, sent for him. One of the gentlemen asked him how many seconds a man of seventy years, some odd months, weeks, and days, had lived, he gave the exact number in a minute and a half. The gentleman took a pen, and after some figuring told Tom he must be mistaken, as the number was too great." 'Top, massa!" exclaimed Tom, "you hab left out de leap-years!" And sure enough, on including the leap-years in the calculation, the number given by Tom was correct.

> "He was visited by William Hartshorn and Samuel Coates," says Mr. Needles, "of this city (Philadelphia), and gave correct answers to all their questions such as, How many seconds there are in a year and a half? In two minutes he answered 47,304,000. How many seconds in seventy years,

seventeen days, twelve hours? In one minute and a half, 2,110,500,800.[617]

That he was a prodigy, no one will question.[618] He was the wonder of the age. The following appeared in several newspapers at the time of his death:—

"Died,—Negro Tom, the famous African calculator, aged 80 years. He was the property of Mrs. Elizabeth Cox, of Alexandria. Tom was a very black man. He was brought to this country at the age of fourteen, and was sold as a slave with many of his unfortunate countrymen. This man was a prodigy. Though he could neither read nor write, he had perfectly acquired the use of enumeration. He could give the number of months, days, weeks, hours, minutes, and seconds, for any period of time that a person chose to mention, allowing in his calculations for all the leap years that happened in the time. He would give the number of poles, yards, feet, inches, and barley-corns in a given distance—say, the diameter of the earth's orbit—and in every calculation he would produce the true answer in less time than ninety-nine out of a hundred men would take with their pens. And what was, perhaps, more extraordinary, though interrupted in the progress of his calculations, and engaged in discourse upon any other subject, his operations were not thereby in the least deranged; he would go on where he left off, and could give any and all of the stages through which the calculation had passed.

"Thus died Negro Tom, this untaught arithmetician, this untutored scholar. Had his opportunities of improvement been equal to those of thousands of his fellow-men, neither the Royal Society of London, the Academy of Science at Paris, nor even a Newton himself need have been ashamed to acknowledge him a brother in science."[619]

DERHAM THE PHYSICIAN.

Through all time the science of medicine has been regarded as ranking among the most intricate and delicate pursuits man could follow. Our Saviour was called "the Great Physician," and St. Luke "the beloved physician." No profession brings a man so near to humanity, and no other class of men have a higher social standing than those who are consecrated to the "art of healing." Such a position demands of a man not only profound research in the field of medicine, but the rarest intellectual and social gifts and accomplishments. For a Negro to gain such a position in the nineteenth century would require merit of unusual order. But in the eighteenth century, when slavery had cast its long, dark shadows over the entire life of the nation, for a Negro, born and reared a slave, to obtain fame in medicine second to none on the continent, was an achievement that justly challenged the admiration of the civilized world.

Dr. James Derham was born a slave in Philadelphia in 1762. His master was a physician. James was taught to read and write, and early rendered valuable assistance to his master in compounding medicines. Endowed with more than average intelligence, he took a great liking to the science of medicine, and absorbed all the information that came within his observation. On the death of his master he was sold to the surgeon of the Sixteenth British Regiment, at that time stationed in Philadelphia. At the close of the war he was sold to Dr. Robert Dove of New Orleans, a humane and intelligent man, who employed him as his assistant in a large business. He grew in a knowledge of his profession every day, was prompt and faithful in the discharge of the trusts reposed in him, and thereby gained the confidence of his master. Dr. Dove was so much pleased with him, that he offered him his freedom upon very easy terms, requiring only two or three years' service. At the end of the time designated, Dr. Derham entered into the practice of medicine upon his own account. He acquired the English, French, and Spanish languages so as to speak them fluently, and built up a practice in a short time worth three thousand dollars a year.[620] He married, and attached himself to the Episcopal Church, in 1788, and at twenty-six years of age was regarded as one of the most eminent physicians in New Orleans.

Dr. Rush of Philadelphia, in "The American Museum" for January, 1789, gave an interesting account of this distinguished "Negro physician." Says Dr. Rush,—

> "I have conversed with him upon most of the acute and epidemic diseases of the country where he lives. I expected to have suggested some new medicines to him, but he suggested many more to me. He is very modest and engaging in his manners. He speaks French fluently, and has some knowledge of the Spanish."[621]

Phillis Wheatley has been mentioned already. So, in the midst of darkness and oppression, the Negro race in America, without the use of the Christian church, schoolhouse, or printing-press, produced a *poetess*, an *astronomer*, a *mathematician*, and a *physician*, who, had they been white, would have received monuments and grateful memorials at the hands of their countrymen. But even their color cannot rob them of the immortality their genius earned.

FOOTNOTES:

[611] William Wells Brown, William C Nell, and all the Colored men whose efforts I have seen, have made a number of very serious mistakes respecting Banneker's parentage, age, accomplishments, etc. He was of mixed blood. His mother's name was not Molly Morton, but one of his sisters bore that name.

I have used the Memoirs of Banneker, prepared by J.H.B. Latrobe and J. Saurin Norris, and other valuable material from the Maryland Historical Society.

[612] In the most remote records the name was written Banneky.

[613] J. Saurin Norris's sketch.

[614] Jefferson's Works, vol. iii. p. 291.

[615] See Norris, paper on Banneker.

[616] All of Banneker's literary remains were published by J.H.B. Latrobe in the Maryland Historical Society, and in the Maryland Colonization Journal in 1845. The Memoir of Banneker was somewhat marred by a too precipitous and zealous attempt to preach the doctrine of colonization.

[617] Needles's Hist. Memoir of the Penn. Society for Promoting the Abolition of Slavery, p 32.

[618] J.P. Brissot de Warville's Travels in the U.S., vol. i p. 243.

[619] Columbian Centinal of Boston, Dec. 29, 1790.

[620] Brissot de Warville's New Travels in the U.S., ed. 1794, vol. i. p. 242.

[621] For an account of Fuller and Derham, see De la Littérature des Nègres, ou Recherches sur leurs Facultés intellectuelles, leurs Qualités morales et leur Littérature; suivies de Notices sur la Vie et les Ouvrages des Nègres qui se sont distingués dans les Sciences, les Lettres et les Arts. Par H. Grégoire, ancien Évêque de Blois, membre du Sénat conservateur, de l'Institut national, de la Société royale des Sciences de Göttingue, etc. Paris: MDCCCVIII.

CHAPTER XXX
SLAVERY DURING THE REVOLUTION

1775-1783.

Progress of the Slave-Trade.—A Great War for the Emancipation of the Colonies from Political Bondage.—Condition of the Southern States during the War.—The Virginia Declaration of Rights.—Immediate Legislation against Slavery demanded.—Advertisement from "The Independent Chronicle."—Petition of Massachusetts Slaves.—An Act preventing the Practice of holding Persons in Slavery.—Advertisements from "The Continental Journal."—A Law passed in Virginia limiting the Rights of Slaves.—Law emancipating all Slaves who served in the Army.—New York promises her Negro Soldiers Freedom.—A Conscientious Minority in Favor of the Abolition of the Slave-Trade.—Slavery flourishes during the Entire Revolutionary Period.

THE thunder of the guns of the Revolution did not drown the voice of the auctioneer. The slave-trade went on. A great war for the emancipation of the colonies from the political bondage into which the British Parliament fain would precipitate them did not depreciate the market value of human flesh. Those whose hearts were not enlisted in the war skulked in the rear, and gloated over the blood-stained shekels they wrung from the domestic slave-trade. While the precarious condition of the Southern States during the war made legislation in support of the institution of slavery impolitic, there were, nevertheless, many severe laws in force during this entire period. In the New England and Middle States there was heard an occasional voice for the oppressed; but it was generally strangled at the earliest moment of its being by that hell-born child, avarice. On the 21st of September, 1776, William Gordon of Roxbury, Mass., wrote,—

> The Virginians begin their Declaration of Rights with saying,'that all men are born equally free and independent, and have certain inherent natural rights, of which they

cannot, by any compact, deprive themselves or their posterity; among which are the enjoyment of life and liberty.' The Congress declare that they 'hold these truths to be self-evident, that all men are created equal, that they are endowed by their Creator with certain inalienable rights, that among these are life, liberty and pursuit of happiness.' The Continent has rung with affirmations of the like import. If these, Gentlemen, are our genuine sentiments, and we are not provoking the Deity, by acting hypocritically to serve a turn, let us apply earnestly and heartily to the extirpation of slavery from among ourselves. Let the State allow of nothing beyond servitude for a stipulated number of years, and that only for seven or eight, when persons are of age, or till they are of age: and let the descendants of the Africans born among us, be viewed as free-born; and be wholly at their own disposal when one-and-twenty, the latter part of which age will compensate for the expense of infancy, education, and so on."

No one gave heed. Two months later, Nov. 14, there appeared in "The Independent Chronicle" of Boston a plan for gradual emancipation; and on the 28th of the same month, in the same paper there appeared a communication demanding specific and immediate legislation against slavery. But all seemed vain: there were few moral giants among the friends of "liberty for all;" and the comparative silence of the press and pulpit gave the advocates of human slavery an easy victory.

Boston, the home of Warren, and the city that witnessed the first holy offering to liberty, busied herself through all the perilous years of the war in buying and selling human beings. The following are but a few of the many advertisements that appeared in the papers of the city of Boston during the war:—[622]

From "The Independent Chronicle," Oct. 3, 1776:—

"*To be* SOLD A stout, hearty, likely Negro Girl, fit for either Town or Country. Inquire of Mr. *Andrew Gillespie, Dorchester, Octo., 1., 1776.*"

From the same, Oct. 10:—

"A hearty Negro Man, with a small sum of Money to be given away."

From the same, Nov. 28:—

"To Sell—A Hearty likely Negro Wench about 12 or 13 Years of Age, has had the Small Pox, can wash, iron, card, and spin, etc., for no other Fault but for want of Employ."

From the same, Feb. 27, 1777:—

"WANTED a Negro Girl between 12 and 20 Years of Age, for which a good Price will be given, if she can be recommended."

From "The Continental Journal," April 3, 1777:—

"*To be* SOLD, a likely Negro Man, twenty-two years old, has had the small-pox, can do any sort of business; sold for want of employment."

To be SOLD, a large, commodious Dwelling House, Barn, and Outhouses, with any quantity of land from 1 to 50 acres, as the Purchaser shall choose within 5 miles of Boston. Also a smart well-tempered Negro Boy of 14 years old, not to go out of this State and *sold for* 15 *years only, if he continues to behave well."*

From "The Independent Chronicle," May 8, 1777:—

"*To be* SOLD, for want of employ, a likely strong Negro Girl, about 18 years old, understands all sorts of household business, and can be well recommended."

The strange and trying vicissitudes through which the colonies had passed exposed their hypocrisy, revealed the weakness of their government, and forced them to another attempt at the extirpation of slavery. The valorous conduct of the Negro soldiers in the army had greatly encouraged their friends and emboldened their brethren, who still suffered from the curse of slavery. The latter were not silent when an opportunity presented to claim the rights they felt their due. On the 18th of March, 1777, the following petition was addressed, by the slaves in Boston, to the Legislature:—

"PETITION OF MASSACHUSETTS SLAVES.

"The petition of a great number of negroes, who are detained in a state of slavery in the very bowels of a free and Christian country, humbly showing,—

"That your petitioners apprehend that they have, in common with all other men, a natural and inalienable right to that freedom, which the great Parent of the universe hath bestowed equally on all mankind, and which they have never forfeited by any compact or agreement whatever. But they were unjustly dragged by the cruel hand of power from their dearest friends, and some of them even torn from the embraces of their tender parents,—from a populous, pleasant and plentiful country, and in violation of the laws of nature and of nations, and in defiance of all the tender feelings of humanity, brought hither to be sold like beasts of burthen, and, like them, condemned to slavery for life—among a people possessing the mild religion of Jesus—a people not insensible of the sweets of national freedom, nor without a spirit to resent the unjust endeavors of others to reduce them to a state of bondage and subjection.

"Your Honors need not to be informed that a life of slavery like that of your petitioners, deprived of every social privilege, of every thing requisite to render life even tolerable, is far worse than non-existence.

"In imitation of the laudable example of the good people of these States, your petitioners have long and patiently waited the event of petition after petition, by them presented to the legislative body of this State, and cannot but with grief reflect that their success has been but too similar.

"They cannot but express their astonishment that it has never been considered, that every principle from which America has acted, in the course of her unhappy difficulties with Great Britain, bears stronger than a thousand arguments in favor of your humble petitioners. They therefore humbly beseech Your Honors to give their petition its due weight and consideration, and cause an act of the legislature to be passed, whereby they may be restored to the enjoyment of that freedom, which is the natural right of all men, and their children (who were born in this land of liberty) may not be held as slaves after they arrive at the age of twenty-one years. So may the inhabitants of this State (no longer chargeable with the inconsistency of acting themselves the part which they condemn and oppose in others) be prospered in their glorious struggles for liberty, and have those blessings secured to them by Heaven, of which benevolent minds cannot wish to deprive their fellow men.

"And your petitioners, as in duty bound, shall ever pray:—

Lancaster Hill,
Peter Bess,
Brister Slenfen,
Prince Hall,
Jack Pierpont, [his X mark.]
Nero Funelo, [his X mark.]
Newport Sumner, [his X mark.]"

The following entry, bearing the same date, was made:—

"A petition of Lancaster Hill, and a number of other Negroes praying the Court to take into consideration their state of bondage, and pass an act whereby they may be restored to the enjoyment of that freedom which is the natural right of all men. Read and committed to Judge Sargent, Mr. Dalton, Mr. Appleton, Col. Brooks, and Mr. Story."

There is no record of the action of the committee, if any were ever had; but at the afternoon session of the Legislature, Monday, June 9, 1777, a bill was introduced to prevent "the Practice of holding persons in Slavery." It was "read a first time, and ordered to be read again on Friday next, at 10 o'clock A.M." Accordingly, on the 13th of June, the bill was "read a second time, and after Debate thereon, it was moved and seconded, That the same lie upon the Table, and that Application be made to Congress on the subject thereof; and the Question being put, it passed in the affirmative, and Mr. Speaker, Mr. Wendell, and Col. Orne, were appointed a Committee to prepare a letter to Congress accordingly, and report." The last action, as far as indicated by the journal, was had on Saturday, June 14, when "the Committee appointed to prepare a Letter to Congress, on the subject of the Bill for preventing the Practice of holding Persons in Slavery, reported." It was "Read and ordered to lie."[623] And so it did "lie," for that was the end of the matter.

Judge Sargent, who was chairman of the committee appointed on the 18th of March, 1777, was doubtless the author of the following bill:—

"State of Massachusetts Bay. In the Year of our Lord, 1777.

"An Act for preventing the practice of holding persons in Slavery.

"Whereas, the practice of holding Africans and the children born of them, or any other persons, in Slavery, is unjustifiable in a civil government, at a time when they are asserting their natural freedom; wherefore, for preventing such a practice for the future, and establishing to every person residing within the State the invaluable blessing of liberty.

"*Be it Enacted*, by the Council and House of Representatives, in General Court assembled, and by the authority of the same,—That all persons, whether black or of other complexion, above 21 years of age, now held in Slavery, shall, from and after the —— day of —— next, be free from any subjection to any master or mistress, who have claimed their servitude by right of purchase, heirship, free gift, or otherwise, and they are hereby entitled to all the freedom, rights, privileges and immunities that do, or ought of right to belong to any of the subjects of this State, any usage or custom to the contrary notwithstanding.

"*And be it Enacted*, by the authority aforesaid, that all written deeds, bargains, sales or conveyances, or contracts without writing, whatsoever, for conveying or transferring any property in any person, or to the service and labor of any person whatsoever, of more than twenty-one years of age, to a third person, except by order of some court of record for some crime, that has been, or hereafter shall be made, or by their own voluntary contract for a term not exceeding seven years, shall be and hereby are declared null and void.

"And Whereas, divers persons now have in their service negroes, mulattoes or others who have been deemed their slaves or property, and who are now incapable of earning their living by reason of age or infirmities, and may be desirous of continuing in the service of their masters or mistresses,—*be it therefore Enacted*, by the authority aforesaid, that whatever negro or mulatto, who shall be desirous of continuing in the service of his master or mistress, and shall voluntarily declare the same before two justices of the County in which said master or mistress resides, shall have a right to continue in the service, and to a maintenance from their master or mistress, and if they are incapable of earning their living, shall be supported by the said master or mistress, or their heirs, during the lives of said servants, any thing in this act to the contrary notwithstanding.

> "Provided, nevertheless, that nothing in this act shall be understood to prevent any master of a vessel or other person from bringing into this State any persons, not Africans, from any other part of the world, except the United States of America, and selling their service for a term of time not exceeding five years, if twenty-one years of age, or, if under twenty-one, not exceeding the time when he or she so brought into the State shall be twenty-six years of age, to pay for and in consideration of the transportation and other charges said master of vessel or other person may have been at, agreeable to contracts made with the persons so transported, or their patents or guardians in their behalf, before they are brought from their own country."[624]

On the back of the bill the following indorsement was written by some officer of the Legislature: "Ordered to lie till the second Wednesday of the next Session of the General Court." This might have ended the struggle for the extinction of slavery in Massachusetts, had not the people at this time made an earnest demand for a State constitution. As the character of the constitution was discussed, the question of slavery divided public sentiment. If it were left out of the constitution, then the claims of the master would forever lack the force of law; if it were inserted as part of the constitution, it would evidence the insincerity of the people in their talk about the equality of the rights of man, etc. The Legislature—Convention of 1777-78—prepared, debated, and finally approved and submitted to the people, a draught of a constitution for the State, on the 28th of February, 1778. The framers of the constitution seemed to lack the courage necessary to declare in favor of the freedom of the faithful blacks who had rendered such efficient aid to the cause of the colonists. The prevailing sentiment of the people demanded an article in the constitution denying Negroes the right of citizens. It may be fortunate for the fame of the Commonwealth that the record of the debates on the article denying Negroes the right of suffrage has not been preserved. The article is here given:—

"V. Every male inhabitant of any town in this State, being *free*, and twenty-one years of age, *excepting Negroes, Indians and Mulattoes*, shall be intitled to vote for a Representative or Representatives, as the case may be," etc.

By this article three classes of inhabitants were excluded from the rights, blessings, and duties of citizenship; and the institution of slavery was recognized as existing by sanction of law. But the constitution was rejected by the people, by an overwhelming majority; not, however, on account of the fifth article, but because the instrument was obnoxious to them on general principles.

The defeat of the constitution did not temper public sentiment on the question of Negro slavery, for the very next year the domestic trade seemed to receive a fresh impetus. The following advertisements furnish abundant proof of the undiminished vigor of the enterprise.

From "The Continental Journal," Nov. 25, 1779:—

"*To be* SOLD A likely Negro Girl, 16 years of Age, for no fault, but want of employ."

From the same, Dec. 16, 1779:—

"*To be* SOLD, A Strong likely Negro Girl," etc.

From "The Independent Chronicle," March 9, 1780:—

"*To be* SOLD, for want of employment, an exceeding likely Negro Girl, aged sixteen."

From the same, March 30 and April 6, 1780:—

"*To be* SOLD, very Cheap, for no other Reason than for want of Employ, an exceeding Active Negro Boy, aged fifteen. Also, a likely Negro Girl, aged seventeen."

From "The Continental Journal," Aug. 17, 1780:—

"*To be* SOLD, a likely Negro Boy."

From the same, Aug. 24 and Sept. 7:—

"*To be* SOLD or LETT, for a term of years, a strong, hearty, likely Negro Girl."

From the same, Oct. 19 and 26, and Nov. 2:—

"*To be* SOLD, a likely Negro Boy, about eighteen years of Age, fit for to serve a Gentleman, to tend horses or to work in the Country."

From the same, Oct. 26, 1780:—

"*To be* SOLD, a likely Negro Boy, about 13 years old, well calculated to wait on a Gentleman. Inquire of the Printer."

"*To be* SOLD, a likely young Cow and Calf. Inquire of the Printer."

"Independent Chronicle," Dec. 14, 21, 28, 1780:—

"A Negro Child, *soon expected, of a good breed*, may be owned by any Person inclining to take it, and Money with it."

"Continental Journal," Dec. 21, 1780, and Jan. 4, 1781:—

"*To be* SOLD, a hearty, strong Negro Wench, about 29 years of age, fit for town or country."

From "The Continental Journal," March 1, 1781:—

"*To be* SOLD, an extraordinary likely Negro Wench, 17 years old, she can be warranted to be strong, healthy and good-natured, *has no notion of Freedom*, has been always used to a Farmer's Kitchen and dairy, and is not known to have any failing, but being with Child, which is the only cause of her being sold."

It is evident, from the wording of the last advertisement quoted, that the Negroes were sniffing the air of freedom that occasionally blew from the victorious battle-fields, where many of their race had distinguished themselves by the most intrepid valor. They began to get "*notions of freedom*," and this depreciated their market value.

Dr. William Gordon, the steadfast, earnest, and intelligent friend of the Negro, was deposed as chaplain of both branches of the Legislature on account of his vehement protest against the adoption of the fifth article of the constitution by that body. But his zeal was not thereby abated. He continued to address able articles to the public, and wrought a good work upon the public conscience.

In Virginia, notwithstanding Negroes were among the State's most gallant defenders, a law was passed in October, 1776, "declaring tenants of lands or slaves in taille to hold the same in fee simple." Under the circumstances, after the war had begun, and after the declaration by the State of national independence, it was a most remarkable law.

> "That any person who now hath, or hereafter may have, any estate in fee taille, general or special, in any lands or slaves in possession, or in the use or trust of any lands or slaves in possession, or who now is or hereafter may be entitled to any such estate taille in reversion or remainder, after the determination of any estate for life or lives, or of any lesser estate, whether such estate taille hath been or shall be created by deeds, will, act of assembly, or by any other ways or means, shall from henceforth, or from the commencement of such estate taille, stand ipso facto seized, possessed, or entitled of, in, or to such lands or slaves, or use in lands or slaves, so held or to be held as aforesaid, in possession, reversion, or remainder, in full and absolute fee simple, in like manner as if such deed, will, act of assembly, or other instrument, had conveyed the same to him in fee simple; any words, limitations, or conditions, in the said deed, will, act of assembly, or other instrument, to the contrary notwithstanding."[625]

But the valor of the Negro soldier had great influence upon the public mind, and inspired the people in many of the States to demand public recognition of deserving Negroes. It has been noted already, that in South Carolina, if a Negro, having been captured by the enemy, made good his escape back into the State, he was emancipated; and, if wounded in the line of duty, was rewarded with his freedom. Rhode Island purchased her Negroes for the army, and presented them with fifty dollars bounty and a certificate of freedom at the close of the war. Even Virginia, the mother of slavery, remembered, at the close of the war, the brave Negroes who had fought in her regiments. In October, 1783, the following Act was passed emancipating all slaves who had served in the army with the permission of their masters. It is to be regretted, however, that *all* slaves who had served in the army were not rewarded with their freedom.

"I. WHEREAS it hath been represented to the present general assembly, that during the course of the war, many persons in this state had caused their slaves to enlist in certain regiments or corps raised within the same, having tendered such slaves to the officers appointed to recruit forces within the state, as substitutes for free persons, whose lot or duty it was to serve in such regiments or corps, at the same time representing to such recruiting officers that the slaves so enlisted by their direction and concurrence were freemen; and it appearing further to this assembly, that on the expiration of the term of enlistment of such slaves that the former owners have attempted again to force them to return to a state of servitude, contrary to the principles of justice, and to then own solemn promise.

> "II. And whereas it appears just and reasonable that all persons enlisted as aforesaid, who have faithfully served agreeable to the terms of their enlistment, and have thereby of course contributed towards the establishment of American liberty and independence, should enjoy the blessings of freedom as a reward for their toils and labours; Be it therefore enacted, That each and every slave who by the appointment and direction of his owner, hath enlisted in any regiment or corps raised within this state, either on continental or state establishment, and hath been received as a substitute for any free person whose duty or lot it was to serve in such regiment or corps, and hath served faithfully during the term of such enlistment, or hath been discharged from such service by some officer duly authorized to grant such discharge, shall from and after the passing of this act, be fully and compleatly emancipated, and shall be held and deemed free in as full and ample a manner as if each and every of them were specially named in this act; and the attorney-general for the commonwealth, is hereby required to commence an action, in forma pauperis, in behalf of any of the persons above described who shall after the passing of this act be detained in servitude by any person whatsoever; and if upon such prosecution it shall appeal that the pauper is entitled to his freedom in consequence of this act, a jury shall be empanelled to assess the damages for his detention."[626]

New York enlisted her Negro soldiers under a statutory promise of freedom. They were required to serve three years, or until regularly discharged. Several other States emancipated a few slaves who had served faithfully in the army; and the recital of the noble deeds of black soldiers was listened to with great interest, had an excellent effect upon many white men after the war, and went far towards mollifying public sentiment on the slavery question.

If Massachusetts were ever moved by the valor of her black soldiers to take any action recognizing their services, the record has not been found up to the present time. After commemorating the 5th of March for a long time, as a day on which to inflame the public zeal for the cause of freedom, her Legislature refused to mark the grave of the first martyr of the Revolution, Crispus Attucks!

Slavery flourished during the entire Revolutionary period. It enjoyed the silent acquiescence of the pulpit, the support of the public journals, the sanction of the courts, and the endorsement of the military establishment. In a free land (?), under the flag of the government Negroes fought, bled, sacrificed, and died to establish, slavery held undisputed sway. The colonial government, built by the cruel and voracious avarice of Britain, crumbled under the master-stroke of men who desired political and religious liberty more than jewelled crowns; but the slave institution stood unharmed by the shock of embattled arms. The colonists asked freedom for themselves and children, but forged chains for Negroes and their children. And while a few individual Negro slaves were made a present of themselves at the close of the war, on account of their gallant service, hundreds of thousands of their brethren were still retained in bondage

FOOTNOTES:

[622] See Slavery in Mass., p. 178.

[623] House Journal, pp. 19, 25.

[624] Mass. Archives; Revolutionary Resolves, vol. vii. p. 133.

[625] Hening, vol. ix. p. 226.

[626] Hening, vol. xi pp. 308, 309.

CHAPTER XXXI
SLAVERY AS A POLITICAL AND LEGAL PROBLEM

1775-1800.

British Colonies in North America declare their Independence.—A New Government established.—Slavery the Bane of American Civilization.—The Tory Party accept the Doctrine of Property in Man.—The Doctrine of the Locke Constitution in the South.—The Whig Party the Dominant Political Organization in the Northern States.—Slavery recognized under the New Government.—Anti Slavery Agitation in the States.—Attempted Legislation against Slavery.—Articles of Confederation.—Then Adoption in 1778.—Discussion concerning the Disposal of the Western Territory.—Mr. Jefferson's Recommendation.—Amendment by Mr. Spaight.—Congress in New York in 1787.—Discussion respecting the Government of the Western Territory.—Convention at Philadelphia to frame the Federal Constitution.—Proceedings of the Convention.—The Southern States still advocate Slavery.—Speeches on the Slavery Question by Leading Statesmen.—Constitution adopted by the Convention in 1787.—First Session of Congress under the Federal Constitution held in New York in 1789.—The Introduction of a Tariff-Bill.—An Attempt to amend it by inserting a Clause levying a Tax on Slaves brought by Water.—Extinction of Slavery in Massachusetts.—A Change in the Public Opinion of the Middle and Eastern States on the Subject of Slavery.—Dr. Benjamin Franklin's Address to the Public for promoting the Abolition of Slavery.—Memorial to the United-States Congress.—Congress in 1790.—Bitter Discussion on the Restriction of the Slave-Trade.—Slave-Population.—Vermont and Kentucky admitted into the Union.—A Law providing for the Return of Fugitives from "Labor and Service."—Convention of Friends held in Philadelphia.—An Act against the Foreign Slave-Trade.—Mississippi Territory.—Constitution of Georgia revised.—New York passes a Bill for the Gradual Extinction of Slavery.—Constitution of Kentucky revised.—Slavery as an Institution firmly established.

THE charge that the mother-country forced slavery upon the British colonies in North America held good until the colonies threw off the yoke, declared their independence, and built a new government, on the 4th of July, 1776. After the promulgation of the gospel of human liberty, the United States of America could no longer point to England as the "first man Adam" of the accursed sin of slavery. Henceforth the American government, under the new dispensation of peace and the equality of all men, was responsible for the continuance of slavery, both as a political and legal problem

Slavery did not escheat to the English government upon the expiration of its authority in North America. It became the dreadful inheritance of the new government, and the eyesore of American civilization. Instead of expelling it from the political institutions of the country, it gradually became a factor of great power. Instead of ruling it out of the courts, it was clothed with the ample garments of judicial respectability.

The first article of the immortal Declaration of Independence was a mighty shield of beautifully wrought truths, that the authors intended should protect every human being on the American Continent.

"We hold these truths to be self-evident:—that all men are created equal, that they are endowed by their Creator with certain inalienable rights; that among these are life, liberty, and the pursuit of happiness. That to secure these rights, governments are instituted among men, deriving their just powers from the consent of the governed; that whenever any form of government becomes destructive of these ends, it is the right of the people to alter or to abolish it, and to institute a new government, laying its foundation on such principles, and organizing its powers in such form, as to them shall seem most likely to effect their safety and happiness."

It was to be expected, that, after such a declaration of principles, the United States would have abolished slavery and the slave-trade forever. While the magic words of the Declaration of Independence were not the empty "palaver" of a few ambitious leaders, yet the practices of the local and the national government belied the grand sentiments of that instrument. From the earliest moment of the birth of the United-States government, slavery began to receive political support and encouragement. Though it was the cruel and depraved offspring of the British government, it nevertheless was adopted by the *free government* of America. Political policy seemed to dictate the methods of a political recognition of the institution. And the fact that the slave-trade was prohibited by Congress at an early day, and by many of the colonies also, did not affect the institution in a local sense.

The Tory party accepted the doctrine of property in man, without hesitation or reservation. Their political fealty to the Crown, their party exclusiveness, and their earnest desire to co-operate with the Royal African Company in the establishment of the slave institution in America, made them, as per necessity, the political guardians of slavery. The institution once planted, property in man having been acquired, it was found to be a difficult task to uproot it. Moreover, the loss of the colonies to the British Crown did not imply death to the Tory party. It doubtless suffered organically; but its individual members did not forfeit their political convictions, nor suffer their interest in the slave-trade to abate. The new States were ambitious to acquire political power. The white population of the South was small when compared with that of the North; but the slave population, added to the former, swelled it to alarming proportions.

The local governments of the South had been organized upon the fundamental principles of the Locke Constitution. The government was lodged with the few, and their rights were built upon landed estates and political titles and favors. Slaves in the Carolinas and Virginias answered to the vassals and villeins of England. This aristocratic element in Tory politics was in harmony, even in a republic, with the later wish of the South to build a great political "government upon Slavery as its chief corner-stone." Added to this was the desire to abrogate the law of indenture of white servants, and thus to the odium of slavery to loan the powerful influence of caste,—ranging the Caucasian against the Ethiopian, the intelligent against the ignorant, the strong against the weak.

New England had better ideas of popular government for and of the people, but her practical position on slavery was no better than any State in the South. The Whig party was the dominant political organization throughout the Northern States; but the universality of slavery made dealers in human flesh members of all parties.

The men who wrote the Declaration of Independence deprecated slavery, as they were pronounced Whigs; but nevertheless many of them owned slaves. They wished the evil exterminated, but confessed themselves ignorant of a plan by which to carry their desire into effect. The good desires of many of the people, born out of the early days of the struggle for independent existence, perished in their very infancy; and, as has been shown, all the States, and the Congress of the United States, recognized slavery as existing under the new political government.

But public sentiment changes in a country where the intellect is unfettered. First, on the eve of the Revolutionary War, Congress and nearly all the States pronounced against slavery; a few years later they all recognized the sacredness of slave property; and still later all sections of the United States seemed to have been agitated by anti-slavery sentiments. In 1780 the Legislature of Pennsylvania prohibited the further introduction of slaves, and gave freedom to the children of all slaves born in the State. Delaware resolved "that no person hereafter imported from Africa ought to be held in slavery under any pretense whatever." In 1784 Connecticut and Rhode Island modified their slave-code, and forbade further importations of slaves. In 1778 Virginia passed a law prohibiting the importation of slaves, and in 1782 repealed the law that confined the power of emancipating to the Legislature, only on account of meritorious conduct. Private emancipations became very numerous, and the sentiment in its favor pronounced. But the restriction was re-enacted in about ten years. The eloquence of Patrick Henry and the logic of Thomas Jefferson went far to enlighten public sentiment; but the political influence of the institution grew so rapidly that in 1785, but two years after the war, Washington wrote LaFayette, "petitions for the abolition of slavery, presented to the Virginia Legislature, could scarcely obtain a hearing." Maryland, New York, and New Jersey prohibited the slave-trade; but the institution held its place among the people until 1830. North Carolina attempted to prohibit in 1777, but-failed; but in 1786 declared the slave-trade "of evil consequences and highly impolitic." South Carolina and Georgia refused to act, and the slave-trade continued along their shores.

After the adoption of the Articles of Confederation in 1778, the Continental Congress found itself charged with the responsibility of deciding the conflicting claims of the various States to the vast territory stretching westward from the Ohio River. The war over, the payment of the public debt thus incurred demanded the consideration of the people and of their representatives. Massachusetts, Connecticut, New York, Virginia, North Carolina, and Georgia laid claim to boundless tracts of lands outside of their State boundaries. But New Hampshire, Rhode Island, New Jersey, Maryland, Delaware, and South Carolina, making no such claims, and lacking the resources to pay their share of the war debt, suggested that the other States should cede all the territory outside of their State lines, to the United States Government, to be used towards liquidating the entire debt. The proposition was accepted by the States named; but not, however, without some modification. Virginia reserved a large territory beyond the Ohio with which to pay the bounties of her soldiers, while Connecticut retained a portion of the Reserve since so famous in the history of Ohio. The duty of framing an ordinance for the government of the Western territory was referred to a select committee by Congress, consisting of Mr. Jefferson of Virginia (chairman), Mr. Chase of Maryland, and Mr. Howell of Rhode Island. The plan reported by the committee contemplated the whole region included within our boundaries west of the old thirteen States, and as far south as our thirty-first degree north latitude. The plan proposed the ultimate division of this territory into seventeen States; eight of which were to be located below the parallel of the Falls of the Ohio (now Louisville), and nine above it. But the most interesting rule reported by Mr. Jefferson was the following, on the 19th of April, 1784:—

"That after the year 1800, of the Christian era, there shall be neither slavery nor involuntary servitude in any part of the said *states*, otherwise than in punishment of crimes, whereof the part shall have been convicted to be personally guilty."

Mr. Spaight of North Carolina moved to amend the report by striking out the above clause, which was seconded by Mr. Reed of South Carolina. The question, upon a demand for the yeas and nays, was put: "Shall the words moved to be stricken out stand?" The question was lost, and the words were stricken out. The ordinance was further amended, and finally adopted on the 23d of April

The last Continental Congress was held in the city of New York in 1787. The question of the government of the Western territory came up. A committee was appointed on this subject, with Nathan Dane of Massachusetts as chairman On the 11th of July the committee reported "An Ordinance for the government of the Territory of the United States, Northwest of the Ohio." It embodied many of the features of Mr. Jefferson's bill, concluding with six unalterable articles of perpetual compact, the last being the following: "There shall be neither slavery nor involuntary servitude in the said territory, otherwise than in punishment of crimes, whereof the parties shall be duly convicted." When upon its passage, a stipulation was added for the delivery of fugitives from "labor or service:"[627] and in this shape the entire ordinance passed on the 13th of July, 1787.

Thus it is clear that under the Confederation slavery existed, a part of the political government, as a legal fact. There was no effort made by Congress to abolish it. Mr. Jefferson simply sought to arrest its progress, and confine it to the original thirteen States.

On the 25th of May, 1787, the convention to frame the Federal Constitution met at Philadelphia, although the day appointed was the 14th. George Washington was chosen president, a committee chosen to report rules of proceeding, and a secretary appointed. The sessions were held with closed doors, and all the proceedings were secret. It contained the most eminent men in the United States,—generals of the army, statesmen, lawyers, and men of broad scholarship. The question of congressional apportionment was early before them, and there was great diversity of opinion. But, as there was no census, therefore there could be no just apportionment until an enumeration of the people was taken. Until that was accomplished, the number of delegates was fixed at sixty-five. Massachusetts was the only State in the Union where slavery did not exist. The Northern States desired representation according to the free inhabitants only; while all of the Southern States, where the great mass of slaves was, wanted representation according to the entire population, bond and free. Some of the Northern delegates urged their view with great force and eloquence. Mr. Patterson of New Jersey said he regarded slaves as mere property. They were not represented in the States: why should they be in the general government? They were not allowed to vote: why should they be represented? He regarded it as an encouragement to the slave-trade. Mr. Wilson of Pennsylvania said, "Are they admitted as citizens? then, why not on an equality with citizens? Are they admitted as property? then, why is not other property admitted into the computation?" It was evident that neither extreme view could carry: so the proposition carried to reckon three-fifths of the slaves in estimating taxes, and to make taxation the basis of representation. New Jersey and Delaware voted Nay; Massachusetts and South Carolina were divided; and New York was not represented, her delegates having failed to arrive.

It was apparent during the early stages of the debates, that a constitution had to be made that would be acceptable to the Southern delegates. A clause was inserted relieving the Southern States from duties on exports, and upon the importation of slaves; and that no navigation act should be passed except by a two-thirds vote. By denying Congress the authority of giving preference to American over foreign shipping, it was designed to secure cheap transportation for Southern exports; but, as the shipping was largely owned in the Eastern States, their delegates were zealous in their efforts to prevent any restriction of the power of Congress to enact navigation laws. It has been already shown that all the States, with the exception of North Carolina, South Carolina, and Georgia, had prohibited the importation of slaves. The prohibition of duties on the importation of slaves was demanded by the delegates from South Carolina and Georgia. They assured the Convention that without such a provision they could never give their assent to the constitution. This declaration dragooned some Northern delegates into a support of the restriction, but provoked some very plain remarks concerning slavery. Mr. Pinckney said, that, "If the Southern States were let alone, they would probably of themselves stop importations. He would himself, as a citizen of South Carolina, vote for it."

Mr. Sherman remarked that "the abolition of slavery seemed to be going on in the United States, and that the good sense of the several states would probably by degrees complete it;" and Mr. Ellsworth thought that "slavery, in time, will not be a speck in our country." Mr. Madison said "he thought it *wrong* to admit in the Constitution the idea of property in men."

Slavery, notwithstanding the high-sounding words just quoted, was recognized in and by three separate clauses of the Constitution The word "slave" was excluded, but the language does not admit of any doubt.

> "Art. I. Sect. 2.... Representatives and direct taxes shall be apportioned among the several States which may be included within this Union, according to their respective numbers; which shall be determined by adding to the whole number of free persons, including those bound to service for a term of years, and excluding Indians not taxed, three-fifths of all other persons.[628] ...

"Art I. Sect. 9. The migration or importation of such *persons* as any of the States now existing shall think proper to admit, shall not be prohibited by the Congress prior to the year one thousand eight hundred and eight; but a tax or duty may be imposed on such importation, not exceeding ten dollars for each person....

"Art. IV. Sect. 2.... No *person* held to service or labor in one State, under the laws thereof, escaping into another, shall, in consequence of any law or regulation therein, be discharged from such service or labor, but shall be delivered up on claim of the party to whom such service or labor may be due."

The debate on the above was exciting and interesting, as the subject of slavery was examined in all its bearings. Finally the Constitution was submitted to Gouverneur Morris of Pennsylvania, to receive the finishing touches of his facile pen. On the 8th of August, 1787, during the debate, he delivered the following speech:—

> "He never would concur in upholding domestic slavery. It was a nefarious institution. It was the curse of Heaven on the States where it prevailed. Compare the free regions of the Middle States, where a rich and noble cultivation marks the prosperity and happiness of the people, with the misery and poverty which overspread the barren wastes of Virginia, Maryland, and the other States having slaves. Travel through

the whole continent, and you behold the prospect continually varying with the appearance and disappearance of slavery. The moment you leave the Eastern States, and enter New York, the effects of the institution become visible. Passing through the Jerseys, and entering Pennsylvania, every criterion of superior improvement witnesses the change. Proceed southwardly, and every step you take through the great regions of slaves presents a desert, increasing with the increasing proportion of these wretched beings. Upon what principle it is that the slaves shall be computed in the representation? Are they men? Then make them citizens, and let them vote. Are they property? Why, then, is no other property included? The houses in this city (Philadelphia) are worth more than all the wretched slaves who cover the rice-swamps of South Carolina. The admission of slaves into the representation, when fairly explained, comes to this,— that the inhabitant of Georgia and South Carolina, who goes to the coast of Africa, and, in defiance of the most sacred laws of humanity, tears away his fellow-creatures from their dearest connections, and damns them to the most cruel bondage, shall have more votes in a government instituted for the protection of the rights of mankind than the citizen of Pennsylvania or New Jersey, who views with a laudable horror so nefarious a practice. He would add, that domestic slavery is the most prominent feature in the aristocratic countenance of the proposed Constitution. The vassalage of the poor has ever been the favorite offspring of aristocracy. And what is the proposed compensation to the Northern States for a sacrifice of every principle of right, of every impulse of humanity? They are to bind themselves to march their militia for the defence of the Southern States, for their defence against those very slaves of whom they complain. They must supply vessels and seamen in case of foreign attack. The Legislature will have indefinite power to tax them by excises and duties on imports, both of which will fall heavier on them than on the Southern inhabitants; for the bohea tea used by a Northern freeman will pay more tax than the whole consumption of the miserable slave, which consists of nothing more than his physical subsistence and the rag that covers his nakedness. On the other side, the Southern States are not to be restrained from importing fresh supplies of wretched Africans, at once to increase the danger of attack and the difficulty of defence: nay, they are to be encouraged to it by an assurance of having their votes in the National Government increased in proportion: and are, it the same time, to have their exports and their slaves exempt from all contributions for the public service. Let it not be said that direct taxation is to be proportioned to representation. It is idle to suppose that the General Government can stretch its hand directly into the pockets of the people scattered over so vast a country. They can only do it through the medium of exports, imports, and excises. For what, then, are all the sacrifices to be made? He would sooner submit himself to a tax for paying for all the negroes in the United States than saddle posterity with such a Constitution."[629]

Mr. Rufus King of Massachusetts in the same debate said,—

"The admission of slaves was a most grating circumstance to his mind, and he believed would be so to a great part of the people of America. He had not made a strenuous opposition to it heretofore, because he had hoped that this concession would have produced a readiness, which had not been manifested, to strengthen the General Government, and to mark a full confidence in it. The report under consideration had, by the tenor of it, put an end to all those hopes. In two great points, the hands of the Legislature were absolutely tied. The importation of slaves could not be prohibited. Exports could not be taxed. Is this reasonable? What are the great objects of the general system? First, defence against foreign invasion; secondly, against internal sedition. Shall all the States, then, be bound to defend each, and shall each be at liberty to introduce a weakness which will render defence more difficult? Shall one part of the United States be bound to defend another part, and that other part be at liberty, not only to increase its own danger, but to withhold the compensation for the burden? If slaves are to be imported, shall not the exports produced by their labor supply a revenue, the better to enable the General Government to defend their masters? There was so much inequality and unreasonableness in all this, that the people of the Northern States could never be reconciled to it. No candid man could undertake to justify it to them. He had hoped that some accommodation would have taken place on this subject; that, at least, a time would have been limited for the importation of slaves. He never could agree to let them be imported without limitation, and then be represented in the National Legislature. Indeed, he could so little persuade himself of the rectitude of such a practice, that he was not sure he could assent to it under any circumstances. At all events, either slaves should not be represented, or exports should be taxable."

Mr. Roger Sherman of Connecticut, —

"Regarded the slave-trade as iniquitous: but the point of representation having been settled after much difficulty and deliberation, he did not think himself bound to make opposition; especially as the present article, as amended, did not preclude any arrangement whatever on that point, in another place of the report."[630]

Mr. Luther Martin of Maryland, in the debate, Tuesday, Aug. 21, —

"Proposed to vary Art. 7, Sect. 4, so as to allow a prohibition or tax on the importation of slaves. In the first place, as five slaves are to be counted as three free men in the apportionment of representatives, such a clause would leave an encouragement to this traffic. In the second place, slaves weakened one part of the Union, which the other parts were bound to protect: the privilege of importing them was therefore unreasonable. And, in the third place, it was inconsistent with the principles of the Revolution, and dishonorable to the American character, to have such a feature in the Constitution.

"Mr. Rutledge did not see how the importation of slaves could be encouraged by this section. He was not apprehensive of insurrections, and would readily exempt the other States from the obligation to protect the Southern against them. Religion and humanity had nothing to do with this question: interest alone is the governing principle with nations. The true question at present is, whether the Southern States shall or shall not be parties to the Union. If the Northern States consult their interest, they will not oppose the increase of slaves, which will increase the commodities of which they will become the carriers.

"Mr. Ellsworth was for leaving the clause as it stands. Let every State import what it pleases. The morality or wisdom of slavery are considerations belonging to the States themselves. What enriches a part enriches the whole, and the States are the best judges of their particular interest. The old Confederation had not meddled with this point; and he did not see any greater necessity for bringing it within the policy of the new one.

"Mr. Pinckney. South Carolina can never receive the plan if it prohibits the slave trade. In every proposed extension of the powers of Congress, that State has expressly and watchfully excepted that of meddling with the importation of Negroes, *If the States be all left at liberty on this subject, South Carolina may perhaps, by degrees, do of herself what is wished, as Virginia and Maryland have already done.*

"Adjourned.

"WEDNESDAY, AUG. 22.

"*In Convention.*—Art. 7, Sect. 4, was resumed.

"Mr. Sherman was for leaving the clause as it stands. He disapproved of the slave-trade; yet, as the States were now possessed of the right to import slaves, as the public good did not require it to be taken from them, and as it was expedient to have as few objections as possible to the proposed scheme of government, he thought it best to leave the matter as we find it. ... He urged on the Convention the necessity of despatching its business.

"Col. Mason. This infernal traffic originated in the avarice of British merchants. The British Government constantly checked the attempts of Virginia to put a stop to it. The present question concerns, not the importing States alone, but the whole Union. The evil of having slaves was experienced during the late war. Had slaves been treated as they might have been by the enemy, they would have proved dangerous instruments in their hands. But their folly dealt by the slaves as it did by the Tories. He mentioned the dangerous insurrections of the slaves in Greece and Sicily, and the instructions given by Cromwell to the commissioners sent to Virginia,—to arm the servants and slaves, in case other means of obtaining its submission should fail. Maryland and Virginia, he said, had already prohibited the importation of slaves expressly. North Carolina had done the same in substance. All this would be in vain, if South Carolina and Georgia be at liberty to import. The Western people are already calling out for slaves for their new lands; and will fill that country with slaves, if they can be got through South Carolina and Georgia. Slavery discourages arts and manufactures. The poor despise labor when performed by slaves. They prevent the emigration of whites, who really enrich and strengthen a country. They produce the most pernicious effect on manners. Every master of slaves is born a petty tyrant. They bring the judgment of heaven on a country. As nations cannot be rewarded or punished in the next world, they must be in this. By an inevitable chain of causes and effects, Providence punishes national sins by national calamities. He lamented that some of our Eastern brethren had, from a lust of gain, embarked in this nefarious traffic. As to the States being in possession of the right to import, this was the case with many other rights, now to be properly given up. He held it essential, in every point of view, that the General Government should have power to prevent the increase of slavery.

"Mr. Ellsworth, as he had never owned a slave, could not judge of the effects of slavery on character. He said, however, that, if it was to be considered in a moral light, we ought to go further, and free those already in the country. As slaves also multiply so fast in Virginia and Maryland, that it is cheaper to raise than import them, whilst in the sickly rice-swamps foreign supplies are necessary, if we go no further than is urged, we shall be unjust towards South Carolina and Georgia. Let us not intermeddle. As population increases, poor laborers will be so plenty as to render slaves useless. *Slavery, in time, will not be a speck in our county.* Provision is already made in Connecticut for abolishing it; and the abolition has already taken place in Massachusetts. As to the danger of insurrections from foreign influence, that will become a motive to kind treatment of the slaves.

"Gen. Pinckney declared it to be his firm opinion, that if himself and all his colleagues were to sign the Constitution, and use their personal influence, it would be of no avail towards obtaining the assent of their constituents. South Carolina and Georgia cannot do without slaves. As to Virginia, she will gain more by stopping the importations. Her slaves will rise in value, and she has more than she wants. It would be unequal to require South Carolina and Georgia to confederate on such unequal terms. He said, the royal assent, before the Revolution, had never been refused to South Carolina as to Virginia. He contended, that the importation of slaves would be for the interest of the whole Union. The more slaves, the more produce to employ the carrying-trade: the more consumption also; and, the more of this, the more revenue for the common treasury. He admitted it to be reasonable, that slaves should be dutied like other imports; but should consider a rejection of the clause as an exclusion of South Carolina from the Union.

"Mr. Baldwin had conceived national objects alone to be before the Convention: not such as, like the present, were of a local nature. Georgia was decided on this point. That State has always hitherto supposed a General Government to be the pursuit of the Central States, who wished to have a vortex for every thing; that her distance would preclude her from equal advantage; and that she could not prudently purchase it by yielding national powers. From this it might be understood in what light she would view an attempt to abridge one of her favorite prerogatives. If left to herself, she may probably put a stop to the evil. As one ground for this conjecture, he took notice of the sect of — —, which, he said, was a respectable class of people, who carried their ethics beyond the mere equality of men,—extending their humanity to the claims of the whole animal creation.

"Mr. Wilson observed, that, *if South Carolina and Georgia were themselves disposed to get rid of the importation of slaves in a short time, as had been suggested, they would never refuse to unite because the importation might be prohibited.* As the section now stands, all articles imported are to be taxed. Slaves alone are exempt. This is, in fact, a bounty on that article.

"Mr. Gerry thought we had nothing to do with the conduct of the States as to slaves, but ought to be careful not to give any sanction to it.

"Mr. Dickinson considered it as inadmissible, on every principle of honor and safety, that the importation of slaves should be authorized to the States by the Constitution. The true question was, whether the national happiness would be promoted or impeded by the importation; and this question ought to be left to the National Government, not to the States particularly interested. If England and France permit slavery, slaves are, at the same time, excluded from both those kingdoms. Greece and Rome were made unhappy by their slaves. He could not believe that the Southern States would refuse to confederate on the account apprehended; especially as the power was not likely to be immediately exercised by the General Government.

"Mr. Williamson stated the law of North Carolina on the subject; to wit, that it did not directly prohibit the importation of slaves. It imposed a duty of £5 on each slave imported from Africa, £10 on each from elsewhere, and £50 on each from a State licensing manumission. He thought the Southern States could not be members of the Union, if the clause should be rejected: and it was wrong to force any thing down not absolutely necessary, and which any State must disagree to.

"Mr. King thought the subject should be considered in a political light only. If two States will not agree to the Constitution, as stated on one side, he could affirm with equal belief, on the other, that great and equal opposition would be experienced from the other States. He remarked on the exemption of slaves from duty, whilst every other import was subjected to it, as an inequality that could not fail to strike the commercial sagacity of the Northern and Middle States.

"Mr. Langdon was strenuous for giving the power to the General Government. He could not, with a good conscience, leave it with the States, who could then go on with the traffic, without being restrained by the opinions here given, *that they will themselves cease to import slaves.*

"Gen. Pinckney thought himself bound to declare candidly, that he did not think South Carolina would stop her importations of slaves in any short time; but only stop them occasionally, as she now does. He moved to commit the clause, that slaves might be made liable to an equal tax with other imports, which he thought right, and which would remove one difficulty that had been started.

"Mr. Rutledge. If the Convention thinks that North Carolina, South Carolina, and Georgia will ever agree to the plan, unless their right to import slaves be untouched, the expectation is vain. The people of those States will never be such fools as to give up so important an interest. He was strenuous against striking out the section, and seconded the motion of Gen. Pinckney for a commitment.

"Mr. Gouverneur Morris wished the whole subject to be committed, including the clauses relating to taxes on export and to a navigation act. These things may form a bargain among the Northern and Southern States.

"Mr. Butler declared, that he never would agree to the power of taxing exports.

"Mr. Sherman said it was better to let the Southern States import slaves than to part with them, if they made that a *sine qua non*. He was opposed to a tax on slaves imported, as making the matter worse, because it implied they were *property*. He acknowledged, that, if the power of prohibiting the importation should be given to the General Government, it would be exercised. He thought it would be its duty to exercise the power.

'Mr. Read was for the commitment, provided the clause concerning taxes on exports should also be committed.

"Mr. Sherman observed, that that clause had been agreed to, and therefore could not be committed.

> "Mr. Randolph was for committing, in order that some middle ground might, if possible, be found. He could never agree to the clause as it stands. He would sooner risk the Constitution. He dwelt on the dilemma to which the Convention was exposed. By agreeing to the clause, it would revolt the Quakers, the Methodists, and many others in the States having no slaves. On the other hand, two States might be lost to the Union. Let us then, he said, try the chance of a commitment."[631]

Three days later (Saturday, Aug. 25) the debate on the subject was resumed, and the report of the committee of eleven was taken up. It was in the following words:—

"Strike out so much of the fourth section as was referred to the Committee, and insert 'The migration or importation of such persons as the several States, now existing, think proper to admit, shall not be prohibited by the Legislature prior to the year 1800; but a tax or duty may be imposed on such migration or importation, at a rate not exceeding the average of the duties laid on imports.'

"Gen. Pinckney moved to strike out the words 'the year eighteen hundred' as the year limiting the importation of slaves, and to insert the words 'the year eighteen hundred and eight.'

"Mr. Gorham seconded the motion.

> "Mr. Madison. Twenty years will produce all the mischief that can be apprehended from the liberty to import slaves. So long a term will be more dishonorable to the American character than to say nothing about it in the Constitution.

"On the motion, which passed in the affirmative, —

"New Hampshire, Massachusetts, Connecticut, Maryland, North Carolina, South Carolina, Georgia, ay, —7, New Jersey, Pennsylvania, Delaware, Virginia, no, —4.

"Mr. Gouvernour Morris was for making the clause read at once, —

"The importation of slaves into North Carolina, South Carolina, and Georgia, shall not be prohibited,' &c. This, he said, would be most fair, and would avoid the ambiguity by which, under the power with regard to naturalization, the liberty reserved to the States might be defeated. He wished it to be known, also, that this part of the Constitution was a compliance with those States. If the change of language, however, should be objected to by the members from those States, he should not urge it.

"Col. Mason was not against using the term 'slaves,' but against naming North Carolina, South Carolina, and Georgia, lest it should give offence to the people of those States.

"Mr. Sherman liked a description better than the terms proposed, which had been declined by the old Congress, and were not pleasing to some people.

"Mr. Clymer concurred with Mr. Sherman.

"Mr. Williamson said, that, both in opinion and practice, he was against slavery; but thought it more in favor of humanity, from a view of all circumstances, to let in South Carolina and Georgia on those terms, than to exclude them from the Union.

"Mr. Gouverneur Morris withdrew his motion.

"Mr. Dickinson wished the clause to be confined to the States which had not themselves prohibited the importation of slaves; and, for that purpose, moved to amend the clause so as to read.—

"'The importation of slaves into such of the States as shall permit the same shall not be prohibited by the Legislature of the United States until the year 1808;'—

"which was disagreed to, *nem. con.*

"The first part of the Report was then agreed to, amended as follows:—

"'The migration or importation of such persons as the several States now existing shall think proper to admit shall not be prohibited by the Legislature prior to the year 1808.'

> "New Hampshire, Massachusetts, Connecticut, Maryland, North Carolina, South Carolina, Georgia, ay,—7; New Jersey, Pennsylvania, Delaware, Virginia, no,—4."[632]

The above specimens of the speeches on the slavery question, during the debate, are sufficient to furnish a fair idea of the personal opinion of the great thinkers of that time on slavery. It is clear that it was the wish of the great majority of the Northern delegates to abolish the institution, in a domestic as well as in a foreign sense; but they were not strong enough to resist the temptation to compromise their profoundest convictions on a question as broad and far-reaching as the Union that they were met to launch anew. Thus by an understanding, or, as Gouverneur Morris called it, "a bargain," between the commercial representatives of the Northern States and the delegates of South Carolina and Georgia, and in spite of the opposition of Maryland and Virginia, the unrestricted power of Congress to enact navigation-laws was conceded to the Northern merchants; and to the Carolina rice-planters, as an equivalent, twenty years' continuance of the African slave-trade. This was the third great "compromise" of the Constitution. The other two were the concession to the smaller States of an equal representation in the Senate; and, to the slaveholders, the counting three-fifths of the slaves in determining the ratio of representation. If this third compromise differed from the other two by involving not merely a political but a moral sacrifice, there was this partial compensation about it, that it was not permanent like the others, but expired, by limitation, at the end of twenty years.[633]

The Constitution was adopted by the Convention, and signed, on the 17th of September, 1787. It was then forwarded to Congress, then in session in New-York City, with the recommendation that that body submit it to the State conventions for ratification; which was accordingly done. Delaware adopted it on the 7th of December, 1787; Pennsylvania, Dec. 12; New Jersey, Dec. 18; Georgia, Jan. 2, 1788; Connecticut, Jan. 9; Massachusetts, Feb. 7; Maryland, April 28; South Carolina, May 23; New Hampshire, June 21 (and, being the ninth ratifying, gave effect to the Constitution); Virginia ratified June 27; New York, July 26. North Carolina gave a conditional ratification on the 7th of August, but Congress did not receive it until January, 1790; nor that of Rhode Island, until June of the same year.

At the conclusion of the deliberations of the convention that framed the Constitution, it was voted that its journal be intrusted to the custody of George Washington. He finally deposited it in the State Department, and it was printed in 1818 by order of Congress.

The first session of Congress, under the new Constitution, was held in the city of New York, in 1789. A quorum was obtained on the 6th of April; and the first measure brought up for consideration was a tariff-bill which Mr. Parker of Virginia sought to amend by inserting a clause levying an impost-tax of ten dollars upon every slave brought by water. "He was sorry the Constitution prevented Congress from prohibiting the importation altogether. It was contrary to revolution principles, and ought not to be permitted." Thus the question of slavery made its appearance early at the first session of the first Congress under the present Constitution. At that time Georgia was the only State in the Union that seemed to retain a pecuniary interest in the importation of slaves. Even South Carolina had passed an Act prohibiting for one year the importation of slaves. In this, as on several occasions before, she was actuated on account of the low prices of produce,—too low to be remunerative. But, notwithstanding this, Mr. Smith, the member from the Charleston district, grew quite captious over the proposition of the gentleman from Virginia. He

'Hoped that such an important and serious proposition would not be hastily adopted. It was rather a late moment for the first introduction of a subject so big with serious consequences. No one topic had been yet introduced so important to South Carolina and the welfare of the Union."

Mr. Sherman got the floor, and said he

"Approved the object of the motion, but did not think it a fit subject to be embraced in this bill. He could not reconcile himself to the insertion of human beings, as a subject of impost, among goods, wares, and merchandise. He hoped the motion would be withdrawn for the present, and taken up afterwards as an independent subject."

Mr. Jackson of Georgia

"Was not surprised, however others might be so, at the quarter whence this motion came. Virginia, as an old settled State, had her complement of slaves, and the natural increase being sufficient for her purpose, she was careless of recruiting her numbers by importation. But gentlemen ought to let their neighbors get supplied before they imposed such a burden. He knew this business was viewed in an odious light at the Eastward, because the people there were capable of doing their own work, and had no occasion for slaves. But gentlemen ought to have some feeling for others. Surely they do not mean to tax us for every comfort and enjoyment of life, and, at the same time, to take from us the means of procuring them! He was sure, from the unsuitableness of the motion to the business now before the house, and the want of time to consider it, the gentleman's candor would induce him to withdraw it. Should it ever be brought forward again, he hoped it would comprehend the white slaves as well as the black, imported from all the jails of Europe; wretches convicted of the most flagrant crimes, who were brought in and sold without any duty whatever. They ought to be taxed equally with Africans, and he had no doubt of the equal constitutionality and propriety of such a course."

Mr. Parker of Virginia obtained the floor again, and proceeded to reply to the remarks offered upon his amendment by Sherman, Jackson, and Smith. He declared,—

"That, having introduced the motion on mature reflection, he did not like to withdraw it. The gentleman from Connecticut had said that human beings ought not to be enumerated with goods, wares, and merchandise. Yet he believed they were looked upon by African traders in that light. He hoped Congress would do all in their power to restore to human nature its inherent privileges; to wipe off, if possible, the stigma under which America labored; to do away with the inconsistence in our principles justly charged upon us; and to show, by our actions, the pure beneficence of the doctrine held out to the world in our Declaration of Independence."

Mr. Ames of Massachusetts

"Detested slavery from his soul; but he had some doubts whether imposing a duty on their importation would not have an appearance of countenancing the practice."

Mr. Madison made an eloquent speech in support of Mr. Parker's amendment. He said,—

"The confounding men with merchandise might be easily avoided by altering the title of the bill; it was, in fact, the very object of the motion to prevent men, so far as the power of Congress extended, from being confounded with merchandise. The clause in the Constitution allowing a tax to be imposed, though the traffic could not be prohibited for twenty years, was inserted, he believed, for the very purpose of enabling Congress to give some testimony of the sense of America with respect to the African trade. By expressing a national disapprobation of that trade, it is to be hoped we may destroy it, and so save ourselves from reproaches, and our posterity from the imbecility ever attendant on a country filled with slaves. This was as much the interest of South Carolina and Georgia as of any other States. Every addition they received to their number of slaves tended to weakness, and rendered them less capable of self-defence. In case of hostilities with foreign nations, their slave population would be a means, not of repelling invasions, but of inviting attack. It was the duty of the general government to protect every part of the Union against danger, as well internal as external. Every thing, therefore, which tended to increase this danger, though it might be a local affair, yet, if it involved national expense or safety, became of concern to every part of the Union, and a proper subject for the consideration of those charged with the general administration of the government."

Mr. Bland approved the position taken by Mr. Madison, while Mr. Burke of South Carolina charged the gentlemen with having wasted the time of Congress upon a useless proposition. He contended, that, while slaves were not mentioned in the Constitution, they would come under the general five per cent *ad valorem* duty on all unenumerated articles, which would be equivalent to the proposition of the gentleman from Virginia. Mr. Madison replied by saying, that no collector of customs would presume to apply the terms "goods," "wares," and "merchandise" to persons. Mr. Sherman followed him in the same strain, and denied that persons were anywhere recognised as property in the Constitution. Finally, at the suggestion of Mr. Madison, Mr. Parker consented to withdraw his motion with the understanding that a separate bill should be brought in. A committee was appointed to discharge that duty, but the noble resolve found a quiet grave in the committee-room.

The failure of this first attempt, under the new Constitution, to restrict slavery, did not lame the cause to any great extent. It was rather accelerated. The manner and spirit of the debate on the subject quickened public thought, animated the friends of the Negro, and provoked many people to good works. Slavery had ceased to exist in Massachusetts. Several suits, entered by slaves against their masters for restraining their liberty, had been won. The case of Elizabeth Freeman, better known as "Mum Bet," was regarded as the first-fruits of the Massachusetts Declaration of Rights in the new Constitution of 1780. The Duke de la Rochefoucault Laincort gives the following interesting account of the extinction of slavery in Massachusetts: —

> "In 1781, some negroes, prompted by private suggestion, maintained that they were not slaves: they found advocates, among whom was Mr. Sedgwick, now a member of the Senate of the United States; and the cause was carried before the Supreme Court. Their counsel pleaded, 1°. That no antecedent law had established slavery, and that the laws which seemed to suppose it were the offspring of error in the legislators, who had no authority to enact them; —2°, That such laws, even if they had existed, were annulled by the new Constitution. They gained the cause under both aspects: and the solution of this first question that was brought forward set the negroes entirely at liberty, and at the same time precluded their pretended owners from all claim to indemnification, since they were proved to have possessed and held them in slavery without any right. As there were only a few slaves in Massachusetts, the decision passed without opposition, and banished all further idea of slavery."[634]

Mr. Nell gives an account of the legal death of slavery in Massachusetts, but unfortunately does not cite any authority. John Quincey Adams, in reply to a question put by John C. Spencer, stated that, "a note had been given for the price of a slave in 1787. This note was sued, and the Court ruled that the maker had received no consideration, as a man could not be sold. From that time forward, slavery died in the Old Bay State." There were several suits instituted by slaves against their reputed masters in 1781-82; but there are strong evidences that slavery died a much slower death in Massachusetts than many are willing to admit. James Sullivan wrote to Dr. Belknap in 1795: —

> "In 1781, at the Court in Worcester County, an indictment was found against a white man named Jennison for assaulting,

beating, and imprisoning Quock Walker, a black. He was tried at the Supreme Judicial Court in 1783. His defence was, that the black was his slave, and that the beating, etc., was the necessary restraint and correction of the master. This was answered by citing the aforesaid clause in the declaration of rights. The judges and jury were of opinion that he had no right to imprison or beat the negro. He was found guilty and fined 40 shillings. This decision put an end to the idea of slavery in Massachusetts."[635]

There are two things in the above that throw considerable uncertainty about the subject as to the precise date of the end of slavery in the Commonwealth. First, the suit referred to was tried in 1783, three years after the adoption of the new Constitution. Second, the good doctor does not say that the decision sealed the fate of slavery, but only that it "was a mortal wound to slavery in Massachusetts."

From 1785-1790, there was a wonderful change in the public opinion of the Middle and Eastern States on the subject of slavery. Most of them had passed laws providing for gradual emancipation. The Friends of New York, New Jersey, and Pennsylvania began to organize a crusade against domestic slavery. In the fall of 1789, while the Congressional debates were still fresh in the minds of the people, the venerable Dr. Benjamin Franklin, as president of the "Pennsylvania Society for Promoting the Abolition of Slavery," etc., issued the following letter:—

"AN ADDRESS TO THE PUBLIC.

From the Pennsylvania Society for Promoting the Abolition of Slavery, and the Relief of Free Negroes unlawfully held in Bondage.

It is with peculiar satisfaction we assure, the friends of humanity, that, in prosecuting the design of our association, our endeavors have proved successful, far beyond our most sanguine expectations.

"Encouraged by this success, and by the daily progress of that luminous and benign spirit of liberty which is diffusing itself throughout the world, and humbly hoping for the continuance of the divine blessing on our labors, we have ventured to make an important addition to our original plan; and do therefore earnestly solicit the support and assistance of all who can feel the tender emotions of sympathy and compassion, or relish the exalted pleasure of beneficence.

"Slavery is such an atrocious debasement of human nature, that its very extirpation, if not performed with solicitous care, may sometimes open a source of serious evils.

"The unhappy man, who has long been treated as a brute animal, too frequently sinks beneath the common standard of the human species. The galling chains that bind his body do also fetter his intellectual faculties, and impair the social affections of his heart. Accustomed to move like a mere machine, by the will of a master, reflection is suspended; he has not the power of choice; and reason and conscience have but little influence over his conduct, because he is chiefly governed by the passion of fear. He is poor and friendless; perhaps worn out by extreme labor, age, and disease.

"Under such circumstances, freedom may often prove a misfortune to himself, and prejudicial to society.

"Attention to emancipated black people, it is therefore to be hoped, will become a branch of our national police; but, as far as we contribute to promote this emancipation, so far that attention is evidently a serious duty incumbent on us, and which we mean to discharge to the best of our judgement and abilities.

"To instruct, to advise, to qualify those who have been restored to freedom, for the exercise and enjoyment of civil liberty; to promote in them habits of industry; to furnish them with employments suited to their age, sex, talents, and other circumstances; and to procure their children an education calculated for their future situation in life,—these are the great outlines of the annexed plan which we have adopted, and which we conceive will essentially promote the public good, and the happiness of these our hitherto too much neglected fellow-creatures.

"A plan so extensive cannot be carried into execution without considerable pecuniary resources, beyond the present ordinary funds of the Society. We hope much from the generosity of enlightened and benevolent freemen, and will gratefully receive any donations or subscriptions for this purpose which may be made to our Treasurer, James Starr, or to James Pemberton, Chairman of our Committee of Correspondence.

"Signed by order of the Society,

"B. Franklin, President.

"Philadelphia, 9th of November, 1789."

And as his last public act, Franklin gave his signature to the subjoined memorial to the United States Congress:—

"The memorial respectfully showeth,—

"That, from a regard for the happiness of mankind, an association was formed several years since in this State, by a number of her citizens, of various religious denominations, for promoting the abolition of slavery, and for the relief of those unlawfully held in bondage. A just and acute conception of the true principles of liberty, as it spread through the land, produced accessions to their numbers, many friends to their cause, and a legislative co-operation with their views, which, by the blessing of Divine Providence, have been successfully directed to the relieving from bondage a large number of their fellow-creatures of the African race. They have also the satisfaction to observe, that, in consequence of that spirit of philanthropy and genuine liberty which is generally diffusing its beneficial influence, similar institutions are forming at home and abroad.

"That mankind are all formed by the same Almighty Being, alike objects of his care, and equally designed for the enjoyment of happiness, the Christian religion teaches us to believe, and the political creed of Americans fully coincides with the position. Your memorialists, particularly engaged in attending to the distresses arising from slavery, believe it their indispensable duty to present this subject to your notice. They have observed, with real satisfaction, that many important and salutary powers are vested in you for 'promoting the welfare and securing the blessings of liberty to the people of the United States'; and as they conceive that these blessings ought rightfully to be administered, without distinction of color, to all descriptions of people, so they indulge themselves in the pleasing expectation, that nothing which can be done for the relief of the unhappy objects of their care, will be either omitted or delayed.

"From a persuasion that equal liberty was originally the portion, and is still the birth-right, of all men; and influenced by the strong ties of humanity, and the principles of their institution, your memorialists conceive themselves bound to use all justifiable endeavors to loosen the bands of slavery, and promote a general enjoyment of the blessings of freedom. Under these impressions, they earnestly entreat your serious attention to the subject of slavery; that you will be pleased to countenance the restoration of liberty to those unhappy men, who alone, in this land of freedom, are degraded into perpetual bondage, and who, amidst the general joy of surrounding freemen, are groaning in servile subjection; that you will devise means for removing this inconsistency from the character of the American people; that you will promote mercy and justice towards this distressed race; and that you will step to the very verge of the power vested in you for discouraging every species of traffic in the persons of our fellow-men.

"BENJ. FRANKLIN, PRESIDENT.

"PHILADELPHIA, FEBRUARY 3, 1790."

The session of Congress held in 1790 was stormy. The slavery question came back to haunt the members. On the 12th of February, the memorial from the Pennsylvania society was read. It provoked fresh discussion, and greatly angered many of the Southern members. As soon as its reading was completed, the "Quaker Memorial," that had been read the day previous, was called up; and Mr. Hartley moved its commitment. A long and spirited debate ensued. It was charged that the memorial was "a mischievous attempt, an improper interference, at the best, an act of imprudence;" and that it "would sound an alarm and blow the trumpet of sedition through the Southern States." Mr. Scott of Pennsylvania replied by saying, "I cannot entertain a doubt that the memorial is strictly agreeable to the Constitution. It respects a part of the duty particularly assigned to us by that instrument." Mr. Sherman was in favor of the commitment of the memorial, and gave his reasons in extenso. Mr. Smith of South Carolina said, "Notwithstanding all the calmness with which some gentlemen have viewed the subject, they will find that the mere discussion of it will create alarm. We have been told that, if so, we should have avoided discussion by saying nothing. But it was not for that purpose we were sent here. We look upon this measure as an attack upon property; it is, therefore, our duty to oppose it by every means in our power. When we entered into a political connection with the other States, this property was there. It had been acquired under a former government conformably to the laws and constitution, and every attempt to deprive us of it must be in the nature of an ex post facto law, and, as such, forbidden by our political compact." Following the unwise and undignified example set by the gentlemen who had preceded him on that side of the question, he slurred the Quakers. "His constituents wanted no lessons in religion and morality, and least of all from such teachers."

Madison, Gerry, Boudinot, and Page favored commitment. Upon the question to commit, the yeas and nays being demanded, the reference was made by a vote of forty-three to eleven. Of the latter, six were from Georgia and South Carolina, two from Virginia, two from Maryland, and one from New York. A special committee was announced, to whom the memorial was referred, consisting of one member from each of the following States: New Hampshire, Massachusetts, Connecticut, New York, New Jersey, Pennsylvania, and Virginia. At the end of a month, the committee made the following report to Congress:—

"1st. That the general government was expressly restrained, until the year 1808, from prohibiting the importation of any persons whom any of the existing states might till that time think proper to admit. 2d. That, by a fair construction of the constitution, congress was equally restrained from interfering to emancipate slaves within the states, such slaves having been born there, or having been imported within the period mentioned. 3d. That congress had no power to interfere in the internal regulation of particular states relative to the instruction of slaves in the principles of morality and religion, to their comfortable clothing, accommodation, and subsistence, to the regulation of marriages or the violation of marital rights, to the separation of children and parents, to a comfortable provision in cases of age or infirmity, or to the seizure, transportation, and sale of free negroes; but entertained the fullest confidence in the wisdom and humanity of the state legislature that, from time to time, they would revise their laws, and promote these and all other measures tending to the happiness of the slaves. The fourth asserted that congress had authority to levy a tax of ten dollars, should they see fit to exact it, upon every person imported under the special permission of any of the states. The fifth declared the authority of congress to interdict or to regulate the African slave-trade, so far as it might be carried on by citizens of the United States for the supply of foreign countries, and also to provide for the humane treatment of slaves while on their passage to any ports of the United States into which they might be admitted. The sixth asserted the right of congress to prohibit foreigners from fitting out vessels in the United States to be employed in the supply of foreign countries with slaves from Africa. The seventh expressed an intention on the part of congress to exercise their authority to its full extent to promote the humane objects aimed at in the Quaker's memorial."

Mr. Tucker took the floor against the report of the committee, and, after a bitter speech upon the unconstitutionality of meddling with the slavery question in any manner, moved a substitute for the whole, in which he pronounced the recommendations of the committee "as unconstitutional, and tending to injure some of the States of the Union." Mr. Jackson seconded the motion in a rather intemperate speech, which was replied to by Mr. Vining. The substitute of Mr. Tucker was declared out of order. Mr. Benson moved to recommit in hopes of getting rid of the subject, but the motion was overwhelmingly voted down. The report was taken up article by article. The three first resolutions (those relating to the authority of Congress over slavery in the States) were adopted; while the second and third were merged into one, stripped of its objectionable features. But on the fourth the debate was carried to a high pitch. This one related to the ten-dollar tax. Mr. Tucker moved to amend by striking out the fourth resolution.

Considerable discussion followed; and, upon the question being put, it was carried by one vote. The fifth resolution, affirming the power of Congress to regulate the slave-trade, drew the fire of Jackson, Smith, and Tucker. Mr. Madison offered to modify it somewhat. It was argued by the opponents of this resolution, that Congress, under the plea of regulating the trade, might prohibit it entirely. Mr. Vining of Delaware, somewhat out of patience with the demands of the Southern members, told those gentlemen very plainly that they ought to be satisfied with the changes already made to gratify them; that they should show some respect to the committee; that all the States from Virginia to New Hampshire had passed laws prohibiting the slave-trade; and then delivered an eloquent defence of the Quakers. The resolution, as modified by Mr. Madison, carried.

The sixth resolution, relating to the foreign slave-trade carried on from ports of the United States, received considerable attention. Mr. Scott made an elaborate speech upon it, in which he claimed, that, if it were a question as to the power of Congress to regulate the foreign slave-trade, he had no doubts as to the authority of that body. "I desire," said that gentleman, "that the world should know, I desire that those people in the gallery, about whom so much has been said, should know, that there is at least one member on this floor who believes that Congress have ample powers to do all they have asked respecting the African slave-trade. Nor do I doubt that Congress will, whenever necessity or policy dictates the measure, exercise those powers." Mr. Jackson attempted to reply. He started out with a labored argument showing the divine origin of slavery, quoting Scriptures; showed that the Greeks and Romans had held slaves, etc. He was followed and supported by Smith of South Carolina. Boudinot obtained the floor, and, after defending the Quakers and praising Franklin, declared that there was nothing unreasonable in the memorial; that it simply requested them "to go to the utmost verge of the Constitution," and not beyond it. Further debate was had, when the sixth resolution was adopted.

The seventh resolution, pledging Congress to exert their full powers for the restriction of the slave-trade—and, as some understood it, to discountenance slavery—was struck out. The committee then arose and reported the resolutions to the house. The next day, the 23d March, 1790, after some preliminary business was disposed of, a motion was made to take up the report of the committee. Ames, Madison, and others thought the matter, having occupied so much of the time of the house, should be left where it was; or rather, as Mr. Madison expressed it, simply entered on the Journals as a matter of public record. After some little discussion, this motion prevailed by a vote of twenty-nine to twenty-five. The entry was accordingly made as follows:—

"That the migration or importation of such persons as any of the states now existing shall think proper to admit, can not be prohibited by congress prior to the year 1808.

"That congress have no right to interfere in the emancipation of slaves, or in the treatment of them, in any of the states, it remaining with the several states alone to provide any regulations therein which humanity and true policy require.

"That congress have authority to restrain the citizens of the United States from carrying on the African slave-trade for the purpose of supplying foreigners with slaves, and of providing by proper regulations for the humane treatment, during their passage, of slaves imported by the said citizens into the said states admitting such importation.

"That congress have also authority to prohibit foreigners from fitting out vessels in any port of the United States for transporting persons from Africa to any foreign port."

The census of 1790 gave the slave population of the States as follows:—

SLAVE POPULATION.--CENSUS OF 1790.

State	Slaves
Connecticut	2,759
Delaware	8,887
Georgia	29,264
Kentucky	11,830
Maryland	103,036
New Hampshire	158
New Jersey	11,423
New York	21,324
North Carolina	100,572
Pennsylvania	3,737
Rhode Island	952
South Carolina	107,094
Vermont	17
Virginia	293,427

Territory south of Ohio   3,417

Aggregate, 697,897.

Vermont was admitted into the Union on the 18th of February, 1791; and the first article of the Bill of Rights declared that "no male person born in this country, or brought from over sea, ought to be bound by law to serve any person as a servant, slave, or apprentice after he arrives at the age of twenty-one years, nor female, in like manner, after she arrives at the age of twenty-one years, unless they are bound by their own consent after they arrive at such age, or are bound by law for the payment of debts, damages, fines, costs, or the like." This provision was contained in the first Constitution of that State, and, therefore, it was the first one to abolish and prohibit slavery in North America.

On the 4th of February, 1791, Kentucky was admitted into the Union by Act of Congress, though it had no Constitution. But the next year a Constitution was framed. By it the Legislature was denied the right to emancipate slaves without the consent of the owner, nor without paying the full price of the slaves before emancipating them; nor could any laws be passed prohibiting emigrants from other states from bringing with them persons deemed slaves by the laws of any other states in the Union, so long as such persons should be continued as slaves in Kentucky. The Legislature had power to prohibit the bringing into the state slaves for the purpose of sale. Masters were required to treat their slaves with humanity, to properly feed and clothe them, and to abstain from inflicting any punishment extending to life and limb. Laws could be passed granting owners the right to emancipate their slaves, but requiring security that the slaves thus emancipated should not become a charge upon the county.

During the session of Congress in 1791, the Pennsylvania Society for the Abolition of Slavery presented another memorial, calling upon Congress to exercise the powers they had been declared to possess by the report of the committee which had been spread upon the Journals of the house. Thus emboldened, other anti-slavery societies, of Rhode Island, Connecticut, New York, Virginia, and a few local societies of Maryland, presented memorials praying for the suppression of slavery in the United States. They were referred to a select committee; and, as they made no report, New Hampshire and Massachusetts, the next year, called the attention of Congress to the subject. On the 24th of November, 1792, a Mr. Warner Mifflin, an anti-slavery Quaker from Delaware, addressed a memorial to Congress on the general subject of slavery, which was read and laid upon the table without debate. On the 26th of November, Mr. Stute of North Carolina offered some sharp remarks upon the presumption of the Quaker, and moved that the petition be returned to the petitioner, and that the clerk be instructed to erase the entry from the Journal. This provoked a heated discussion; but at length the petition was returned to the author, and the motion to erase the record from the Journal was withdrawn by the mover.

In 1793 a law was passed providing for the return of fugitives from justice and from service, "In case of the escape out of any state or territory of any person held to service or labor under the laws thereof, the person to whom such labor was due, his agent, or attorney, might seize the fugitive and carry him before any United States judge, or before any magistrate of the city, town, or county in which the arrest was made; and such judge or magistrate, on proof to his satisfaction, either oral or by affidavit before any other magistrate, that the person seized was really a fugitive, and did owe labor as alleged, was to grant a certificate to that effect to the claimant, this certificate to serve as sufficient warrant for the removal of the fugitive to the state whence he had fled. Any person obstructing in any way such seizure or removal, or harboring or concealing any fugitive after notice, was liable to a penalty of $500, to be recovered by the claimant."

In 1794 an anti-slavery convention was held in Philadelphia, in which nearly all of the abolition societies of the country were represented. A memorial, carefully avoiding constitutional objections, was drawn and addressed to Congress to do whatever they could toward the suppression of the slave-trade. This memorial, with several other petitions, was referred to a special committee. In due time they reported a bill, which passed without much opposition. It was the first act of the government toward repressing the slave-trade, and was as mild as a summer's day. On Wednesday, the 7th of January, 1795, another meeting was held in Philadelphia, the second, to consider anti-slavery measures. The Act of Congress was read.

> "*An Act to prohibit the carrying on the Slave-trade from the United States to any foreign place or country.*
>
> "Section I. BE it enacted by the Senate and House of Representatives of the United States of America, in Congress assembled, That no citizen or citizens of the United States, or foreigner, or any other person coming into, or residing within the same, shall, for himself or any other person whatsoever, either as master, factor or owner, build, fit, equip, load or otherwise prepare any ship or vessel, within any port or place of the said United States, nor shall cause any ship or vessel to sail from any port or place within the same, for the

purpose of carrying on any trade or traffic in slaves, to any foreign country; or for the purpose of procuring, from any foreign kingdom, place or country, the inhabitants of such kingdom, place or country, to be transported to any foreign country, port or place whatever, to be sold or disposed of, as slaves: And if any ship or vessel shall be so fitted out, as aforesaid, for the said purposes, or shall be caused to sail, so as aforesaid, every such ship or vessel, her tackle, furniture, apparel and other appurtenances, shall be forfeited to the United States; and shall be liable to be seized, prosecuted and condemned, in any of the circuit courts or district court for the district, where the said ship or vessel may be found and seized.

"Section II. *And be it further enacted*, That all and every person, so building, fitting out, equipping, loading, or otherwise preparing, or sending away, any ship or vessel, knowing, or intending, that the same shall be employed in such trade or business, contrary to the true intent and meaning of this act, or any ways aiding or abetting therein, shall severally forfeit and pay the sum of two thousand dollars, one moiety thereof, to the use of the United States, and the other moiety thereof, to the use of him or her, who shall sue for and prosecute the same.

"Section III. *And be it further enacted*, That the owner, master or factor of each and every foreign ship or vessel, clearing out for any of the coasts or kingdoms of Africa, or suspected to be intended for the slave-trade, and the suspicion being declared to the officer of the customs, by any citizen, on oath or affirmation, and such information being to the satisfaction of the said officer, shall first give bond with sufficient sureties, to the Treasurer of the United States, that none of the natives of Africa, or any other foreign country or place, shall be taken on board the said ship or vessel, to be transported, or sold as slaves, in any other foreign port or place whatever, within nine months thereafter.

"Section IV. *And be it further enacted*, That if any citizen or citizens of the United States shall, contrary to the true intent and meaning of this act, take on board, receive or transport any such persons, as above described, in this act, for the purpose of selling them as slaves, as aforesaid, he or they shall forfeit and pay, for each and every person, so received on board, transported, or sold as aforesaid, the sum of two hundred dollars, to be recovered in any court of the United States proper to try the same; the one moiety thereof, to the use of the United States, and the other moiety to the use of such person or persons, who shall sue for and prosecute the same.

"Frederick Augustus Muhlenberg,

Speaker of the House of Representatives.

"John Adams,

Vice-President of the United States, and
President of the Senate.

"Approved—March the twenty-second, 1794.

Go: Washington, President of the United States."

In 1797 Congress again found themselves confronted by the dark problem of slavery, that would not down at their bidding. The Yearly Meeting of the Quakers of Philadelphia sent a memorial to Congress, complaining that about one hundred and thirty-four Negroes, and others whom they knew not of, having been lawfully emancipated, were afterwards reduced to bondage by an ex post facto law passed by North Carolina, in 1777, for that cruel purpose. After considerable debate, the memorial went to a committee, who subsequently reported that the matter complained of was purely of judicial cognizance, and that Congress had no authority in the premises.

During the same session a bill was introduced creating all that portion of the late British Province of West Florida, within the jurisdiction of the United States, into a government to be called the Mississippi Territory. It was to be conducted in all respects like the territory north-west of the Ohio, with the single exception that slavery should not be prohibited. During the discussion of this section of the bill, Mr. Thatcher of Massachusetts moved to amend by striking out the exception as to slavery, so as to make it conform to the ideas expressed by Mr. Jefferson a few years before in reference to the Western Territory. But, after a warm debate, Mr. Thatcher's motion was lost, having received only twelve votes. An amendment of Mr. Harper of South Carolina, offered a few days later, prohibiting the introduction of slaves into the new Mississippi Territory, from without the limits of the United States, carried without opposition.

Georgia revised her Constitution in 1798, and prohibited the importation of slaves "from Africa or any foreign place." Her slave-code was greatly moderated. Any person maliciously killing or dismembering a slave was to suffer the same punishment as if the act had been committed upon a free white person, except in case of insurrection, or "unless such death should happen by accident, in giving such slave moderate correction." But, like

Kentucky, the Georgia constitution forbade the emancipation of slaves without the consent of the individual owner; and encouraged emigrants to bring slaves into the State.

In 1799, after three failures, the Legislature of New York passed a bill for the gradual extinction of slavery. It provided that all persons in slavery at the time of the passage of the bill should remain in bondage for life, but all their children, born after the fourth day of July next following, were to be free, but were required to remain under the direction of the owner of their parents, males until twenty-eight, and females until twenty-five. Exportation of slaves was disallowed; and if the attempt were made, and the parties apprehended, the slaves were to be free instanter. Persons moving into the State were not allowed to bring slaves, except they had owned them for a year previous to coming into the State.

In 1799 Kentucky revised her Constitution to meet the wants of a growing State. An attempt was made to secure a provision providing for gradual emancipation. It was supported by Henry Clay, who, as a young lawyer and promising orator, began on that occasion a brilliant political career that lasted for a half-century. But not even his magic eloquence could secure the passage of the humane amendment, and in regard to the question of slavery the Constitution received no change.

As the shadows gathered about the expiring days of the eighteenth century, it was clear to be seen that slavery, as an institution, had rooted itself into the political and legal life of the American Republic. An estate prolific of evil, fraught with danger to the new government, abhorred and rejected at first, was at length adopted with great political sagacity and deliberateness, and then guarded by the solemn forms of constitutional law and legislative enactments.

FOOTNOTES:

[627] St. Clair Papers, vol. i. p. 120.

[628] The clause "three fifths of all other persons" refers to Negro slaves. The Italics are our own. The Negro is referred to as person all through the Constitution.

[629] Madison Papers, Elliot, vol. v. pp. 392, 393.

[630] Ibid., vol. v pp. 391, 392.

[631] Madison Papers, Elliot, vol. v. pp. 457-461.

[632] Madison Papers, Elliot, vol. v. pp. 477, 478.

[633] Examine Hildreth and the Secret Debates on the subject of the "compromises."

[634] Travels, etc., vol. ii. p. 166.

[635] M.H.S. Coll., 5th Series, III., p. 403.

APPENDIX

Part I
PRELIMINARY CONSIDERATIONS.

CHAPTER I
THE UNITY OF MANKIND

In Acts xvii. 26 the apostle says, "And God hath made of one blood all nations of men to dwell on the face of the earth, and hath determined the times before appointed, and the bounds of their habitation." In Mark xvi. 15, 16, is recorded that remarkable command of our Saviour, "Go ye into all the world, and preach the gospel to every creature. He that believeth and is baptized shall be saved; but he that believeth not shall be damned." (See also Matt. xxviii. 18, 20.) Now there is a very close connection between the statement here made by the apostle, and the command here given by our Lord Jesus Christ; for it was in obedience to this command that the apostle was at that time at Athens. There, amid the proud and conceited philosophers of Greece, in the centre of their resplendent capital, surrounded on every hand by their noblest works of art and their proudest monuments of learning, the apostle proclaims the equality of all men, their common origin, guilt, and danger, and their universal obligations to receive and embrace the gospel. The Athenians, like other ancient nations, and like them, too, in opposition to their own mythology, regarded themselves as a peculiar and distinct race, created upon the very soil which they inhabited, and pre-eminently elevated above the barbarians of the earth,—as they regarded the other races of men. Paul, however, as an inspired and infallible teacher, authoritatively declares that "God who made the world and all things therein," "hath made of one blood," and caused to descend from one original pair the whole species of men, who are now by His providential direction so propagated as to inhabit "all the face of the earth," having marked out in his eternal and unerring counsel the determinate periods for their inhabiting, and the boundaries of the regions they should inhabit.

The apostle in this passage refers very evidently to the record of the early colonization and settling of the earth contained in the books of Moses.

Some Greek copies preserve only the word ενος, leaving out αιματος, a reading which the vulgar Latin follows. The Arabic version, to explain both, has ex homine, or as De Dieu renders it, ex Adamo uno, there being but the difference of one letter in the Eastern languages between dam and adam, the one denoting blood, and the other man. But if we take this passage as our more ordinary copies read it, εξενος αιματος, it is still equally plain that the meaning is not that all mankind were made of the same uniform matter, as the author of the work styled Pre-Adamites weakly imagined, for on that ground, not only mankind, but the whole world might be said to be ex henos haimatos, i.e., of the same blood, since all things in the world were at first formed out of the same matter. The word αιμα therefore must be here rendered in the same sense as that in which it occurs in the best Greek authors—the stock out of which men come Thus Homer says,—

"Ετ ετεου γ εμος εστι και αιματος ημετεροιο."

In like manner those who are near relations, are called by Sophocles οι προς αιματος. And hence the term *consanguinity*, employed to denote nearness of relation. Virgil uses *sanguis* in the same sense.

"*Trojano a sanguine duci.*"

So that the apostle's meaning is, that however men now are dispersed in their habitations, and however much they differ in language and customs from each other, yet they were all originally of the same stock, and derived their succession from the first man whom God created, that is, from Adam, from which name the Hebrew word for blood—i.e.—*dam*—is a derivative.

Neither can it be conceived on what account Adam in the Scripture is called "the first man," and said to be "made a living soul," and "of the earth earthy," unless it is to denote that he was absolutely the first of his kind, and was, therefore, designed to be the standard and measure of all the races of men. And thus when our Saviour would trace up all things to the beginning, he illustrates his doctrine by quoting those words which were pronounced after Eve was formed. "But from the beginning of the creation, God made them male and female, for this cause shall a man leave father and mother and cleave unto his wife" Now nothing can be more plain and incontrovertible than that those of whom these words were spoken, were the first male and female which were made in "the beginning of the creation." It is equally evident that these words were spoken of Adam and Eve for "Adam said, This is now bone of my bone, and flesh of my flesh; therefore shall a man leave his father and his mother, and shall cleave unto his wife" If the Scriptures then of the New Testament be true, it is most plain and evident that all mankind are descended from Adam.[636]

THE CURSE OF CANAAN

It is not necessary—nay, it is not admissible—to take the words of Noah, as to Shem and Japheth, as prophetic We shall presently see that, as prophetic, they have failed. Let us not, in expounding Scripture, introduce the supernatural when the natural is adequate. Noah had now known the peculiarities of his sons long enough, and well enough, to be able to make some probable conjecture as to their future course, and then success or failure in life. It is what parents do now a-days. They say of one son, He will succeed,—he is so dutiful, so economical, so industrious. They say of another, This one will make a good lawyer—he is so sharp in an argument. Of another, they say, We will educate him for the ministry, for he has suitable qualifications While of another they may be constrained to predict that he will not succeed, because he is indolent, and selfish, and sensual. Does it require special inspiration for a father, having ordinary common sense, to discover the peculiar talents and dispositions of his children, and to predict the probable future of each of them? Some times they hit it sometimes they miss it. Shall it not be conceded to Noah that he could make as probable a conjecture, as to his sons, as your father made as to you, or as you think yourselves competent to make for either of your sons? Noah made a good hit. What he said as to the future of his sons, and of their posterity, has turned out, in some respects, as he said it would, but not exactly,—not so exactly as to authorize our calling his words an inspired prophecy, as we shall presently show.

But, if we set out to establish or to justify slavery upon these words of Noah, on the assumption God *spake* by Noah as to the curse and blessings here recorded, we have a right to expect to find the facts of history to correspond. If the facts of history do not correspond with these words of Noah, then God did not speak them by Noah as his own. Let us face this matter. It is said, by those who interpret the curse of Canaan as divine authority for slavery, that God *has hereby ordained that the descendants of Ham shall be slaves*. The descendants of Shem are not, of course, doomed to that curse. Now, upon the supposition that these are the words of God, and not the denunciations of an irritated father just awaking from his drunkenness, we ought not to find any of *Canaan's descendants out of a condition of slavery, nor any of the descendants of Shem in it*. If we do, then either these are not God's words, or God's words have not come true.

But it is a fact that not all of Ham's entire descendants, nor even of Canaan's descendants (on whom alone, and not at all on Ham, nor on his three other sons, Noah's curse fell), are now, nor ever have been, as a whole, in a state of bondage. The Canaanites were not slaves, but free and powerful tribes, when the Hebrews entered their territory. The Carthaginians, it is generally admitted, were descended from Canaan. They certainly were free and powerful when, in frequent wars, they contended, often with success, against the formidable Romans. If the curse of Noah was intended for all the descendants of Ham, it signally failed in the case of the first military hero mentioned in the Bible, who was the founder of a world-renowned city and empire. I refer to Nimrod, who was a son of Cush, the oldest son of Ham. Of this Nimrod the record is, "He began to be a mighty one in the earth: he was a mighty hunter before the Lord: and the beginning of his Kingdom was Babel, and Erech, and Accad, and Calneh, in the land of Shinar. Out of that land went forth Asshur and builded Nineveh, and the city Rehoboth, and Calah, and Resen, between Nineveh and Calah; the same is a great city." This is Bible authority, informing us that the grandson of Ham (Nimrod, the son of Cush) was a mighty man—the great man of the world, in his day—the founder of the Babylonian empire, and the ancestor of the founder of the city of Nineveh, one of the grandest cities of the ancient world. We are not led to conclude, from these wonderful achievements by the posterity of Cush (who was the progenitor of the Negroes), that this line of Ham's descendants was so weak in intellect as to be unable to set up and maintain a government.[637]

FOOTNOTES

[636] The Unity of the Human Races, pp. 14-17.

[637] Curse of Canaan, pp. 5-7. By Rev. C.H. Edgar.

CHAPTER III-NEGRO CIVILIZATION

Dr. Wiseman has also shown that both Aristotle and Herodotus describe the Egyptians—to whom Homer, Lycurgus, Solon, Pythagoras, and Plato resorted for wisdom—as having the black skin, the crooked legs, the distorted feet and the woolly hair of the Negro, from which we do not wish, or feel it necessary to infer that the Egyptians were Negroes, but first that the ideas of degradation and not-human, associated with the dark-colored African races of people now, were not attached to them at an early period of their history; and secondly, that while depicted as Negroes, the Egyptians were regarded by these profound ancients—the one a naturalist and the other a historian—as one of the branches of the human family, and as identified with a nation of whose descent from Ham there is no question. [638] Egyptian antiquity, not claiming priority of social existence for itself, often pointed to the regions of Habesh, or high African Ethiopia, and sometimes to the North, for the seat of the gods and demigods, because both were the intermediate stations of the progenitor tribes.[639]

There is, therefore, every reason to believe that the primitive Egyptians were conformed much more to the African than to the European form and physiognomy, and therefore that there was a time when learning, commerce, arts, manufactures, etc., were all associated with a form and character of the human race now regarded as the evidence only of degradation and barbarous ignorance.

But why question this fact when we can refer to the ancient and once glorious kingdoms of Meroe, Nubia, and Ethiopia, and to the prowess and skill of other ancient and interior African Nations? And among the existing nations of interior Africa, there is seen a manifold diversity as regards the blackest races. The characteristics of the most truly Negro race are not found in *all*, nor to the same degree in *many*.

Clapperton and other travellers among the Negro tribes of interior Africa, attest the superiority of the pure Negroes above the mixed races around them, in all moral characteristics, and describe also large and populous kingdoms with numerous towns, well cultivated fields, and various manufactures, such as weaving, dyeing, tanning, working in iron and other metals, and in pottery.[640]

From the facts we have adduced it seems to follow, that one of the earliest races of men of whose existence, civilization and physiognomy, we have any remaining proofs, were dark or black colored. "We must," says Prichard, "for the present look upon the black races as the aborigines of Kelænonesia, or Oceanica,—that is as the immemorial and primitive inhabitants. There is no reason to doubt that they were spread over the Austral island long before the same or the contiguous regions were approached by the Malayo-Polynesians. We cannot say definitely how far back this will carry us, but as the distant colonizations of the Polynesians probably happened before the island of Java received arts and civilization from Hindustan, it must be supposed to have preceded by some ages the Javan era of Batara Guru, and therefore to have happened before the Christian era."

The Negro race is known to have existed 3,345 years, says Dr. Morton, 268 years later than the earliest notice of the white race, of which we have distinct mention B.C. 2200. This makes the existence of a Negro race certain about 842 years after the flood, according to the Hebrew chronology, or 1650 years after the flood, according to the Septuagint chronology, which may very possibly have been the original Hebrew chronology. There is thus ample time given for the multiplication and diffusion of man over the earth, and for the formation—either by natural or supernatural causes, in combination with the anomalous and altogether extraordinary condition of the earth—of all the various races of men.

It is also apparent from the architecture, and other historical evidences of their character, that dark or black races, with more or less of the Negro physiognomy, were in the earliest period of their known history cultivated and intelligent, having kingdoms, arts, and manufactures. And Mr. Pickering assures us that there is no fact to show that Negro slavery is not of modern origin. The degradation of this race of men therefore, must be regarded as the result of external causes, and not of natural, inherent and original incapacity.[641]

FOOTNOTES:

[638] See Dr. Wiseman's Lectures on the connection between Science and Revealed Religion, Am. ed., pp. 95-98

[639] See Nat. Hist. Human Species p. 373.

[640] See British Encyclopædia, vol. ii. pp. 237, 238

[641] Tiedeman, on the Brain of the Negro, in the Phil. Trans., 1838, p. 497

CHAPTER VI-NEGRO TYPE

It has often been said that, independently of the woolly hair and the complexion of the Negroes, there are sufficient differences between them and the rest of mankind to mark them as a very peculiar tribe. This is true, and yet the principal differences are perhaps not so constant as many persons imagine. In our West Indian colonies very many Negroes, especially females, are seen, whose figures strike Europeans as remarkably beautiful. This would not be the case if they deviated much from the idea prevalent in Europe, or from the European standard of beauty. Yet the slaves in the colonies, particularly in those of England, were brought from the west coast of intertropical Africa, where the peculiarities of figure, which in our eyes constitute deformity in the Negro, are chiefly prevalent. The black people imported into the French and to some of the Portuguese colonies, from the eastern coast of the African continent, and from Congo, are much better made. The most degraded and savage nations are the ugliest. Among the most improved and the partially civilized, as the Ashantees, and other interior States, the figure and the features of the native people approach much more to the European. The ugliest Negro tribes are confined to the equatorial countries; and on both sides of the equator, as we advance towards the temperate zones, the persons of the inhabitants are most handsome and well formed.

In a later period of this work I shall cite authors who have proved that many races belonging to this department of mankind are noted for the beauty of their features, and their fine stature and proportions. Adanson has made this observation of the Negroes on the Senegal. He thus describes the men. "Leur taille est pour l'ordinaire au-dessus de la mediocre, bien prise et sans défaut. Ils sont forts, robustes, et d'un tempérament propre à la fatigue. Ils ont les yeux noirs et bien fendus, peu de barbe, les traits du visage assez agréables." They are complete Negroes, for it is added that their complexion is of a fine black, that their hair is black, frizzled, cottony, and of extreme fineness. The women are said to be of nearly equal stature with the men, and equally well made. "Leur visage est d'une douceur extrême. Elles ont les yeux noirs, bien fendus, la bouche et les lèvres petites, et les traits du visage bien proportionnés. Il s'en trouve plusieurs d'une beauté parfaite." Mr. Rankin, a highly intelligent traveller, who reports accurately and without prejudice the results of his personal observation, has recently given a similar testimony in regard to some of the numerous tribes of northern Negro-land, who frequent the English colony of Sierra Leone. In the skull of the more improved and civilized nations among the woolly-haired blacks of Africa, there is comparatively slight deviation from the form which may be looked upon as the common type of the human head. We are assured, for example, by M. Golberry, that the Ioloffs, whose colour is a deep transparent black, and who have woolly hair, are robust and well made, and have regular features. Their countenances, he says, are ingenuous, and inspire confidence: they are honest, hospitable, generous, and faithful. The women are mild, very pretty, well made, and of agreeable manners. On the other side of the equinoctial line, the Congo Negroes, as Pigafetta declares, have not thick lips or ugly features; except in colour they are very like the Portuguese. Kafirs in South Africa frequently resemble Europeans, as many late travellers have declared. It has been the opinion of many that the Kafirs ought to be separated from the Negroes as a distinct branch of the human family. This has been proved to be an error. In the conformation of the skull, which is the leading character, the Kafirs associate themselves with the great majority of woolly African nations.[642]

THE NEGROES

The Negroes inhabit Africa from the southern margin of the Sahara as far as the territory of the Hottentots and Bushmen, and from the Atlantic to the Indian Ocean, although the extreme east of their domain has been wrested from them by intrusive Hamites and Semites. Most negroes have high and narrow skulls. According to Welcker the average percentage of width begins at 68 and rises to 78. The variations are so great that, among eighteen heads from Equatorial Africa, Barnard Davis found no less than four brachyrephals. In the majority dolichocephalism is combined with a prominence of the upper jaw and an oblique position of the teeth, yet there are whole nations which are purely mesognathous. It is to be regretted that in the opinion of certain mistaken ethnologists, the negro was the ideal of every thing barbarous and beast-like. They endeavoured to deny him any capability of improvement, and even disputed his position as a man. The negro was said to have an oval skull, a flat forehead, snout-like jaws, swollen lips, a broad flat nose, short crimped hair, falsely called wool, long arms, meagre thighs, calfless legs, highly elongated heels, and flat feet. No single tribe, however, possesses all these deformities. The colour of the skin passes through every gradation, from ebony black, as in the Joloffers, to the light tint of the mulattoes, as in the Wakilema, and Barth even describes copper-coloured negroes in Marghi. As to the skull in many tribes, as in the above mentioned Joloffers, the jaws are not prominent, and the lips are not swollen. In some tribes the nose is pointed, straight, or hooked; even "Grecian profiles" are spoken of, and travellers say with surprise that they cannot perceive anything of the so-called negro type among the negroes.

According to Paul Broca, the upper limbs of the negro are comparatively much shorter than the lower, and therefore less ape-like than in Europeans, and, although in the length of the femur the negro may approximate to the proportions of the ape, he differs from them by the shortness of the humerus more than is the case with Europeans. Undoubtedly narrow and more or less high skulls are prevalent among the negroes. But the only persistent character which can be adduced as common to all is greater or less darkness of skin, that is to say, yellow, copper-red, olive, or dark brown, passing into ebony black. The colour is always browner than that of Southern Europe. The hair is generally short, elliptic in section, often split longitudinally, and much crimped. That of the negroes of South Africa, especially of the Kaffirs and Betshuans, is matted into tufts, although not in the same degree as that of the Hottentots. The hair is black, and in old age white, but there are also negroes with red hair, red eye-brows, and eye-lashes, and among the Monbuttoo, on the Uelle, Schweinfurth even discovered negroes with ashy fair hair. Hair on the body and beards exist, though not abundantly; whiskers are rare although not quite unknown.

The negroes form but a single race, for the predominant as well as the constant characters recur in Southern as well as in Central Africa, and it was therefore a mistake to separate the Bantu negroes into a peculiar race. But, according to language, the South Africans can well be separated, as a great family, from the Soudan negroes.[643]

FOOTNOTES:

[642] Prichard's Physical History of Mankind, vol. i. pp. 247-249.

THE RELATION OF PHYSICAL CHARACTER TO CLIMATE

We shall now find, on comparing these several departments with each other, that marked differences of physical character, and particularly of complexion, distinguished the human races which respectively inhabit them, and that these differences are successive or by gradations.

First, Among the people of level countries within the Mediterranean region, including Spaniards, Italians, Greeks, Moors, and the Mediterranean islanders, black hair with dark eyes is almost universal, scarcely, one person in some hundreds presenting an exception to this remark with this colour of the hair and eyes is conjoined a complexion of brownish white, which the French call the colour of brunettes. We must observe, that throughout all the zones into which we have divided the European region, similar complexions to this of the Mediterranean countries are occasionally seen The qualities, indeed, of climate are not so diverse, but that even the same plants are found sporadically, in the North of Europe as in the Alps and Pyrenees. But if we make a comparison between the prevalent colours of great numbers, we can easily trace a succession of shades or of different hues.

Secondly, In the southernmost of the three zones, to the northward of the Pyreno-Alpine line, namely, in the latitude of France, the prevalent colour of the hair is a chestnut brown, to which the complexion and the colour of the eyes bear a certain relation.

Thirdly, In the northern parts of Germany, England, in Denmark, Finland and a great part of Russia, the xanthous variety, strongly marked, is prevalent The Danes have always been known as a people of florid complexion, blue eyes, and yellow hair The Hollanders were termed by Silius Italicus, "Auricomi Batavi," the golden haired Batavians, and Linnæus has defined the Finns as a tribe distinguished by "capillis flavis prolixis."

Fourthly, In the northern division we find the Norwegians and Swedes to be generally tall, white haired men, with light gray eyes characters so frequent to the northward of the Baltic, that Linnæus has specified them in a definition of the inhabitants of Swedish Gothland. We have then to the northward of Mount Atlas, four well marked varieties of human complexion succeeding each other, and in exact accordance with the gradations of latitude and of climate from south to north. The people are thus far nearly white in the colour of their skin, but in the more southerly of the three regions above defined, with a mixture of brown, or of the complexion of brunettes, or such as we term swarthy or sallow persons.

Fifthly, In the next region, to the southward of Atlas, the native inhabitants, are the "gentes sub fusci coloris" of Leo, and the immigrant Arabs in the same country are, as we have seen by abundant testimonies, of a similar high brown hue, but varying between that and a perfect black.

Sixthly, With the tropic and the latitude of the Senegal, begins the region of predominant and almost universal black, and this continues, if we confine ourselves to the low and plain countries, through all inter tropical Africa.

Seventhly, Beyond this is the country of copper coloured and red people, who, in Kafirland, are the majority, while in inter-tropical Africa there are but few such tribes, and those in countries of mountainous elevation.

Lastly, Towards the Cape are the tawny Hottentots, scarcely darker than the Mongoles, whom they resemble in many other particulars besides colour.

It has long been well known, that as travellers ascend mountains, in whatever region, they find the vegetation at every successive level altering its character, and assuming a more northern aspect, thus indicating that the state of the atmosphere, temperature and physical agencies in general, assimilate as we approach alpine regions, to the peculiarities locally connected with high latitudes. If therefore, complexions and other bodily qualities belonging to races of men depend upon climate and external conditions, we should expect to find them varying in reference to elevation of surface, and if they should be found actually to undergo such variations, this will be a strong argument that these external characters do, in fact, depend upon local conditions. Now, if we inquire respecting the physical characters of the tribes inhabiting high tracts within either of the regions above marked out, we shall find that they coincide with those which prevail in the level or low parts of more northern tracts. The Swiss, in the high mountains above the plains of Lombardy, have sandy or brown hair. What a contrast presents itself to the traveller who descends into the Milanese, where the peasants have black hair and eyes, with strongly-marked Italian and almost Oriental features. In the higher parts of the Biscayan country, instead of the swarthy complexion and black hair of the Castilians, the natives have a fair complexion with light-blue eyes and flaxen or auburn hair. And in Atlantica, while the Berbers of the plains are of brown complexion with black hair, we have seen that the Shuluh mountaineers are fair, and that the inhabitants of the high tracts of Mons Aurasius are completely xanthous, having red or yellow hair and blue eyes, which fancifully, and without the shadow of any proof, they have been conjectured to have derived from the Vandal troops of Genseric.

Even in the inter-tropical region, high elevations of surface, as they produce a cooler climate, seem to occasion the appearance of light complexions. In the high parts of Senegambia, which front the Atlantic, and are cooled by winds from the Western Ocean, where, in fact, the temperature is known to be moderate and even cool at times, the light copper-coloured Frelahs are found surrounded on every side by Negro nations inhabiting lower districts; and nearly in the same parallel, but at the opposite side of Africa, are the high plains of Enarea and Kaffa, where the inhabitants are said to be fairer than the natives of southern Europe. The Galla and the Abyssinians themselves are, in proportion to the elevation of the country inhabited by them, fairer than the natives of low countries; and lest an exception should be taken to a comparison of straight-haired races with woolly Negroes or Shungalla, they bear the same comparison with the Danakil, Hazorta, and the Bishari tribes, resembling them in their hair and features, who inhabit the low tracts between the mountains of Tigre and the shores of the Red Sea, and who are equally or nearly as black as Negroes.

We may find occasion to observe that an equally decided relation exists between local conditions and the existence of other characters of human races in Africa. Those races who have the Negro character in an exaggerated degree, and who may be said to approach to deformity in person—the ugliest blacks with depressed foreheads, flat noses, crooked legs—are in many instances inhabitants of low countries, often of swampy tracts near the sea-coast, where many of them, as the Papels, have scarcely any other means of subsistence than shell fish, and the accidental gifts of the sea. In many places similar Negro tribes occupy thick forests in the hollows beneath high chains of mountains, the summits of which are inhabited by Abyssinian or Ethiopian races. The high table-lands of Africa are chiefly, as far as they are known, the abode or the wandering places of tribes of this character, or of nations who, like the Kafirs, recede very considerably from the Negro type. The Mandingos are, indeed, a Negro race inhabiting a high region; but they have neither the depressed forehead nor the projecting features considered as characteristic of the Negro race.[644]

FOOTNOTES:

[643] Peschel, The Races of Man, pp. 462-464.

CHAPTER VII—CITIES OF AFRICA

Carthage. The foundation of this celebrated city is ascribed to Elissa, a Tyrian princess, better known as Dido; it may therefore be fixed at the year of the world 3158; when Joash was king of Judah; 98 years before the building of Rome, and 846 years before Christ. The king of Tyre, father of the famous Jezebel, called in Scripture Ethbaal, was her great grandfather. She married her near relation Acerbas, also called Sicharbas, or Sichæus, an extremely rich prince, Pygmalion, king of Tyre, was her brother. Pygmalion put Sichæus to death in order that he might have an opportunity to seize his immense treasures, but Dido eluded her brother's cruel avarice, by secretly conveying away her deceased husband's possessions. With a large train of followers she left her country, and after wandering some time, landed on the coast of the Mediterranean, in Africa, and located her settlement at the bottom of the gulf, on a peninsula, near the spot where Tunis now stands. Many of the neighboring people, allured by the prospect of gain, repaired thither to sell to those foreigners the necessities of life, and soon became incorporated with them. The people thus gathered from different places soon grew very numerous. And the citizens of Utica, an African city about fifteen miles distant, considering them as their countrymen, as descended from the same common stock, advised them to build a city where they had settled. The other natives of the country, from their natural esteem and respect for strangers, likewise encouraged them to the same object. Thus all things conspiring with Dido's views, she built her city, which was appointed to pay in annual tribute to the Africans for the ground it stood upon, and called it Carthage—a name that in the Phoenician and Hebrew languages, [which have a great affinity,] signifies the "New City." It is said that in digging the foundation, a horse's head was found, which was thought to be a good omen, and a presage of the future warlike genius of that people. Carthage had the same language and national character as its parent state—Tyre. It became at length, particularly at the period of the Punic War, one of the most splendid cities in the world, and had under its dominion 300 cities bordering upon the Mediterranean. From the small beginning we have described, Carthage increased till her population numbered 700,000, and the number of her temples and other public buildings was immense. Her dominion was not long confined to Africa. Her ambitious inhabitants extended their conquest into Europe, by invading Sardinia, seizing a great part of Sicily, and subduing almost all of Spain. Having sent powerful colonies everywhere, they enjoyed the empire of the seas for more than six hundred years and formed a State which was able to dispute pre-eminence with the greatest empire of the world, by their wealth, their commerce, their numerous armies, their formidable fleets, and above all by the courage and ability of their commanders, and she extended her commerce over every part of the known world. A colony of Phoenicians or Ethiopians, known in Scripture as Canaanites, settled in Carthage. The Carthaginians settled in Spain and Portugal. The first inhabitants of Spain were the Celts, a people of Gaul, after them the Phoenicians possessed themselves of the most southern parts of the country, and may well be supposed to have been the first civilizers of this kingdom, and the founders of the most ancient cities. After these, followed the Grecians, then the Carthaginians.

Portugal was anciently called Lusitania, and inhabited by tribes of wandering people, till it became subject to the Carthaginians and Phoenicians, who were dispossessed by the Romans 250 years before Christ. (Rollin.)

The Carthaginians were masters of all the coast which lies on the Mediterranean, and all the country as far as the river Iberus. Their dominions, at the time when Hannibal the Great set out for Italy, all the coast of Africa from the Aræ Phileanorum, by the great Syrtis, to the pillars of Hercules was subject to the Carthaginians, who had maintained three great wars against the Romans. But the Romans finally prevailed by carrying the war into Africa, and the last Punic war terminated with the overthrow of Carthage (Nepos, *in Vita Annibalis*, liv.)

The celebrated Cyrene was a very powerful city, situated on the Mediterranean, towards the greater Syrtis, in Africa, and had been built by Battus, the Lacedæmonian. (Rollin.)

Cyrene—(Acts xi. 20.) A province and city of Libya. There was anciently a Phoenician colony called Cyrenaica, or "Libya, about Cyrene." (Acts ii. 10.).

Cyrene—A country west of Egypt, and the birthplace of Callimachus the poet, Eratosthenes the historian, and Simon who bore the Saviour's cross. Many Jews from hence were at the Pentecost, and were converted under Peter's sermon (Acts ii.). The region, now under the Turkish power, and has become almost a desert. It is now called Cairoan. Some of the Cyrenians were among the earliest Christians (Acts xi. 20); and one of them, it is supposed, was a preacher at Antioch (Acts xiii. 1). We find also, that among the most violent opposers of Christianity were the Cyrenians, who had a synagogue at Jerusalem, as had those of many other nations. It is said there were four hundred and eighty synagogues in Jerusalem.

Lybia, or Libya (Acts ii. 10), was anciently among the Greeks, a general name for Africa, but properly it embraced only so much of Africa as lay west of Egypt, on the southern coast of the Mediterranean. Profane geographers call it Libya Cyrenaica, because Cyrene was its capitol. It was the country of the Lubims (2 Chron. xii. 3), or Lehabims, of the Old Testament, from which it is supposed to have derived its name.

The ancient city of Cyrene is now called Cyreune, Cairoan, or Cayran and lies in the dominion of Tripoli. This district of the earth has lately occasioned much interest among Italian and French geographers. Great numbers of Jews resided here (Matt. xxvii. 32).

Libya, a part of Africa, bordering on Egypt, famous for its armed chariots and horses (2 Chron. xvi. 8).

Ophir, the son of Joktan, gave name to a country in Africa, famous for gold, which was renowned even in the time of Job (Job xxi. 24, xxviii. 16); and from the time of David to the time of Jehoshaphat the Hebrews traded with it, and Uzziah revived this trade when he made himself master of Elath, a noted port on the Red Sea. In Solomon's time, the Hebrew fleet took up three years in their voyage to Ophir, and brought home gold, apes, peacocks, spices, ivory, ebony and almug-trees (1 Kings ix. 28, x. 11, xxii. 48, 2 Chron. ix. 10).

Tarshish (Isa. xxiii. 1), or Tharsish (1 Kings x. 22). It is supposed that some place of this name existed on the eastern coast of Africa or among the southern ports of Asia, with which the ships of Hiram and Solomon traded in gold and silver, ivory, and apes and peacocks (2 Chron. ix. 21). It is said that once in every three years these ships completed a voyage, and brought home their merchandise. Hence, it is inferred, the place with which they traded must have been distant from Judea.

The vessels given by Hiram to Solomon, and those built by Jehoshaphat, to go to Tarshish, were all launched at Eziongeber, it the northern extremity of the eastern gulf of the Red Sea, now called the Gulf of Ahaba (2 Chron xx. 36). The name of Tarshish was from one of the sons of Javan (Gen. x. 4).

Phut (Gen. x. 6), or Put (Nah. iii. 9), was the third son of Ham, and his descendants, sometimes called Libyans, are supposed to be the Mauritanians, or Moors of modern times. They served the Egyptians and Tyrians as soldiers (Jer. xlvi. 9; Ezek. xxvii. 10, xxx. 5, xxxviii. 5).

Pul. A district in Africa, thought by Bochart to be an island in the Nile, not far from Syene (Isa. lxvi. 19).

Seba (Isa. xliii. 3) A peninsular district of African Ethiopia, deriving its name from the eldest son of Cush (Gen. x. 7), who is supposed to have been the progenitor of the Ethiopians. It is called Seba by the Hebrews.

FOOTNOTES:

[644] Prichard. vol. ii pp. 334-338.

CITIES OF ETHIOPIA

Ethiopian is a name derived from the "land of Ethiopia," the first settled country before the flood. "The second river that went out of Eden, to water the garden, or earth, was Gihon; the same that encompasseth the whole land, or country, of *Ethiopia*" (Gen. ii. 13). Here Adam and his posterity built their tents and tilled the ground (Gen. iii. 23, 24).

The first city was Enoch, built before the flood in the land of Nod on the east of Eden,—a country now called Arabia. Cain the son of Adam, went out of Eden and dwelt in the land of Nod. We suppose, according to an ancient custom he married his sister and she bare Enoch. And Cain built a city and called the name of the city after the name of his son, Enoch, (Gen. iv. 16, 17). We know there must have been more than Cain and his son Enoch in the land of Nod to build a city but who were they?... (Malcom's *Bible Dictionary*.)

The first great city described in ancient and sacred history was built by the Cushites, or Ethiopians. They surrounded it with walls which, according to Rollin, were eighty-seven feet in thickness, three hundred and fifty feet in height and four hundred and eighty furlongs in circumference. And even this stupendous work they shortly after eclipsed by another, of which Diodorus says, "Never did any city come up to the greatness and magnificence of this."

It is a fact well attested by history, that the Ethiopians once bore sway, not only in all Africa, but over almost all Asia; and it is said that even two continents, could not afford field enough for the expansion of their energies.

"They found their way into Europe, and built a city on the western coast of Spain, called by them Iberian Ethiopia." "And," says a distinguished writer, "wherever they went, they were rewarded for their *wisdom*."

The Tower of Babel—Nimrod, the son of Cush, an Ethiopian, attempted to build the Tower of Babel (Gen. x. 8-10 xi. 4-9). One hundred and two years after the flood, in the land of Shinar—an extensive and fertile plain, lying between Mesopotamia on the west and Persia on the east, and watered by the Euphrates,—mankind being all of one language, one color, and one religion,—they agree to erect a tower of prodigious extent and height. Their design was not to secure themselves against a second deluge, or they would have built their tower on a high mountain, but to get themselves a famous character, and to prevent their dispersion by the erection of a monument which should be visible from a great distance. No quarries being found in that alluvial soil, they made bricks for stone, and used slime for mortar. Their haughty and rebellious attempt displeased the Lord; and after they had worked, it is said, twenty-two years, he confounded their language.

This effectually stopped the building, procured it the name of *Babel*, or *Confusion*, and obliged some of the offspring of Noah to disperse themselves and replenish the world. The tower of Babel was in sight from the great city of Babylon. Nimrod was a hunter and monarch of vast ambition. When he rose to be king of Babylon he re-peopled Babel, which had been desolate since the confusion of tongues, but did not dare to attempt the finishing of the tower. The Scriptures inform us, he became "mighty upon earth;" but the extent of his conquests is not known. (Malcom's *Bible Dictionary*.)

The private houses, in most of the ancient cities, were simple in external appearance, but exhibited, in the interior, all the splendor and elegance of refined luxury. The floors were of marble; alabaster and gilding were displayed on every side. In every great house there were several fountains, playing in magnificent basins. The smallest house had three pipes,—one for the kitchen, another for the garden, and a third for washing. The same magnificence was displayed in the mosques, churches, and coffee houses. The environs presented, at all seasons of the year, a pleasing verdure, and contained extensive series of gardens and villas.

The Great and Splendid City of Babylon.—This city was founded by Nimrod, about 2,247 years B.C., in the land of Shinar, or Chaldea, and made the capital of his kingdom. It was probably an inconsiderable place, until it was enlarged and embellished by Semiramis; it then became the most magnificent city in the world, surpassing even Nineveh in glory. The circumference of both these cities was the same, but the walls which surrounded Babylon were twice as broad as the walls of Nineveh, and having a hundred brass gates. The city of Babylon stood on the river Euphrates, by which it was divided into two parts, eastern and western; and these were connected by a cedar bridge of wonderful construction, uniting the two divisions. Quays of beautiful marble adorned the banks of the river; and on one bank stood the magnificent Temple of Belus, and on the other the Queen's Palace. These two edifices were connected by a passage under the bed of the river. This city was at least forty-five miles in circumference; and would, of course, include eight cities as large as London and its appendages. It was laid out in six hundred and twenty five squares, formed by the intersection of twenty-five streets at right angles The walls, which were of brick, were three hundred and fifty feet high, and eighty-seven feet broad. A trench surrounded the city, the sides of which were lined with brick and waterproof cement. This city was famous for its hanging gardens, constructed by one of its kings, to please his queen. She was a Persian, and was desirous of seeing meadows on mountains, as in her own country. She prevailed on him to raise artificial gardens, adorned with meadows and trees. For this purpose, vaulted arches were raised from the ground, one above another, to an almost inconceivable height, and of a magnificence and strength sufficient to support the vast weight of the whole garden Babylon was a great commercial city, and traded to all parts of the earth then known, in all kinds of merchandise, and she likewise traded in slaves, and the souls of men. For her sins she has been blotted from existence,—even her location is a matter of supposition. Great was Babylon of old; in merchandise did she trade, and in souls. For her sins she thus became blotted from the sight of men.

THE ETHIOPIAN KINGS OF EGYPT

1. *Menes* was the first king of Egypt. We have accounts of but one of his successors—Timans, during the first period, a space of more than two centuries.

2. *Shishak* was king of Ethiopia, and doubtless of Egypt. After his death

3. *Zerah* the son of Judah became king of Ethiopia, and made himself master of Egypt and Libya; and intending to add Judea to his dominions made war upon Asa king of Judea. His army consisted of a million of men, and three hundred chariots of war (2 Chron. xiv. 9).

4. *Sabachus*, an Ethiopian, king of Ethiopia, being encouraged by an oracle, entered Egypt with a numerous army, and possessed himself of the country. He reigned with great clemency and justice. It is believed, that this Sabachus was the same with Solomon, whose aid was implored by Hosea king of Israel, against Salmanaser king of Assyria.

5. *Sethon* reigned fourteen years. He is the same with Sabachus, or Savechus the son of Sabacan or Saul the Ethiopian who reigned so long over Egypt.

6. *Tharaca*, an Ethiopian, joined Sethon, with an Ethiopian army to relieve Jerusalem. After the death of Sethon, who had filled the Egyptian throne fourteen years, Tharaca ascended the throne and reigned eight years over Egypt.

7. Sesach or Shishak was the king of Egypt to whom Jeroboam fled to avoid death at the hands of king Solomon. Jeroboam was entertained till the death of Solomon, when he returned to Judea and was made king of Israel. (2 Chron. xi. and xii.)

This Sesach, in the fifth year of the reign of Rehoboam marched against Jerusalem, because the Jews had transgressed against the Lord. He came with twelve hundred chariots of war, and sixty thousand horses. He had brought numberless multitudes of people, who were all Libyans, Troglodytes, and Ethiopians. He seized upon all the strongest cities of Judah, and advanced as far as Jerusalem. Then the king, and the princes of Israel, having humbled themselves, and implored the protection of the God of Israel, he told them, by his prophet Shemaiah, that, because they humbled themselves, he would not utterly destroy them, as they had deserved but that they should be the servants of Sesach, in order *that they might know* the difference of *his service, and the service of the kingdoms of the country.* Sesach retired from Jerusalem, after having plundered the treasures of the house of the Lord, and of the king's house, he carried off every thing with him, *and even also the three hundred shields of gold which Salomon had made.*

The following are the kings of Egypt mentioned in Scripture by the common appellation of Pharaoh:—

8. *Psammetichus.*—As this prince owed his preservation to the Ionians and Carians, he settled them in Egypt, from which all foreigners hitherto had been excluded; and, by assigning them sufficient lands and fixed revenues, he made them forget their native country. By his order, Egyptian children were put under their care to learn the Greek tongue; and on this occasion, and by this means, the Egyptians began to have a correspondence with the Greeks, and, from that era, the Egyptian history, which till then had been intermixed with pompous fables, by the artifice of the priests, begins, according to Herodotus, to speak with greater truth and certainty.

As soon as Psammetichus was settled on the throne, he engaged in a war against the king of Assyria, on account of the limits of the two empires. This war was of long continuance. Ever since Syria had been conquered by the Assyrians, Palestine, being the only country that separated the two kingdoms, was the subject of continual discord; as afterwards it was between the Ptolemies and the Seleucidæ. They were perpetually contending for it, and it was alternately won by the stronger. Psammetichus, seeing himself the peaceable possessor of all Egypt, and having restored the ancient form of government, thought it high time for him to look to his frontiers, and to secure them against the Assyrian, his neighbour, whose power increased daily. For this purpose he entered Palestine at the head of an army.

Perhaps we are to refer to the beginning of this war, an incident related by Diodorus; that the Egyptians, provoked to see the Greeks posted on the right wing by the king himself in preference to them, quitted the service, being upwards of two hundred thousand men, and retired into Ethiopia, where they met with an advantageous settlement

Be this as it will, Psammetichus entered Palestine, where his career was stopped by Azotus, one of the principal cities of the country, which gave him so much trouble, that he was forced to besiege it twenty nine years before he could take it. This is the longest siege mentioned in ancient history.

Psammetichus died in the 24th year of the reign of Josiah king of Judah; and was succeeded by his son Nechoa or Necho—in Scriptures frequently called Pharaoh Necho.

9. *Nechao* or *Pharaoh-Necho* reigned sixteen years king of Egypt, (2 Chron. xxxv. 20,) whose expeditions are often mentioned in profane history

The Babylonians and Medes having destroyed Nineveh, and with it the empire of the Assyrians, were thereby become so formidable, that they drew upon themselves the jealousy of all their neighbours. Nechao, alarmed at the danger, advanced to the Euphrates, at the head of a powerful army, in order to check their progress. Josiah, king of Judah, so famous for his uncommon piety, observing that he took his route through Judea, resolved to oppose his passage. With this view he raised all the forces of his kingdom, and posted himself in the valley of Megiddo (a city on this side of Jordan, belonging to the tribe of Manasseh, and called Magdolus by Herodotus). Nechao informed him by a herald, that his enterprise was not designed against him; that he had other enemies in view, and that he had undertaken this war in the name of God, who was with him; that for this reason he advised Josiah not to concern himself with this war for fear it otherwise should turn to his disadvantage. However, Josiah was not moved by these reasons; he was sensible that the bare march of so powerful an army through Judea would entirely ruin it. And besides, he feared that the victor, after the defeat of the Babylonians, would fall upon him and dispossess him of part of his dominions. He therefore marched to engage Nechao; and was not only overthrown by him, but unfortunately received a wound of which he died at Jerusalem, whither he had ordered himself to be carried.

Nechao, animated by this victory, continued his march and advanced towards the Euphrates. He defeated the Babylonians; took Carchemish, a large city in that country; and securing to himself the possession of it by a strong garrison, returned to his own kingdom after having been absent three months.

Being informed in his march homeward, that Jehoaz had caused himself to be proclaimed king at Jerusalem, without first asking his consent, he commanded him to meet him at Riblah in Syria. The unhappy prince was no sooner arrived there than he was put in chains by Nechao's order, and sent prisoner to Egypt, where he died. From thence, pursuing his march, he came to Jerusalem, where he gave the sceptre to Eliakim (called by him Jehoiakim), another of Josiah's sons, in the room of his brother; and imposed an annual tribute on the land, of a hundred talents of silver, and one talent of gold. This being done, he returned in triumph to Egypt.

Herodotus, mentioning this king's expedition, and the victory gained by him at Magdolus, (as he calls it,) says that he afterwards took the city Cadytis, which he represents as situated in the mountains of Palestine, and equal in extent to Sardis, the capital at that time not only of Lydia, but of all Asia Minor. This description can suit only Jerusalem, which was situated in the manner above described, and was then the only city in those parts that could be compared to Sardis. It appears besides, from Scripture, that Nechao, after his victory, made himself master of this capital of Judea; for he was there in person, when he gave the crown to Jehoiakim. The very name Cadytis, which in Hebrew, signifies the holy, points clearly to the city of Jerusalem, as is proved by the learned dean Prideaux.

10. *Psammis.*—His reign was but of six years' duration, and history has left us nothing memorable concerning him, except that he made an expedition into Ethiopia.

11. *Apries.*—In Scripture he is called Pharaoh-Hophra; and, succeeding his father Psammis, reigned twenty-five years.

During the first year of his reign, he was as happy as any of his predecessors. He carried his arms into Cyprus; besieged the city of Sidon by sea and land; took it, and made himself master of all Phoenicia and Palestine.

So rapid a success elated his heart to a prodigious degree, and, as Herodotus informs us, swelled him with so much pride and infatuation, that he boasted it was not in the power of the gods themselves to dethrone him; so great was the idea he had formed to himself of the firm establishment of his own power. It was with a view to these arrogant conceits, that Ezekiel put the vain and impious words following into his mouth: *My river is mine own, and I have made it for myself.* But the true God proved to him afterwards that he had a master, and that he was a mere man; and he had threatened him long before, by his prophets, with all the calamities he was resolved to bring upon him, in order to punish him for his pride.

12. *Amasis.*—After the death of Apries, Amasis became peaceable possessor of Egypt, and reigned over it forty years. He was, according to Plato, a native of the city of Sais.

As he was but of mean extraction, he met with no respect, and was contemned by his subjects in the beginning of his reign. He was not insensible of this; but nevertheless thought it his interest to subdue their tempers by an artful carriage, and to win their affection by gentleness and reason. He had a golden cistern, in which himself, and those persons who were admitted to his table, used to wash their feet, he melted it down, and had it cast into a statue, and then exposed the new god to public worship. The people hastened in crowds to pay their adorations to the statue. The king, having assembled the people, informed them of the vile uses to which this statue had once been put, which nevertheless was now the object of their religious prostrations; the application was easy, and had the desired success; the people thenceforward paid the king all the respect that is due to majesty.

He always used to devote the whole morning to public affairs, in order to receive petitions, give audience, pronounce sentences, and hold his councils; the rest of the day was given to pleasure, and as Amasis, in hours of diversion, was extremely gay, and seemed to carry his mirth beyond due bounds, his courtiers took the liberty to represent to him the unsuitableness of such a behaviour; when he answered that it was impossible for the mind to be always serious and intent upon business, as for a bow to continue always bent.

It was this king who obliged the inhabitants of every town to enter their names in a book kept by the magistrates for that purpose, with their profession and manner of living. Solon inserted this custom among his laws.

He built many magnificent temples, especially at Sais the place of his birth. Herodotus admired especially a chapel there, formed of one single stone, and which was twenty-one cubits in front, fourteen in depth, and eight in height; its dimensions within were not quite so large; it had been brought from Elephantina, and two thousand men were employed three years in conveying it along the Nile.

Amasis had a great esteem for the Greeks. He granted them large privileges; and permitted such of them as were desirous of settling in Egypt to live in the city of Naucratis, so famous for its harbour. When the rebuilding of the temple of Delphi, which had been burnt, was debated on, and the expense was computed at three hundred talents, Amasis furnished the Delphians with a very considerable sum towards discharging their quota, which was the fourth part of the whole charge.

He made an alliance with the Cyrenians, and married a wife from among them. He is the only king of Egypt who conquered the island of Cyprus, and made it tributary. Under his reign Pythagorus came into Egypt, being recommended to that monarch by the famous Polycrates, tyrant of Samos, who had contracted a friendship with Amasis, and will be mentioned hereafter. Pythagoras, during his stay in Egypt, was initiated in all the mysteries of the country, and instructed by the priests in whatever was most abstruse and important in their religion. It was here he imbibed his doctrine of the metempsychosis, or transmigration of souls.

In the expedition in which Cyrus conquered so great a part of the world, Egypt doubtless was subdued, like the rest of the provinces, and Xenophon positively declares this in the beginning of his Cyropædia, or institution of that prince. Probably, after that the forty years of desolation, which had been foretold by the prophet, were expired, Egypt beginning gradually to recover itself, Amasis shook off the yoke, and recovered his liberty.

Accordingly we find, that one of the first cares of Cambyses, the son of Cyrus, after he had ascended the throne, was to carry his arms into Egypt. On his arrival there, Amasis was just dead, and succeeded by his son Psammetus.

13. Rameses Miamun, according to Archbishop Usher, was the name of this king, who is called Pharaoh in Scripture. He reigned sixty-six years, and oppressed the Israelites in a most grievous manner. He set over them taskmasters, to afflict them with their burdens, and they built for Pharaoh treasure cities, Pithon and Raamses. And the Egyptians made the children of Israel serve with rigour, and they made their lives bitter with hard bondage, in mortar and in brick, and in all manner of service in the field; all their service wherein they made them serve, was with rigour. This king had two sons, Amenophis and Busiris.

14. *Amenophis*, the eldest, succeeded him. He was the Pharaoh under whose reign the Israelites departed out of Egypt, and who was drowned in his passage through the Red Sea. Archbishop Usher says, that Amenophis left two sons, one called Sesothis, or Seaostris, and the other Armais. The Greeks call him Belus, and his two sons, Egyptus and Danaus.

15. *Sesostris* was not only one of the most powerful kings of Egypt, but one of the greatest conquerors that antiquity boasts of. He was at an advanced age sent by his father against the Arabians, in order that, by fighting with them, he might acquire military knowledge. Here the young prince learned to bear hunger and thirst, and subdued a nation which till then had never been conquered. The youth educated with him, attended him in all his campaigns.

Accustomed by this conquest to martial toils he was next sent by his father to try his fortune westward. He invaded Libya, and subdued the greatest part of that vast continent.

His army consisted of six hundred thousand foot, and twenty thousand horse, besides twenty thousand armed chariots.

He invaded Ethiopia, and obliged the nations of it to furnish him annually with a certain quantity of ebony, ivory, and gold.

He had fitted out a fleet of four hundred sail, and ordering it to sail to the Red Sea, made himself master of the isles and cities lying on the coast of that sea. After having spread desolation through the world for nine years, he returned, laden with the spoils of the vanquished nations. A hundred famous temples, raised as so many monuments of gratitude to the tutelar gods of all the cities, were the first, as well as the most illustrious testimonies of his victories.

16. *Pheron* succeeded Sesostris in his kingdom, but not in his glory. He probably reigned fifty years.

17. *Proteus* was son of Memphis, and according to Herodotus, must have succeeded the first—since Proteus lived at the time of the siege of Troy, which, according to Usher, was taken An. Mun. 2820.

18. *Rhampsinitus* who was richer than any of his predecessors, built a treasury. Till the reign of this king, there had been some shadow at least of justice and moderation in Egypt; but, in the two following reigns, violence and cruelty usurped their place.

19, 20. Cheops and Cephrenus, reigned in all one hundred and six years. Cheops reigned fifty years, and his brother Cephrenus fifty-six years after him. They kept the temples closed during the whole time of their long reign; and forbid the offerings of sacrifice under the severest penalties. They oppressed their subjects.

21. *Mycerinus* the son of Cheops, reigned but seven years. He opened the temples; restored the sacrifices; and did all in his power to comfort his subjects, and make them forget their past miseries.

22. *Asychis* one of the kings of Egypt. He valued himself for having surpassed all his predecessors, by building a pyramid of brick, more magnificent, than any hitherto seen.

23. *Busiris*, built the famous city of Thebes, and made it the seat of his empire. This prince is not to be confounded with Busirus, so infamous for his cruelties.

24. *Osymandyas*, raised many magnificent edifices, in which were exhibited sculptures and paintings of exquisite beauty.

25. *Uchoreus*, one of the successors of Osymandyas, built the city of Memphis. This city was 150 furlongs, or more than seven leagues in circumference, and stood at the point of the Delta, in that part where the Nile divides itself into several branches or streams. A city so advantageously situated, and so strongly fortified, became soon the usual residence of the Egyptian kings.

26. *Thethmosis* or *Amosis*, having expelled the Shepherd kings, reigned in Lower Egypt.[645]

FOOTNOTES:

[645] Rollin, vol. i. pp. 129-147.

CHAPTER VIII-AFRICAN LANGUAGES

In the language of the Kafirs, for example, not only the cases but the numbers and genders of nouns are formed entirely by prefixes, analogous to articles. The prefixes vary according to number, gender and case, while the nouns remain unaltered except by a merely euphonic change of the initial letters. Thus, in Coptic, from *sheri*, a son, comes the plural *neu-sheri*, the sons; from *sori*, accusation, *hau-sori*, accusations. Analogous to this we have in the Kafir *ama* marking the plural, as *amakosah* the plural of *kosah*, *amahashe* the plural of *ihashe*, *insana* the plural of *usana*. The Kafir has a great variety of similar prefixes; they are equally numerous in the language of Kongo, in which, as in the Coptic and the Kafir, the genders, numbers, and cases of nouns are almost solely distinguished by similar prefixes.

"The Kafir language is distinguished by one peculiarity which immediately strikes a student whose views of language have been formed upon the examples afforded by the inflected languages of ancient and modern Europe. With the exception of a change of termination in the ablative case of the noun, and five changes of which the verb is susceptible in its principal tenses, the whole business of declension, conjugation, &c., is carried on by prefixes, and by the changes which take place in the initial letters or syllables of words subjected to grammatical government."[646]

Resources are not yet in existence for instituting a general comparison of the languages of Africa. Many years will probably elapse before it will be possible to produce such an analysis of these languages, investigated in their grammatical structure, as it is desirable to possess, or even to compare them by extensive collections of well-arranged vocabularies, after the manner of Klaproth's Asia Polyglotta. Sufficient data however are extant, and I trust that I have adduced evidence to render it extremely probable that a principle of analogy in structure prevails extensively among the native idioms of Africa. They are probably allied, not in the manner or degree in which Semitic or Indo-European idioms resemble each other, but by strong analogies in their general principles of structure, which may be compared to those discoverable between the individual members of two other great classes of languages, by no means connected among themselves by what is called family relation. I allude to the monosyllabic and the polysynthetic languages, the former prevalent in Eastern Asia, the latter throughout the vast regions of the New World. If we have sufficient evidence for constituting such a class of dialects under the title of African languages, we have likewise reason—and it is equal in degree—for associating in this class the language of the ancient Egyptians.[647]

That the written Abyssinian language, which we call Ethiopick, is a dialect of old Chaldean, and sister of Arabick and Hebrew; we know with certainty, not only from the great multitude of identical words, but (which is a far stronger proof) from the similar grammatical arrangement of the several idioms: we know at the same time, that it is written like all the Indian characters, from the left hand to the right, and that the vowels are annexed, as in Devanagari, to the consonants; with which they form a syllabick system extremely clear and convenient, but disposed in a less artificial order than the system of letters now exhibited in the Sanscrit grammars; whence it may justly be inferred, that the order contrived by Panini or his disciples is comparatively modern; and I have no doubt, from a cursory examination of many old inscriptions on pillars and in caves, which have obligingly been sent to me from all parts of India, that the Nagari and Ethiopean letters had at first a similar form. It has long been my opinion, that the Abyssinians of the Arabian stock, having no symbols of their own to represent articulate sounds, borrowed those of the black pagans, whom the Greeks call Troglodytes, from their primeval habitations in natural caverns, or in mountains excavated by their own labour: they were probably the first inhabitants of Africa, where they became in time the builders of magnificent cities, the founders of seminaries for the advancement of science and philosophy, and the inventors (if they were not rather the importers) of symbolical characters. I believe on the whole, that the Ethiops of Meroe were the same people with the first Egyptians, and consequently, as it might easily be shown, with the original Hindus. To the ardent and intrepid Mr. Bruce, whose travels are to my taste, uniformally agreeable and satisfactory, though he thinks very differently from me on the language and genius of the Arabs, we are indebted for more important, and, I believe, more accurate information concerning the nations established near the Nile, from its fountains to its mouths, than all Europe united could before have supplied; but, since he has not been at the pains to compare the seven languages, of which he has exhibited a specimen, and since I have not leisure to make the comparison, I must be satisfied with observing, on his authority, that the dialects of the Gafots and the Gallas, the Agows of both races, and the Falashas, who must originally have used a Chaldean idiom, were never preserved in writing, and the Amharick only in modern times: they must, therefore, have been for ages in fluctuation, and can lead, perhaps, to no certain conclusion as to the origin of the several tribes who anciently spoke them. It is very remarkable, as Mr. Bruce and Mr. Bryan have proved, that the Greeks gave the appellation of Indians both to the southern nations of Africk and to the people, among whom we now live; nor is it less observable, that, according to Ephorus, quoted by Strabo, they called all the southern nations in the world Ethiopians, thus using Indian and Ethiop as convertible terms: but we must leave the gymnosophists of Ethiopia, who seemed to have professed the doctrines of Buddha, and enter the great Indian ocean, of which their Asiatick and African brethren were probably the first navigators.[648]

FOOTNOTES:

[646] Kafir Grammar, p. 3.

[647] Prichard, vol. ii. pp. 216, 217.

SHERBRO MISSION-DISTRICT, WESTERN AFRICA

Western Africa is one of the most difficult mission-fields in the entire heathen world. The low condition of the people, civilly, socially, and religiously, and the deadly climate to foreigners, make it indeed a hard field to cultivate. I am fully prepared to indorse what Rev. F. Fletcher, in charge of Wesleyan District, Gold Coast, wrote a few months ago in the following language: "The Lord's work in western Africa is as wonderful as it is deadly. In the last forty years more than 120 missionaries have fallen victims to that climate; but to-day the converts to Christianity number at least 30,000, many of whom are true Christians. In this district we have 6,000 church members, and though they are poor, last year they gave over 5,000 dollars for evangelistic and educational work.

"*Sherbro Mission* now has four stations and chapels and over forty appointments, 112 church members, 164 seekers of religion, 75 acres of clear land, with carpenter, blacksmith, and tailor shops, in and upon which, twenty five boys are taught to labor, and where eleven girls are taught to do all ordinary house work and sewing, with its four day and Sunday schools, 212 in the former and more than that number in the latter, and with an influence for good that now reaches the whole Sherbro tribe, embracing a country at least fifty miles square and containing about 15,000 people. The seed sown is taking deep root there, and the harvest is rapidly ripening, when thousands of souls will be garnered for heaven. Surely we ought to thank God for past success and resolve to do much more for that needy country in the future.

"We now have Revs. Corner, Wilberforce, Evans, and their wives, all excellent missionaries, from America; then Revs. Sawyer, Hero, Pratt, and their wives, Mrs. Lucy Caulker, and other native laborers, all of whom are doing us good service. With these six ordained ministers, and twice that number of teachers and helpers, who are devoting all their time to the mission, the work is going forward gloriously. Still, there should be new stations opened and more laborers sent out immediately."[649]

FOOTNOTES:

[648] Asiatic Researches, vol. iii. pp. 4, 5.

[649] Twenty fifth Annual Report, United Brethren, 1881.

PART II
SLAVERY IN THE COLONIES.

CHAPTER XV
CONDITION OF SLAVES IN MASSACHUSETTS

The following memorandum in Judge Sewall's letter book was called forth by Samuel Smith, murderer of his Negro slave at Sandwich. It illustrates the deplorable condition of servants at that time in Massachusetts, and shows Judge Sewall to have been a man of great humanity.

"The poorest Boys and Girls in this Province, such as are of the lowest Condition; whether they be English, or Indians, or Ethiopians: They have the same Right to Religion and Life, that the Richest Heirs have.

"And they who go about to deprive them of this Right, they attempt the bombarding of HEAVEN, and the Shells they throw, will fall down upon their own heads.

"Mr. Justice Davenport, Sir, upon your desire, I have sent you these *Quotations*, and my *own Sentiment*. I pray GOD, the Giver and Guardian of Life, to give his gracious Direction to you, and the other Justices, and take leave, who am your brother and most humble servant,

"Samuel Sewall.

"Boston, July 20, 1719.

"I inclosed also the *selling of Joseph*, and my Extract out of the *Athenian Oracle*.

"To Addington Davenport, Esq., etc., going to Judge Sam'l Smith of Sandwitch, for killing his Negro."[650]

Petition of Slaves in Boston.

On the 23d of June, 1773, the following petition was presented to the General Court of Massachusetts, which was read, and referred to the next session:—

PETITION OF SLAVES IN BOSTON.

Province of Massachusetts Bay.

To His Excellency, Thomas Hutchinson, Esq., Governor—

"To the Honorable, His Majesty's Council, and to the Honorable House of Representatives, in general court assembled at Boston, the 6th day of January, 1773:—The humble petition of many slaves living in the town of Boston, and other towns in the province, is this, namely:—

That Your Excellency and Honors, and the Honorable the Representatives, would be pleased to take their unhappy state and condition under your wise and just consideration.

We desire to bless God, who loves mankind, who sent his Son to die for their salvation, and who is no respecter of persons, that he hath lately put it into the hearts of multitudes, on both sides of the water, to bear our burthens, some of whom are men of great note and influence, who have pleaded our cause with arguments, which we hope will have their weight with this Honorable Court.

We presume not to dictate to Your Excellency and Honors, being willing to rest our cause on your humanity and justice, yet would beg leave to say a word or two on the subject.

Although some of the negroes are vicious, (who, doubtless, may be punished and restrained by the same laws which are in force against others of the King's subjects,) there are many others of a quite different character, and who, if made free, would soon be able, as well as willing, to bear a part in the public charges. Many of them, of good natural parts, are discreet, sober, honest and industrious; and may it not be said of many, that they are virtuous and religious, although their condition is in itself so unfriendly to religion, and every moral virtue, except *patience*? How many of that number have there been and now are, in this province, who had every day of their lives embittered with this most intolerable reflection, that, let their behavior be what it will, neither they nor their children, to all generations, shall ever be able to do or to possess and enjoy any thing—no, not even *life itself*—but in a manner as the *beasts* that perish!

We have no property! we have no wives! we have no children! we have no city! no country! But we have a Father in heaven, and we are determined, as far as his grace shall enable us, and as far as our degraded condition and contemptuous life will admit, to keep all his commandments; especially will we be obedient to our masters, so long as God, in his, sovereign providence, shall *suffer* us to be holden in bondage.

It would be impudent, if not presumptuous, in us to suggest to Your Excellency and Honors, any law or laws proper to be made in relation to our unhappy state, which although our greatest unhappiness, is not our *fault*; and this gives us great encouragement to pray and hope for such relief as is consistent with your wisdom, justice and goodness.

We think ourselves very happy, that we may thus address the great and general court of this province, which great and good court is to us the best judge, under God, of what is wise, just and good.

> We humbly beg leave to add but this one thing more we pray for such relief only, which by no possibility can ever be productive of the least wrong or injury to our masters, but to us will be as life from the dead.[651]

FOOTNOTES:

[650] Slavery in Mass., pp 96, 97.

[651] Neil, pp. 39-41.

CHAPTER XIII-THE COLONY OF NEW YORK

1693, August 21st—All Indians, Negroes, and others not "listed in the militia," are ordered to work on the fortification for repairing the same, to be under the command of the captains of the wards they inhabit. And £100 to be raised for the fortifications.

1722, February 20th.—A law passed by the common council of New York, "restraining slaves, negroes, and Indians from gaming with moneys." If found gaming with any sort of money, "copper pennies, copper halfpence, or copper farthings," they shall be publickly whipped at the publick whipping-post of this city, at the discretion of the mayor, recorder, and aldermen, or any one of them, unless the owner pay to the church wardens for the poor, 3s.

1731, November 18th—If more than three negro, mulatto, or Indian slaves assemble on Sunday and play or make noise, (or at any other time at any place from their master's service,) they are to be publickly whipped fifteen lashes at the publick whipping-post.

NEW YORK

Negro slavery, a favorite measure with England, was rapidly extending its baneful influence in the colonies. The American Register, of 1769, gives the number of negroes brought in slavery from the coast of Africa, between Cape Blanco and the river Congo, by different nations in one year, thus: Great Britain, 53,100; British Americans, 6,300; France, 23,520; Holland, 11,300; Portugal, 1,700; Denmark, 1,200; in all, 104,100, bought by barter for European and Indian manufacturers,—£15 sterling being the average price given for each negro. Thus we see that more than one half of the wretches who were kidnapped, or torn by force from their homes by the agents of European merchants (for such those who supply the market must be considered), were sacrificed to the cupidity of the merchants of Great Britain; the traffic encouraged by the government at the same time that the boast is sounded through the world, that the moment a slave touches the sacred soil, governed by those who encourage the slavemakers, and inhabited by those who revel in the profits derived from murder, he is free. Somerset, the negro, is liberated by the court of king's bench, in 1772, and the world is filled with the fame of English justice and humanity! James Grahame tells us that Somerset's case was not the first in which the judges of Great Britain counteracted in one or two cases the practical inhumanity of the government and the people: he says, that in 1762, his grandfather, Thomas Grahame, judge of the admiralty court of Glasgow, liberated a negro slave imported into Scotland.

It was in vain that the colonists of America protested against the practice of slave dealing. The governors appointed by England were instructed to encourage it, and when the assemblies enacted laws to prohibit the inhuman traffic, they were annulled by the vetoes of the governors. With such encouragement, the reckless and avaricious among the colonists engaged in the trade, and the slaves were purchased when brought to the colonies by those who were blind to the evil, or preferred present ease or profit to all future good. Paley, the moralist, thought the American Revolution was designed by Providence, to put an end to the slave trade, and to show that a nation encouraging it was not fit to be intrusted with the government of extensive colonies. But the planter of the Southern States have discovered, since made free by that revolution, that slavery is no evil; and better moralists than Paley, that the increase of slaves, and their extension over new regions, is the duty of every good democrat. The men who lived in 1773, to whom America owes her liberty, did not think so.

Although resistance to the English policy of increasing the number of negro slaves in America agitated many minds in the colonies, opposition to the system of taxation was the principal source of action; and this opposition now centered in a determination to baffle the designs of Great Britain in respect to the duties on tea. Seventeen millions of pounds of tea were now accumulated in the warehouses of the East-India Company. The government was determined, for reasons I have before given, to assist this mercantile company, as well as the African merchants, at the expense of the colonists of America. The East-India Company were now authorized to export their tea free of all duty. Thus the venders being enabled to offer it cheaper than hitherto to the colonists, it was expected that it would find a welcome market. But the Americans saw the ultimate intent of the whole scheme, and their disgust towards the mother country was proportionably increased.

INDEX

Abbott, Granville S., verses by,

Adams, Abigail, views on slavery,

Adams, John,

views on slavery,

letter to Jonathan Sewall on emancipation,

Adams, Samuel, urges the consideration of the memorial of Massachusetts Negroes,

Adgai, see Crowther

Africa,

described,

Negro tribes,

Negro kingdoms,

natives engage in the slave-trade,

laws,

religion,

war between the different tribes,

war with England,

patriarchal government,

villages described,

architecture,

women reign in,

marriage,

polygamy,

status of the natives,

warfare,

agriculture,
mechanic arts,
languages,
literature,
colony founded at Sierra Leone,,
and Liberia,
first emigrants to,
republican government established,
first constitution abolishing slavery in Liberia,
weaker tribes chief source of slavery,
early Christianity in,
earliest commerce for slaves between America and,
slaves from Angola,
shipload of slaves from Sierra Leone sold at Hispaniola,
number of Negroes stolen from annually,
slaves from, sold at Barbadoes,
cities of, described,
number of slaves brought from,
See Negroes
African Company,
their charter abolished,
see Royal African Company
Akwasi Osai, king of Ashantee,
invades Dahomey,
his defeat and death,
Alexander, James, volunteers to prosecute the Negroes in New York,
Alricks, Peter, resident of New York 1657,
Amasis, king of Egypt,
Amenophis, king of Egypt,
America,
introduction of Negro slaves,

colonies declare independence,
slavery in,
slaves imported to British America,
American Colonization Society locate a colony at Monrovia,
American Revolution,
service of Negroes in the army of the,
slavery during the,
Ames, Edward B., remarks in favor of the government of Liberia,
Angola, Africa, slaves imported from,
Anne, queen of England, encourages the slave-trade,
Anti-slavery societies,
memorials to Congress,
convention held at Philadelphia,
Apoko, Osai, king of Ashantee,
Appleton, Nathaniel,
defends the doctrine of freedom for all,
author of "Consideration on Slavery,"
Apries, king of Egypt,
Argall, Samuel, engaged in the slave-trade,
Ashantee Empire,
described,
wars of,
revolt in,
troubles with England,,
massacre of women,
government,
Asia,
idols with Negro features in,
traces of the race,
Asychis, king of Egypt,

Attucks, Crispus,
advertised as a runaway slave,
figures in the Boston Massacre,
his death and funeral,
letter to Gov. Hutchinson,
Aviia, tribe in Africa,
Aviro, Alfonso de, discovers Benin in Africa,
Babel, the tower of, built by an Ethiopian,
Babylon, description of,
Bancroft, George, views on slavery,
Banneker, Benjamin,
astronomer and philosopher,
farmer and inventor,
mathematician,
his first calculation of an eclipse,
letter to George Ellicott,
character of,
his business transactions,
verses addressed to,
letter to Mrs. Mason,
his first almanac,
letter to Thomas Jefferson,
accompanies commissioners to run the lines of District of Columbia,
his habits of studying the heavenly bodies,
his death,
Baptist missionaries in Liberia,
Barbadoes,
Negro slaves exchanged for Indians,
a slave-market for New-England traders,
Rhode Island supplied with slaves from,
Barrère, Peter, treatise on the color of the skin,

Barton, Col. William, captures Gen. Prescott,

Bates, John, a slave-trader,

Belknap, Jeremy, remarks on the slave-trials in Massachusetts,

Benin, a kingdom in Africa,

supplies America with slaves,

discovered by the Portuguese and colonized,

the king contracts to Christianize his subjects for a white wife,

the kingdom divided, and slave-trade suppressed,

Berkeley, Sir William, opposed to education and printing,

Bermuda Islands,

slaves placed on Warwick's plantation,

Pequod Indians exchanged for Negroes at,

Bernard, John, governor of the Bermudas,

Beverley, Robert, correction of his History of Virginia,

Bill, Jacob, a slave-trader,

Billing, Joseph, sued by his slave Amos Newport,

Blumenbach, Jean Frederic, opinion in regard to the color of the skin,

Blyden, Edward W.,

defines the term "Negro,"

president of Liberia College,

Board of Trade,

circular to the governors of the English colonies, relative to Negro slaves,

reply of Gov. Cranston of Rhode Island,

Bolzius, Henry, favors the introduction of slavery into Georgia,

Boombo, a Negro chief of Liberia,

Borden, Cuff, a Negro slave in Massachusetts, sued for trespass and ordered to be sold to satisfy judgment,

Boston,

a slave-trader from,

Negro prohibited from employment in manufacturing hoops,

number of slaves in,

instructs the representatives to vote against the slave-trade,

Negroes charged with firing the town,

articles for the regulation of Negroes passed,

massacre in, 1770,

Negroes on Castle Island,

Bowditch, Thomas Edward, commissioner to treat with the Ashantees,

Bradley, Richard, attorney-general of New York, prosecutes the Negroes,

Bradstreet, Ann, frees her slave,

Brazil, slaves sold to the Dutch,

Brewster, Capt. Edward, banished by Capt. Argall,

Brewster, Thomas, a slave-trader,

Bristol County, Mass., a slave ordered to be sold, to satisfy judgment against him for trespass,

British army, Negroes in the,

Brown, John, reproved by Virginia committee of 1775 for purchasing slaves,

Brown, Joseph, effect of climate on man,

Bruce, James, discovers the ruins of the city of Meroe,

Bunker Hill, Negroes in the battle of,

Burgess, Ebenezer, missionary to Monrovia,

Burton, Mary,

testifies in the Negro plot at New York, 1741,

recompensed by the government,

Busiris, king of Egypt,

Butler, Nathaniel, commissioner for Virginia Company,

Cade, Elizabeth, a witness in the Somersett case,

Calanee, image of Buddha at,

Caldwell, Jonas, killed at the Boston Massacre,

Campbell, Sir Neill, determines the war with Ashantees,

Canaan, the curse of,

Canada, expedition from New York against,

Candace, queen of the Ethiopians,

Carey, Lot, vice-agent of Liberia,

Carey, Peggy,

implicated with Negro plot in New York, 1741,

trial,

found guilty,

her evidence,

sentenced to be hanged,

Carr, Patrick, wounded at the Boston Massacre,

Cartel, Edwin, a slave-trader,

Carthage, description of,

Castle Island, Boston,

Negroes sent to the barracks at,

list of the same,

Cepharenus, king of Egypt,

Ceylon, image of Buddha at,

Chaillu, Paul B. Du,

description of the Obongos,

of the villages of Mandji and Ishogo,,

Chambers, John, volunteers to prosecute the Negroes in New York,

Charles V., grants a patent to import Negroes to America,

Charleston, S.C.,

slave-market at,

Negroes from, recaptured,

list of,

claimed by owners,

Charlestown, Mass., Negro slaves executed at, in 1755,

Chastellux, Marquis de, describes the bravery of Col. Greene's Negro regiment at the battle of Rhode Island,

Cheops, king of Egypt,

Chibbu, Kudjoh, captured by the English,
Chisholm, Major J, services in Ashantee mentioned,
Christy, David, describes the colony of Liberia,
Cintra, Piedro de, discoverer of Sierra Leone,
Clinton, Sir Henry, proclamation concerning fugitive Negroes, 1779,
Codman, John, poisoned by his slave,
Coleman, Elihu, author of "Testimony against making Slaves of Men,"
Coney Island, N.Y., slave captured at,
Congo Empire, Shinga queen of,
Congress, see United-States Congress
Connecticut,
slavery in,
Negro slaves introduced,
number of Negroes in 1680,
purchase and treatment of slaves and free persons,
persons manumitting slaves, to maintain them,
commerce with slaves prohibited,
punishment of insubordinate slaves,
social conduct regulated,
punished for using profane language,
number of slaves in 1730,
Indian slaves prohibited,
Indian and Negro slavery legalized,
limited rights of free Negroes,
Negro population in 1762,
importation of slaves prohibited,
number of slaves in 1715,
enlistment of Negroes prohibited,
enlisted,
a Colored company recruited by David Humphreys,
slave population in 1790,

Continental army,
condition of the,
Negroes in the,
Negro regiment raised for the,
number of men supplied to the,
return of Negroes in 1778,
Continental Congress,
prohibits the importation of Negroes,
debate on the discharge of Negroes from the army,
action on the enlistment of Negroes,
resolution to establish courts to decide cases of captured slaves,
action of the, relative to Negroes captured at sea,
discussion on the, Western territory,
last meeting,

Cooke, Nicholas, governor of Rhode Island, letters to Washington on the enlistment of Negroes,

Cornwallis, Lord, proclamation offering protection to fugitive Negroes,

Cox, Melville B., missionary to Monrovia,

Cranston, Samuel, letter to the board of trade, relative to Negro slaves in Rhode Island,

Croker, John, testimony in the Negro plot at New York,

Crowther,
Negro sold into slavery,
set at liberty by the English,
fitted for the ministry, returns to Africa as a missionary,

Cuffe, John, sketch of,

Cuffe, Paul, a distinguished Negro,

Cush,
ancestor of the Negro race,
meaning of the term,

Cushing, Nathan, his opinion, 1783, relative to the South-Carolina Negroes,

Cuvier, Baron, varieties of the human form,

Cyrene, Africa,

mentioned,

described,

Dahomey, a Negro kingdom of Africa,

described,

women serve in the army,

laws,

invaded by King Akwasi,

Dalton, Richard, his slave reads Greek,

Davis, Hugh, a white servant, flogged in Virginia, for consorting with a Negro woman,

Deane, Thomas, mentioned,

Delaware,

slavery in,

settled by Danes and Swedes,

slavery not allowed by the Swedes,

conveyed to William Penn,

granted a separate government,

slavery introduced,

first legislation on slavery,

law for the regulation of servants,

act restraining manumission of slaves,

number of slaves in 1715,

slave population in 1790,

Denmark, engaged in the slave-trade,

Denny, Thomas, representative of Leicester, Mass., instructed to vote against slavery,

Derham, James, a Negro physician of New Orleans,

Desbrosses, Elias, testimony in the Negro plot in New York, 1741,

"Desire," ship built for the slave-trade,

Dodge, Caleb, of Beverly, Mass., sued by his slave,

Dorsey, Charles W., character of Banneker, the Negro astronomer,

Duchet, Sir Lionel, engaged in the slave-trade,

Dummer, William, proclamation against Negroes of Boston,

Dunmore, Lord,

proclamation in regard to fugitive Negroes,

condemned by the Virginia convention,

his failure to enlist Negroes,

Dupuis, M., appointed English consul to the court of Ashantee,

Dutch man-of-war

lands the first Negroes in Virginia,

engage in the slave-trade,

import slaves to New Netherlands,

encourage the trade,

settlement on the Delaware,

Earl, John, his connection with the Negro plot at New York,

East Greenwich, R.I., bridge built at, by Negro impost-tax,

Egmont, Earl of, opposed to slavery in Georgia,

Egypt,

first settlers of,

Negro and Mulatto races in,

slavery in,

Negro civilization imitated by,

the Ethiopian kings of,

Elizabeth, Queen, of England, encourages the slave-trade,

Elizabeth, N.J., police regulations,

England,

suppresses the slave-trade,

sends agricultural implements, machinery, and missionaries to Africa,

conduct in the Ashantee war,,,

treaty with Ashantee,

founds a colony in Sierra Leone,

all slaves declared free on reaching British soil,

declares slave-trade piracy,

establishes a mission at Sierra Leone,

women sent to Virginia,

laws relating to slavery,

sanctions the slave-trade,

courts decide in 1677 that a Negro slave is property,

slavery recognized in,

agrees to furnish Negroes to the West Indies,

treaty with United States,

Enoch, description of the city of,

Ethiopia,

war with Cæsar,

natives same race as Egyptians,

meaning of,

cities of, described,

kings rule Egypt,

Fairfax, Va., meeting at, in 1774, pass resolutions against slavery,

"Fanny," brig, arrives at Norfolk, Va., with slaves,

Federal Constitution, proceedings of convention to frame the,

Ferguson, Dr., describes character of the inhabitants of Sierra Leone,

Folger, Elisha, captain of ship "Friendship," sued for recovery of a slave,

Forbes, Archibald, mentions Africans nine feet in height,

Fox, George, views concerning slaves,

France engaged in the slave-trade,

Franklin, Benjamin,

letter to Dean Woodward on the abolition of slavery,

address to the public on the abolition of slavery,

Friends, see Quakers

Fuller, Thomas, a Negro mathematician,

Gage, Thomas, refuses to sign the bill to prevent the importation of Negroes into Massachusetts,

Gates, Gen. Horatio, his order not to enlist Negroes,

George III. in 1751 repeals the act declaring slaves real estate,

Georgia,

slavery in,

colony of, established,

slavery prohibited in,

discussion in regard to the admission of slavery,

clandestine importation of Negroes,

slavery established,

history of slavery,

number of slaves in 1715,

importation of slaves prohibited,

slave population in 1790,

Germantown, Penn., memorial of Quakers against slavery in 1688,

Glasgow, Scotland, a slave liberated in 1762,

Goddard, Benjamin, protests against enlisting Negroes in Grafton, Mass.,

Godfrey family of South Carolina, killed by a Negro mob,

Gordon, William,

letter on the emancipation of slaves,

deposed as chaplain of the legislature of Massachusetts,

Grafton, Mass., protest in 1778 against the enlistment of Negroes,

Grahame, Judge Thomas, liberates Negro slave in Glasgow, Scotland,

Gray, Samuel, killed at the Boston Massacre,

Greece, Negro civilization imitated by,

Greene, Col. Christopher,

commands a Negro regiment in 1778 at battle of Rhode Island, his death,

Greene, Gen. Nathanael,

letters to Washington on the raising of a Negro regiment,

on the enlistment of Negroes, the British army,

at battle of Rhode Island,

Greenleaf, Richard, sued by his slave,

Guerard, Benjamin, governor of South Carolina, letter to Gov. Hancock relative to slaves recaptured from the British,

Guyot, Arnold H., opinion on the diversity of the human race,

Habersham, James, favors slavery in Georgia,

Ham,

the progenitor of the Negro race,

family of,

founder of the Babylonian empire,

Hamilton, Alexander,

letter to John Jay on the enlistment of Negroes,

opinion in regard to slaves captured by the British,

Hamilton, Dr., his connection with the Negro plot at New York,

Hancock, John, letter on the condition of the South-Carolina Negroes recaptured from the British,

"Hannibal," sloop, Negroes captured from,

Harcourt, Col. William, captures Gen. Charles Lee,

Harper, ——, one of the founders of the colony at Cape Palmas, Liberia,

Harris, Rev. Samuel, describes bravery of Negro regiment at battle of Rhode Island,

Hawkins, Sir John, a slave-trader,

"Hazard," armed vessel, recaptures Negroes,

Hendrick, Cæsar, a slave, sues for his freedom,,

Hessian officer, letter on the employment of Negroes in the army,

Hillgroue, Nicholas, engaged in the slave-trade,

Hispaniola, slaves from Sierra Leone sold at,

Hobby, Mr. Negro in the army claimed by,

Hogg, Robert, a merchant of New York, robbed by Negroes,

Holbrook, Felix, petition of, for freedom,

Holland,

growth of slavery in New Netherlands,

children of manumitted Negroes held as slaves to serve the government of,

slaves exchanged for tobacco,

engaged in the slave-trade,

Holt, Lord, his opinion that slavery was unknown to English law,

Hopkins, John H., views of slavery,

Hopkins, Samuel, necessity of employing the Negroes in the American army,

Horsmanden, Daniel, one of the judges in the trial of the Negro plot at New York, 1741,

Hotham, Sir Charles, testimony in regard to the abolishment of slavery in Liberia,

Hughson, John,

his tavern at New York a resort for Negroes,

his connection with the Negro plot,

trial,

sentenced to be hanged,

executed,

Hughson, Sarah,

her connection with the New York Negro plot,

trial,

respited,

testimony,

Human race, the unity of,

Humphreys, David, recruits a company of colored infantry in Connecticut,

Hutchinson, a commissioner to treat with king of Ashantee,

Hutchinson, Gov. Thomas, refuses to sign bill to prevent the importation of slaves from Africa,

Indians,

taxable,

not treated as slaves,

declared slaves,

denied the right to appear as witnesses,

act to baptize,

proclamation against the harboring,

alarmed on seeing a Negro,

exchanged for Negroes,

sent to Bermudas,

held in perpetual bondage,

marriage with Negroes,

introduction of, as slaves, prohibited in Massachusetts,

importation of, prohibited,

slavery of, legalized,

Ishogo villages in Africa described,

Jacksonburgh, S.C., Negro insurrection at,

Jamaica, slaves from, sold in Virginia,

James, Gov., commissioner to treat with king of Ashantee,

James City, Va., buildings destroyed,

Jameson, David, volunteers to prosecute the negroes in New York,

Japan, negro idols in,

Jefferson, Thomas,

author of instructions to the Virginia delegation in Congress, 1774, on the abolition of slavery,

letters to Dr. Gordon relative to the treatment of Negroes in Cornwallis's army,

to Benjamin Banneker,

his recommendation in regard to slavery in the Western Territory,

Jeffries, John P., declares there are no reliable data of the Negro race,

Johnson, David, accused of conspiracy in New York,

Jones, William, his genealogy of Noah,

Joseph, the selling of,

a memorial by Samuel Sewall,

answered by John Saffin,

Josselyn, John, describes attempt to breed slaves in Massachusetts,

Kane, William,

accused of conspiracy in New York,

testimony of, in the Negro plot,

Kench, Thomas, letters to the General Assembly of Massachusetts on the enlistment of Negroes,

Kendall, Capt. Miles,

deputy governor of Virginia, receives Negro slaves in exchange for supplies,

dispossessed of the same, returns to England to seek equity,

portion of the Negroes allotted to him,

none of which he receives,

Kentucky,

admitted into the Union,

constitution revised,

Keyser, Elizur, emancipates his slave,

Knowls, John, confines James Sommersett on board his ship "Mary and Ann,"

Knox, Thomas, South Carolina, recaptured slaves delivered to,

Kudjoh Osai, king of Ashantee,

Kwamina Osai, succeeds his father Kudjoh as king of Ashantee,

"Lady Gage," a prize-ship with Negroes,

Laing, Capt., his services in Ashantee,

Latrobe, J.H.B., one of the founders of the colony at Cape Palmas, Liberia,

Laurens, Henry, letter to Washington on arming of the Negroes of South Carolina,

Laurens, John,
 endeavors to raise Negro troops in South Carolina,
 sails for France,
 letters to Washington on his return, urging the enlistment of Negroes,
 Lawrence, Major Samuel, commands a company of Negro soldiers,
 Lechmere, Richard, sued by his slave,
 Lee, Gen. Charles, captured by the British,
 Leicester, Mass., representative of, instructed to vote against slavery,
 Liberia,
 founded by Colored people from Maryland,
 population,
 refuge for Colored people,
 native tribes,
 Christian mission founded,
 government,
 a republic,
 school and college established,
 churches,
 trade,
 first constitution,
 slavery and slave-trade abolished,
 treaty with England in regard to slavery,
 testimony of officers of the Royal Navy in regard to the slave-trade at,
 revolt in, subdued,
 Lincoln, Gen. Benjamin, letter to Gov. Rutledge of South Carolina, on the enlistment of Negroes,
 Livingstone, David,
 describes African wars,
 status of the Africans,
 skilful in the mechanic arts,
 Locke, John,

constitution prepared by, adopted in North Carolina,
local governments of the South organised on his plan,
Lodge, Abraham, volunteers to prosecute the Negroes in New York,
Lodge, Sir Thomas, a slave-trader,
Lowell, John, sues for the freedom of a slave in Newburyport, Mass.
Lybia, Africa, description of,
MacBrair, R.M., author of a Mandingo grammar,
McCarthy, Charles,
appointed governor-general of Western Africa,
war with the Ashantees,
his defeat and death,
Madison, James, letter to Joseph Jones, on the arming of the Negroes,
Mahoney, Lieut., his description of a Negro idol at Calanee,
Mandji, a village in Africa described,
Mankind,
unity of,
varieties of,
Mansfield, Lord, decision in the case of the Negro Sommersett,
Marlow, John, affidavit in the Sommersett case,
Maryland,
appropriates money for the colony at Cape Palmas,
slaves purchased to evade tax,
slavery in,
under the laws of Virginia,
first legislation on slavery,
population of,
slavery established by statute,
Act passed encouraging the importation of Negroes and slaves,
impost on Negroes, slaves, and white persons imported into,
duties on rum and wine,
treatment of slaves and papists,

convicts imported into,
convict trade condemned,
defended,
slave-code,
rights of slaves,
law against manumission of slaves,
Negro population,
white population,
increase of slavery,
number of slaves in 1715,
Negroes enlist in the army,
slave population in 1790,

Maryland Colonization Society, found colony of Negroes at Cape Palmas, Liberia,

Mason, George, author of the Virginia resolutions of 1774 against slavery,

Mason, Susanna, addresses a poetical letter to Benjamin Banneker,

Massachusetts,
slavery in,
earliest mention of the Negro in,
Moore's history of slavery in,
Pequod War the cause of slavery,
slaves imported to,
ship "Desire" arrives with slaves,,
slavery established,
first statute establishing slavery,
made hereditary,
kidnapped Negroes,
number of slaves,
tax on slaves,
Negro population,

introduction of Indian slaves prohibited,

Negroes rated with cattle,

denied baptism,

Act in relation to marriage of Negro slaves,

slave-marriage ceremony,

condition of free Negro,

Act to abolish slavery,

slave awarded a verdict against his master,

emancipation of slaves,

legislation favoring the importation of white servants, and prohibiting the clandestine bringing-in of Negroes,

importation of Negroes not as profitable as white servants,

prohibitory legislation against slavery,

proclamation against Negroes,

slaves executed,

transported and exchanged for small Negroes,

slaves sue for freedom,

Negroes petition for freedom,

bill passed for the suppression of the slave-trade,

vetoed by Gov. Gage,

number of slaves in,

emancipation of slaves,

enlistment of Negroes and emancipation of slaves prohibited,

enlistment of Negroes opposed,

mode of enlisting Negroes,

Negroes serve with white troops,

number of men furnished to the army,

act relative to captured Negroes,

sale of captured Negroes prohibited,

armed vessels from, recapture Negroes,

act relative to prisoners of war,

slaves petition for freedom,

act against slavery,

extinction of slavery,

lawsuits brought by slaves,

condition of slaves,

Maverick, Samuel, attempts to breed slaves in Massachusetts,

Maverick, Samuel, mortally wounded at the Boston Massacre,

Mede, Joseph, his statement in regard to Ham corrected,

Medford, Mass., representative of, instructed to vote against slavery,

Melville, John, his sermon on Simon mentioned,

Menes, first king of Egypt,

Meroe, Egypt, capital of African Ethiopia and chief city of the Negroes,

Methodist Episcopal Church, establishes a mission in Liberia,

Methodist Missionary Society appropriate money for the mission at Monrovia,

Mifflin, Warner, presents a memorial to Congress in 1792 for the abolition of slavery,

Mills, James,

missionary to Monrovia,

death,

Missah Kwanta, son of the king of Ashantee, sent to England as a hostage,

Mississippi, slavery in Territory of, prohibited, 1797,

Monroe, James, town of Monrovia named in honor of,

Monrovia, Africa,

founded,

population,

Christian mission established,

Moore, George H.,

his history of slavery in Massachusetts commended,

mentioned,

remarks on the bill to prohibit the importation of slaves from Africa,

Morton, Samuel G., the sphinx a shrine of the Negro,

Murphy, Edward, accused of conspiracy in New York,

Murray, Joseph, volunteers to prosecute the Negroes in New York,

Mycerinus, king of Egypt,

"Nautilus," ship arrives at Sierra Leone with colony of Negroes,

Nechao, king of Egypt,

Negro plot in New York City, 1741,

Negroes,

members of the human family,

descendants of Ham,

represented in pictures of the crucifixion of Christ,

an Ethiopian eunuch becomes a Christian,

same race as Egyptian,

Cush an ancestor,

use of the term "Negro,"

antiquity of the race,

early military service,

figured in a Theban tomb,

political and social condition,

the Sphinx a shrine of,

idols,

origin of color and hair,

primitive civilization,

decline,

kingdoms,

engage in the slave trade,

women in the army,

laws, religion,

different tribes at war,

war with England,

the Negro type,

physical and mental character affected by climate,

longevity,

slaves the lower class,

habits,

susceptible to Christianity,

idiosyncrasies of the,

patriarchal government,

villages,

pursuits

architecture,

women as rulers,

priests,

laws,

marriage,

status,

nine feet in height,

beauty of the,

warfare,

agriculture,

mechanic arts,

languages,

literature,

religion,

free, leave for England,

colony of, at Sierra Leone,

serve in the British army,

their condition in America,

found colony at Liberia,

first importance of,

military abilities,

early Christianity,

earliest importation to America,
in Virginia,
number of, in Virginia,
prohibition against,
tax on female,
law of Virginia declares them slaves,
repeal of the Act declaring them real estate,
duty on slaves in Virginia,
traffic encouraged in Virginia,
no political or military rights in Virginia,
denied the right to appear as witnesses,
revolt of free, in Virginia,
pay taxes,
in the military service,
intermarriage of, prohibited,
denied education,
children of manumitted, made slaves,
not allowed to hold real estate in New York,
earliest mention of, in Massachusetts,
held in perpetual bondage,
condition of free, in Massachusetts,
importation of, not so profitable as white servants,
Act encouraging the importation of, into Maryland,
condition of free, in Maryland,
limited lights of free,
prohibited the use of the streets in Rhode Island,
military employment of,
excluded from the Continental Army,
allowed to re-enlist,
in Virginia join the British Army,
cautioned against joining the latter,

serve in the army with white troops in Massachusetts,
efforts to enlist in South Carolina,
company of, enlisted in Connecticut,
return of, in the army, 1778,
as soldiers, 1775-1783,
at the battle of Bunker Hill,
at battle of Rhode Island,
valor of,
sale of two captured, prohibited in Massachusetts,
disposal of recaptured,
education of, prohibited,
Newburyport, Mass, a slave sues for freedom,
New England
Negroes leave for England,
engaged in the slave trade,,
see Massachusetts
New Hampshire,
Massachusetts exercises authority over,
slavery in,
Negro slave emancipated,
instruction against importation of slaves,
conduct of servants regulated,
ill treatment of slaves,
importation of Indian servants prohibited,
ill treatment of servants and slaves prohibited,
duration of slaves in,
number of slaves in,
slave population in 1790,
New Jersey,
slavery in,
Act in regard to slaves,

the colony divided, with separate governments,
entertaining of fugitive servants, or trading with Negroes, prohibited,
Negroes and other slaves allowed trial by a jury,
publicity in judicial proceedings,
rights of government of surrendered to the queen,
conduct of slaves regulated,
impost tax on imported Negroes,
trials of slaves regulated,
security required
for manumitted slaves,
slaves prohibited from joining the militia,
population, 1738-45,
number of slaves in,
slave population in 1790,
New Netherlands, see New York
Newport, Amos, a slave, sues for his freedom,
Newport, R.I.,
Negroes and Indians prohibited the use of the streets,
Negro slaves arrive,
part of them sold,
vessels fitted out for the slave-trade,
streets repaired from the impost-tax on Negroes,
New York,
slavery in,
slaves imported from Brazil,
laws relative to slavery,
slaves the property of West-India Company,
supply of slaves,
Act for regulating slaves,
Act to baptize slaves,
expedition against Canada,

governor of, claims jurisdiction over Pennsylvania,
number of slaves in,
Act for raising Negro troops,
Negro soldiers promised freedom,
slave population in 1790,
bill for the gradual extinction of slavery,
laws in regard to slaves,
New York City,
settled by the Dutch,
growth of slavery under the Holland government,
children of manumitted Negroes made slaves,
slaves imported from Brazil,
captured by the English,
laws on slavery,
identical with Massachusetts,
Gov. Dongan arrives,
General Assembly meet,
proclamation against the harboring of slaves,
slaves forbidden the streets after nightfall,
slave-market erected,
Negro riot,
Negro plot,
house of Robert Hogg robbed,
population,
fire at Fort George,
fires in,
crew of Spanish vessel adjudged slaves,
charged with firing houses,
house of John Hughson, resort for Negroes,
act against entertaining slaves,
council meet, request governor to offer reward for incendiaries,

Negroes deny all knowledge of the fires and plot,
Supreme Court convened, trial of Negroes,
Negroes hanged,
fast observed in,
Negroes arrested,
chained to a stake, and burned,
proclamation granting freedom to conspirators who would confess,
Spanish Negroes sentenced to be hung,
Hughson executed,
Negroes hanged,
thanksgiving,
Rev. John Ury executed,
arrests for conspiracy,
first session of Congress held at, in 1789,
Nicoll, Benjamin, volunteers to prosecute the Negroes in New York,
Nineveh, the city of, founded,
Noddle's Island, Mass., slaves on,
Non-Importation Act passed by Congress,
Norfolk, Va., arrival of slaves at,
North Carolina,
slaves purchased in, to evade the tax,
slavery in,
situation of, favorable to the slave-trade,
the Locke Constitution adopted,
William Sayle commissioned governor,
Negro slaves eligible to membership in the church,
Church of England established in,
rights of Negroes controlled by their masters,
act respecting conspiracies,
form of trying Negroes,
ill treatment of Negroes,

emancipation of slaves prohibited,

limited rights of free Negroes,

number of slaves in,

slave population in 1790,

Nott, John C.,

antiquity of the Negro,

his social condition,

Oates, Titus, his connection with the Popish plot,

Obongos of Africa described,

Ockote, Osai, king of Ashantee, his war with the English,

Oglethorpe, John, first governor of Georgia, opposed to slavery,

Ophir, Africa, description of,

Opoko, Osai, king of Ashantee,

Osymandyas, king of Egypt,

Otis, James, speech in favor of freedom to the Negroes,

Parsons, Theophilus,

is opinion on the existence of slavery in Massachusetts,

decision in the case of Winchendon *vs.* Hatfield,

Pastorius, Francis Daniel, his memorial against slavery, 1688,

Payne, John, missionary bishop of Africa,

Pendleton, Edmund, letter to Richard Lee on the slaves of Virginia joining the British army,

Penn, William,

Delaware conveyed to,

grants the privilege of separate government,

introduces bill for the regulation of servants,

opposed to slavery,

Pennsylvania,

slavery in,

government organized,

Swedes and Dutch settlement,

governor of New York claims jurisdiction over,

first laws of,

memorial against slavery,

Penn presents bill for the better regulation of servants,

tax on imported slaves,

importation of Negroes and Indians prohibited,

petition for the freedom of slaves denied,

rights of the Negroes,

tax on Negroes and Mulatto slaves,

fears for the conduct of the slaves,

number of slaves in,

slave population in 1790,

Pennsylvania Society for promoting the abolition of slavery, address of the, 1789,

Pequod Indians

captured in war exchanged for Negroes,

as slaves,

Peters, John, married to Phillis Wheatley,

Peters, Phillis, see Wheatley, Phillis

Pheron, king of Egypt,

Philadelphia,

Federal Convention meet at,

Anti-slavery Convention held at,

see Pennsylvania

Phut, Africa, description of,

Pickering, Timothy, representative of Salem, Mass., instructed to vote against the importation of slaves,

Pinny, J.B., missionary to Liberia,

Pitcairn, John, killed at Bunker Hill by a Negro soldier,

Plant, Matthias, missionary of the Propagation Society in Mass,

Po, Fernando, locates Portuguese colony in Africa,

Poor, Salem, a Negro soldier, his bravery at Bunker Hill,
Popish plot in England concocted by Titus Gates,
Portugal,
engages in the slave-trade,
locates colony at Benin, Africa,
Prescott, Richard, captured by Lieut.-Col. Barton,
Presbyterian Board of Missions establish missions in Liberia,
Price, Arthur,
arrested for theft in New York,
testimony in the Negro plot,154
Prichard, John C., varieties of the human race,
Prince, a Negro, assists in the capture of Gen. Prescott,
Protestant Episcopal Church
establishes first mission at Sierra Leone,
in Liberia,
Proteus, king of Egypt,
Psammetichus, king of Egypt,
Psammis, king of Egypt,
Pul, Africa, description of,
Quakers,
opposed to slavery,
memorial of, against slavery in Pennsylvania,
the friends of the Negroes,
memorial to Congress relative to slavery,
Rameses, Miamun, king of Egypt,
Raffles, T. Stanford, his researches on the Negro race,
Reade, W. Winwood,
describes patriarchal government of Africa,
beauty of the Negro,
people of Sierra Leone,
Revere, Paul, Negroes placed in his charge at Castle Island, Mass.,

Rhampsinitus, king of Egypt,

Rhode Island,

slavery in,

colonial government,

Act of 1652 to abolish slavery not enforced,

Negroes and Indians prohibited the use of the streets,

impost-tax on slaves,

entertainment of slaves prohibited,

Negro slaves sold in,

supply of Negroes from Barbadoes,

vessels fitted out for the slave-trade,

value of Negro slaves,

list of militia-men, including white and black servants,

clandestine importations and exportations of passengers, Negroes, or Indian slaves prohibited,

masters of vessels required to report the names and number of passengers,

penalties for violating the impost-tax law on slaves,

portion of the impost-tax on imported Negroes appropriated to repair streets of Newport,

disposition of the money raised by impost-tax,

slaves imported into,

impost-tax repealed,

manumission of aged and helpless slaves regulated,

Negro slaves rated as chattel property,

masters of vessels prohibited from carrying slaves out of,

importation of Negroes prohibited,

population from 1730-1774,

number of slaves in,

act emancipating slaves on joining the army,

protest against the enlistment of slaves,

Negro troops engaged in the battle of,

slave population in 1790,
Ricketts, Capt., services in the Ashantee war,
Roberts, J.J., president of Liberia, proclamation regarding passports,
Rockwell, Charles, describes Liberia,
Roman Catholics
denied the right to appear as witnesses in Virginia,
treatment of, in Maryland,
denounced by Oates,
suspected in New York,
Rome, Negro civilization imitated by,
Rommes, John,
charged with burglary at New York,
accused of being in the Negro plot,
Royal African Company,
charter abolished,
ordered to send supply of slaves to New York,
has sole right to trade on the coast of Africa,
Royall, Jacob, imports Negro slaves into Rhode Island,
Ruffin, Robert, a slave of, declared free for revealing plot of free Negroes in Virginia,
Rush, Benjamin, his opinion of James Derham the Negro physician,
Ryase, Andrew, accused of conspiracy in New York,
Sabachus, king of Ethiopia,
Saffin, John, reply to Judge Sewall's tract, "The Selling of Joseph,"
St. George's Bay Company
organized,
succeeded by the Sierra Leone Company,
Salem, Mass,
representative of, instructed to vote against the importation of slaves,,
Negro conspiracy,
slaves sent to,

petition of slaves in,

Negroes captured at sea advertised for sale,

Salem, Peter, a Negro soldier, his bravery at Bunker Hill,

Salisbury, Samuel Webster, author of an address on slavery, 1769,

Saltonstall, Richard, petitions the General Court of Massachusetts against stealing Negroes for slaves,

Sandwich, Mass, representative of, instructed to vote against slavery,

Sargent, Nathaniel P., opinion, 1783, relative to South-Carolina Negroes,

Savage, Samuel P., letter, 1763, in regard to South Carolina Negroes,

Sayle, William, commissioned governor of North Carolina,

Schultz, John, testimony in the Negro plot at New York, 1741,

Scotland, a Negro slave liberated in 1762,

Scott, Bishop, letter on the government of Liberia,

"Seaflower," ship, arrives at Newport, R.I., from Africa, with slaves,

Seba, Africa, description of,

Sesach, king of Egypt,

Sesostris, king of Egypt,

Sethon, king of Egypt,

Sewall, Jonathan, letter to John Adams on the emancipation of slaves,

Sewall, Joseph, sermon on the fires in Boston, 1723,

Sewall, Samuel,

protests against rating Negroes with cattle,

his hatred of slavery,

publishes his tract "The Selling of Joseph,"

father of the anti-slavery movement in Massachusetts,

letter to Addington Davenport on the murder of Smith's slave, 1719,

Shaftesbury, Earl of, in favor of introducing slavery into Georgia,

Sharp, Granville, one of the founders of Sierra Leone colony,

Sherbro, mission district, Western Africa, described,

Shinga, queen of Congo,

Shishak, king of Ethiopia,
Shodeke, king of Yoruba, Africa,
Siam, negro idols in,
Sicana, chief of the Kaffir tribe, a Christian and a poet,
Sierra Leone,
sends colony to Yoruba, Africa,
discovered,
Negro colony founded,
attacked by French squadron,
England takes possession of,
population,
trade,
Christian missions at,
languages of colony,
character of the inhabitants described by Gov. Ferguson,
slaves from, sold at Hispaniola,
Sierra Leone Company,
organized,
objects of,
Simon, a negro, bears the cross of Jesus,
Slavery,
Hopkins's Bible views of,
in Egypt,
in Africa,
Lord Manfield's decision in the Sommersett case,
colonization, the solution of,
abolished in Liberia,
weaker tribes of Africa, chief source of,
introduced in Virginia,
made legal in Virginia,
growth of, in Virginia,

growth in New York,
sanctioned by the English,
New York laws,
made legal in New York,
in Massachusetts,
established,
first statute establishing, in United States,
sanctioned by the church and courts,
made hereditary in Massachusetts,
growth of, in Massachusetts,
recognized in England,
act to abolish in Massachusetts,
prohibitory legislation against,
first legislation in Maryland,
established by statute,
increased in Maryland,
introduced in Delaware,
first legislation on,
Indian and Negro, legalized in Connecticut,
in New Jersey,
established in South Carolina,
perpetual,
in New Hampshire
memorial against, in Pennsylvania,
prohibited in Georgia,
Gov. Oglethorpe's opinion on,
discussion on the admission of, in Georgia,
established in Georgia,
Washington prevents resolutions against,
legislation against, demanded,
act against, in Massachusetts,

progress of, during the Revolution,
as a political and legal problem,
recognized under the new government of United States,
attempted legislation against,
advocated by the Southern States,
speeches delivered in the convention at Philadelphia on,
in the Federal Congress,
extinction of, in Massachusetts,
Franklin's address for the abolition of,
memorials to Congress for the abolition of,
bill for the gradual extinction of, in New York,
firmly established,
Slaves,
social condition of white and black,
the lower class of negroes,
Lord Mansfield's decision in the Sommersett case,
declared free on reaching British soil,
introduced in America,
first introduced in Virginia,,
on Somer Islands,
number of, in Virginia,
prohibition against,
special tax on female,
sold for tobacco,
laws of Virginia in regard to,
act repealed declaring them real estate,
duty on,
purchased in Maryland and Carolina to evade the tax,
tax on sales of, in Virginia,
reduced,
repealed,

revived,

traffic in, encouraged in Virginia,

no political or military rights,

laws in Virginia,

value fixed on, when executed,

laws of Virginia in regard to freedom of,

presented to clergymen,

prohibition against instructing,

denied education,

introduced in New York,

West India Company trade in,

manumitted in New York,

children of the latter held as,

imported from Brazil to New York,

exchanged for tobacco,

intermarry in New York,

New York to have constant supply,

Act to regulate,

Act to baptizse,

against the harboring of,

forbidden the streets in New York,

Negro riot,

Negro plot,

executed,

burned,

Negroes exchanged for Indians,

Indians sent to Bermudas,

imported from Barbadoes to Massachusetts,

ship "Desire" arrives with,

attempt to breed, in Massachusetts,

sold in Massachusetts,

issue of female, the property of their master,
marriage of,
sold at Barbadoes and West Indies,
number in Massachusetts,
tax on,
rated as cattle,
denied baptism,
marriage-ceremony,
verdict awarded to a slave in Massachusetts,
number in Boston,
emancipated,
executed in Massachusetts,
transported and exchanged for small negroes,
sue for freedom in Massachusetts,
emancipated by England,
slave-code of Maryland,
laws against manumission of,
introduced in Connecticut,
purchase and treatment of,
persons manumitting to maintain them,
commerce with, prohibited,
importation of, prohibited,
impost-tax on, in Rhode Island,
entertainment of, prohibited,
letter of the board of trade relative to,
Rhode Island supplied with, from Barbadoes,
slaves sold in Rhode Island,
value of,
clandestine importation and exportation of, prohibited,
Act relative to freeing Mulatto and Negro, in Rhode Island,
rated as chattel property,

masters of vessels prohibited from carrying Negro out of Rhode Island,

importation of, prohibited,

allowed trial by jury, in New Jersey,

impost-tax on,

prohibited from joining militia,

regarded as chattel property in South Carolina,

branded,

life of, regarded as of little consequence,

education of, prohibited,

overworking of, prohibited,

insurrection,

enlistment of,

masters compensated for the loss of,

rights of, controlled by the master in North Carolina,

emancipation of, prohibited,

New Hampshire opposed to the importation of,

ill treatment of, prohibited,

duration of, in New Hampshire,

tax on, imported into Pennsylvania,

petition for freedom of, denied,

number of slaves in the colonies 1715 and 1775,

arrival of, at Virginia, from Jamaica,

severe treatment of, modified,

the Boston Massacre,

in the Continental army,

excluded from the army,

allowed to re-enlist,

Lord Dunmore's proclamation freeing,

join the British army,

prohibited from enlisting in Connecticut,

Rhode Island emancipates, on joining the army,
protest against the same,
masters of enlisted, recompensed,
serve in the army with white troops,
Act to enlist, in New York,
efforts to enlist, in South Carolina,
treatment of, by Cornwallis,
exchanged for merchandise,
disposal of recaptured,
recaptured, sent to Boston,
list of recaptured,
held as personal property,
education of, prohibited,
sale of, advertised,
in Massachusetts petition for freedom,
rights of, limited in Virginia,
who served in the army emancipated,
promised their freedom in New York,
impost-tax on, introduced in Federal Congress,
lawsuits instituted by, in Massachusetts,
number of, in United States, 1790,
law for the return of fugitive,
introduction of, prohibited into the Mississippi Territory,
importation of, prohibited in Georgia,
condition of, in Massachusetts,
petition of, in Boston,
Massachusetts laws in regard to,
Slave-trade,
commenced at Benin, Africa,
natives of Africa engage in,
suppressed by England,

at Yoruba, Africa,

declared piracy by England,

abolished in Liberia,

earliest commerce for slaves between Africa and America,

introduced first in Virginia,

Dutch engage in the,

tax on the subjects of Great Britain in the,

encouraged in Virginia,

with Angola, Africa,

encouraged by the Dutch,

sanctioned by the English,

encouraged by Queen Elizabeth,

growth in New York,

slave-market erected in New York,

Indians exchanged for Negroes,

in New England,

ship "Desire" built for the,

arrives with cargo of slaves,

on the coast of Guinea,

increased in Massachusetts,

abolished by England,

bill for the suppression of, in Massachusetts,

sanctioned in Rhode Island,

vessels fitted out for the,

slave-market at Charleston, S.C.,

the situation of South Carolina favorable to the,

progress during the Revolution,

discussion in Congress on the restriction of the,

act against the foreign,

Slew, Jenny, a slave, sues for her freedom,

Smeatham, Dr., one of the founders of the Sierra Leone colony,

Smith, Hamilton, antiquity of the Negro race,

Smith, Samuel, murders his Negro slave,

Smith, William, volunteers to prosecute the Negroes in New York,

Sommersett, James,

a Negro slave, brought to England and abandoned by his master,

discharged,

Sorubiero, Margaret, connected with the New-York Negro plot, 1741,

South Carolina,

slaves purchased in, to evade the tax,

slavery in,

receives two charters from Great Britain,

Negro slaves in,

slavery legislation,

slavery established,

perpetual bondage of the Negro,

slaves regarded as chattel property,

trial of slaves,

increase of slave population,

growth of the rice-trade,

trade with Negroes prohibited,

conduct of slaves regulated,

punishment of slaves,

branded,

life of slaves regarded as of little consequence,

fine for killing slaves,

education of slaves prohibited,

permitted to be baptized,

inquiry into the treatment of slaves,
overworking of slaves prohibited,
hours of labor,
slave-market at Charleston,
Negro insurrection,
whites authorized to carry fire-arms,
enlistment of slaves,
Negroes admitted to the militia service,
masters compensated for the loss of slaves,
few slaves manumitted,
little legislation on slavery from 1754-1776,
effect of the threatened war with England,
number of slaves in 1715 and 1775,
efforts to raise Negro troops,
Negroes desert from,
recapture of Negroes from the British,
slave population, 1790,
Spain
engaged in the slave-trade,
her colonies in the West Indies to be furnished with Negroes,
Stanley, Henry M., description of a journey through Africa,
Staten Island, N.Y., a Negro regiment to be raised there,
Stephens, Thomas,
favors the introduction of slavery in Georgia,
reprimanded,
Stewart, Charles, owner of the Negro slave James Sommersett,
Stone, S.C., a Negro insurrection at,
Swain, John, suit to recover a slave,
Swan, James, advocate of liberty for all,

Swedes, settle on the Delaware River,

Tacudons, king of Dahomey,

Tarshish, Africa, description of,

Taylor, Comfort, sues a slave for trespass,

Teage, Collin, missionary to Liberia,

Tembandumba, queen of the Jagas,

Tharaca, king of Egypt,

Thethmosis, king of Egypt,

Thomas, John, letter to John Adams, 1775, on the employment of Negroes in the army,

Thompson, Capt, of ship "Nautilus," arrives at Sierra Leone with Negroes,

Timans, second king of Egypt,

Tutu Osai, king of Ashantee,

"Treasurer," ship,

sails to West Indies for Negroes,

arrives at Virginia,

"Tyrannicide," armed vessel, re-captures Negroes,

Uchoreus, king of Egypt,

Undi, African chief,

United States,

condition of the Colored population before the war of 1861,

first statute establishing slavery in,

slave population, 1715 and 1775,

confederation of the,

treaty with England,

the Tory party in favor of slavery,

the Whigs the dominant party in the Northern States,

slavery recognized under the new government of the,

anti-slavery agitation in,

plan for the disposal of the Western Territory,

proceedings of Federal Convention,

slave population in 1790,

United-States Congress,

action on the disposal of recaptured Negroes,

first session at New York, 1789,

proceedings,

memorials to, for the abolition of slavery,

discussion in, on the restriction of the slave-trade,

prohibits the introduction of slaves into the Mississippi Territory,

Upton, Samuel and William, emancipate their father's slave,

Ury, John,

his connection with the New-York Negro plot, 1741,

executed,

Utrecht, the treaty of, to provide Negroes for the Spanish West Indies,

Van Twiller, Wouter,

charged with neglect of public affairs in New Netherlands,

owner of Negro slaves,

Varick, Cæsar, charged with burglary at New York,

Varnum, Gen. J.M., letter to Washington on the enlistment of Negroes,

Vaughan, Col. James, Legislature of Rhode Island refund tax on two child slaves imported by,

Vermont,

slave population, 1790

admitted into the Union,

"Victoria," ship, captures British privateer with Negroes,

Virginia,

slavery in,

slaves first introduced,

number of,

forced on the colony,

the first to purchase slaves,

women purchased in England and sent to,

number of slaves,

population,

Assembly pass prohibition against Negroes,

slavery legalized,

Indians declared slaves,

Assembly protest against the repeal of the Act declaring Negroes real estate,

impose duty on slaves and servants imported,,

tax on slaves sold,

reduced,, repealed,

revived,

prohibit Catholics, Indians, and Negro slaves to appear as witnesses,

pass act to value slave when executed,

threatened revolt of the free Negroes,

Act in regard to the freedom of slaves,

number of slaves in 1715 and 1775,

arrival of slaves in 1775,

purchaser of the same reproved,

instructions to delegation to Congress relative to the abolition of slavery,

Lord Dunmore's proclamation freeing slaves,

Negroes join the British army,,

declaration of convention against Dunmore's proclamation,

number of slaves in Cornwallis's army,

rights of slaves limited,

slaves who served in the army emancipated,

slave population, 1790,

Walklin, Thomas, testimony in the Sommersett case,

Warren, Joseph, oration on human liberty,

Warwick, Earl of, slaves on his plantation at the Bermudas,

Washburn, Emory, views on the slavery laws of Massachusetts,

Washington, George,

acknowledges verses written by Phillis Wheatley,

presents Virginia resolutions of 1774 against slavery,

takes command of the army,

forbids the enlistment of Negroes,

instructed to discharge all Negroes and slaves in the army,

order of, against Negro enlistments,

letter to Congress on admitting Negroes to the army,

letter to Joseph Reed on Lord Dunmore's proclamation,

letter to Gov. Cooke,

letter to Henry Laurens, on the arming of the Negroes,

letter to John Laurens on the failure to enlist Negroes in the South,

letter to Sir Guy Carleton relative to Negroes,

to Gen. Putnam in regard to a Negro in the army claimed by his owner,

president of the Federal Convention,

Watson, Capt., arrives at Norfolk, Va., with slaves,

Wayne, Anthony, letter to Lieut.-Col. Meigs relative to Negroes captured by him,

Wesleyan Methodists establish mission at Sierra Leone,

West India Company,

trade in slaves,

children of manumitted Negroes held as slaves by the,

cost of the government of New Netherland to the,

encourage commerce in slaves,

slaves in New York the property of the,

West Indies,

Negroes captured and made slaves,,

slaves sold at,

England furnishes Negroes to the,

Western Territory,

plan for the disposal of the,

slave population, 1790,

Wheatley, Phillis,

an African poetess,

visits England,

publishes her poems,

marries John Peters,

death of,

poem to Washington,

Washington's letter of acknowledgment,

Whipple, John, sued by Jenny Slew, a slave,

Whitefield, Rev. George, his plantation and Negroes in Georgia,

Williams, George W.,

orations on "The Footsteps of the Nation," "Early Christianity in Africa,"

first colored graduate from Newton Seminary,

ordination poem by Rev. Dr. Abbott,

Wilson, D.A., principal of school at Liberia,

Wilson, Jacob, on African languages,

Wilkinson, Gardiner,

discovers a Theban tomb with Negro scenes,

condition of white and black slaves,

Willson, Capt. John, charged with exciting slaves,

Windsor, Thomas, master of ship "Seaflower," arrives at Newport, R.I., with slaves from Africa,

Winter, Sir William, a slave-trader,

Worcester, Mass, representative instructed to vote against slavery,

York, Duke of, conveys Delaware to William Penn,

Yoruba, Africa,

Negro kingdom,

slave trade stopped,

Zerah, king of Ethiopia,